SQL Server
Query Performance Tuning
Distilled

Second Edition

SAJAL DAM

Apress®

SQL Server Query Performance Tuning Distilled, Second Edition

Copyright © 2004 by Sajal Dam

ISBN (pbk): 1-59059-421-5

Printed and bound in the United States of America 9 8 7 6 5 4 3 2 1

Lead Editor: Tony Davis
Technical Reviewer: Michael Ask
Editorial Board: Steve Anglin, Dan Appleman, Ewan Buckingham, Gary Cornell, Tony Davis, John Franklin, Jason Gilmore, Chris Mills, Dominic Shakeshaft, Jim Sumser
Project Manager: Kylie Johnston
Copy Edit Manager: Nicole LeClerc
Copy Editors: Nicole LeClerc, Ami Knox
Production Manager: Kari Brooks-Copony
Production Editor: Ellie Fountain
Compositor and Artist: Diana Van Winkle, Van Winkle Design Group
Proofreader: Greg Teague
Indexer: John Collin
Interior Designer: Diana Van Winkle, Van Winkle Design Group
Cover Designer: Kurt Krames
Manufacturing Manager: Tom Debolski

Distributed to the book trade in the United States by Springer-Verlag New York, LLC, 233 Spring Street, Sixth Floor, New York, NY 10013 and outside the United States by Springer-Verlag GmbH & Co. KG, Tiergartenstr. 17, 69112 Heidelberg, Germany.

In the United States: phone 1-800-SPRINGER, fax 201-348-4505, e-mail orders@springer-ny.com, or visit http://www.springer-ny.com. Outside the United States: fax +49 6221 345229, e-mail orders@springer.de, or visit http://www.springer.de.

For information on translations, please contact Apress directly at 2560 Ninth Street, Suite 219, Berkeley, CA 94710. Phone 510-549-5930, fax 510-549-5939, e-mail info@apress.com, or visit http://www.apress.com.

The source code for this book is available to readers at http://www.apress.com in the Downloads section.

Contents at a Glance

Contents

About the Author

SAJAL DAM holds a Master's of Technology degree in computer science from the Indian Institute of Science, Bangalore, and has been working with Microsoft technologies for over 12 years. He has developed an extensive background in designing database applications and managing software development. Sajal also possesses significant experience in troubleshooting and optimizing the performance of Microsoft-based applications, from front-end web pages to back-end databases.

While working at Microsoft Corporation, Sajal helped many Fortune 500 companies design scalable database solutions and maximize the performance of their database environments. Currently an IT strategist at Dell, Sajal manages Dell's vast database infrastructure by optimizing not only the databases, but also the database management processes, tools, and use of best practices. He also closely works with the application development teams and vendors, including Microsoft, in analyzing and resolving performance bottlenecks.

About the Technical Reviewer

MICHAEL ASK has worked in the IT industry since graduating from the University of Iowa in 1995. Michael has worked as a consultant for the majority of his career, including three years with Microsoft Consulting Services. He now works for Data Transmission Network (http://www.dtn.com) in Omaha, Nebraska, specializing in SQL Server and .NET application development.

Between technical reviews and programming assignments, he enjoys spending as much time as possible with his kids, Emily and Kaleb. He also enjoys cheering for Hawkeye football games in the land of the Huskers! You can reach him at admin@askwaresolutions.com.

Acknowledgments

Many special thanks to my parents and siblings, who made me capable of mastering my field and helped me cultivate an interest in sharing my knowledge with others. Without their continued support, I wouldn't have been able to concentrate on this endeavor.

I would also like to thank some special people, Neeraj Srivastava, Rajesh Patel, and Soumendra Paik, who kept me going through my roller-coaster highs and lows. It wouldn't have been possible for me to get over the humps without their encouragement and motivation. My special thanks to Gene Daigle and Kelvin Yund, who had to put up with me through my odyssey—thanks for all the cooperation and understanding!

I'm equally thankful to the Apress team, especially Tony Davis and Kylie Johnston, for giving very high importance to my book. Without Kylie's positive remarks and considerations, I wouldn't have been able to balance my endless responsibilities at Dell, hectic book schedule, and passion for knowledge.

Introduction

Every time I work on a poorly performing database, I feel the importance of analyzing the behavior of the database not just from indexing aspect, but also from every other aspect that can be a big performance killer. Whatever the configurations of the database may be, it is important to analyze the behavior of the database and the queries that correlate to the slowness symptoms, and concentrate on determining the root cause and possible solutions. During a performance bottleneck, there is usually a huge amount of diagnostic data to go through, which not only makes the analysis itself quite a daunting task, but also makes it very easy to get lost in the diagnostic data.

I like almost every performance-tuning book and article on the market. However, the irony is that when I face a performance issue, I don't find many good articles that help me analyze the bottleneck and correlate it to a small list of possible root causes without bothering too much about the best practices that aren't related to the performance issue at hand. If everything in a database application and its queries were perfect, then there probably wouldn't have been a performance issue in the first place.

Seeing the importance of analyzing the performance of a database from a practical point of view, I decided to share my knowledge with you. My intention is not to simply dump some performance-tuning concepts on you; rather, my aim is to teach you how to fish for yourself, so that you can analyze and resolve the bottlenecks every time you face a poorly performing database. Therefore, I present not only the right ways of implementing a scalable database application, but also the caveats associated with the performance tips and the impacts of the other possible options.

What This Book Covers

The beauty of performance tuning is that, in many cases, an appropriate change to an index or a SQL query can result in a far more efficient application. However, it is challenging to identify the root cause of a costly query, and there are many pitfalls for the unwary. Therefore, to help you properly identify and resolve performance bottlenecks, I cover the performance aspects outlined in the sections that follow in this book, with the help of simple, yet real-world examples.

Chapter 1: SQL Query Performance Tuning

This chapter presents performance-tuning principles and processes. The chapter also covers the importance of defining the baseline performance of a database.

Chapter 2: System Performance Analysis

Although a poorly written SQL query can create unsustainable pressure on the system resources and make the hardware resources look bad, it is important to understand how to analyze and resolve system bottlenecks that can affect query performance. This chapter also covers how to generate a database baseline.

Chapter 3: SQL Query Performance Analysis

This chapter shows you how to examine database performance and identify problematic SQL queries. To help you examine database performance, I explain how to use the performance-tuning tools and cover the strengths of the tools in analyzing the execution plans and the different costs of the bad queries. I also describe how to analyze the effectiveness of indexing and joining strategies of the costly queries.

Chapter 4: Index Analysis

Indexes usually make the biggest impact on query performance. Therefore, in this chapter, I discuss in detail how to evaluate the effectiveness of the existing indexes and the benefits of new indexes. Since there are different indexing options, I cover in depth the benefits and drawbacks of the different options, and how to choose the best indexing option.

Chapter 5: Index Tuning Wizard

One of the cool performance-tuning tools in SQL Server 2000 is the Index Tuning Wizard. In this chapter, I cover how to get the best index advice from this tool as well as the limitations of the tool.

Chapter 6: Bookmark Lookup Analysis

Often, one of the costly steps in the execution plan of a query that can be optimized by proper indexing is bookmark lookup. In this chapter, I present the concepts of bookmark lookup, and discuss how to analyze and resolve costly bookmark lookup operations.

Chapter 7: Statistics Analysis

This chapter covers the role of statistics in query execution. It covers not only how to maintain up-to-date statistics, but also how to evaluate the effectiveness of the current statistics on query performance.

Chapter 8: Fragmentation Analysis

One of the database aspects that can affect query performance, and yet is not directly related to the query design, is fragmentation. In this chapter, I cover the causes of fragmentation, how to analyze and resolve the impact of fragmentation on query performance, and how to minimize the overhead of defragmentation.

Chapter 9: Execution Plan Cache Analysis

Since a query can't be executed without having an execution plan first, and the process of generating an execution plan can be costly enough, in this chapter I discuss the process of execution plan creation and caching, and how to analyze and optimize execution plan caching and reuse.

Chapter 10: Stored Procedure Recompilation

One of the main causes of poor reusability of execution plans is plan recompilation. This chapter covers the causes of stored procedure recompilation, and how to analyze and avoid stored procedure recompilations.

Chapter 11: Query Design Analysis

Irrespective of the query optimizer's "intelligence," if a query is written without any performance consideration, you will end up running short of hardware resources, and the optimizer won't be able to provide an efficient execution plan. Therefore, in this chapter, I cover the design aspects of resource-friendly queries.

Chapter 12: Blocking Analysis

A database may perform well when used by a limited number of users, but it may not scale up as the load is increased. One of the biggest performance killers in a multiuser database is database blocking. In this chapter, I detail the ACID properties of a database, the principles of database locks, and the fundamentals of transaction isolation levels. I explain how to analyze and minimize blocking, and thereby increase database concurrency.

Chapter 13: Deadlock Analysis

One of the outcomes of blocking is deadlock. This issue is tricky to analyze because by the time you see the problem, one of the SQL Server processes will have been victimized and the problem will have disappeared. In this chapter, I cover how to analyze a complex deadlock scenario, how to identify all the participants and the contended resources in the deadlock scenario, and how to avoid/minimize deadlocks.

Chapter 14: Cursor Cost Analysis

In this chapter, I discuss how to examine and optimize the cost of using different cursor types.

Chapter 15: Database Connection Performance Issues

This chapter covers the costs associated with database connections, the performance impact of connection pooling, and the recommendations for optimizing database connection costs.

Chapter 16: Database Workload Optimization

It is important to learn not only the individual performance concepts, but also how to apply those concepts to a poorly performing database workload. In this chapter, I describe how to examine the performance of a SQL workload and optimize the performance of the workload by using the right tools and performance tips.

Chapter 17: Scalability Scenarios

Besides learning the performance aspects of individual queries, you must also know how to design application features using a set of SQL queries and application-design principles that will perform well even under heavy loads. In this chapter, I use a number of real-world examples to show how to design scalable application features.

Chapter 18: SQL Server Optimization Checklist

This chapter provides a performance-monitoring checklist that can serve as a quick reference for database developers and DBAs when they're out in the field.

Who This Book Is For

The book is targeted toward SQL Server optimizer geeks and database developers/administrators who want to become optimization gurus. For database developers and DBAs involved in database performance, this book's in-depth coverage of performance analysis and resolutions make it an invaluable reference. The presentation of performance concepts using numerous, lucid, and yet practical examples provides hands-on experience to developers interested in mastering database performance concepts.

Source Code

In spite of all the praise and positive comments the first edition of this book received, I learned from many readers that they weren't able to locate the source code and, in some cases, chapters were missing from the book. This time, Apress has done an excellent job shaping the book and making the source code available from the Downloads section of the Apress website at http://www.apress.com. As a backup measure, you may reach me at sajaldam1@hotmail.com.

CHAPTER 1

■ ■ ■

SQL Query Performance Tuning

Performance tuning is an important part of today's database applications. Very often, large savings in both time and money can be achieved with proper performance tuning. The beauty of performance tuning is that, in many cases, a small change to an index or a SQL query can result in a far more efficient application.

There are, however, many pitfalls for the unwary. As a result, a proven process is required to ensure that you correctly identify and resolve performance bottlenecks.

To whet your appetite for the types of topics essential to honing your query optimization skills, here is a quick list of the query optimization aspects I will cover in this book:

- Identifying problematic SQL queries

- Analyzing a query execution plan

- Evaluating the effectiveness of the current indexes

- Avoiding bookmark lookups

- Evaluating the effectiveness of the current statistics

- Analyzing and resolving fragmentation

- Optimizing execution plan caching

- Analyzing and avoiding stored procedure recompilation

- Minimizing blocking and deadlocks

- Examining the cost of using a specific cursor type

- Optimizing database connection cost

- Applying performance tuning processes, tools, and optimization techniques to optimize SQL workload

Before jumping straight in to these topics, let's first examine why we go about performance tuning the way we do. In this chapter, I discuss the basic concepts of performance tuning for a SQL Server database system. I detail the main performance bottlenecks and show just how important it is to design a database-friendly application, which is the consumer of the data, as well as optimize the database. Specifically, I cover the following topics:

- The performance tuning process

- Performance versus price

- The performance baseline

- Where to focus efforts in tuning

- The top 11 SQL Server performance killers

So, without further ado, let's begin.

The Performance Tuning Process

The performance tuning process consists of identifying performance bottlenecks, troubleshooting their cause, applying different resolutions, and then quantifying performance improvements. It is necessary to be a little creative, since most of the time there is no one silver bullet to improve performance. The challenge is to narrow down the list of possible reasons and evaluate the effects of different resolutions. You may even undo modifications as you iterate through the tuning process.

During the tuning process, you must examine various hardware and software factors that can affect the performance of a SQL Server–based application. A few of the general questions you should be asking yourself during the performance analysis are as follows:

- Is any other resource-intensive application running on the same server?

- Is the hardware subsystem capable of withstanding the maximum workload?

- Is SQL Server configured properly?

- Is the database connection between SQL Server and the database application efficient?

- Does the database design support the fastest data retrieval (and modification for an updateable database)?

- Is the user workload, consisting of SQL queries, optimized to reduce the load on SQL Server?

- Does the workload support the maximum concurrency?

If any of these factors is not configured properly, then the overall system performance may suffer. Let's briefly examine these factors.

Having another resource-intensive application on the same server can limit the resources available to SQL Server. Even an application running as a service can consume a good part of the system resources, limiting the resources available to SQL Server. Consider that even running Windows Task Manager continuously on the server is not recommended. Windows

Task Manager is also an application, `taskmgr.exe`, which runs at a higher priority than the SQL Server process. To determine the priority of a process, follow these steps:

1. Launch Windows Task Manager.

2. Select View ➤ Select Columns.

3. Select the Base Priority check box.

4. Click the OK button.

These steps will add the Base Priority column to the list of processes. Subsequently, you will be able to determine that the SQL Server process (`sqlservr.exe`) by default runs at Normal priority, whereas the Windows Task Manager process (`taskmgr.exe`) runs at High priority. Therefore, to allow SQL Server to maximize the use of available resources, you should look for all the nonessential applications/services running on the SQL Server machine and ensure that they are not acting as resource hogs.

Improper configuration of the hardware can prevent SQL Server from gaining the maximum benefit from the available resources. The main hardware resources to be considered are processor, memory, disk, and network. For example, in a server with more than 4GB of memory, an improper memory configuration will prevent SQL Server from using the memory beyond 4GB. Furthermore, if the capacity of a particular resource is small, then it can soon become a performance bottleneck for SQL Server. Chapter 2 covers these hardware bottlenecks in detail.

You should also look at the configuration of SQL Server, since proper configuration is essential for an optimized application. There is a long list of SQL Server configurations that define the generic behavior of a SQL Server installation. These configurations can be viewed and modified using a system stored procedure, `sp_configure`. Many of these configurations can be managed interactively through SQL Server Enterprise Manager.

Since the SQL Server configurations are applicable for the complete SQL Server installation, a standard configuration is generally preferred. The good news is that, generally, you need not modify these configurations; the default settings work best for most situations. In fact, the general recommendation is to keep the SQL Server configurations at the default values. I discuss the configuration parameters in detail throughout the book.

Poor connectivity between SQL Server and the database application can hurt application performance. One of the questions you should ask yourself is "How good is the database connection?" For example, the query executed by the application may be highly optimized, but the database connection used to submit this query may add considerable overhead to the query performance. Based on the distribution of the application and the database, different network protocols should be used to reduce the network overhead. Additionally, the data access layer used to manage the database connectivity above the network connection may not be efficient. The data access layer technology or the way the data access layer is used by the application may not be optimal. Chapter 15 covers the database connection aspects in detail.

The design of the database should also be analyzed while troubleshooting performance. This helps you understand not only the entity-relationship model of the database, but also why a query may be written in a certain way. Although it may not always be possible to modify a database design because of wider implications on the database application, a good understanding of the database design helps you to focus in the right direction and to understand the impact of a resolution.

If the previous configurations are quite normal or have to be the way they are, then the question becomes "Is the application slow because of poorly designed or indexed queries?" The workload may contain resource-intensive or nonoptimized queries, which may hurt the performance of the queries and that of other queries in the workload. I cover index optimization in depth in Chapters 3, 4, 5, and 6. The next question at this stage should be "Is a query slow because of its resource intensiveness or because of concurrency issues with other queries?" You can find in-depth information on blocking analysis in Chapter 12.

The challenge is to find out which factor is causing the performance bottleneck. For example, with slow-running SQL queries and high pressure on the hardware resources, you may find that both poor database design and nonoptimized workload are to blame. In such a case, you must diagnose the symptoms further and correlate the findings with possible causes. As performance tuning can be time-consuming and tiresome, you should ideally take a preventive approach by designing the system for optimum performance from the outset.

To strengthen the preventive approach, every lesson that you learn during the optimization of poor performance should be considered an optimization guideline when implementing new database applications. There are also proven best practices that you should consider while implementing database applications. I present these best practices in detail throughout the book, and Chapter 18 is dedicated to optimization best practices.

Please ensure that you take the performance optimization techniques into consideration at the early stages of your database application development. Doing so will help you roll out your database projects without big surprises later.

Unfortunately, we rarely live up to this ideal and often find database applications needing performance tuning. Therefore, it is important to understand not only how to improve the performance of a SQL Server–based application, but also how to diagnose the causes of poor performance.

An Iterative Process

Performance tuning is an *iterative process*, where you identify major bottlenecks, attempt to resolve them, measure the impact of your changes, and return to the first step until performance is acceptable. While applying your solutions, you should follow the golden rule of making only one change at a time. Any change usually affects other parts of the system, so you must re-evaluate the effect of each change on the performance of the overall system.

As an example, the addition of an index may fix the performance of a specific query, but it could cause other queries to run more slowly, as explained in Chapter 4. Consequently, it is preferable to conduct performance analysis in a test environment, to shield users from your diagnosis attempts and intermediate optimization steps. In such a case, evaluating one change at a time also helps in prioritizing the implementation order of the changes on the production server, based on their relative contributions.

You can keep on chipping away at performance bottlenecks and improving the system performance gradually. Initially, you will be able to resolve big performance bottlenecks and achieve significant performance improvements, but as you proceed through the iterations, your returns will gradually diminish. Therefore, to use your time efficiently, it is worthwhile to quantify the performance objectives first (for example, an 80% reduction in the time taken for a certain query, with no adverse effect anywhere else on the server), and then work toward them.

The performance of a SQL Server application is highly dependent on the amount and distribution of user activity (or workload) and data. Both the amount and distribution of workload and data change over time, and differing data can cause SQL Server to execute SQL queries differently. The performance resolution applicable for a certain workload and data may lose its effect over a period of time. Therefore, to ensure an optimum system performance on a continuing basis, you will need to analyze performance at regular intervals. Performance tuning is a never-ending process, as shown in Figure 1-1.

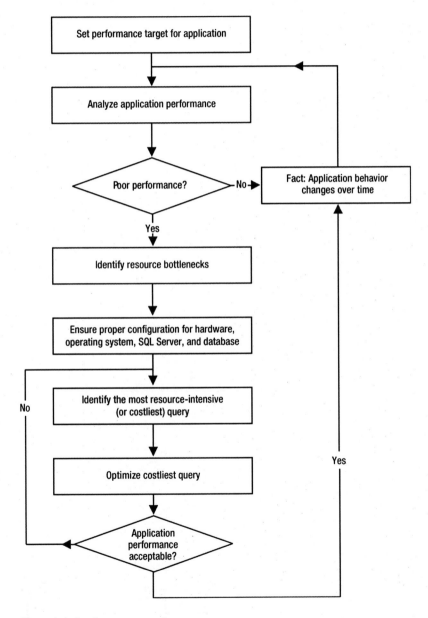

Figure 1-1. *Performance tuning process*

You can see that the steps to optimize the costliest query make for a complex process, which also requires multiple iterations to troubleshoot the performance issues within the query and apply one change at a time. The steps involved in the optimization of the costliest query are shown in Figure 1-2.

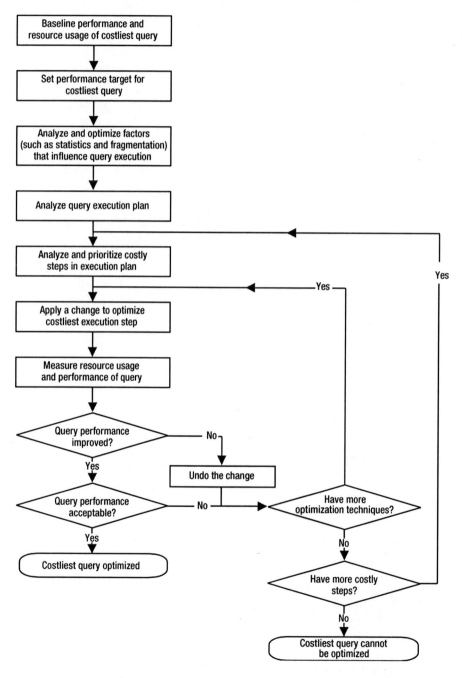

Figure 1-2. *Optimization of the costliest query*

As you can see from this process, there is quite a lot to do to ensure that you correctly tune the performance of a given query. It is important to use a solid process like this in performance tuning, to focus on the main identified issues.

Having said this, it also helps to try and keep a broader perspective about the problem as a whole, since sometimes you may believe that you are trying to solve the correct performance bottleneck, when in reality something else is causing the problem.

Performance vs. Price

One of the points I touched on earlier is that to gain increasingly small performance increments, you need to spend increasingly large amounts of time and money. Therefore, to ensure the best return on your investment, you should be very objective while optimizing performance. Always consider the following two aspects:

- What is the acceptable performance for your application?

- Is the investment worth the performance gain?

To derive maximum efficiency, you must realistically estimate your performance requirements. There are many best practices that you can follow to improve performance—for example, you can have your database files on the most efficient disk subsystem. However, before applying a best practice, you should consider how much you may gain from it and whether the gain will be worth the investment.

Sometimes it is really difficult to estimate the performance gain without actually making the enhancement. A practical approach can be to increase a resource in increments and analyze the application's scalability with the added resource. A scalable application will proportionately benefit from an incremental increase of the resource, if the resource was truly causing the scalability bottleneck. If the results appear to be satisfactory, then you can commit to the full enhancement. Experience also plays a very important role here.

"Good Enough" Tuning

Instead of tuning a system to the theoretical maximum performance, the goal should be to tune until the system performance is "good enough." This is a commonly adopted performance tuning approach. The cost investment after such a point usually increases exponentially in comparison to the performance gain. The 80:20 rule works very well: by investing 20% of your resources, you may get 80% of the possible performance enhancement, but for the remaining 20% possible performance gain, you may have to invest an additional 80% of resources, as shown in Figure 1-3. It is therefore important to be realistic when setting your performance objectives.

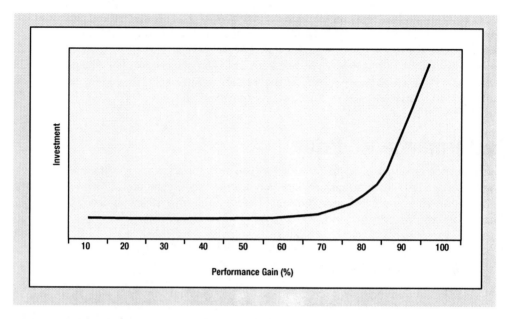

Figure 1-3. *Performance gain vs. investment*

A business benefits not by considering pure performance, but by considering price performance. However, if the target is to find the scalability limit of your application (for various reasons, including marketing the product against its competitors), then it may be worthwhile investing as much as you can. Even in such cases, using a third-party stress test lab may be a better investment decision.

Performance Baseline

One of the main objectives of performance analysis is to understand the underlying level of system use or pressure on different hardware and software subsystems. This knowledge helps you in the following ways:

- Allows you to analyze resource bottlenecks.

- Enables you to troubleshoot by comparing system utilization patterns with a pre-established baseline.

- Assists you in making accurate estimates in capacity planning and scheduling hardware upgrades.

- Aids you in identifying low-utilization periods, when the database administrative activities can be executed.

- Helps you to estimate the nature of possible hardware downsizing. This sounds interesting—why would a company downsize? Well, in the past, some companies leased very high-end systems expecting strong growth, but due to poor growth, they are now forced to downsize their system setups.

Therefore, to better understand your application's resource requirements, you should create a *baseline* for your application's hardware and software usage. A baseline serves as a statistic of your system's current usage pattern and as a reference with which to compare future statistics. Baseline analysis helps you to understand your application's behavior during a stable period, how hardware resources are used during such periods, and what the software characteristics are. With a baseline in place, you can

- Measure current performance and express your application's performance goals.

- Compare other hardware or software combinations against the baseline.

- Measure how the workload and/or data changes over time.

- Evaluate the peak and nonpeak usage pattern of the application. This information can be used to effectively distribute database administration activities, such as full database backup and database defragmentation during nonpeak hours.

You can use the System Monitor tool (also referred to as Performance Monitor) to create a baseline for SQL Server's hardware and software resource utilization. Similarly, you may baseline the SQL Server workload using the SQL Profiler tool, which can help you to understand the average resource utilization and execution time of SQL queries when conditions are stable. You will learn in detail how to use these tools in Chapters 2 and 3.

Where to Focus Efforts

When you tune a particular system, pay special attention to the application layer (the database queries and stored procedures executed by Visual Basic/ADO or otherwise that are used to access the database). You will usually find that you can positively affect performance in the application layer far more than if you spend an equal amount of time figuring out how to tune the hardware, operating system, or SQL Server configuration. Although a proper configuration of hardware, operating system, and SQL Server is essential for the best performance of a database application, these fields have standardized so much that you usually need to spend only a limited amount of time configuring them properly for performance. Application design issues such as query design and indexing strategies, on the other hand, are application dependent. Consequently, there is usually more to optimize in the application layer than in the hardware, operating system, or SQL Server configuration. Thus, for a unit of time spent in each area, work in the application layer usually yields the maximum performance benefit, as illustrated in Figure 1-4.

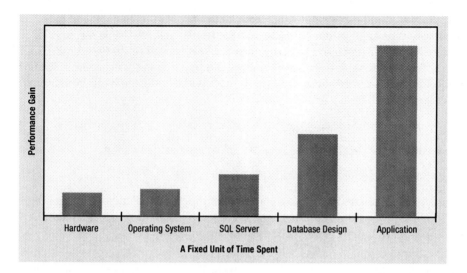

Figure 1-4. *Time spent vs. performance gain*

In my experience, the greatest improvement in database application performance can be obtained by looking first at the area of application design, including logical/physical database design, query design, and index design.

Sure, if you concentrate on hardware configuration and upgrades, you may obtain a satisfactory performance gain. However, a bad SQL query sent by the application can consume all the hardware resources available, no matter how much you have. Therefore, a poor application design can make the hardware upgrade requirements very high, or even beyond your limits. In the presence of a heavy SQL workload, concentrating on hardware configurations and upgrades usually produces a poor return on investment.

You should analyze the stress created by an application on a SQL Server database at two levels:

- *High level*: Analyze how much stress the database application is creating on individual hardware resources and what the overall behavior of the SQL Server installation is. This information can help you in two ways. First, it helps you to identify the area to concentrate on within a SQL Server application where there is poor performance. Second, it helps you to identify any lack of proper configuration at the higher levels. You can then decide which hardware resource may be upgraded, if you are not able to tune the application, using the Performance Monitor tool, as explained in Chapter 2.

- *Low level*: Identify the exact culprits within the application—in other words, the SQL queries that are creating most of the pressure visible at the overall higher level. This can be done using the SQL Profiler tool, as explained in Chapter 3.

SQL Server Performance Killers

Let's now consider the major problem areas that can degrade SQL Server performance. By being aware of the main performance killers in SQL Server in advance, you will be able to focus your tuning efforts on the likely causes.

Once you have optimized the hardware, operating system, and SQL Server settings, the main performance killers in SQL Server are as follows, in a rough order (with the worst appearing first):

- Poor indexing

- Inaccurate statistics

- Excessive blocking and deadlocks

- Poor query design

- Poor database design

- Excessive fragmentation

- Nonreusable execution plans

- Frequent recompilation of execution plans

- Improper use of cursors

- Improper configuration of the database log

- Ineffective connection pooling

Let's take a quick look at each of these, before considering them in more depth in later chapters.

Poor Indexing

Poor indexing is usually one of the biggest performance killers in SQL Server. In the absence of proper indexing for a query, SQL Server has to retrieve and process much more data while executing the query. This causes high amounts of stress on the disk, memory, and CPU, increasing the query execution time significantly. Increased query execution time then leads to excessive blocking and deadlocks in SQL Server. You will learn how to determine the indexing strategies and resolve indexing problems in Chapters 4, 5, and 6.

Generally, indexes are considered to be the responsibility of the database administrator (DBA). However, the DBA cannot define how to use the indexes, since the use of indexes is determined by the database queries and stored procedures written by the developers. Therefore, defining the indexes should be the responsibility of the developers. Indexes created without the knowledge of the queries serve little purpose.

■NOTE Because indexes created without the knowledge of the queries serve little purpose, database developers ought to understand the indexes as much as the DBAs.

Inaccurate Statistics

As SQL Server relies heavily on cost-based optimization, accurate data-distribution statistics are extremely important for the effective use of indexes. Without accurate statistics, SQL Server's built-in query optimizer cannot accurately estimate the number of rows affected by a query. As the amount of data to be retrieved from a table is highly important in deciding how to optimize the query execution, the query optimizer is much less effective if the data distribution statistics are not maintained accurately. You will look at how to analyze statistics in Chapter 7.

Excessive Blocking and Deadlocks

Because SQL Server is fully Atomicity, Consistency, Isolation, Durability (ACID) compliant, the database engine ensures that modifications made by concurrent transactions are properly isolated from one another. By default, a transaction sees the data either in the state before another concurrent transaction modified the data or after the other transaction completed—it does not see an intermediate state.

Because of this isolation, when multiple transactions try to access a common resource concurrently in a noncompatible way, *blocking* occurs in the database. A *deadlock*, which is an outcome of blocking, aborts the victimized database request that faced the deadlock. This requires that the database request be resubmitted for successful execution. The execution time of a query is adversely affected by the amount of blocking and deadlock it faces.

For scalable performance of a multiuser database application, properly controlling the isolation levels and transaction scopes of the queries to minimize blocking and deadlock is critical; otherwise, the execution time of the queries will increase significantly, even though the hardware resources may be highly underutilized. I will cover this problem in depth in Chapters 12 and 13.

Poor Query Design

The effectiveness of indexes depends entirely on the way you write SQL queries. Retrieving excessively large numbers of rows from a table, or specifying a filter criterion that returns a larger result set from a table than is required, renders the indexes ineffective. To improve performance, you must ensure that the SQL queries are written to make the best use of new or existing indexes. Failing to write cost-effective SQL queries may prevent SQL Server from choosing proper indexes, which increases query execution time and database blocking. Chapter 11 covers how to write effective queries.

Query design covers not only single queries, but also sets of queries often used to implement database functionalities such as a queue management among queue readers and writers. Even when the performance of individual queries used in the design is fine, the overall performance of the database can be very poor. Resolving this kind of bottleneck requires a broad understanding of different characteristics of SQL Server, which can affect the performance of database functionalities. You will see how to design effective database functionality using SQL queries in Chapter 17.

Poor Database Design

A database should be adequately normalized to increase the performance of data retrieval and reduce blocking. For example, if you have an undernormalized database with customer and order information in the same table, then the customer information will be repeated in all the order rows of the customer. This repetition of information in every row will increase the I/Os required to fetch all the orders placed by a customer. At the same time, a data writer working on a customer's order will reserve all the rows that include the customer information and thus block all other data writers/data readers trying to access the customer profile.

Overnormalization of a database is as bad as undernormalization. Overnormalization increases the number and complexity of joins required to retrieve data. An overnormalized database contains a large number of tables with a very small number of columns. As a *very* general rule of thumb, you may continue the normalization process unless it causes lots of queries to have four-way or greater joins.

Having too many joins in a query may also be due to the fact that database entities have not been partitioned very distinctly or the query is serving a very complex set of requirements that could perhaps be better served by creating a new view or stored procedure.

Database design is a large subject, and I will not cover it any further in this book. However, if you want to read a book on database design, with an emphasis on introducing the subject, I recommend reading *Data Modeling for Everyone* by Sharon Allen (Apress, 2003).

Excessive Fragmentation

While analyzing data retrieval operations, you can usually assume that the data is organized in an orderly way, as indicated by the index used by the data retrieval operation. However, if the pages containing the data are fragmented in a nonorderly fashion, or if they contain a small amount of data due to frequent page splits, then the number of read operations required by the data retrieval operation will be much higher than might otherwise be required. The increase in the number of read operations caused by fragmentation hurts query performance. In Chapter 8, you will learn how to analyze and remove fragmentation.

Nonreusable Execution Plans

To execute a query in an efficient way, SQL Server's query optimizer spends a fair amount of CPU cycles creating a cost-effective execution plan. The good news is that the plan is cached in memory, so you can reuse it once created. However, if the plan is designed so that you cannot plug variable values into it, SQL Server creates a new execution plan every time the same query is resubmitted with different variable values. So, for better performance, it is extremely important to submit SQL queries in forms that help SQL Server cache and reuse the execution plans. You will see in detail how to improve the reusability of execution plans in Chapter 9.

Frequent Recompilation of Execution Plans

One of the standard ways of ensuring a reusable execution plan, independent of variable values used in a query, is to use a stored procedure. Using a stored procedure to execute a set of SQL queries allows SQL Server to create a *parameterized execution plan*.

A parameterized execution plan is independent of the parameter values supplied during the execution of the stored procedure, and it is consequently highly reusable. However, the execution plan of the stored procedure can be reused only if SQL Server does not have to recompile the execution plan every time the stored procedure is run. Frequent recompilation of a stored procedure increases pressure on the CPU and the query execution time. I will discuss in detail the various causes and resolutions of stored procedure recompilation in Chapter 10.

Improper Use of Cursors

By preferring a cursor-based (row-at-a-time) result set instead of a regular set-based SQL query, you add a fair amount of overhead on SQL Server. Use set-based queries whenever possible, but if you are forced to use cursors, be sure to use efficient cursor types such as fast forward–only. Excessive use of inefficient cursors increases stress on SQL Server resources, slowing down system performance. I discuss how to use cursors properly in Chapter 14.

Improper Configuration of the Database Log

By failing to follow the general recommendations in configuring a database log, you can adversely affect the performance of an Online Transaction Processing (OLTP)–based SQL Server database. For optimal performance, SQL Server heavily relies on accessing the database logs effectively.

Chapter 2 covers how to configure the database log properly.

Ineffective Connection Pooling

If you don't use connection pooling, or if you don't have enough connections in your pool, then each database connection request goes across the network to establish a database connection. This network latency increases the query execution time. Poor use of the connection pool will also increase the amount of memory used in SQL Server, since a large number of connections require a large amount of memory on the SQL Server. You will learn how to use connections efficiently in Chapter 15.

Summary

In this introductory chapter, you have seen that SQL Server performance tuning is an iterative process, consisting of identifying performance bottlenecks, troubleshooting their cause, applying different resolutions, quantifying performance improvements, and then going back to the start until your required performance level is reached.

To assist in this process, you should create a system baseline to compare with your modifications. Throughout the performance tuning process, you need to be very objective about the amount of tuning you would like to perform—you can always make a query run a little bit faster, but is the effort worth the cost? Finally, since performance depends on the pattern of user activity and data, you must re-evaluate the database server performance on a regular basis.

To derive the optimal performance from a SQL Server database system, it is extremely important that you understand the stresses on the server created by the database application. In the next two chapters, I will discuss how to analyze these stresses, both at a higher system level and at a lower SQL Server activities level.

In the rest of the book, you will examine in depth the biggest SQL Server performance killers, as mentioned earlier in the chapter. You will learn how these individual factors can affect performance if used incorrectly, and how to resolve or avoid these traps.

System Performance Analysis

In the first chapter, I stressed the importance of having a performance baseline that you can use to measure performance changes. In fact, this is one of the first things you should do when starting the performance tuning process, since without a baseline you will not be able to quantify improvements. In this chapter, you will learn how to use the System Monitor tool to accomplish this, and how to use the different performance counters that are required to create a baseline.

Specifically, I cover the following topics:

- The basics of the System Monitor tool

- How to analyze hardware resource bottlenecks using System Monitor

- How to resolve hardware resource bottlenecks

- How to analyze the overall performance of SQL Server

- Steps to create a baseline for the system

System Monitor Tool

Windows 2000 provides a tool called *System Monitor* that monitors in detail the utilization of operating system resources. It allows you to track nearly every aspect of system performance, including memory, disk, processor, and the network. In addition, SQL Server 2000 provides extensions to the System Monitor tool, to track a variety of functional areas within SQL Server. The older version of this tool in Windows NT 4.0 is called Performance Monitor (or perfmon), and the tool is still commonly referred to by that name.

System Monitor tracks resource behavior by capturing performance data generated by hardware and software components of the system such as a processor, a process, a thread, and so on. The performance data generated by a system component is represented by a *performance object*. A performance object provides *counters* that represent specific aspects of a component, such as % Processor Time for a Processor object.

There can be multiple instances of a system component. For instance, the `Processor` object in a computer with two processors will have two instances represented as instances 0 and 1. Performance objects with multiple instances may also have an instance called `_Total` to represent the total value for all the instances. For example, the processor usage of a computer with four processors can be determined using the following performance object, counter, and instance (as shown in Figure 2-1):

- *Performance object*: `Processor`

- *Counter*: `% Processor Time`

- *Instance*: `_Total`

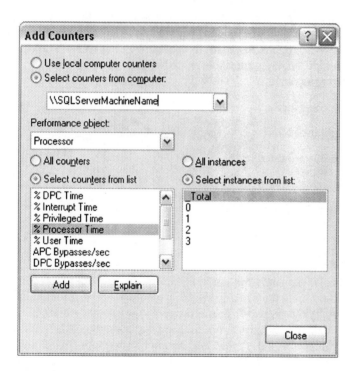

Figure 2-1. *Adding a perfmon counter*

System behavior can be either tracked in real time in the form of graphs or captured as a log (called a *counter log*) for offline analysis.

To run the System Monitor tool, either execute `perfmon` from a command prompt or navigate through the Start menu appropriately (for Windows 2000, go to Control Panel ➤ Administrative Tools ➤ Performance).

You will look at how to set up the individual counters in the "Creating a Baseline" section at the end of the chapter. First, you will examine which counters you should choose to identify system bottlenecks, and also how you can resolve some of these bottlenecks.

System Resource Utilization

Typically, SQL Server OLTP database performance is affected by stress on the following hardware resources:

- Memory

- Disk I/O

- Processor

- Network

Stress beyond the capacity of a hardware resource forms a bottleneck. To address the overall performance of a system, you need to identify these bottlenecks, as they form the limit on overall system performance.

Identifying Bottlenecks

There is usually a relationship between resource bottlenecks. For example, a processor bottleneck may be a symptom of excessive paging (memory bottleneck) or a slow disk (disk bottleneck). If a system is low on memory, causing excessive paging, and has a slow disk, then one of the end results will be a processor with high utilization since the processor has to spend a significant number of CPU cycles to swap pages in and out of the memory and to manage the resultant high number of I/O requests. Replacing the processor with a faster one may help a little, but it would not be the best overall solution. In a case like this, increasing memory is a more appropriate solution, because it will decrease pressure on the disk and processor as well. Even upgrading the disk will probably be a better solution than upgrading the processor.

NOTE A limit in memory stresses both the disk and the processor. A limit in the disk subsystem in turn stresses the processor. Therefore, you should first evaluate memory, then disk utilization, and finally the stress on the processor.

One of the best ways of locating a bottleneck is to identify resources that are experiencing *queuing*. The response time of a request served by a resource includes the time the request had to wait in the resource queue, as well as the time taken to execute the request, so end user response time is directly proportional to the amount of queuing in a system.

For example, consider that the disk subsystem has a disk queue length of 10. Since the disk subsystem already has pending disk requests on it, a new disk request has to wait until the previous disk requests complete. If the time taken by an average disk transfer is 1 second, then the new disk request has to wait for around 10 seconds before getting the attention of the disk subsystem. Therefore, the total response time of the disk request will be 10 seconds wait time, plus 1 second disk transfer time.

Be aware that the absence of a queue does not mean that there is no bottleneck. When queue lengths start growing, however, it is a sure sign that the system is not able to keep up with the demand.

Not all resources have specific counters that show queuing levels, but most resources have some counters that represent an overcommittal of that resource. For example, memory has no such counter, but the amount of hard page faults represents overcommittal of physical memory (*hard page fault* is explained later in the chapter in the section entitled "Pages and Page Fault Counters"). Other resources, such as the processor and the disk, have specific counters to indicate the level of queuing.

You will see which counters to use in analyzing each type of bottleneck shortly.

Bottleneck Resolution

Once you have identified bottlenecks, you can resolve them in two ways:

- Increase resource throughput.

- Decrease arrival rate of requests to the resource.

Increasing the throughput usually requires extra resources such as memory, disks, processors, or network adapters. Decreasing the arrival rate can be accomplished by being more selective on the requests to a resource. For example, when you have a disk subsystem bottleneck, you can either increase throughput of the disk subsystem or decrease the amount of I/O requests.

Increasing throughput means adding more disks or upgrading to faster disks. Decreasing the arrival rate means identifying the cause of high I/O requests to the disk subsystem and applying resolutions to decrease their number. You may be able to decrease the I/O requests, for example, by adding appropriate indexes on a table to limit the amount of data accessed.

Memory Bottleneck Analysis

Memory is the most common bottleneck. Furthermore, a bottleneck in memory will manifest on other resources, too. This is particularly true for a system running SQL Server. When SQL Server runs out of cache (or memory), a process within SQL Server (called *lazy writer*) has to work extensively to maintain enough free internal memory pages within SQL Server. This consumes extra CPU cycles and performs additional physical disk I/O to write memory pages back to disk.

SQL Server Memory Management

SQL Server manages memory for databases, including memory requirements for data and query execution plans, in a large pool of memory called the *memory pool*. The memory pool consists of a collection of 8KB buffers to manage data pages and plan cache pages, free pages, and so forth. The memory pool is usually the largest portion of SQL Server memory. By default, SQL Server manages memory by growing or shrinking its memory pool size dynamically, maintaining free physical memory between 4MB and 10MB.

SQL Server can be configured for dynamic memory management from Enterprise Manager. This can be done from the memory folder of the SQL Server Properties (Configure) dialog box, as shown in Figure 2-2.

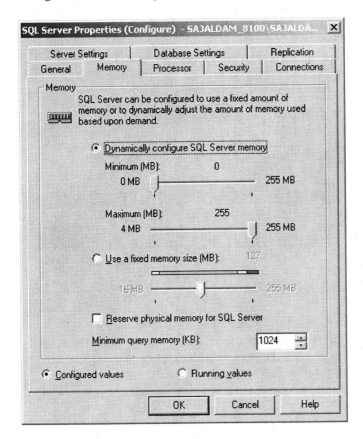

Figure 2-2. *SQL Server memory configuration*

The dynamic memory range is controlled through two configuration properties: `Minimum(MB)` and `Maximum(MB)`.

- `Minimum(MB)`, also known as `min server memory`, works as a floor value for the memory pool. Once the memory pool reaches the same size as the floor value, SQL Server can continue committing pages in the memory pool, but it cannot be shrunk below the floor value. Note that SQL Server does not start with the `min server memory` configuration value, but commits memory dynamically, as needed.

- `Maximum(MB)`, also known as `max server memory`, serves as a ceiling value to limit the maximum growth of the memory pool. These configuration settings take effect immediately and do not require a restart.

It is usually recommended that you use dynamic memory configuration for SQL Server, where min server memory will be 0 and max server memory will be the maximum physical memory of the system. You should not run other memory-intensive applications on the same server as SQL Server, but if you do, it is recommended that you configure min server memory to a good enough value, say 50% of the max server memory value, to prevent the other applications from starving SQL Server of memory.

The configuration values for min server memory and max server memory can also be managed using the sp_configure system stored procedure. To see the configuration values for these parameters, execute the sp_configure stored procedure as follows:

```
exec sp_configure 'min server memory (MB)'
exec sp_configure 'max server memory (MB)'
```

Figure 2-3 shows the result of running these commands.

name	minimum	maximum	config_value	run_value
min server memory (MB)	0	2147483647	0	0

name	minimum	maximum	config_value	run_value
max server memory (MB)	4	2147483647	2147483647	21474...

Figure 2-3. *SQL Server memory configuration properties*

Note that the default value for the min server memory setting is 0MB and for the max server memory setting it is 2147483647MB. Also, max server memory cannot be set below 4MB.

These configuration values can also be modified using the sp_configure stored procedure. For example, to set max server memory to 200MB and min server memory to 100MB, execute the following set of statements (set_memory.sql in the download):

```
USE master
EXEC sp_configure 'show advanced option', '1'
RECONFIGURE
exec sp_configure 'min server memory (MB)', 100
exec sp_configure 'max server memory (MB)', 200
RECONFIGURE WITH OVERRIDE
```

The min server memory and max server memory configurations are classified as advanced options. By default, the sp_configure stored procedure does not affect/display the advanced options. Setting show advanced option to 1 as shown previously enables the sp_configure stored procedure to affect/display the advanced options.

The RECONFIGURE statement updates the memory configuration values set by sp_configure. Since ad hoc updates to the system catalog containing the memory configuration values are not recommended, the OVERRIDE flag is used with the RECONFIGURE statement to force the memory configuration. If the memory configuration is done through Enterprise Manager, Enterprise Manager automatically executes the RECONFIGURE WITH OVERRIDE statement after the configuration setting.

In some rare circumstances, you may need to use a fixed memory size for SQL Server instead of the dynamic memory behavior. To elaborate, consider a computer with SQL Server and Exchange Server running on it. Both servers are heavy users of memory, and thus keep pushing each other for memory. The dynamic-memory behavior of SQL Server allows it to release memory to Exchange Server at one instance and grab it back as Exchange Server releases it. This dynamic-memory management overhead can be avoided by configuring SQL Server for fixed memory size. In such a case, you use the set working set size option of SQL Server, which fixes the physical memory space reserved for SQL Server. However, please keep in mind that since SQL Server is an extremely resource-intensive process, it is highly recommended that you run a production SQL Server on a dedicated machine.

Enabling this option means the operating system does not swap out the memory pages of SQL Server, even though those memory pages are not used for a long time and could be effectively used by another process. This option requires setting both min server memory and max server memory to the same value.

Now that you understand SQL Server memory management, let's consider the performance counters that we can use to analyze stress on memory, as shown in Table 2-1.

Table 2-1. *Perfmon Counters to Analyze Memory Pressure*

Object(Instance[,InstanceN])	Counter	Description	Values
Memory	Available MB	Free physical memory	Average value > 10MB.
	Pages/sec	Rate of hard page faults	Average value < 50.
	Page Faults/sec Pages Input/sec Pages Output/sec	Rate of total page faults Rate of input page faults Rate of output page faults	Compare with its baseline value for trend analysis.
SQLServer:Buffer Manager	Buffer cache hit ratio	Percentage of requests served out of buffer cache	Average value >= 90%.
	Free pages	Total number of free pages	Minimum value > 640.
SQLServer:Memory Manager	Memory Grants Pending	Number of processes waiting for memory grant	Average value = 0.
	Target Server Memory (KB)	Maximum physical memory SQL Server can consume on the box	Close to size of physical memory.
	Total Server Memory (KB)	Physical memory currently assigned to SQL Server	Close to Target Server Memory.

Let's walk through these counters to get a better idea of what you can use them for.

Available MB

This counter represents free physical memory in the system. For good performance, this counter value should not be too low. If SQL Server is configured for dynamic memory usage, then this value may be close to 4 to 10MB. Windows 2000 attempts to prevent this value from falling below 4MB. It often trims the working set of processes to maintain the 4MB minimum available memory.

Any value below 4MB is a big issue. If the value is less than 4MB but not under 2.5MB, it may be OK for very short time periods, but the cause of the memory stress still needs to be investigated. Extended periods below 4MB indicate that the system is out of physical memory; extensive paging will occur at that point (also called *memory thrashing*) and the system will drastically slow down.

Pages and Page Fault Counters

To understand the importance of these counters, you first need to learn about *page faults*. A page fault occurs when a process requires code or data that is not in its *working set* (its space in physical memory). It may lead to a *soft page fault* or a *hard page fault*. If the faulted page is found elsewhere in physical memory, then it is called soft page fault. A hard page fault occurs when a process requires code or data that is not in its working set or elsewhere in physical memory and must be retrieved from disk.

The speed of a disk access is in the order of milliseconds, whereas a memory access is in the order of nanoseconds. This huge difference in the speed between a disk access and a memory access makes the effect of hard page faults significant compared to that of soft page faults.

The Pages/sec counter represents the number of pages read from or written to disk per second to resolve hard page faults. The Page Faults/sec performance counter indicates total page faults per second—soft page faults plus hard page faults—handled by the system.

Hard page faults, indicated by Pages/sec, should not be consistently high. If this counter is very high, then SQL Server is probably starving other applications. As a general rule of thumb in Windows 2000, the rate of hard page faults should be below 50 per second on a system with a slow disk. On a fast disk subsystem, a hard page fault rate of even up to 300 per second may not be an issue.

If this counter is very high, then you may break it up into Pages Input/sec and Pages Output/sec:

- Pages Input/sec: An application will wait only on an input page, not on an output page.

- Pages Output/sec: Page output will stress the system, but an application usually does not see this stress. Pages output are usually represented by the application's dirty pages that need to be backed out to the disk. Pages Output/sec is an issue only when disk load become an issue.

Also, check Process:Page Faults/sec to find out which process is causing excessive paging in case of high Pages/sec. The Process object is the system component that provides performance data for the processes running on the system, which are individually represented by their corresponding instance name.

For example, the SQL Server process is represented by the sqlservr instance of the Process object. High numbers for this counter usually do not mean much unless Pages/sec is high. Page Faults/sec can range all over the spectrum with normal application behavior, with values from 0 to 1,000 per second within an acceptable range. This is where a baseline is essential to determine the expected normal behavior.

Buffer Cache Hit Ratio

Buffer cache is the pool of buffer pages into which data pages are read, and it is the biggest part of the SQL Server memory pool. This counter value should be 90% or more for OLTP applications. It is extremely common to find this counter value as 99% or more for most production servers. A Buffer cache hit ratio value of less than 90% indicates that only 90% of requests could be served out of the buffer cache, with the rest of the requests being served from disk.

When this happens, either SQL Server is still warming up or the memory requirement of the buffer cache cache is more than the maximum memory available for its growth.

Free Pages

If this counter value is well below 640 pages (about 5MB), then SQL Server is either running low on physical memory or the active portion of the buffer cache is very large. Note that this counter value is expressed in the number of 8KB pages in the cache that are not currently being used.

Memory Grants Pending

This counter represents the number of processes pending for a memory grant within SQL Server memory. If this counter value is high, then SQL Server is short of memory. Under normal conditions, this counter value should consistently be 0 for most of the production servers.

Target Server Memory (KB) and Total Server Memory (KB)

Target Server Memory indicates the total amount of dynamic memory SQL Server is willing to consume. Total Server Memory indicates the amount of memory currently assigned to SQL Server. The Total Server Memory counter value can be very high if the system is dedicated to SQL Server. If Total Server Memory is much less than Target Server Memory, then either the SQL Server memory requirement is low, the max server memory configuration parameter of SQL Server is set at too low a value, or the system is in *warm-up phase*. Warm-up phase is the period after SQL Server is started when the database server is in the process of expanding its memory allocation dynamically as more datasets are accessed, bringing more data pages into memory.

A low memory requirement from SQL Server can be confirmed by the presence of a large number of free pages, usually 5,000 or more.

Memory Bottleneck Resolutions

When there is high stress on memory, indicated by a large number of hard page faults, you can resolve memory bottleneck using the flowchart shown in Figure 2-4.

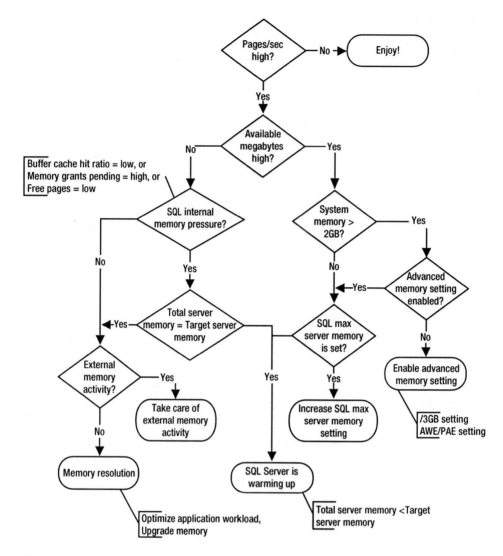

Figure 2-4. *Memory bottleneck resolution chart*

A few of the common resolutions for memory bottlenecks are as follows:

- Optimizing application workload

- Allocating more memory to SQL Server

- Increasing system memory

- Enabling 3GB of process space

- Using extended memory within SQL Server

Let's take a look at each of these in turn.

Optimizing Application Workload

Optimizing application workload is the most effective resolution most of the time, but because of the complexity and challenges involved in this process, it is usually considered last. To identify the memory-intensive queries, capture all the SQL queries using SQL Profiler (which you will learn how to use in Chapter 3), and then group the trace output on the Reads column. The queries with highest number of logical reads contribute to most of the memory stress. You will see how to optimize those queries in more detail throughout this book.

Allocating More Memory to SQL Server

As you learned in the "SQL Server Memory Management" section, the max server memory configuration can limit the maximum size of the SQL Server memory pool. If the memory requirement of SQL Server is more than the max server memory value, which you can tell through the number of hard page faults, then increasing the value will allow the memory pool to grow. To benefit from increasing the max server memory value, ensure that enough physical memory is available in the system.

Increasing System Memory

The memory requirement of SQL Server is dependent on the total amount of data processed by SQL activities. It is not directly correlated to the size of the database or the number of incoming SQL queries. For example, if a memory-intensive query performs a cross join between two small tables without any filter criteria to narrow down the result set, it can cause high stress on the system memory.

   One of the easiest and cheapest resolutions is to simply increase system memory. However, it is still important to find out what is consuming the physical memory, because if the application workload is extremely memory intensive, you will soon be limited by the maximum amount of memory a system can access.

Enabling 3GB of Process Space

Standard 32-bit addresses can map a maximum of 4GB of memory. The standard address spaces of 32-bit Microsoft Windows NT 4.0 and Windows 2000 processes are therefore limited to 4GB. Out of this 4GB process space, by default the upper 2GB is reserved for the operating system, and the lower 2GB is made available to the application. If you specify a /3GB switch in the boot.ini file of Windows NT 4.0 Enterprise Edition, Windows 2000 Advanced Server, or Windows 2000 Datacenter Server, the operating system reserves only 1GB of the address space, and the application can access up to 3GB. This is also called *4-Gig Tuning* (4GT). No new APIs are required for this purpose.

   Therefore, on a machine with 4GB of physical memory and the default Windows configuration, you will find available megabytes of around 2GB or more. To let SQL Server use up to 3GB of the available memory, we can add the /3GB switch in the boot.ini file as follows:

```
[boot loader]
timeout=30
default=multi(0)disk(0)rdisk(0)partition(1)\WINNT
[operating systems]
multi(0)disk(0)rdisk(0)partition(1)\WINNT="Microsoft Windows 2000 Advanced Server" ⏎
/fastdetect /3GB
```

   The /3GB switch should not be used for systems with more than 16GB of physical memory, as explained in the following section.

Using Extended Memory Within SQL Server

All processors based on the IA-32 architecture, beginning with the Intel Pentium Pro, support a new 36-bit physical addressing mode called Physical Address Extension (PAE). PAE allows up to 64GB of physical memory, depending upon the operating system. The PAE mode kernel requires an Intel Architecture processor (Pentium Pro or later), more than 4GB of RAM, and either Windows 2000 Advanced Server or Windows 2000 Datacenter Server.

Windows 2000 Advanced Server and Datacenter Server implement Address Windowing Extensions (AWE) to access up to 64GB of physical memory with the PAE addressing mode. Windows NT Server 4.0 Enterprise Edition uses a different mechanism to access extended memory beyond 4GB. It uses a feature known as PSE36 on Intel platforms. The PSE36 driver, by default, requires Intel Pentium II Xeon processors. The Windows 2000 kernel does not support the PSE36 driver.

SQL Server 2000 dropped SQL Server 7.0's driver model (PSE36 driver) in favor of directly supporting AWE. This allows SQL Server 2000 to manage the extended memory and the lower memory as a single buffer cache, unlike SQL Server 7.0. Therefore, SQL Server 2000 on Windows 2000 Advanced Server or Datacenter Server will be able to access memory beyond 4GB. On the negative side, SQL Server 2000 on Windows NT 4.0 Enterprise Edition will be limited to 4GB of memory addressing, including 1GB of system (or kernel) space reserved within its process space, since the Windows NT 4.0 kernel does not have the AWE feature.

From the preceding discussion, it can also be inferred that SQL Server 7.0 can access memory beyond 4GB on Windows NT 4.0 using the PSE36 driver, but since SQL Server 7.0 does not support AWE, it will be limited to 4GB memory addressing on Windows 2000, including the 1GB of system space reserved within its process space.

Accessing memory beyond 4GB in Windows 2000 requires configuration at two levels: the operating system level and the application level. To enable the operating system to access more than 4GB of physical memory, add a /PAE switch in the boot.ini file as follows:

```
[boot loader]
timeout=30
default=multi(0)disk(0)rdisk(0)partition(1)\WINNT
[operating systems]
multi(0)disk(0)rdisk(0)partition(1)\WINNT="Microsoft Windows 2000 Advanced Server"↵
/fastdetect /PAE
```

Once you have modified boot.ini, you can use sp_configure to enable SQL Server 2000 to access more than 4GB of physical memory. The following example (set_5GigMemory.sql in the download) shows how to enable 5GB:

```
sp_configure 'show advanced options', 1
RECONFIGURE
GO
sp_configure 'awe enabled', 1
RECONFIGURE
GO
sp_configure 'max server memory', 5120
RECONFIGURE
GO
```

The operating system must be restarted for the /PAE switch to take effect. The associated restart of SQL Server puts the AWE configuration into effect.

Instances of SQL Server 2000 do not dynamically manage the size of the address space when AWE memory is enabled; therefore, setting the max server memory configuration parameter of SQL Server is mandatory while using AWE memory. On a dedicated SQL Server machine, max server memory may be set to (total physical memory – 200MB) so that enough physical memory is kept aside for the operating system and other essential tools/applications.

While running multiple instances of SQL Server 2000 on the same computer, with each instance using AWE memory, you must ensure the following:

- Each instance has a max server memory setting.

- The sum of the max server memory values for all the instances is less than the amount of physical memory in the computer.

Considering the preceding factors, in a SQL Server 2000 cluster environment with two nodes and AWE/PAE enabled, the max server memory value on each node should be less than half of the system physical memory.

NOTE If you use the /3GB feature along with AWE/PAE, then an instance of SQL Server will be limited to a maximum of 16GB of extended memory.

This limitation is due to the internal design of the Windows 2000 operating system. Limiting the system space within the process space to 1GB using the /3GB switch allows the Windows 2000 operating system to manage physical memory up to 16GB. Therefore, to access memory beyond 16GB, the /3GB switch should not be used.

Disk Bottleneck Analysis

SQL Server is a heavy user of the hard disk, and since disk speeds are comparatively much slower than memory and processor speeds, a contention in disk resources can significantly degrade SQL Server performance. Analysis and resolution of any disk resource bottleneck can improve SQL Server performance significantly.

Disk Counters

To analyze disk performance, you can use the counters shown in Table 2-2.

Table 2-2. *Perfmon Counters to Analyze I/O Pressure*

Object(Instance[,InstanceN])	Counter	Description	Value
PhysicalDisk(Data-disk, Log-disk)	% Disk Time	Percentage of time disk was busy	Average value < 5%
	Current Disk Queue Length	Number of outstanding disk requests at the time performance data is collected	Average value < 2 per disk
	Avg. Disk Queue Length	Average number of queued disk requests during the sample interval	Average value < 2 per disk
	Disk Transfers/sec	Rate of read/write operations on disk	Maximum value < 100 per disk
	Disk Bytes/sec	Amount of data transfer to/from disk per second	Maximum value < 10MB/sec. per disk

Prior to analyzing disk utilization, make sure that disk counters are enabled by running `diskperf -y` from a command prompt to enable both logical and physical disk counters:

```
C:\>diskperf -y
```

The `diskperf` settings become effective on the next system restart. You can check that the counters are running by verifying the presence of nonzero values for the `% Disk Time` counter for the `PhysicalDisk` or `LogicalDisk` objects as required.

The `PhysicalDisk` counters represent the activities on a physical disk. `LogicalDisk` counters represent logical subunits (or partitions) created on a physical disk. If you create two partitions, say `C:` and `D:` on a physical disk, then you can monitor the disk activities of the individual logical disks using logical disk counters. However, as a disk bottleneck ultimately occurs on the physical disk, not on the logical disk, it is usually preferable to use the `PhysicalDisk` counters.

In Windows 2000, `PhysicalDisk` counters are enabled by default. In Windows NT 4.0, considering the overhead physical-disk counters may add to system utilization, they were disabled by default. However, even though enabling the disk counters does consume some resources on the database server, it is still worth running the `diskperf -y` command on all production SQL Servers, so that disk queuing problems can be confirmed immediately and all the performance monitor counters are immediately available to diagnose disk I/O issues. To obtain help on `diskperf`, execute `diskperf /?`.

Note that for a hardware redundant array of independent disks (RAID) subsystem (see the "RAID Array" section for more on RAID), the counters treat the array as a single physical disk. For example, even if you have ten disks in a RAID configuration, they will all be represented as one physical disk to the operating system, and subsequently you will have only one set of `PhysicalDisk` counters for that RAID subsystem.

% Disk Time

This counter monitors the percentage of time the disk is busy with read/write activities. It should not be continuously high. If this counter value is consistently more than 85%, then you must take steps to bring it down. You could upgrade the disk subsystem, but a more effective solution would be to avoid going to the data disk as much as possible. Even a consistent disk usage of 5% may adversely affect performance.

For performance, it is always beneficial to cache the disk contents in memory since disk access is in the order of milliseconds, whereas memory access is in the order of nanoseconds. SQL Server adopts this strategy by caching the data pages in its buffer cache. But if SQL Server has to go to disk often, as indicated by a high % Disk Time value, then the slow access time of the disk compared to that of the memory will hurt the performance of the database.

Current Disk Queue Length

Current Disk Queue Length is the number of requests outstanding on the disk subsystem at the time the performance data is collected. It includes requests in service at the time of the snapshot. A disk subsystem will have only one disk queue. This counter value should be used to support the conclusion made from the % Disk Time counter. A consistent disk queue length of 2 per disk indicates a bottleneck on the disk.

For example, in a RAID configuration with 10 disks, a consistent disk queue length of 2 per disk or 20 (= 10 disks × 2 per disks) for the complete disk subsystem is an indication of a disk bottleneck. RAID controllers usually distribute disk I/Os uniformly across all disks in the disk subsystem, but due to the obvious chances of nonuniform disk I/O, consider the following range of values for the Current Disk Queue Length counter:

- Less than (2 + # of spindles) is an excellent value to see. In the worst case, the two requests in the queue may be pending on the same disk.

- Less than (2 × # of spindles) is a fair value to see. In the best case, the queued requests may be uniformly distributed across all the disks in the disk subsystem with two requests pending per disk.

If you do not suspect dynamic variation in disk loads, then you may use the Avg. Disk Queue Length counter since this counter represents the average of the instantaneous values provided by the Current Disk Queue Length counter.

Disk Transfers/sec

This counter monitors the rate of read and write operations on the disk. A typical disk today can do around 180 disk transfers per second for sequential I/O and 100 disk transfers per second for random I/O. In the case of random I/O, Disk Transfers/sec is lower because more disk arm and head movements are involved. OLTP workloads, which are workloads for doing mainly singleton operations, small operations, and random access, are typically constrained by disk transfers per second. So in the case of an OLTP workload, you are more constrained by the fact that a disk can do only 100 disk transfers per second than by its throughput specification of 10MB per second.

Due to the inherent slowness of a disk, it is recommended that you keep disk transfers per second as low as possible. You will see how to do this next.

Disk Bytes/sec

This counter monitors the rate at which bytes are transferred to or from the disk during read or write operations. A typical disk can transfer around 10MB per second. Generally, OLTP applications are not constrained by the disk transfer capacity of the disk subsystem since the OLTP applications access small amounts of data in individual database requests. If the amount of data transfer exceeds the capacity of the disk subsystem, then a backlog starts developing on the disk subsystem, as reflected by the disk queue length counters.

Disk Bottleneck Resolutions

A few of the common disk bottleneck resolutions are as follows:

- Optimizing application workload

- Using a faster disk drive

- Using a RAID array

- Using a battery-backed controller cache

- Adding system memory

- Creating multiple files and filegroups

- Placing the table and the index for that table on different disks

- Saving the log file to a separate physical drive

- Creating the `tempdb` on RAID 0

Let's consider each of these resolutions in turn.

Optimizing Application Workload

I cannot stress enough how important it is to optimize an application's workload in resolving a performance issue. The queries with highest number of reads will be the ones that cause a great deal of disk I/O. The strategies for optimizing those queries are covered in more detail throughout the rest of this book.

Using a Faster Disk Drive

One of the easiest resolutions, and one that you will adopt most of the time, is to use disk drives with higher disk transfers per second speeds. However, you should not just upgrade disk drives without further investigation; you need to find out what is causing the stress on the disk.

Using a RAID Array

One way of obtaining disk I/O parallelism is to create a single pool of drives to serve all SQL Server database files, excluding transaction log files. The pool can be a single RAID array, which is represented in Windows NT/2000 as a single physical disk drive. The effectiveness of a drive pool depends on the configuration of the RAID disks.

Out of all available RAID configurations, the most commonly used RAID configurations are the following (see Figure 2-5):

- *RAID 0*: Striping with no fault tolerance

- *RAID 1*: Mirroring

- *RAID 5*: Striping with parity

- *RAID 0+1*: Striping with mirroring

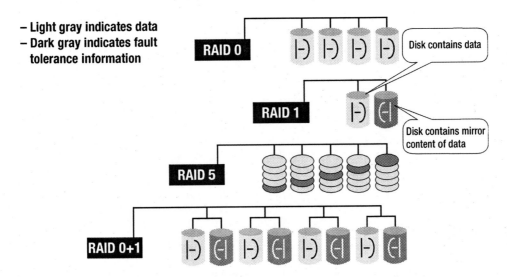

Figure 2-5. *RAID configurations*

RAID 0

Since this RAID configuration has no fault tolerance, it can be used only in situations where reliability of data is not a concern. The failure of any disk in the array will cause complete data loss in the disk subsystem. Therefore, it cannot be used for any data file or transaction log file that constitutes a database, except for the system temporary database called tempdb.

The number of I/Os per disk in RAID 0 is represented by the following equation:

I/Os per disk = (Reads + Writes) / Number of disks in the array

In this equation, "Reads" is the number of read requests to the disk subsystem, and "Writes" is the number of write requests to the disk subsystem.

I discuss using RAID 0 for tempdb later in this chapter.

RAID 1

RAID 1 provides high fault tolerance for critical data by mirroring the data disk onto a separate disk. It can be used where the complete data can be accommodated in one disk only. Database transaction log files for user databases, operating system files, and SQL Server system databases (master and msdb) are usually small enough to use RAID 1.

The number of I/Os per disk in RAID 1 is represented by the following equation:

$$\text{I/Os per disk} = (\text{Reads} + 2 \times \text{Writes}) / 2$$

RAID 5

This configuration is a good option in many cases. It provides reasonable fault tolerance by effectively using only one extra disk to save the computed parity of the data in other disks, as shown in Figure 2-5. When there is a disk failure in a RAID 5 configuration, I/O performance becomes terrible, although the system does remain usable while operating with the failed drive.

Any data where writes make up more than 10% of total disk requests is not a good candidate for RAID 5. Thus, use RAID 5 on read-only volumes or volumes with a low percentage of disk writes.

The number of I/Os per disk in RAID 5 is represented by the following equation:

$$\text{I/Os per disk} = (\text{Reads} + 4 \times \text{Writes}) / \text{Number of disks in the array}$$

As shown in the preceding equation, the write operations on RAID 5 disk subsystem are magnified four times. For each incoming write request, the following are the four corresponding I/O requests on the disk subsystem:

- One read I/O to read existing data from the data disk whose content is to be modified

- One read I/O to read existing parity information from the corresponding parity disk

- One write I/O to write the new data to the data disk whose content is to be modified

- One write I/O to write the new parity information to the corresponding parity disk

Therefore, the four I/Os for each write request consist of two read I/Os and two write I/Os.

In an OLTP database, all the data modifications are immediately written to the transaction log file as a part of the database transaction, but the data in the data file itself is synchronized with the transaction log file content asynchronously in batch operations. This operation is managed by an internal process of SQL Server called the *checkpoint* process. The frequency of this operation can be controlled by using the recovery interval (min) configuration parameter of SQL Server.

Because of the continuous write operation in the transaction log file for a highly transactional OLTP database, placing transaction log files on a RAID 5 array will significantly degrade the array's performance. Although you should not place the transactional log files on a RAID 5 array, the data files may be placed on RAID 5, since the write operations to the data files are intermittent and batched together to improve efficiency of the write operation.

RAID 0+1

RAID 0+1 (also referred to as 1+0 and 10) configuration offers a high degree of fault tolerance by mirroring each and every data disk in the array. It is a much more expensive solution than RAID 5, since double the number of data disks are required to provide fault tolerance. This RAID configuration should be used where a large volume is required to save data and more than 10% of disk requests are writes. Since RAID 0+1 supports *split seeks* (the ability to distribute the read operations onto the data disk and the mirror disk and then converge the two data streams), read performance is also very good. Thus, use RAID 0+1 wherever performance is critical.

The number of I/Os per disk in RAID 0+1 is represented by the following equation:

$$\text{I/Os per disk} = (\text{Reads} + 2 \times \text{Writes}) / \text{Number of disks in the array}$$

Using a Battery-Backed Controller Cache

For best performance, use a caching RAID controller for SQL Server files, because the controller guarantees that data entrusted to it is written to disk eventually, no matter how large the queue is, or even if power fails. When using a controller cache, the write requests to the RAID controller are written to the controller cache, and the subsequent disk operations are scheduled asynchronously. This asynchronous technique of doing I/Os for the write requests improves the performance of database queries significantly. The amount of performance improvement depends on the size of the controller cache and number of write requests.

When there is an unreliable battery backup, a power disruption will cause a loss of new/modified data (i.e., dirty data) in the controller cache that was not flushed to the disk. If this dirty data belonged to a committed transaction, then the consistency of the data will be compromised.

For example, if a user commits a database transaction, the dirty data for the transaction will be written to the controller cache, and the user will be informed about a successful completion of the transaction. But should the power go down before this committed data is written to the disk, then all the data in the cache will be lost unless the controller has a reliable battery backup.

To avoid data inconsistency, ensure from your disk vendor that the controller cache has a reliable battery backup.

Adding System Memory

When physical memory is scarce, the system starts writing the contents of memory back to disk and reading smaller blocks of data more frequently, causing a lot of paging. The less memory the system has, the more the disk subsystem is used. This can be resolved using the memory bottleneck resolutions enumerated in the previous section.

Creating Multiple Files and Filegroups

In SQL Server, each user database consists of one or more data files and one or more transaction log files. The data files belonging to a database can be grouped together in one or more filegroups for administrative and data allocation/placement purposes. For example, if a data file is placed in a separate filegroup, then write access to all the tables in the filegroup can be controlled collectively by making the filegroup read-only. (Transaction log files do not belong to any filegroup.)

A filegroup for a database can be created from SQL Server Enterprise Manager as shown in Figure 2-6. The filegroups of a database are presented in the Filegroups pane of the database Properties dialog box.

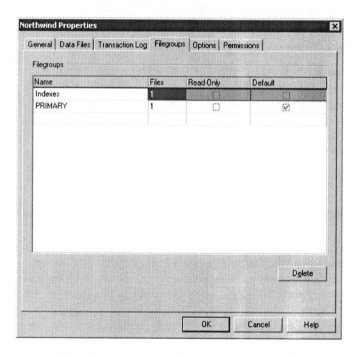

Figure 2-6. *Filegroups configuration*

In Figure 2-6, you can see that the index and the primary data file are in separate filegroups. These separate filegroups can now be saved onto separate disks, and a system with multiple processors can perform parallel scans on the different filegroups.

You can add a data file to a filegroup from the Data Files pane by clicking the Location ellipsis, as shown in Figure 2-7.

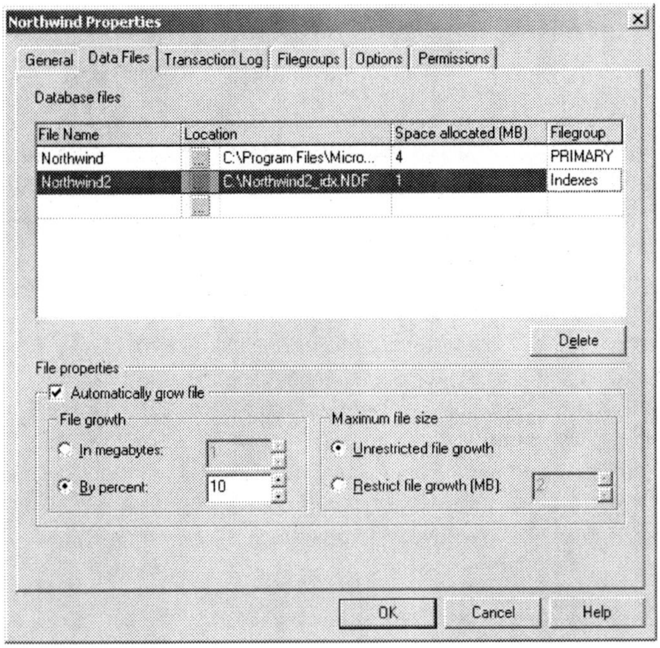

Figure 2-7. *Data files configuration*

You can also do this programmatically, as follows (`filegroup.sql` in the download):

```
ALTER DATABASE Northwind
ADD FILEGROUP Indexes
GO
ALTER DATABASE Northwind
ADD FILE
(NAME = Northwind2,
  FILENAME = 'C:\Northwind2_idx.ndf',
  SIZE = 1MB,
  FILEGROWTH = 10%)
TO FILEGROUP Indexes
```

In a system with multiple processors, SQL Server can take advantage of multiple files and filegroups by performing multiple parallel scans on the data files. As tables in a file are accessed sequentially, a thread is created to read the associated data file. If a filegroup consists of four data files, then four threads will be created to read data in parallel. If the data files are placed on four different physical disks, then all the disk spindles can work simultaneously. Therefore, in a multidisk subsystem, it is usually advantageous to have multiple files in the filegroup.

Using multiple files and filegroups also enables you to improve the performance of join operations. By separating tables that are frequently joined into separate filegroups, you allow each table to be read in parallel, improving query performance. For example, consider the following query:

```
SELECT * FROM t1, t2
WHERE t1.c1 = t2.c2
```

If the tables t1 and t2 are placed in separate filegroups containing one file each, then on a multiple processor system a separate thread will be created for each table. With the files of the two filegroups on different physical disks, data from both the tables can be retrieved simultaneously.

It is recommended for performance and recovery purposes that, if multiple filegroups are to be used, the primary filegroup should be used only for system objects, and secondary filegroups should be used only for user objects. This approach improves disk I/O and the ability to recover from corruption. The recoverability of a database is higher if the primary data file and the log files are intact. Use the primary filegroup for system databases only, and store all user-related databases on a secondary filegroup.

Spreading a database into multiple files, even onto the same drive, makes it easy to move the database files onto separate drives, making future disk upgrades easier. For example, to move a user database file (Northwind_idx.ndf) to a new disk subsystem (F:), you may follow these steps:

1. Detach the user database as follows (file_move.sql in the code download):

   ```
   USE master
   GO
   sp_detach_db 'northwind'
   GO
   ```

2. Copy the data file Northwind_idx.ndf to a folder F:\Data\ on the new disk subsystem.

3. Reattach the user database by referring files at appropriate locations as shown here:

   ```
   USE master
   GO
   sp_attach_db 'northwind'
   , 'D:\Data\Northwind_Data.mdf'
   , 'F:\Data\Northwind_idx.ndf'
   , 'E:\Log\Northwind_Log.ldf'
   GO
   ```

4. To verify the files belonging to a database, execute the following commands:

   ```
   USE northwind
   GO
   sp_helpfile
   GO
   ```

Placing the Table and Index on Separate Disks

If a system has multiple processors, SQL Server can take advantage of multiple filegroups by accessing tables and corresponding nonclustered indexes in parallel. A nonclustered index can be created on a specific filegroup as follows:

```
CREATE INDEX i1 ON t1 (c1) ON Indexes
```

▧**TIP** The nonclustered index and other types of indexes are explained in Chapter 4.

Saving Log Files to a Separate Physical Disk

SQL Server log files should always, where possible, be located on a separate hard disk drive from all other SQL Server database files. Transaction log activity primarily consists of sequential write I/O, unlike the nonsequential (or random) I/O required for the data files. Separating transaction log activity from other nonsequential disk I/O activity can result in I/O performance improvements, as it allows the hard disk drives containing log files to concentrate on sequential I/O.

The major portion of time required to access data from a hard disk is spent on the physical movement of the disk spindle head to locate the data. Once the data is located, the data is read electronically, which is much faster than the physical movement of the head. With only sequential I/O operations on the log disk, the spindle head of the log disk can write to the log disk with a minimum of physical movement. If the same disk is used for data files, however, the spindle head has to move to the correct location before writing to the log file. This increases the time required to write to the log file and thereby hurts performance.

Furthermore, for SQL Server with multiple OLTP databases, the transaction log files should be physically separated from each other on different physical drives to improve performance.

An exception to this requirement is a read-only database or a database with very few database changes. Since no online changes are made to the read-only database, no write operations are performed on the log file. Therefore, having the log file on a separate disk is not required for the read-only databases.

Creating tempdb on RAID 0

Besides the user databases that you create, a SQL Server system contains the following system databases:

- `master`: Serves as a systemwide catalog that includes system-level information on configuration settings, login accounts, and so on. Without a `master` database, no user database can be accessed.

- `msdb`: Maintains information about SQL alerts and jobs.

- `model`: Template used by SQL Server to create a new database.

- tempdb: Serves as a global space to manage all temporary resources such as temporary tables, temporary stored procedures, worktables used intermediately while executing a query, and so forth. SQL Server cannot work without the tempdb. This system database is rebuilt (to its initial size) from scratch from the model template every time SQL Server is restarted.

Because tempdb is write-intensive, RAID 5 is not as good a choice for tempdb as RAID 1 or 0+1. Since the tempdb database only contains temporary resources and is rebuilt every time SQL Server is restarted, the fault tolerance for tempdb content is not very critical. So, RAID 0 is a possibility for obtaining the best RAID performance for the tempdb database. The concern with using RAID 0 for tempdb is that the SQL Server machine must be restarted if any disk in the RAID 0 array fails. A system restart allows the RAID controller to rebuild the RAID 0 array by excluding the failed disk. A system restart is not required if tempdb is placed on a RAID 1 or 0+1 array.

Processor Bottleneck Analysis

SQL Server 2000 makes heavy use of any processor resource available. You can use the system monitor counters in Table 2-3 to analyze pressure on the processor resource.

Table 2-3. *Perfmon Counters to Analyze CPU Pressure*

Object(Instance[,InstanceN])	Counter	Description	Value
Processor(_Total)	% Processor Time	Percentage of time processor was busy	Average value < 80%
	% Privileged Time	Percentage of processor time spent in privileged mode	Average value < 10%
System	Processor Queue Length	Number of requests outstanding on the processor	Average value < 2
	Context Switches/sec	Rate at which processor is switched from one thread to another	Average value < 1,000 per processor

Let's look at these counters in more detail.

% Processor Time

% Processor Time should not be consistently high (> 80%). The effect of any sustained processor time over 90% is the same as that with 100%. If % Processor Time is consistently high, and disk and network counter values are low, your first priority must be to optimize the stress on the processor.

For example, if the % Processor Time is 85% and the % Disk Time is 50%, then it is quite likely that a major part of the processor time is spent on managing the disk activities. This will be reflected in the `% Privileged Time` of the processor as explained in the next section. In that case, it will be advantageous to optimize the disk bottleneck first. Further, remember that the disk bottleneck in turn can be because of a memory bottleneck, as explained earlier in the chapter.

% Privileged Time

Processing on a Windows server is done in two modes: *user mode* and *privileged* (or *kernel*) mode. All system-level activities, including disk access, are done in privileged mode. If you find a `% Privileged Time` on a dedicated SQL Server system of 20–25% or more, then the system is probably doing a lot of I/O—likely more than you need. The `% Privileged Time` on a dedicated SQL Server system should be at most 5–10%.

Processor Queue Length

`Processor Queue Length` is the number of threads in the processor queue. (There is a single processor queue, even on computers with multiple processors.) Unlike the disk counters, this counter does not read threads that are already running. On systems with lower CPU utilization, the `Processor Queue Length` is typically 0 or 1. In SQL Server 2000 with the `lightweight pooling` configuration parameter `ON`, the typical processor queue length will range between 0 and 1, because there is a single thread on each processor that schedules fibers within the thread.

> ▓**NOTE** I cover the `lightweight pooling` feature of SQL Server in the "Processor Bottleneck Resolutions" section of this chapter.

A sustained `Processor Queue Length` of > 2 generally indicates processor congestion. Although a high `% Processor Time` indicates a busy processor, a sustained high `Processor Queue Length` is a more certain indicator. If the recommended value is exceeded, this generally indicates that there are more threads ready to run than the current number of processors can service in an optimal way.

Context Switches/sec

This counter monitors the combined rate at which all processors on the computer are switched from one thread to another. A context switch occurs when a running thread voluntarily relinquishes the processor, is preempted by a higher priority ready thread, or switches between user mode and privileged mode to use an executive or subsystem service. It is the sum of `Thread:Context Switches/sec` for all threads running on all processors in the computer, and it is measured in numbers of switches.

A figure of 300 to 1,000 `Context Switches/sec` per processor is excellent to fair. Abnormally high rates can be caused by page faults due to memory starvation.

Processor Bottleneck Resolutions

A few of the common processor bottleneck resolutions are as follows:

- Optimizing application workload

- Using more or faster processors

- Using a large L2 cache

- Running with more efficient controllers/drivers

- Not running a screen saver

- Using lightweight pooling or NT fibers

Let's consider each of these resolutions in turn.

Optimizing Application Workload

To identify the processor-intensive queries, capture all the SQL queries using SQL Profiler (which I will discuss in the next chapter), and then group the Profiler trace output on the CPU column. The queries with the highest amount of CPU time contribute the most to the CPU stress. You should then analyze and optimize those queries to reduce stress on the CPU. Most of the rest of the chapters in this book are concerned with optimizing application workload.

Using More or Faster Processors

One of the easiest resolutions, and one that you will adopt most of the time, is to increase system processing power. However, due to the high cost involved in a processor upgrade, you should first optimize CPU-intensive operations as much as possible.

The system's processing power can be increased by increasing the power of individual processors or by adding more processors. When you have a high % Processor Time and a low Processor Queue Length, it makes sense to increase the power of individual processors. In the case of both a high % Processor Time and a high Processor Queue Length, you should consider adding more processors. Increasing the number of processors allows the system to execute more requests simultaneously.

Using a Large L2 Cache

Modern processors have become so much faster than memory that they need at least two levels of memory cache to reduce latency. On Pentium-class machines, the fast L1 cache holds 8KB of data and 8KB of instructions, while the slower L2 cache holds several hundred kilobytes of mixed code and data. A reference to content found in the L1 cache costs one cycle, and references to the L2 cache cost four to seven cycles, whereas references to the main memory cost dozens of processor cycles. With the increase in processing power, the latter figure will soon exceed 100 cycles. In many ways, the caches are like a small, fast, virtual memory inside the processor.

Database engines like L2 caches because they keep processing off the system bus. The processor does not have to go through the system bus to access memory; it can work out of the L2 cache. Not having enough L2 cache can cause the processor to wait a longer period of time for the data/code to move from the main memory to the L2 cache. A processor with a high clock speed but a low L2 cache may waste a large number of CPU cycles waiting on the small L2 cache. A large L2 cache helps maximize the use of CPU cycles for actual processing instead of waiting on the L2 cache.

Today, it is very common to have megabyte caches on four-way systems. With new four- and eight-way systems, you will often get a 2MB L2 cache. For example, sometimes you may get a performance improvement of 20% or more, simply by using a 512KB L2 cache instead of a 256KB L2 cache.

Running More Efficient Controllers/Drivers

There is a big difference in `% Privileged Time` consumption between different controllers and controller drivers on the market today. The techniques used by controller drivers to do I/O are quite different and consume different amounts of CPU time. If you can change to a controller that frees up 4–5% of `% Privileged Time`, you can improve performance.

Not Running a Screen Saver

If you have screen savers running on your system, they may use a large amount of processor time. This is particularly true of screen savers that use OpenGL (a software interface that supports production of high-quality, three-dimensional color imaging), as they can easily take away 15% of processor time on a server that lacks an OpenGL graphics card. As you can run your servers with the monitor switched off for the majority of the time, simply disable any screen savers on your server or, as a preventive measure, use the blank screen saver. Please do remember to lock your server for security.

Using Lightweight Pooling or NT Fibers

The part of the operating system that manages threads for multitasking executes in the kernel mode. Switching threads for multitasking requires transitions between user mode and kernel mode, which is a moderately expensive operation. The fibers in the Windows operating system are a subcomponent of threads and are managed in user mode. Switching fibers for multitasking does not require the user mode to kernel mode transition needed to switch threads. Each thread can have multiple fibers. The scheduling of the fibers is managed by the application, and the thread scheduling is managed by the operating system.

The `lightweight pooling` feature of SQL Server uses Windows NT fiber support to essentially run several user activities within a single thread. In theory, this can reduce thread context switches and help performance. Enabling lightweight pooling is beneficial only if all of the following conditions are met:

- Large, multi-CPU server

- All processors running near maximum capacity

- A lot of context switches per second (over 1,000 per processor)

To enable `lightweight pooling` in SQL Server 2000, execute the following SQL commands:

```
sp_configure 'show advanced options', 1
RECONFIGURE
GO
sp_configure 'lightweight pooling', 1
RECONFIGURE
GO
```

This setting takes effect after stopping and restarting SQL server.

Since the fiber scheduling has to be done by SQL Server instead of the operating system, it adds overhead on SQL Server. Therefore, whether or not enabling lightweight pooling will be actually beneficial must be determined through careful, controlled testing. Actual production experience shows that taking this step is not necessary under most conditions, unless the overhead of switching thread contexts is very high. You may get up to a 5% performance benefit on a system with a large number of CPUs and a high number of context switches per second.

Network Bottleneck Analysis

In SQL Server OLTP production environments, you find few performance issues due to problems with the network. Most of the network issues you face in the OLTP environment are in fact hardware or driver limitations, or issues with switches or routers. Most of these issues can be best diagnosed with the Network Monitor tool. However, System Monitor also provides objects that collect data on network activity, as shown in Table 2-4.

Table 2-4. *Perfmon Counter to Analyze Network Pressure*

Object(Instance[,InstanceN])	Counter	Description	Value
Network Interface(Network card)	Bytes Total/sec	Rate at which bytes are transferred on the NIC	Average value < 50% of NIC capacity
Network Segment	% Net Utilization	Percentage of network bandwidth in use on a network segment	Average value < 80% of network bandwidth

Bytes Total/sec

You can use this counter to determine how the network interface card (NIC) or network adapter is performing. The `Bytes Total/sec` counter should report high values, to indicate a large number of successful transmissions. Compare this value with that reported by the `Network Interface\Current Bandwidth` performance counter, which reflects each adapter's bandwidth.

To allow headroom for spikes in traffic, you should usually average no more than 50% of capacity. If this number is close to the capacity of the connection, and processor and memory use are moderate, then the connection may well be a problem.

% Net Utilization

This counter represents the percentage of network bandwidth in use on a network segment. The threshold for this counter depends on the type of network. For Ethernet networks, for example, 30% is the recommended threshold when SQL Server is on a shared network hub. For SQL Server on a dedicated full-duplex network, even though near 100% usage of the network is acceptable, it is advantageous to keep the network utilization below an acceptable threshold to keep room for the spikes in the load.

NOTE You must install the Network Monitor Driver to collect performance data using the Network Segment object counters.

In Windows 2000, the Network Monitor Driver can be installed from the local area connection properties for the network adapter. The Network Monitor Driver is available in the network protocol list of network components for the network adapter.

Network Bottleneck Resolutions

A few of the common network bottleneck resolutions are as follows:

- Optimizing application workload

- Adding network adapters

- Moderating and avoiding interruptions

Let's consider these resolutions in more detail.

Optimizing Application Workload

To optimize network traffic between a database application and a database server, make the following design changes in the application:

- Instead of sending a long SQL string, create a stored procedure for the SQL query. Then, you just need to send over the network the name of the stored procedure and its parameters.

- Group multiple database requests into one stored procedure. Then, only one database request will be required across the network for the set of SQL queries implemented in the stored procedure.

- Request a small dataset. Do not request table columns that are not used in the application logic.

- Move data-intensive business logic into the database as stored procedures or database triggers, to reduce network round-trips.

Adding Network Adapters

You may add network adapters so that you have one network adapter per processor. Generally, you should add a network adapter only if you need the increased bandwidth, because each additional network adapter has some intrinsic overhead. However, if one of the processors is nearly always active (that is, Processor\% Processor Time consistently equals 100%) and more than half of its time is spent servicing deferred procedure calls (that is, Processor\% DPC Time exceeds 50%), then adding a network card is likely to improve system performance.

If a network adapter does not use Network Driver Interface Specification (NDIS) miniport drivers, you cannot modify the distribution of deferred procedure calls (DPCs) for better performance. An NDIS miniport driver (also called a *miniport driver*) manages a NIC and interfaces with higher-level drivers. It communicates with its NIC and higher-level drivers through the NDIS library.

To be able to modify the distribution of DPCs, and because other NDIS optimizations might be unavailable, you may consider upgrading an individual network adapter instead of adding a new adapter.

Moderating and Avoiding Interruptions

When adding or upgrading network adapters, choose adapters with drivers that support *interrupt moderation* and/or *interrupt avoidance*. Interrupt moderation allows a processor to process interrupts more efficiently by grouping several interrupts into a single hardware interrupt. Interrupt avoidance allows a processor to continue processing interrupts without new interrupts queued until all pending interrupts are completed.

SQL Server Overall Performance

To analyze the overall performance of a SQL Server, besides examining hardware resource utilization, you should also examine some general aspects of SQL Server itself. You may use the performance counters presented in Table 2-5.

Table 2-5. *Perfmon Counters to Analyze Generic SQL Pressure*

Object(Instance[,InstanceN])	Counter
SQLServer:Access Methods	FreeSpace Scans/sec Full Scans/sec
SQLServer:Latches	Total Latch Wait Time (ms)
SQLServer:Locks(_Total)	Lock Timeouts/sec Lock Wait Time (ms) Number of Deadlocks/sec
SQLServer:SQL Statistics	Batch Requests/sec SQL Re-Compilations/sec
SQLServer:General Statistics	User Connections

Let's take a look at each of these counters in context.

Missing Indexes

To analyze the possibility of missing indexes causing table scans or large dataset retrievals, you can look at the counters in Table 2-6.

Table 2-6. *Perfmon Counter to Analyze Excessive Data Scans*

Object(Instance[,InstanceN])	Counter
SQLServer:Access Methods	FreeSpace Scans/sec Full Scans/sec

FreeSpace Scans/sec

This counter represents inserts into a table with no physical ordering of its rows—such a table is also called a *heap table*. Inserts into a heap table are usually subjected to performance problems due to the space allocation algorithm used by SQL Server 2000. Therefore, it is usually recommended that you physically order the table rows by using a clustered index on the table. You will learn about heap tables and clustered indexes in Chapter 5.

Full Scans/sec

This counter monitors the number of unrestricted full scans on base tables or indexes. A few of the main causes of high Full Scans/sec are

- Missing indexes

- Too many rows requested

To further investigate queries producing the preceding problems, use SQL Profiler to identify the queries (I will cover this tool in the next chapter). Queries with missing indexes or too many rows requested will have a large number of logical reads and an increased CPU time.

Be aware of the fact that full scans may be performed for the temporary tables used in a stored procedure, because most of the time you will not have indexes (or you will not need indexes) on temporary tables. Still, adding this counter to the baseline helps identify the possible increase in the use of temporary tables, which are usually not good for performance.

Database Blocking

To analyze the impact of database blocking on the performance of SQL Server, you can use the counters shown in Table 2-7.

Table 2-7. *Perfmon Counters to Analyze SQL Server Locking*

Object(Instance[,InstanceN])	Counter
SQLServer:Latches	Total Latch Wait Time (ms)
SQLServer:Locks(_Total)	Lock Timeouts/sec Lock Wait Time (ms) Number of Deadlocks/sec

Total Latch Wait Time (ms)

Latches are used internally by SQL Server to protect the integrity of internal structures, such as a table row, and are not directly controlled by users. This counter monitors total latch wait time (in milliseconds) for latch requests that had to wait in the last second. A high value for this counter indicates that SQL Server is spending too much time waiting on its internal synchronization mechanism.

When you have a SQL Server 7.0 database, upgrading to SQL Server 2000 is an applicable solution, since a lot of design and implementation enhancements have been made in SQL Server 2000 to reduce latch overheads.

Lock Timeouts/sec and Lock Wait Time (ms)

You should expect Lock Timeouts/sec to be 0 and Lock Wait Time to be very low. A nonzero value for Lock Timeouts/sec and a high value for Lock Wait Time indicate that excessive blocking is occurring in the database.

Two approaches can be adopted in this case:

- First, you can identify the costly queries using SQL Profiler and optimize them appropriately.

- Second, you can use blocking analysis to diagnose the cause of excessive blocking. It is usually advantageous to concentrate on optimizing the costly queries first, because this, in turn, reduces blocking for others. In Chapter 12, you will learn how to analyze and resolve blocking.

Number of Deadlocks/sec

You should expect to see a 0 value for this counter. If you find a nonzero value, then you should identify the victimized request and either resubmit the database request automatically suggest that the user do so. More importantly, an attempt should be made to troubleshoot and resolve the deadlock. Again, Chapter 12 shows how to do this.

Nonreusable Execution Plans

Since generating an execution plan for a stored procedure query requires CPU cycles, the stress on the CPU can be reduced by reusing the execution plan. To analyze the nonreusability of a stored procedure execution plan, you can look at the counter in Table 2-8.

Table 2-8. *Perfmon Counter to Analyze Execution Plan Reusability*

Object(Instance[,InstanceN])	Counter
SQLServer:SQL Statistics	SQL Re-Compilations/se c

SQL Re-Compilations/sec

Recompilations of stored procedures add overhead on the processor. You should see a value close to zero for this counter. If you consistently see nonzero values, then you should use SQL Profiler to further investigate the stored procedures undergoing recompilations. Once you identify the relevant stored procedures, an attempt should be made to analyze and resolve the cause of recompilations. In Chapter 10, you will learn how to analyze and resolve various causes of recompilation.

General Behavior

SQL Server provides additional performance counters to track some general aspects of a SQL Server system. A few of the most commonly used counters are shown in Table 2-9.

Table 2-9. *Perfmon Counters to Analyze Volume of Incoming Requests*

Object(Instance[,InstanceN])	Counter
SQLServer:General Statistics	User Connections
SQLServer:SQL Statistics	Batch Requests/sec

User Connections

Multiple read-only SQL Servers can work together in a load-balancing environment (where SQL Server is spread over several machines) to support a large number of database requests. In such cases, it is better to monitor the User Connections counter to evaluate the distribution of user connections across multiple SQL Servers. User Connections can range all over the spectrum with normal application behavior. This is where a normal baseline is essential to determine the expected behavior. You will see how you can establish this baseline shortly.

Batch Requests/sec

This counter is a good indicator of the load on SQL Server. Based on the level of system resource utilization and Batch Requests/sec, you can estimate the number of users the SQL Server may be able to take without developing resource bottlenecks. This counter value, at different load cycles, also helps you understand its relationship with the number of database connections. You may also understand SQL Server's relationship with Web Request/sec (that is, Active Server Pages.Requests/Sec for web applications using Microsoft Internet Information Server [IIS] and Active Server Pages [ASP]). All this analysis helps you to better understand and predict system behavior as the user load changes.

The value of this counter can range over a wide spectrum with normal application behavior. A normal baseline is essential to determine the expected behavior. Let's move on to look at creating one now.

Creating a Baseline

Now that you have looked at a few of the main performance counters, let's see how to bring these counters together to create a system baseline. These are the steps you need to follow:

1. Create a reusable list of performance counters.

2. Create a counter log using your list of performance counters.

3. Minimize System Monitor overhead.

Create a Reusable List of Performance Counters

Run the System Monitor tool (or perfmon) on a Windows 2000 machine connected to the same network as that of the SQL Server system. Add performance counters to the View Chart display of the System Monitor through the Properties ➤ Data ➤ Add Counters dialog box, as shown in Figure 2-8.

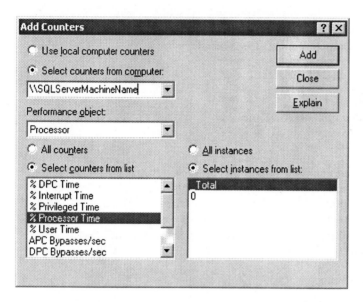

Figure 2-8. *Adding perfmon counters*

For example, to add the performance counter `Processor(_Total)\% Processor Time`, follow these steps:

1. Select the option "Select counters from computer" and specify the computer name running the SQL Server in the corresponding entry field.

2. Select the performance object Processor from the Performance object drop-down list.

3. Select the option "Select counters from list" and choose the % Processor Time counter from the corresponding list of performance counters.

4. Select the option "Select instances from list" and choose the instance _Total from the corresponding list of instances.

5. Click the Add button to add this performance counter.

When creating a reusable list for your baseline, you can repeat the preceding steps to add all the performance counters listed in Table 2-10.

Table 2-10. *Perfmon Counters to Analyze SQL Server Performance*

Object(Instance[,InstanceN])	Counter
Memory	Available MBytes Pages/sec
PhysicalDisk(Data-disk, Log-disk)	% Disk Time Current Disk Queue Length Disk Transfers/sec Disk Bytes/sec
Processor(_Total)	% Processor Time % Privileged Time
System	Processor Queue Length Context Switches/sec
Network Interface(Network card)	Bytes Total/sec
Network Segment	% Net Utilization
SQLServer:Access Methods	FreeSpace Scans/sec Full Scans/sec
SQLServer:Buffer Manager	Buffer cache hit ratio Free pages
SQLServer:Latches	Total Latch Wait Time (ms)
SQLServer:Locks(_Total)	Lock Timeouts/sec Lock Wait Time (ms) Number of Deadlocks/sec
SQLServer:Memory Manager	Memory Grants Pending Target Server Memory (KB) Total Server Memory (KB)
SQLServer:SQL Statistics	Batch Requests/sec SQL Re-Compilations/sec
SQLServer:General Statistics	User Connections

Once you have added all the performance counters, close the Add Counters dialog box and save the list of counters as an .htm file through the context menu (right-click anywhere in the right frame of System Monitor to see the Save As menu item).

The .htm file contains a list of all the performance counters that can be used as a base set of counters to create a counter log, or view System Monitor graphs interactively, for the same SQL Server machine. To also use this list of counters for other SQL Server machines, open the .htm file in an editor such as Notepad and replace all instances of "\\SQLServerMachineName" with "" (a blank string), without the double quotes.

You can also use this counter list file to view System Monitor graphs interactively in an Internet browser, as shown in Figure 2-9.

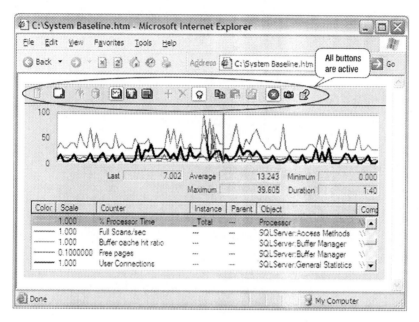

Figure 2-9. *Perfmon in Internet browser*

Create a Counter Log Using the List of Performance Counters

System Monitor provides a counter log facility to save the performance data of multiple counters over a period of time. The saved counter log can be viewed using System Monitor to analyze the performance data. It is usually convenient to create a counter log from a defined list of performance counters.

You can use your new .htm file in the System Monitor tool to create a counter log as follows: From the context menu of Performance Log and Alerts ➤ Counter Logs, select New Log Settings From, and select the .htm file saved earlier. This will add all the counters from the .htm file into the new counter log, as shown in Figure 2-10.

You can add more performance counters, if needed, through this dialog box by clicking the Add button and then following the steps listed previously. The destination folder and filename for the counter log can be specified in the Log Files pane. The counter log can be scheduled to automatically start at a specific time and stop after a certain time period or at a specific time. These settings can be configured through the Schedule pane. Keep all other settings in the Log Files and Schedule panes the same.

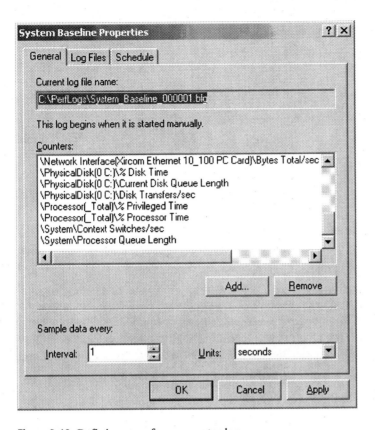

Figure 2-10. *Defining a perfmon counter log*

■**TIP** Additional suggestions for these settings are mentioned in the section that follows.

For additional information on how to create counter logs using System Monitor, please refer to the following Microsoft Knowledge Base articles:

- "How to Create a Log Using System Monitor in Windows 2000" (Q248345):
  http://support.microsoft.com/default.aspx?scid=kb;en-us;Q248345

- "How to Create a Performance Monitor Log for NT Troubleshooting" (Q150934):
  http://support.microsoft.com/default.aspx?scid=kb;en-us;Q150934

Minimize Performance Monitor Overhead

The System Monitor tool is designed to add as little overhead as possible, if used correctly. To minimize the impact of using this tool on a system, consider the following suggestions:

- Limit the number of counters, specifically performance objects.

- Use counter logs instead of viewing System Monitor graphs interactively.

- Run System Monitor remotely while viewing graphs interactively.

- Save the counter log file to a different local disk.

- Increase the sampling interval.

Let's consider each of these points in more detail.

Limit the Number of Counters

Monitoring large numbers of performance counters with small sampling intervals can incur a high amount of overhead on the system. The bulk of this overhead comes from the number of performance objects you are monitoring, so selecting them wisely is important. The number of counters for the selected performance objects does not add much overhead, because it gives only an attribute of the object itself. Therefore, it is important to know what objects you want to monitor and why.

Prefer Counter Logs

Use counter logs instead of viewing a System Monitor graph interactively, as System Monitor graphing is more costly in terms of overhead. Monitoring current activities should be limited to short-term viewing of data, troubleshooting, and diagnosis. Performance data reported via a counter log is *sampled*, meaning that data is collected periodically rather than traced, whereas the System Monitor graph is updated in real time as events occur. Using counter logs will reduce that overhead.

View System Monitor Graphs Remotely

Since viewing the live performance data using System Monitor graphs creates a fair amount of overhead on the system, run the tool remotely on a different machine and connect to the SQL Server system through the tool. To remotely connect to the SQL Server machine, run the Performance Monitor tool on a machine connected to the network to which the SQL Server machine is connected.

As shown in Figure 2-8, type the computer name (or IP address) of the SQL Server machine in the "Select counters from computer" combo box. Be aware that if you connect to the production server through a Windows 2000 terminal service session, the major part of the tool will still run on the server.

Save Counter Log Locally

Collecting the performance data for the counter log does not incur the overhead of displaying any graph. So, while using counter log mode, it is more efficient to log counter values locally on the SQL Server system instead of transferring the performance data across the network. Put the counter log file on a local disk other than the ones that are monitored.

Increase the Sampling Interval

As you are mainly interested in the resource utilization pattern during baseline monitoring, the performance data sampling interval can be easily increased to 60 seconds or more to decrease the log file size and reduce demand on disk I/Os. A short sampling interval may be used to detect and diagnose timing issues. Even while viewing System Monitor graphs interactively, increase the sampling interval from the default value of 1 second per sample.

System Behavior Analysis Against Baseline

The default behavior of a database application changes over time due to various factors such as the following:

- Change of data

- Change of user group

- Change in usage pattern of the application

- Addition to or change in application functionalities

- Change in software environment due to installation of new service packs or software upgrades

- Change in hardware environment

Due to the preceding changes, the baseline created for the database server slowly loses its significance. It may not always be accurate to compare the current behavior of the system with an old baseline. Therefore, it is important to keep the baseline up to date by creating a new baseline at regular time intervals. It is also beneficial to archive the previous baseline logs, so that they can be referred to later, if required.

The counter log for the baseline or the current behavior of the system can be analyzed using the System Monitor tool by following these steps:

1. Open the counter log. Use System Monitor's toolbar item View Log File Data and select the log filename.

2. Add all the performance counters to analyze the performance data. Note that only the performance objects, counters, and instances selected during the counter log creation are shown in the selection lists. The counters can be added quickly by selecting All Counters and All Instances for the performance objects with multiple counters and/or instances, as shown in Figure 2-11.

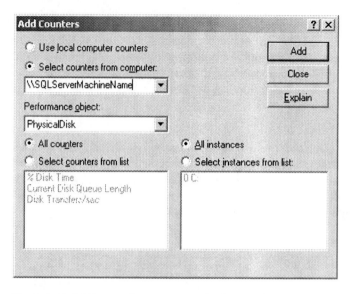

Figure 2-11. *Adding perfmon counters for log analysis*

3. Analyze the system behavior at different parts of the day by adjusting the time range accordingly, as shown in Figure 2-12.

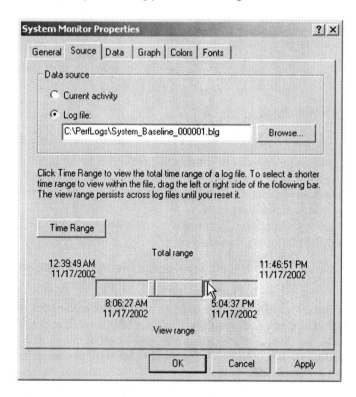

Figure 2-12. *Defining time range for log analysis*

During a performance review, you can analyze the system-level behavior of the database by comparing the current value of performance counters with the latest baseline. Take the following considerations into account while comparing the performance data:

- Use the same set of performance counters in both the cases. Having the list of performance counters in the form of an .htm file helps in reusing the list of counters.

- Compare the minimum, maximum, or average value of the counters as applicable for the individual counters. The specific values for the counters were explained earlier.

- Some counters have an absolute good/bad value as mentioned previously. The current value of these counters need not be compared with the baseline values. For example, if the current average value of the Pages/sec counter is 100, then it indicates that the system has developed a memory bottleneck. Even though it does not require a comparison with the baseline, it is still advantageous to review the corresponding baseline value, as the memory bottleneck might have existed for a long time. Having the archived baseline logs helps detect the first occurrence of the memory bottleneck.

- Some counters do not have a definitive good/bad value. As their value depends on the application, a relative comparison with the corresponding baseline counters is a must. For example, the current value of the User Connections counter for SQL Server does not signify anything good or bad with the application. But comparing it with the corresponding baseline value may reveal a big increase in the number of user connections, indicating an increase in the workload.

- Compare a range of value for the counters from the current and the baseline counter logs. The fluctuation in the individual values of the counters will be normalized by the range of values.

- Compare logs from the same part of the day. For most applications, the usage pattern varies during different parts of the day. To obtain the minimum, maximum, and average value of the counters for a specific time, adjust the time range of the counter logs as shown previously.

Once the system-level bottleneck is identified, the internal behavior of the application should be analyzed to determine the cause of the bottleneck. Identifying and optimizing the source of the bottleneck will help use the system resources efficiently.

Summary

In this chapter, you learned that you can use the System Monitor tool to analyze the effect on system resources of a slow-performing database application, as well as the overall behavior of SQL Server. For every resultant system bottleneck, there are two types of resolutions: hardware resolutions and application optimization. Of course, it is always beneficial to optimize the database application before considering a hardware upgrade.

In the next chapter, you will learn how to analyze the workload of a database application for performance tuning.

■ ■ ■

CHAPTER 3

SQL Query Performance Analysis

A common cause of slow SQL Server performance is a heavy database application workload: the nature of the queries themselves. Thus, to analyze the cause of a system bottleneck, it is important to examine the database application workload and identify the SQL queries causing the most stress on system resources. To do this, you use the SQL Profiler and Query Analyzer tools.

In this chapter, I cover the following topics:

- The basics of the SQL Profiler tool

- How to analyze SQL Server workload and identify costly SQL queries using SQL Profiler

- How to analyze the processing strategy of a costly SQL query using Query Analyzer

- How to analyze the effectiveness of index and join strategies for a SQL query

- How to measure the cost of a SQL query using SQL utilities

The SQL Profiler Tool

SQL Profiler is a graphical tool that can be used to

- Monitor SQL Server activities.

- Analyze performance.

- Diagnose problems such as deadlocks.

- Debug a Transact-SQL (T-SQL) statement.

- Replay SQL Server activity in a simulation.

This tool can also be used to capture activities performed on a SQL Server. Such a capture is called a *Profiler trace*. A Profiler trace can be used to capture events generated by various subsystems within SQL Server. Before you see how to run a trace, let's look in more detail at what you *can* trace using Profiler.

Events

An *event* represents various activities performed inside SQL Server. These are categorized for easy classification into *event classes*; cursor events, lock events, stored procedure events, and T-SQL events are a few common event classes.

For performance analysis, you are mainly interested in the events that help you judge levels of resource stress for various activities performed on SQL Server. By *resource stress,* I mean things like the following:

- What kind of CPU utilization was involved for the SQL activity?

- How much memory was used?

- How much I/O was involved?

- How long did the SQL activity take to execute?

- How frequently was a particular query executed?

- What kind of errors and warnings were faced by the queries?

The resource stress of a SQL activity can be calculated after the completion of an event, so the main events you use for performance analysis are those that represent completion of a SQL activity. Table 3-1 describes these events.

Table 3-1. *Events to Trace Query Completion*

Event Class	Event	Description
Stored Procedures	RPC:Completed	An RPC completion event
	SP:Completed	A stored procedure completion event
	SP:StmtCompleted	A SQL statement completion event within a stored procedure
TSQL	SQL:BatchCompleted	A T-SQL batch completion event
	SQL:StmtCompleted	A T-SQL statement completion event

Let's discuss some of these events in more detail.

An RPC event indicates that the stored procedure was executed using the Remote Procedure Call (RPC) mechanism. When a stored procedure is executed using the ODBC CALL escape clause, the ODBC driver for SQL Server sends the stored procedure to SQL Server using RPC. You can submit a stored procedure using RPC by following these steps:

1. Prepare a SQL statement that uses the ODBC CALL escape sequence as follows:

   ```
   {? = CALL StoredProcedureName (?,?)}
   ```

   The statement uses parameter markers for all the parameters and for the stored procedure return value, if any.

2. Call the SQLBindParameter ODBC API for each parameter and for the stored procedure return value, if any.

3. Submit the prepared statement to SQL Server using the SQLExecDirect ODBC API.

If a database application executes a stored procedure using the T-SQL EXECUTE statement instead of the ODBC CALL escape sequence, the ODBC driver submits the stored procedure as a SQL statement rather than as an RPC. RPC requests are generally faster than EXECUTE requests, since they bypass much of the statement parsing and parameter processing in SQL Server.

A *T-SQL batch* is a set of SQL queries that are submitted together to SQL Server. A T-SQL batch is usually terminated by a GO command. The GO command is not a T-SQL statement. It is recognized by the osql and isql utilities, as well as Query Analyzer, and signals the end of a batch. Each SQL query in the batch is considered a T-SQL statement. Thus, a T-SQL batch consists of one or more T-SQL statements.

To add the preceding events to a Profiler trace, open the Profiler tool from the Start ➤ Programs ➤ Microsoft SQL Server menu, and select File ➤ New ➤ Trace or press Ctrl+N. On connecting to the SQL Server to be monitored, a Trace Properties dialog box will appear. Switch to the Events tab as shown in Figure 3-1 to add the list of events in Table 3-1. Select an event under an event class in the "Available event classes" list, and click the Add button to add the event to the "Selected event classes" list. To remove events not required in the "Selected event classes" list, select the specific event and click the Remove button.

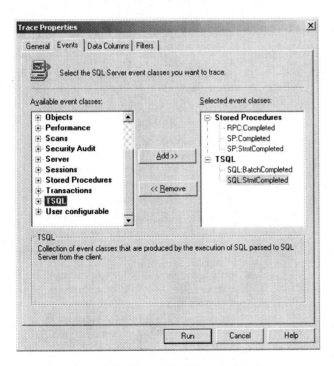

Figure 3-1. *Trace definition with SQL completed events*

Although the list in Table 3-1 represents the main events, there are a number of additional events that you may sometimes use to diagnose the cause of poor performance. For example, as mentioned in Chapter 1, repeated recompilation of a stored procedure adds processing overhead, which hurts the performance of the database request. The Stored Procedures event class of the Profiler tool includes an event, SP:Recompile, to indicate the recompilation of a stored procedure (this event is explained in depth in Chapter 10). Similarly, Profiler includes additional events to indicate other performance-related issues with a database workload. Table 3-2 shows a few of these events.

Table 3-2. *Events to Trace Query Performance*

Event Class	Event	Description
Security Audit	Audit Login Audit Logout	Keeps track of database connections when users connect to and disconnect from SQL Server.
Sessions	ExistingConnection	Represents all the users connected to SQL Server before the trace was started.
Cursors	CursorImplicitConversion	Indicates that the cursor type created is different from the requested type.
Errors and Warnings	Attention	Represents intermediate termination of a request caused by actions such as query cancellation by a client or a broken database connection.
	Exception	Indicates the occurrence of an exception in SQL Server.
	Execution Warnings	Indicates the occurrence of any warning during the execution of a query or a stored procedure.
	Hash Warning	Indicates the occurrence of error in a hashing operation.
	Missing Column Statistics	Indicates that the statistics of a column, required by the optimizer to decide a processing strategy, are missing.
	Missing Join Predicate	Indicates that a query is executed with no joining predicate between two tables.
	Sort Warnings	Indicates that a sort operation performed in a query such as SELECT did not fit into memory.
Locks	Lock:Deadlock Lock:Deadlock Chain	Flags the presence of a deadlock. Additionally, Deadlock Chain shows a trace of the chain of queries creating the deadlock.
	Lock:Timeout	Signifies that the lock has exceeded the timeout parameter, which is set by SET LOCK_TIMEOUT timeout_period(ms).
Stored Procedures	SP:Recompile	Indicates that an execution plan for a stored procedure had to be recompiled, because one did not exist, a recompilation was forced, or the existing execution plan could not be reused.

Event Class	Event	Description
	SP:Starting SP:StmtStarting	Represents the starting of a stored procedure and a SQL statement within a stored procedure, respectively. They are useful to identify queries that started but could not finish due to an operation that caused an Attention event.
Transactions	SQLTransaction	Provides information about a database transaction, including information such as when a transaction started/completed, the duration of the transaction, and so on.

Data Columns

Events are represented by different attributes called *data columns*. The data columns represent different attributes of an event, such as the class of the event, the SQL statement for the event, the resource cost of the event, and the source of the event.

The data columns that represent the resource cost of an event are CPU, Reads, Writes, and Duration. As a result, for performance analysis, the data columns you will use most are shown in Table 3-3.

Table 3-3. *Data Columns to Trace Query Completion*

Data Column	Description
EventClass	Type of event, for example, SQL:StatementCompleted.
TextData	SQL statement for an event, such as SELECT * FROM sysobjects.
CPU	CPU cost of an event in milliseconds (ms). For example, CPU = 100 for a SELECT statement indicates that the statement took 100 ms to execute.
Reads	Number of logical reads performed for an event. For example, Reads = 800 for a SELECT statement indicates that the statement required a total of 800 reads.
Writes	Number of logical writes performed for an event.
Duration	Execution time of an event in milliseconds (ms).
SPID	SQL Server process identifier user for the event.
StartTime	Start time of an event.

Each logical read and write consists of an 8KB page activity in memory, which may require zero or more physical I/O operations. To find the number of physical I/O operations on a disk subsystem, use the System Monitor tool. In general, the value of the Reads and Writes data columns represents the amount of memory activity and possible disk activities.

The data columns can be added to a Profiler trace using the Data Columns tab of the Trace Properties dialog box. The list of data columns in Table 3-3 added to a Profiler trace is shown in Figure 3-2. To arrange the order of data columns in the Profiler trace output, move the data columns up and down using the Up and Down buttons.

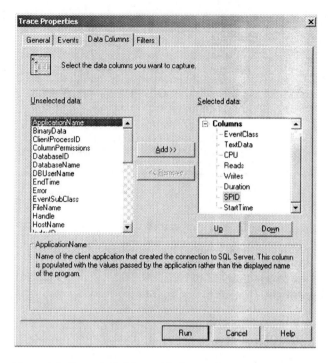

Figure 3-2. *Trace definition with data columns*

In addition to the previous list of data columns, you may use additional data columns from time to time to diagnose the cause of poor performance. For example, in the case of a stored procedure recompilation, the Profiler tool indicates the cause of the recompilation through the EventSubClass data column. (This data column is explained in depth in Chapter 10.) A few of the commonly used additional data columns are as follows:

- BinaryData

- IntegerData

- EventSubClass

- DatabaseID

- ObjectID

- IndexID

- TransactionID

- Error

- EndTime

The `BinaryData` and `IntegerData` data columns provide specific information about a given SQL Server activity. For example, in the case of a cursor, they specify the type of cursor requested and the type of cursor created. Although the names of these additional data columns indicate their purpose to a great extent, I will explain the usefulness of these data columns in later chapters as we use them.

Filters

In addition to defining events and data columns for a Profiler trace, you can also define various filter criteria. These help to keep the trace output small, which is usually a good idea. Table 3-4 describes the filter criteria that you will commonly use during performance analysis.

Table 3-4. *SQL Trace Filters*

Events	Filter Criteria Example	Use
ApplicationName	Not like: SQL Profiler	To filter out the events generated by Profiler itself. This is the default behavior.
DatabaseID	Equals: <ID of the database to monitor>	To filter out events generated by a particular database. You can determine the ID of a database from its name as follows: `SELECT DB_ID('Northwind')`
Duration	Greater than or equal: 2	For performance analysis, you will often capture a trace for a large workload. In a large trace, there will be many event logs with a `Duration` of 0 or 1 ms. Filter out these event logs, as there is hardly any scope for optimizing these SQL activities.
Reads	Greater than or equal: 2	Similar to the criterion on the `Duration` data column.
SPID	Equals: <Database users to monitor>	To troubleshoot queries sent by a specific database user.

Figure 3-3 shows a snippet of the preceding filter criteria selection in SQL Profiler.

■**NOTE** For a complete list of filters available in SQL Profiler, please refer to the MSDN article "Limiting Traces" (http://msdn.microsoft.com/library/default.asp?url=/library/en-us/adminsql/ad_mon_perf_6nxd.asp).

Now that you have seen what events and data columns to trace, as well as what to filter out, let's move on to set up a new trace.

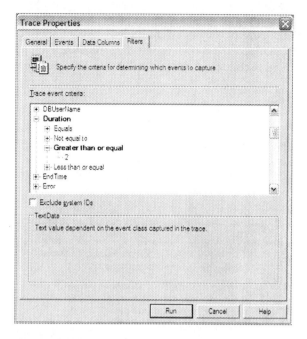

Figure 3-3. *Trace definition with filters*

Trace Template

In the previous section, you learned how to define a new Profiler trace to monitor activities on a SQL Server. However, instead of defining a new trace every time you want to use one, you can create a trace template with your customized events, data columns, and filters, and then reuse the trace template to capture a trace (you can find this particular template in the code download as PerformanceTrace.tdf). The procedure for defining a new trace template is very similar to that of defining a new trace:

1. Instead of using the SQL Profiler menu items File ➤ New ➤ Trace, use File ➤ New ➤ Trace Template.

2. Define the events, data columns, and filters exactly the same way as shown earlier.

3. Save the trace definition as a trace template from the General tab. If you save it to the default Templates folder, Profiler will automatically populate its Templates list with your new template.

You will see how to use this trace template next.

A New Trace

Once your new Profiler trace is designed, you can use it to capture the activities performed on SQL Server for further analysis. To capture a Profiler trace, follow these steps:

1. Select File ➤ New ➤ Trace in SQL Profiler.

2. Connect to the required server.

3. Select the trace template you want to use as shown in Figure 3-4.

4. Customization is required, since filter criteria such as DatabaseID and SPID are not constants. To customize a trace, remove the event, data column, or filter criterion that is not needed.

5. Start capturing SQL activities by clicking the Run button in the General tab.

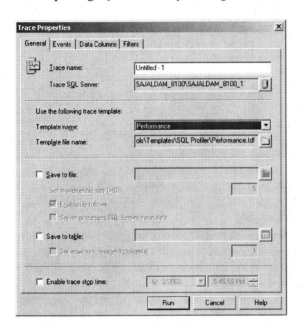

Figure 3-4. *Trace definition for a new trace*

Once you finish capturing your SQL Server activities, you can save the trace output to a *trace file* or a *trace table*. The trace output saved to a trace file is in a native format and can be opened by Profiler to analyze the SQL queries. Saving the trace output to a trace table allows the SQL queries in the trace output to be analyzed by Profiler as well as by SELECT statements on the trace table.

Profiler creates a trace table dynamically as per the definition of the data columns in the trace output. The ability to analyze the trace output using SELECT statements adds great flexibility to the analysis process. For example, if you want to find out the number of query executions with a response time of less than 500 ms, you can execute a SELECT statement on the trace table as follows:

```
SELECT COUNT(*) FROM <Trace Table>
WHERE Duration > 500
```

You will look at some sample queries in the "Identifying Costly Queries" section later in the chapter, but first let's discuss how to minimize Profiler's footprint.

SQL Profiler Recommendations

To help minimize the impact of Profiler on system resources, you have already set some filters on your trace. To further minimize the impact, consider the following suggestions:

- Limit the number of events and data columns.

- Discard start events for performance analysis.

- Limit trace output size.

- Avoid online data column sorting.

- Run Profiler remotely.

- Capture traces using stored procedures.

In the following sections, I cover each of these suggestions in more depth.

Limiting the Number of Events and Data Columns

While tracing SQL queries, you can decide the SQL activities to be captured by filtering events and data columns. Choosing extra events contributes to the bulk of tracing overhead. Data columns do not add much overhead, since they are only attributes of an event class itself. Therefore, it is extremely important to know why you want to trace each event selected and to select your events based only on necessity.

Minimizing the number of events to be captured prevents SQL Server from wasting the bandwidth of valuable resources generating all those events. Capturing events such as locks and execution plans should be done with caution, because these events make the trace output very large and degrade SQL Server's performance.

It's important to reduce the number of events while analyzing a production server, since you don't want the profiler to add a large amount of load to the production server. On a test server, the amount of load contributed by Profiler is a lesser consideration than the ability to analyze every activity on SQL Server. Therefore, on a test server, you need not compromise so much with the information you might be interested in.

Filtering Stages

There are two stages of filtering: prefiltering, which is performed by SQL Server, and postfiltering, which is performed by the user.

- *Prefiltering* is the online stage of capturing the SQL Server activities. Prefiltering offers many advantages:

    - It reduces the impact on the performance of SQL Server itself, since a limited number of events are generated.

    - It reduces trace output size.

    - It simplifies postfiltering operations, due to fewer events being captured in the first place.

- The only disadvantage to prefiltering is that you may miss some vital information that might be required for thorough analysis.

- *Postfiltering* is the stage where you analyze the captured trace file. It is an offline stage, incurring no overhead on SQL Server. Once you filter an existing trace file, you can save the postfiltered information to a new trace file. For example, while identifying the problematic queries, you might be interested in queries with an execution time greater than 500 ms. To identify such queries, you can apply a postfilter on the trace output for Duration greater than or equal to 500 and save this filtered trace output as a separate trace file. This means that the next time you need to look at the same criteria, you do not have to load the original trace file and do filtering again; you can just use the new trace file.

Discarding Start Events for Performance Analysis

The information you want for performance analysis revolves around the resource cost of a query. Start events, such as SP:StmtStarting, do not provide this information, because it is only after an event completes that you can compute the amount of I/O, the CPU load, and the duration of the query. Therefore, while tracking slow-running queries for performance analysis, you need not capture the start events. This information is provided by the corresponding completion events.

So when should you capture start events? When you don't expect some SQL queries to finish execution due to error conditions, or when you find frequent Attention events. An Attention event usually indicates that the user cancelled the query midway or the query timeout expired, probably because the query was running for a long time.

Limiting the Trace Output Size

Besides prefiltering events and data columns, there are other filtering criteria that limit the trace output size. On the Filters tab of the Trace Properties dialog box, consider the following settings:

- *Duration – Greater than or equal: 2*. SQL queries with a Duration equal to 0 or 1 ms cannot be further optimized.

- *Reads – Greater than or equal: 2*. SQL queries with number of logical reads equal to 0 or 1 ms cannot be further optimized.

Avoiding Online Data Column Sorting

During performance analysis, you usually sort a trace output on different data columns (such as Duration, CPU, and Reads) to identify queries with the largest corresponding figures. If you sort these offline, you reduce the activities Profiler has to perform while interacting with SQL Server. This is how to sort a captured SQL trace output:

1. Capture the trace without any sorting (or grouping).

2. Save the trace output to a trace file.

3. Open the trace file and sort (or group) the trace file output on specific data columns as required.

Running Profiler Remotely

It is usually not a good practice to run test tools directly on the production server. Profiler has a heavy user interface; therefore, it is better to run it on another machine. Similar to System Monitor, Profiler should not be run through a terminal service session, because a major part of the tool still runs on the server. When collecting a trace output directly to a file, save the file locally where Profiler is being run.

Capturing a Trace Using Stored Procedures

Although you can use Profiler to capture SQL activities, a further lightweight approach is to use SQL trace-related system stored procedures provided with SQL Server 2000. You can use the following stored procedures to define which SQL activities should be captured:

- sp_trace_create: Create a trace definition.

- sp_trace_setevent: Add events and event columns to the trace.

- sp_trace_setfilter: Apply filters to the trace.

Once the SQL trace has been defined, you can run the trace using the following stored procedure:

- sp_trace_setstatus: Start the trace.

The tracing of SQL activities continues until the trace is stopped.

The problem with this technique is that it requires an extensive amount of SQL scripting. You can simplify the SQL scripting process by following these steps:

1. Start SQL Profiler.

2. Connect to SQL Server.

3. Open an existing trace template or define a new trace definition.

4. Temporarily start capturing SQL activities by clicking the Run button.

5. Immediately stop the trace by selecting File ➤ Stop Trace.

6. Script the trace definition and the step to run the trace to a SQL script file by selecting File ➤ Script Trace ➤ For SQL Server 2000.

7. Open the SQL script file in Query Analyzer.

8. Modify the InsertFileNameHere parameter of sp_trace_create to a meaningful filename.

9. Execute the SQL script, which starts the SQL trace as a background process. It also returns the ID of the trace as traceid, which is required to stop the trace later on.

You can find the resultant SQL script file in the code download as `PerformanceTrace.sql`. It includes the appropriate modifications to close the current trace file and create a new trace file when the size of the current trace file reaches 500MB.

Since the SQL tracing continues as a back-end process, the Query Analyzer session need not be kept open. You can identify the running traces by using the SQL Server 2000 built-in function as follows:

```
SELECT * FROM ::fn_trace_getinfo(default)
```

Figure 3-5 shows the output of the function `fn_trace_getinfo`.

	traceid	property	value
1	1	1	2
2	1	2	C:\PerformanceTrace
3	1	3	500
4	1	4	NULL
5	1	5	1

Figure 3-5. *Output of fn_trace_getinfo*

The number of unique `traceids` in the output of the function `fn_trace_getinfo` shows the number of traces active on SQL Server. The data value of the column `value` for the property of 5 indicates whether the trace is running (value = 1) or stopped (value = 0). A specific trace, say `traceid` = 1, can be stopped by executing the stored procedure `sp_trace_setstatus`:

```
EXEC sp_trace_setstatus 1, 0
```

After a trace is stopped, its definition must be closed and deleted from the server by executing `sp_trace_setstatus`:

```
EXEC sp_trace_setstatus 1, 2
```

To verify that the trace is stopped successfully, re-execute the function `fn_trace_getinfo` and ensure that the output of the function doesn't contain the `traceid`.

The format of trace file created by this technique is same as that of the trace file created by Profiler. Therefore, this trace file can be analyzed in exactly the same way as a trace file created by Profiler.

This technique of capturing a SQL trace using stored procedures avoids the overheads associated with Profiler. It also provides greater flexibility in managing the tracing schedule of a SQL trace than is provided by the Profiler tool. In Chapter 16, you will learn how to control the schedule of a SQL trace while capturing the activities of a SQL workload over an extended period of time.

Costly Queries

Now that you have seen what you need to consider when using the Profiler tool, let's look at what it represents: the costly queries themselves. When the performance of SQL Server goes bad, two things are most likely happening:

- First, certain queries create high stress on system resources. These queries affect the performance of the overall system, as the server becomes incapable of serving other SQL queries fast enough.

- Additionally, the costly queries block all other queries requesting the same database resources, further degrading the performance of those queries. Optimizing the costly queries improves not only their own performance, but also the performance of other queries by reducing database blocking and pressure on SQL Server resources.

NOTE Create the od table using the script od.sql provided in the download.

You can use Profiler to capture the SQL Server workload, as explained in the preceding section. Open the file Performance.tdf that you saved earlier, or open the one from the code download, and then run the queries in trace_queries.sql. Figure 3-6 shows a sample trace output. On a live production server, the trace output may be quite large; the solution is to use filter criteria, as explained in the "Filters" section, to limit the size of the trace output.

EventClass	TextData	CPU	Reads	Writes	Duration
SQL:BatchCompleted	select * from [Region]	0	6	0	10
SQL:StmtCompleted	select distinct p.productid, p...	991	3575	0	1082
SQL:BatchCompleted	select distinct p.productid, p...	991	3575	0	1113
SQL:StmtCompleted	select * from [Territories]	0	6	0	0
SQL:BatchCompleted	select * from [Territories]	0	6	0	20
SQL:StmtCompleted	select * from [EmployeeTerrito...	0	1	0	0
SQL:BatchCompleted	select * from [EmployeeTerrito...	0	1	0	20
SQL:StmtCompleted	select * from [Employees]	0	141	0	40
SQL:BatchCompleted	select * from [Employees]	0	141	0	100
SQL:StmtCompleted	select * from [Categories]	10	91	0	40
SQL:BatchCompleted	select * from [Categories]	10	91	0	60
SQL:StmtCompleted	select * from [Customers]	0	5	0	40
SQL:BatchCompleted	select * from [Customers]	10	5	0	80
SQL:StmtCompleted	select * from [Shippers]	0	2	0	0
SQL:BatchCompleted	select * from [Shippers]	0	2	0	20
SQL:StmtCompleted	select * from [Suppliers]	0	20	0	10
SQL:BatchCompleted	select * from [Suppliers]	0	20	0	10

select * from [Suppliers]

Figure 3-6. *A sample trace output*

The trace output in Figure 3-6 contains the `SQL:BatchCompleted` event for every SQL query batch and the `SQL:StmtCompleted` event for every query within the batch. If the `SQL:BatchCompleted` event contains only one query, then this event, and the corresponding `SQL:StmtCompleted` event, represents the same query.

Once you have captured the set of SQL queries representing a complete workload, you should analyze the trace to identify two sets of queries:

- Costly queries that are causing a great deal of pressure on the system resources

- Queries that are slowed down the most

Identifying Costly Queries

The goal of SQL Server is to return result sets to the user in the shortest time. To do this, SQL Server has a built-in, cost-based optimizer called the *query optimizer*, which generates a cost-effective strategy called a *query execution plan*. The query optimizer weighs many factors, including (but not limited to) the usage of CPU, memory, and disk I/O required to execute a query, and it then creates a cost-effective execution plan. Although minimizing the number of I/Os is not a requirement for a cost-effective plan, you will often find that the least costly plan has the fewest I/Os because I/O operations are expensive.

The `CPU` and `Reads` columns also show where a query costs you. The `CPU` column represents the CPU time used to execute the query. The `Reads` column represents the number of logical pages (8KB in size) a query operated on, and thereby indicates the amount of memory stress caused by the query. It also provides an indication of disk stress, since memory pages have to be backed up in the case of action queries, populated during first-time data access, and displaced to disk during memory bottlenecks. The higher the number of logical reads for a query, the higher the stress on the disk is likely to be. An excessive number of logical pages also increases load on the CPU in managing those pages.

The queries that cause a large number of logical reads usually acquire locks on a correspondingly large set of data. Even reading (as opposed to writing) requires share locks on all the data. These queries block all other queries requesting this data (or a part of the data) in an incompatible lock mode. Since these queries are inherently costly and require a long time to execute, they block other queries for an extended period of time. The blocked queries then cause blocks on further queries, introducing a chain of blocking in the database. (Chapter 12 covers lock modes.)

As a result, it makes sense to identify the costly queries and optimize them first, thereby

- Improving performance of the costly queries themselves

- Reducing the overall stress on system resources

- Reducing database blocking

The costly queries can be categorized into the following two types:

- *Single execution*: An individual execution of the query is costly.

- *Multiple executions*: A query itself may not be costly, but the repeated execution of the query causes pressure on the system resources.

These two types of costly queries can be identified using different approaches, as explained in the following sections.

Costly Queries with a Single Execution

You can identify the costly queries by analyzing a SQL Profiler trace output file. Since you are interested in identifying queries that perform a large number of logical reads, you should sort the trace output on the Reads data column. You do this by following these steps:

1. Capture a Profiler trace that represents a typical workload.

2. Save the trace output to a trace file.

3. Open the trace file for analysis.

4. Sort the trace output on Reads column. To do this, move the Reads column under the Groups section, as shown in Figure 3-7.

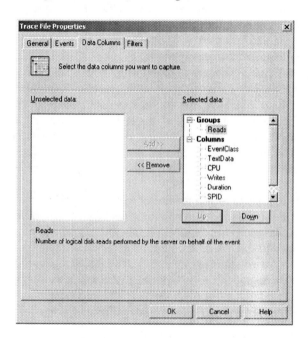

Figure 3-7. *Trace definition sorted on the Reads column*

This will sort the trace output on the Reads column, as shown in Figure 3-8. The trace output is sorted on Reads in ascending order. From this, you can select a few of the costliest queries, and analyze and optimize them appropriately.

In some cases, you may have identified a large stress on the CPU from the System Monitor output. The pressure on the CPU may be due to a large number of CPU-intensive operations, such as stored procedure recompilations, aggregate functions, data sorting, hash joins, and so on. In such cases, you should sort the Profiler trace output on the CPU column, to identify the queries taking up a large number of processor cycles.

Reads	EventClass	TextData	CPU	Writes	Duration
6	SQL:BatchCompleted	select * from [Territories]	0	0	20
14	SQL:StmtCompleted	select * from [Order Details]	0	0	350
14	SQL:BatchCompleted	select * from [Order Details]	0	0	400
20	SQL:StmtCompleted	select * from [Suppliers]	0	0	10
20	SQL:BatchCompleted	select * from [Suppliers]	0	0	10
23	SQL:StmtCompleted	select * from [Orders]	10	0	271
23	SQL:BatchCompleted	select * from [Orders]	10	0	280
91	SQL:StmtCompleted	select * from [Categories]	10	0	40
91	SQL:BatchCompleted	select * from [Categories]	10	0	60
141	SQL:StmtCompleted	select * from [Employees]	0	0	40
141	SQL:BatchCompleted	select * from [Employees]	0	0	100
3575	SQL:StmtCompleted	select distinct p.productid, p...	991	0	1082
3575	SQL:BatchCompleted	select distinct p.productid, p...	991	0	1113

```
select distinct p.productid, p.productname, p.unitprice, od.quantity, p.unitsins
    from products p, [od] od
    where p.productid = od.productid
    and od.quantity = (select min(odSub.quantity) from [od] odSub)
    order by p.productid
```

Figure 3-8. *Trace output sorted on the Reads column*

Costly Queries with Multiple Executions

As I mentioned earlier, sometimes a query may not be costly by itself, but the cumulative effect of multiple executions of the same query might put pressure on the system resources. In this case, sorting on the Reads column won't help you identify this type of costly query. You would instead like to know the total number of reads performed by the multiple executions of the query. Unfortunately, Profiler doesn't help here directly, but you can still get this information in the following two ways:

- Group the trace output in Profiler on the following columns: EventClass, TextData, and Reads. For the group of rows with same EventClass and TextData, manually calculate the total of all the corresponding Reads. This approach doesn't sound very user-friendly!

- Save the trace output to a trace table by selecting File ➤ Save As ➤ Trace Table in Profiler. Also, you can import the trace file output of Profiler to a trace table by using the built-in function fn_trace_gettable:

```
SELECT * INTO Trace_Table
FROM ::fn_trace_gettable('C:\PerformanceTrace.trc', default)
```

Once the SQL trace is imported into a database table, execute a SELECT statement to find the total number of Reads performed by the multiple executions of the same query as follows (reads.sql in the download):

```
SELECT COUNT(*) AS TotalExecutions, EventClass, TextData
  , SUM(Duration) AS Duration_Total
  , SUM(CPU) AS CPU_Total
  , SUM(Reads) AS Reads_Total
  , SUM(Writes) AS Writes_Total
FROM Trace_Table
GROUP BY EventClass, TextData
ORDER BY Reads_Total DESC
```

The TotalExecutions column in the preceding script indicates the number of times a query was executed. The Reads_Total column indicates the total number of Reads performed by the multiple executions of the query.

However, there is a little problem. The data type of the TextData column for the trace table created by Profiler is NTEXT, which can't be specified in the GROUP BY clause—SQL Server 2000 doesn't support grouping on a column with the NTEXT data type. Therefore, you may create a table similar to the trace table, with the only exception being that the data type of the TextData column should be NVARCHAR(<size>) instead of NTEXT. The maximum data size for the TextData column can be used for the size of the NVARCHAR data type, which can be determined using the following SELECT statement:

```
SELECT MAX(DATALENGTH(TextData)) FROM <Trace Table>
```

Another approach is to use the CAST function as follows:

```
SELECT COUNT(*) AS TotalExecutions, EventClass
  , CAST(TextData AS NVARCHAR(500)) TextData
  , SUM(Duration) AS Duration_Total
  , SUM(CPU) AS CPU_Total
  , SUM(Reads) AS Reads_Total
  , SUM(Writes) AS Writes_Total
FROM Trace_Table
GROUP BY EventClass, CAST(TextData AS NVARCHAR(500))
ORDER BY Reads_Total DESC
```

The costly queries identified by this approach are a better indication of load than the costly queries (with single execution) identified by Profiler. For example, a query that requires 50 reads might be executed 1,000 times. The query itself may be considered cheap enough, but the total number of reads performed by the query turns out to be 50,000 (= 50 × 1,000), which cannot be considered cheap. Optimizing this query to reduce the reads by even 10 for individual execution reduces the total number of reads by 10,000 (= 10 × 1,000), which can be more beneficial than optimizing a single query with 5,000 reads.

The problem with this approach is that it is not as simple as the first approach of identifying the costly single execution queries. As a result, the usual practice is to identify the costly single execution queries first, optimize them, and only then identify the costly multiple-execution queries.

Identifying Slow-Running Queries

Because a user's experience is highly influenced by the response time of his or her requests, you should regularly monitor the execution time of incoming SQL queries and find out the response time of slow-running queries. If the response time (or duration) of slow-running queries becomes unacceptable, then you should analyze the cause of performance degradation.

To discover the slow-running SQL queries, group a trace output on the Duration column. This will sort the trace output as shown in Figure 3-9.

Duration	EventClass	TextData	CPU	Reads	Writes
20	SQL:BatchCompleted	select * from [Shippers]	0	2	0
40	SQL:StmtCompleted	select * from [Employees]	0	141	0
40	SQL:StmtCompleted	select * from [Categories]	10	91	0
40	SQL:StmtCompleted	select * from [Customers]	0	5	0
60	SQL:BatchCompleted	select * from [Categories]	10	91	0
80	SQL:BatchCompleted	select * from [Customers]	10	5	0
100	SQL:BatchCompleted	select * from [Employees]	0	141	0
271	SQL:StmtCompleted	select * from [Orders]	10	23	0
280	SQL:BatchCompleted	select * from [Orders]	10	23	0
350	SQL:StmtCompleted	select * from [Order Details]	0	14	0
400	SQL:BatchCompleted	select * from [Order Details]	0	14	0
1082	SQL:StmtCompleted	select distinct p.productid, p...	991	3575	0
1113	SQL:BatchCompleted	select distinct p.productid, p...	991	3575	0

```
select distinct p.productid, p.productname, p.unitprice, od.quantity, p.unitsins
   from products p, [od] od
   where p.productid = od.productid
   and od.quantity = (select min(odSub.quantity) from [od] odSub)
   order by p.productid
```

Figure 3-9. *Trace output sorted on the Duration column*

For a slow-running system, you should note the duration of slow-running queries before and after the optimization process. After you apply optimization techniques, you should then work out the overall effect on the system. It is possible that your optimization steps may have adversely affected other queries, making them slower.

Execution Plan

Once you have identified a costly query, you need to find out *why* it is so costly. You can identify the costly query from SQL Profiler, rerun it in Query Analyzer, and look at the execution plan used by the query optimizer. An execution plan shows the processing strategy (including multiple intermediate steps) used by the query optimizer to execute a query.

To create an execution plan, the query optimizer evaluates various permutations of indexes and join strategies. Due to the possibility of a large number of potential plans, this optimization process may take a long time to generate the most cost-effective execution plan. To prevent overoptimization of an execution plan, the optimization process is broken into multiple phases. Each phase is a set of transformation rules that evaluate various permutations of indexes and join strategies.

After going through a phase, the query optimizer examines the cost of the resulting plan. If the query optimizer determines that the plan is cheap enough, it will use the plan without going through the remaining optimization phases. However, if the plan is not cheap enough, the optimizer will go through the next optimization phase. I will cover execution plan generation in more depth in Chapter 9.

SQL Server displays a query execution plan in two forms, namely *graphical* and *textual.* The graphical execution plan uses icons to represent the processing strategy of a query. To obtain a graphical execution plan, go to Query ➤ Show Execution Plan. A textual execution plan describes the processing strategy of a query using a tabular representation. A textual execution plan is produced by the `SET SHOWPLAN_ALL`, `SET SHOWPLAN_TEXT`, and `SET STATISTICS PROFILE` statements.

The textual execution plan for the costliest query identified previously can be obtained using the `SET SHOWPLAN_TEXT` command as follows (`set_showplan.sql` in the download):

```
USE Northwind
GO
SET SHOWPLAN_TEXT ON
GO
SELECT DISTINCT p.ProductID, p.ProductName, p.UnitPrice,
                od.Quantity, p.UnitsInStock
  FROM [Products] p, [od] od
  WHERE p.ProductID = od.ProductID
  AND od.Quantity = (SELECT Min(odSub.Quantity)
                     FROM [od] odSub)
  ORDER BY p.ProductID
GO
SET SHOWPLAN_TEXT OFF
GO
```

Figure 3-10 shows the textual execution plan output.

```
  StmtText
1 |--Nested Loops(Inner Join, OUTER REFERENCES:([od].[ProductID]))
2      |--Stream Aggregate(GROUP BY:([od].[ProductID]) DEFINE:([od].[Quantity]=ANY([od].[Quantity])))
3      |    |--Nested Loops(Inner Join, WHERE:([od].[Quantity]=[Expr1001]))
4      |         |--Stream Aggregate(DEFINE:([Expr1001]=MIN([odSub].[Quantity])))
5      |         |    |--Clustered Index Scan(OBJECT:([NWTest].[dbo].[od].[ProductID] AS [odSub]))
6      |         |--Clustered Index Scan(OBJECT:([NWTest].[dbo].[od].[ProductID] AS [od]), ORDERED FORWARD)
7      |--Clustered Index Seek(OBJECT:([NWTest].[dbo].[Products].[PK_Products] AS [p]), SEEK:([p].[ProductID]=[od].[ProductID]) ORDERED F
```

Figure 3-10. *Textual execution plan output*

The procedures to obtain the textual execution plan by the other two commands and the graphical execution plan are explained later in the chapter.

Analyzing the Query Execution Plan

Let's start with the costly query identified in set_showplan.sql. Copy it (minus the
SET SHOWPLAN_TEXT statements) into Query Analyzer and turn Show Execution Plan on.
Now, on executing this query, you see the execution plan in Figure 3-11.

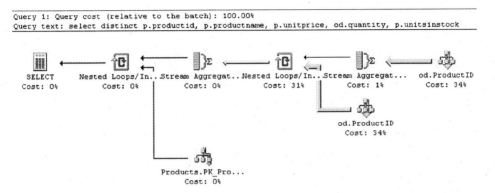

```
Query 1: Query cost (relative to the batch): 100.00%
Query text: select distinct p.productid, p.productname, p.unitprice, od.quantity, p.unitsinstock
```

Figure 3-11. *Query execution plan*

The execution plan is read from right to left and from top to bottom. Each step represents
an operation performed to get the final output of the query. Some of the aspects of a query
execution represented by an execution plan are as follows:

- If a query consists of a batch of multiple queries, the execution plan for each query
  will be displayed in the order of execution. Each execution plan in the batch will have
  a relative cost, with the total cost of the whole batch being 100%.

- Every node in an execution plan will have a relative cost, with the total cost of all the
  nodes in an execution plan being 100%.

- Usually a starting node in an execution represents a data-retrieval mechanism from a
  database object (a table or an index). For example, in the execution plan in Figure 3-11,
  the three starting points represent two data retrievals from the od table and one data
  retrieval from the Products table.

- Data retrieval will be either a table operation or an index operation. For example, in the
  execution plan in Figure 3-11, all three data retrieval steps are index operations.

- Data retrieval on an index will be either an *index scan* or an *index seek*. An index scan is
  represented by a thick arrow traversing across the node; an index seek is represented by
  a thin, twisted arrow traversing through the node. For example, the first two index operations in Figure 3-11 are index scans and the last one is an index seek.

- The naming convention for a data retrieval operation on an index is
  [Table Name].[Index Name].

- Data flows from right to left between two nodes and is indicated by a connecting arrow
  between the two nodes.

- The thickness of a connecting arrow between nodes represents the number of rows transferred.

- The joining mechanism between two nodes in the same column will be either a *nested loop join*, a *hash join*, or a *merge join*. For example, in the execution plan shown in Figure 3-11, there are two nested-loop joins.

- Running the mouse over a node in an execution plan shows its details, as you can see from Figure 3-12.

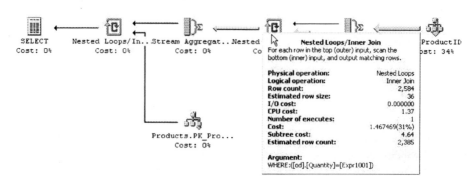

Query 1: Query cost (relative to the batch): 100.00%
Query text: select distinct p.productid, p.productname, p.unitprice, od.quantity, p.unitsinstock

Figure 3-12. *Execution plan node detail*

- A node detail shows both physical and logical operation types at the top. If logical and physical operations are the same, then only the physical operation is shown. It also displays other useful information, such as row count, I/O cost, CPU cost, and so on.

- The Argument section in a node detail pop-up is especially useful in analysis, as it shows the filter or join criterion used by the optimizer.

Identifying the Costly Steps in an Execution Plan

Your main interest in the execution plan is to find out which steps are relatively costly. These steps are the starting point for your query optimization. You can choose the starting steps by adopting the following techniques:

- Each node in an execution plan shows its relative cost in the complete execution plan, with the total cost of the whole plan being 100%. Therefore, focus attention on the node(s) with highest relative cost. For example, the execution plan in Figure 3-11 has two steps with 34% cost each.

- Observe the thickness of the connecting arrows between nodes. A very thick connecting arrow indicates a large number of rows being transferred between the corresponding nodes. Analyze the node to the left of the arrow to understand why it requires so many rows.

- Look for hash join operations. For small result sets, a nested loop join is usually the pre-ferred join technique. You will learn more about hash joins compared to nested loop joins later in this chapter.

- Look for bookmark lookup operations. A bookmark operation for a large result set can cause a large number of logical reads. I will cover bookmark lookups in more detail in Chapter 6.

- Look for steps performing a sort operation. This indicates that the data was not retrieved in the correct sort order.

Analyzing Index Effectiveness

To examine a costly step in an execution plan further, you should analyze the data-retrieval mechanism for the relevant table or index. First, you should check whether an index opera-tion is a seek or a scan. Usually, for best performance, you should retrieve as few rows as pos-sible from a table, and an index seek is usually the most efficient way of accessing a small number of rows. A scan operation usually indicates that a large number of rows have been accessed. Therefore, it is generally preferable to seek rather than scan.

Next, you want to ensure that the indexing mechanism is properly set up. The query opti-mizer evaluates the available indexes to discover which index will retrieve data from the table in the most efficient way. If a desired index is not available, the optimizer uses the next best index. For best performance, you should always ensure that the best index is used in a data-retrieval operation. You can judge the index effectiveness (whether the best index is used or not) by analyzing the Argument section of a node detail for the following:

- A data-retrieval operation

- A join operation

Let's look at the data-retrieval mechanism for the Products table in the previous execution plan. Figure 3-13 shows the node detail.

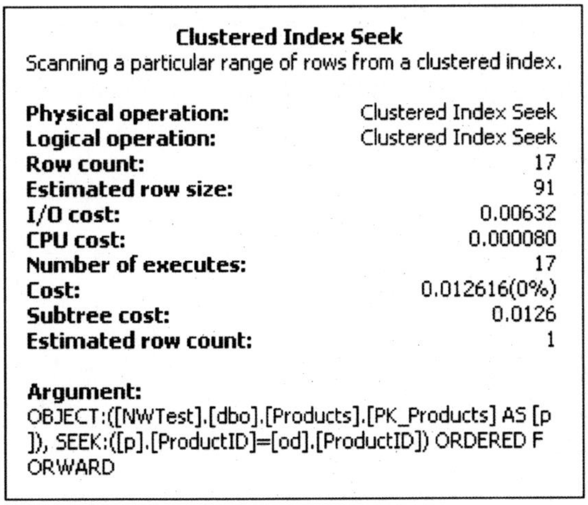

```
Clustered Index Seek
Scanning a particular range of rows from a clustered index.

Physical operation:            Clustered Index Seek
Logical operation:             Clustered Index Seek
Row count:                                       17
Estimated row size:                              91
I/O cost:                                   0.00632
CPU cost:                                  0.000080
Number of executes:                              17
Cost:                                 0.012616(0%)
Subtree cost:                                0.0126
Estimated row count:                              1

Argument:
OBJECT:([NWTest].[dbo].[Products].[PK_Products] AS [p
]), SEEK:([p].[ProductID]=[od].[ProductID]) ORDERED F
ORWARD
```

Figure 3-13. *Data-retrieval mechanism for the Products table*

In the node detail for the Products table, the OBJECT part of the Argument section specifies the index used. It uses the following naming convention: [Database].[Owner].[Table Name].[Index Name]. The SEEK part specifies the column used to seek into the index. Therefore, from Figure 3-13, you can infer that the index used to retrieve data from the Products table is PK_Products. It is joined with the od table on the ProductID column. The SEEK part confirms that the column on which the table is joined with another table matches the prefix ordering of columns in the index used. For example, from Figure 3-13, you can infer that ProductID is the first column in the PK_Products index.

Sometimes, you may have a different data-retrieval mechanism, as shown in Figure 3-14.

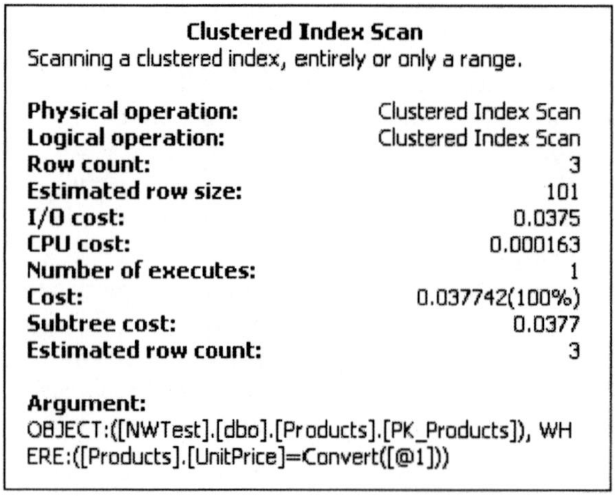

```
             Clustered Index Scan
Scanning a clustered index, entirely or only a range.

Physical operation:            Clustered Index Scan
Logical operation:             Clustered Index Scan
Row count:                                        3
Estimated row size:                             101
I/O cost:                                    0.0375
CPU cost:                                  0.000163
Number of executes:                               1
Cost:                            0.037742(100%)
Subtree cost:                                0.0377
Estimated row count:                              3

Argument:
OBJECT:([NWTest].[dbo].[Products].[PK_Products]), WH
ERE:([Products].[UnitPrice]=Convert([@1]))
```

Figure 3-14. *A variation of the data-retrieval mechanism*

In the node detail in Figure 3-14, you have WHERE in place of SEEK. This signifies that the column requirement for a filter (or join) criterion doesn't match the prefix ordering of columns in the index used. This mismatch increases the cost of data retrieval. To increase the effectiveness of the index, you should analyze the index used, and if possible add the filter (or join) criteria column as the first column in the index. If adding or reordering columns in an existing index isn't possible, then you can create a new index on the filter (or join) criteria columns. Since this will change the data-retrieval mechanism, you should analyze its effect on other steps in the execution plan.

Analyzing Join Effectiveness

In addition to analyzing the indexes used, you should examine the effectiveness of join strategies decided by the optimizer. SQL Server uses three types of joins, namely

- Nested loop joins

- Merge joins

- Hash joins

In many simple queries affecting a small set of rows, nested loop joins are far superior to both hash and merge joins. The join types to be used in a query are decided dynamically by the optimizer.

To understand SQL Server's join strategy, consider the following simple query (plan.sql in the download):

■**NOTE** Create the od table using the script od_join.sql provided in the download.

```
SELECT p.*
  FROM [Products] p, [od] od
  WHERE p.ProductID = od.ProductID
```

Table 3-5 shows the two tables' indexes and number of rows.

Table 3-5. *Indexes and Number of Rows of the Products and od Tables*

Table	Indexes	Number of Rows
Products	Clustered index on ProductID	77
od	Clustered index on OrderID	327,560

Hash Join

Figure 3-15 shows the execution plan for the preceding query.

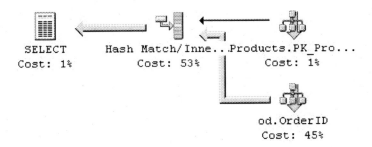

Figure 3-15. *Execution plan with a hash join*

You can see that the optimizer used a hash join between the two tables.

A hash join uses the two join inputs as a *build input* and a *probe input*. The build input is shown as the top input in the execution plan, and the probe input is shown as the bottom input. The smaller of the two inputs serves as the build input.

The hash join performs its operation in two phases: the *build phase* and *probe phase*. In the most commonly used form of the hash join, the *in-memory hash join*, the entire build input is scanned or computed, and then a hash table is built in memory. Each row is inserted into a hash bucket depending on the hash value computed for the *hash key* (the set of columns in the equality predicate).

This build phase is followed by the probe phase. The entire probe input is scanned or computed one row at a time, and for each probe row a hash key value is computed. The corresponding hash bucket is scanned for the hash key value from the probe input, and the matches are produced. Figure 3-16 illustrates the process of an in-memory hash join.

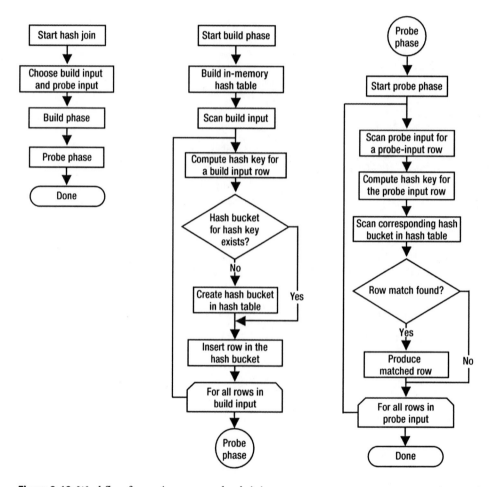

Figure 3-16. *Workflow for an in-memory hash join*

The query optimizer uses hash joins to process large, unsorted, nonindexed inputs effi-ciently. Let's now look at the next type of join: the merge join.

Merge Join

In the previous case, input from the od table is large and the table is not indexed on the joining column (ProductID). Since the join criterion is on the ProductID column, to improve perform-ance, you can create an index on [od].[ProductID]:

```
USE Northwind
GO
CREATE INDEX [ProductID] ON [od]([ProductID])
```

Figure 3-17 shows the resultant execution plan for the preceding query.

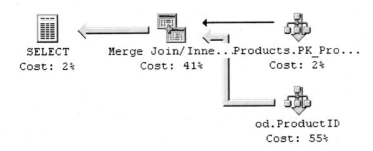

Figure 3-17. *Execution plan with a merge join*

As shown previously, this time the optimizer used a merge join between the two tables.

A merge join requires both join inputs to be sorted on the merge columns, as defined by the join criterion. If indexes are available on both joining columns, then the join inputs are sorted by the index. Since each join input is sorted, the merge join gets a row from each input and compares them for equality. A matching row is produced if they are equal. This process is repeated until all rows are processed.

In this case, the query optimizer found that the join inputs were not small, and both the join inputs were sorted (or indexed) on their join column. As a result, the merge join turns out to be a faster join strategy than the hash join. Previously, not having an index on the [od].[ProductID] column caused the optimizer to select a hash join strategy.

The final type of join we will look at here is the nested loop join.

Nested Loop Join

For better performance, you should always access a limited number of rows from individual tables. To understand the effect of using a smaller result set, decrease the join inputs in your query as follows:

```
SELECT TOP 1000 p.*
  FROM [Products] p, [od] od
  WHERE p.ProductID = od.ProductID
```

Figure 3-18 shows the resultant execution plan of the modified query.

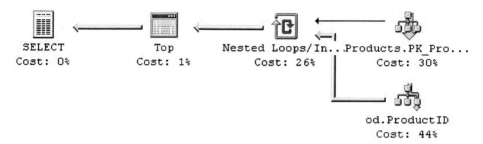

Figure 3-18. *Execution plan with a nested loop join*

As you can see, the optimizer used a nested loop join between the two tables.

A nested loop join uses one join input as the outer input table, and the other as the inner input table. The outer input table is shown as the top input in the execution plan, and the inner input table is shown as the bottom input table. The outer loop consumes the outer input table row by row. The inner loop, executed for each outer row, searches for matching rows in the inner input table.

Nested loop joins are highly effective if the outer input is quite small and the inner input is large but indexed. In many simple queries affecting a small set of rows, nested loop joins are far superior to both hash and merge joins.

Even for small join inputs as in the previous modified query, it's important to have an index on the joining columns. As you saw in the preceding execution plan, for a small set of rows, indexes on joining columns allow the query optimizer to consider a nested loop join strategy. A missing index on the joining column of an input will force the query optimizer to use a hash join instead. Let's verify this behavior for the preceding query (retrieving the smaller result set) by dropping the [od].[ProductID] index:

```
DROP INDEX [od].[ProductID]
```

Figure 3-19 shows that the resultant execution plan uses a hash join.

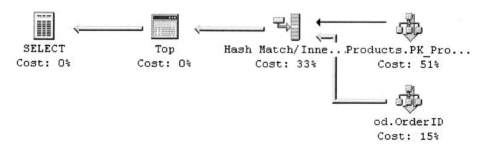

Figure 3-19. *Execution plan back to a hash join*

Therefore, whenever you find a hash join in an execution plan, you should evaluate the availability of indexes on the join columns between the two tables participating in the join operation.

Table 3-6 summarizes the use of the three join types.

Table 3-6. *Characteristics of the Three Join Types*

Join Type	Index on Joining Columns	Usual Size of Joining Tables	Presorted	Join Clause
Nested loop	Inner table: Must Outer table: Preferable	Small	Optional	All
Merge	Both tables: Must Optimal condition: Clustered or covering index on both	Large	Yes	Equi-join
Hash	Inner table: Not indexed Outer table: Optional	Any Optimal condition: Small outer table, large inner table	No	Equi-join

NOTE The outer table is usually the smaller of the two joining tables.

I will cover index types, including clustered and covering indexes, in Chapter 4.

SHOWPLAN_ALL vs. STATISTICS PROFILE

Both SET SHOWPLAN_ALL and SET STATISTICS PROFILE generate a textual execution plan for a query:

- SHOWPLAN_ALL describes the processing strategy decided by the query optimizer without executing the query. It shows an estimated execution plan.

- STATISTICS PROFILE executes the query and returns the regular result set output along with an additional output that represents the processing strategy used for the query execution.

Let's examine a situation where using STATISTICS PROFILE is preferable to using SHOWPLAN_ALL. Consider the following stored procedure (create_p1.sql in the download):

```
IF(SELECT OBJECT_ID('p1')) IS NOT NULL
   DROP PROC p1
GO
CREATE PROC p1
AS
CREATE TABLE #t1(c1 INTEGER)
INSERT INTO #t1 SELECT ProductID FROM Products
SELECT * FROM #t1
GO
```

You may try to use SHOWPLAN_ALL to obtain a textual execution plan for the query as follows (showplan.sql in the download):

```
SET SHOWPLAN_ALL ON
GO
EXEC p1
GO
SET SHOWPLAN_ALL OFF
GO
```

But this fails with the following error:

```
Server: Msg 208, Level 16, State 1, Procedure p1, Line 4
Invalid object name '#t1'.
```

Since SHOWPLAN_ALL doesn't actually execute the query, the query optimizer can't generate an execution plan for INSERT and SELECT statements on the temporary table (#t1). One workaround is to create the temporary table first:

```
CREATE TABLE #t1(c1 INTEGER)
GO
SET SHOWPLAN_ALL ON
GO
EXEC p1
GO
SET SHOWPLAN_ALL OFF
GO
```

Instead, you can use STATISTICS PROFILE as follows:

```
SET STATISTICS PROFILE ON
GO
EXEC p1
GO
SET STATISTICS PROFILE OFF
GO
```

Since STATISTICS PROFILE executes the query, you need not create the temporary table separately. A part of the textual execution plan provided by STATISTICS PROFILE is shown in Figure 3-20.

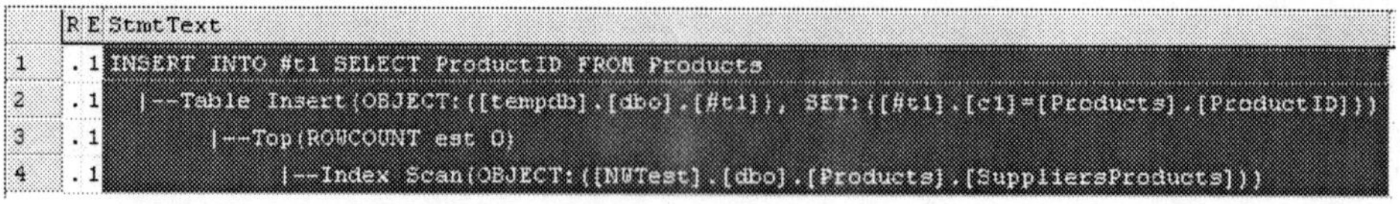

Figure 3-20. *STATISTICS PROFILE output*

STATISTICS PROFILE is also useful in analyzing the effectiveness of the statistics for a query. I will cover this in more depth in Chapter 7.

Query Cost

Even though the execution plan for a query provides a detailed processing strategy and the relative costs of the individual steps involved, it doesn't provide the overall cost of the query in terms of CPU usage, reads/writes to disk, or query duration. While optimizing a query, you may add an index to reduce the relative cost of a step. This may adversely affect a dependent step in the execution plan, or sometimes it may even modify the execution plan itself. Thus, if you only look at the execution plan, you can't be sure that your query optimization benefits the query as a whole, as opposed to that one step in the execution plan. You can analyze the overall cost of a query in different ways; let's examine how to do this next.

Server Trace Information

You should monitor the overall cost of a query while optimizing it. As explained previously, you can use SQL Profiler to monitor the Duration, CPU, Reads, and Writes information for the query. To reduce the overhead of Profiler on SQL Server, you should set a filter criterion on SPID (for example, an identifier inside SQL Server to identify a database user) equal to the SPID of your Query Analyzer window. However, using Profiler still adds a consistent overhead on SQL Server in filtering out the events for other database users or SPIDs. I will explain SPID in more depth in Chapter 12.

The *Server Trace* option provides you with the cost of a query in the Query Analyzer window itself while optimizing the query, and it doesn't add any consistent overhead on SQL Server. The work is done only when the query is executed from the Query Analyzer window. To turn the Server Trace option on, select the Query ➤ Show Server Trace option in Query Analyzer.

For example, consider this query:

```
SELECT TOP 1000 p.*
  FROM [Products] p, [od] od
  WHERE p.ProductID = od.ProductID
```

The server trace information for the query should look something like that shown in Figure 3-21.

Text	Event Class	Duration	CPU	Reads	Writes
set noexec off set parse...	SQL:StmtCompleted	0	0	0	0
select IS_SRVROLEMEMBER ...	SQL:StmtCompleted	0	0	0	0
SELECT TOP 1000 p.* F...	SQL:StmtCompleted	80	10	158	0

Figure 3-21. *Server trace output*

This server trace information usually matches the corresponding cost figures captured by SQL Profiler, as shown in Figure 3-22.

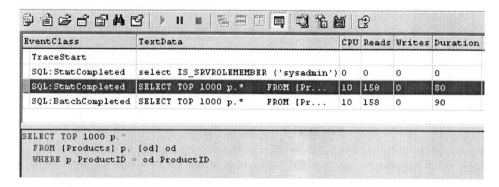

Figure 3-22. *Profiler trace output*

Execution Time

Both Duration and CPU represent the time factor of a query. To obtain detailed information on the amount of time (in milliseconds) required to parse, compile, and execute a query, use SET STATISTICS TIME as follows (timestats.sql in the download):

```
SET STATISTICS TIME ON
GO
SELECT TOP 1000 p.*
  FROM [Products] p, [od] od
  WHERE p.ProductID = od.ProductID
GO
SET STATISTICS TIME OFF
GO
```

The output of STATISTICS TIME for the preceding SELECT statement is as follows:

```
SQL Server Execution Times:
   CPU time = 0 ms,  elapsed time = 0 ms.
SQL Server parse and compile time:
   CPU time = 0 ms, elapsed time = 0 ms.


(1000 row(s) affected)


SQL Server Execution Times:
   CPU time = 10 ms,  elapsed time = 80 ms.
SQL Server parse and compile time:
   CPU time = 0 ms, elapsed time = 0 ms.
```

The CPU time = 10 ms part of the Execution Times represents the CPU value provided by the Profiler tool and the Server Trace option. Similarly, the corresponding Elapsed time = 80 ms represents the Duration value provided by the other mechanisms.

A 0 ms parse and compile time signifies that the optimizer reused the existing execution plan for this query, and therefore didn't have to spend any time parsing and compiling the query again. If the query is executed for the first time, then the optimizer has to parse the query first for syntax, and then compile it to produce the execution plan. This can be easily verified by dropping and re-creating the clustered index on [od].[OrderID]. The resultant output of the STATISTICS TIME for the SELECT statement is as follows:

```
SQL Server Execution Times:
   CPU time = 0 ms,  elapsed time = 0 ms.
SQL Server parse and compile time:
   CPU time = 10 ms, elapsed time = 11 ms.


(1000 row(s) affected)

SQL Server Execution Times:
   CPU time = 10 ms,  elapsed time = 84 ms.
SQL Server parse and compile time:
   CPU time = 0 ms, elapsed time = 0 ms.
```

This time, SQL Server spent 10 ms of CPU time, and a total of 11 ms parsing and compiling the query.

STATISTICS IO

As discussed in the "Identifying Costly Queries" section presented earlier in the chapter, the number of Reads is usually the most significant cost factor among Duration, CPU, Reads, and Writes. The total number of Reads performed by a query consists of the sum of the number of Reads performed on all tables involved in the query. The Reads performed on the individual tables may vary significantly, depending on the size of the result set requested from the individual table and the indexes available.

To reduce the total number of Reads, it will be useful to find all the tables accessed in the query and their corresponding number of Reads. This detailed information helps you concentrate on optimizing data access on the tables with a large number of Reads. The number of Reads per table also helps you evaluate the impact of the optimization step (implemented for one table) on the other tables referred to in the query.

In a simple query, you determine the individual tables accessed by taking a close look at the query. This becomes increasingly difficult the more complex the query becomes. In the case of a stored procedure, database views, or functions, it becomes more difficult to identify all the tables actually accessed by the optimizer. You can use STATISTICS IO to get this information, irrespective of query complexity.

To turn STATISTICS IO on, navigate to Query ➤ Current Connection Properties ➤ Set Statistics IO in Query Analyzer. You may also get this information programmatically as follows (statisticsio.sql in the download):

```
SET STATISTICS IO ON
GO
SELECT p.*
  FROM [Products] p, [od] od
  WHERE p.ProductID = od.ProductID
GO
SET STATISTICS IO OFF
GO
```

While analyzing the effectiveness of a join strategy in the "Analyzing Join Effectiveness" section, you found that the optimizer uses a hash join for the preceding query with no index on [od].[ProductID]. On having an index on the [od].[ProductID] column, the optimizer uses the merge join instead. That's an interesting fact—but you don't know how it affects the query cost! You can use SET STATISTICS IO as shown previously to compare the cost of the query (in terms of logical reads) between the two processing strategies used by the optimizer.

You get following STATISTICS IO output when the query uses the hash join:

```
Table 'od'. Scan count 1, logical reads 1585, physical reads 0, read-ahead reads 0.
Table 'Products'. Scan count 1, logical reads 2, physical reads 0,
 read-ahead reads 0.
```

Now when you add the [od].[ProductID] index to allow the optimizer to use the merge join, the resultant STATISTICS IO output turns out to be this:

```
Table 'od'. Scan count 1, logical reads 892, physical reads 0, read-ahead reads 0.
Table 'Products'. Scan count 1, logical reads 2, physical reads 0,
 read-ahead reads 0.
```

Logical reads for the od table have been almost halved with a merge join compared to that with a hash join. It also hasn't affected the data retrieval cost of the Products table. This indicates the cost benefit of using a merge join over a hash join in this case.

While interpreting the output of STATISTICS IO, you mostly refer to the number of logical reads. Sometimes you also refer to the scan count, but even if you perform few logical reads per scan, the total number of logical reads provided by STATISTICS IO can still be high. If the number of logical reads per scan is small for a specific table, then you may not be able to improve the indexing mechanism of the table any further. The number of physical reads and read-ahead reads will be nonzero when the data is not found in the memory, but once the data is populated in-memory, the physical reads and read-ahead reads will tend to be zero.

There is another advantage to knowing all the tables used and their corresponding Reads for a query. Both Duration and CPU values may fluctuate significantly on re-executing the same query with no change in table schema (including indexes) or data because the essential services and background applications running on the SQL Server machine usually affect the processing time of the query under observation.

During optimization steps, you need a nonfluctuating cost figure as a reference. The Reads (or logical reads) don't vary between multiple executions of a query with fixed table schema and data. For example, if you execute the previous SELECT statement ten times, you will probably get ten different figures for Duration and CPU, but Reads will remain the same each time. Therefore, during optimization, you can refer to the number of Reads for an individual table to ensure that you really have reduced the data access cost of the table.

Even though the number of logical Reads can also be obtained from Profiler or the Server Trace option, there is another benefit to using STATISTICS IO. The number of logical Reads for a query shown by Profiler or the Server Trace option increases as you use different SET statements (mentioned previously) along with the query. But the number of logical Reads shown by STATISTICS IO doesn't include the additional pages that are accessed as SET statements are used with a query. Thus, STATISTICS IO provides a consistent figure for the number of logical reads.

To illustrate this point, let's examine the number of logical reads for the preceding query using SET STATISTICS IO and Profiler simultaneously. Figure 3-23 shows the number of logical Reads indicated by Profiler for the query.

EventClass	TextData	CPU	Reads	Writes
TraceStart				
SQL:StmtCompleted	SET STATISTICS IO ON	0	0	0
SQL:BatchCompleted	SET STATISTICS IO ON	0	0	0
SQL:StmtCompleted	SELECT p.* FROM [Products] p, [od...	...	919	0
SQL:BatchCompleted	SELECT p.* FROM [Products] p, [od...	...	989	0
SQL:StmtCompleted	SET STATISTICS IO OFF	0	0	0
SQL:BatchCompleted	SET STATISTICS IO OFF	0	0	0

```
SELECT p.*
  FROM [Products] p, [od] od
  WHERE p.ProductID = od.ProductID
```

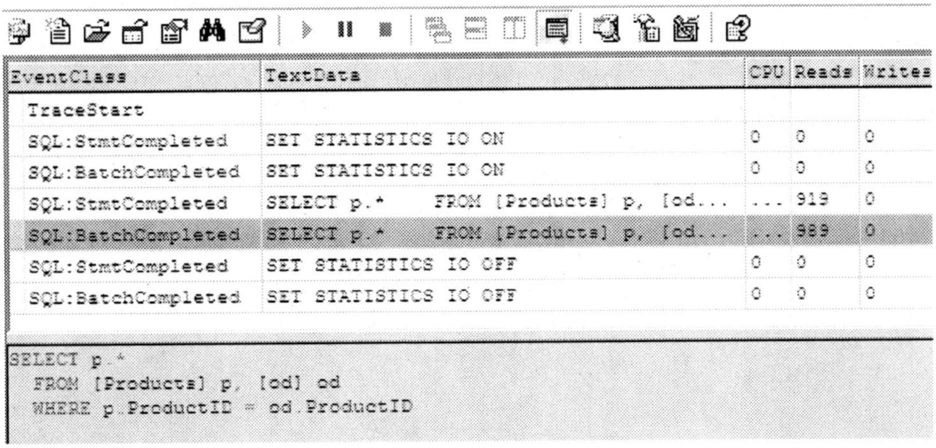

Figure 3-23. *Reads without SET STATISTICS PROFILE*

On using SET STATISTICS PROFILE along with the query, the number of logical Reads indicated by Profiler for the query increases as shown in Figure 3-24. However, in both cases (with and without STATISTICS PROFILE), the number of logical reads indicated by STATISTICS IO remains the same (892).

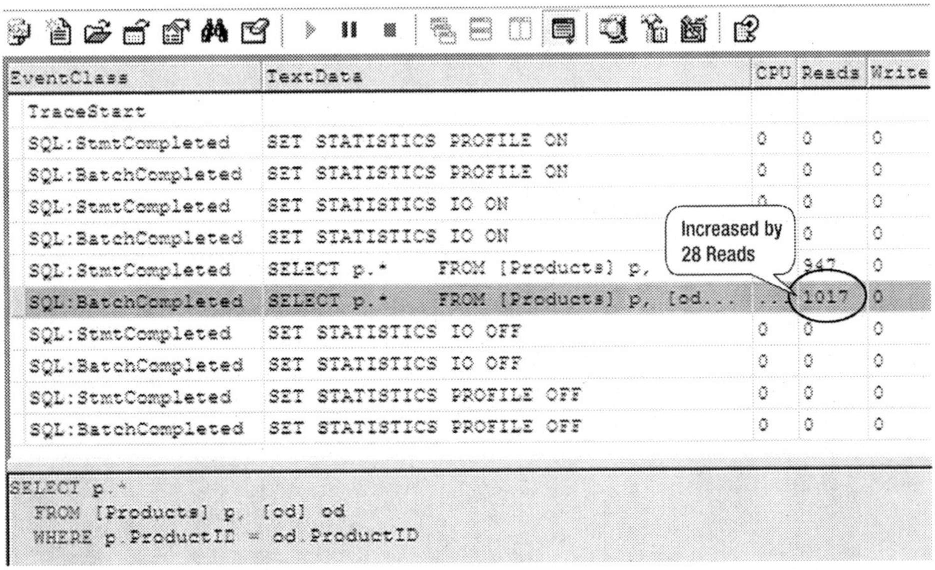

EventClass	TextData	CPU	Reads	Write
TraceStart				
SQL:StmtCompleted	SET STATISTICS PROFILE ON	0	0	0
SQL:BatchCompleted	SET STATISTICS PROFILE ON	0	0	0
SQL:StmtCompleted	SET STATISTICS IO ON	0	0	0
SQL:BatchCompleted	SET STATISTICS IO ON	0	0	0
SQL:StmtCompleted	SELECT p.* FROM [Products] p,		947	0
SQL:BatchCompleted	SELECT p.* FROM [Products] p, [od...	...	1017	0
SQL:StmtCompleted	SET STATISTICS IO OFF	0	0	0
SQL:BatchCompleted	SET STATISTICS IO OFF	0	0	0
SQL:StmtCompleted	SET STATISTICS PROFILE OFF	0	0	0
SQL:BatchCompleted	SET STATISTICS PROFILE OFF	0	0	0

Increased by 28 Reads

```
SELECT p.*
  FROM [Products] p, [od] od
  WHERE p.ProductID = od.ProductID
```

Figure 3-24. *Reads with SET STATISTICS PROFILE*

Therefore, using STATISTICS IO is usually your best option for measuring logical reads.

Summary

In this chapter, you saw that you can use the Profiler tool or SQL tracing to identify the queries causing a high amount of stress on the system resources in a SQL workload. These queries can be further analyzed with Query Analyzer to find the costly steps in the processing strategy of the query. For better performance, it is important to consider both the index and join mechanisms used in an execution plan while analyzing a query. The number of data retrievals (or Reads) for the individual tables provided by SET STATISTICS IO helps concentrate on the data access mechanism of the tables with most number of Reads.

Once you identify a costly query and finish the initial analysis, the next step should be to optimize the query for performance. As indexing is one of the most commonly used performance tuning techniques, in the next chapter I will discuss in depth the various indexing mechanisms available in SQL Server.

CHAPTER 4

Index Analysis

A good index is one of your best allies in reducing the stress caused by a SQL query on the system resources. Conversely, having no indexes, or not having the right ones, can adversely affect the performance of a query by retrieving far more rows from the table than is necessary. For this reason, it is extremely important for everyone—not just the DBA—to understand the different indexing techniques that can be used to optimize a query.

In this chapter, I cover the following topics:

- What an index is

- The benefits and overheads of an index

- General recommendations for index design

- Clustered and nonclustered index behavior and comparisons

- Recommendations for clustered and nonclustered indexes

- Advanced indexing techniques: covering index, index intersection, index join, and indexed view

- Additional characteristics of indexes

What Is an Index?

One of the best ways to reduce disk I/O and logical reads is to use an index. An index allows SQL Server to find data in a table without scanning the entire table. An index in a database is analogous to an index in a book. Say, for example, that you wanted to look up "ADO" in this book. Without the index at the back of the book, you would have to scan through the entire book to find the text you needed. With the index, you know exactly where to go.

While tuning a database for performance, you create indexes on the different columns used in a query to help SQL Server find data quickly. For example, consider the Product table shown in Figure 4-1.

Name	Manufacturer	Description	Quantity	Price	RowID
Product1	M2	...	...	...	1
Product2	M3	...	...	...	2
Product3	M1	...	...	...	3
Product4	M4	...	...	...	4
Product5	M5	...	...	...	5

Figure 4-1. *Sample product table*

Suppose you want to retrieve all the products supplied by the manufacturer M1. This requires a scan through all the rows of the table to identify the rows with Manufacturer = M1. To speed up this search process, you can index the content of the Product table on the Manufacturer column. You can do this in the following two ways:

- *Like a book's index*: The ordered list of manufacturers is created without altering the layout of the Product table, similar to the way the index of a book is created. As the keyword index of a book lists the keywords in a separate section with a page number to refer to the main content of the book, the list of manufacturers (or index on the Manufacturer column) is created as a separate structure and refers to the corresponding row in the Product table. Table 4-1 shows the structure of the manufacturer index.

Table 4-1. *Structure of the Manufacturer Index*

Manufacturer	RowID
M1	3
M2	1
M3	2
M4	4
M5	5

SQL Server can scan the manufacturer index to find rows with Manufacturer = 1. Since the manufacturers are arranged in a sorted order, SQL Server can stop scanning as soon as it encounters the row with value M2. This type of index is called a *nonclustered index*, and it is explained in detail later in the chapter.

- *Like a dictionary*: Unlike a book, the content of a dictionary is indexed by arranging the content of the dictionary itself in a sorted order. The keywords are not duplicated to create the index. Similarly, the contents of the Product table itself can be rearranged so that the rows are ordered on the Manufacturer column as shown in Figure 4-2.

Name	Manufacturer	Description	Quantity	Price	RowID
Product3	M1	...	...	...	3
Product1	M2	...	...	...	1
Product2	M3	...	...	...	2
Product4	M4	...	...	...	4
Product5	M5	...	...	...	5

Figure 4-2. *Dictionary sorting of products*

Once again, SQL Server can go through the ordered content of the Manufacturer column and stop scanning as soon as it encounters the row with value M2. This type of index is called a *clustered index*, and it is explained in detail later in the chapter.

In either case, SQL Server will be able to find all the products supplied by the manufacturer M1 more quickly than without an index.

You can create indexes on either a single column (as shown previously) or a combination of columns in a table. SQL Server automatically creates indexes for certain types of constraints (for example, PRIMARY KEY and UNIQUE constraints).

The Benefit of Indexes

Since a page has a limited amount of space, it can store a larger number of rows if the rows contain a fewer number of columns. The first index form mentioned in the list in the previous section, the nonclustered index, doesn't contain all the columns of the table, but only a limited number of the columns. Therefore, a page will be able to store more rows of a nonclustered index than rows of the table itself, which contains all the columns. Consequently, SQL Server will be able to read more values for a column from a page representing a nonclustered index on the column than from a page representing the table that contains the column.

Another benefit of the nonclustered index is that, because it is in a separate structure from the data table, it can be put in a different filegroup, as explained in Chapter 2. This means that SQL Server can access the index and table concurrently, making searches even faster.

Indexes store their information in a B-tree structure, so the number of reads required to find a particular row is minimized. The benefit of a B-tree structure can be seen in the following example.

Consider a single column table with 27 rows in a random order and only three rows per leaf page. Suppose the layout of the rows in the pages is as shown in Figure 4-3.

24,14,12		11,20,9		25,15,10		16,13,7		2,26,17		21,18,22		19,6,5		1,8,3		27,4,23

Figure 4-3. *Initial layout of 27 rows*

To search the row (or rows) for the column value of 5, SQL Server has to scan all the rows and the pages, since even the last row in the last page may have the value 5. As the number of reads depends on the number of pages accessed, nine read operations have to be performed without an index on the column. This content can be ordered by creating an index on the column, with the resultant layout of the rows and pages shown in Figure 4-4.

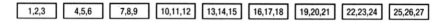

Figure 4-4. *Ordered layout of 27 rows*

Indexing the column arranges the content in a sorted. This allows SQL Server to determine the possible value for a row position in the column with respect to the value of another row position in the column. For example, in Figure 4-4, when SQL Server finds the first row with the column value 6, it can be sure that there are no more rows with the column value 5. Thus, only two read operations are required to fetch the rows with the value 5 when the content is indexed. However, what happens if you want to search for the column value 25? This will require nine read operations! This problem is solved by implementing indexes using the B-tree structure.

A B-tree consists of a starting node (or page) called a *root node* with *branch nodes* (or pages) growing out of it (or linked to it). All keys are stored in the leaves. Contained in each interior node (above the leaf nodes) are pointers to its branch nodes and values representing the smallest value found in the branch node. Keys are kept in sorted order within each node. B-trees use a balanced tree structure for efficient record retrieval—a B-tree is balanced when the leaf nodes are all at the same level from the root node. For example, creating an index on the preceding content will generate the balanced B-tree structure shown in Figure 4-5.

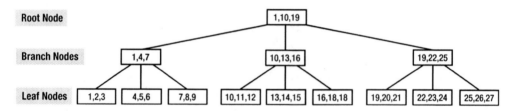

Figure 4-5. *B-tree layout of 27 rows*

The B-tree algorithm minimizes the number of pages to be accessed to locate a desired key, thereby speeding up the data access process. For example, in Figure 4-5, the search for the key value 5 starts at the top root node. Since the key value is between 1 and 10, the search process follows the left branch to the next node. As the key value 5 falls between the values 4 and 7, the search process follows the middle branch to the next node with the starting key value of 4. The search process retrieves the key value 5 from this leaf page. If the key value 5 doesn't exist in this page, the search process will stop since it's the leaf page. Similarly, the key value 25 can also be searched using the same number of reads.

Index Overhead

The performance benefit of indexes, however, does come at a cost. Tables with indexes require more storage and memory space for the index pages in addition to the data pages of the table. Action queries (INSERT, UPDATE, and DELETE statements) can take longer, and more processing time is required to maintain the indexes of constantly changing tables. This is because, unlike a SELECT statement, action queries modify the data content of a table. If an INSERT statement adds a row to the table, then it also has to add a row in the nonclustered index structure. If the index is a clustered index, the overhead is greater still, as the row has to be added to the data pages themselves in the right order, which may require other data rows to be repositioned below the entry position of the new row. The UPDATE and DELETE action queries manipulate the index pages in a similar manner.

When designing indexes, then, you should ensure that the performance benefits of an index outweigh the extra cost in processing resources. You can do this by using the Profiler tool (explained in Chapter 3) to do an overall workload optimization (explained in Chapter 16).

To understand the overhead cost of an index on action queries, consider the following example. First, create a test table with 10,000 rows (create_test.sql in the download):

```
IF(SELECT OBJECT_ID('t1')) IS NOT NULL
   DROP TABLE t1
GO
CREATE TABLE t1(c1 INT, c2 INT, c3 CHAR(50))
DECLARE @n INT
SET @n = 1
WHILE @n <= 10000
BEGIN
   INSERT INTO t1 VALUES(@n, @n,'c3')
   SET @n = @n + 1
END
```

If you then run an UPDATE statement

```
UPDATE t1 SET c1 = 1, c2 = 1 WHERE c2 = 1
```

the number of logical reads reported by SET STATISTICS IO is

```
Table 't1'. Scan count 1, logical reads 87
```

On adding an index on column c1

```
CREATE INDEX i1 ON t1(c1)
```

the resultant number of logical reads for the same UPDATE statement increases from 87 to 93:

```
Table 't1'. Scan count 1, logical reads 93
```

Even though it is true that the amount of overhead required to maintain indexes increases for action queries, be aware that SQL Server must first find a row before it can update or delete it; therefore, indexes can be helpful for UPDATE and DELETE statements with complex WHERE clauses as well. The increased efficiency in using the index to locate a row usually offsets the extra overhead needed to update the indexes, unless the table has a lot of indexes.

To understand how an index can benefit even action queries, let's build on the example. Create another index on table t1. This time, create the index on column c2 referred to in the WHERE clause of the UPDATE statement:

```
CREATE INDEX i2 ON t1(c2)
```

After adding this new index, run the UPDATE command again:

```
UPDATE t1 SET c1 = 1, c2 = 1 WHERE c2 = 1
```

The total number of logical reads for this UPDATE statement decreases from 93 to 18 (= 15 + 3):

```
Table 't1'. Scan count 1, logical reads 15
Table 'Worktable'. Scan count 1, logical reads 3
```

NOTE A *worktable* is a temporary table used internally by SQL Server to process the intermediate results of a query. Worktables are created in the tempdb database and are dropped automatically after query execution.

The examples in this section have demonstrated that, although having an index adds some overhead cost to action queries, the overall result is a decrease in cost due to the beneficial effect of indexes on searching.

Index Design Recommendations

The main recommendations for index design are as follows:

- Examine the WHERE clause and join criteria columns.

- Use narrow indexes.

- Examine column uniqueness.

- Examine the column data type.

- Consider column order.

- Consider the type of index (clustered versus nonclustered).

Let's consider each of these recommendations in turn.

Examine the WHERE Clause and Join Criteria Columns

When a query is submitted to SQL Server, the query optimizer tries to find the best data access mechanism for every table referred to in the query. Here is how it does this:

1. The optimizer identifies the columns included in the WHERE clause and the join criteria.

2. The optimizer then examines indexes on those columns.

3. The optimizer assesses the usefulness of each index by determining the selectivity of the clause (i.e., how many rows will be returned) from statistics.

4. Finally, the optimizer estimates the least costly method of retrieving the qualifying rows, based on the information gathered in the previous steps.

■**NOTE** Chapter 7 covers statistics in more depth.

To understand the significance of a WHERE clause column in a query, let's consider an example. Create a test table with an index and just one row (create_t1.sql in the download):

```
IF(SELECT OBJECT_ID('t1')) IS NOT NULL
  DROP TABLE t1
GO
CREATE TABLE t1(c1 INT, c2 INT)
CREATE INDEX i1 ON t1(c1)
INSERT INTO t1 VALUES(11, 12)
```

To read the only row in the table, you can execute a SELECT statement without any WHERE clause as follows:

```
SELECT * FROM t1
```

The query optimizer performs a table scan to read the row directly from the table as shown in Figure 4-6 (switch on the Show Execution Plan option from Query Analyzer's Query menu and the Set Statistics IO option from Query Analyzer's Tools ➤ Options menu).

```
   SELECT           Table Scan
  Cost: 0%         Cost: 100%
```

Figure 4-6. *Execution plan with no WHERE clause*

The number of logical reads reported by SET STATISTICS IO for the SELECT statement is

```
Table 't1'. Scan count 1, logical reads 1
```

To understand the effect of a WHERE clause column on the query optimizer's decision, let's add a WHERE clause to retrieve the same row as retrieved previously:

```
SELECT * FROM t1 WHERE c1 = 11
```

With the WHERE clause in place, the query optimizer examines the WHERE clause column c1, identifies the availability of index i1 on column c1, assesses a high selectivity (that is, only one row will be returned) for the WHERE clause from the statistics on index i1, and decides to use index i1 on column c1, as shown in Figure 4-7.

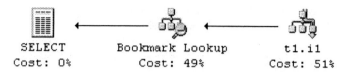

SELECT   Bookmark Lookup   t1.i1
Cost: 0%   Cost: 49%   Cost: 51%

Figure 4-7. *Execution plan with a* WHERE *clause*

The resultant number of logical reads is

`Table 't1'. Scan count 1, logical reads 2`

The cost of this execution plan is so cheap that the query optimizer determined that it would cost more to cycle through the various options than it would to simply execute the first plan it came to, even though the table scan is the slightly cheaper (one logical read instead of two) option. This is one of the improvements of SQL Server 2000 over SQL Server 7.0; sometimes, 7.0's optimizer spends a longer time optimizing queries than it would require to execute the first plan that it came to.

In the real world, you rarely have such small tables, where accessing a row through an index will be costlier than scanning the complete table. However, if you do have very small tables (where all the rows fit within a single 8KB data page), performance may be better from a table scan, rather than an index on the WHERE clause column.

The earlier behavior of the query optimizer shows that the WHERE clause column helps the optimizer choose the indexing operation for a query. This is also applicable for a column used in the join criterion between two tables. The optimizer looks for the indexes on the WHERE clause column or the join criterion column and, if available, considers the index to retrieve the rows from the table. The query optimizer considers index(es) on WHERE clause column(s) and the join criteria column(s) while executing a query. Therefore, having indexes on the frequently used columns in the WHERE clause and the join criteria of a SQL query helps the optimizer avoid scanning a base table.

Use Narrow Indexes

Indexes can be created on a combination of columns in a table. For the best performance, avoid using too many columns in an index. For tables with fewer than 20 columns, examine carefully the performance of indexes with more than four columns (tables with significantly more than 20 columns may have more columns in their indexes). You should also avoid very wide (many-character) columns in an index. Columns with string data types (CHAR, VARCHAR, NCHAR, and NVARCHAR) sometimes can be quite wide; unless they are necessary, minimize the use of string columns with large sizes in an index.

A narrow index can accommodate more rows into an 8KB index page than a wide index. This has the following effects:

- Reduces I/O (through having to read fewer 8 KB pages)

- Makes database caching more effective, because SQL Server can cache fewer index pages, consequently reducing the logical reads required for the index pages in the memory

- Reduces the storage space for the database

To understand how a narrow index can reduce the number of logical reads, consider the following example. Create a test table with 20 rows and an index (narrowIDX_t1.sql in the download):

```
IF(SELECT OBJECT_ID('t1')) IS NOT NULL
  DROP TABLE t1
GO
CREATE TABLE t1(c1 INT, c2 INT)
DECLARE @n INT
SET @n = 1
WHILE @n <= 20
BEGIN
  INSERT INTO t1 VALUES(@n, 2)
  SET @n = @n + 1
END
CREATE INDEX i1 ON t1(c1)
```

Since the indexed column is narrow (the INT data type is 4 bytes), all the index rows can be accommodated in one 8KB index page. As shown in Figure 4-8, you can confirm this in the sysindexes system table (sysindex_select.sql in the download):

```
SELECT Name=name
    , CASE indid
          WHEN 0 THEN 'Table'
          WHEN 1 THEN 'Clustered Index'
          ELSE 'Nonclustered Index'
      END AS Type
    , Pages=dpages, Rows=rowcnt
FROM sysindexes
WHERE id = OBJECT_ID('t1')
```

Name	Type	Pages	Rows
t1	Table	1	20
i1	Nonclustered Index	1	20

Figure 4-8. *Number of pages for a narrow, nonclustered index*

The sysindexes system table is stored in each database and contains useful information on every index in the database. The indid column in sysindexes represents the type of the index, with indid = 0 for a table without a clustered index, indid = 1 for a clustered index, and indid > 1 for nonclustered indexes and statistics. To understand the disadvantage of a wide index key, modify the data type of the indexed column c1 from INT to CHAR(500) (narrow_alter.sql in the download):

```
DROP INDEX t1.i1
ALTER TABLE t1 ALTER COLUMN c1 CHAR(500)
CREATE INDEX i1 ON t1(c1)
```

The width of a column with the INT data type is 4 bytes, and the width of a column with the CHAR(500) data type is 500 bytes. Due to the large width of the indexed column, two index pages are required to contain all 20 index rows. You can confirm this in the sysindexes system table by running sysindex_select.sql again (see Figure 4-9).

Name	Type	Pages	Rows
t1	Heap	2	20
i1	Nonclustered	2	20

Figure 4-9. *Number of pages for a wide, nonclustered index*

A large index key size increases the number of index pages, thereby increasing the amount of memory and disk activities required for the index. It is always recommended to have the index key size as narrow as possible.

Examine Column Uniqueness

Creating an index on columns with a very low range of possible values (such as gender) does not usually benefit performance, as the query optimizer will not be able to use the index to effectively narrow down the rows to be returned. Consider a gender column with only two unique values: male and female. When you execute a query with the gender column in the WHERE clause, you end up with a large number of rows from the table (assuming the distribution of male and female is even), making the query implicitly very costly. It is always preferable to have columns in the WHERE clause with lots of unique rows (or *high selectivity*) to limit the number of rows accessed. You should create an index on those column(s) to help the optimizer access a small result set.

Furthermore, while creating an index on multiple columns, which is also referred to as *composite index*, use the most selective columns first. This will help filter the index rows more efficiently.

▓**NOTE** The importance of column order in a composite index is explained later in the chapter.

From this, you can see that it is important to know the selectivity of a column before creating an index on it. You can find this by executing

```
SELECT COUNT(DISTINCT ColumnName) FROM TableName
```

To compare the output with total number of rows in the table, execute

```
SELECT COUNT(*) FROM TableName
```

The column with the highest number of unique values (or selectivity) is the best candidate for indexing, when referred to in a WHERE clause or a join criterion.

To understand how the selectivity of an index key column affects the use of the index, consider the following example. Create a test table with 2,000 rows (create_unique.sql in the download). The modulo operation (@n%2) provides only two outputs (0 and 1) for every positive value of the variable @n. Therefore, in the following table, the first column (c1) will have all unique values, whereas the second column (c2) will have two unique values (0 and 1) only, alternating between the two unique values for the consecutive rows.

```
IF(SELECT OBJECT_ID('t1')) IS NOT NULL
  DROP TABLE t1
GO
CREATE TABLE t1(c1 INT, c2 INT, c3 CHAR(50))
DECLARE @n INT
SET @n = 1
WHILE @n <= 2000
BEGIN
  INSERT INTO t1 VALUES(@n, @n%2, 'c3')
  SET @n = @n + 1
END
```

Now let's execute a SELECT statement, with both columns c1 and c2 in the WHERE clause:

```
SELECT * FROM t1 WHERE c1 = 1 AND c2 = 1
```

This returns the following (see Figure 4-10):

```
Table 't1'. Scan count 1, logical reads 18
```

   SELECT   Table Scan
  Cost: 1%   Cost: 99%

Figure 4-10. *Execution plan with no index*

Since the SELECT statement has both columns c1 and c2 in the WHERE clause, you can have an index on c1, c2, or a combination of both. To keep the index key width small, you can use a single column index on either c1 or c2. To decide which column is a better candidate for the index, find the uniqueness of these two columns as follows:

```
SELECT COUNT(DISTINCT c1) FROM t1
SELECT COUNT(DISTINCT c2) FROM t1
```

Figure 4-11 shows the result.

(No column name)
2000

(No column name)
2

Figure 4-11. *Number of distinct values for the WHERE clause columns*

The number of unique values for column c1 is 2,000, and that for column c2 is 2. From this, it is apparent that column c1 has many more unique values than column c2. Therefore, column c1 is a better candidate for the index. So, create an index on column c1 as follows:

```
CREATE INDEX i1 ON t1(c1)
```

With the index on column c1 in place, you can now reissue your SELECT command:

```
SELECT * FROM t1 WHERE c1 = 1 AND c2 = 1
```

The index will be used by the optimizer navigating from the index page to the corresponding row in the base table (through a bookmark operation), as shown in the execution plan in Figure 4-12.

```
Table 't1'. Scan count 1, logical reads 3
```

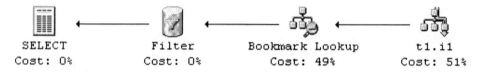

Figure 4-12. *Execution plan with an index on a high selectivity column*

▓**NOTE** You will learn more about bookmark lookups in Chapter 6.

To observe the effect of creating an index on a column with very low selectivity, change the index column from column c1 to c2:

```
CREATE INDEX i1 ON t1(c2) WITH DROP_EXISTING
```

With the index on column c2 in place, you can again reissue your SELECT command:

```
SELECT * FROM t1 WHERE c1 = 1 AND c2 = 1
```

The resultant execution plan for the SELECT statement is shown in Figure 4-13.

```
Table 't1'. Scan count 1, logical reads 18
```

Figure 4-13. *Execution plan with an index on a low selectivity column*

Since the selectivity of column c2 is very low (only two unique values in 2,000 rows), the optimizer found no benefit in using the index on column c2 and preferred a table scan instead.

To find whether it would have been really disadvantageous to use the index on column c2, compare the number of logical reads for the query between two scenarios: the preceding case, where the query plan uses a table scan, and the following case, where you force it to use the index on c2 using an index hint:

```
SELECT * FROM t1 WITH(INDEX(i1)) WHERE c1 = 1 AND c2 = 1
```

The resultant number of logical reads for the SELECT statement is this (see Figure 4-14):

```
Table 't1'. Scan count 1, logical reads 1004
```

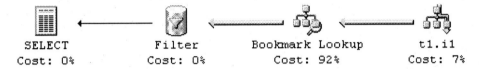

Figure 4-14. *Execution plan with an index on a low selectivity column, plus an index hint*

You can see that the number of logical reads required for a forced index is much greater than for a direct table scan.

▓**NOTE** To make the best use of your indexes, it is highly recommended that you create the index on a column (or set of columns) with very high selectivity.

Examine the Column Data Type

An index search on integer keys is very fast, due to the small size and easy arithmetic manipulation of the INTEGER (or INT) data type. You may also use other variations of integer data types (BIGINT, SMALLINT, and TINYINT) for index columns. Avoid using string data types where possible (CHAR, VARCHAR, NCHAR, and NVARCHAR), because a string match operation is usually costlier than an integer match operation.

Suppose you want to create an index on one column, and you have two candidate columns: one with an INTEGER data type and the other with a CHAR(4) data type. Even though the size of both data types is 4 bytes in SQL Server 2000, you will still prefer the INTEGER data type index. Look at arithmetic operations as an example. The value 1 in the CHAR(4) data type is actually stored as 1 followed by three spaces, a combination of the following four bytes: 0x35, 0x20, 0x20, and 0x20. The CPU doesn't understand how to perform arithmetic operations on this data, and therefore it converts to an integer data type before the arithmetic operations, whereas the value 1 in an INTEGER data type is saved as 0x00000001. The CPU can easily perform arithmetic operations on this data.

Consider Column Order

An index key is sorted on the first column of the index and then subsorted on the next column within each value of the previous column. For example, consider Table 4-2.

Table 4-2. *Sample Table*

c1	c2
1	1
2	1
3	1
1	2
2	2
3	2

If a composite index is created on the columns (c1, c2), then the index will be ordered as shown in Table 4-3.

Table 4-3. *Composite Index on Column (c1, c2)*

c1	c2
1	1
1	2
2	1
2	2
3	1
3	2

As shown in Table 4-3, the data is sorted on the first column (c1) in the composite index. Within each value of the first column, the data is further sorted on the second column (c2).

Therefore, the column order in a composite index is an important factor in the effectiveness of the index. You can see this by considering

- Column uniqueness

- Column width

- Column data type

For example, suppose most of your queries on table t1 are similar to the following:

```
SELECT * FROM t1 WHERE c2=12
SELECT * FROM t1 WHERE c2=12 AND c1=11
```

An index on (c2, c1) will benefit both the queries. But an index on (c1, c2) will not be appropriate, because it will sort the data mainly on column c1, whereas the first SELECT statement needs the data to be sorted on column c2.

To understand the importance of column ordering in an index, consider the following example. Create a test table (create_order.sql in the download) with an index and a small number of rows:

```
IF(SELECT OBJECT_ID('t1')) IS NOT NULL
  DROP TABLE t1
GO
CREATE TABLE t1(c1 INT, c2 INT IDENTITY, c3 CHAR(50))
CREATE INDEX i1 ON t1(c1, c2)
DECLARE @n INT
SET @n = 1
WHILE @n <= 15
BEGIN
  INSERT INTO t1 (c1, c3) VALUES(@n, 'c3')
  SET @n = @n + 1
END
```

The order of columns in the index is c1, c2. The IDENTITY property of column c2 instructs SQL Server to automatically generate a unique incremental value for column c2. The initial value (or *seed*) of an IDENTITY column and the incremental value can be specified by using IDENTITY(Seed, Increment). If neither of the values is specified, then the default is (1, 1).

A SELECT statement with a filter criterion on column c1 in the WHERE clause as follows will be able to use the preceding index:

```
SELECT * FROM t1 WHERE c1 = 12
```

with the result

```
Table 't1'. Scan count 1, logical reads 2
```

You can confirm this in the execution plan shown in Figure 4-15.

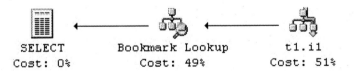

```
  SELECT        Bookmark Lookup        t1.i1
 Cost: 0%          Cost: 49%         Cost: 51%
```

Figure 4-15. *Execution plan with an index on the correct column order*

To understand the disadvantage of having the wrong column order in an index, use column c2 (instead of c1) in the WHERE clause of the SELECT statement:

```
SELECT * FROM t1 WHERE c2 = 12
```

The first column of the composite index on (c1, c2) is different from the column (c2) used in the WHERE clause. The resultant execution plan is shown in Figure 4-16.

```
Table 't1'. Scan count 1, logical reads 1
```

```
   SELECT              Table Scan
   Cost: 0%            Cost: 100%
```

Figure 4-16. *Execution plan with an index on the incorrect column order*

The rows in the index pages of the composite index on multiple columns (c1, c2) are sorted on column c1. Within each value of c1, the index rows are further sorted on column c2. Since the index pages are not mainly sorted on column c2, using the index would require scanning all the index pages first to identify the matching rows for the value of c2, and then navigating from the matching index rows to the base table. Realizing the cost overhead of using the index, the optimizer decided to scan the table directly as shown in Figure 4-16.

For a large table, the cost of scanning the leaf pages of an index to identify matching rows and then navigating to the base table for the matching rows only can be cheaper than scanning the complete table instead. This is especially valid if the index key size is narrow and the number of rows requested is small. The SQL Server optimizer can evaluate this relative cost (from statistics) to decide whether using the index (containing the candidate column in the noninitial position) will be a more efficient processing strategy than a table scan.

▓**NOTE** Chapter 7 covers statistics in more depth.

To demonstrate this feature of SQL Server, let's add a large number of rows in the test table (row_add.sql in the download):

```
DECLARE @n INT
SET @n = 1
WHILE @n <= 2000
BEGIN
  INSERT INTO t1 (c1, c3) VALUES(@n%100, 'c3')
  SET @n = @n + 1
END
```

Re-execute the previous SELECT statement that uses column c2 in the WHERE clause:

```
SELECT * FROM t1 WHERE c2 = 12
```

The resultant execution plan is shown in Figure 4-17.

```
Table 't1'. Scan count 1, logical reads 10
```

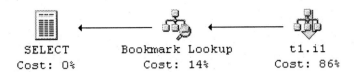

Figure 4-17. *Another scenario of an execution plan with an index on the incorrect column order*

In this case, statistics on the index key (c1, c2) indicate that only one row will satisfy the WHERE clause criterion ([c2] = 12). Based on the information that only one redirection is required to the base table from the index, the optimizer decided to scan the index leaf pages, since this is cheaper than scanning the table. The link (or bookmark) for the matching index row is then followed to retrieve the actual data from the table.

▓**NOTE** Chapter 7 covers index key statistics in more depth.

Even though the optimizer used the index effectively, it is still preferable to have the index with c2 as the first column. The STATISTICS IO output for the SELECT statement with the current index on (c1, c2) is

Table 't1'. Scan count 1, logical reads **10**

If you modify the column order of the index to have column c2 at the first position:

CREATE INDEX i1 ON t1(c2, c1) WITH DROP_EXISTING

you can then rerun your SELECT query:

SELECT * FROM t1 WHERE c2 = 12

and the number of logical reads decreases to three with an index SEEK (see Figure 4-18):

Table 't1'. Scan count 1, logical reads **3**

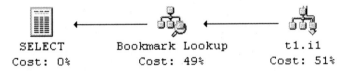

Figure 4-18. *Another scenario of an execution plan with an index on the correct column order*

▓**NOTE** The examples in this section have demonstrated that even though SQL Server 2000 can analyze index statistics and use an index even when the filter (or join) column is not the first column in the index, for the best performance it is extremely important to specify the correct column order in the index.

Consider the Type of Index

In SQL Server, you have two main index types: *clustered* and *nonclustered*. Both types have a B-tree structure. The main difference between the two types is that the leaf pages in a clustered index are the data pages of the table and are therefore in the same order as the data they point to. As you proceed, you will see that the difference at the leaf level between the two index types becomes very important in determining the type of index to use.

Clustered Index

The leaf pages of a clustered index and the data pages of the table the index is on are one and the same. Because of this, table rows are physically sorted on the clustered index column, and since there can be only one physical order of the table data, a table can have only one clustered index.

▓**TIP** Note that when you create a primary key constraint, SQL Server automatically creates a unique clustered index on the primary key if one does not already exist and it is not explicitly specified that the index should be a unique nonclustered index.

Heap Table

A table with no clustered index is called a *heap table*. The data rows of a heap table are not stored in any particular order or linked to the adjacent pages in the table. This unorganized structure of the heap table usually increases the overhead of accessing a large heap table, when compared to accessing a large nonheap table (a table with clustered index).

Relationship with Nonclustered Indexes

There is an interesting relationship between a clustered index and the nonclustered indexes in SQL Server. An index row of a nonclustered index contains a pointer to the corresponding data row of the table. This pointer is called a *row locator*. The value of the row locator depends on whether the data pages are stored in a heap or are clustered. For a nonclustered index, the row locator is a pointer to the data row. For a table with a clustered index, the row locator is the clustered index key value.

For example, say you have a heap table with no clustered index, as shown in Table 4-4.

Table 4-4. *Data Page for a Sample Table*

RowID (Not a Real Column)	c1	c2	c3
1	A1	A2	A3
2	B1	B2	B3

A nonclustered index on column c1 will cause the row locator for the index rows to contain a pointer to the corresponding data row in the database table, as shown in Table 4-5.

Table 4-5. *Nonclustered Index Page with No Clustered Index*

c1	Row Locator
A1	Pointer to RowID = 1
B1	Pointer to RowID = 2

On creating a clustered index on column c2, the row locator values of the nonclustered index rows are changed. The new value of the row locator will contain the clustered index key value, as shown in Table 4-6.

Table 4-6. *Nonclustered Index Page with a Clustered Index on c2*

c1	Row Locator
A1	A2
B1	B2

To verify this dependency between a clustered and a nonclustered index, consider this example. Create a test table with only one row and a nonclustered index (clustered.sql in the download):

```
IF(SELECT OBJECT_ID('t1')) IS NOT NULL
  DROP TABLE t1
GO
CREATE TABLE t1(c1 INT, c2 INT)
INSERT INTO t1 VALUES(11, 12)
CREATE NONCLUSTERED INDEX inc1 ON t1(c1)
```

Since the table has no clustered index, the row locator value of the nonclustered index row will be a pointer to the corresponding data row. Therefore, if you request column c2 in addition to the nonclustered index column c1, then a navigation (or bookmark) is required from the index row to the data row to fetch the value of column c2. You can verify this using the following SELECT statement:

```
SELECT c1, c2 FROM t1 WHERE c1 = 11
```

and its corresponding execution plan (shown in Figure 4-19):

```
Table 't1'. Scan count 1, logical reads 2
```

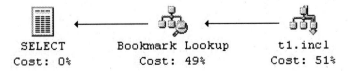

Figure 4-19. *Execution plan with no clustered index*

If you create a clustered index on column c2 as follows, then the row locator of the non-clustered index will be automatically changed to contain the value of the cluster key column c2:

```
CREATE CLUSTERED INDEX icl ON t1(c2)
```

With the row locator containing the value of column c2, you can rerun your SELECT statement:

```
SELECT c1, c2 FROM t1 WHERE c1 = 11
```

The optimizer can then find the value of both columns (c1 and c2) for the SELECT statement in the nonclustered index itself as shown in Figure 4-20:

```
Table 't1'. Scan count 1, logical reads 1
```

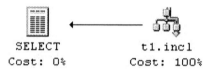

```
  SELECT              t1.incl
  Cost: 0%          Cost: 100%
```

Figure 4-20. *Execution plan with a clustered index*

You can also see from the STATISTICS IO result that navigation from the index page to the data page is not required to fetch the value of column c2.

To navigate from a nonclustered index row to a data row, this relationship between the two index types requires an additional indirection for navigating the B-tree structure of the clustered index. Without the clustered index, the row locator of the nonclustered index would be able to navigate directly from the nonclustered index row to the data row in the base table. The presence of the clustered index causes the navigation from the nonclustered index row to the data row to go through the B-tree structure of the clustered index, since the new row locator value points to the clustered index key. However, the associated cost of this indirection is insignificant since the index B-tree pages are mainly maintained in memory.

On the other hand, consider inserting an intermediate row in the clustered index key order or expanding the content of an intermediate row. For example, imagine a clustered index table containing four rows per page, with clustered index column values of 1, 2, 4, and 5. Adding a new row in the table with the clustered index value 3 will require space in the page between values 2 and 4. If enough space is not available in that position, a page split will occur on the data page (or clustered index leaf page). Even though the data page split will cause relocation of the data rows, the nonclustered index row locator values need not be updated. These row locators continue to point to the same logical key values of the clustered index key, even though the data rows have physically moved to a different location. In the case of a data page split, the row locators of the nonclustered indexes need not be updated. This is an important point, since tables often have a large number of nonclustered indexes.

▓**NOTE** Page splits and their effect on performance are explained in more detail in Chapter 8.

Clustered Index Recommendations

The relationship between a clustered index and a nonclustered index imposes some considerations on the clustered index, which are explained in the sections that follow.

Create the Clustered Index First

Since all nonclustered indexes hold clustered index keys within their index rows, the order of
nonclustered and clustered index creation is very important. For example, if the nonclustered
indexes are built before the clustered index is created, then the nonclustered index row locator
will contain a pointer to the corresponding data row of the table. Creating the clustered index
later will modify all the nonclustered indexes to contain clustered index keys as the new row
locator value. This effectively rebuilds all the nonclustered indexes.

For the best performance, I recommend that you create the clustered index *before* you
create any nonclustered index. This allows the nonclustered indexes to have their row locator
set to the clustered index keys at the time of creation. This does not have any effect on the
final performance, but rebuilding the indexes may be quite a large job.

Keep Indexes Narrow

Since all nonclustered indexes hold the clustered keys as their row locator, for the best performance, keep the overall byte size of the clustered index as small as possible. If you create a
wide clustered index, say CHAR(500), this will add 500 bytes to every nonclustered index. Thus,
keep the number of columns in the clustered index to a minimum, and carefully consider the
byte size of each column to be included in the clustered index. A column of the integer data
type usually makes a good candidate for a clustered index, whereas a string data type column
will be a less-than-optimal choice.

To understand the effect of a wide clustered index on a nonclustered index, consider
this example. Create a small test table with a clustered index and a nonclustered index
(clust_nonclust.sql in the download):

```
IF(SELECT OBJECT_ID('t1')) IS NOT NULL
  DROP TABLE t1
GO
CREATE TABLE t1(c1 INT, c2 INT)
DECLARE @n INT
SET @n = 1
WHILE @n <= 20
BEGIN
  INSERT INTO t1 VALUES(@n, @n+1)
  SET @n = @n + 1
END
CREATE CLUSTERED INDEX icl ON t1(c2)
CREATE NONCLUSTERED INDEX incl ON t1(c1)
```

Since the table has a clustered index, the row locator of the nonclustered index contains the clustered index key value, therefore

Width of the nonclustered index row
= Width of the nonclustered index column + Width of the clustered index column
= Size of INT data type + Size of INT data type
= 4 bytes + 4 bytes = 8 bytes

With this small size of a nonclustered index row, all the nonclustered index rows can be compressed in one index page. You can confirm this in the sysindexes system table (sysindex_select2.sql in the download) as shown in Figure 4-21:

```
SELECT Name=name
    , CASE indid
        WHEN 0 THEN 'Table'
        WHEN 1 THEN 'Clustered'
        ELSE 'Nonclustered'
      END AS Type
    , Pages=dpages, Rows=rowcnt
FROM sysindexes
WHERE id = OBJECT_ID('t1')
```

Name	Type	Pages	Rows
icl	Clustered	1	20
incl	Nonclustered	1	20

Figure 4-21. *Number of index pages for a narrow index*

To understand the effect of a wide clustered index on a nonclustered index, modify the data type of the clustered indexed column c2 from INT to CHAR(500):

```
DROP INDEX t1.icl
ALTER TABLE t1 ALTER COLUMN c2 CHAR(500)
CREATE CLUSTERED INDEX icl ON t1(c2)
```

Running sysindex_select2.sql again returns the result in Figure 4-22.

Name	Type	Pages	Rows
icl	Clustered	2	20
incl	Nonclustered	2	20

Figure 4-22. *Number of index pages for a wide index*

You can see that a wide clustered index increases the width of the nonclustered index row size. Due to the large width of the nonclustered index row, one 8KB index page can't accommodate all the index rows. Instead, two index pages will be required to store all 20 index rows.

In the case of a large table, an unreasonable expansion in the size of the nonclustered indexes due to a large clustered index key size can significantly increase the number of pages of the nonclustered indexes.

Therefore, a large clustered index key size not only affects its own width, but also widens all nonclustered indexes on the table. This increases the number of index pages for all the indexes on the table, increasing the logical reads and disk I/Os required for the indexes.

▓**TIP** For the best performance, I always recommend keeping the clustered index key as narrow as possible.

Rebuild the Clustered Index in a Single Step

Due to the dependency of nonclustered indexes on the clustered index, rebuilding the clustered index as separate DROP INDEX and CREATE INDEX statements causes all the nonclustered indexes to be rebuilt twice. To avoid this, use the DROP_EXISTING clause of the CREATE INDEX statement to rebuild the clustered index in a single atomic step. Similarly, the DROP_EXISTING clause can also be used with a nonclustered index.

When to Use a Clustered Index

In certain situations, the use of a clustered index is very helpful. I discuss these in the sections that follow.

Retrieving a Range of Data

Since the leaf pages of a clustered index and the data pages of the table are the same, the order of the clustered index column not only orders the rows of the clustered index, but also physically orders the data rows of the base table. If the physical order of the data rows matches the order of data requested by a query, then the disk head can read all the rows sequentially, without much disk head movement. For example, if a query requests all the employee records belonging to the database group, and the corresponding employee table has a clustered index on the group column, then all the relevant employee rows will be physically arranged together on the disk. This allows the disk head to move to the position of the first row on the disk and then electronically read all the data sequentially with minimal physical movement of the disk head. On the other hand, if the rows are not sorted on the disk in the correct physical order, the disk head has to move randomly from one location to another to fetch all the relevant rows. Since physical movement of the disk head constitutes a major portion of the cost of a disk operation, sorting the rows in the proper physical order on the disk (using a clustered index) optimizes the I/O cost.

Retrieving Presorted Data

Clustered indexes are particularly efficient when the data retrieval needs to be sorted. If you create a clustered index on the column or columns that you may need to sort by, then the rows will be physically stored in that order, eliminating the overhead of sorting the data after it is retrieved.

Let's see this in action. Create a test table as follows (create_sort.sql in the download):

```
IF(SELECT OBJECT_ID('od')) IS NOT NULL
  DROP TABLE od
GO
SELECT * INTO od FROM Northwind.dbo.[Order Details]
```

The new table od is created with data only. It doesn't have any indexes. You can verify the indexes on the table by executing

```
sp_helpindex od
```

which returns nothing.

To understand the use of a clustered index, fetch a large range of rows ordered on a certain column:

```
SELECT * FROM od
WHERE ProductID BETWEEN 30 AND 70
ORDER BY ProductID
```

The cost of executing this query (without any indexes) can be obtained from the STATISTICS IO output:

```
Table 'od'. Scan count 1, logical reads 11
```

To improve the performance of this query, you should create an index on the WHERE clause column. This query requires both a range of rows and a sorted output. The result set requirement of this query meets the recommendations for a clustered index. Therefore, create a clustered index as follows, and re-examine the cost of the query:

```
CREATE CLUSTERED INDEX i1 ON od(ProductID)
```

When you run the query again, the resultant cost of the query (with a clustered index) is

```
Table 'od'. Scan count 1, logical reads 8
```

Creating the clustered index reduced the number of logical reads and therefore should contribute to the query performance improvement.

On the other hand, if you create a nonclustered index (instead of a clustered index) on the candidate column, then the query performance may be affected adversely. Let's verify the effect of a nonclustered index in this case:

```
DROP INDEX od.i1
CREATE NONCLUSTERED INDEX i1 on od(ProductID)
```

The resultant cost of the query (with a nonclustered index) is

```
Table 'od'. Scan count 1, logical reads 1185
```

The nonclustered index significantly increases the number of logical reads, affecting the query performance accordingly.

> **NOTE** For a query that retrieves a large range of rows and/or an ordered output, a clustered index is usually a better choice than a nonclustered index.

When Not to Use a Clustered Index

In certain situations, you are better off not using a clustered index. I discuss these in the sections that follow.

Frequently Updateable Columns

If the clustered index columns are frequently updated, this will cause the row locator of all the nonclustered indexes to be updated accordingly, significantly increasing the cost of the relevant action queries. This also affects database concurrency by blocking all other queries referring to the same part of the table and the nonclustered indexes during that period. Therefore, avoid creating a clustered index on columns that are highly updateable.

> **NOTE** Chapter 12 covers blocking in more depth.

To understand how the cost of an UPDATE statement that modifies only a clustered key column is increased by the presence of nonclustered indexes on the table, consider the following example. Create a small test table with a clustered index (freq_update.sql in the download):

```
IF(SELECT OBJECT_ID('t1')) IS NOT NULL
  DROP TABLE t1
GO
CREATE TABLE t1(c1 INT, c2 INT)
CREATE CLUSTERED INDEX icl ON t1(c1)
INSERT INTO t1 VALUES(11, 12)
```

Update the clustered key column using the following UPDATE statement:

```
UPDATE t1 SET c1 = 11 WHERE c1 = 11
```

The STATISTICS IO output indicates that 6 logical reads are performed on table t1:

```
Table 't1'. Scan count 1, logical reads 6
Table 'Worktable'. Scan count 1, logical reads 3
```

To understand how the cost of the UPDATE statement is increased by the nonclustered index on a different column of the table, create a nonclustered index:

```
CREATE NONCLUSTERED INDEX incl1 ON t1(c2)
```

Note that column c2 is neither referred to by the UPDATE statement nor included in the clustered key. Bearing this in mind, you might mistakenly assume that the nonclustered index will not affect the performance of the UPDATE statement, which is based on column c1 only. In reality, this is not true!

You can then run the UPDATE command again:

```
UPDATE t1 SET c1 = 11 WHERE c1 = 11
```

The output of STATISTICS IO for the preceding UPDATE statement indicates that 8 logical reads are performed on table t1:

```
Table 't1'. Scan count 1, logical reads 8
Table 'Worktable'. Scan count 1, logical reads 3
```

In fact, if you add two more nonclustered indexes on column c2, the logical reads for the UPDATE statement increase to 12.

Even though the UPDATE statement refers to (and updates) the clustered key column only, adding a nonclustered index on a different column increases the cost of the UPDATE statement.

Wide Keys

Since all nonclustered indexes hold the clustered keys as their row locator, for performance reasons, avoid creating a clustered index on a very wide column (or columns) or on too many columns. As explained in the preceding section, a clustered index must be very narrow.

Too Many Concurrent Inserts in Sequential Order

If you want to add many new rows concurrently, then it may be better for performance to distribute them across the data pages of the table. However, if you add all the rows in the same order as that imposed by the clustered index, then all the inserts will be attempted on the last page of the table. This may cause a huge "hotspot" on the corresponding sector of the disk. To avoid this disk hotspot, you should not arrange the data rows in the same order as their physical location. The inserts can be randomized throughout the table by creating a clustered index on another column that doesn't arrange the rows in the same order as that of the new rows. This is an issue only with a large number of simultaneous inserts.

There is a caveat to this recommendation. Allowing inserts on the bottom of the table prevents page splits on the intermediate pages required to accommodate the new rows in those pages. If the number of concurrent inserts is low, then ordering the data rows (using a clustered index) in the order of the new rows will prevent intermediate page splits. However, if the disk hotspot becomes a performance bottleneck, then new rows can be accommodated in intermediate pages without causing page splits, by reducing the *fill factor* of the table.

■**NOTE** Chapter 8 covers the fill factor in depth.

Nonclustered Index

A nonclustered index does not affect the order of the data in the table pages, as the leaf pages of a nonclustered index and the data pages of the table are separate. A pointer (the row locator) is required to navigate from an index row to the data row. As you learned in the earlier "Clustered Index" section, the structure of the row locator depends on whether the data pages are stored in a heap or are clustered. For a heap, the row locator is a pointer to the data row; for a table with a clustered index, the row locator is the clustered index key.

Nonclustered Index Maintenance

Using a clustered index value as the row locator in a nonclustered index decreases the maintenance cost of the nonclustered indexes. When a data page splits, the nonclustered indexes of a table that have a clustered index as their row locator need not be updated. The row locator value of the nonclustered indexes continue to have the same clustered index value, even when the clustered index rows are physically relocated. But in the case of a heap table (with no clustered index), the row locators of the nonclustered indexes have to be updated to point to the new physical location of the data row when a data page splits.

To optimize this maintenance cost, SQL Server adds a pointer to the old data page to point to the new data page after a page split, instead of updating the row locator of all the relevant nonclustered indexes. Although this reduces the maintenance cost of the nonclustered indexes, it increases the navigation cost from the nonclustered index row to the data row, since an extra link is added between the old data page and the new data page. Therefore, having a clustered index as the row locator decreases these overheads associated with the nonclustered index.

Introducing the Bookmark Lookup

When a query requests columns that are not part of the nonclustered index chosen by the optimizer, a *bookmark lookup* is required. This fetches the corresponding data row from the table by following the row locator value from the index row, requiring a logical read on the data page besides the logical read on the index page. However, if all the columns required by the query are available in the index itself, then access to the data page is not required.

These bookmark lookups are the reason that large result sets are better served with a clustered index. A clustered index doesn't require a bookmark lookup, since the leaf pages and data pages for a clustered index are the same.

▓**NOTE** Chapter 6 covers bookmark lookups in more detail.

Nonclustered Index Recommendations

Since a table can have only one clustered index, you depend upon the nonclustered indexes to improve performance. I explain the factors that decide the use of a nonclustered index in the following sections.

When to Use a Nonclustered Index

In certain situations, the use of a nonclustered index is very helpful. I discuss these in the sections that follow.

Retrieving a Few Rows

A nonclustered index is most useful when all you want to do is retrieve a small number of rows from a large table. As the number of rows to be retrieved increases, the overhead cost of the bookmark lookup rises proportionately. To retrieve a small number of rows from a table, the indexed column should have a very high selectivity.

Furthermore, there will be indexing requirements that won't be suitable for a clustered index, as explained in the "Clustered Index" section:

- Frequently updateable columns

- Wide keys

In these cases, a nonclustered index can be used, since unlike a clustered index, it doesn't affect other indexes in the table. A nonclustered index on a frequently updateable column isn't as costly as having a clustered index on that column. The UPDATE operation on a nonclustered index is limited to the base table and the nonclustered index. It doesn't affect any other nonclustered indexes on the table. Similarly, a nonclustered index on a wide column (or set of columns) doesn't increase the size of any other index, unlike that with a clustered index. However, remain cautious, even while creating a nonclustered index on a highly updateable column or a wide column (or set of columns), since this can increase the cost of action queries, as explained earlier in the chapter.

> ▓**TIP** A nonclustered index can also help resolve blocking and deadlock issues. I will cover this in more depth in Chapters 12 and 13.

When Not to Use a Nonclustered Index

Nonclustered indexes are not suitable for queries that retrieve a large number of rows. Such queries are better served with a clustered index, as it doesn't require a separate bookmark lookup to retrieve a data row. Since a bookmark lookup requires an additional logical read on the data page besides the logical read on the nonclustered index page, the cost of a query using a nonclustered index increases significantly for a large number of rows. The SQL Server query optimizer takes this cost into effect, and accordingly discards the nonclustered index when retrieving a large result set.

If your requirement is to retrieve a large result set from a table, then having a nonclustered index on the filter criterion (or the join criterion) column will not be useful unless you use a special type of nonclustered index called a *covering index*. I describe this index type in detail later in the chapter.

Clustered vs. Nonclustered Index

The main considerations in choosing between a clustered and a nonclustered index are as follows:

- Number of rows to be retrieved

- Data-ordering requirement

- Index key width

- Column update frequency

- Bookmark cost

- Any disk hotspots

Benefits of a Clustered Index over a Nonclustered Index

When deciding upon a type of index on a table with no indexes, the clustered index is usually the preferred choice. Even the situation best suited for a nonclustered index—that of retrieving a small number of rows—can be better served by the clustered index. As the index page and the data pages are the same, the clustered index doesn't have to jump from the index row to the base row as required in the case of a nonclustered index.

To understand how a clustered index can outperform a nonclustered index even in retrieving small number of rows, consider the following example. Create a large test table with a high selectivity for one column (`cluster_bene.sql` in the download):

```
IF(SELECT OBJECT_ID('t1')) IS NOT NULL
  DROP TABLE t1
GO
CREATE TABLE t1(c1 INT, c2 CHAR(50))
DECLARE @n INT
SET @n = 1
WHILE @n <= 10000
BEGIN
  INSERT INTO t1 VALUES(@n%2000, @n)
  SET @n = @n + 1
END
```

▓**TIP** Switching the graphic execution plan off will make this script run much faster.

The following SELECT statement fetches only 5 out of 10,000 rows from the table:

SELECT c1, c2 FROM t1 WHERE c1 = 1

with the graphical execution plan shown in Figure 4-23 and the output of SET STATISTICS IO:

Table 't1'. Scan count 1, logical reads **82**

SELECT   Table Scan
Cost: 2%   Cost: 98%

Figure 4-23. *Execution plan with no index*

Considering the small size of the result set retrieved by the preceding SELECT statement, a nonclustered column on c1 can be a good choice:

CREATE NONCLUSTERED INDEX inc1 ON t1(c1)

You can run the SELECT command again:

SELECT c1, c2 FROM t1 WHERE c1 = 1

Since retrieving a small number of rows through a nonclustered index is more economical than table scan, the optimizer used the nonclustered index on column c1, as shown in Figure 4-24. The number of logical reads reported by STATISTICS IO is

Table 't1'. Scan count 1, logical reads **7**

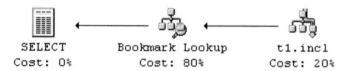

SELECT   Bookmark Lookup   t1.inc1
Cost: 0%   Cost: 80%   Cost: 20%

Figure 4-24. *Execution plan with a nonclustered index*

Even though retrieving a small result set using a column with high selectivity is a good pointer toward creating a nonclustered index on the column, a clustered index on the same column can be equally beneficial or even better. To evaluate how the clustered index can be more beneficial than the nonclustered index, create a clustered index on the same column:

CREATE CLUSTERED INDEX ic1 ON t1(c1)

You can run the SELECT command again:

SELECT c1, c2 FROM t1 WHERE c1 = 1

From the resultant execution plan (see Figure 4-25) of the preceding SELECT statement, you can see that the optimizer used the clustered index (instead of the nonclustered index) even for a small result set. The number of logical reads for the SELECT statement decreased from seven to two:

Table 't1'. Scan count 1, logical reads **2**

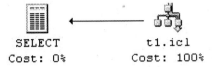

SELECT   t1.icl
Cost: 0%   Cost: 100%

Figure 4-25. *Execution plan with a clustered index*

■**NOTE** Even though a clustered index can usually outperform a nonclustered index in data retrieval, a table can have only one clustered index. Therefore, reserve the clustered index for a situation in which it can be of the greatest benefit.

Benefits of a Nonclustered Index over a Clustered Index

As you learned in the previous section, a nonclustered index is preferred over a clustered index for the following conditions:

- When the index key size is large.

- To avoid the overhead cost associated with a clustered index since rebuilding the clustered index rebuilds all the nonclustered indexes of the table.

- To resolve blocking by having a database reader work on the pages of a nonclustered index, while a database writer modifies other columns (not included in the nonclustered index) in the data page. In this case, the writer working on the data page won't block a reader who can get all the required column values from the nonclustered index without hitting the base table. I'll explain this in detail in Chapter 12.

- When all the columns (from a table) referred to by a query can be safely accommodated in the nonclustered index itself, as explained in this section.

As already established, the data retrieval performance when using a nonclustered index is poorer than that when using a clustered index, due to the cost associated in jumping from the nonclustered index rows to the data rows in the base table. In cases where the jump to the data rows is not required, the performance of a nonclustered index should be just as good as—or even better than—a clustered index. This is possible if the nonclustered index key includes all the columns required from the table.

To understand the situation where a nonclustered index can outperform a clustered index, consider the following example. Create a large test table (noncluster_bene.sql in the download):

```
IF(SELECT OBJECT_ID('t1')) IS NOT NULL
  DROP TABLE t1
GO
CREATE TABLE t1(c1 INT, c2 INT, c3 CHAR(250))
DECLARE @n INT
SET @n = 1
WHILE @n <= 10000
BEGIN
  INSERT INTO t1 VALUES(@n, @n, @n)
  SET @n = @n + 1
END
```

TIP Again, you may want to temporarily switch the graphical execution plan off to run this script quickly.

The following SELECT statement fetches a large range of rows and requires a sorted output as shown in Figure 4-26:

```
SELECT c1, c2 FROM t1
  WHERE c1 between 5000 and 6000
  ORDER BY c1, c2
```

The result is

```
Table 't1'. Scan count 1, logical reads 345
```

Figure 4-26. *Execution plan with no index*

Considering that the requirements of the preceding SELECT statement match the preferred conditions for a clustered index, create a clustered index:

```
CREATE CLUSTERED INDEX icl ON t1(c1, c2)
```

If you run your SELECT command again

```
SELECT c1, c2 FROM t1
  WHERE c1 between 5000 and 6000
  ORDER BY c1, c2
```

the resultant execution plan is shown in Figure 4-27 and the number of logical reads reported by STATISTICS IO is

```
Table 't1'. Scan count 1, logical reads 36
```

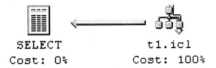

SELECT
Cost: 0%

t1.icl
Cost: 100%

Figure 4-27. *Execution plan with a clustered index*

Even though the query requirements are highly suitable for a clustered index, in this case, as all the columns required by the query can be included in the index itself, a nonclustered index is preferable. To verify this behavior, convert the clustered index to a nonclustered index:

```
DROP INDEX t1.icl
CREATE NONCLUSTERED INDEX incl ON t1(c1, c2)
```

and then rerun your SELECT command:

```
SELECT c1, c2 FROM t1
  WHERE c1 between 5000 and 6000
  ORDER BY c1, c2
```

The number of logical reads for the SELECT statement decreased from 36 to 5:

```
Table 't1'. Scan count 1, logical reads 5
```

Figure 4-28 shows the corresponding execution plan.

SELECT
Cost: 1%

t1.incl
Cost: 99%

Figure 4-28. *Execution plan with a nonclustered index*

In this case, the SELECT statement doesn't include any column that requires a jump from the nonclustered index page to the data page of the table, which is what usually makes a nonclustered index costlier than a clustered index for a large result set and/or sorted output. This kind of nonclustered index is called a *covering index*. You can see that, irrespective of the number of rows requested, if a query refers to a limited set of columns that already have a nonclustered index on them, then fewer logical reads are required when compared to a clustered index on those columns.

Advanced Indexing Techniques

A few of the more advanced indexing techniques that you can also consider are as follows:

- *Covering index*: This was introduced in the preceding section.

- *Index intersection*: Use multiple nonclustered indexes to satisfy all the column requirements (from a table) for a query.

- *Index join*: Use the index intersection and covering index techniques to avoid hitting the base table.

- *Indexed view*: Materializes the output of a view on disk.

I cover these topics in more detail in the following sections.

Covering Index

A *covering index* is a nonclustered index built upon all the columns required to satisfy a SQL query without going to the base table. If a query encounters an index and does not need to refer to the underlying data table at all, then the index can be considered a covering index. For example, in the following SELECT statement, irrespective of where the columns are referred, all the columns (c1 to c6) should be included in the nonclustered index to cover the query fully:

```
SELECT c1, AVG(c2)
  FROM t1
  WHERE c3 = 1
  GROUP BY c4, c1
  HAVING MAX(c5) > 0
  ORDER BY MIN(c6)
```

Then all the required data for the query can be obtained from the nonclustered index page, without accessing the data page. This helps SQL Server save logical and physical reads. To understand the benefit of covering index, consider the following example. Create a test table (covering.sql in the download):

```
IF(SELECT OBJECT_ID('t1')) IS NOT NULL
  DROP TABLE t1
GO
CREATE TABLE t1(c1 INT, c2 INT, c3 CHAR(250))
DECLARE @n INT
SET @n = 1
WHILE @n <= 1000
BEGIN
  INSERT INTO t1 VALUES(@n%200, @n, @n)
  SET @n = @n + 1
END
```

For the following SELECT statement retrieving a small number of rows

```
SELECT c1, c2 FROM t1 WHERE c1 = 1
```

with the following result

```
Table 't1'. Scan count 1, logical reads 35
```

a nonclustered index should be created on the WHERE clause column c1 to improve performance:

```
CREATE NONCLUSTERED INDEX i1 ON t1(c1)
```

After creating the index, you can run your SELECT command again:

```
SELECT c1, c2 FROM t1 WHERE c1 = 1
```

As shown in Figure 4-29, a jump (bookmark lookup) from the nonclustered index to the table is performed, fetching the value of column c2 that is in the SELECT list but is not in the nonclustered index key. The resultant number of logical reads for the query as reported by STATISTICS IO is

```
Table 't1'. Scan count 1, logical reads 7
```

SELECT   Bookmark Lookup   t1.i1
Cost: 0%   Cost: 80%   Cost: 20%

Figure 4-29. *Execution plan with a bookmark lookup*

To avoid hitting the base table, modify the nonclustered index to serve as a covering index by including all the columns (c1, c2) referred to in the preceding SELECT statement:

```
CREATE NONCLUSTERED INDEX i1 ON t1(c1, c2) WITH DROP_EXISTING
```

and then run your SELECT command again:

```
SELECT c1, c2 FROM t1 WHERE c1 = 1
```

From the resultant execution plan shown in Figure 4-30, you can see that the nonclustered index satisfies all the column requirements of the query. Subsequently, the number of logical reads decreases from seven to two:

```
Table 't1'. Scan count 1, logical reads 2
```

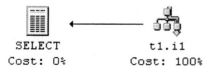

SELECT   t1.i1
Cost: 0%   Cost: 100%

Figure 4-30. *Execution plan with no bookmark lookup*

A covering index is a useful technique for reducing the number of logical reads of a query. In a clustered index, the leaf page (being same as the data page) always contains all the columns of the table. Therefore, a clustered index is a natural covering index. However, since the rows of a clustered index contain all the columns, a clustered index is always the widest covering index.

A Pseudo-Clustered Index

The covering index physically organizes the data of all the indexed columns in a sequential order. Thus, from a disk I/O perspective, a covering index becomes a clustered index for all queries satisfied completely by the columns in the covering index. If the result set of a query requires a sorted output, then the covering index can be used to physically maintain the column data in the same order as required by the result set—it can then be used in the same way as a clustered index for sorted output. As shown in the previous example, covering indexes give better performance than clustered indexes for queries requesting a range of rows and/or sorted output.

Recommendations

To take advantage of covering indexes, be careful with the column list in SELECT statements. Use as few columns as possible to keep the index key size small for the covering indexes. Since a covering index includes all columns used in a query, it has a tendency to be very wide, increasing the maintenance cost of the covering indexes. You must balance the maintenance cost with the performance gain that the covering index brings. If the number of bytes from all the columns in the index is small compared to the number of bytes in a single data row of that table, and you are certain the query taking advantage of the covered index will be executed frequently, then it may be beneficial to use a covering index.

▨**TIP** Covering indexes can also help resolve blocking and deadlocks, as you will see in Chapters 12 and 13.

Before building a lot of covering indexes, consider how SQL Server can effectively and automatically create covering indexes for queries on the fly using index intersection.

Index Intersection

If a table has multiple indexes, then SQL Server can use multiple indexes to execute a query. SQL Server can take advantage of multiple indexes, selecting small subsets of data based on each index and then performing an intersection of the two subsets (that is, returning only those rows that meet all the criteria). SQL Server can exploit multiple indexes on a table and then employ a join algorithm to obtain the *index intersection* between the two subsets.

Let's see this indexing technique in work. Create a sample table (`intersection.sql` in the download):

```
IF(SELECT OBJECT_ID('t1')) IS NOT NULL
  DROP TABLE t1
GO
SELECT * INTO t1 FROM Northwind.dbo.Orders
CREATE CLUSTERED INDEX icl ON t1(OrderID)
CREATE NONCLUSTERED INDEX CustID ON t1(CustomerID)
```

In the following SELECT statement, for the WHERE clause columns the table has a nonclustered index on the CustomerID column, but it has no index on the RequiredDate column:

```
SELECT COUNT(*)
  FROM t1
  WHERE CustomerID BETWEEN 'G' AND 'H'
    AND RequiredDate BETWEEN '1/1/97' AND '12/31/97'
```

Figure 4-31 shows the execution plan for this query.

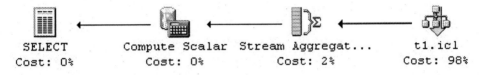

Figure 4-31. *Execution plan with no index on the RequiredDate column*

As you can see, the optimizer didn't use the nonclustered index on the CustomerID column. Since the value of the RequiredDate column is also required, the optimizer chose the clustered index to fetch the value of all the referred columns.

To improve the performance of the query, the RequiredDate column can be included in the nonclustered index on the CustomerID column. But in this real-world scenario, you may have to consider the following while modifying an existing index:

- It may not be permissible to modify an existing index for various reasons.

- The existing nonclustered index key may be already quite wide.

- The cost of the queries using the existing index will be affected by the modification.

In such cases, you can create a new nonclustered index on the RequiredDate column:

```
CREATE NONCLUSTERED INDEX RDate ON t1(RequiredDate)
```

Run your SELECT command again:

```
SELECT COUNT(*)
  FROM t1
  WHERE CustomerID BETWEEN 'G' AND 'H'
    AND RequiredDate BETWEEN '1/1/97' AND '12/31/97'
```

Figure 4-32 shows the resultant execution plan of the SELECT statement.

Figure 4-32. *Execution plan with an index on the RequiredDate column*

As you can see, SQL Server exploited both the nonclustered indexes as index seeks (rather than scans) and then employed an intersection algorithm to obtain the index intersection of the two subsets.

To improve the performance of a query, SQL Server can use multiple indexes on a table. Therefore, instead of creating wide index keys, consider creating multiple narrow indexes. SQL Server will be able to use them together where required and, when not required, queries benefit from narrow indexes. While creating a covering index, determine whether or not the width of the index will be acceptable. If not, then identify the existing nonclustered indexes that include most of the columns required by the covering index. You may already have two existing nonclustered indexes that jointly serve all the columns required by the covering index. If it is possible, rearrange the column order of the existing nonclustered indexes appropriately, allowing the optimizer to consider an index intersection between the two nonclustered indexes.

At times, it is possible that you may have to create a separate nonclustered index for the following reasons:

- Reordering the columns in one of the existing indexes is not allowed.

- Some of the columns required by the covering index may not be included in the existing nonclustered indexes.

- The total number of columns in the two existing nonclustered indexes may be more than the number of columns required by the covering index.

In such cases, you can create a nonclustered index on the remaining columns. If the combined column order of the new index and an existing nonclustered index meets the requirement of the covering index, the optimizer will be able to use index intersection. While identifying the columns and their order for the new index, try to maximize their benefit by keeping an eye on other queries, too.

Index Join

The *index join* is a variation of index intersection, where the covering index technique is applied to the index intersection. If no single index covers a query, but multiple indexes together can cover the query, SQL Server can use an index join to satisfy the query fully without going to the base table.

Let's look at this indexing technique at work. Create a sample table (`joins.sql` in the download):

```
IF(SELECT OBJECT_ID('t1')) IS NOT NULL
  DROP TABLE t1
GO
SELECT * INTO t1 FROM Northwind.dbo.Orders
CREATE CLUSTERED INDEX icl ON t1(OrderID)
CREATE NONCLUSTERED INDEX CustID ON t1(CustomerID)
CREATE NONCLUSTERED INDEX ODate ON t1(OrderDate)
```

For the following `SELECT` statement, the table has a nonclustered index on column `OrderDate`:

```
SELECT CustomerID, OrderDate
  FROM t1
  WHERE OrderDate BETWEEN '1/1/97' AND '12/31/97'
```

The execution plan for this query is shown in Figure 4-33.

```
Table 't1'. Scan count 1, logical reads 23
```

```
SELECT              t1.icl
Cost: 1%          Cost: 99%
```

Figure 4-33. *Execution plan with no index join*

As shown in Figure 4-33, the optimizer didn't use the nonclustered index on the `OrderDate` column. Since the query requires the value of the `CustomerID` column also, the optimizer selected the clustered index to retrieve values for all the columns referred to in the query. Note that there is a nonclustered index on the `CustomerID` column also. If this index can be used along with the index on the `OrderDate` column, then the query can be fully satisfied using the index join technique. This can be done in the following two ways:

- Modify the query to include the `CustomerID` column in the `WHERE` clause without affecting its functionality:

```
SELECT CustomerID, OrderDate
  FROM t1
  WHERE OrderDate BETWEEN '1/1/97' AND '12/31/97'
    AND CustomerID > ''
```

Including the indexed columns in the `WHERE` clause influences the optimizer to consider indexes on both the `OrderDate` and `CustomerID` columns. The resultant execution plan is shown in Figure 4-34.

```
Table 't1'. Scan count 2, logical reads 7
```

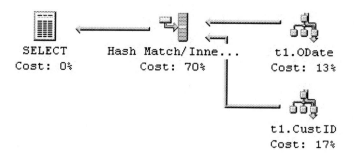

Figure 4-34. *Execution plan with an index join*

As shown in Figure 4-34, the optimizer used index intersection to cover the query fully.

- Use an index hint as follows to force the optimizer use both the nonclustered indexes, and thereby satisfy the query fully from the two nonclustered indexes without going to the base table.

```
SELECT CustomerID, OrderDate
  FROM t1 WITH(INDEX(ODate, CustID))
  WHERE OrderDate BETWEEN '1/1/97' AND '12/31/97'
```

with the following result
Table 't1'. Scan count 2, logical reads **7**

Figure 4-35 shows the corresponding execution plan.

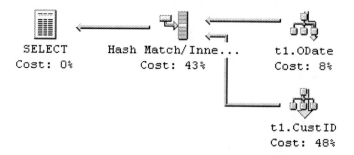

Figure 4-35. *Execution plan with an index join forced using an index hint*

The obvious question is, which technique is better?

To evaluate which of the previous two techniques is better, execute both the variations of the query together, and find from the execution plan which query has the higher relative cost in the batch. The relative costs of these techniques are as follows:

- Technique 1: 38.37%

- Technique 2: 61.63%

The second technique, forcing the optimizer with an index hint, is much costlier than the first technique. Therefore, instead of overriding the optimizer's decision, leave the optimizer to determine the most cost-effective processing strategy. Note that while you may be able to modify the query to aid the optimizer, try to avoid index hints. These restrict the optimizer from choosing a better index if the one in the hint turns out to be less effective as the data changes over time.

▓**NOTE** While generating a query execution plan, the SQL Server optimizer goes through the optimization phases not only to determine the type of index and join strategy to be used, but also to evaluate the advanced indexing techniques such as index intersection and index join. Therefore, instead of creating wide covering indexes, consider creating multiple narrow indexes. SQL Server can use them together to serve as a covering index, yet use them separately where required.

Indexed View

A database view in SQL Server is like a virtual table that represents the output of a SELECT statement. A view is created using the CREATE VIEW statement, and it can be queried exactly like a table. In general, a view doesn't store any data—only the SELECT statement associated with it. Every time a view is queried, it further queries the underlying tables by executing its associated SELECT statement.

In SQL Server 2000 Enterprise Edition (not Standard Edition), a database view can be materialized on the disk by creating a unique clustered index on the view. Such a view is referred to as an *indexed view*. After a unique clustered index is created on the view, the view's result set is materialized immediately and persisted in physical storage in the database, saving the overhead of performing costly operations during query execution. After the view is materialized, multiple nonclustered indexes can be created on the indexed view.

Benefit

An indexed view can be used to increase the performance of a query in the following ways:

- Aggregations can be precomputed and stored in the indexed view to minimize expensive computations during query execution.

- Tables can be prejoined and the resulting data set can be materialized.

- Combinations of joins or aggregations can be materialized.

Overhead

Indexed views have a major overhead on an OLTP database. Some of the overheads of indexed views are as follows:

- Any change in the base table(s) has to be reflected in the indexed view by executing the view's SELECT statement.

- Any changes to a base table on which an indexed view is defined may initiate one or more changes in the nonclustered indexes of the indexed view. The clustered index will also have to be changed if the clustering key is updated.

- The indexed view adds to the ongoing maintenance overhead of the database.

- Additional storage is required in the database.

The restrictions on creating an indexed view include the following:

- The first index on the view must be a unique clustered index.

- Nonclustered indexes on an indexed view can be created only after the unique clustered index is created.

- The view definition must be *deterministic*—that is, it is able to return only one possible result for a given query. (A list of deterministic and nondeterministic functions is provided in SQL Server Books Online.)

- The indexed view must reference only base tables in the same database, not other views.

- The indexed view may contain float columns. However, such columns cannot be included in the clustered index key.

- The indexed view must be schema bound to the tables referred to in the view, to prevent modifications of the table schema.

- There are several restrictions on the syntax of the view definition. (A list of the syntax limitations on the view definition is provided in SQL Server Books Online.)

- The list of SET options that must be fixed are

    - ON: ARITHABORT, CONCAT_NULL_YIELDS_NULL, QUOTED_IDENTIFIER, ANSI_NULLS, ANSI_PADDING, and ANSI_WARNING

    - OFF: NUMERIC_ROUNDABORT

Usage Scenarios

Analysis Service systems (or read-only database systems) benefit the most from the implementation of indexed views. OLTP systems with frequent writes may not be able to take advantage of the indexed views because of the increased maintenance cost associated with updating both the view and underlying base tables. The net performance improvement provided by an indexed view is the difference between the total query execution savings offered by the view and the cost of storing and maintaining the view.

An indexed view need not be referenced in the query for the query optimizer to use it during query execution. This allows existing applications to benefit from the newly created indexed views without changing those applications. The query optimizer considers indexed views only for queries with nontrivial cost.

Let's see how indexed views work with the following example. Consider the following three queries in Listings 4-1 through 4-3.

Listing 4-1. *Query1.sql*

```sql
SELECT ProductName,
       od.ProductID,
       AVG(od.UnitPrice*(1.00-Discount)) AS AvgPrice,
       SUM(od.Quantity) AS Units
  FROM Northwind.dbo.[Order Details] od, Northwind.dbo.Products p
  WHERE od.ProductID = p.ProductID
  GROUP BY ProductName, od.ProductID
GO
```

Listing 4-2. *Query2.sql*

```sql
SELECT ProductName,
       od.ProductID,
       AVG(od.UnitPrice*(1.00-Discount)) AS AvgPrice,
       SUM(od.Quantity) AS Units
  FROM Northwind.dbo.[Order Details] od, Northwind.dbo.Products p
  WHERE od.ProductID = p.ProductID
    AND p.ProductName LIKE '%Tofu%'
  GROUP BY ProductName, od.ProductID
GO
```

Listing 4-3. *Query3.sql*

```sql
SELECT ProductName,
       od.ProductID,
       AVG(od.UnitPrice*(1.00-Discount)) AS AvgPrice,
       SUM(od.Quantity) AS Units
  FROM Northwind.dbo.[Order Details] od, Northwind.dbo.Products p
  WHERE od.ProductID = p.ProductID
    AND od.ProductID IN (1,2,13,41)
  GROUP BY ProductName, od.ProductID
```

All the three queries use the aggregation functions AVG and SUM on columns of the Order Details table. Therefore, you can create an indexed view on the Order Details table to precompute these aggregations and minimize the cost of these complex computations during query execution.

The number of logical reads performed by these queries to access the Order Details table are shown in Listings 4-4 through 4-6.

Listing 4-4. *Logical Reads by Query1*

```
Table 'Products'. Scan count 77, logical reads 154
Table 'Order Details'. Scan count 1, logical reads 10
```

Listing 4-5. *Logical Reads by Query2*

```
Table 'Products'. Scan count 77, logical reads 154
Table 'Order Details'. Scan count 1, logical reads 10
```

Listing 4-6. *Logical Reads by Query3*

```
Table 'Products'. Scan count 4, logical reads 8
Table 'Order Details'. Scan count 4, logical reads 347
```

Create an indexed view to precompute the costly computations on the Order Details table (odView.sql in the download):

```
USE Northwind
GO
IF(SELECT OBJECT_ID('IndexedView')) IS NOT NULL
  DROP VIEW IndexedView
GO
CREATE VIEW IndexedView WITH SCHEMABINDING
AS
  SELECT ProductID,
         SUM(UnitPrice*(1.00-Discount)) AS Price,
         COUNT_BIG(*) AS [Count],
         SUM(Quantity) AS Units
    FROM dbo.[Order Details]
    GROUP BY ProductID
GO
CREATE UNIQUE CLUSTERED INDEX iv ON IndexedView(ProductID)
```

Since AVG is a disallowed construct in indexed view, a combination of SUM and COUNT could be used. However, since COUNT is a disallowed construct, SUM and COUNT_BIG are used instead. (For the complete list of disallowed constructs, refer the SQL Server Books Online.)

The indexed view materializes the output of the aggregate functions on the disk. This eliminates the need for computing the aggregate functions during the execution of a query interested in the aggregate outputs. For example, Query3.sql requests the AvgPrice and Units for certain products from the Order Details table. As these values are materialized in the indexed view for every product in the Order Details table, you can fetch these preaggregated values using the following SELECT statement on the indexed view:

```
SELECT ProductID,
       Price/[Count] AS AvgPrice,
       Units
  FROM IndexedView
```

As shown in the execution plan in Figure 4-36, the SELECT statement retrieves the values directly from the indexed view without accessing the base table (Order Details).

Figure 4-36. *Execution plan with an indexed view*

The indexed view benefits not only the queries based on the view directly, but also other queries that may be interested in the materialized data. For example, with the indexed view in place, the resultant number of logical reads for the three queries on Order Details decreases as shown in Listings 4-7 through 4-9.

Listing 4-7. *Logical Reads by Query1 with an Indexed View*

```
Table 'Products'. Scan count 77, logical reads 154
Table 'Order Details'. Scan count 1, logical reads 2
```

Listing 4-8. *Logical Reads by Query2 with an Indexed View*

```
Table 'Products'. Scan count 77, logical reads 154
Table 'Order Details'. Scan count 1, logical reads 2
```

Listing 4-9. *Logical Reads by Query3 with an Indexed View*

```
Table 'Products'. Scan count 4, logical reads 8
Table 'Order Details'. Scan count 4, logical reads 8
```

Even though the queries are not modified to refer to the new indexed view, the optimizer still uses the indexed view to improve performance. Thus even existing queries in the database application can benefit from new indexed views without any modifications to the queries.

Additional Characteristics of Indexes

SQL Server 2000 has some enhancements in indexing over SQL Server 7.0. A few of these are explained in the sections that follow.

Different Column Sort Order

SQL Server 2000 supports creating a composite index with a different sort order for the different columns of the index. Suppose you want an index with the first column sorted in ascending order and the second column sorted in descending order. You could achieve this as follows:

```
CREATE NONCLUSTERED INDEX i1 ON t1(c1 ASC, c2 DESC)
```

Index on Computed Columns

In SQL Server 2000, you can create an index on a computed column, as long as the expression defined for the computed column meets certain restrictions, such as that it only references columns from the table containing the computed column and is deterministic.

Index on BIT Data Type Columns

SQL Server 2000 allows the creation of an index on columns with the BIT data type. The ability to create an index on a BIT data type column by itself is not a big advantage since such a column can have only two unique values. As mentioned previously, columns with such low selectivity (number of unique values) are not usually good candidates for indexing. However, this feature comes into its own when you consider covering indexes. Because covering indexes require including all the columns in the index, the ability to add the BIT data type column to an index allows covering indexes to include such a column, if required.

CREATE INDEX Statement Processed As a Query

In SQL Server 2000, the CREATE INDEX operation is integrated into the query processor. The optimizer can use existing index(es) to reduce scan cost and sort while creating an index.

Consider a table with an index as follows (create_index.sql in the download):

```
IF(SELECT OBJECT_ID('t1')) IS NOT NULL
  DROP TABLE t1
GO
CREATE TABLE t1(c1 INT, c2 INT, c3 INT)
CREATE NONCLUSTERED INDEX i1 ON t1(c1, c2)
```

To understand how the creation of an index can take advantage of existing indexes, let's create two new indexes:

```
CREATE NONCLUSTERED INDEX i2 ON t1(c1)
CREATE NONCLUSTERED INDEX i3 ON t1(c2)
```

Figure 4-37 shows the execution plan for these two index creation statements.

As shown in Figure 4-37, to create the new indexes, the optimizer decides to scan the existing index instead of the base table. As the existing index contains the columns for the new indexes, scanning the existing index provides all the required values for the new indexes. Thus, if creation of one index can take advantage of another index, create them in the appropriate order.

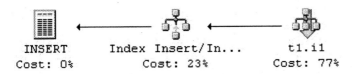

Query 1: Query cost (relative to the batch): 5(
Query text: insert [NWTest].[dbo].[t1] select

INSERT   Index Insert/In...   t1.i1
Cost: 0%   Cost: 23%   Cost: 77%

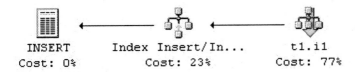

Query 2: Query cost (relative to the batch): 5(
Query text: insert [NWTest].[dbo].[t1] select

INSERT   Index Insert/In...   t1.i1
Cost: 0%   Cost: 23%   Cost: 77%

Figure 4-37. *Execution plan for CREATE INDEX*

Parallel Index Creation

SQL Server 2000 supports parallel plans for a CREATE INDEX statement, as supported in other SQL queries. On a multiprocessor machine, index creation won't be restricted to a single processor, but will benefit from the multiple processors. The number of processors to be used in a CREATE INDEX statement can be controlled by the max degree of parallelism configuration parameter of SQL Server. The default value for this parameter is 0, as you can see by executing the sp_configure stored procedure:

EXEC sp_configure 'max degree of parallelism'

The default value of 0 means that SQL Server can use all the available CPUs in the system for the parallel execution of a T-SQL statement. On a system with four processors, the maximum degree of parallelism can be set to 2 by executing sp_configure:

EXEC sp_configure 'max degree of parallelism', 2
RECONFIGURE WITH OVERRIDE

This allows SQL Server to use up to two CPUs for the parallel execution of a T-SQL statement. This configuration setting takes effect immediately, without a server restart.

The query hint MAXDOP can't be used for the CREATE INDEX statement. Also, be aware of the fact that the parallel CREATE INDEX feature is available in SQL Server 2000 Enterprise Edition, but it is not available in the Standard Edition.

Considering the Index Tuning Wizard

A simple approach to indexing is to use the Index Tuning Wizard tool provided by SQL Server. This wizard is a usage-based tool that looks at a particular workload and works with the query optimizer to determine the costs associated with various index combinations. Based on the wizard's analysis, you can add or drop indexes as appropriate.

▒**NOTE** I will cover the Index Tuning Wizard tool in more depth in Chapter 5.

Summary

In this chapter, you learned that indexing is an effective method for reducing the number of logical reads and disk I/O for a query. Although an index may add overhead to action queries, even action queries such as UPDATE and DELETE can benefit from an index.

To decide the index key columns for a particular query, evaluate the WHERE clause and the join criteria of the query. Factors such as column selectivity, width, data type, and column order are important in deciding the columns in an index key. Since an index is mainly useful in retrieving a small number of rows, the selectivity of an indexed column should be very high. It is important to note that nonclustered indexes contain the value of a clustered index key as their row locator, because this behavior greatly influences the selection of an index type.

For better performance, try to cover a query fully using a covering index. Since SQL Server can benefit from multiple indexes, use the index intersection and index join techniques, and consider having multiple narrow indexes instead of one very wide index.

In the next chapter, you will learn more about the Index Tuning Wizard, the SQL Server-provided tool that can help you determine the correct indexes in a database for a given SQL workload.

CHAPTER 5

■■■

Index Tuning Wizard

SQL Server's performance largely depends upon having proper indexes on the database tables. However, as the workload and data change over time, the existing indexes may not be entirely appropriate, and new indexes may be required. The task of deciding upon the correct indexes is complicated by the fact that an index change that benefits one set of queries may be detrimental to another set of queries.

To help you through this process, SQL Server provides a handy tool called the Index Tuning Wizard. This tool helps identify an optimal set of indexes and statistics for a given workload without requiring an expert understanding of the database schema, workload, or SQL Server internals. It can also recommend tuning options for a small set of problem queries. In addition to the wizard's benefits, I cover its limitations in this chapter, because it is a tool that can cause more harm than good if used incorrectly.

In this chapter, I cover the following topics:

- The architecture of the Index Tuning Wizard

- How to use the Index Tuning Wizard on a set of problematic queries for index recommendations

- How to choose a SQL trace for the Index Tuning Wizard

- The limitations of the Index Tuning Wizard

Index Tuning Architecture

Figure 5-1 shows a simple architecture of index tuning.

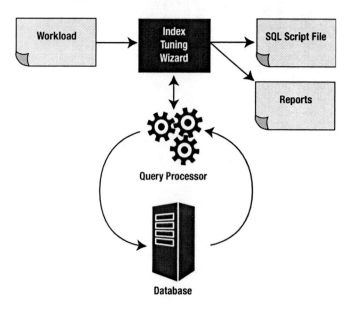

Figure 5-1. *Index tuning architecture*

You can run the Index Tuning Wizard from the command prompt (`itwiz.exe`) or from either SQL Profiler (Tools ➤ Index Tuning Wizard) or Query Analyzer (highlight the required query and select Query ➤ Index Tuning Wizard). Once the tool is opened, you should see a window like the one in Figure 5-2.

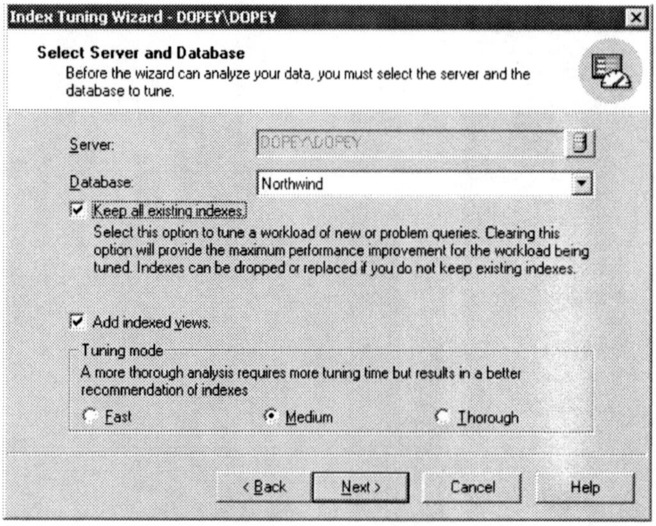

Figure 5-2. *Selecting the server and database in the Index Tuning Wizard*

Note the option to keep all existing indexes. If the sample SQL workload you feed to the wizard doesn't represent a typical workload, then it is advisable to leave this option checked, thus avoiding dropping indexes that may be used by full-workload queries. Also note that the index tuning process can recommend indexed views, if they are found to be beneficial.

TIP The Index Tuning Wizard recommends indexed views only for platforms that support them. SQL Server 2000 Enterprise Edition does, but the Standard and Professional Editions don't.

Once you've selected the database and check boxes, you can provide a SQL workload, as shown in Figure 5-3. The index tuning architecture takes this SQL workload and recommends adding new indexes or dropping existing indexes, as appropriate for the workload. You can input the SQL workload in one of three forms:

- SQL trace saved to a trace file (.trc)

- SQL trace saved to a trace table

- SQL script (.sql)

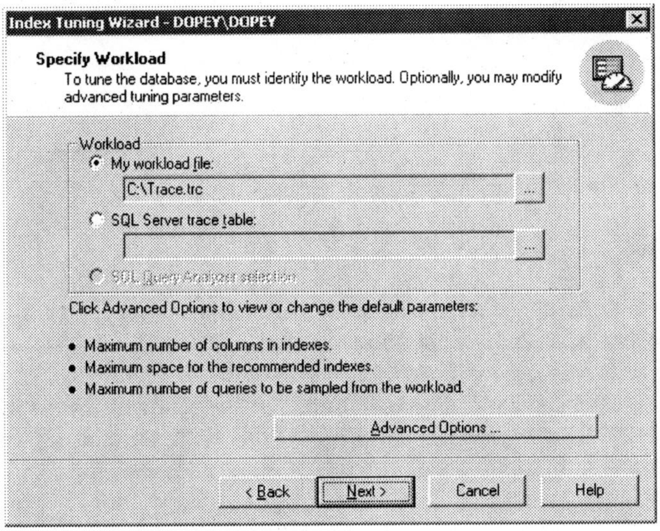

Figure 5-3. *Specifying the workload in the Index Tuning Wizard*

The input options for the SQL workload depend upon from where the wizard is launched. When the Index Tuning Wizard is launched from the Profiler tool (as shown in Figure 5-3), you can use the first workload option to input either a SQL trace file or a SQL script file. When using a trace file, the SQL:BatchCompleted counter should be included in the list of captured events, since the Index Tuning Wizard currently (SQL Server 2000 SP3a) doesn't analyze SQL:StmtCompleted events.

▓**NOTE** See Chapter 3 to learn how to create a SQL trace file.

If the SQL trace is available in trace table form, then you can use the second workload option. A third option, grayed out in Figure 5-3, is enabled when the tool is launched from Query Analyzer. This option allows the set of problematic queries being worked upon in Query Analyzer to be supplied as input to the Index Tuning Wizard.

Note the Advanced Options button. Figure 5-4 displays these options.

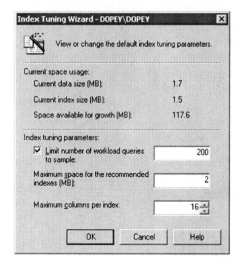

Figure 5-4. *Advanced options in the Index Tuning Wizard*

You may configure these options as follows:

- If the workload is not fully represented within 200 queries (the default value), then increase this number realistically or uncheck the corresponding check box. If index tuning is done in a test environment, it may be appropriate to limit the number of workload queries, since you will mostly run a limited number of test scripts and rerun them multiple times in the same order. However, if the input for the index tuning is from a production environment, this approach may not be appropriate, since the queries may not form a repetitive pattern.

- If disk space is a constraint, then decrease the maximum space for recommended indexes. The Index Tuning Wizard recommends only the best combination of indexes, not all possible indexes.

- Since indexes with many columns increase the index maintenance cost for action queries, you should be wary of adding an index with as many as 16 columns unless your tables also have a large number of columns. Reduce the maximum columns per index to something more acceptable, say to 6 (or even less than that). Reducing this setting decreases the number of column combinations that the index tuning process has to analyze, and so makes the tuning process faster as well.

The Index Tuning Wizard also allows you to select specific tables in the database you are interested in analyzing for indexing. If the input represents a typical workload, then all the tables may be selected for index analysis, as shown in Figure 5-5.

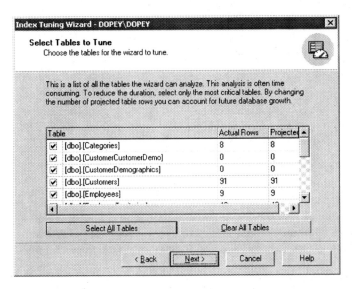

Figure 5-5. *Selecting tables to tune in the Index Tuning Wizard*

The index tuning process uses the query processor to run the queries from the input workload, with appropriate settings to obtain just their execution plan. The tool iterates through several alternative sets of indexes called *configurations*, taking into account aspects such as single-column indexes, composite indexes, and the order of columns in composite indexes. For each index configuration, the resultant execution plan resource (I/O and CPU) cost is computed, and based on these computations the tuning process provides its indexing recommendations.

Note that the index configurations considered by the index tuning process are not materialized (or physically created), which is a good thing because this would require creating and dropping indexes on the fly, a resource-intensive process. The simulation of the index configurations reduces the cost overhead of the index tuning process. However, as the resultant resource costs are computed without an actual creation of the index, there can be some differences between the *suggested* cost improvement and the *actual* improvement. For this reason, I recommend that you *always check* the cost improvement of the workload after the Index Tuning Wizard recommendations are applied.

After you click Next in the dialog box shown in Figure 5-5, the wizard runs through its cycles until the recommendations appear, as shown in Figure 5-6.

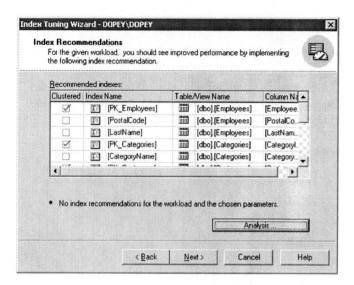

Figure 5-6. *Index recommendations in the Index Tuning Wizard*

For recommendations, the wizard not only specifies the new indexes to be created, but also provides the list of existing indexes that are degrading the database performance or occupying unnecessary space. These recommendations can be saved in a .sql file to be analyzed and executed later. By clicking the Analysis button, you can access various reports with statistics from the tuning process and the effect of various recommendations. Table 5-1 enumerates these reports.

Table 5-1. *Index Tuning Wizard Reports*

Report Name	Report Description
Index Usage Report (current versus recommended configuration)	Percentage of queries in the workload that use an index, and the space requirement of the index
Table Analysis Report	Top 100 tables heavily used by the workload with the current indexes and with the recommendations
View – Table Relations Report	Indexed views recommended and the tables referred to in the view
Query – Index Relations Report	Indexes used by individual queries in a workload with current indexes and with the recommendations
Query Cost Report	Cost improvement in the top 100 queries with recommended indexes
Workload Analysis Report	Distribution of queries within different cost groups with current indexes and with the recommendations
Tuning Summary Report	Overview of the index tuning analysis

Index Tuning Wizard Recommendations

You can use the Index Tuning Wizard to recommend indexes for a complete database by using a workload that fairly represents all SQL activities. You can also use it to recommend indexes for a set of problematic queries.

To learn how you can use the Index Tuning Wizard to get index recommendations on a set of problematic queries, consider the following example. Create a test table emp with different data distributions for the individual columns (create_emp.sql in the download):

```
IF(SELECT OBJECT_ID('emp')) IS NOT NULL
  DROP TABLE emp
GO
CREATE TABLE emp (
empID INT IDENTITY
, address CHAR(300)
, [name] CHAR(4)
)

--Load the table with 10,000 rows of test data:
DECLARE @counter INT
SET @counter = 1
WHILE (@counter <= 2000)
BEGIN
  INSERT emp(address, [name]) VALUES('Charlotte, NC', 'Andy')
  INSERT emp(address, [name]) VALUES('Charlotte, NC', 'Dave')
  INSERT emp(address, [name]) VALUES('Charlotte, NC', 'John')
  INSERT emp(address, [name]) VALUES('Charlotte, NC', 'Kate')
  INSERT emp(address, [name]) VALUES('Charlotte, NC', 'Pete')
  SET @counter = @counter + 1
END
```

The three columns of the table have three different levels of selectivity:

- *Column 1* (INT IDENTITY): Very high selectivity (all unique values)

- *Column 2* (Charlotte, NC): Very low selectivity (one unique value only)

- *Column 3* (Andy, Dave, John, Kate, or Pete): Low selectivity (five unique values only)

Suppose you have two queries accessing this dataset as follows (problem_queries.sql in the download):

```
SELECT empID, [name], address FROM emp WHERE [name] = 'Andy'
GO
SELECT empID, [name], address FROM emp WHERE empID = 10000
```

To decide upon suitable indexes for these problem queries, let's use the Index Tuning Wizard:

1. Highlight the two queries in the Query Analyzer window, if there are other queries besides the problem queries in the Query Analyzer window.

2. Select Query ➤ Index Tuning Wizard.

3. In the Select Server and Database dialog box

   • Select the database containing the emp table.

   • Keep the option "Keep all existing indexes" checked, since the queries don't represent a complete workload.

   • Keep the option "Add indexed views" checked, since indexed views can optimize existing queries even if they aren't referred to by the existing queries.

   • Keep the option "Tuning mode" at Medium to balance between the tuning time and the tuning recommendations.

4. In the Specify Workload dialog box

   • Select the "SQL Query Analyzer selection" option.

   • Leave the default values for the advanced options.

5. In the Select Tables to Tune dialog box, choose the [emp] table, and then start the index tuning process by clicking Next.

Figure 5-7 shows the index recommendations for the preceding two queries.

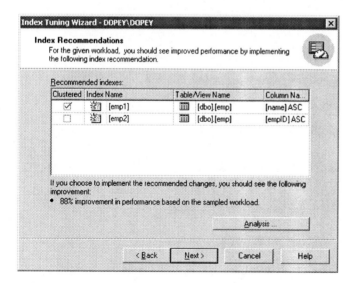

Figure 5-7. *Index recommendations*

As you can see, the Index Tuning Wizard recommended the following two indexes:

- A clustered index on the name column.

- A nonclustered index on the empID column. You can tell it is nonclustered because the Clustered check box is blank.

The star symbol on an index name indicates the recommendation of new index. The absence of the star symbol indicates that the Index Tuning Wizard found the existing index to be useful. In Figure 5-7, the star symbol on both index recommendations suggests the creation of two new indexes.

To save the index recommendations of the wizard in a script file, click Next and select the "Save script file" option in the resulting dialog box. The following is an excerpt from the resulting SQL script file (tuning_recommendations.sql in the download):

```
USE [Northwind]
go

SET QUOTED_IDENTIFIER ON
SET ARITHABORT ON
SET CONCAT_NULL_YIELDS_NULL ON
SET ANSI_NULLS ON
SET ANSI_PADDING ON
SET ANSI_WARNINGS ON
SET NUMERIC_ROUNDABORT OFF
go

DECLARE @bErrors as bit

BEGIN TRANSACTION
SET @bErrors = 0

CREATE CLUSTERED INDEX [emp1] ON [dbo].[emp] ([name] ASC )
IF( @@error <> 0 ) SET @bErrors = 1

CREATE NONCLUSTERED INDEX [emp2] ON [dbo].[emp] ([empID] ASC )
IF( @@error <> 0 ) SET @bErrors = 1

IF( @bErrors = 0 )
  COMMIT TRANSACTION
ELSE
  ROLLBACK TRANSACTION
```

Note that besides the index recommendations, the wizard recommendation script contains additional settings to enforce the rules of the SQL-92 standard and the recommended settings for SQL Server. Per the recommended settings for SQL Server, the following six SET options must be set to ON:

- QUOTED_IDENTIFIER

- ARITHABORT

- CONCAT_NULL_YIELDS_NULL

- ANSI_NULLS

- ANSI_PADDING

- ANSI_WARNINGS

Also, the NUMERIC_ROUNDABORT option must be set to OFF. These SET options must be set correctly for any connection that creates an indexed view or index on a computed column. The OLEDB provider and ODBC driver for SQL Server automatically set these seven session options to the required settings. For detailed descriptions of these settings, please refer to the following MSDN articles:

- "SET Options" at http://msdn.microsoft.com/library/en-us/acdata/ ac_8_qd_03_35df.asp

- "SET Options That Affect Results" at http://msdn.microsoft.com/library/en-us/ createdb/cm_8_des_05_1ng3.asp

The Index Tuning Wizard estimates the overall performance improvement by its recommendations for the input workload. For the current set of problem queries, the wizard estimates that the recommendations will provide a reduction in cost of 88%, as shown in Figure 5-7. (Although the dialog box uses the phrase "improvement in performance," you can see that if you time an example, it is actually a reduction in cost.) For a detailed analysis of the recommendations, the wizard generates a number of reports, which were enumerated in Table 5-1 earlier in the chapter.

Knowing the total reduction in cost helps, but as a DBA you would be further interested to know the reduction in cost of the individual queries. For this purpose, you can refer to the Query Cost Report. As shown in Figure 5-8, the first query is likely to have a cost reduction of 80%, and the cost reduction for the second query is estimated to be 96%.

The next aspect of the recommendation to determine is which indexes are recommended for these individual queries as, based on the performance improvement of the individual queries, you may decide to apply the recommendations for only the queries that will benefit the most in the first phase. You can obtain this information from the Query – Index Relations Report (Recommended Configuration). As shown in Figure 5-9, only one index, emp1, is recommended for the first query. Similarly, only one index, emp2, is recommended for the second query.

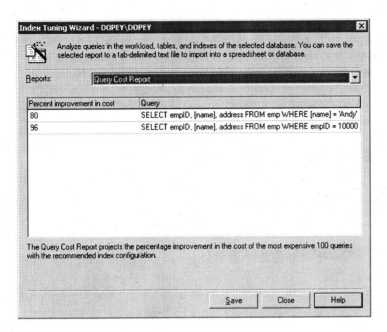

Figure 5-8. *Query Cost Report*

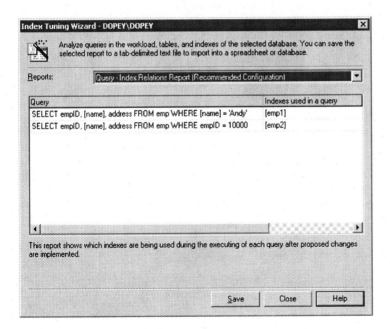

Figure 5-9. *Query-Index Relations Report*

Based on the reports for the performance improvement of the individual queries and their corresponding indexes, in the first phase you may decide to create the indexes for the query that provides the greatest performance benefit. These indexes may be used by other queries in the workload, too. An index used by many queries in the workload will benefit the overall workload. To determine the usage of those indexes by the overall workload, refer to the Index Usage Report (Recommended Configurations). As shown in Figure 5-10, index emp1 serves 50% of the total workload. Similarly, index emp2 serves 50% of the workload.

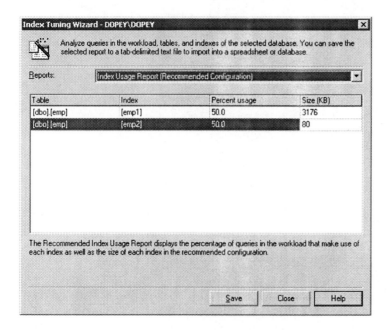

Figure 5-10. *Index Usage Report, first scenario*

If the first problem query is repeated three times as follows:

```
SELECT empID, [name], address FROM emp WHERE [name] = 'Andy'
GO
SELECT empID, [name], address FROM emp WHERE empID = 10000
GO
SELECT empID, [name], address FROM emp WHERE [name] = 'Dave'
GO
SELECT empID, [name], address FROM emp WHERE [name] = 'John'
```

then the Index Usage Report (Recommended Configuration) would represent this, as shown in Figure 5-11.

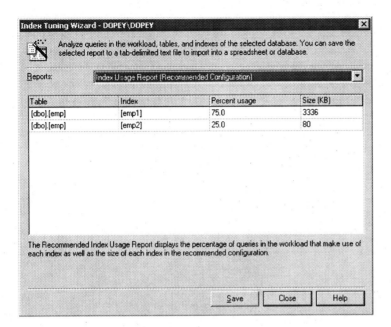

Figure 5-11. *Index Usage Report, second scenario*

Figure 5-11 indicates that index emp1 serves three out of four queries in the workload, and index emp2 serves one out of four queries in the workload. This reflects the percent usage of the recommended indexes and the distribution of the corresponding queries in the workload.

The Index Usage Report (Recommended Configuration) window also indicates the amount of disk space required to create the individual indexes, which will be useful in determining the additional disk space requirement. Based on all this information, you can decide which indexes to create in the first phase, the affected queries, and the amount of performance improvement expected for those queries.

Now let's analyze the basis of the previous recommendations. The first SELECT statement requires data retrieval from the table based on one of the values in the name column. There are only five unique values for the name column, with each repeating 2,000 times. Thus the first query retrieves a large range of rows. As you learned in the previous chapter, a clustered index is suitable to retrieve a range of rows. Therefore, it is appropriate to create a clustered index on the name column.

The second SELECT statement retrieves only one row based on the value of the empID column. The empID column contains all unique values, and there are a total of 10,000 rows in the table. Once again, as you learned in the previous chapter, a nonclustered index is suitable to retrieve a small set of rows. Therefore, it is appropriate to create a nonclustered index on the empID column.

Choosing a SQL Trace for the Index Tuning Wizard

As mentioned previously, you can supply a saved SQL trace as an input to the Index Tuning Wizard for index recommendations on the workload. The Index Tuning Wizard passes the queries from the saved trace output to its tuning process to determine the right indexes for the individual queries. It doesn't analyze the different attributes of the queries in the trace output; for example, irrespective of the number of reads/writes for the query in the trace output, the wizard passes the query to the index tuning process. The Index Tuning Wizard needs the minimum set of events and data columns in the trace output shown in Tables 5-2 and 5-3.

Table 5-2. *Trace Events for the Index Tuning Wizard*

Event	Remarks
SQL:BatchCompleted	The wizard requires this event to identify the queries in the workload.

Table 5-3. *Trace Data Columns for the Index Tuning Wizard*

Data Column	Remarks
EventClass	The wizard looks for the SQL:BatchCompleted event in this column.
TextData	The wizard determines the T-SQL statement for the queries from this column.
SPID	Profiler doesn't allow this column to be removed.

Limiting the set of events and data columns reduces the impact of SQL tracing on the database server, which is especially important if the database under review is a production server. It also keeps the size of the trace output comparatively small. To further reduce the overhead of SQL tracing on the database server, follow the other recommendations for the Profiler tool outlined in Chapter 3.

As mentioned previously, the Index Tuning Wizard won't be able to identify the queries in the trace output without the inclusion of the SQL:BatchCompleted event. The trace for the workload to be analyzed can be captured using the Profiler tool as explained in Chapter 3. The trace output may be saved either in a trace file or in a trace table, and then later fed to the Index Tuning Wizard for index analysis.

Index Tuning Wizard Limitations

The Index Tuning Wizard recommendations are based on the input workload. If the input workload is not a true representation of the actual workload, then the recommended indexes may sometimes have a *negative* effect on some queries that are missing in the workload.

For a production server, you should ensure that the SQL trace includes a complete representation of the database workload. For most database applications, capturing a trace for a complete day usually includes most of the queries executed on the database. A few of the other considerations/limitations with the Index Tuning Wizard are as follows:

- *Trace input without the* `SQL:BatchCompleted` *event*: As mentioned earlier, the SQL trace input to the Index Tuning Wizard must include the `SQL:BatchCompleted` event; otherwise, the wizard won't be able to identify the queries in the workload. For example, let's use the `SQL:StmtCompleted` event instead of the `SQL:BatchCompleted` event while capturing the trace output for the preceding problem queries. Figure 5-12 shows the corresponding trace output.

EventClass	TextData	SPID
TraceStart		
SQL:StmtCompleted	SELECT empID, [name], address FROM emp WHERE [name] = 'Andy'	51
SQL:StmtCompleted	SELECT empID, [name], address FROM emp WHERE empID = 10000	51
TraceStop		

Figure 5-12. *Trace output without the SQL:BatchCompleted event*

If this trace output is saved as a trace file and then supplied as an input to the Index Tuning Wizard, the wizard won't be able to identify the problem queries in the trace. Consequently, the wizard may display the error message in Figure 5-13.

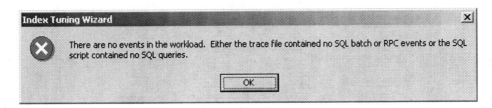

Figure 5-13. *Index Tuning Wizard error*

Or it may just say "No index recommendations for the workload and the chosen parameters." To avoid this problem, always include the `SQL:BatchCompleted` event while capturing the SQL trace. Also, remember to include this event even for stored procedures.

- *Query distribution in the workload*: In a workload, a query may be executed multiple times with the same parameter value. Even a small performance improvement to the most common query can make a bigger contribution to the performance of the overall workload, compared to a large improvement in performance of a query that is executed only once. For example, consider that the problem set of queries includes three executions of the first problem query as follows:

```
SELECT empID, [name], address FROM emp WHERE [name] = 'Andy'
GO
SELECT empID, [name], address FROM emp WHERE empID = 10000
GO
SELECT empID, [name], address FROM emp WHERE [name] = 'Andy'
GO
SELECT empID, [name], address FROM emp WHERE [name] = 'Andy'
```

Even though the per-query percentage improvement of index emp1 is less (i.e., 80%) than that for index emp2 (i.e., 96%), index emp1 serves 75% of the workload. Thus, overall, index emp1 should be more useful to the total workload than index emp2. However, since the three instances of first problem query are exactly the same (including the parameter value), the Index Usage Report (Recommended Configuration) indicates that the percent usage of index emp1 is 50% instead of the expected 75%.

- *Multiple SQL queries in a batch*: If multiple SQL queries are submitted together as a part of a query batch, then the wizard analyzes only the first query in the batch. For example, in the preceding problem set of queries, if you remove the GO statement between the two queries, as follows, and submit them together from the Query Analyzer session, then both queries will be submitted as a part of one query batch to SQL Server:

```
SELECT empID, [name], address FROM emp WHERE [name] = 'Andy'
SELECT empID, [name], address FROM emp WHERE empID = 10000
```

Consequently, the Index Tuning Wizard will recommend the clustered index required for the first query, but not the nonclustered index required for the second query, as shown in Figure 5-14.

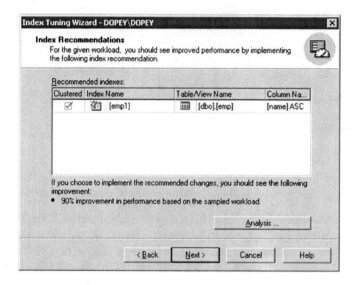

Figure 5-14. *Index recommendations for multiple SQL queries in a batch*

To avoid this problem, include the GO statement between every query.

- *Index hints*: Index hints in a SQL query can prevent the Index Tuning Wizard from choosing a better execution plan. The wizard includes all index hints used in a SQL query as a part of its recommendations. As these indexes may not be optimal for the table, remove all index hints from queries before submitting the workload to the wizard, bearing in mind that you need to add them back to see if they do actually improve performance.

- *Stored procedures with temporary tables*: Since the Index Tuning Wizard only simulates the execution of queries, temporary tables used within stored procedures are not created. This prevents the wizard from properly analyzing stored procedure statements referring these temporary tables. Thus, the Index Tuning Wizard cannot effectively tune stored procedures that use temporary tables.

- *Triggers*: The wizard doesn't analyze SQL statements belonging to a trigger. A trigger statement in a SQL trace is captured as a `SQL:StmtCompleted` event. As stated earlier, the Index Tuning Wizard currently analyzes only the `SQL:BatchCompleted` events, not the `SQL:StmtCompleted` events.

Summary

As you learned in this chapter, the Index Tuning Wizard is a useful tool for analyzing the effectiveness of existing indexes and recommending new indexes for a SQL workload. As the SQL workload changes over time, you can use this tool to determine which existing indexes are no longer in use and which new indexes are required to improve performance. It is a good idea to run the wizard occasionally, just to check that your existing indexes really are the best fit for your current workload. It also provides many useful reports for analyzing the SQL workload and the effectiveness of its own recommendations.

Most of the time, you will rely on nonclustered indexes to improve the performance of a SQL workload. As the performance of a nonclustered index is highly dependent on the cost of the bookmark lookup associated with the nonclustered index, you will see in the next chapter how to analyze and resolve a bookmark lookup.

■ ■ ■

CHAPTER 6

Bookmark Lookup Analysis

To maximize the benefit from nonclustered indexes, you must minimize the cost of the data retrieval as much as possible. One of the major overheads associated with nonclustered indexes is the cost of excessive *bookmark lookups*, which are a mechanism to navigate from a nonclustered index row to the corresponding data row in the base table. Therefore, it makes sense to look at the cause of bookmark lookups and to evaluate how to avoid this cost.

In this chapter, I cover the following topics:

- The purpose of a bookmark lookup

- Drawbacks of using a bookmark lookup

- Analysis of the cause of bookmark lookups

- Techniques to resolve bookmark lookups

Purpose of a Bookmark Lookup

When a SQL query requests a small number of rows, the optimizer can use the nonclustered index, if available, on the column(s) in the WHERE clause to retrieve the data. If the query refers to columns that are not part of the nonclustered index used to retrieve the data, then navigation is required from the index row to the corresponding data row in the table to access these columns.

For example, in the following SELECT statement, if the nonclustered index used by the optimizer doesn't include all the columns, navigation will be required from a nonclustered index row to the data row in the base table to retrieve the value of those columns:

```
SELECT c1, AVG(c2)
  FROM t1
  WHERE c3 = 1
  GROUP BY c4, c1
  HAVING MAX(c5) > 0
  ORDER BY MIN(c6)
```

Suppose table t1 has a nonclustered index on column c3. The optimizer can use the index to filter the rows from the table. Considering the table has no clustered index, the nonclustered index contains column c3 only. The other columns (c1, c2, c4, c5, and c6) referred to by the SELECT statement are not available in the nonclustered index. To fetch the values for those columns, navigation from the nonclustered index row to the corresponding data row is required. This operation is called a bookmark lookup.

To better understand how a nonclustered index can cause a bookmark lookup, consider the following example. Create a test table (create_t1.sql in the download code) with 1,000 rows and a nonclustered index:

```
IF(SELECT OBJECT_ID('t1')) IS NOT NULL
   DROP TABLE t1
GO
CREATE TABLE t1(c1 INT, c2 CHAR(50))
DECLARE @n INT
SET @n = 1
WHILE @n <= 1000
BEGIN
   INSERT INTO t1 VALUES(@n, @n)
   SET @n = @n + 1
END
CREATE NONCLUSTERED INDEX incl ON t1(c1)
```

The following SELECT statement requests only one row from the table by using a filter criterion on column c1:

```
SELECT * FROM t1 WHERE c1 = 1
```

The optimizer evaluates the WHERE clause and finds that the column c1 included in the WHERE clause has a nonclustered index on it that filters the number of rows to one. Since only one row is requested, retrieving the data through the nonclustered index will be cheaper than scanning the complete table (containing 1,000 rows) to identify the matching row. The non-clustered index on column c1 will help identify the matching row quickly. The nonclustered index includes column c1 only; column c2 is not included. Therefore, as you may have guessed, to retrieve column c2 while using the nonclustered index, a bookmark lookup is required.

This is shown in the following execution plan (see Figure 6-1; you can turn STATISTICS IO on from the Query ➤ Current Connections Properties menu):

```
Table 't1'. Scan count 1, logical reads 3
```

SELECT   Bookmark Lookup   t1.incl
Cost: 0%   Cost: 49%   Cost: 51%

Figure 6-1. *Execution plan with a bookmark lookup*

Drawbacks of a Bookmark Lookup

A bookmark lookup requires data page access in addition to index page access. Accessing two set of pages increases the number of logical reads for the query. Additionally, if the pages are not available in memory, a bookmark lookup will probably require a random (or nonsequential) I/O operation on the disk to jump from the index page to the data page. This is because, for a large table, the index page and the corresponding data page usually won't be close to each other on the disk.

The increased logical reads and costly physical reads (if required) make the data retrieval operation of the bookmark lookup quite costly. This cost factor is the reason that nonclustered indexes are better suited for queries that return a small set of rows from the table. As the number of rows retrieved by a query increases, the overhead cost of a bookmark lookup becomes unacceptable.

Queries that require many rows to be returned are better served with a clustered index, which doesn't require a bookmark lookup. However, you can have only one clustered index on a table, which can't always serve every filter and join criteria on the table. As a result of this, you have to use nonclustered indexes to filter rows for queries not served by the clustered index and face the overhead of a bookmark lookup.

To understand how a bookmark lookup makes a nonclustered index ineffective as the number of rows retrieved increases, let's look at an example. Create a small test table (create_t1_2.sql in the download) with a nonclustered index as follows:

```
IF(SELECT OBJECT_ID('t1')) IS NOT NULL
    DROP TABLE t1
GO
CREATE TABLE t1(c1 INT, c2 CHAR(50))
CREATE NONCLUSTERED INDEX incl ON t1(c1)
INSERT INTO t1 VALUES(1, '1')
```

The following SELECT statement retrieves only one row filtered on column c1, and the table has a nonclustered index on that column:

```
SELECT * FROM t1 WHERE c1 >= 1
```

Consequently, the optimizer uses the nonclustered index on the WHERE clause column c1 as shown in the following execution plan (see Figure 6-2):

```
Table 't1'. Scan count 1, logical reads 2
```

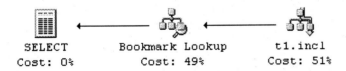

Figure 6-2. *Execution plan for fetching one row*

Add a large number of rows to the table (with `row_add.sql`), so that the preceding `SELECT` statement retrieves a large number of rows.

```
DECLARE @n INT
SET @n = 2
WHILE @n <= 1000
BEGIN
  INSERT INTO t1 VALUES(@n, @n)
  SET @n = @n + 1
END
```

You can then run your `SELECT` statement again:

```
SELECT * FROM t1 WHERE c1 >= 1
```

Here the optimizer discards the nonclustered index and scans the table directly as shown in the following execution plan (see Figure 6-3):

```
Table 't1'. Scan count 1, logical reads 9
```

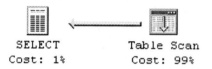

```
  SELECT           Table Scan
Cost: 1%          Cost: 99%
```

Figure 6-3. *Execution plan for fetching 1,000+ rows*

To determine how costly it will be to use the nonclustered index, consider the number of logical reads (9) performed by the query during the table scan. If you force the optimizer to use the nonclustered index by using an index hint

```
SELECT * FROM t1 WITH(INDEX(incl)) WHERE c1 >= 1
```

the number of logical reads increases from 9 to 1,004:

```
Table 't1'. Scan count 1, logical reads 1004
```

Figure 6-4 shows the corresponding execution plan.

```
  SELECT        Bookmark Lookup        t1.incl
Cost: 0%          Cost: 86%          Cost: 14%
```

Figure 6-4. *Execution plan for fetching 1,000+ rows with an index hint*

From the resultant execution plan, you can see that the cost of a bookmark lookup (86%) is more than six times the cost of retrieving data from the nonclustered index (14%). When you were retrieving only one row in the first query in this chapter, the bookmark lookup cost (49%) was less than the cost of retrieving data from the nonclustered index (51%).

Therefore, the optimizer discards the nonclustered index while retrieving a large number of rows. To benefit from nonclustered indexes, queries should request a very small number of rows. Application design plays an important role for the requirements that handle large result sets. For example, search engines on the Web mostly return a limited number of articles at a time, even if the search criterion returns thousands of matching articles. If the queries request a large number of rows, then the increased overhead cost of a bookmark lookup makes the nonclustered index unsuitable; subsequently, you have to consider the possibilities of avoiding the bookmark lookup operation.

Analyzing the Cause of a Bookmark Lookup

Since a bookmark lookup can be a costly operation, you should analyze what causes a query plan to choose a bookmark step in an execution plan. You may find that you are able to avoid the bookmark lookup by including the missing columns in the nonclustered index key, and thereby avoid the cost overhead associated with the bookmark lookup.

To learn how to identify the columns not included in the nonclustered index, consider the following example. Create a small test table with a nonclustered index (create_t1_3.sql in the download):

```
IF(SELECT OBJECT_ID('t1')) IS NOT NULL
  DROP TABLE t1
GO
CREATE TABLE t1(c1 INT, c2 INT, c3 INT)
CREATE NONCLUSTERED INDEX incl ON t1(c1)
INSERT INTO t1 VALUES(11, 12, 13)
```

Suppose you want to execute the following query:

```
SELECT c1, c2, c3 FROM t1 WHERE c1 = 11
```

This produces the following execution plan (see Figure 6-5):

```
Table 't1'. Scan count 1, logical reads 2
```

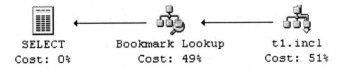

Figure 6-5. *Execution plan with a bookmark lookup*

As shown in the execution plan, you have a bookmark lookup. The SELECT statement refers to columns c1, c2, and c3. The nonclustered index on column c1 doesn't provide values for columns c2 and c3, so a bookmark lookup operation was required to retrieve those columns from base table. However, in the real world, it usually won't be this easy to identify all the columns used by a query. Remember that a bookmark lookup operation will be caused if all the columns referred to in any part of the query (not just the selection list) aren't included in the nonclustered index used.

In the case of a complex query based on views and user-defined functions, it may be too difficult to find all the columns referred to by the query. As a result, you need a standard mechanism to find the columns returned by the bookmark lookup that are not included in the nonclustered index.

The graphical execution plan doesn't show you these columns. To find this, the textual execution plan will be useful. You can use the SET SHOWPLAN_ALL statement along with the SELECT statement as follows (showplan.sql in the download) to obtain the textual execution plan for the query:

```
SET SHOWPLAN_ALL ON
GO
SELECT c1, c2, c3 FROM t1 WHERE c1 = 11
GO
SET SHOWPLAN_ALL OFF
GO
```

The output of SET SHOWPLAN_ALL includes a column called OutputList. This column lists all the columns output of the corresponding execution step. Therefore, the value of the OutputList column for the bookmark lookup provides the list of columns outputted by the bookmark lookup, as shown in Figure 6-6.

StmtText	S	N	P	P	L	A	D	E	E	E	A	T	OutputList
SELECT c1, c2, c3 FR...	.	1	0	.	.	1	.	.	.	.	.	.	NULL
|--Bookmark Lookup...	.	3	1	.	.	.	.	.	.	.	.	.	[t1].[c3], [t1].[c2], [t1].[c1]
|--Index Seek...	.	4	3	.	.	.	.	.	.	.	.	.	[Bmk1000]

Figure 6-6. *Columns output by a bookmark lookup*

From the OutputList column for the bookmark lookup step, you can see that the bookmark lookup returned columns c2 and c3 in addition to column c1 included in the nonclustered index. This mechanism of identifying columns causing a bookmark lookup can be used even for complex queries.

You can find the columns missing from the nonclustered index using index hints. As shown in the preceding section, you can use an index hint to force the optimizer to use the index(es) specified in the index hint. The index hint may specify the name of an index or the identifier of the index maintained by SQL Server. The identifier of the nonclustered index incl can be determined from the sysindexes system table (indexes.sql in the download):

```
SELECT name AS IndexName
     , indid AS IndexID
     , OBJECT_NAME(id) AS TableName
FROM sysindexes
WHERE id = OBJECT_ID('t1')
  AND name = 'incl'
```

Figure 6-7 shows the result.

IndexName	IndexID	TableName
incl	2	t1

Figure 6-7. *IndexID of an index from sysindexes*

Accordingly, the index hint in the preceding SELECT statement can be modified to use the identifier of the nonclustered index instead of the index name:

```
SELECT * FROM t1 WITH(INDEX(2)) WHERE c1 >= 1
```

TIP Instead of using the index ID, you can use the index name.

By using an index hint, you are able to force the optimizer to use the nonclustered index and thereby introduce the bookmark lookup. On analyzing the bookmark lookup, you will be able to find the required columns that are not included in the nonclustered index.

Resolving a Bookmark Lookup

Since the relative cost of a bookmark lookup can be very high, you should, wherever possible, try to get rid of bookmark lookup operations. In the preceding section, you needed to obtain the values of columns c2 and c3 without navigating from the index row to the data row. You can do this in three different ways, as explained in the following sections.

Using a Clustered Index

For a clustered index, the leaf page of the index is the same as the data page of the table. Therefore, when reading the values of the clustered index key columns, the database engine can also read the values of other columns without any navigation from the index row. In the previous example, if you convert the nonclustered index to a clustered index, for a particular row, SQL Server can retrieve values of all the columns from the same page itself.

To evaluate the role of a clustered index in avoiding a bookmark lookup, let's convert the nonclustered index in the preceding example to a clustered index:

```
DROP INDEX t1.incl
CREATE CLUSTERED INDEX icl ON t1(c1)
```

Now if you rerun the query

```
SELECT c1, c2, c3 FROM t1 WHERE c1 = 11
```

the bookmark lookup is eliminated (see Figure 6-8):

```
Table 't1'. Scan count 1, logical reads 2
```

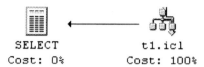

Figure 6-8. *Execution plan with a clustered index*

Converting a nonclustered index to a clustered index is an easy technique for avoiding a bookmark lookup. However, in many cases it won't be possible to do so, since the table may already have a clustered index in place; remember that a table can have only one clustered index.

Using a Covering Index

In Chapter 4, you learned that a covering index is like a pseudo-clustered index for the queries, since it can return results without recourse to the table data. So you can also use a covering index to avoid a bookmark lookup.

To understand how you can use a covering index to avoid a bookmark lookup, consider the following example. Create a small test table (create_t1_4.sql in the download) with a nonclustered index as follows. Considering that the test table already has a clustered index in place on c3, you cannot use it to filter rows on column c1, if required. To filter rows on column c1, you require an index on that column. Since the clustered index is already used on column c3, you have to use a nonclustered index on column c1.

```
IF(SELECT OBJECT_ID('t1')) IS NOT NULL
  DROP TABLE t1
GO
CREATE TABLE t1(c1 INT, c2 INT, c3 INT)
CREATE CLUSTERED INDEX icl ON t1(c3)
CREATE NONCLUSTERED INDEX incl ON t1(c1)
INSERT INTO t1 VALUES(11, 12, 13)
```

The following SELECT statement that filters rows on column c1

```
SELECT c1, c3, c2 FROM t1 WHERE c1 = 11
```

will have a bookmark lookup as shown in the preceding section.

To avoid this bookmark lookup, you can add the columns retrieved by the bookmark lookup (c2, c3) to the nonclustered index on column c1 as follows. This makes the nonclustered index a covering index for this query, and therefore all the columns requested by the query can be served by the nonclustered index without a bookmark lookup.

```
CREATE NONCLUSTERED INDEX incl ON t1(c1, c2, c3)
WITH DROP_EXISTING
```

If you run the SELECT statement again

```
SELECT c1, c3, c2 FROM t1 WHERE c1 = 11
```

the following execution plan is returned (see Figure 6-9):

```
Table 't1'. Scan count 1, logical reads 1
```

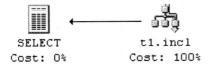

Figure 6-9. *Execution plan with a covering index*

There is a caveat to using a covering index, however. If you add too many columns to a nonclustered index, it becomes too wide, and the index maintenance cost associated with the action queries can increase, as discussed in Chapter 4. Therefore, evaluate closely the number of columns (for size and data type) to be added to the nonclustered index key. If the total width of the additional columns is not too large (usually up to 20% of the table width), then those columns can be added in the nonclustered index key to be used as a covering index.

There is one more interesting aspect of the covering index. In the current example, what will happen if you remove the last column, c3, from the nonclustered index key? While you are thinking (at least I hope so!), let me go ahead and modify the nonclustered index like so:

```
CREATE NONCLUSTERED INDEX incl ON t1(c1, c2) WITH DROP_EXISTING
```

Now run the SELECT statement again:

```
SELECT c1, c3, c2 FROM t1 WHERE c1 = 11
```

The resultant execution plan is as follows (Figure 6-10):

```
Table 't1'. Scan count 1, logical reads 1
```

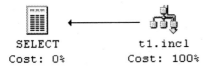

Figure 6-10. *Execution plan with a "narrower" covering index*

Note that the resultant execution plan doesn't have a bookmark lookup. In fact, the execution plan looks exactly the same as the execution plan for the full covered index. The obvious question is, where is the value of column c3 coming from?

Remember that you have a clustered index on column c3. From your understanding of the relationship between a clustered and a nonclustered index on a table, you know that the row locator of a nonclustered index contains the clustered index key value, if the table contains a clustered index. All the columns of the clustered index are appended to the columns of all nonclustered indexes on the same table. Therefore, in this case, the nonclustered index has the value of column c3 in its row locator.

This means that you do not need to add clustered index columns to your nonclustered indexes on the same table. However, because the clustered index columns are appended to the end of the nonclustered index columns as a row locator, the resultant column order of the nonclustered index may not always be appropriate.

If a certain column order in the nonclustered index including the clustered index columns is required, then explicitly add those columns to the nonclustered index. For instance, in the preceding SELECT statement, suppose you wanted the following column order:

```
SELECT c1, c3, c2 FROM t1 WHERE c1 = 11
   ORDER BY c1, c3, c2
```

Then, with the current nonclustered index on (c1, c2), and clustered index on c3, the resultant execution plan won't have any bookmark lookup, but it will have a sort step, as shown here (see Figure 6-11):

```
Table 't1'. Scan count 1, logical reads 1
```

Figure 6-11. *A variation on the execution plan with a "narrower" covering index*

On adding the clustered index column c3 explicitly to the nonclustered index in the desired order as follows, the overhead of the sort operation can be eliminated:

```
CREATE NONCLUSTERED INDEX incl ON t1(c1, c3, c2)
WITH DROP_EXISTING
```

Run the SELECT command again:

```
SELECT c1, c3, c2 FROM t1 WHERE c1 = 11
   ORDER BY c1, c3, c2
```

This is shown in the resultant execution plan (see Figure 6-12):

```
Table 't1'. Scan count 1, logical reads 1
```

Figure 6-12. *Execution plan with a reordered covering index*

Adding a clustered index column (or columns) to a nonclustered index key doesn't increase the width of a nonclustered index. It only affects the order of columns in the nonclustered index key. This can be confirmed from the output of DBCC SHOW_STATISTICS for the nonclustered index with and without the explicit addition of the clustered index column:

```
DBCC SHOW_STATISTICS(t1, incl)
```

The DBCC SHOW_STATISTICS output for the nonclustered index on the columns (c1, c2)—that is, without an explicit addition of the clustered index column c3—is shown in Figure 6-13.

	Updated	Rows	Rows Sampled	Steps	Density	Average key length
1	Jul 24 2004 10:13PM	1	1	1	0.0	12.0

	All density	Average Length	Columns
1	1.0	4.0	c1
2	1.0	8.0	c1, c2
3	1.0	12.0	c1, c2, c3

Column c3 is appended to the nonclustered index

	RANGE_HI_KEY	RANGE_ROWS	EQ_ROWS	DISTINCT_RANGE_ROWS	AVG_RANGE_ROWS
1	11	0.0	1.0	0	0.0

Figure 6-13. *DBCC SHOW_STATISTICS output for a "narrower" covering index*

You can see from the DBCC SHOW_STATISTICS output that even though the nonclustered index doesn't include column c3, it has been appended to the (c1, c2) column combination. Consequently, the size of the nonclustered index as indicated by the "Average key length" value is 12 bytes.

You can calculate the "Average key length" of the index as follows:

Average key length of the nonclustered index

= (Width of nonclustered index columns) + (Width of clustered index columns, if not included in the nonclustered index)

= (Combined size of c1 and c2) + (Size of c3)
= (Size of INT data type + Size of INT data type) + (Size of INT data type)
= (4 bytes + 4 bytes) + (4 bytes) = 12 bytes

The DBCC SHOW_STATISTICS output for the nonclustered index on the columns (c1, c3, c2)—that is, with an explicit addition of the clustered index column c3—is shown in Figure 6-14.

As shown in the preceding DBCC SHOW_STATISTICS output, for the nonclustered index on columns (c1, c3, c2), the order of column c3 in the index followed the column order specified for the index. Also, note that the size of the nonclustered index remained the same—in other words, the average key length equals 12 bytes.

	Updated	Rows	Rows Sampled	Steps	Density	Average key length
1	Jul 24 2004 10:32PM	1	1	1	0.0	12.0

	All density	Average Length	Columns
1	1.0	4.0	c1
2	1.0	8.0	c1, c3
3	1.0	12.0	c1, c3, c2

> Order of column c3 followed the column order specified for the index

	RANGE_HI_KEY	RANGE_ROWS	EQ_ROWS	DISTINCT_RANGE_ROWS	AVG_RANGE_ROWS
1	11	0.0	1.0	0	0.0

Figure 6-14. *DBCC SHOW_STATISTICS output for a reordered covering index*

NOTE I will cover the DBCC SHOW_STATISTICS command in depth in Chapter 7.

As shown in the preceding DBCC SHOW_STATISTICS outputs, the addition of the clustered key column(s) in the nonclustered index is not required unless a specific column order for the nonclustered index is required. In addition, as long as all the columns referred to by a query are included in the nonclustered index used by the optimizer, a bookmark lookup operation won't be needed for the query.

Using an Index Join

If the covering index becomes very wide, then you may consider an index join technique. As explained in Chapter 4, the index join technique uses an index intersection between two or more indexes to cover a query fully. Since the index join technique requires access to more than one index, it has to perform logical reads on all the indexes used in the index join. Consequently, it requires a higher number of logical reads than the covering index. But since the multiple narrow indexes used for the index join can serve more queries than a wide covering index (as explained in Chapter 4), you can certainly consider the index join as a technique to avoid bookmark lookups.

To better understand how an index join can be used to avoid bookmark lookups, consider the following example. Create a test table (index_join.sql in the download) with a clustered index already reserved on another column, like so:

```
IF(SELECT OBJECT_ID('t1')) IS NOT NULL
  DROP TABLE t1
GO
CREATE TABLE t1(c1 INT, c2 INT, c3 INT, c4 CHAR(500), c5
CHAR(500))
CREATE CLUSTERED INDEX icl ON t1(c3)
CREATE NONCLUSTERED INDEX incl1 ON t1(c1)
--Add 1000 rows to the test table
```

```
DECLARE @n INT
SET @n = 1
WHILE @n <= 1000
BEGIN
  INSERT INTO t1 VALUES(@n, @n, @n, 'C4', 'C5')
  SET @n = @n + 1
END
```

This still leaves you with the option of using nonclustered indexes only on other columns, yet you want to prevent the overhead of bookmark lookups associated with the nonclustered indexes.

The following SELECT statement

```
SELECT c1, c2 FROM t1 WHERE c1 BETWEEN 1 AND 20
```

will have a bookmark lookup as shown in the preceding section and a corresponding STATISTICS IO output as follows:

```
Table 't1'. Scan count 1, logical reads 50
```

The bookmark lookup is caused since all the columns referred to by the SELECT statement are not included in the nonclustered index on column c1. Using the nonclustered index is still better than not using it, since that will require a scan on the table (in this case, a clustered index scan) with the number of logical reads being 144.

To avoid the bookmark lookup, you can consider a covering index on columns (c1, c2) as explained in the previous section. But in addition to the covering index solution, you can consider an index join. As you learned, an index join requires narrower indexes than the covering index and thereby provides the following two benefits:

- Multiple narrow indexes can serve a larger number of queries than the wide covering index.

- Narrow indexes require less maintenance overhead than the wide covering index.

To avoid the bookmark lookup using an index join, create a narrow nonclustered index on column c2 that is not included in the existing nonclustered index:

```
CREATE NONCLUSTERED INDEX incl2 ON t1(c2)
```

If you run the SELECT statement again

```
SELECT c1, c2 FROM t1 WHERE c1 BETWEEN 1 AND 20
```

the following execution plan is returned (see Figure 6-15):

```
Table 't1'. Scan count 2, logical reads 5
```

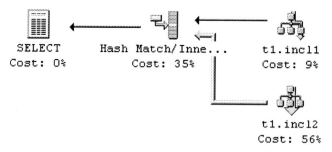

SELECT   Hash Match/Inne...   t1.incl1
Cost: 0%   Cost: 35%   Cost: 9%

                                             t1.incl2
                                             Cost: 56%

Figure 6-15. *Execution plan without a bookmark lookup*

From the preceding execution plan, you can see that the optimizer used the nonclustered index (incl1) on column c1 and the new nonclustered index (incl2) on column c2 to serve the query fully without hitting the base table. This index join operation avoided the bookmark lookup and consequently decreased the number of logical reads from 50 to 5.

It is true that a covering index on columns (c1, c2) will reduce the number of logical reads further. But it may not always be possible to use covering indexes, since they tend to be wide and have their associated overheads. In such cases, index join can be a good alternative.

Summary

As demonstrated in this chapter, the bookmark lookup step associated with a nonclustered index makes data retrieval through a nonclustered index very costly. The SQL Server optimizer takes this into account when generating an execution plan, and if it finds the overhead cost of using a nonclustered index to be very high, it discards the index and performs a table scan (or a clustered index scan if the table contains a clustered index). Therefore, to improve the effectiveness of a nonclustered index, it makes sense to analyze the cause of a bookmark lookup and consider whether you can avoid it completely with either a clustered index or a covering index (or index join).

Up to this point, you have concentrated on indexing techniques and presumed that the SQL Server optimizer will be able to determine the effectiveness of an index for a query. In the next chapter, you will see the importance of statistics in helping the optimizer determine the effectiveness of an index.

CHAPTER 7

■ ■ ■

Statistics Analysis

By now, you should have a good understanding of the importance of indexes. It is equally important that the optimizer have the necessary *statistics* on the data distribution, enabling the query optimizer to choose indexes effectively. In SQL Server, this information is maintained in the form of statistics on the index key.

In this chapter, you'll learn the importance of statistics in query optimization. Specifically, I cover the following topics:

- The role of statistics in query optimization

- The importance of statistics on columns with indexes

- The importance of statistics on nonindexed columns used in join and filter criteria

- Analysis of single column and multicolumn statistics, including computation of selectivity of a column for indexing

- Statistics maintenance

- Effective evaluation of statistics used in a query execution

The Importance of Statistics

SQL Server's query optimizer is a cost-based optimizer, deciding upon the best data access mechanism and join strategy by identifying indexes on WHERE clause columns (and/or join columns) and assessing the usefulness of the indexes available. As you learned in Chapter 4, you should use a nonclustered index to retrieve a small result set, whereas for a large result set, going to the base table (or clustered index) directly is usually more beneficial.

Up-to-date information on data distribution in the indexed column helps the optimizer determine the indexing strategy to be used. In SQL Server, this information is maintained in the form of statistics. These statistics are essential for the cost-based optimizer to create an effective query execution plan. As long as you ensure that the default statistical settings for the database are used, the optimizer will be able to do its best in determining effective processing strategies dynamically. Also, as a safety measure, while troubleshooting performance, you should ensure that the automatic statistics maintenance routine is doing its job as desired.

Statistics on an Indexed Column

The usefulness of an index is fully dependent on the statistics of the indexed columns; without statistics, SQL Server's cost-based query optimizer can't decide upon the most effective way of using an index. To meet this requirement, SQL Server automatically stores the statistics of an index key whenever the index is created. It isn't possible to turn this feature off.

As data changes, the data-retrieval mechanism required to keep the cost of a query low may also change. For example, if a table has only one matching row for a certain column value, then it makes sense to retrieve the matching rows from the table by going through the nonclustered index on the column. But if the data in the table changes, so that a large number of rows are added with the same column value, then using the nonclustered index no longer makes sense. To let SQL Server decide this change in processing strategy as the data changes over time, it is vital to have up-to-date statistics.

SQL Server can keep the statistics on an index updated as the contents of the indexed column are modified. By default, this feature is turned on and is configurable through the Properties ➤ Options ➤ Auto update statistics setting of a database. Updating statistics consumes extra CPU cycles. To optimize the update process, SQL Server uses an efficient algorithm to decide when to execute the update statistics procedure, based on factors such as the number of modifications and the size of the table. For example, on a small table with only 10 rows, the addition of 1,000 rows causes the statistics on an index key to be automatically updated when a query is executed that references the indexed column in the WHERE clause. If the same number of rows is added to a large table with 10,000 rows, then considering the relatively small number of changes, the statistics are not updated automatically. This built-in intelligence keeps the CPU utilization by the process very low.

You can manually disable (or enable) the auto update statistics feature by using the ALTER DATABASE command or the sp_dboption system stored procedure. By default, this feature is enabled, and it is strongly recommended that you keep it enabled.

NOTE I explain ALTER DATABASE and sp_dboption later in this chapter, in the "Manual Maintenance" section.

Benefits of Updated Statistics

The benefits of performing an auto update usually outweigh its cost on the system resources.

To better understand the benefit of having updated statistics, consider the following example. Create a test table (create_t1.sql in the download) with only three rows and a nonclustered index:

```
IF(SELECT OBJECT_ID('t1')) IS NOT NULL
   DROP TABLE t1
GO
CREATE TABLE t1(c1 INT, c2 INT IDENTITY)
INSERT INTO t1 (c1) VALUES(1)
INSERT INTO t1 (c1) VALUES(2)
INSERT INTO t1 (c1) VALUES(3)
CREATE NONCLUSTERED INDEX i1 ON t1(c1)
```

If you execute a SELECT statement, as shown in the following line of code, with a very selective filter criterion on the indexed column to retrieve only one row, then the optimizer uses a nonclustered index SEEK, as shown in the execution plan in Figure 7-1:

```
SELECT * FROM t1 WHERE c1 = 2 --Retrieve 1 row
```

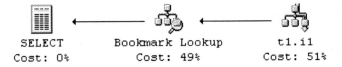

SELECT   Bookmark Lookup   t1.i1
Cost: 0%   Cost: 49%   Cost: 51%

Figure 7-1. *Execution plan for a very small result set*

To understand the effect of small data modifications on a statistics update, add only one row to the table:

```
INSERT INTO t1 (c1) VALUES(2)
```

On re-executing the preceding SELECT statement, you get the same execution plan as shown in Figure 7-1. The Auto Update Statistics event in SQL Server can be tracked by the Profiler tool by using the Auto Stats event (under the Objects event class). The Profiler trace output with all completed events and the Auto Stats event for this query is shown in Figure 7-2.

EventClass	TextData	CPU	Reads	Writes	Duration
TraceStart					
SQL:StmtCompleted	SELECT * FROM t1 WHERE c1 = 2 ...	10	31	0	10
SQL:BatchCompleted	SELECT * FROM t1 WHERE c1 = 2 ...	10	31	0	10

Figure 7-2. *Trace output on the addition of a small number of rows*

The trace output doesn't contain any SQL activity representing a statistics update.

■TIP To keep the profiler trace output compact, I have used a prefilter on TextData Not like SET%. This filters the SET statements used to show the graphical execution plan.

To understand the effect of large data modification on statistics update, add 10,000 rows to the table (add_rows.sql in the download):

```
DECLARE @n INT
SET @n = 1
WHILE @n <= 10000
BEGIN
  INSERT INTO t1 (c1) VALUES(2)
  SET @n = @n + 1
END
```

■**TIP** Remember to keep the Show Execution Plan option off while inserting a large number of rows; otherwise, Query Analyzer will have trouble displaying the large number of execution plans.

Now, if you re-execute the SELECT statement

SELECT * FROM t1 WHERE c1 = 2

then a large result set (10,002 rows out of 10,004 rows) will be retrieved. Since a large result set is requested, scanning the base table directly is preferable to going through the nonclustered index to the base table 10,002 times. Accessing the base table directly will prevent the overhead cost of bookmark lookup associated with the nonclustered index. This is represented in the resultant execution plan (see Figure 7-3).

Table 't1'. Scan count 1, logical reads **23**

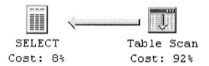

```
SELECT          Table Scan
Cost: 8%        Cost: 92%
```

Figure 7-3. *Execution plan for a large result set*

Figure 7-4 shows the resultant Profiler trace output.

EventClass	TextData	CPU	Reads	Writes	Duration
SQL:StmtCompleted	INSERT INTO t1 (c1) VALUES(2) SET	0	18	0	10
SP:StmtCompleted	SELECT statman([c1],@PSTATMAN) ...	20	48	0	20
Auto Stats	Updated				40
SQL:StmtCompleted	SELECT * FROM t1 WHERE c1 = 2	20	50	0	140
SQL:BatchCompleted	SELECT * FROM t1 WHERE c1 = 2	40	179	2	180

Figure 7-4. *Trace output on the addition of a large number of rows*

The Profiler trace output includes an Auto Stats event and a SQL statement above it to take care of the outdated statistics. These SQL activities consume some extra CPU cycles. However, by doing this, the optimizer determines a better data-processing strategy, keeping the overall cost of the query low.

Drawbacks of Outdated Statistics

As explained in the preceding section, the auto update statistics feature allows the optimizer to decide on an efficient processing strategy for a query as the data changes. If the statistics become outdated, however, then the processing strategies decided by the optimizer may not be applicable for the current dataset, and thereby will degrade performance.

To understand the detrimental effect of having outdated statistics, follow these steps:

1. Re-create the preceding test table with three rows only and the corresponding non-clustered index.

2. Prevent SQL Server from updating statistics automatically as the data changes. To do so, disable the auto update statistics feature by executing the following SQL statement:

```
ALTER DATABASE Northwind SET AUTO_UPDATE_STATISTICS OFF
```

3. Add 10,000 rows to the table as before.

Now, re-execute the SELECT statement to understand the effect of the outdated statistics on the query optimizer. The query is repeated here for clarity:

```
SELECT * FROM t1 WHERE c1 = 2
```

Figure 7-5 and Figure 7-6 show the resultant execution plan and the Profiler trace output for this query, respectively.

```
SELECT          Bookmark Lookup        t1.i1
Cost: 0%          Cost: 49%          Cost: 51%
```

Figure 7-5. *Execution plan with AUTO_UPDATE_STATISTICS OFF*

EventClass	TextData	CPU	Reads	Writes	Duration
SQL:StmtCompleted	INSERT INTO t1 (c1) VALUES(2) SET	10	18	0	10
SQL:StmtCompleted	SELECT * FROM t1 WHERE c1 = 2	90	10066	0	200
SQL:BatchCompleted	SELECT * FROM t1 WHERE c1 = 2	90	10089	0	240

Figure 7-6. *Trace output with AUTO_UPDATE_STATISTICS OFF*

With the auto update statistics feature switched off, the query optimizer has selected a different execution plan from the one it selected with this feature on. Based on the outdated statistics, which have only one row for the filter criterion (c1 = 2), the optimizer decided to use a nonclustered index SEEK. The optimizer couldn't make its decision based on the current data distribution in the column. For performance reasons, it would have been better to hit the base table directly instead of going through the nonclustered index, since a large result set (10,001 rows out of 10,003 rows) is requested.

You can see that turning off the auto update statistics feature has a negative effect on performance by comparing the cost of this query with and without updated statistics. Table 7-1 shows the difference in the cost of this query.

Table 7-1. *Cost of the Query With and Without Updated Statistics*

Statistics Update Status	Figure	Cost (SQL:Batch Completed Event)	
		CPU (ms)	Number of Reads
Updated	Figure 7-4	40	179
Not updated	Figure 7-6	90	10,089

The number of logical reads and the CPU utilization is significantly higher when the statistics are out of date. Therefore, it is recommended that you keep the auto update statistics feature on. The benefits of keeping statistics updated outweigh the costs of performing the update.

Statistics on a Nonindexed Column

Sometimes you may have columns in join or filter criteria without any index. Even for such nonindexed columns, the query optimizer is more likely to make the best choice if the data distribution (or statistics) of those columns is known.

In addition to statistics on indexes, SQL Server can build statistics on columns with no indexes. The information on data distribution, or the likelihood of a particular value occurring in a nonindexed column, can help the query optimizer determine an optimal processing strategy. This benefits the query optimizer even if it can't use an index to actually locate the values. SQL Server automatically builds statistics on nonindexed columns if it deems this information valuable in creating a better plan. By default, this feature is turned on, and it's configurable through the Properties ➤ Options ➤ Auto create statistics setting of a database. You can override this setting programmatically by using the ALTER DATABASE command or the sp_dboption system stored procedure. However, for better performance, it is strongly recommended that you keep this feature on.

In general, automatic creation of statistics on nonindexed columns should not be disabled. One of the scenarios in which you may consider disabling this feature is while executing a series of ad hoc SQL activities that you will not execute again. In such a case, you must decide whether or not you want to pay the cost of automatic statistics creation to get a better plan in this one case and affect the performance of other SQL Server activities. It is worthwhile noting that SQL Server eventually removes statistics on realizing that they have not been used for a while. So, in general, you should keep this feature on and not be concerned about it.

Benefits of Statistics on a Nonindexed Column

To understand the benefit of having statistics on a column with no index, consider the following example. Create two test tables with disproportionate data distributions, as shown in the following code (create_t1_t2.sql in the download). Both tables contain 10,001 rows. Table t1 contains only one row for a value of the second column (t1_c2) equal to 1, and the remaining 10,000 rows contain this column value as 2. Table t2 contains exactly the opposite data distribution.

```
--Create first table with 10001 rows
IF(SELECT OBJECT_ID('t1')) IS NOT NULL
  DROP TABLE t1
GO
CREATE TABLE t1(t1_c1 INT IDENTITY, t1_c2 INT)
INSERT INTO t1 (t1_c2) VALUES(1)
DECLARE @n INT
SET @n = 0
WHILE @n < 10000
BEGIN
  INSERT INTO t1 (t1_c2) VALUES(2)
  SET @n = @n + 1
END
GO
CREATE CLUSTERED INDEX i1 ON t1(t1_c1)

--Create second table with 10001 rows,
--  but opposite data distribution
IF(SELECT OBJECT_ID('t2')) IS NOT NULL
  DROP TABLE t2
GO
CREATE TABLE t2(t2_c1 INT IDENTITY, t2_c2 INT)
INSERT INTO t2 (t2_c2) VALUES(2)
DECLARE @n INT
SET @n = 0
WHILE @n < 10000
BEGIN
  INSERT INTO t2 (t2_c2) VALUES(1)
  SET @n = @n + 1
END
GO
CREATE CLUSTERED INDEX i1 ON t2(t2_c1)
```

Table 7-2 illustrates how the tables will look.

Table 7-2. *Sample Tables*

	Table t1		Table t2	
Column	t1_c1	t1_c2	t2_c1	t2_c2
Row1	1	1	1	2
Row2	2	2	2	1
RowN	N	2	N	1
Row10001	10001	2	10001	1

To understand the importance of statistics on a nonindexed column, use the default setting for the auto create statistics feature. By default, this feature is on. You can verify this using the DATABASEPROPERTYEX function:

```
SELECT DATABASEPROPERTYEX('Northwind', 'IsAutoCreateStatistics')
```

■**NOTE** You can find a detailed description of configuring the auto create statistics feature later in this chapter.

Use the following SELECT statement (nonindexed_select.sql in the download) to access a large result set from table t1 and a small result set from table t2. Table t1 has 10,000 rows for the column value of t1_c2 = 2, and table t2 has 1 row for t2_c2 = 2. Note that these columns used in the join and filter criteria have no index on either table.

```
SELECT t1.t1_c2, t2.t2_c2 FROM t1, t2
  WHERE t1.t1_c2 = t2.t2_c2
    AND t1.t1_c2 = 2
```

Figure 7-7 shows the execution plan for this query.

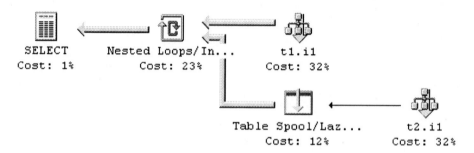

Figure 7-7. *Execution plan with AUTO_CREATE_STATISTICS ON*

The Profiler trace output with all completed events and the Auto Stats event for this query are shown in Figure 7-8. You can use this to evaluate the cost of the query.

■**TIP** To keep the Profiler trace output compact, I have used a prefilter on TextData Not like SET%. This filters the SET statements used to show the graphical execution plan.

The Profiler trace output shown in Figure 7-8 includes two Auto Stats events and, above each event, a corresponding SQL statement creating statistics on the nonindexed columns referred to in the WHERE clause, t2_c2 and t1_c2, respectively. This activity consumes extra CPU cycles, but by consuming these extra CPU cycles, the optimizer decides upon a better processing strategy for keeping the overall cost of the query low.

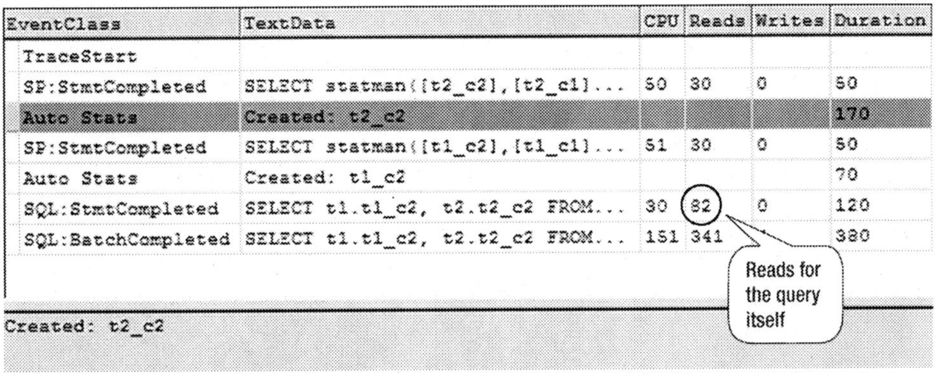
EventClass
TextData
CPU
Reads
Writes
Duration
TraceStart
SP:StmtCompleted
SELECT statman([t2_c2],[t2_c1]...
50
30
0
50
Auto Stats
Created: t2_c2
170
SP:StmtCompleted
SELECT statman([t1_c2],[t1_c1]...
51
30
0
50
Auto Stats
Created: t1_c2
70
SQL:StmtCompleted
SELECT t1.t1_c2, t2.t2_c2 FROM...
30
82
0
120
SQL:BatchCompleted
SELECT t1.t1_c2, t2.t2_c2 FROM...
151
341
380
Reads for the query itself
Created: t2_c2

Figure 7-8. *Trace output with AUTO_CREATE_STATISTICS ON*

To verify the statistics automatically created by SQL Server on the nonindexed columns of each table, right-click the data-retrieval node for the corresponding table in the execution plan and select Manage Statistics. This shows all statistics automatically created by SQL Server on nonindexed columns and any you may have created manually (using the `sp_createstats` system stored procedure or the `CREATE STATISTICS` command). Figure 7-9 shows the automatic statistics created for table `t1`.

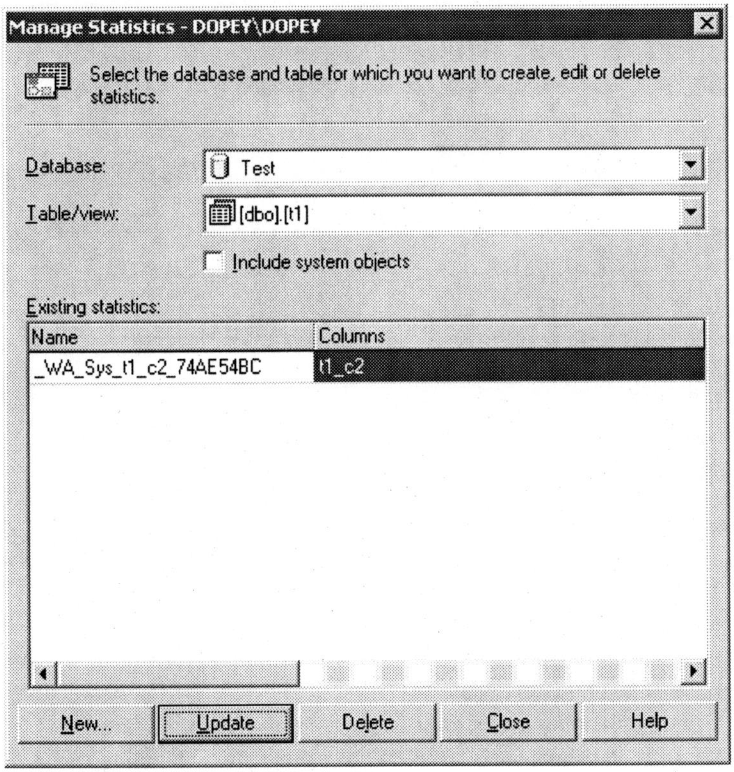
Manage Statistics - DOPEY\DOPEY
Select the database and table for which you want to create, edit or delete statistics.
Database:
Test
Table/view:
[dbo].[t1]
Include system objects
Existing statistics:
Name
Columns
_WA_Sys_t1_c2_74AE54BC
t1_c2
New...
Update
Delete
Close
Help

Figure 7-9. *Automatic statistics for table t1*

To verify how a different result set size from the two tables influences the decision of the query optimizer, modify the filter criteria of nonindexed_select.sql to access an opposite result set size from the two tables (small from t1 and large from t2). Instead of filtering on t1.t1_c2 = 2, change it to filter on 1:

```
SELECT t1.t1_c2, t2.t2_c2 FROM t1, t2
  WHERE t1.t1_c2 = t2.t2_c2
    AND t1.t1_c2 = 1
```

Figure 7-10 shows the resultant execution plan, and Figure 7-11 shows the Profiler trace output of this query.

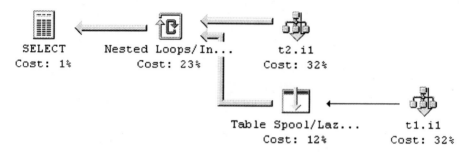

Figure 7-10. *Execution plan for a different result set*

EventClass	TextData	CPU	Reads	Writes	Duration
TraceStart					
SQL:StmtCompleted	SELECT t1.t1_c2, t2.t2_c2 FROM...	50	80	0	121
SQL:BatchCompleted	SELECT t1.t1_c2, t2.t2_c2 FROM...	60	130	0	140

Reads for the query itself

```
SELECT t1.t1_c2, t2.t2_c2 FROM t1, t2
  WHERE t1.t1_c2 = t2.t2_c2
    AND t1.t1_c2 = 1
```

Figure 7-11. *Trace output for a different result set*

The resultant Profiler trace output doesn't perform any additional SQL activities to manage statistics. The statistics on the nonindexed columns (t1.t1_c2 and t2.t2_c2) had already been created during the previous execution of the query.

For effective cost optimization, in each case the query optimizer selected different processing strategies, depending upon the statistics on the nonindexed columns (t1.t1_c2 and t2.t2_c2). You can see this from the last two execution plans. In the first, table t1 is the outer table for the nested loop join, whereas in the latest one, table t2 is the outer table. By having statistics on the nonindexed columns (t1.t1_c2 and t2.t2_c2), the query optimizer can create a cost-effective plan suitable for each individual case.

An even better solution would be to have an index on the column. This would not only create the statistics on the column, but also allow fast data retrieval through an index SEEK operation, while retrieving a small result set. However, in the case of a database application with queries referring to nonindexed columns in the WHERE clause, keeping the auto create statistics feature on still allows the optimizer to determine the best processing strategy for the existing data distribution in the column.

Drawback of Missing Statistics on a Nonindexed Column

To understand the detrimental effect of not having statistics on nonindexed columns, drop the statistics automatically created by SQL Server and prevent SQL Server from automatically creating statistics on columns with no index by following these steps:

1. Drop the automatic statistics created on column t1.t1_c2 through the Manage Statistics dialog box as shown in the section "Benefits of Statistics on a Nonindexed Column," or use the following SQL command:

   ```
   DROP STATISTICS [t1].StatisticsName
   ```

2. Similarly, drop the corresponding statistics on column t2.t2_c2.

3. Disable the auto create statistics feature by unchecking the "Auto create statistics" check box for the corresponding database or by executing the following SQL command:

   ```
   ALTER DATABASE Northwind SET AUTO_CREATE_STATISTICS OFF
   ```

   Now re-execute the SELECT statement nonindexed_select.sql:

```
SELECT t1.t1_c2, t2.t2_c2 FROM t1, t2
  WHERE t1.t1_c2 = t2.t2_c2
    AND t1.t1_c2 = 1
```

The resultant execution plan and Profiler trace output are shown in Figure 7-12 and Figure 7-13, respectively.

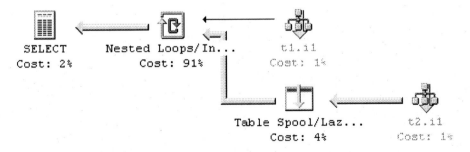

Figure 7-12. *Execution plan with AUTO_CREATE_STATISTICS OFF*

NOTE Again, a prefilter on TextData Not like SET% was used.

EventClass	TextData	CPU	Reads	Writes	Durat
TraceStart					
SQL:StmtCompleted	SELECT t1.t1_c2, t2.t2_c2 FROM t1...	241	10136	0	550
SQL:BatchCompleted	SELECT t1.t1_c2, t2.t2_c2 FROM t1...	241	10136	0	560

```
SELECT t1.t1_c2, t2.t2_c2 FROM t1, t2
  WHERE t1.t1_c2 = t2.t2_c2
    AND t1.t1_c2 = 1
```

Figure 7-13. *Trace output with AUTO_CREATE_STATISTICS OFF*

With the auto create statistics feature off, the query optimizer selected a different execution plan compared to the one it selected with the auto create statistics feature on. On not finding statistics on the relevant columns, the optimizer chose the first table (t1) in the FROM clause as the outer table of the nested loop join operation. The optimizer couldn't make its decision based on the actual data distribution in the column. For example, if you modify the query to refer table t2 as the first table in the FROM clause:

SELECT t1.t1_c2, t2.t2_c2 FROM t2, t1
  WHERE t1.t1_c2 = t2.t2_c2
    AND t1.t1_c2 = 1

then the optimizer selects table t2 as the outer table of the nested loop join operation. Figure 7-14 shows the execution plan.

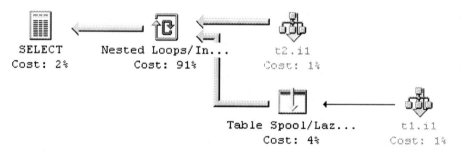

Figure 7-14. *Execution plan with AUTO_CREATE_STATISTICS OFF (a variation)*

You can see that turning off the auto create statistics feature has a negative effect on performance by comparing the cost of this query with and without statistics on a nonindexed column. Table 7-3 shows the difference in the cost of this query.

Table 7-3. *Cost Comparison of a Query With and Without Statistics on a Nonindexed Column*

Statistics on Nonindexed Column	Figure	Cost (SQL:Batch Completed Event)	
		CPU (ms)	**Number of Reads**
With statistics	Figure 7-11	60	130
Without statistics	Figure 7-13	241	10,136

The number of logical reads and the CPU utilization are very high with no statistics on the nonindexed columns. Without these statistics, the optimizer can't create a cost-effective plan.

A query execution plan highlights the missing statistics in red. You can see this in the table names in the previous execution plan, as well as in the detailed description for a node in a graphical execution plan, as shown in Figure 7-15 for table t2.

```
                 Clustered Index Scan
Warning: Statistics missing for this table. Choose 'Create
Missing Statistics' from the context (right click) menu.

Scanning a clustered index, entirely or only a range.

Physical operation:            Clustered Index Scan
Logical operation:             Clustered Index Scan
Row count:                               10,000
Estimated row size:                          36
I/O cost:                                0.0531
CPU cost:                                0.0110
Number of executes:                           1
Cost:                           0.064214(1%)
Subtree cost:                            0.0642
Estimated row count:                      1,000

Argument:
OBJECT:([NWTest].[dbo].[t2].[i1]), WHERE:([t2].[t2_c2]
=1)
```

Figure 7-15. *Missing statistics indication in a graphical plan*

The textual execution plan provides the missing statistics information under the Warnings column, as shown in Figure 7-16. Remember that you can obtain the textual execution plan by re-executing the query with the SET SHOWPLAN_ALL statement as follows:

```
SET SHOWPLAN_ALL ON
GO
SELECT t1.t1_c2, t2.t2_c2 FROM t1, t2
  WHERE t1.t1_c2 = t2.t2_c2
    AND t1.t1_c2 = 1
GO
SET SHOWPLAN_ALL OFF
GO
```

	StmtText	S	N	P	P	L	A	D	E	E	E	A	T	O	Warnings
1	SELECT t1.t1_c2, t2...	.	1	0	.	.	1	.	.	.	.	.	.	.	NULL
2	|--Nested Loops(I...	.	3	1	.	.	.	.	.	.	.	.	.	.	NO JOIN PREDICATE
3	|--Clustered...	.	4	3	.	.	.	.	.	.	.	.	.	.	NO STATS:([t1].[t1_c2])
4	|--Table Spool	.	5	3	.	.	.	.	.	.	.	.	.	.	NULL
5	|--Clus...	.	6	5	.	.	.	.	.	.	.	.	.	.	NO STATS:([t2].[t2_c2])

Figure 7-16. *Missing statistics indication in a textual plan*

You can create the missing statistics manually by right-clicking the pertinent node in the graphical execution plan and selecting Create Missing Statistics.

NOTE In a database application, there is always the possibility of queries using columns with no indexes. Therefore, for performance reasons, leaving the auto create statistics feature of SQL Server databases on is recommended.

Analyzing Statistics

Statistics are histograms, consisting of a sampling of data distribution for a column or an index key (or the first column of a multicolumn index key). The information on the range of index key values between two consecutive samples is called a *step*. A step provides the following information:

- Value of the current sample (RANGE_HI_KEY).

- Number of rows equal to the current sample (EQ_ROWS).

- Range of rows between previous sample and the current sample, without counting either of these samples (RANGE_ROWS).

- Number of distinct rows in the range (DISTINCT_RANGE_ROWS). If all values in the range are unique, then RANGE_ROWS equals DISTINCT_RANGE_ROWS.

- Average number of rows equal to a key value within a range (AVG_RANGE_ROWS).

The value of EQ_ROWS for an index key value (RANGE_HI_KEY) helps the optimizer decide how (and whether) to use the index when the indexed column is referred to in a WHERE clause. As the optimizer can perform a SEEK or a SCAN operation to retrieve rows from a table, the optimizer can decide which operation to perform based on the number of matching rows (EQ_ROWS) for the index key value.

To understand how the optimizer's data-retrieval strategy depends on the number of matching rows, consider the following example. Create a test table (create_t3.sql in the download) with different data distributions on an indexed column:

```
IF(SELECT OBJECT_ID('t1')) IS NOT NULL
  DROP TABLE t1
GO
CREATE TABLE t1(c1 INT, c2 INT IDENTITY)
INSERT INTO t1 (c1) VALUES(1)
DECLARE @n INT
SET @n = 0
WHILE @n < 10000
BEGIN
  INSERT INTO t1 (c1) VALUES(2)
  SET @n = @n + 1
END
GO
CREATE NONCLUSTERED INDEX i1 ON t1(c1)
```

When the preceding nonclustered index is created, SQL Server automatically creates statistics on the index key. You can obtain statistics for this nonclustered index key (i1) by executing the DBCC SHOW_STATISTICS command:

DBCC SHOW_STATISTICS(t1, i1)

Figure 7-17 shows the statistics output.

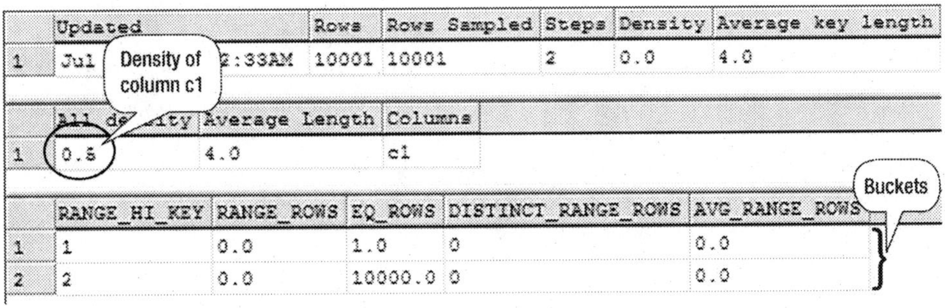

	Updated	Rows	Rows Sampled	Steps	Density	Average key length
1	Jul (Density of column c1) 2:33AM	10001	10001	2	0.0	4.0

	All density	Average Length	Columns
1	0.5	4.0	c1

	RANGE_HI_KEY	RANGE_ROWS	EQ_ROWS	DISTINCT_RANGE_ROWS	AVG_RANGE_ROWS
1	1	0.0	1.0	0	0.0
2	2	0.0	10000.0	0	0.0

Figure 7-17. *Statistics on index i1*

Now, to understand how effectively the optimizer decides upon different data-retrieval strategies based on statistics, execute the following two queries requesting different numbers of rows:

```
SELECT * FROM t1 WHERE c1 = 1 --Retrieve 1 row
SELECT * FROM t1 WHERE c1 = 2 --Retrieve 10000 rows
```

Figure 7-18 shows execution plans of these queries.

```
Query 1: Query cost (relative to the batch): 15.18%
Query text: SELECT * FROM [t1] WHERE [c1]=@1
```

```
 SELECT          Bookmark Lookup            t1.i1
Cost: 0%             Cost: 49%           Cost: 51%
```

```
Query 2: Query cost (relative to the batch): 84.82%
Query text: SELECT * FROM [t1] WHERE [c1]=@1
```

```
 SELECT            Table Scan
Cost: 8%            Cost: 92%
```

Figure 7-18. *Execution plans of small and large result set queries*

From the statistics, the optimizer can find the number of rows affected by the preceding two queries. Understanding that there is only one row to be retrieved for the first query, the optimizer chose an index SEEK operation. For the second query, the optimizer knows that a large number of rows (10,000 rows) will be affected and therefore avoided the index to improve performance. (Chapter 4 explains indexing strategies in detail.)

SQL Server maintains statistical information on the data stored in the indexed columns by dividing the data into small, manageable parts. Each part represents a subrange of the data and is stored separately in structures called *buckets*. In SQL Server 2000, statistics mainte-nance has improved compared to that available in SQL Server 7.0. SQL Server 2000 merges identical or similar buckets, and uses more buckets for larger variances in data.

Besides the information on steps, other useful information in the statistics includes the following:

- The time statistics were last updated

- The number of rows in the table

- The average index key length

- Densities for combinations of columns

Information on the time of the last update can help you decide whether or not you should manually update the statistics. The average key length represents the average size of the data in the index key column(s). It helps you understand the width of the index key, which is an important measure in determining the effectiveness of the index. As explained in Chapter 4, a wide index is usually costly to maintain, and requires more disk space and memory pages. I will present different techniques to calculate the average size of data in a table in Chapter 17.

Density

When creating an execution plan, the query optimizer analyzes the statistics of the columns used in the filter and join clauses. A filter criterion with high selectivity limits the number of rows from a table to a small result set and helps the optimizer keep the query cost low. A column with a unique index will have a very high selectivity, since it can limit the number of matching rows to one.

On the other hand, a filter criterion with low selectivity will return a large result set from the table. A filter criterion with very low selectivity makes a nonclustered index on the column ineffective. Navigating through a nonclustered index to the base table for a large result set is usually costlier than scanning the base table (or clustered index) directly due to the cost overhead of bookmark lookups associated with nonclustered index. You can observe this behavior in the execution plan in Figure 7-18.

Statistics track the selectivity of a column in the form of a density ratio. A column with high selectivity (or uniqueness) will have low density. A column with low density (that is, high selectivity) is suitable for a nonclustered index, because it helps the optimizer retrieve a small number of rows very fast.

Density Calculation

Density can be expressed as follows:

Density = Average number of rows for a column value / Total number of rows

where

Average number of rows for a column value =
Total number of rows / Number of distinct values for a column

therefore

Density = 1 / Number of distinct values for a column

You can note from the preceding equation that the density value for a column ranges between 0 and 1. The lower the column density, the more suitable it is for use in a nonclustered index.

For a column with a unique index

Density = 1 / Total number of rows

where

Total number of rows = Number of distinct values for a column =
```
SELECT COUNT(*) FROM <TableName>
```

For a column with a nonunique index

Density = 1 / Number of distinct values for a column

where

Number of distinct values for a column =
SELECT COUNT(DISTINCT <ColumnName>) FROM <TableName>

Let's calculate the density of column c1 for the test table built by create_t3.sql (rerun this script to build the table again):

Number of distinct values for column c1 = 2

You can calculate this by using the following query:

SELECT COUNT(DISTINCT c1) FROM t1

Therefore

Density of column c1
= 1 / Number of distinct values for column c1
= 1 / 2 = 0.5

You can confirm this from the statistics output found by executing DBCC SHOW_STATISTICS (t1, i1). This relatively high-density value of a column makes it a less suitable candidate for a nonclustered index. However, the statistics of the index key values maintained in the individual bucket help the query optimizer use the index for the predicate c1 = 1, as shown in the previous execution plan.

Statistics on a Multicolumn Index

In the case of an index with one column, statistics consist of a histogram and a density value for that column. Statistics for a composite index with multiple columns consist of one histogram for the first column only and multiple density values. The density values include the density for the first column and for each prefix combination of the index key columns. Multiple density values help the optimizer find the selectivity of the composite index when multiple columns are referred to in the WHERE clause.

To better understand the density values maintained for a multicolumn index, let's modify the nonclustered index used in the early part of the section to include two columns:

CREATE NONCLUSTERED INDEX i1 ON t1(c1, c2) WITH DROP_EXISTING

Figure 7-19 shows the resultant statistics provided by DBCC SHOW_STATISTICS.

	Updated		Rows	Rows Sampled	Steps	Density	Average key length
1	Jun 3 2002 2:26AM		10001	10001	2	0.0	8.0

	All density	Average Length	Columns
1	0.5	4.0	c1
2	0.00009999	8.0	c1, c2

	RANGE_HI_KEY	RANGE_ROWS	EQ_ROWS	DISTINCT_RANGE_ROWS	AVG_RANGE_ROWS
1	1	0.0	1.0	0	0.0
2	2	0.0	10000.0	0	0.0

Figure 7-19. *Statistics on the multicolumn index i1*

As you can see, there are two density values under the All density column:

- The density of the first column

- The density of the (first + second) columns

For a multicolumn index with three columns, the statistics for the index would also contain the density value of the (first + second + third) columns. The statistics won't contain a density value for any other combination of columns. Therefore, this index ([i1]) won't be very useful for filtering rows only on the second column (c2), because the density value of the second column (c2) alone isn't maintained in the statistics.

You can compute the second density value (0.00009999) shown in Figure 7-19 through the following steps. This is the number of distinct values for a column combination of (c1, c2):

```
= SELECT COUNT(*)
    FROM (SELECT DISTINCT c1, c2 FROM t1) DistinctRows
= 10001
```

therefore

Density
= 1 / Number of distinct values for a column combination of (c1, c2)
= 1 / 10001 = 0.00009999

Statistics Maintenance

SQL Server allows a user to manually override the maintenance of statistics in an individual database. The three main configurations controlling automatic statistics maintenance behavior of SQL Server are as follows:

- New statistics on columns with no index (auto create statistics)

- Updating existing statistics (auto update statistics)

- The degree of sampling used to collect statistics

The preceding configurations can be controlled at the levels of a database (all indexes and statistics on a table) or on a case-by-case basis on individual indexes or statistics. The auto create statistics setting is applicable for nonindexed columns only, as SQL Server always creates statistics for an index key when the index is created. The auto update statistics setting is applicable for statistics on both indexes and WHERE clause columns with no index.

Automatic Maintenance

By default, SQL Server automatically takes care of statistics. Both the auto create statistics and auto update statistics features are on by default. These two features together are referred as *Autostats*. As explained previously, it is usually better to keep these settings on.

Statistics consist of an even sampling of column values from the table. To minimize performance overhead, SQL Server uses an efficient algorithm to limit the number of samples on a table based on the table size.

As shown previously, the Profiler tool has an Auto Stats event (under the Objects event class) to track the automatic creation and update of statistics. Also, DBCC Trace Flag 8721 can be used as follows to provide the Autostats information in SQL Server's error log:

```
DBCC TRACEON(8721)
```

The preceding DBCC statement turns on logging of Autostats information only for the database connection on which it is executed. It remains effective until the connection is closed or is turned off by executing the following DBCC command:

```
DBCC TRACEOFF(8721)
```

Auto Create Statistics

The auto create statistics feature automatically creates statistics on nonindexed columns when referred to in the WHERE clause of a query. For example, consider the following small table (create_t4.sql in the download):

```
IF(SELECT OBJECT_ID('t1')) IS NOT NULL
  DROP TABLE t1
GO
CREATE TABLE t1(c1 INT)
INSERT INTO t1 VALUES(1)
INSERT INTO t1 VALUES(2)
```

If the following SELECT statement is executed with no index on the column c1 referred to in the WHERE clause

SELECT * FROM t1 WHERE c1 = 1

then the auto create statistics feature (make sure it is turned back on if you have turned it off) automatically creates statistics on column c1. You can see this in the Profiler trace output in Figure 7-20.

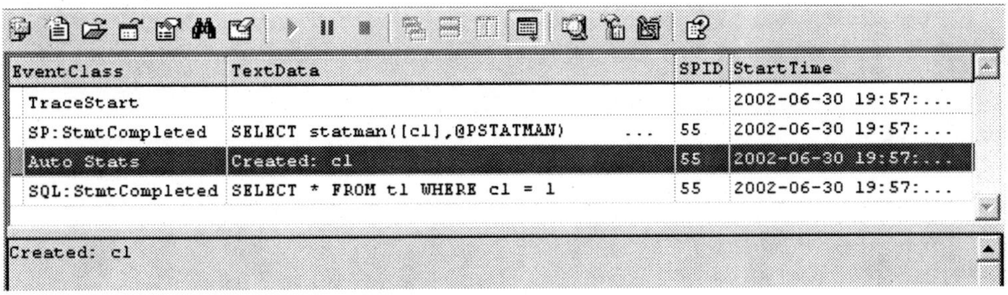

EventClass	TextData	SPID	StartTime
TraceStart			2002-06-30 19:57:...
SP:StmtCompleted	SELECT statman([c1],@PSTATMAN) ...	55	2002-06-30 19:57:...
Auto Stats	Created: c1	55	2002-06-30 19:57:...
SQL:StmtCompleted	SELECT * FROM t1 WHERE c1 = 1	55	2002-06-30 19:57:...

Created: c1

Figure 7-20. *Trace output with AUTO_CREATE_STATISTICS ON*

The corresponding output of DBCC TRACEON(8721) from SQL Server's error log is as follows:

```
2002-06-30 19:57:24.69 spid55    AUTOSTATS: CREATED Dbid = 6 Tbl: t1(c1) Rows: 2
CrtCnt: 1 Dur: 80ms
```

TIP The default location of the SQL Server ERRORLOG file is C:\Program Files\Microsoft SQL Server\ MSSQL\LOG.

This tells you that the Autostats feature was executed to create statistics on column c1 of table t1. It also provides other information, such as that there are two rows in the table and it took 80 ms to create the statistics.

Auto Update Statistics

The auto update statistics feature automatically updates existing statistics on the indexes and columns of a permanent table when the table is referred to in a query, provided the number of changes made to the table exceeds a threshold value. The types of changes are action statements, such as INSERT, UPDATE, and DELETE. The number of changes made in a permanent table is maintained in the rowmodctr column of sysindexes system table. The threshold for the number of changes depends on the number of rows in the table, as shown in Table 7-4.

Table 7-4. *Update Statistics Threshold for Number of Changes*

Number of Rows	Threshold for Number of Changes
Empty	>= 500 changes
Not empty	>= 500 + (20% of cardinality) changes

In the table, the empty condition is true if the number of rows is fewer than 500. In SQL Server, cardinality is counted as the number of rows in the table.

The use of a threshold reduces the frequency of automatic update of statistics. For example, consider the following table (create_t5.sql in the download):

```
IF(SELECT OBJECT_ID('t1')) IS NOT NULL
  DROP TABLE t1
GO
CREATE TABLE t1(c1 INT)
CREATE NONCLUSTERED INDEX i1 ON t1(c1)
DECLARE @n INT
SET @n = 1
WHILE @n <= 500
BEGIN
  INSERT INTO t1 VALUES(@n)
  SET @n = @n + 1
END
```

After the nonclustered index is created, 500 rows are added to the table. This outdates the existing statistics on the nonclustered index. The number of changes to the table is maintained in the rowmodctr column of the sysindexes system table, as shown in Figure 7-21.

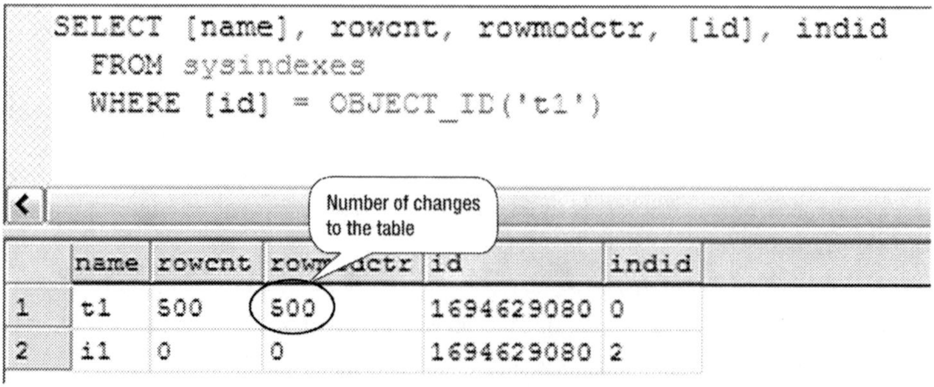

Figure 7-21. *The number of changes to the table is not reflected in the statistics.*

If the following SELECT statement is executed, with a reference to the indexed column in the WHERE clause

SELECT * FROM t1 WHERE c1 = 1

then the auto update statistics feature automatically updates statistics on the nonclustered index, as shown in the Profiler trace output in Figure 7-22.

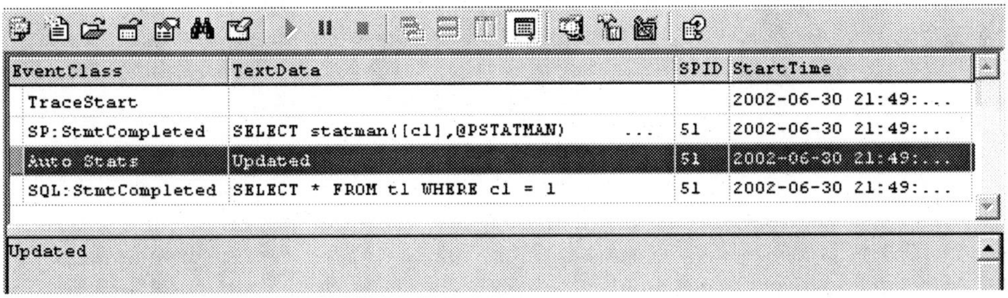

Figure 7-22. *Trace output with AUTO_UPDATE_STATISTICS ON*

This is the corresponding output of DBCC TRACEON(8721):

```
2002-06-30 21:49:24.49 spid51    AUTOSTATS: UPDATED Stats: t1..i1 Dbid = 6 Indid = 2
 Rows: 500 Duration: 10ms
2002-06-30 21:49:24.49 spid51    AUTOSTATS: SUMMARY Tbl: t1 Objid:1154103152
 UpdCount: 1 Rows: 500 Mods: 500 Bound: 500 Duration: 321ms LStatsSchema: 0
```

The first line in the output indicates that Autostats was executed on index i1 of table t1. Indid = 2 can also be used to identify the index from the sysindexes table output shown in Figure 7-22. Some of the useful information provided by the second line is as follows:

- Number of rows in the table (Rows: 500)

- Number of changes to the table (Mods: 500)

- Threshold for number of changes that, when exceeded, executes the automatic update of statistics (Bound: 500)

- Time required to update the statistics (Duration: 321ms)

Once the statistics are updated, the rowmodctr values for the corresponding tables are set to 0. This way, SQL Server keeps track of the number of changes to the tables and manages the frequency of automatic updates of statistics.

Manual Maintenance

There are rare situations in which you need to interfere with the automatic maintenance of statistics:

- *When experimenting with statistics.* Just a friendly suggestion: please spare your production servers from experiments such as the ones you are doing in this book.

- *After upgrading from SQL Server 7.0 to SQL Server 2000.* Since the statistics maintenance of SQL Server 2000 has been upgraded, you should manually update the statistics of the complete database immediately after the upgrade instead of waiting for SQL Server to update it over time with the help of automatic statistics.

- *While executing a series of ad hoc SQL activities that you won't execute again.* In such cases, you must decide whether or not you want to pay the cost of automatic statistics maintenance to get a better plan in that one case and affect the performance of other SQL Server activities. It is worthwhile noting that SQL Server eventually removes unused statistics on realizing that they haven't been used for a while. So, in general, you need not be concerned with such one-timers.

- *When you come upon an issue with the automatic statistics maintenance and the only workaround for the time being is to keep the automatic statistics maintenance feature off.* Even in such cases, you can turn the feature off for the specific database table that faces the problem instead of disabling it for the complete database.

- *While analyzing the performance of a query, you realize that the statistics are missing for few of the database objects referred to by the query.* This can be evaluated from the graphical and textual execution plans, as explained earlier in the chapter.

- *While analyzing the effectiveness of statistics for a query, you realize that the statistics are out of date for a few of the database objects referred to by the query.* This can be analyzed from the textual execution plan, as explained later in the chapter.

SQL Server allows a user to control many of its automatic statistics maintenance features. You can enable (or disable) the automatic statistics creation and update features by using the auto create statistics and auto update statistics settings, respectively, and then you can get your hands dirty.

Manage Statistics Settings

The auto create statistics setting can be controlled at a database level. To disable this setting, use the ALTER DATABASE command:

```
ALTER DATABASE Northwind SET AUTO_CREATE_STATISTICS OFF
```

The auto update statistics setting can be controlled at different levels of a database, all indexes and statistics on a table, or at the individual index or statistics level. To disable auto update statistics at the database level, use the ALTER DATABASE command:

```
ALTER DATABASE Northwind SET AUTO_UPDATE_STATISTICS OFF
```

Disabling this setting at the database level overrides individual settings at lower levels.

To configure auto update statistics for all indexes and statistics on a table in the current database, use the `sp_autostats` system stored procedure:

```
USE Northwind
EXEC sp_autostats [Order Details], 'OFF'
```

You can also use the same stored procedure to configure this setting for individual indexes or statistics. To disable this setting for the `OrderID` index on `Northwind.dbo.Order Details`, execute the following statements:

```
USE Northwind
EXEC sp_autostats [Order Details], 'OFF', OrderID
```

You can also use the `UPDATE STATISTICS` command's `WITH NORECOMPUTE` option to disable this setting for all or individual indexes and statistics on a table in the current database. The `sp_createstats` stored procedure also has the `NORECOMPUTE` option.

Avoid disabling the automatic statistics features, unless you have confirmed through testing that this brings a performance benefit. If the automatic statistics features are disabled, then you should manually identify and create missing statistics on the columns that are not indexed, and then keep the existing statistics up to date.

Generate Statistics

To create statistics manually, use one of the following options:

- `CREATE STATISTICS`: You can use this option to create statistics on single or multiple columns of a table or indexed view. Unlike the `CREATE INDEX` command, `CREATE STATISTICS` uses sampling by default.

- `sp_createstats`: Use this stored procedure to create single-column statistics for all eligible columns for all user tables in the current database. This includes all columns except computed columns and columns with the `NTEXT`, `TEXT`, or `IMAGE` data type, and columns that already have statistics or are the first column of an index.

Similarly, to update statistics manually, use one of the following options:

- `UPDATE STATISTICS`: You can use this option to update the statistics of individual or all index keys and nonindexed columns of a table or indexed view.

- `sp_updatestats`: Use this stored procedure to update statistics of all user tables in the current database.

Leaving the default sampling rates for statistics is recommended. However, if you want, you can manually control the amount of sampling using the `FULLSCAN` or `SAMPLE` options of the `UPDATE STATISTICS` and `CREATE STATISTICS` commands, to specify the amount of sampling preferred. The `sp_createstats` stored procedure also has the `FULLSCAN` option. For further explanation of these commands, please refer to SQL Server Books Online.

▓**NOTE** In general, you should always use the default settings for automatic statistics. Consider modifying these settings only after identifying that the default settings appear to detract from performance.

Statistics Maintenance Status

You can verify the current settings for the Autostats feature using the following function/stored procedures:

- DATABASEPROPERTYEX

- sp_autostats

- sp_dboption

Status of Auto Create Statistics

You can verify the current setting for auto create statistics using the function DATABASEPROPERTYEX:

```
SELECT DATABASEPROPERTYEX('Northwind', 'IsAutoCreateStatistics')
```

A return value of 1 means enabled, and a value of 0 means disabled.

You can also verify the status of this feature using the sp_autostats system stored procedure as shown in the following code. Supplying any table name to the stored procedure will provide the configuration value of auto create statistics for the current database under the Output section of global statistics settings:

```
USE Northwind
EXEC sp_autostats [Order Details]
```

An excerpt of the preceding sp_autostats statement's output is as follows:

```
Global statistics settings for [Northwind]:
  Automatic update statistics: ON
  Automatic create statistics: ON
```

A return value of ON means enabled, and a value of OFF means disabled.

This stored procedure is more useful when verifying the status of auto update statistics, as explained later in this chapter.

The status of auto create statistics can also be verified using the sp_dboption system stored procedure as follows:

```
sp_dboption 'Northwind', 'auto create statistics'
```

A return value of ON means enabled, and a value of OFF means disabled.

This stored procedure in SQL Server 2000 is provided for backward compatibility. You should, in general, use the DATABASEPROPERTYEX function to verify the setting for auto create statistics.

Status of Auto Update Statistics

You can verify the current setting for auto update statistics in a similar manner to auto create statistics. Here's how to do it using the function DATABASEPROPERTYEX:

```
SELECT DATABASEPROPERTYEX('Northwind', 'IsAutoUpdateStatistics')
```

Here's how to do it using sp_autostats:

```
USE Northwind
EXEC sp_autostats [Order Details]
```

And here's how to do it using sp_dboption:

```
sp_dboption 'Northwind', 'auto update statistics'
```

Analyzing the Effectiveness of Statistics for a Query

For performance reasons, it is extremely important to maintain proper statistics on your database objects. It's true that statistics issues are rare, but it may not be appropriate to keep your eyes closed to statistical aspects while analyzing the performance of a query because, if an issue does arise (mostly due to bugs), then it can really take you for a ride. In this section, you'll see what you can do should you find statistics to be missing or out of date.

While analyzing an execution plan for a query, look for the following points to ensure a cost-effective processing strategy:

- Indexes are available on the columns referred to in the filter and join criteria.

- In the case of a missing index, statistics should be available on the columns with no index. It is preferable to have the index itself.

- Since outdated statistics are of no use and can even be misleading, it is important that the estimates used by the optimizer from the statistics are up to date.

You analyzed the use of a proper index in Chapter 4. In this section, you will analyze the effectiveness of statistics for a query.

Resolving a Missing Statistics Issue

To see how to identify and resolve a missing statistics issue, consider the following example. First, disable both auto create statistics and auto update statistics using the ALTER DATABASE command:

```
ALTER DATABASE Northwind SET AUTO_CREATE_STATISTICS OFF
ALTER DATABASE Northwind SET AUTO_UPDATE_STATISTICS OFF
```

Create a test table with a large number of rows and a nonclustered index (create_t6.sql in the download):

```
IF(SELECT OBJECT_ID('t1')) IS NOT NULL
   DROP TABLE t1
GO
CREATE TABLE t1(c1 INT, c2 INT, c3 CHAR(50))
INSERT INTO t1 VALUES(51, 1, 'c3')
INSERT INTO t1 VALUES(52, 1, 'c3')
CREATE NONCLUSTERED INDEX i1 ON t1(c1, c2)
DECLARE @n INT
SET @n = 0
WHILE @n < 10000
BEGIN
   INSERT INTO t1 VALUES(@n%50, @n, 'c3')
   SET @n = @n + 1
END
```

Since the index is created on (c1, c2), the statistics on the index contain a histogram for the first column c1 and density values for the prefixed column combinations (c1, and c1 + c2). There are no histograms or density values for column c2.

To understand how to identify missing statistics on a column with no index, execute the following SELECT statement. Since the auto create statistics feature is off, the optimizer won't be able to find the data distribution for the column c2 used in the WHERE clause. You can see this through the use of the SET SHOWPLAN_ALL statement as follows (showplan.sql in the download):

```
SET SHOWPLAN_ALL ON
GO
SELECT * FROM t1 WHERE t1.c2 = 1
GO
SET SHOWPLAN_ALL OFF
GO
```

As shown in Figure 7-23, the textual execution plan indicates missing statistics for a particular execution step under its Warnings column. This shows that the statistics on column t1.c2 are missing for the Table Scan execution step.

	StmtText	S	N	P	P	L	A	D	E	E	E	A	T	O	Warnings
1	SELECT * FROM t1 WHERE...	.	1	0	.	.	1	.	.	.	.	.	.	.	NULL
2	|--Table Scan(OBJECT...	.	3	1	.	.	.	.	.	.	.	.	.	.	NO STATS:([t1].[c2])

Figure 7-23. *Missing statistics indication in a textual plan*

The information on missing statistics is also provided by the graphical execution plan, as shown in Figure 7-24.

SELECT
Cost: 4%
Table Scan
Cost: 96%

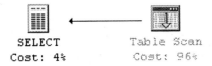

Figure 7-24. *Missing statistics indication in a graphical plan*

The graphical execution plan contains a node with red-colored text. This is an indication of some problem with the data-retrieval mechanism (usually missing statistics). You can obtain a detailed description of the error by moving your mouse over the corresponding node of the execution plan, as shown in Figure 7-25.

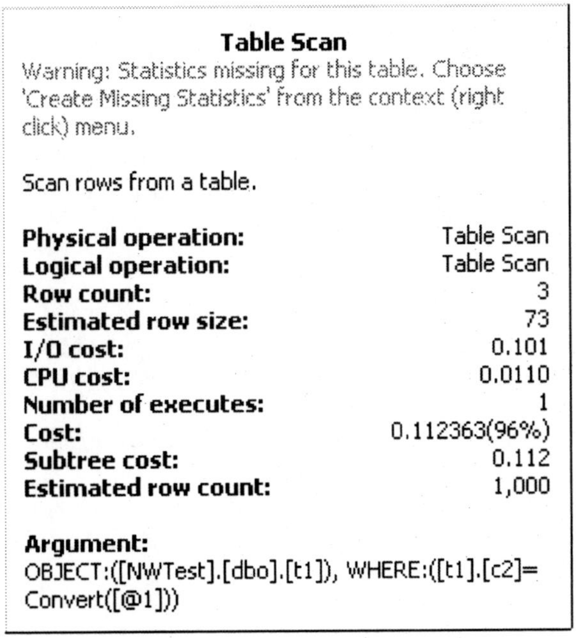
Table Scan
Warning: Statistics missing for this table. Choose 'Create Missing Statistics' from the context (right click) menu.
Scan rows from a table.
Physical operation: Table Scan
Logical operation: Table Scan
Row count: 3
Estimated row size: 73
I/O cost: 0.101
CPU cost: 0.0110
Number of executes: 1
Cost: 0.112363(96%)
Subtree cost: 0.112
Estimated row count: 1,000
Argument:
OBJECT:([NWTest].[dbo].[t1]), WHERE:([t1].[c2]=Convert([@1]))

Figure 7-25. *Detailed description of a graphical plan's node*

Figure 7-25 shows that the statistics for this table are missing. This may prevent the optimizer from selecting the best processing strategy. The current cost of this query in terms of logical reads as shown by `SET STATISTICS IO` is as follows:

```
Table 't1'. Scan count 1, logical reads 87
```

To resolve this missing statistics issue, you can create the statistics on column t1.c2 by using the CREATE STATISTICS statement:

CREATE STATISTICS s1 ON t1(c2)

The resultant execution plan with statistics created on column c2 is shown in Figure 7-26.

Table 't1'. Scan count 1, logical reads **42**

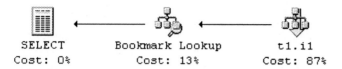

SELECT   Bookmark Lookup   t1.i1
Cost: 0%   Cost: 13%   Cost: 87%

Figure 7-26. *Execution plan with statistics in-place*

The query optimizer uses statistics on a noninitial column in a composite index to determine if scanning the leaf level of the composite index to obtain the bookmarks will be a more efficient processing strategy than scanning the whole table. In this case, creating statistics on column c2 allows the optimizer to determine that instead of scanning the base table, it will be less costly to scan the composite index on (c1, c2) and bookmark lookup to the base table for the few matching rows. Consequently, the number of logical reads has decreased from 87 to 42.

Resolving an Outdated Statistics Issue

Sometimes outdated statistics can be more damaging than missing statistics. Based on old statistics, the optimizer may decide upon a particular indexing strategy, which may be highly inappropriate for the current data distribution. Unfortunately, the execution plans don't show the same glaring warnings for outdated statistics as they do for missing statistics.

To identify outdated statistics, you should examine how close the optimizer's estimation of the number of rows affected is to the actual number of rows affected.

The following example shows you how to identify and resolve an outdated statistics issue. The statistics on the nonclustered index key on column c1 provided by DBCC SHOW_STATISTICS is shown in Figure 7-27.

DBCC SHOW_STATISTICS(t1, i1)

These results say that the density value for column c1 is 0.5. Now consider the following SELECT statement:

SELECT * FROM t1 WHERE c1 = 51

Since the total number of rows in the table is currently 10,002, the number of matching rows for the filter criteria c1 = 51 can be estimated to be 5,001 (= 0.5 × 10,002). This estimated number of rows (5,001) is way off the actual number of matching rows for this column value. The table actually contains only one row for c1 = 51.

	Updated		Rows	Rows Sampled	Steps	Density	Average key length
1	Jun 3 2002 1:47AM	2	2		2	0.0	8.0

	All density	Average Length	Columns
1	0.5	4.0	c1
2	0.5	8.0	c1, c2

	RANGE_HI_KEY	RANGE_ROWS	EQ_ROWS	DISTINCT_RANGE_ROWS	AVG_RANGE_ROWS
1	51	0.0	1.0	0	0.0
2	52	0.0	1.0	0	0.0

Figure 7-27. *Statistics on index i1*

You can get the information on both the estimated and actual number of rows from the textual plan provided by the SET STATISTICS PROFILE statement. As you know by now, you can also obtain a textual execution plan from the SET SHOWPLAN_ALL statement. But unlike SET SHOWPLAN_ALL, SET STATISTICS PROFILE executes the query and can therefore collect the *actual* number of rows affected by individual execution steps.

Execute the SELECT statement with SET STATISTICS PROFILE as follows (statistics.sql in the download):

```
SET STATISTICS PROFILE ON
GO
SELECT * FROM t1 WHERE c1 = 51
GO
SET STATISTICS PROFILE OFF
GO
```

▓TIP To get the output of SET STATISTICS PROFILE, turn the Show Execution Plan option off.

Figure 7-28 shows the textual plan output of SET STATISTICS PROFILE.

	Rows	Executes	StmtText	S	N	P	P	L	A	D	EstimateRows
1	1	1	SELECT * FROM [t1] WHERE [c1]=@1	.	1	0	.	.	.	.	4984.0
2	1	1	|--Table Scan(OBJECT:([Nort...	.	3	1	.	.	.	.	4984.0

To compute actual rows

Figure 7-28. *Actual and estimated number of rows with outdated statistics*

Estimated rows for individual execution steps = 4,984
Actual rows affected by individual execution steps = (Rows) × (Executes) = 1 × 1 = 1

From the estimated rows value versus the actual rows value, it's clear that the optimizer made an incorrect estimation based on out-of-date statistics. If the difference between the estimated rows and actual rows is more than a factor of 10, then it's quite possible that the processing strategy chosen may not be very cost-effective for the current data distribution. An inaccurate estimation may misguide the optimizer in deciding the processing strategy. The graphical execution plan for this query is shown in Figure 7-29.

```
Table 't1'. Scan count 1, logical reads 87
```

```
  SELECT              Table Scan
  Cost: 5%            Cost: 95%
```

Figure 7-29. *Execution plan with outdated statistics*

To help the optimizer make an accurate estimation, you should update the statistics on the nonclustered index key on column c1 (alternatively, of course, you can just leave the auto update statistics feature on):

UPDATE STATISTICS t1 i1

If you run the query again

```
SET STATISTICS PROFILE ON
GO
SELECT * FROM t1 WHERE c1 = 51
GO
SET STATISTICS PROFILE OFF
GO
```

the resultant output is as shown in Figure 7-30.

	Rows	Executes	StmtText	S	N	P	P	L	A	D	EstimateRows	
1	1	1	SELECT * FROM [t1] WHE...	.	1	0	.	.	.	.	1.0	ℕ
2	1	1	|--Bookmark Lookup(B...	.	3	1	.	.	.	.	1.0	(
3	1	1	|--Index Seek(O...	.	4	3	.	.	.	.	1.0	(

Figure 7-30. *Actual and estimated number of rows with up-to-date statistics*

As shown in the textual execution plan in Figure 7-30, the optimizer accurately estimated the number of rows using updated statistics. Since the estimated number of rows is 1, it makes sense to retrieve the row through the nonclustered index on c1 instead of scanning the base table. The graphical execution plan used by the optimizer for this query is shown in Figure 7-31.

```
Table 't1'. Scan count 1, logical reads 3
```

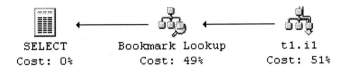

SELECT   Bookmark Lookup   t1.i1
Cost: 0%   Cost: 49%   Cost: 51%

Figure 7-31. *Execution plan with up-to-date statistics*

Updated, accurate statistics on the index key column help the optimizer come to a better decision on the processing strategy, and thereby reduce the number of logical reads from 87 to 3.

Recommendations

Throughout this chapter, I covered various recommendations for statistics. For easy reference, I've consolidated and expanded upon these recommendations in the sections that follow.

Backward Compatibility of Statistics

Statistical information in SQL Server 2000 is different from that in SQL Server 7.0. However, SQL Server 2000 understands the statistics of SQL Server 7.0, transfers the statistics during upgrade and, by default, automatically updates these statistics over time. For the best performance, however, manually update the statistics immediately after an upgrade, so that they are all in SQL Server 2000's preferred format.

Auto Create Statistics

This feature should usually be left on. With the default setting, during the creation of an execution plan, SQL Server determines if statistics on a nonindexed column will be useful. If this is deemed beneficial, SQL Server creates statistics on the nonindexed column. However, if you plan to create statistics on nonindexed columns manually, then you have to identify exactly for which nonindexed columns statistics will be beneficial.

Auto Update Statistics

This feature should usually be left on, allowing SQL Server to decide on the appropriate execution plan as the data distribution changes over time. Usually the performance benefit provided by this feature outweighs the cost overhead. As I mentioned previously, it's rarely required to interfere with the automatic maintenance of statistics, and such requirements are usually identified during a problem troubleshooting or performance analysis. To ensure that you aren't facing surprises from the automatic statistics features, it's important to analyze the effectiveness of statistics while diagnosing SQL Server issues.

Unfortunately, if you come across an issue with the auto update statistics feature and have to turn it off, make sure to create a SQL Server job to update the statistics, and schedule it to run at regular intervals. For performance reasons, ensure that the SQL job is scheduled to run during off-peak hours.

You can create a SQL Server job to update the statistics from SQL Server Enterprise Manager by following these simple steps:

1. Select *ServerName* ➤ Management ➤ SQL Server Agent ➤ Jobs ➤ New Job.

2. In the General tab of the New Job Properties dialog box, enter the job name and other details, as shown in Figure 7-32.

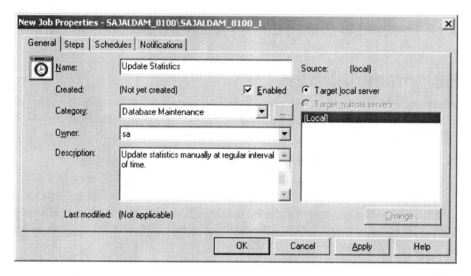

Figure 7-32. *Entering new job information*

3. Choose the Steps tab, click New, and enter the SQL command for the user database, as shown in Figure 7-33.

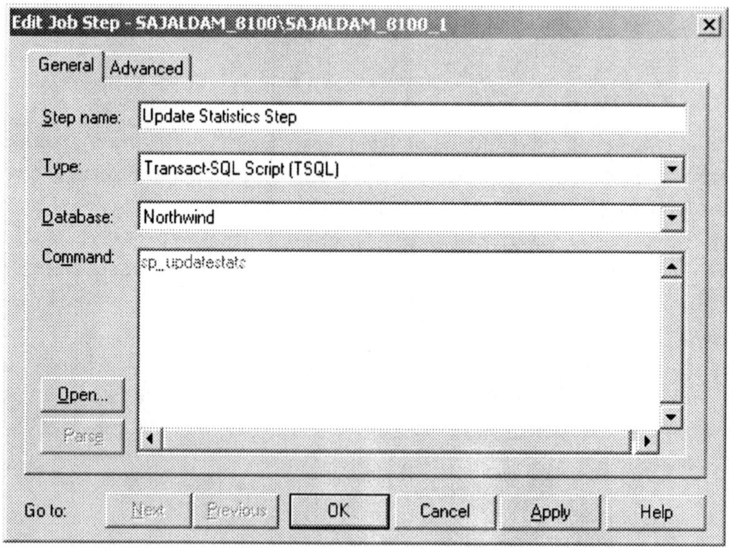

Figure 7-33. *Entering the SQL command for the user database*

4. Return to the New Job Properties dialog box by clicking the OK button.

5. In the Schedules tab of the New Job Properties dialog box, click New Schedule and enter an appropriate schedule to run the SQL Server job, as shown in Figure 7-34.

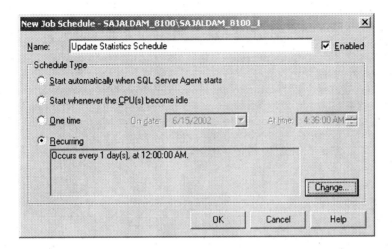

Figure 7-34. *Scheduling the SQL Server job*

6. Return to the New Job Properties dialog box by clicking the OK button.

7. Once you've entered all the information, click OK in the New Job Properties dialog box to create the SQL Server job.

8. Ensure that SQL Server Agent is running so that the SQL Server job is run automatically at the set schedule.

Amount of Sampling to Collect Statistics

It is generally recommended that you use the default sampling rate. This rate is decided by an efficient algorithm based on the data size and number of modifications. Although the default sampling rate turns out to be best in most cases, if for a particular query you find that the statistics are not very accurate, then you can manually update them with FULLSCAN.

If this is required repeatedly, then you can add a SQL Server job to take care of it. For performance reasons, ensure that the SQL job is scheduled to run during off-peak hours. To identify cases in which the default sampling rate doesn't turn out to be the best, analyze the statistics effectiveness for costly queries while troubleshooting the database performance.

Summary

As discussed in this chapter, SQL Server's cost-based optimizer requires accurate statistics on columns used in filter and join criteria to determine an efficient processing strategy. Statistics on an index key are always created during the creation of the index and, by default, SQL Server also keeps the statistics on indexed and nonindexed columns updated as the data changes.

This enables it to determine the best processing strategies applicable to the current data distribution.

Even though you can disable both the auto create statistics and auto update statistics features, it is recommended that you leave these features *on*, since their benefit to the optimizer is almost always more than their overhead cost. For a costly query, analyze the statistics to ensure that the automatic statistics maintenance lives up to its promise. The best news is that you can rest easy with a little vigilance, since automatic statistics do their job well most of the time. If manual statistics maintenance procedures are used, then you may use SQL Server jobs to automate these procedures.

Even with proper indexes and statistics in place, a heavily fragmented database will incur an increased data-retrieval cost. In the next chapter, you will see how fragmentation in an index can affect query performance, and how to analyze and resolve fragmentation.

■■■

CHAPTER 8

Fragmentation Analysis

As explained in Chapter 4, index column values are stored in the leaf pages of an index's B-tree structure. When you create an index (clustered or nonclustered) on a table, the cost of data retrieval is reduced by properly ordering the leaf pages of the index and the rows within the leaf pages. In an OLTP database, data changes continually, causing fragmentation of the indexes. As a result, the number of reads required to return multiple rows increases over time.

In this chapter, I cover the following topics:

- The causes of index fragmentation, including an analysis of page splits caused by INSERT and UPDATE statements

- The overhead costs associated with fragmentation

- How to analyze the amount of fragmentation

- Techniques used to resolve fragmentation

- T   ignificance of the fill factor in controlling fragmentation

- Automating the fragmentation analysis process

Causes of Fragmentation

Fragmentation occurs when data is modified in a table. When you INSERT or UPDATE data in a table, the table's corresponding clustered indexes and the affected nonclustered indexes are modified. This causes an index leaf page split if the modification to an index can't be accommodated in the same page. A new leaf page will then be added that contains a part of the original page and maintains the logical order of the rows in the index key. Although the new leaf page maintains the *logical* order of the data rows in the original page, this new page usually won't be *physically* adjacent to the original page on the disk.

For example, suppose an index has nine key values (or index rows), and the average size of the index rows allows a maximum of four index rows in a leaf page. As explained in Chapter 4, the 8KB leaf pages are connected to the previous and the next leaf pages to maintain the logical order of the index. Figure 8-1 illustrates the layout of the leaf pages for the index.

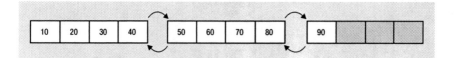

Figure 8-1. *Leaf pages layout*

Since the index key values in the leaf pages are always sorted, a new index row with a key value of 25 has to occupy a place between the existing key values 20 and 30. As the leaf page containing these existing index key values is full with the four index rows, the new index row will cause the corresponding leaf page to split. A new leaf page will be assigned to the index and a part of the first leaf page will be moved to this new leaf page, so that the new index key can be inserted in the correct logical order. The links between the index pages will also be updated so that the pages are logically connected in the order of the index. As shown in Figure 8-2, the new leaf page, even though linked to the other pages in the correct logical order, can be physically out of order.

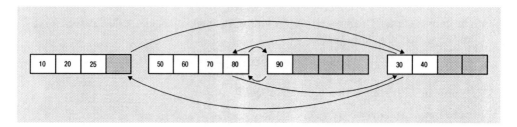

Figure 8-2. *Out-of-order leaf pages*

The pages are grouped together in bigger units called *extents*, which can contain up to eight pages. SQL Server uses extents as a physical unit of allocation on the disk. Ideally, the physical order of the extents containing the leaf pages of an index should be the same as the logical order of the index. This reduces the number of switches required between extents when retrieving a range of index rows. However, page splits can physically disorder the pages within the extents, and they can also physically disorder the extents themselves. For example, suppose the first two leaf pages of the index are in extent 1, and the third leaf page is in extent 2. If extent 2 contains free space, then the new leaf page allocated to the index due to the page split will be in extent 2, as shown in Figure 8-3.

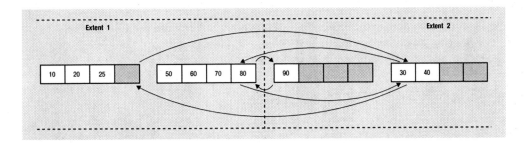

Figure 8-3. *Out-of-order leaf pages distributed across extents*

With the leaf pages distributed between two extents, ideally you expect to read a range of index rows with a maximum of one switch between the two extents. However, the disorganization of pages between the extents can cause more than one extent switch while retrieving a range of index rows. For example, to retrieve a range of index rows between 25 and 90, you will need three extent switches between the two extents, as follows:

- First extent switch to retrieve the key value 30 after the key value 25

- Second extent switch to retrieve the key value 50 after the key value 40

- Third extent switch to retrieve the key value 90 after the key value 80

This type of fragmentation is called *external fragmentation*. External fragmentation is always undesirable.

Fragmentation can also happen within an index page. If an INSERT or UPDATE operation creates a page split, then free space will be left behind in the original leaf page. Free space can also be caused by a DELETE operation. The net effect is to reduce the number of rows included in a leaf page. For example, in Figure 8-3, the page split caused by the INSERT operation has created an empty space within the first leaf page. This is known as *internal fragmentation*.

For a highly transactional database, it is desirable to deliberately leave some free space within your leaf pages, so that you can add new rows, or change the size of existing rows, without causing a page split. In Figure 8-3, the free space within the first leaf page allows an index key value of 26 to be added to the leaf page without causing a page split.

NOTE Note that this index fragmentation is different from disk fragmentation. It cannot be fixed simply by running the disk defragmentation tool, as the order of pages within a SQL Server file is understood only by SQL Server, not by the operating system.

You can obtain the number of leaf pages assigned to an index (or the data pages assigned to a heap table) through the DBCC SHOWCONTIG command. You can also use this command to analyze the amount of fragmentation in an index or a table.

Let's now take a look at the mechanics of fragmentation.

Page Split by an UPDATE Statement

To see what happens when a page split is caused by an UPDATE statement, let's walk through a simple example. Create a small test table with a clustered index, ordering the rows within one leaf (or data) page as follows (you'll find this code in create_t1.sql in the code download):

```
IF(SELECT OBJECT_ID('t1')) IS NOT NULL
  DROP TABLE t1
GO

CREATE TABLE t1(c1 INT, c2 CHAR(999), c3 VARCHAR(10))
INSERT INTO t1 VALUES(100, 'c2', '')
INSERT INTO t1 VALUES(200, 'c2', '')
INSERT INTO t1 VALUES(300, 'c2', '')
INSERT INTO t1 VALUES(400, 'c2', '')
INSERT INTO t1 VALUES(500, 'c2', '')
INSERT INTO t1 VALUES(600, 'c2', '')
INSERT INTO t1 VALUES(700, 'c2', '')
INSERT INTO t1 VALUES(800, 'c2', '')

CREATE CLUSTERED INDEX i1 ON t1(c1)
```

The average size of a row in the clustered index leaf page (excluding internal overhead) is not just the sum of the average size of the clustered index columns, but the sum of the average size of all the columns in the table, since the leaf page of the clustered index and the data page of table are the same. Therefore, the average size of a row in the clustered index is as follows:

$$= \text{(Average size of } [c1]) + \text{(Average size of } [c2]) + \text{(Average size of } [c3]) \text{ bytes}$$
$$= \text{(Size of INT)} + \text{(Size of CHAR(999))} + \text{(Average size of data in } [c3]) \text{ bytes}$$
$$= 4 + 999 + 0 = 1{,}003 \text{ bytes}$$

The maximum size of a row in SQL Server 2000 is 8,060 bytes. Therefore, if the internal overhead is not very high, all eight rows can be accommodated in a single 8KB page.

To determine the number of leaf pages assigned to the i1 clustered index, execute the DBCC SHOWCONTIG statement as follows:

```
DBCC SHOWCONTIG(t1, i1)
```

The output of DBCC SHOWCONTIG is

```
DBCC SHOWCONTIG scanning 't1' table...
Table: 't1' (1364199910); index ID: 1, database ID: 7
TABLE level scan performed.
- Pages Scanned...............................: 1
- Extents Scanned............................: 1
- Extent Switches............................: 0
- Avg. Pages per Extent......................: 1.0
- Scan Density [Best Count:Actual Count].......: 100.00% [1:1]
- Logical Scan Fragmentation .................: 0.00%
- Extent Scan Fragmentation ...................: 0.00%
- Avg. Bytes Free per Page....................: 0.0
- Avg. Page Density (full)....................: 100.00%
DBCC execution completed. If DBCC printed error messages, contact your system
 administrator.
```

From the preceding output, you can see that the number of pages assigned to the clustered index is equal to Pages Scanned, which is equal to 1. You can also see that the number of free bytes in the page is equal to Avg. Bytes Free per Page, which is equal to 0. From this information, you can infer that the page has no free space left to expand the content of column c3, which is of type VARCHAR(10) and is currently empty.

▓NOTE I analyze the other information provided by DBCC SHOWCONTIG later in the chapter.

Therefore, if you attempt to expand the content of column c3 for one of the rows as follows, it should cause a page split:

UPDATE t1 SET c3 = 'Add data' WHERE c1 = 200

Running DBCC SHOWCONTIG(t1, i1) again returns the following result:

```
- Pages Scanned...............................: 2
- Extents Scanned............................: 1
- Extent Switches............................: 0
- Avg. Pages per Extent......................: 2.0
- Scan Density [Best Count:Actual Count].......: 100.00% [1:1]
- Logical Scan Fragmentation .................: 0.00%
- Extent Scan Fragmentation ...................: 0.00%
- Avg. Bytes Free per Page....................: 4041.0
- Avg. Page Density (full)....................: 50.07%
```

From the preceding output, you can see that SQL Server has added a new page to the index. On a page split, SQL Server generally moves half the total number of rows in the original page to the new page. Therefore, the rows in the two pages are distributed as shown in Figure 8-4.

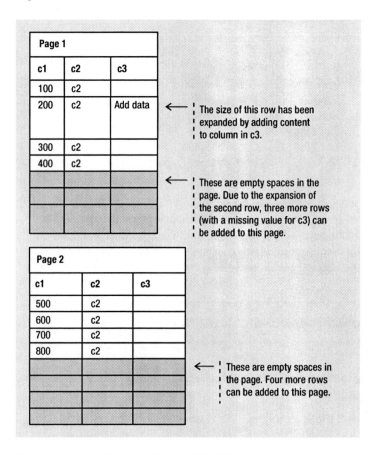

Figure 8-4. *Page split caused by an UPDATE statement*

From the preceding tables, you can see that the page split caused by the UPDATE statement results in an internal fragmentation of data in the leaf pages. If the new leaf page can't be written physically next to the original leaf page, there will be external fragmentation as well. For a large table with a high amount of fragmentation, a larger number of leaf pages will be required to hold all the index rows.

To confirm the resultant distribution of rows shown in the previous pages, you can add three trailing rows to the first leaf page and four trailing rows to the second page (t1_update.sql in the download):

```
INSERT INTO t1 VALUES(410, 'c2', '')
INSERT INTO t1 VALUES(420, 'c2', '')
INSERT INTO t1 VALUES(430, 'c2', '')
INSERT INTO t1 VALUES(900, 'c2', '')
```

```
INSERT INTO t1 VALUES(1000, 'c2', '')
INSERT INTO t1 VALUES(1100, 'c2', '')
INSERT INTO t1 VALUES(1200, 'c2', '')
```

These seven new rows are accommodated in the existing two leaf pages without causing a page split. You can confirm this by executing DBCC SHOWCONTIG(t1, i1) again:

```
- Pages Scanned...............................: 2
- Extents Scanned.............................: 1
- Extent Switches.............................: 0
- Avg. Pages per Extent.......................: 2.0
- Scan Density [Best Count:Actual Count].......: 100.00% [1:1]
- Logical Scan Fragmentation ..................: 0.00%
- Extent Scan Fragmentation ...................: 0.00%
- Avg. Bytes Free per Page....................: 499.0
- Avg. Page Density (full)....................: 93.83%
```

In the worst case, the two pages (Pages Scanned = 2) may be assigned to two different extents, affecting the other values:

```
- Extents Scanned.............................: 2
- Extent Switches.............................: 1
- Avg. Pages per Extent.......................: 1.0
- Scan Density [Best Count:Actual Count].......: 50.00% [1:2]
```

Page Split by an INSERT Statement

To understand how a page split can be caused by an INSERT statement, consider the following example. Create the same test table (create_t1.sql) as you did previously, with the eight initial rows and the clustered index. Since the single index leaf page is completely filled, any attempt to add an intermediate row as follows should cause a page split in the leaf page:

```
INSERT INTO t1 VALUES(110, 'c2', '')
```

You can verify this by examining the output of DBCC SHOWCONTIG(t1, i1):

```
- Pages Scanned...............................: 2
- Extents Scanned.............................: 1
- Extent Switches.............................: 0
- Avg. Pages per Extent.......................: 2.0
- Scan Density [Best Count:Actual Count].......: 100.00% [1:1]
- Logical Scan Fragmentation ..................: 50.00%
- Extent Scan Fragmentation ...................: 0.00%
- Avg. Bytes Free per Page....................: 3542.0
- Avg. Page Density (full)....................: 56.24%
```

As explained previously, half the rows from the original leaf page are moved to the new page. Once space is cleared in the original leaf page, the new row is added in the appropriate order to the original leaf page. Be aware that a row is associated with only one page; it cannot span multiple pages. Figure 8-5 shows the resultant distribution of rows in the two pages.

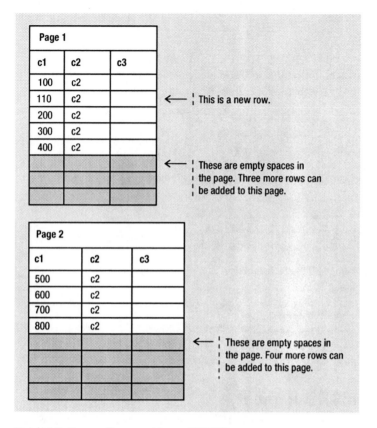

Figure 8-5. *Page split caused by an INSERT statement*

From the previous index pages, you can see that the page split caused by the INSERT statement spreads the rows sparsely across the leaf pages, causing internal fragmentation. It often causes external fragmentation also, since the new leaf page may not be physically adjacent to the original page. For a large table with a high amount of fragmentation, the page splits caused by the INSERT statement will require a larger number of leaf pages to accommodate all the index rows.

To verify the row distribution shown in the index pages, you can run t1_insert.sql again, adding three more rows to the first page and four more rows to the second page:

```
INSERT INTO t1 VALUES(120, 'c2', '')
INSERT INTO t1 VALUES(130, 'c2', '')
INSERT INTO t1 VALUES(140, 'c2', '')
INSERT INTO t1 VALUES(900, 'c2', '')
INSERT INTO t1 VALUES(1000, 'c2', '')
INSERT INTO t1 VALUES(1100, 'c2', '')
INSERT INTO t1 VALUES(1200, 'c2', '')
```

The result is the same as for the previous example: these seven new rows can be accommodated in the two existing leaf pages without causing any page split. Note that in the first page, new rows are added in between the other rows existing in the page. This won't cause a page split, since free space is available in the page.

What about when you have to add rows to the trailing end of an index? In this case, even if a new page is required, it won't split any existing page. For example, adding a new row with c1 equal to 1,300 will require a new page, but it won't cause a page split since the row isn't added in an intermediate position. Therefore, if new rows are added in the order of the clustered index, then the index rows will be always added at the trailing end of the index, preventing the page splits otherwise caused by the INSERT statements.

Fragmentation caused by page splits hurts data-retrieval performance, as you will see next.

Fragmentation Overhead

Both internal and external fragmentations adversely affect data-retrieval performance. External fragmentation causes a noncontiguous sequence of index pages on the disk, with new leaf pages far from the original leaf pages, and their physical ordering different from their logical ordering. Consequently, a range scan on an index will need more switches between the corresponding extents than ideally required, as explained earlier in the chapter. Also, a range scan on an index will be unable to benefit from read-ahead operations performed on the disk. If the pages are arranged contiguously, then a read-ahead operation can read pages in advance without much head movement.

For better performance, it is preferable to use sequential I/O, since this can read a whole extent (eight 8KB pages together) in a single disk I/O operation. By contrast, a noncontiguous layout of pages requires nonsequential or random I/O operations to retrieve the index pages from the disk, and a random I/O operation can read only 8KB of data in a single disk operation (this may be acceptable, however, if you are retrieving only one row).

In the case of internal fragmentation, rows are distributed sparsely across a large number of pages, increasing the number of disk I/O operations required to read the index pages into memory and the number of logical reads required to retrieve multiple index rows from memory. As mentioned earlier, even though it increases the cost of data retrieval, a little internal fragmentation can be beneficial, as it allows you to perform INSERT and UPDATE queries without causing page splits.

To understand how fragmentation affects the cost of a query, consider the following example. Create a test table with a clustered index, and insert a highly fragmented dataset in the table. Since an INSERT operation in between an ordered dataset can cause a page split, you can easily create the fragmented dataset by adding rows in an order as follows (create_t1_fragmented.sql in the code download):

```
IF(SELECT OBJECT_ID('t1')) IS NOT NULL
  DROP TABLE t1
GO
CREATE TABLE t1(c1 INT, c2 INT, c3 INT, c4 CHAR(2000))
CREATE CLUSTERED INDEX i1 ON t1(c1)
DECLARE @n INT
SET @n = 1
WHILE @n < 21
BEGIN
  INSERT INTO t1 VALUES(@n, @n, @n, 'a')
  INSERT INTO t1 VALUES(41-@n, @n, @n, 'a')
  SET @n = @n + 1
END
```

To determine the number of logical reads required to retrieve a small result set and a large result set from this fragmented table, execute the two SELECT statements with STATISTICS IO ON (statistics.sql in the download):

```
SET STATISTICS IO ON
GO
SELECT * FROM t1 WHERE c1 BETWEEN 21 AND 25 --Reads 5 rows
SELECT * FROM t1 WHERE c1 BETWEEN 1 AND 40  --Reads all rows
GO
SET STATISTICS IO OFF
GO
```

The number of logical reads performed by the individual queries is, respectively, as follows:

```
Table 't1'. Scan count 1, logical reads 5
Table 't1'. Scan count 1, logical reads 26
```

To evaluate how the fragmented dataset affects the number of logical reads, rearrange the index leaf pages physically by re-creating the clustered index:

```
DROP INDEX t1.i1
CREATE CLUSTERED INDEX i1 ON t1(c1)
```

With the index leaf pages rearranged in the proper order, rerun statistics.sql. The number of logical reads required by the preceding two SELECT statements reduces to 4 and 11, respectively:

```
Table 't1'. Scan count 1, logical reads 4
Table 't1'. Scan count 1, logical reads 11
```

The cost overhead due to fragmentation usually increases in line with the number of rows retrieved, as this involves reading a greater number of out-of-order pages. For *point queries* (queries retrieving only one row), fragmentation doesn't usually matter, since the row is retrieved from one leaf page only, but this isn't always the case. Because of the internal structure of the index, fragmentation may increase the cost of even a point query. For instance, the following SELECT statement (singlestat.sql in the download) performs two logical reads with the leaf pages rearranged properly, but it requires four logical reads on the fragmented dataset:

```
SET STATISTICS IO ON
GO
SELECT * FROM t1 WHERE c1 = 10 --Read 1 row
GO
SET STATISTICS IO OFF
GO
```

The resulting message in Query Analyzer for this script is

```
Table 't1'. Scan count 1, logical reads 2
```

> **NOTE** The lesson from this section is that, for better query performance, it is important to analyze the amount of fragmentation in an index and rearrange it if required.

Analyzing the Amount of Fragmentation

The fragmentation ratio of an index can be analyzed using the DBCC SHOWCONTIG statement. For a table with a clustered index, the fragmentation of the clustered index is congruous with the fragmentation of the data pages, since the leaf pages of the clustered index and data pages are the same. DBCC SHOWCONTIG also indicates the amount of fragmentation in a heap table (or a table with no clustered index). Since a heap table doesn't require any row ordering, the logical order of the pages isn't relevant for the heap table.

The output of DBCC SHOWCONTIG shows information on the pages and extents of an index (or a table). As explained earlier, in SQL Server, eight contiguous 8KB pages are grouped together in an extent that is 64KB in size. For very small tables (much less than 64KB), the pages in an extent can belong to more than one index or table—these are called *mixed extents*. If there are too many small tables in the database, mixed extents help SQL Server conserve disk space.

As a table (or index) grows and requests more than eight pages, SQL Server creates an extent dedicated to the table (or index) and assigns the pages from this extent. Such an extent is called a *uniform extent*, and it serves up to eight page requests for the same table (or index). Uniform extents help SQL Server lay out the pages of a table (or an index) contiguously. They also reduce the number of page creation requests by one-eighth, since a set of eight pages is created in the form of an extent.

To analyze the fragmentation of an index, let's re-create the table with the fragmented dataset used in the "Fragmentation Overhead" section (create_t1_fragmented.sql). You can obtain the fragmentation detail of the clustered index by executing the DBCC SHOWCONTIG statement:

DBCC SHOWCONTIG(t1, i1)

The output of the DBCC SHOWCONTIG statement is as follows:

```
DBCC SHOWCONTIG scanning 't1' table...
Table: 't1' (541244983); index ID: 1, database ID: 7
TABLE level scan performed.
- Pages Scanned...............................: 25
- Extents Scanned.............................: 5
- Extent Switches.............................: 10
- Avg. Pages per Extent.......................: 5.0
- Scan Density [Best Count:Actual Count].......: 36.36% [4:11]
- Logical Scan Fragmentation ..................: 48.00%
- Extent Scan Fragmentation ...................: 40.00%
- Avg. Bytes Free per Page.....................: 4862.4
- Avg. Page Density (full)....................: 39.93%
DBCC execution completed. If DBCC printed error messages, contact your system
  administrator.
```

This output represents the following:

- Pages Scanned: This is the number of pages in the index or the table. In the preceding example, four rows can fit on one page, since the average row size, with three INTs and one CHAR(2000), is 2012 (= 4 + 4 + 4 + 2,000) bytes. As there are 40 rows, then ideally the number of pages should be 10 (= 40 / 4). A high value of 25 indicates a large amount of internal fragmentation.

- Extents Scanned: This is the number of extents for the index or the table. In the preceding example there are 25 pages. Therefore, the minimum number of extents should be 4 (= 25 / 8, rounded to the higher integer value). A value of 5 indicates that there is some, but not a significant amount of, fragmentation within the extents.

- Extent Switches: This is the number of switches required between the extents to access pages in the logical order of the index. In an ideal situation, if all the pages of an index (or table) are laid out in the same order as that of the index, then Extent Switches = Extents Scanned – 1.

  In the preceding example, the ideal number of Extent Switches = (Extents Scanned – 1) = (5 – 1) = 4. A value greater than 4 indicates that the pages in the extents are not in the same order as the logical order of the index. The current high value of 10 is a sign of a large amount of external fragmentation.

- Avg. Pages per Extent: The average number of pages in an extent is equal to Pages Scanned / Extents Scanned. For a large table with minimal external fragmentation, Avg. Pages per Extent should be close to 8. For large tables, anything less than 8 indicates external fragmentation. For small tables, however, Avg. Pages per Extent can be less than 8. For example, a small table with only two pages will have Avg. Pages per Extent as 2, which should not be considered as an external fragmentation since the small number in this case is not due to fragmented content, but a small amount of content.

- Scan Density [Best Count:Actual Count]: This is the ratio of the Best Count of extents to the Actual Counts, and it is one of the most useful indicators of fragmentation.

  The Best Count represents the number of extents required for the number of Pages Scanned. It is equal to Pages Scanned / 8, rounded to the higher integer number. For example, if Pages Scanned is 9, then Best Count is 9 / 8, which rounded to the higher integer number is 2.

  The Actual Count is an indicator of how many extents can ideally cause the current number of Extent Switches. As mentioned in the preceding description of the Extent Switches, Actual Count = Extent Switches + 1.

  In the best case, the Actual Count should be equal to the Best Count. Therefore, ideally, Scan Density should be 100%. A value less than 100% indicates that the pages are non-contiguously distributed between the extents. An index with a Scan Density of less than 40% can be considered a candidate for defragmentation.

In the preceding example

$$\text{Best Count} = \text{Pages Scanned} \textbf{ / 8, rounded to the higher integer value}$$
$$\textbf{= 25 / 8, rounded to the higher integer value}$$
$$\textbf{= 4}$$

and

$$\text{Actual Count} = \text{Extent Switches} \textbf{ + 1 = 10 + 1 = 11}$$

Therefore

$$\text{Scan Density} \textbf{ = 4:11 = 36.36\%}$$

A low value of 36.36% indicates a high amount of external fragmentation.

- `Logical Scan Fragmentation`: This shows the ratio of pages with a different physical order from the logical order of the index. A range between 0% and 10% is considered an acceptable value.

In the preceding example, the high value of 48.00% indicates that 12 out of 25 pages are out of order, which is a sign of high external fragmentation.

- `Extent Scan Fragmentation`: This indicates the gaps between the extents. Ideally, all the extents used by an index should be side by side on the disk. If a gap exists between two adjacent extents, then the next extent can't be retrieved by the read-ahead operation on the disk. The value of `Extent Scan Fragmentation` represents the ratio of the total number of gaps between extents to the total number of extents. For instance, if two adjacent extents aren't side by side, then it represents one gap. For a large table using uniform extents, a high `Extent Scan Fragmentation` value is a sign of high external fragmentation. Ideally, the value of `Extent Scan Fragmentation` should be 0%, indicating that there are no gaps between the extents.

In the preceding example, a value of 40.00% indicates that out of the five extents, two have gaps from their adjacent extents. This is a sign of high external fragmentation.

- `Avg. Bytes Free per Page`: This is the average number of free bytes in a page. A high value may be due to a large amount of internal fragmentation. This value can also be high if you intentionally maintain lots of free space per page, using the *fill factor* to reduce page splits caused by INSERT and UPDATE queries. You'll learn about the fill factor later in the chapter.

In the preceding example, a high value of 4,862.4 bytes indicates that, on average, more than half of the pages are empty. This is a sign of high internal fragmentation.

- `Avg. Page Density (full)`: This is the inverse of `Avg. Bytes Free per Page` expressed as percentage. A high percentage value indicates that a greater number of rows have been compressed in the pages.

In the preceding example, the low value of 39.93% represents the same information as represented by the high value of Avg. Bytes Free per Page. It is an indication of a high amount of internal fragmentation.

For a large table, DBCC SHOWCONTIG may take a long time to provide the detailed fragmentation report. To get a quick report on the fragmentation status, you can execute the DBCC SHOWCONTIG statement with the FAST option:

```
DBCC SHOWCONTIG(t1, i1) WITH FAST
```

This provides a short report:

```
DBCC SHOWCONTIG scanning 't1' table...
Table: 't1' (541244983); index ID: 1, database ID: 7
TABLE level scan performed.
- Pages Scanned...............................: 25
- Extent Switches............................: 10
- Scan Density [Best Count:Actual Count].......: 36.36% [4:11]
- Logical Scan Fragmentation ..................: 48.00%
DBCC execution completed. If DBCC printed error messages, contact your system
 administrator.
```

You can use this report to decide whether or not a detailed fragmentation analysis is required.

Analyzing the Fragmentation of a Small Table

Don't be overly concerned with the output of DBCC SHOWCONTIG for small tables. For a small table or index with fewer than eight pages, SQL Server uses mixed extents for the pages. For example, if a table (SmallTable1 or its clustered index) contains only two pages, then SQL Server allocates the two pages from a mixed extent instead of dedicating an extent to the table. The mixed extent may contain pages of other small tables/indexes also, as shown in Figure 8-6.

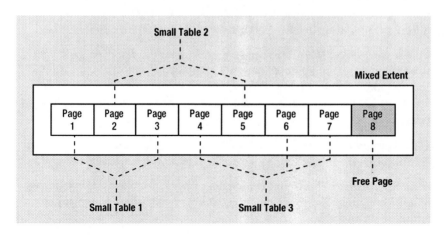

Figure 8-6. *Mixed extent*

The distribution of pages across multiple mixed extents may lead you to believe that there is a high amount of external fragmentation in the table or the index, when in fact this is by design in SQL Server and is therefore perfectly acceptable.

To understand how the fragmentation information of a small table or index may look, consider the following example. Create a small table with a clustered index (create_small_t1_fragmented.sql in the download):

```
IF(SELECT OBJECT_ID('t1')) IS NOT NULL
  DROP TABLE t1
GO
CREATE TABLE t1(c1 INT, c2 INT, c3 INT, c4 CHAR(2000))
DECLARE @n INT
SET @n = 1
WHILE @n <= 28
BEGIN
  INSERT INTO t1 VALUES(@n, @n, @n, 'a')
  SET @n = @n + 1
END
CREATE CLUSTERED INDEX i1 ON t1(c1)
```

In the preceding table, with each INT taking 4 bytes, the average row size is 2,012 (= 4 + 4 + 4 + 2,000) bytes. Therefore, a default 8KB page can contain up to four rows. After all 28 rows are added to the table, a clustered index is created to physically arrange the rows and reduce fragmentation to a minimum. With the minimum internal fragmentation, seven (= 28 / 4) pages are required for the clustered index (or the base table). Since the number of pages is not more than eight, SQL Server uses pages from mixed extents for the clustered index (or the base table). If the mixed extents used for the clustered index are not side by side, then the output of DBCC SHOWCONTIG may express a high amount of external fragmentation. But as a SQL user, you can't reduce the resultant external fragmentation. The output of DBCC SHOWCONTIG is as follows:

```
DBCC SHOWCONTIG scanning 't1' table...
Table: 't1' (205243786); index ID: 1, database ID: 7
TABLE level scan performed.
- Pages Scanned...............................: 7
- Extents Scanned............................: 2
- Extent Switches............................: 1
- Avg. Pages per Extent.......................: 3.5
- Scan Density [Best Count:Actual Count].......: 50.00% [1:2]
- Logical Scan Fragmentation ..................: 0.00%
- Extent Scan Fragmentation ...................: 0.00%
- Avg. Bytes Free per Page....................: 12.0
- Avg. Page Density (full)....................: 99.85%
DBCC execution completed. If DBCC printed error messages, contact your system
  administrator.
```

From the output of DBCC SHOWCONTIG, you can analyze the fragmentation of the small clustered index (or the table) as follows:

- Extents Scanned: Two mixed extents are used for the index. Even though more than one extent for seven pages may be considered as an indication of external fragmentation, SQL Server won't use a single uniform extent for this index with only seven pages. In this case, therefore, it is *not* an indication of external fragmentation caused by page splits.

- Avg. Pages per Extent: As explained previously, the low value of 3.5 for Avg. Pages per Extent doesn't represent a remedial external fragmentation.

- Scan Density: Accordingly, the Scan Density value is also low. Although the value of Best Count is considered to be 1, in practice that is difficult to achieve for an index with only seven pages.

- Extent Scan Fragmentation: Even though currently you are fortunate to have 0% extent scan fragmentation, or no gap between the extents, in general you can't expect the mixed extents to be just next to each other. Therefore, a high value for the extent scan fragmentation can be commonly seen for small tables.

In spite of the preceding misleading values, a small table (or index) with minimum fragmentation should still have the following values:

- Extent Switches: Should be Extents Scanned – 1

- Logical Scan Fragmentation: Should be 0%

- Avg. Bytes Free per Page: Should be close to 0

- Avg. Page Density (full): Should be close to 100%

Once you determine that fragmentation in an index (or a table) needs to be dealt with, you need to decide which defragmentation technique to use. The factors affecting this decision, and the different techniques, are explained in the following section.

Fragmentation Resolutions

Fragmentation in an index can be resolved by rearranging the index rows and pages so that their physical and logical orders match. To reduce external fragmentation, the leaf pages of the index can be physically reordered to follow the logical order of the index. You achieve this through the following techniques:

- Dropping and re-creating the index

- Re-creating the index with the DROP_EXISTING clause

- Executing the DBCC DBREINDEX statement on the index

- Executing the DBCC INDEXDEFRAG statement on the index

Dropping and Re-creating the Index

One of the easiest ways to remove fragmentation in an index is to drop the index and then re-create it. Dropping and re-creating the index reduces fragmentation the most, since it allows SQL Server to use completely new pages for the index and populate them appropriately with the existing data. This avoids both internal and external fragmentation.

This technique of defragmentation adds a high amount of overhead on the system, and it causes blocking. Dropping and re-creating the index blocks all other requests on the table (or on any other index on the table). For this reason, it is not a recommended technique for a production database, at least outside of off-peak times.

To clarify this point, let's consider an example. Create a fragmented test table (create_t1_fragmented_2.sql in the download) with a clustered primary key (pkc1) and two nonclustered indexes (incl_2 and incl_3):

```
IF(SELECT OBJECT_ID('t1')) IS NOT NULL
  DROP TABLE t1
GO
CREATE TABLE t1(c1 INT NOT NULL, c2 INT, c3 INT, c4 CHAR(200))
ALTER TABLE t1 ADD CONSTRAINT pkcl PRIMARY KEY CLUSTERED(c1)
CREATE NONCLUSTERED INDEX incl_c2 ON t1(c2)
CREATE NONCLUSTERED INDEX incl_c3 ON t1(c3)
DECLARE @n INT
SET @n = 1
WHILE @n < 21
BEGIN
  INSERT INTO t1 VALUES(@n, @n, @n, 'a')
  INSERT INTO t1 VALUES(41-@n, 41-@n, 41-@n, 'a')
  SET @n = @n + 1
END
```

As you know, the fragmentation in the nonclustered index incl_c2, if any, can be reduced by executing a set of DROP and CREATE statements:

```
DROP INDEX t1.incl_c2
CREATE NONCLUSTERED INDEX incl_c2 ON t1(c2)
```

To consider how the drop/creation of the index affects the concurrency of other queries, use the following SELECT statement:

```
SELECT c3 FROM t1 WHERE c3 = 1
```

This query can use the nonclustered index incl_c3 on column c3 as a covered index to satisfy the query fully, and it is not dependent on the other nonclustered index incl_c2.

But the preceding defragmentation steps on incl_c2 even block the SELECT statement, which is based on incl_c3 only. To verify this concurrency issue, execute the previous DROP and CREATE statements as a part of an open transaction (open_trans.sql in the download) as follows, so that the locks acquired by them are retained while executing the SELECT statement from another connection:

```
BEGIN TRANSACTION
  DROP INDEX t1.incl_c2
  CREATE NONCLUSTERED INDEX incl_c2 ON t1(c2)
--COMMIT --Intentionally commented to keep the transaction open
```

Now if you execute the preceding SELECT statement from another connection, it faces a block until the open transaction on the first connection is completed. You'll learn how to analyze and resolve blocking in Chapter 12.

The other drawbacks of this defragmentation technique are as follows:

- *Blocking*: Besides blocking other queries, this defragmentation technique can itself be blocked by other queries accessing the table (or any other index on the table).

- *Missing index*: As the index is dropped and then re-created in two separate steps, the index will be missing between the two steps. During that time period, the performance of all queries dependent on the index will be adversely affected.

- *Index with constraints*: The indexes that support either the PRIMARY KEY or UNIQUE constraint cannot be dropped using the DROP INDEX statement. A primary key may be further referred to in other tables as a foreign key to maintain declarative referential integrity between parent and child tables. Thus, to delete the PRIMARY KEY constraint, you need to delete the FOREIGN KEY constraint first. You can use an ALTER TABLE statement to add and drop the constraints:

  ```
  -- Drop the foreign key(s) first
  ALTER TABLE Child DROP CONSTRAINT fkncl
  -- Drop the primary key
  ALTER TABLE Parent DROP CONSTRAINT pkcl
  -- Re-create the primary key
  ALTER TABLE Parent ADD CONSTRAINT pkcl PRIMARY KEY CLUSTERED(c1)
  -- Re-create the foreign key(s)
  ALTER TABLE Child ADD CONSTRAINT fkncl FOREIGN KEY (c2)
    REFERENCES Parent(c1)
  ```

- *Nonclustered indexes rebuild*: Rebuilding the clustered index using DROP and CREATE INDEX causes all nonclustered indexes on the table to be rebuilt twice. As explained previously in Chapter 4, when a clustered index is dropped, the row locators of all the nonclustered indexes on the table are automatically modified to point to the physical location of the data rows. Later, when the clustered index is re-created, the row locators of the nonclustered indexes are again modified to contain the value of clustered index key. To avoid this overhead of re-creating all the nonclustered indexes twice and yet re-create the clustered index, use the DROP_EXISTING clause with the CREATE INDEX statement as explained in the next section.

Re-creating the Index with the DROP_EXISTING Clause

To avoid the overhead of rebuilding the nonclustered indexes twice while rebuilding a clustered index, use the DROP_EXISTING clause of the CREATE INDEX statement. This re-creates the clustered index in one atomic step, avoiding re-creating the nonclustered indexes since the clustered index key values used by the row locators remain the same. To rebuild the previous clustered key in one atomic step using the DROP_EXISTING clause, execute the CREATE INDEX statement as follows:

```
CREATE UNIQUE CLUSTERED INDEX pkcl ON t1(c1)
  WITH DROP_EXISTING
```

You can use the DROP_EXISTING clause for both clustered and nonclustered indexes, and even to convert a nonclustered index to a clustered index. However, you can't use it to convert a clustered index to a nonclustered index.

The drawbacks of this defragmentation technique are as follows:

- *Blocking*: Similar to the DROP and CREATE method, this technique also causes and faces blocking from other queries accessing the table (or any index on the table).

- *Index with constraints*: Unlike the first method, the CREATE INDEX statement with DROP_EXISTING can be used to re-create indexes with constraints, provided the index definition exactly matches the requirements of the constraint. For example, if the index supports a PRIMARY KEY constraint, then the UNIQUE keyword should be used in the CREATE INDEX statement:

```
CREATE UNIQUE CLUSTERED INDEX pkcl ON t1(c1)
  WITH DROP_EXISTING
```

Failing to use the UNIQUE keyword in the preceding statement returns the following error:

```
Server: Msg 1907, Level 16, State 1, Line 1
Cannot re-create index 'pkcl'. The new index definition does not
 match the constraint being enforced by the existing index.
```

- *Table with multiple fragmented indexes*: As table data fragments, the indexes often become fragmented as well. If this defragmentation technique is used, then all the indexes on the table have to be identified and rebuilt individually.

You can avoid the last two limitations associated with this technique by using DBCC DBREINDEX, as explained next.

Executing the DBCC DBREINDEX Statement

DBCC DBREINDEX rebuilds an index in one atomic step, just like CREATE INDEX with the
DROP_EXISTING clause. Since DBCC DBREINDEX also rebuilds the index physically, it allows
SQL Server to assign fresh pages to reduce both internal and external fragmentation to a
minimum. But unlike CREATE INDEX with the DROP_EXISTING clause, it allows an index (supporting either the PRIMARY KEY or UNIQUE constraint) to be rebuilt dynamically without dropping and re-creating the constraints.

To understand the use of DBCC DBREINDEX to defragment an index, consider the fragmented
table used in the "Fragmentation Overhead" and "Analyzing the Amount of Fragmentation"
sections (create_t1_fragmented.sql). This table is repeated here:

```
IF(SELECT OBJECT_ID('t1')) IS NOT NULL
  DROP TABLE t1
GO
CREATE TABLE t1(c1 INT, c2 INT, c3 INT, c4 CHAR(2000))
CREATE CLUSTERED INDEX i1 ON t1(c1)
DECLARE @n INT
SET @n = 1
WHILE @n < 21
BEGIN
  INSERT INTO t1 VALUES(@n, @n, @n, 'a')
  INSERT INTO t1 VALUES(41-@n, @n, @n, 'a')
  SET @n = @n + 1
END
```

You can defragment the clustered index (or the table) by using the DBCC DBREINDEX
statement:

DBCC DBREINDEX(t1, i1)

The resultant output of DBCC SHOWCONTIG(t1, i1) is as follows:

```
DBCC SHOWCONTIG scanning 't1' table...
Table: 't1' (265768004); index ID: 1, database ID: 7
TABLE level scan performed.
- Pages Scanned................................: 10
- Extents Scanned.............................: 2
- Extent Switches.............................: 1
- Avg. Pages per Extent.......................: 5.0
- Scan Density [Best Count:Actual Count].......: 100.00% [2:2]
- Logical Scan Fragmentation ..................: 0.00%
- Extent Scan Fragmentation ...................: 0.00%
- Avg. Bytes Free per Page....................: 12.0
- Avg. Page Density (full)....................: 99.85%
```

Compare the preceding output of DBCC SHOWCONTIG with that from the earlier "Analyzing
the Amount of Fragmentation" section. You can see that both internal and external fragmentation have been reduced efficiently. Here's an analysis of the output:

- *Internal fragmentation*: The table has 40 rows with an average row size (2,012 bytes) that allows a maximum of four rows per page. If the rows are highly compressed to reduce the internal fragmentation to a minimum, then there should be ten data pages in the table (or leaf pages in the clustered index). You can observe the following in the preceding output:

  - Number of leaf (or data) pages = Pages Scanned = 10

  - Average free space in a page = Avg. Bytes Free per Page = 12.0 bytes

  - Amount of compression in a page = Avg. Page Density (full) = 99.85%

- *External fragmentation*: A minimum of two extents is required to hold the ten pages. For a minimum of external fragmentation, there should not be any gap between the two extents, and all pages should be physically arranged in the logical order of the index. You can observe these aspects in the preceding output:

  - Number of extents = Extents Scanned = 2.

  - Amount of gap between the extents = Extent Scan Fragmentation = 0.00%. In case of a nonzero value, determine the number of gaps between the extents. For example, 50% would indicate that one gap exists between the two extents. Compare this number of gaps with the original number of gaps. A lower value is always better.

  - Number of switches between the two extents required to follow the logical order of the pages = Extent Switches = 1.

  - Contiguous distribution of pages across extents = Scan Density [Best Count:Actual Count] = 100.00%.

  - Number of out-of-order pages = Logical Scan Fragmentation = 0.00%. As mentioned previously, a value between 0% and 10% is considered acceptable.

As shown previously, the DBCC DBREINDEX technique effectively reduces fragmentation. You can also use it to rebuild *all* the indexes of a table in one statement:

DBCC DBREINDEX(t1)

Although this is the most effective defragmentation technique, it does have some overhead and limitations:

- *Blocking*: Similar to the previous two index-rebuilding techniques, DBCC DBREINDEX introduces blocking in the system. It blocks all other queries trying to access the table (or any index on the table). It can also be blocked by those queries.

- *Transaction rollback*: Since DBCC DBREINDEX is fully atomic in action, if it is stopped before completion, then all the defragmentation actions performed up to that time are lost.

Executing the DBCC INDEXDEFRAG Statement

DBCC INDEXDEFRAG reduces the fragmentation of an index without rebuilding the index. It reduces external fragmentation by rearranging the existing leaf pages of the index in the logical order of the index key. It compacts the rows within the pages, reducing internal fragmentation, and discards the resultant empty pages. This technique doesn't use any new pages for defragmentation.

To avoid the blocking overhead associated with DBCC DBREINDEX, this technique uses a nonatomic online approach. As it proceeds through its steps, it requests a small number of locks for a short period. Once each step is done, it releases the locks and proceeds to the next step. While trying to access a page, if it finds that the page is being used, it skips that page and never returns to the page again. This allows other queries to run on the table along with the DBCC INDEXDEFRAG operation. Also, if this operation is stopped intermediately, then all the defragmentation steps performed up to then are preserved.

Since DBCC INDEXDEFRAG doesn't use any new pages to reorder the index, and it skips the locked pages, the amount of defragmentation provided by this approach is usually less than that of DBCC DBREINDEX. To observe the relative effectiveness of DBCC INDEXDEFRAG compared to DBCC DBREINDEX, rebuild the (create_t1_fragmented.sql) test table used in the previous section on DBCC DBREINDEX.

Now, to reduce the fragmentation of the clustered index, use DBCC INDEXDEFRAG as follows:

```
DBCC INDEXDEFRAG(0, t1, i1)
```

The first parameter (0) represents the current database. You can use a specific name or ID of the database instead. The resultant output of DBCC SHOWCONTIG(t1, i1) is as follows:

```
DBCC SHOWCONTIG scanning 't1' table...
Table: 't1' (393768460); index ID: 1, database ID: 7
TABLE level scan performed.
- Pages Scanned...............................: 11
- Extents Scanned.............................: 2
- Extent Switches.............................: 4
- Avg. Pages per Extent.......................: 5.5
- Scan Density [Best Count:Actual Count].......: 40.00% [2:5]
- Logical Scan Fragmentation ..................: 18.18%
- Extent Scan Fragmentation ...................: 50.00%
- Avg. Bytes Free per Page....................: 746.9
- Avg. Page Density (full)....................: 90.77%
```

From the output, you can see that DBCC INDEXDEFRAG doesn't reduce fragmentation as effectively as DBCC DBREINDEX, as shown in the previous section. For a highly fragmented index, the DBCC INDEXDEFRAG operation can take much longer than rebuilding the index. Also, if an index spans multiple files, DBCC INDEXDEFRAG doesn't migrate pages between the files. However, the main benefit of using DBCC INDEXDEFRAG is that it allows other queries to access the table (or the indexes) simultaneously.

Table 8-1 summarizes the characteristics of these four defragmentation techniques.

Table 8-1. *Characteristics of Four Defragmentation Techniques*

Characteristics/Issues	Drop and Create Index	Create Index with DROP_EXISTING	DBCC DBREINDEX	DBCC INDEXDEFRAG
Rebuild nonclustered indexes on clustered index defragmentation	Twice	No	No	No
Missing indexes intermediately	Yes	No	No	No
Defragment index with constraints	Highly complex	Moderately complex	Easy	Easy
Defragment multiple indexes together	No	No	Yes	No
Concurrency with others	Low	Low	Low	High
Intermediate cancellation	Dangerous with no transaction	Progress lost	Progress lost	Progress preserved
Degree of defragmentation	High	High	High	Moderate
Apply new fill factor	Yes	Yes	Yes	No
Statistics are updated	Yes	Yes	Yes	No

Internal fragmentation can also be reduced by compressing more rows within a page, reducing free spaces within the pages. The maximum amount of compression that can be done within the leaf pages of an index is controlled by the fill factor, as you will see next.

Significance of the Fill Factor

The internal fragmentation of an index is reduced by compressing more rows per leaf page in an index. Compressing more rows within a leaf page reduces the total number of pages required for the index, decreasing disk I/O and the logical reads required to retrieve a range of index rows. On the other hand, if the index key values are highly transactional, then having fully compressed index pages will cause page splits. Therefore, for a transactional table, a good balance between maximizing the number of rows in a page and avoiding page splits is required.

SQL Server allows you to control the amount of free space within the leaf pages of the index by using the *fill factor*. If you know that there will be enough INSERT queries on the table or UPDATE queries on the index key columns, then you can pre-add free space to the index leaf page using the fill factor to minimize page splits. If the table is read-only, you can create the index with a high fill factor to reduce the number of index pages.

The default fill factor is 0, which means the leaf pages are packed to 100%, although some free space is left in the branch nodes of the B-tree structure. The fill factor for an index is applied only when the index is created. As keys are inserted and updated, the density of rows in the index eventually stabilizes within a narrow range. As you saw in the previous chapter's sections on page splits caused by UPDATE and INSERT, when a page split occurs, generally half of the original page is moved to a new page, which happens irrespective of the fill factor used during the index creation.

To understand the significance of the fill factor, let's use a small test table (create_t1_fill.sql in the download) with 24 rows:

```
IF(SELECT OBJECT_ID('t1')) IS NOT NULL
  DROP TABLE t1
GO
CREATE TABLE t1(c1 INT, c2 CHAR(999))
DECLARE @n INT
SET @n = 1
WHILE @n <= 24
BEGIN
  INSERT INTO t1 VALUES(@n*100, 'a')
  SET @n = @n + 1
END
```

Compress the maximum number of rows in the leaf (or data) page by creating a clustered index with the default fill factor:

```
CREATE CLUSTERED INDEX i1 ON t1(c1)
```

Since the average row size is 1,004 bytes, a clustered index leaf page (or table data page) can contain a maximum of eight rows. Therefore, at least three leaf pages are required for the 24 rows. You can confirm this in the following DBCC SHOWCONTIG(t1, i1) partial output:

```
DBCC SHOWCONTIG scanning 't1' table...
Table: 't1' (489768802); index ID: 1, database ID: 7
TABLE level scan performed.
- Pages Scanned................................: 3
...
- Avg. Bytes Free per Page.....................: 0.0
- Avg. Page Density (full)....................: 100.00%
```

Note that Avg. Page Density (full) is 100%, since the default fill factor allows the maximum number of rows to be compressed in a page. Since a page cannot contain a part row to fill the page fully, Avg. Page Density (full) will be often a little less than 100%, even with the default fill factor.

To prevent page splits caused by INSERT and UPDATE operations, create some free space within the leaf (or data) pages by re-creating the clustered index with fill factor as follows:

```
DROP INDEX t1.i1
CREATE CLUSTERED INDEX i1 ON t1(c1) WITH FILLFACTOR=75
```

As each page has a total space for eight rows, a fill factor of 75% will allow six rows per page. Thus, for 24 rows, the number of leaf pages should increase to four, as shown in the following DBCC SHOWCONTIG(t1, i1) output:

```
DBCC SHOWCONTIG scanning 't1' table...
Table: 't1' (489768802); index ID: 1, database ID: 7
TABLE level scan performed.
- Pages Scanned................................: 4
...
```

```
- Avg. Bytes Free per Page.....................: 2024.0
- Avg. Page Density (full)....................: 74.99%
```

Note that `Avg. Page Density (full)` is around 75%, as set by the fill factor. This allows two more rows to be inserted in each page without causing a page split. You can confirm this by adding two rows to the first set of six rows ($c_1 = 100 - 600$, contained in the first page):

```
INSERT INTO t1 VALUES(110, 'a') --25th row
INSERT INTO t1 VALUES(120, 'a') --26th row
```

The resultant `DBCC SHOWCONTIG(t1, i1)` output is as follows:

```
DBCC SHOWCONTIG scanning 't1' table...
Table: 't1' (489768802); index ID: 1, database ID: 7
TABLE level scan performed.
- Pages Scanned................................: 4
...
- Avg. Bytes Free per Page.....................: 1518.0
- Avg. Page Density (full)....................: 81.25%
```

From the output, you can see that the addition of the two rows has not added any pages to the index. Accordingly, `Avg. Page Density (full)` increased from 74.99% to 81.25%. With the addition of two rows to the set of first six rows, the first page should be completely full (eight rows). Any further addition of rows within the range of the first eight rows should cause a page split and thereby increase the number of index pages to five:

```
INSERT INTO t1 VALUES(130, 'a') --27th row
```

The resultant `DBCC SHOWCONTIG(t1, i1)` output is as follows:

```
DBCC SHOWCONTIG scanning 't1' table...
Table: 't1' (489768802); index ID: 1, database ID: 7
TABLE level scan performed.
- Pages Scanned................................: 5
...
- Avg. Bytes Free per Page.....................: 2631.2
- Avg. Page Density (full)....................: 67.49%
```

Note that even though the fill factor for the index is 75%, `Avg. Page Density (full)` has decreased to 67.49%, which can be computed as follows:

$$\text{Avg. Page Density (full)}$$
$$= \textbf{Average rows per page / Maximum rows per page}$$
$$= (27 / 5) / 8$$
$$= 67.5\%$$

From the preceding example, you can see that the fill factor is applied when the index is created. But later, as the data is modified, it has no significance. Irrespective of the fill factor, whenever a page splits, the rows of the original page are distributed between two pages, and `Avg. Page Density (full)` settles accordingly. Therefore, if you use a nondefault fill factor, you should ensure that the fill factor is reapplied regularly to maintain its effect.

You can reapply a fill factor by re-creating the index as shown previously, or by using DBCC INDEXDEFRAG or DBCC DBREINDEX. DBCC INDEXDEFRAG takes the fill factor specified during the index creation into account. DBCC DBREINDEX also takes the original fill factor into account, but it allows a new fill factor to be specified, if required. To reapply the fill factor specified during the index creation using DBCC DBREINDEX, use this statement:

```
DBCC DBREINDEX(t1, i1, 0)
```

To override the original fill factor, to, say, 80%, execute DBCC DBREINDEX:

```
DBCC DBREINDEX(t1, i1, 80)
```

Without periodic maintenance of the fill factor, for both default and nondefault fill factor settings, Avg. Page Density (full) for an index (or table) eventually settles within a narrow range. Therefore, in most cases, without manual maintenance of the fill factor, the default fill factor is generally good enough.

You should also consider one final aspect when deciding upon the fill factor. Even for a heavy OLTP application, the number of database reads typically outnumbers writes by a factor of 5 to 10. Specifying a fill factor other than the default can degrade read performance by an amount inversely proportional to the fill factor setting, since it spreads keys over a wider area. Before setting the fill factor at a databasewide level, use Performance Monitor to compare the SQL Server:Buffer Manager\Page reads/sec counter to the SQL Server:Buffer Manager\Page writes/sec counter, and use the fill factor option only if writes are a substantial fraction of reads (>30%).

Automatic Maintenance

In a database with a great deal of transactions, tables and indexes become fragmented over time. Thus, to improve performance, you should check the fragmentation of the tables and indexes regularly, and you should defragment the ones with a high amount of fragmentation. You can do this analysis for a database by following these steps:

1. Identify all user tables in the current database to analyze fragmentation.

2. Determine fragmentation of every user table and index.

3. Determine user tables and indexes that require defragmentation by taking into account the following considerations:

   • Low contiguous distribution of pages across extents—that is, Scan Density [Best Count:Actual Count] < 40%

   • Large number of out-of-order pages—that is, Logical Scan Fragmentation > 10%

   • Not a very small table/index—that is, Pages Scanned > 8

4. Defragment tables and indexes with high fragmentation.

A sample SQL stored procedure (sp_FragmentationAnalysis.sql in the download) is included here for easy reference. It performs the following actions:

- Identifies all user tables in the current database and saves them in a temporary table

- Analyzes the fragmentation of the table and all its indexes for every user table identified

- Determines user tables and indexes containing a high amount of fragmentation by taking into account the considerations listed previously

- Defragments the highly fragmented tables and indexes identified

Here's how to analyze and resolve database fragmentation:

```
IF(SELECT OBJECT_ID('sp_FragmentationAnalysis')) IS NOT NULL
  DROP PROC sp_FragmentationAnalysis
GO
CREATE PROC sp_FragmentationAnalysis
AS

SET NOCOUNT ON

--Create temporary table to hold DBCC SHOWCONTIG output
CREATE TABLE #FragmentationResult(
ObjectName VARCHAR(255), ObjectId INT, IndexName VARCHAR(255)
, IndexId INT, [Level] INT, Pages INT, [Rows] INT
, MinimumRecordSize INT, MaximumRecordSize INT
, AverageRecordSize FLOAT, ForwardedRecords INT, Extents INT
, ExtentSwitches INT, AverageFreeBytes FLOAT
, AveragePageDensity FLOAT, ScanDensity FLOAT, BestCount INT
, ActualCount INT, LogicalFragmentation FLOAT
, ExtentFragmentation FLOAT
)

--Create temporary table to hold tables/indexes that require
-- defragmentation
CREATE TABLE #Defragmentation(
[id] INT IDENTITY
, ObjectName VARCHAR(255)
, IndexName VARCHAR(255)
, ScanDensity FLOAT
)

--Identify all user tables in the current database to analyze
-- fragmentation
SELECT [id], [name] INTO #UserTables
  FROM sysobjects
  WHERE type = 'U'
  ORDER BY [id]
```

```
--Determine fragmentation of every user table/index
DECLARE @id INT, @name VARCHAR(255), @TableCnt INT
SET @id = 0
SELECT @TableCnt = COUNT(*) FROM #UserTables
WHILE @TableCnt > 0
BEGIN
  SELECT TOP 1 @id=[id], @name=[name]
    FROM #UserTables
    WHERE [id] > @id
  INSERT INTO #FragmentationResult
    EXEC('DBCC SHOWCONTIG([' + @name + '])
      WITH ALL_INDEXES, TABLERESULTS')
  SET @TableCnt = @TableCnt - 1
END

--Determine user tables/indexes that require defragmentation
INSERT INTO #Defragmentation
  SELECT ObjectName, IndexName, ScanDensity
    FROM #FragmentationResult
    WHERE ScanDensity < 40 --Scan Density is low
      AND LogicalFragmentation > 10 --Logical Scan Fragmentation is high
      AND PAGES > 8 --Not a very small table
DROP TABLE #FragmentationResult

--Defragment tables/indexes with high fragmentation
DECLARE @oname VARCHAR(255), @iname VARCHAR(255), @sdensity FLOAT
SET @id = 0
SELECT @TableCnt = COUNT(*) FROM #Defragmentation
WHILE @TableCnt > 0
BEGIN
  SELECT TOP 1 @id=[id]
    , @oname = ObjectName
    , @iname = IndexName
    , @sdensity = ScanDensity
    FROM #Defragmentation
    WHERE [id] > @id
  PRINT '** De-fragmentation #' + CAST(@id AS VARCHAR(15))+ ' **'
  PRINT 'DBCC DBREINDEX on [' + @oname + '].[' +  @iname
    + '] with ScanDensity = ' + CAST(@sdensity AS VARCHAR(15)) + '%'
  DBCC DBREINDEX(@oname, @iname)
  SET @TableCnt = @TableCnt - 1
END

--Release resources
DROP TABLE #UserTables
DROP TABLE #Defragmentation

SET NOCOUNT OFF
GO
```

To automate the fragmentation analysis process, you can create a SQL Server job from SQL Server Enterprise Manager by following these simple steps:

1. Open Enterprise Manager and select New Job from *ServerName* ➤ Management ➤ SQL Server Agent ➤ Jobs ➤ New Job.

2. On the General tab of the New Job Properties dialog box, enter the job name and other details, as shown in Figure 8-7.

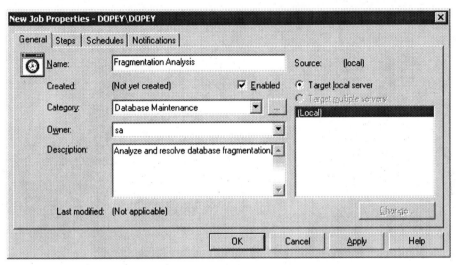

Figure 8-7. *Entering the job name and details*

3. On the Steps tab of the New Job Properties dialog box, click New and enter the SQL command for the user database, as shown in Figure 8-8.

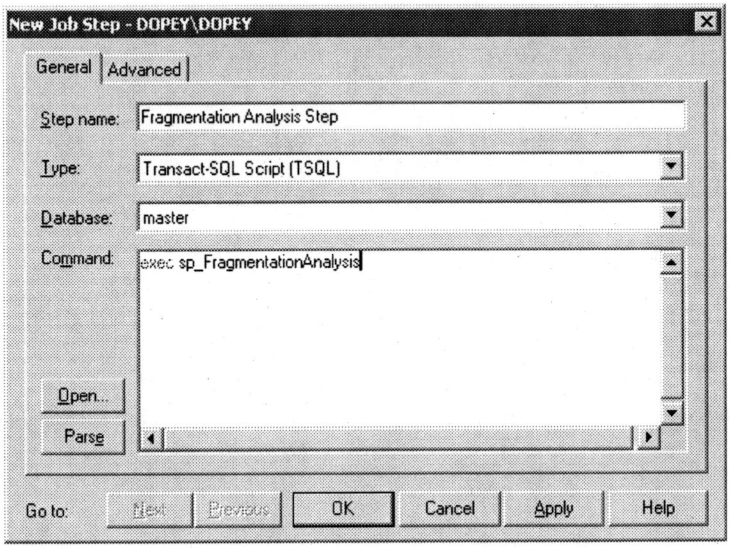

Figure 8-8. *Entering the SQL command for the user database*

4. On the Advanced tab of the New Job Step dialog box, enter an output filename to report the fragmentation analysis outcome, as shown in Figure 8-9.

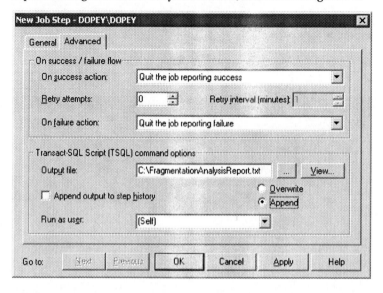

Figure 8-9. *Entering an output filename*

5. Return to the New Job Properties dialog box by clicking OK.

6. On the Schedules tab of the New Job Properties dialog box, click New Schedule and enter an appropriate schedule to run the SQL Server job, as shown in Figure 8-10.

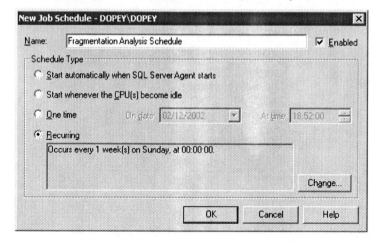

Figure 8-10. *Entering a job schedule*

Schedule this stored procedure to execute during nonpeak hours. Database applications often have a nonpeak load around midnight. To be certain about the usage pattern of your database, log the SQLServer:SQL Statistics\Batch Requests/sec performance counter for a complete day. It will show you the fluctuation in load on the database. This performance counter is explained in Chapter 2.

7. Return to the New Job Properties dialog box by clicking the OK button.

8. Once you've entered all the information, click OK in the New Job Properties dialog box to create the SQL Server job. A SQL Server job is created that schedules the sp_FragmentationAnalysis stored procedure to run at a regular (weekly) time interval.

9. Ensure that SQL Server Agent is running so that the SQL Server job will run automatically according to the set schedule.

The SQL job will automatically analyze and defragment the fragmentation of the user database every Sunday at 00:00:00 a.m. For example, if the Northwind database contains the fragmented table t1 created in the earlier "Fragmentation Overhead" section, then the SQL job created for the Northwind database analyzes the fragmentation of the database, including that of table t1. Figure 8-11 shows the corresponding output of the C:\FragmentationAnalysisReport.txt file.

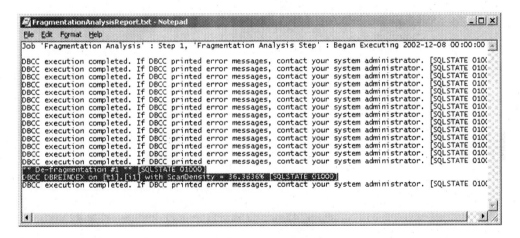

Figure 8-11. *C:\FragmentationAnalysisReport.txt file output*

The output shows that the job analyzed the fragmentation of the database and identified index [t1].[i1] for defragmentation. Subsequently, it defragments index [t1].[i1]. The stored procedure defragmented only the database object that was highly fragmented. Thus, the next run of the SQL job won't identify index [t1].[i1] for defragmentation.

Summary

As you learned in this chapter, in a highly transactional database, page splits caused by INSERT and UPDATE statements fragment the tables and indexes, increasing the cost of data retrieval. You can avoid these page splits by maintaining free spaces within the pages using the fill factor. Since the fill factor is applied only during index creation, you should reapply it at regular intervals to maintain its effectiveness. You can determine the amount of fragmentation in an index (or table) using DBCC SHOWCONTIG. Upon determining a high amount of fragmentation, you can use either DBCC DBREINDEX or DBCC INDEXDEFRAG, depending on the required amount of defragmentation and database concurrency.

Defragmentation rearranges the data so that its physical order on the disk matches its logical order in the table/index, thus improving the performance of queries. However, unless the optimizer decides upon an effective execution plan for the query, query performance even after defragmentation can remain poor. Therefore, it is important that the optimizer use efficient techniques to generate cost-effective execution plans.

In the next chapter, I will delve deeply into execution plan generation and the techniques the optimizer uses to decide upon an effective execution plan.

■ ■ ■

CHAPTER 9

Execution Plan Cache Analysis

The performance of any query depends on the effectiveness of the execution plan decided upon by the optimizer, as you have seen in previous chapters. As the overall time required to execute a query is the sum of the time required to generate the execution plan plus the time required to execute the query based on this execution plan, it is important that the cost of generating the execution plan itself is low. The cost incurred in the generation of the execution plan depends on the process of generating the execution plan, the process of caching the plan, and the reusability of the plan from the plan cache. In this chapter, you will learn how an execution plan is generated and how to analyze the execution plan cache for plan reusability.

In this chapter, I cover the following topics:

- Execution plan generation and caching

- The SQL Server components used to generate an execution plan

- Strategies to optimize the cost of execution plan generation

- Factors affecting parallel plan generation

- An execution plan caching technique

- How to analyze execution plan caching

- Ways to improve the reusability of execution plan caching

Execution Plan Generation

As you know by now, SQL Server uses a cost-based optimization technique to determine the processing strategy of a query. The optimizer takes both the metadata of the database objects and the current distribution statistics of the columns referred to in the query into consideration, to decide which index and join strategies should be used.

In general, the processing strategy chosen by the optimizer for a query is not governed by the exact syntax of the query. For instance, a query may be written in different forms using a different order of tables in the FROM clause and order of filter criteria in the WHERE clause. The cost-based optimizer resolves the syntactical differences and generates the same processing strategy for the different syntaxes of the query.

In the following example (syntax_order.sql in the download), you can see that you can use any order of tables in the FROM clause or any order of filter criteria in the WHERE clause, and the optimizer arrives at the same execution plan (see Figure 9-1):

```
USE Northwind

SELECT * FROM [Order Details] od, Orders o
  WHERE od.OrderID = o.OrderID AND o.CustomerID = 'QUICK'

SELECT * FROM Orders o, [Order Details] od
  WHERE o.CustomerID = 'QUICK' AND o.OrderID = od.OrderID
```

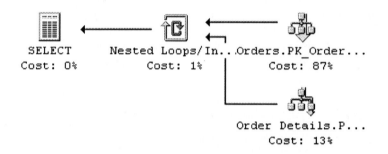

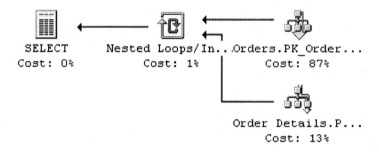

Figure 9-1. *Execution plan shows that the query optimization is independent of query syntax*

▓**TIP** The examples in this chapter use the `Northwind` database. Make sure your version of the database has not been heavily modified, so that you get the same results. If required, you can reinstall your Northwind database by following these steps:

1. At the command prompt, change to the directory `<Directory of SQL Server installation>\ Install`. For example, the default directory of the SQL Server installation is `C:\Program Files\ Microsoft SQL Server\MSSQL`.

2. Use the `osql` utility to run the `instnwnd.sql` script:

   `osql /Usa /Ppassword /Sservername /iinstnwnd.sql /oinstnwnd.rpt`

3. Check `instnwnd.rpt` for reported errors.

The cost-based optimization allows a database developer to concentrate on implementing a business rule, rather than on the exact syntax of the query. At the same time, the process of determining the query processing strategy remains quite complex and can consume a fair amount of resources. SQL Server uses a number of different techniques to optimize resource consumption:

- Syntax-based optimization of the query

- Trivial plan match to avoid in-depth query optimization for simple queries

- Index and join strategies based on current distribution statistics

- Query optimization in multiple phases to control the cost of optimization

- Execution plan caching to avoid the regeneration of query plans

The following techniques are performed in order, as shown in the flowchart in Figure 9-2:

- Command parsing

- Normalization

- Optimization

- Execution plan generation and caching

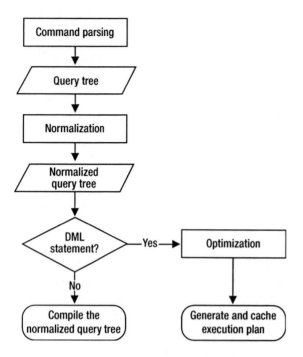

Figure 9-2. *SQL Server techniques to optimize query execution*

Let's take a look at these steps in more detail.

Command Parsing

When a query is submitted, SQL Server passes it to the command processor part of the *relational engine*. (This relational engine is one of the two main parts of SQL Server, with the other being the *storage engine*, which is responsible for data access, modifications, and caching.) The relational engine takes care of command parsing, normalization, and optimization. It also executes a query as per the query execution plan and requests data from the storage engine. The main communication between the relational and storage engines is through OLE DB.

The command parser parses an incoming query, validating it for correct syntax. The query is terminated if a syntax error is detected. If multiple queries are submitted together as a batch as follows (note the error in syntax):

```
CREATE TABLE t1(c1 INT)
INSERT INTO t1 VALUES(1)
CEILEKT * FROM t1 --Error: I meant, SELECT * FROM t1
GO
```

then the command parser parses the complete batch together for syntax and cancels the complete batch on detecting a syntax error. (Note that there may be more than one syntax error in a batch, but the parser goes no further than the first one.) On validating a query for correct syntax, the command parser generates an internal data structure called a *query tree*, for normalization. The command parsing and normalization taken together are called *query compilation.*

Normalization

The query tree generated by the command parser is passed to the query optimizer (which is part of the relational engine) for the *normalization* process. During this process, the optimizer breaks down the query into smaller steps, binding the steps to the database objects. If a batch query is submitted, then the optimizer normalizes the individual queries until it discovers that the database object referred to by a query is missing. The queries normalized up to this point are processed further, whereas the error query and the ones below it are canceled.

For example, if the following batch query (normal_test.sql in the download) is submitted:

```
CREATE TABLE t1(c1 INT)
INSERT INTO t1 VALUES(1)
SELECT 'Before Error', c1 FROM t1
SELECT 'Error',c1 FROM No_t1 --Error: Table doesn't exist
SELECT 'After Error', c1 FROM t1
GO
```

then the first three statements before the error statement are executed, and the errant statement and the one after it are canceled.

The normalization process replaces the database views referred to in a query with the definition of the views. A *database view* is a virtual table that represents the data in one or more tables in an alternative way. You can create it using the CREATE VIEW statement as follows:

```
IF(SELECT OBJECT_ID('vwShippedOrders')) IS NOT NULL
  DROP VIEW vwShippedOrders
GO
CREATE VIEW vwShippedOrders(OrderID, CustomerID, ShippedDate, ShipAddress)
AS
SELECT OrderID, CustomerID, ShippedDate
  , ISNULL(ShipAddress+', ','') + ISNULL(ShipCity+', ','') +
    ISNULL(ShipRegion+' ','') + ISNULL(ShipPostalCode+', ','') +
    ISNULL(ShipCountry,'')
  FROM Orders
  WHERE ShippedDate IS NOT NULL
```

You may refer to this database view in a query as follows:

```
SELECT * FROM vwShippedOrders
```

If a query contains an implicit data conversion, then the normalization process adds an appropriate step to the query tree. The process also performs some syntax-based optimization. For example, if the following query (syntax_optimize.sql in the download) is submitted:

```
USE Northwind
SELECT * FROM [Order Details] od
  WHERE od.OrderID BETWEEN 10200 AND 10250
```

then the syntax-based optimization transforms the syntax of the query as shown in Figure 9-3.

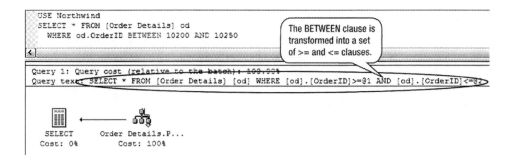

Figure 9-3. *Syntax-based optimization*

For most Data Definition Language (DDL) statements (such as CREATE TABLE, CREATE PROC, etc.), after normalization the query is compiled directly for execution, since the optimizer need not choose among multiple processing strategies. For one DDL statement in particular, CREATE INDEX, an efficient processing strategy can be determined by the optimizer based on other existing indexes on the table, as explained in Chapter 4.

For this reason, you will never see any reference to CREATE TABLE in an execution plan, although you will see reference to CREATE INDEX. If the normalized query is a Data Manipulation Language (DML) statement (such as SELECT, INSERT, UPDATE, or DELETE), then the normalized query tree is passed to the optimizer to decide the processing strategy for the query.

Optimization

Based on the complexity of a query, including the number of tables referred to and the indexes available, there may be several ways to execute the query contained in the query tree. Exhaustively comparing the cost of all the ways of executing a query can take a considerable amount of time, which may sometimes override the benefit of finding the most optimized query. Figure 9-4 shows that, to avoid a high optimization overhead compared to the actual execution cost of the query, the optimizer adopts three or four different techniques, namely:

- Trivial plan match

- Query simplification

- Multiple optimization phases

- Parallel plan optimization

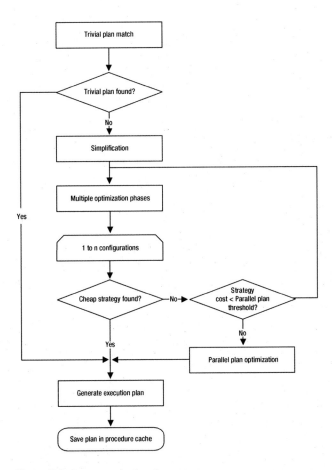

Figure 9-4. *Query optimization steps*

Trivial Plan Match

Sometimes there might be only one way to execute a query. For example, a heap table with no indexes can be accessed in only one way: via a table scan. To avoid the runtime overhead of optimizing such queries, SQL Server maintains a list of trivial plans to choose from. If the optimizer finds a match, then a similar plan is generated for the query without any optimization.

Query Simplification

Usually, there will be multiple ways of executing a query. Therefore, the optimizer needs to evaluate the different processing strategies for the query. Before determining the processing strategies, the optimizer simplifies the query by rearranging the query constructs and operations without affecting the query logic. For example, consider the following query (`simplification.sql` in the download):

```
USE Northwind
SELECT * FROM [Order Details] od, Orders o
  WHERE od.OrderID = o.OrderID AND od.OrderID = 11077
```

Since, as per the commutative theory of mathematics, if a = b and b = c, then a = c, the simplification process can consider od.OrderID = 11077 from the preceding code to be equivalent to o.OrderID = 11077. o.OrderID = 11077 returns only one row compared to the 25 rows returned by od.OrderID = 11077. Figure 9-5 shows this simplification of the query in the detailed graphical execution plan.

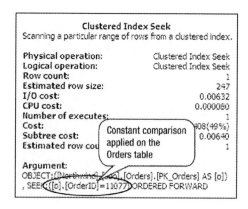

Figure 9-5. *Query simplification in action*

Multiple Optimization Phases

For a complex query, the number of alternative processing strategies to be analyzed can be very high, and it may take a long time to evaluate each option. Therefore, instead of analyzing all the possible processing strategies together, the optimizer breaks them into multiple configurations, each consisting of different index and join techniques.

The index variations consider different indexing aspects, such as single-column index, composite index, index column order, column density, and so forth. Similarly, the join variations consider the different join techniques available in SQL Server: nested loop join, merge join, and hash join. (Chapter 3 covers these join techniques in detail.)

The optimizer considers the statistics of the columns referred to in the WHERE clause to evaluate the effectiveness of the index and the join strategies. Based on the current statistics, it evaluates the cost of the configurations in multiple optimization phases. The cost includes many factors, including (but not limited to) usage of CPU, memory, and disk I/O required to execute the query. After each optimization phase, the optimizer evaluates the cost of the processing strategy. If the cost is found to be cheap enough, then the optimizer stops further iteration through the optimization phases and quits the optimization process. Otherwise, it keeps iterating through the optimization phases to determine a cost-effective processing strategy.

Sometimes a query can be so complex that the optimizer needs to extensively iterate through the optimization phases. While optimizing the query, if it finds that the cost of the processing strategy is more than the cost threshold for parallelism, then it evaluates the cost of processing the query using multiple CPUs. Otherwise, the optimizer proceeds with the serial plan.

Parallel Plan Optimization

The optimizer considers various factors while evaluating the cost of processing a query using a parallel plan. Some of these factors are as follows:

- Number of CPUs available to SQL Server

- SQL Server edition

- Available memory

- Type of query being executed

- Number of rows to be processed in a given stream

- Number of active concurrent connections

If only one CPU is available to SQL Server, then the optimizer won't consider a parallel plan. The number of CPUs available to SQL Server can be restricted using the *affinity mask* setting of the SQL Server configuration. The affinity mask value is a bitmap in which a bit represents a CPU, with the rightmost bit position representing CPU0. For example, to allow SQL Server to use only CPU0 to CPU3 in an 8-way box, execute these statements (affinity_mask.sql in the download):

```
USE master
EXEC sp_configure 'show advanced option', '1'
RECONFIGURE
EXEC sp_configure 'affinity mask', 15 --Bit map: 00001111
RECONFIGURE
```

This configuration takes effect after the server restart. affinity mask is a special setting, and it is recommended that you keep it at its default value of 0, which allows SQL Server to use all the available CPUs in the system based on the operating system and the SQL Server edition.

Even if multiple CPUs are available to SQL Server, if an individual query is not allowed to use more than one CPU for execution, then the optimizer discards the parallel plan option. The maximum number of CPUs that can be used for a parallel query is governed by the max degree of parallelism setting of the SQL Server configuration. The default value is 0, which allows all the CPUs (availed by the affinity mask setting) to be used for a parallel query. If you want to allow parallel queries to use no more than two CPUs out of CPU0 to CPU3, limited by the preceding affinity mask setting, execute the following statements (parallelism.sql in the download):

```
USE master
EXEC sp_configure 'show advanced option', '1'
RECONFIGURE
EXEC sp_configure 'max degree of parallelism', 2
RECONFIGURE
```

This change takes effect immediately, without any restart. The max degree of parallelism setting can also be controlled at a query level using the MAXDOP query hint:

```
SELECT * FROM t1 WHERE c1 = 1 OPTION(MAXDOP 2)
```

Generally, it is recommended that you leave this setting at its default value, allowing parallel queries to benefit from all available CPUs.

Since parallel queries require more memory, the optimizer determines the amount of memory available before choosing a parallel plan. The amount of memory required increases with the degree of parallelism. If the memory requirement of the parallel plan for a given degree of parallelism cannot be satisfied, then SQL Server decreases the degree of parallelism automatically or completely abandons the parallel plan for the query in the given workload context.

Queries with a very high CPU overhead are the best candidates for a parallel plan. Examples include joining large tables, performing substantial aggregations, and sorting large result sets. For simple queries usually found in transaction-processing applications, the additional coordination required to initialize, synchronize, and terminate a parallel plan outweighs the potential performance benefit.

Whether or not a query is simple is determined by comparing the estimated execution time of the query with a cost threshold. This cost threshold is controlled by the cost threshold for parallelism setting of the SQL Server configuration. By default, this setting's value is 5, which means that if the estimated execution time of the serial plan is more than 5 seconds, then the optimizer considers a parallel plan for the query. For example, to modify the cost threshold to 6 seconds, execute the following statements (parallelism_threshold.sql in the download):

```
USE master
EXEC sp_configure 'show advanced option', '1'
RECONFIGURE
EXEC sp_configure 'cost threshold for parallelism', 6
RECONFIGURE
```

This change takes effect immediately, without any restart. If only one CPU is available to SQL Server, then this setting is ignored.

The DML action queries (INSERT, UPDATE, and DELETE) are executed serially. However, the SELECT portion of an INSERT statement and the WHERE clause of an UPDATE or DELETE statement can be executed in parallel. The actual data changes are applied serially to the database. Also, if the optimizer determines that the number of rows affected is too low, it does not introduce parallel operators.

Note that, even at execution time, SQL Server determines whether the current system workload and configuration information allow for parallel query execution. If parallel query execution is allowed, SQL Server determines the optimal number of threads and spreads the execution of the query across those threads. When a query starts a parallel execution, it uses the same number of threads until completion. SQL Server re-examines the optimal number of threads before executing the parallel query the next time.

Once the processing strategy is finalized by using either a serial plan or a parallel plan, the optimizer generates the execution plan for the query. The execution plan contains the detailed processing strategy decided by the optimizer to execute the query. This includes steps such as data retrieval, result set joins, result set ordering, and so on. A detailed explanation of how to analyze the processing steps included in an execution plan is presented in Chapter 3. The execution plan generated for the query is saved in the plan cache for future reuse.

Execution Plan Caching

The execution plan of a query generated by the optimizer is saved in a special part of SQL Server's memory pool called the *plan cache* or *procedure cache*. (The procedure cache is a part of the SQL Server buffer cache and is explained in Chapter 2.) Saving the plan in a cache allows SQL Server to avoid running through the whole query optimization process again when the same query is resubmitted. SQL Server supports different techniques such as *plan cache aging* and *plan cache types* to increase the reusability of the cached plans.

▓**NOTE** I discuss the techniques supported by SQL Server for improving the effectiveness of execution plan reuse later in this chapter.

▓**TIP** On restarting, SQL Server flushes the procedure cache, requiring regeneration of the execution plans. That's probably a good enough reason not to restart your production server every morning!

Components of the Execution Plan

The execution plan generated by the optimizer contains two components:

- *Query plan*: This represents the commands that specify all the physical operations required to execute a query.

- *Execution context*: This maintains the variable parts of a query.

I will cover these components in more detail in the next sections.

Query Plan

The query plan is a re-entrant, read-only data structure, with commands that specify all the physical operations required to execute the query. The re-entrant property allows the query plan to be accessed concurrently by multiple connections. The physical operations include specifications on which tables and indexes to access, how and in what order they should be accessed, the type of join operations to be performed between multiple tables, and so forth. No user context is stored in the query plan. For a single query, there can be two copies of the query plan: the serial plan and the parallel plan (regardless of the degree of parallelism).

Execution Context

The execution context is another data structure that maintains the variable part of the query. While the server keeps track of the execution plans in the procedure cache, these plans are context neutral. Therefore, each user executing the query will have a separate execution context that holds data specific to their execution, such as parameter values and connection details.

Aging of the Execution Plan

The procedure cache is a part of SQL Server's buffer cache, which also holds data pages. As new execution plans are added to the procedure cache, the size of the procedure cache keeps growing, affecting the retention of useful data pages in memory. To avoid this, SQL Server dynamically controls the retention of the execution plans in the procedure cache, retaining the frequently used execution plans and discarding plans that are not used for a certain period of time.

SQL Server keeps track of the frequency of an execution plan reuse by associating an age field to it. When an execution plan is generated, the age field is populated with the cost of generating the plan. A complex query requiring extensive optimization will have an age field value higher than that for a simpler query.

At regular intervals, the age fields of all the execution plans in the procedure cache are decremented by SQL Server's lazy writer process (which manages most of the background processes in SQL Server). If an execution plan is not reused for a long time, then the age field will eventually be reduced to 0. The cheaper the execution plan was to generate, the sooner its age field will be reduced to 0. Once an execution plan's age field reaches 0, the plan becomes a candidate for removal from memory. SQL Server removes all plans with an age field of 0 from the procedure cache when memory pressure increases to such an extent that there is no longer enough free memory to serve new requests. However, if a system has enough memory, and free memory pages are available to serve new requests, execution plans with an age field of 0 can remain in the procedure cache for a long time so that they can be reused later, if required.

As well as aging, execution plans can also find their age field incremented by the cost of generating the plan, every time the plan is reused. For example, suppose you have two execution plans with generation costs equal to 100 and 10. Their starting age field values will therefore be 100 and 10, respectively. If both execution plans are reused immediately, their age fields will be incremented to 200 and 20, respectively. With these age field values, the lazy writer will bring down the cost of the second plan to 0 much earlier than that of the first one, unless the second plan is reused more often. Therefore, even if a costly plan is reused less frequently than a cheaper plan, due to the effect of the cost on the age field, the costly plan can remain at a nonzero age value for a longer period of time.

Analyzing the Execution Plan Cache

You can obtain a lot of information about the execution plans in the procedure cache by accessing the system table `syscacheobjects`:

`SELECT * FROM master.dbo.syscacheobjects`

This is a virtual system table that is formed when accessed and is available in the master database only. Table 9-1 shows some of the useful information provided by `syscacheobjects` (this is easier to read in Grid view).

Table 9-1. *syscacheobjects*

Column Name	Description
sql	Query or object for which an execution plan is saved.
usecounts	Number of times the plan is reused.
bucketid	Entry in an internal hash table to locate the plan. Rows with same bucketid refer to the plan for the same query or object.
cacheobjtype	Type of plan. A *compiled plan* is an execution plan generated by the optimizer. An *executable plan* is the execution environment in which to run the compiled plan. For every executable plan, there must be a compiled plan with the same bucketid. Reusing the executable plan saves the time required to create the execution environment in which to run the compiled plan.
objtype	Type of query or object for which the execution plan is saved: Adhoc: Queries that don't fall under the Prepared or Proc categories Prepared: Queries auto-parameterized by SQL Server or submitted using sp_executesql Proc: Stored procedures or inline functions
objid	For objtype = Proc, it identifies the object in sysobjects system table. For Adhoc and Prepared, it's an internally generated value.
dbid	Database in which the plan was compiled.
uid	USER_ID for whom the plan was compiled. uid = -2 means the plan can be used by any user.
setopts	SET statements that were in effect when the plan was compiled.
langid	Language ID that was in effect when the plan was compiled.
dateformat	Date format that was in effect when the plan was compiled.

In the next section, you will look at the output of `syscacheobjects` to evaluate the reusability of execution plan.

Execution Plan Reuse

When a query is submitted, SQL Server checks the procedure cache for a matching execution plan. If one is not found, then SQL Server performs the query compilation and optimization to generate a new execution plan. However, if the plan exists in the procedure cache, it is reused with the private execution context. This saves the CPU cycles that otherwise would have been spent on the plan generation.

Queries are submitted to SQL Server with filter criteria to limit the size of the result set. The same queries are often resubmitted with different values for the filter criteria. For example, consider the following query:

```
USE Northwind

SELECT * FROM [Order Details] d, Orders o
WHERE d.OrderID = o.OrderID
AND d.ProductID = 1
```

When this query is submitted, the optimizer creates an execution plan and saves it in the procedure cache to reuse in the future. If this query is resubmitted with a different filter criterion value—for example, d.ProductID = 2—it will be beneficial to reuse the existing execution plan for the previously supplied filter criterion value. But whether the execution plan created for one filter criterion value can be reused for another filter criterion value depends on how the query is submitted to SQL Server.

The queries (or workload) submitted to SQL Server can be broadly classified under two categories that determine whether the execution plan will be reusable as the value of the variable parts of the query changes:

- Ad hoc

- Well-defined

Ad Hoc Workload

Queries can be submitted to SQL Server without explicitly isolating the variables from the query. These types of queries executed without explicitly converting the variable parts of the query into parameters are referred to as *ad hoc workloads* (or queries). For example, consider this query:

```
SELECT * FROM [Order Details] d, Orders o
  WHERE d.OrderID = o.OrderID
  AND d.ProductID = 1
```

If the query is submitted as is, without explicitly converting the variable value 1 to a parameter (that can be supplied to the query when executed), then the query is referred to as an ad hoc query.

In this query, the filter criterion value is embedded in the query itself and is not explicitly parameterized to isolate it from the query. This means that you cannot reuse the execution plan for this query unless you use exactly the same variable. However, the variable parts of the queries can be explicitly parameterized in three different ways that are jointly categorized as a well-defined workload.

Well-Defined Workload

Well-defined workloads (or queries) explicitly parameterize the variable parts of the query so that the query plan isn't tied to the value of the variable parts. In SQL Server, queries can be submitted as well-defined workloads using the following three methods:

- *Stored procedures*: Allows saving a collection of SQL statements that can accept and return user-supplied parameters

- sp_executesql: Allows executing a SQL statement or a SQL batch that may contain user-supplied parameters, without saving the SQL statement or batch

- *Prepare/execute model*: Allows a SQL client to request the generation of a query plan that can be reused during subsequent executions of the query with different parameter values, without saving the SQL statement(s) in SQL Server

For example, the SELECT statement shown previously can be explicitly parameterized using a stored procedure as follows (parameterized.sql in the download):

```
IF(SELECT OBJECT_ID('p1')) IS NOT NULL
  DROP PROC p1
GO
CREATE PROC p1
@ProductID INT
AS
  SELECT * FROM [Order Details] d, Orders o
  WHERE d.OrderID = o.OrderID
  AND d.ProductID = @ProductID
GO
```

The plan of the SELECT statement included within the stored procedure will embed the parameter @ProductID, not a variable value. I will cover these methods in more detail shortly.

Plan Reusability of an Ad Hoc Workload

When a query is submitted as an ad hoc workload, SQL Server generates the execution plan and decides whether or not to cache the plan, based upon the cost of generating the execution plan. If the cost of generating the execution plan is very cheap, then SQL Server may not cache the plan to conserve the size of the procedure cache based on the resources available. Instead of flooding the procedure cache with cheap ad hoc queries, SQL Server regenerates the execution plan when the query is resubmitted.

For ad hoc queries with higher execution plan generation costs, SQL Server saves the execution plan in the procedure cache. The values of the variable parts of an ad hoc query are included in the query plan and are not saved separately in the execution context, meaning that you cannot reuse the execution plan for this query unless you use exactly the same variable as you have seen.

To understand this, consider the following ad hoc query (adhoc1.sql in the download):

```
USE Northwind

SELECT * FROM [Order Details] d, Orders o
  WHERE d.OrderID=o.OrderID AND d.ProductID=1
```

The execution plan generated for this ad hoc query is based on the exact text of the query. You can see this by accessing the syscacheobjects system table (syscacheobjects.sql in the download):

```
SELECT sql, usecounts, cacheobjtype, objtype
FROM master.dbo.syscacheobjects
```

■ **TIP** To easily test the output of syscacheobjects for this chapter, you can flush the cached plans in a test environment by executing DBCC FREEPROCCACHE. However, do not execute this command on a production server. Flushing the procedure cache requires all plans to be regenerated as the queries are re-executed, which can significantly degrade performance.

Figure 9-6 shows the output of syscacheobjects.

	sql	usecounts	cacheobjtype	objtype
1	SELECT * FROM [Order Details] d, Orders o WHERE d.OrderID=o.OrderID AND ProductID=1	1	Executable Plan	Adhoc
2	SELECT * FROM [Order Details] d, Orders o WHERE d.OrderID=o.OrderID AND ProductID=1	1	Compiled Plan	Adhoc
3	()SELECT [sql]=[sql],[usecounts]=[usecounts],[cacheobjtype]=[cacheobjtype],[objtype]...	2	Compiled Plan	Prepared

Figure 9-6. *syscacheobjects output*

You can see from Figure 9-6 that a compiled plan is generated and saved in the procedure cache for the preceding ad hoc query. Note that the query (in the sql column) for which the compiled plan is generated is based on the exact text of the query, including the filter criteria value. A corresponding executable plan is also generated for this query and has been used once up until now (usecount = 1). If this ad hoc query is re-executed, SQL Server reuses the existing executable plan from the procedure cache as shown in Figure 9-7.

	sql	usecounts	cacheobjtype	objtype
1	SELECT * FROM [Order Details] d, Orders o WHERE d.OrderID=o.OrderID AND ProductID=1	2	Executable Plan	Adhoc
2	SELECT * FROM [Order Details] d, Orders o WHERE d.OrderID=o.OrderID AND ProductID=1	1	Compiled Plan	Adhoc
3	()SELECT [sql]=[sql],[usecounts]=[usecounts],[cacheobjtype]=[cacheobjtype],[objtype]...	3	Compiled Plan	Prepared

Figure 9-7. *Reusing the executable plan from the procedure cache*

In Figure 9-7, you can see that the usecounts for the preceding query's executable plan has increased to 2, confirming that the existing plan for this query has been reused. If this query is executed repeatedly, the existing plan will be reused every time.

Since the plan generated for the preceding query includes the filter criterion value (see the sql column in the syscacheobjects output), the reusability of the plan is limited to the use of same filter criterion value. Re-execute adhoc1.sql, but change d.ProductID to 2:

```
SELECT * FROM [Order Details] d, Orders o
  WHERE d.OrderID=o.OrderID AND d.ProductID=2
```

The existing plan can't be reused as shown in the syscacheobjects output in Figure 9-8.

	sql	usecounts	cacheobjtype	objtype
1	SELECT * FROM [Order Details] d, Orders o WHERE d.OrderID=o.OrderID AND ProductID=1		Executable Plan	Adhoc
2	SELECT * FROM [Order Details] d, Orders o WHERE d.OrderID=o.OrderID AND ProductID=1	1	Compiled Plan	Adhoc
3	()SELECT [sql]=[sql],[usecounts]=[usecounts],[cacheobjtype]=[cacheobjtype],[objtype]...	4	Compiled Plan	Prepared
4	SELECT * FROM [Order Details] d, Orders o WHERE d.OrderID=o.OrderID AND ProductID=2	1	Executable Plan	Adhoc
5	SELECT * FROM [Order Details] d, Orders o WHERE d.OrderID=o.OrderID AND ProductID=2	1	Compiled Plan	Adhoc

Figure 9-8. *syscacheobjects output showing that the existing plan can't be reused*

From the syscacheobjects output in Figure 9-8, you can see that the previous plan for the query with ProductID=1 hasn't been reused; the corresponding usecounts value remained at the old value of 2. Instead of reusing the existing plan, a new plan is generated for the query with a new filter criterion value (ProductID=2) and is saved in the procedure cache. If this ad hoc query is re-executed repeatedly with different filter criterion values, a new execution plan will be generated every time. The inefficient reuse of the execution plan for this ad hoc query increases the load on CPU by consuming additional CPU cycles to regenerate the plan.

To summarize, ad hoc plan caching uses statement-level caching and is limited to an exact textual match. If an ad hoc query is not complex, SQL Server can implicitly parameterize the query to increase plan reusability by using a feature called auto-parameterization. The definition of a simple query for auto-parameterization is limited to fairly simple cases such as ad hoc queries with only one table. As shown in the previous example, a query requiring a join operation cannot be auto-parameterized.

Auto-Parameterization

When an ad hoc query is submitted, SQL Server analyzes the query to determine which parts of the incoming text might be parameters. It looks at the variable parts of the ad hoc query to determine whether it will be safe to parameterize them automatically and use the parameters (instead of the variable parts) in the query, so that the query plan can be independent of the variable values. This feature of automatically converting the variable part of a query into parameter, even though not parameterized explicitly (using a well-defined workload technique), is called *auto-parameterization.*

During auto-parameterization, SQL Server ensures that, if the ad hoc query is converted to an auto-parameterized template, the changes in the parameter values won't widely change the plan requirement. On determining the auto-parameterization to be safe, SQL Server creates a parameterized template for the ad hoc query and saves the parameterized plan in the procedure cache.

The auto-parameterized plan is not based on the dynamic values used in the query. Since the plan is generated for a parameterized template, it can be reused when the ad hoc query is re-executed with different values for the variable parts.

To understand the auto-parameterization feature of SQL Server, consider the following query (auto_parameterization.sql in the download):

```
SELECT * from [Order Details]
  where OrderID = 10250
```

When this ad hoc query is submitted, SQL Server can treat this query as it is for plan creation. However, before the query is executed, SQL Server tries to determine whether it can be safely auto-parameterized. On determining that the variable part of the query can be parameterized without affecting the basic structure of the query, SQL Server auto-parameterizes the query and generates a plan for the auto-parameterized query. You can observe this from the syscacheobjects output shown in Figure 9-9.

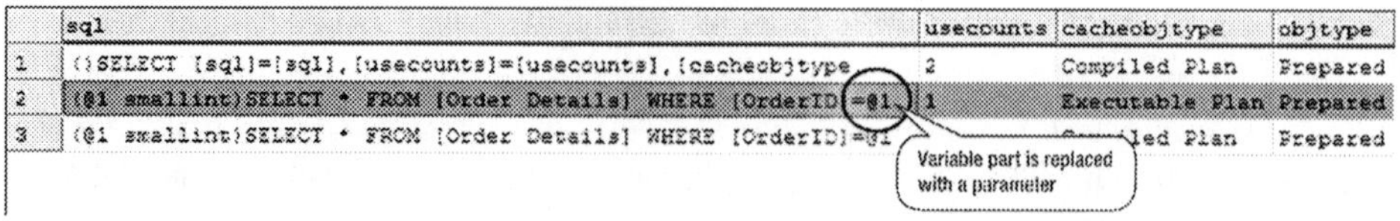

	sql	usecounts	cacheobjtype	objtype
1	(:)SELECT [sql]=[sql],[usecounts]=[usecounts],[cacheobjtype	2	Compiled Plan	Prepared
2	(@1 smallint)SELECT * FROM [Order Details] WHERE [OrderID]=@1	1	Executable Plan	Prepared
3	(@1 smallint)SELECT * FROM [Order Details] WHERE [OrderID]=@1		Compiled Plan	Prepared

Variable part is replaced with a parameter

Figure 9-9. *syscacheobjects output showing an auto-parameterized plan*

The usecounts of the executable plan for the parameterized query appropriately represents the number of reuses as 1. Also, note that the objtype for the auto-parameterized executable plan is no longer Adhoc; it reflects the fact that the plan is for a parameterized query.

The original ad hoc query, even though not executed, gets compiled to create the query tree required for the auto-parameterization of the query. The compiled plan for the ad hoc query may or may not be saved in the plan cache depending on the resources available. But before creating the executable plan for the ad hoc query, SQL Server figured out that it was safe to auto-parameterize, and thus auto-parameterized the query for further processing.

Since this ad hoc query has been auto-parameterized, the existing execution plan can be reused if auto_parameterization.sql is re-executed with a different value for the variable part:

```
SELECT * from [Order Details]
    where OrderID = 10251 -- Previous value was 10250
```

Figure 9-10 shows the output of syscacheobjects.

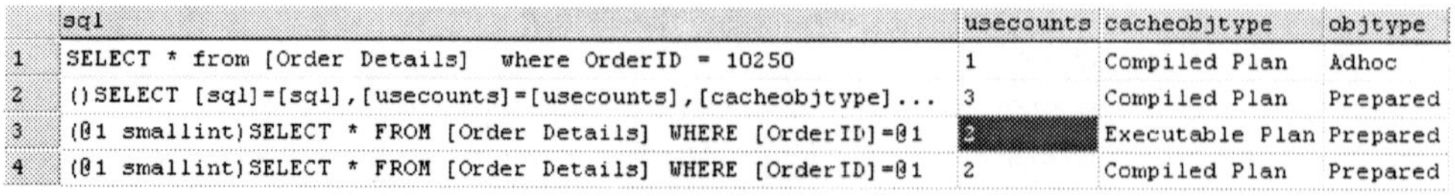

	sql	usecounts	cacheobjtype	objtype
1	SELECT * from [Order Details] where OrderID = 10250	1	Compiled Plan	Adhoc
2	()SELECT [sql]=[sql],[usecounts]=[usecounts],[cacheobjtype]...	3	Compiled Plan	Prepared
3	(@1 smallint)SELECT * FROM [Order Details] WHERE [OrderID]=@1	2	Executable Plan	Prepared
4	(@1 smallint)SELECT * FROM [Order Details] WHERE [OrderID]=@1	2	Compiled Plan	Prepared

Figure 9-10. *syscacheobjects output showing reuse of the auto-parameterized plan*

From Figure 9-10, you can see that no new plan has been generated for this ad hoc query. The existing executable plan is reused as indicated by the increase in the corresponding usecounts value to 2. The ad hoc query can be re-executed repeatedly with different filter criterion values, reusing the existing execution plan.

There is one more aspect to note in the parameterized query for which the execution plan is cached. In Figure 9-10, observe that the body of the parameterized query doesn't exactly match with that of the ad hoc query submitted. For instance, in the ad hoc query, the words from and where are in lowercase, and the OrderID column isn't enclosed in square brackets. On realizing that the ad hoc query can be safely auto-parameterized, SQL Server picks a template that can be used instead of the exact text of the query.

To understand the significance of this, consider the following query:

```
SELECT * FROM [Order Details]
WHERE OrderID BETWEEN 10250 AND 10255
```

Figure 9-11 shows the output of syscacheobjects.

	sql	usecounts	cacheobjtype	objtype
1	()SELECT [sql]=[sql],[usecounts]=[usecounts],[cacheobjtype]=[cacheobjtype],[objty...	2	Compiled Plan	Prepared
2	SELECT * FROM Orders WHERE OrderID BETWEEN 10250 AND 10252	1	Compiled Plan	Adhoc
3	(@1 smallint,@2 smallint)SELECT * FROM [Orders] WHERE [OrderID]>=@1 AND [OrderID]<=@2	1	Executable Plan	Prepared
4	(@1 smallint,@2 smallint)SELECT * FROM [Orders] WHERE [OrderID]>=@1 AND [OrderID]<=@2	2	Compiled Plan	Prepared

Figure 9-11. *syscacheobjects output showing plan auto-parameterization using a template*

From Figure 9-11, you can see that SQL Server auto-parameterized the ad hoc query by picking up a template with a pair of >= and <= operators, which are equivalent to the BETWEEN operator. That means instead of resubmitting the preceding ad hoc query using the BETWEEN clause, if a similar query using a pair of >= and <= is submitted, SQL Server will be able to reuse the existing execution plan. To confirm this behavior, let's modify the ad hoc query follows:

```
SELECT * FROM Orders Details
  WHERE OrderID >= 10250 AND OrderID <= 10252
```

Figure 9-12 shows the output of syscacheobjects.

	sql	usecounts	cacheobjtype	objtype
1	()SELECT [sql]=[sql],[usecounts]=[usecounts],[cacheobjtype]=[cacheobjtype],[objty...	3	Compiled Plan	Prepared
2	SELECT * FROM Orders WHERE OrderID BETWEEN 10250 AND 10252	1	Compiled Plan	Adhoc
3	(@1 smallint,@2 smallint)SELECT * FROM [Orders] WHERE [OrderID]>=@1 AND [OrderID]<=@2	2	Executable Plan	Prepared
4	(@1 smallint,@2 smallint)SELECT * FROM [Orders] WHERE [OrderID]>=@1 AND [OrderID]<=@2	2	Compiled Plan	Prepared

Figure 9-12. *syscacheobjects output showing reuse of the auto-parameterized plan*

From Figure 9-12, you can see that the existing plan is reused, even though the query is syntactically different from the query executed earlier. The auto-parameterized plan generated by SQL Server allows the existing plan to be reused not only when the query is resubmitted with different variable values, but also for queries with same template form.

Auto-Parameterization Limits

SQL Server is highly conservative during auto-parameterization, because the cost of a bad plan can far outweigh the cost of generating a new plan. The conservative approach prevents SQL Server from creating an unsafe auto-parameterized plan. Thus, auto-parameterization is limited to fairly simple cases, such as ad hoc queries with only one table. An ad hoc query with join operation between two (or more) tables (as shown in the early part of the "Plan Reusability of an Ad Hoc Workload" section) is not considered safe for auto-parameterization.

In a scalable system, do not rely on auto-parameterization for plan reusability. The auto-parameterization feature of SQL Server makes an educated guess as to which variables and constants can be parameterized. Instead of relying on SQL Server for auto-parameterization, you should actually specify it programmatically while building your application. To have effective plan reusability, submit queries as well-defined workloads using the techniques explained in the next section.

Plan Reusability of a Well-Defined Workload

Defining queries as a well-defined workload allows the variable parts of the queries to be explicitly parameterized. This enables SQL Server to generate a query plan that is not tied to the variable parts of the query, and it keeps the variable parts separate in an execution context. As you saw in the previous section, SQL Server supports three techniques to submit a well-defined workload:

- Stored procedures

- sp_executesql

- Prepare/execute model

In the sections that follow, I will cover each of these techniques in more depth.

Stored Procedures

Using stored procedures is a standard technique for improving the effectiveness of plan caching. When the stored procedure is compiled, a combined plan is generated for all the SQL statements within the stored procedure. Since the SQL statements within the stored procedure usually don't contain any variables, the execution plan generated for the stored procedure can be reused whenever the stored procedure is re-executed with different parameter values.

In addition to checking syscacheobjects, you can track the execution plan caching for stored procedures using the Profiler tool. Profiler provides the events listed in Table 9-2 to track the plan caching for stored procedures.

Table 9-2. *Events to Analyze Plan Caching*

Event Class	Event	Description
Stored Procedures	SP:CacheHit	Plan is found in the cache
	SP:CacheMiss	Plan is not found in the cache
	SP:ExecContextHit	Execution context for the stored procedure is found in the cache

To track the stored procedure plan caching using Profiler, you can use these events along with the other stored procedure events and data columns as shown in Table 9-3.

Table 9-3. *Data Columns to Analyze Plan Caching*

Events		Data Columns
Event Class	**Event**	
Stored Procedures	SP:CacheHit	EventClass
	SP:CacheMiss	TextData
	SP:Completed	LoginName
	SP:ExecContextHit	SPID
	SP:Starting	StartTime
	SP:StmtCompleted	

To understand how stored procedures can improve plan caching, let's consider the SELECT statement used in the "Plan Reusability of an Ad Hoc Workload" section that wasn't auto-parameterized. The query (adhoc1.sql) is repeated here for clarity:

```
SELECT * FROM [Order Details] d, Orders o
  WHERE d.OrderID=o.OrderID AND d.ProductID=1
```

You can explicitly parameterize this query using a stored procedure (adhoc_sproc.sql in the download):

```
IF(SELECT OBJECT_ID('p1')) IS NOT NULL
  DROP PROC p1
GO
CREATE PROC p1
@ProductID INT
AS
  SELECT * FROM [Order Details] d, Orders o
  WHERE d.OrderID=o.OrderID AND d.ProductID=@ProductID
GO
```

To retrieve a result set for d.ProductID = 1, you can execute the stored procedure like this:

```
EXEC p1 1 --d.ProductID = 1
```

Figure 9-13 shows the output of syscacheobjects.

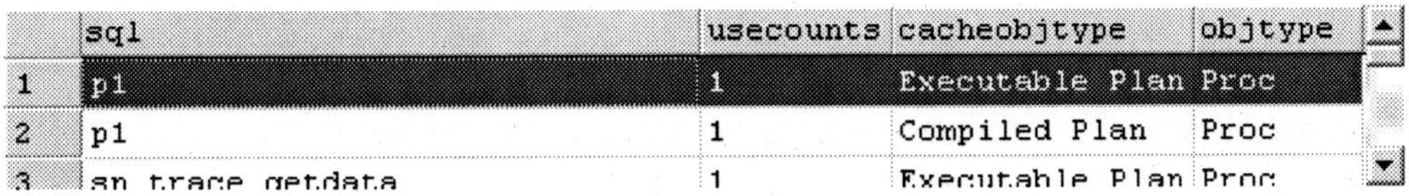

	sql	usecounts	cacheobjtype	objtype	
1	p1	1	Executable Plan	Proc	
2	p1	1	Compiled Plan	Proc	
3	sp_trace_getdata	1	Executable Plan	Proc	

Figure 9-13. *syscacheobjects output showing stored procedure plan caching*

From Figure 9-13, you can see that a compiled plan is generated and cached for the stored procedure. A corresponding executable plan is also created to represent the execution environment for the compiled plan. The usecounts of the executable plan is 1 since the stored procedure is executed only once.

Figure 9-14 shows the Profiler trace output for this stored procedure execution.

EventClass	TextData	LoginName	SPID
TraceStart			
SP:CacheMiss		sa	51
SP:CacheMiss		sa	51
SP:Starting	EXEC p1 1	sa	51
SP:StmtCompleted	-- p1 SELECT * FROM [Order Details...	sa	51
SP:Completed	EXEC p1 1	sa	51
TraceStop			

Figure 9-14. *Profiler trace output showing that the stored procedure plan isn't easily found in the cache*

From the Profiler trace output, you can see that the plan for the stored procedure is not found in the cache. When the stored procedure is executed the first time, SQL Server looks in the procedure cache and fails to find any cache entry for the procedure p1, causing an SP:CacheMiss event. On not finding a cached plan, SQL Server makes arrangements to compile the stored procedure, including resolving the ObjectID of the stored procedure from the name p1. Before compiling the stored procedure, SQL Server uses this ObjectID to perform a precise search in the procedure cache. As the stored procedure is being executed for the first time, SQL Server fails to find any existing plan for the ObjectID, causing another SP:CacheMiss event. Subsequently, SQL Server generates and saves the plan, and proceeds with the execution of the stored procedure.

If this stored procedure is re-executed to retrieve a result set for d.ProductID = 2:

EXEC p1 2 --d.ProductID = 2

then the existing plan is reused as shown in the syscacheobjects output in Figure 9-15.

	sql	usecounts	cacheobjtype	objtype
1	p1	2	Executable Plan	Proc
2	p1	1	Compiled Plan	Proc
3	sp_trace_getdata	2	Executable Plan	Proc

Figure 9-15. *syscacheobjects output showing reuse of the stored procedure plan*

You can also confirm the reuse of the execution plan from the Profiler trace output, as shown in Figure 9-16.

EventClass	TextData	LoginName	SPID
TraceStart			
SP:ExecContextHit		sa	51
SP:Starting	EXEC p1 1	sa	51
SP:StmtCompleted	-- p1 SELECT * FROM [Order Details...	sa	51
SP:Completed	EXEC p1 1	sa	51
TraceStop			

Figure 9-16. *Profiler trace output showing reuse of the stored procedure plan*

From the Profiler trace output, you can see that the existing plan is found in the procedure cache. On searching the cache, SQL Server finds the executable plan for the stored procedure p1 causing an SP:ExecContextHit event. If the stored procedure is executed concurrently by multiple users, then instead of the SP:ExecContextHit event the relevant event may be an SP:CacheHit event. Once the existing execution plan is found, SQL reuses the plan to execute the stored procedure.

There are a few other aspects of stored procedures that are worth considering:

- Stored procedures are compiled on first execution

- Other performance benefits of stored procedures

- Additional benefits of stored procedures

Stored Procedures Are Compiled on First Execution

The execution plan of a stored procedure is generated when it is executed the first time. When the stored procedure is created, it is only parsed and saved in the database. No normalization and optimization processes are performed during the stored procedure creation. This allows a stored procedure to be created before creating all the objects accessed by the stored procedure. For example, you can create the following stored procedure, even when the table no_t1 referred to in the stored procedure does not exist:

```
IF(SELECT OBJECT_ID('p1')) IS NOT NULL
  DROP PROC p1
GO
CREATE PROC p1
AS
  SELECT c1 FROM no_t1 --Table no_t1 doesn't exist
GO
```

The stored procedure will be created successfully, since the normalization process to bind the referred object to the query tree (generated by the command parser during the stored procedure execution) is not performed during the stored procedure creation. The stored procedure will report the error when it is first executed (if table no_t1 is not created by then), since the stored procedure is compiled the first time it is executed.

Other Performance Benefits of Stored Procedures

Besides improving the performance through execution plan reusability, stored procedures provide the following performance benefits:

- *Business logic is close to the data.* The parts of the business logic that perform extensive operations on data stored in the database should be put in stored procedures, since SQL Server's engine is extremely powerful for relational and set theory operations.

- *Network traffic is reduced.* The database application, across the network, sends just the name of the stored procedure and the parameter values. Only the processed result set is returned to the application. The intermediate data need not be passed back and forth between the application and the database.

Additional Benefits of Stored Procedures

Some of the other benefits provided by stored procedures are as follows:

- *The application is isolated from data structure changes.* If all critical data access is made through stored procedures, then when the database schema changes, the stored procedures can be re-created without affecting the application code that accesses the data through the stored procedures. In fact, the application accessing the database need not even be stopped.

- *Security is increased.* User privileges on database tables can be restricted and can be allowed only through the standard business logic implemented in the stored procedure. For example, if you want user u1 to be restricted from physically deleting rows from table t1 and to be allowed to only mark the rows virtually deleted through stored procedure p1 by setting the rows' status as 'Deleted', then you can execute the DENY and GRANT commands as follows:

```
IF(SELECT OBJECT_ID('t1')) IS NOT NULL
  DROP TABLE t1
GO
CREATE TABLE t1(c1 INT, status VARCHAR(7))
INSERT INTO t1 VALUES(1, 'New')
GO
IF(SELECT OBJECT_ID('p1')) IS NOT NULL
  DROP PROC p1
GO
CREATE PROC p1
@c1 INT
AS
  UPDATE t1 SET status = 'Deleted' WHERE c1 = @c1
GO
--Prevent user u1 from deleting rows
DENY DELETE ON t1 TO u1
--Allow user u1 to mark a row as 'deleted'
GRANT EXECUTE ON p1 TO u1
GO
```

Note that if the query within the stored procedure p1 is built dynamically as a string (@sql) as follows, then granting permission to the stored procedure won't grant any permission to the query, since the dynamic query isn't treated as a part of the stored procedure:

```
IF(SELECT OBJECT_ID('p1')) IS NOT NULL
   DROP PROC p1
GO
CREATE PROC p1
@c1 INT
AS
   DECLARE @sql VARCHAR(50)
   SET @sql = 'UPDATE t1 SET status = ''Deleted'' WHERE c1 = ' +
              CAST(@c1 AS VARCHAR(10))
   EXECUTE(@sql)
GO
GRANT EXECUTE ON p1 TO u1
GO
```

Consequently, user u1 won't be able to mark the row as 'Deleted' using the stored procedure p1. I will cover the aspects of using a dynamic query in the stored procedure in the next chapter.

- *There is a single point of administration.* All the business logic implemented in stored procedures is maintained as a part of the database and can be managed centrally on the database itself. Of course, this benefit is highly relative, depending on whom you ask. To get a different opinion, you may ask a non-DBA!

Since stored procedures are saved as database objects, they add maintenance overhead to the database administration. Many times, you may need to execute just one or a few queries from the application. If these singleton queries are executed frequently, you should aim to reuse their execution plans to improve performance. But creating stored procedures for these individual singleton queries adds a large number of stored procedures to the database, increasing the database administrative overhead significantly. To avoid the maintenance overhead of using stored procedures, and yet derive the benefit of plan reuse, submit the singleton queries as a well-defined workload using the sp_executesql system stored procedure.

sp_executesql

sp_executesql is a system stored procedure that provides a mechanism to submit one or more queries as a well-defined workload. It allows the variable parts of the query to be explicitly parameterized, and it can therefore provide execution plan reusability as effective as a stored procedure. The SELECT statement adhoc_sproc.sql can be submitted through sp_executesql as follows (executesql.sql in the download):

```
EXEC sp_executesql
N'SELECT * FROM [Order Details] d, Orders o
WHERE d.OrderID=o.OrderID AND d.ProductID=@1'
, N'@1 INT' --Definition of all parameters
, @1=1      --Assignment to all parameters
```

Note that the strings passed to the sp_executesql stored procedure are submitted with a prefix of N. This is required since sp_executesql uses Unicode strings as the input parameters.

The output of syscacheobjects is shown next (see Figure 9-17):

```
SELECT sql, cacheobjtype, objtype, usecounts
FROM master.dbo.syscacheobjects
```

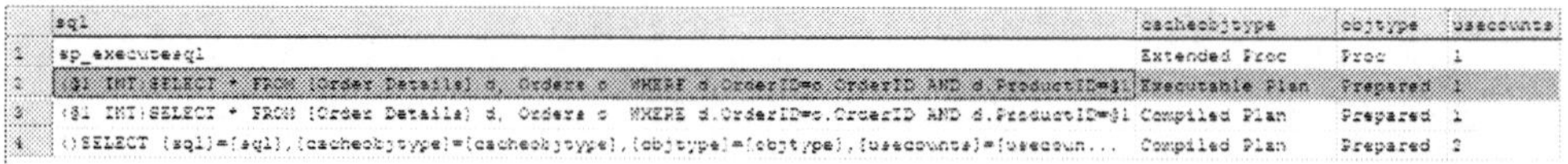

Figure 9-17. *syscacheobjects output showing a parameterized plan generated using sp_executesql*

In Figure 9-17, you can see that the plan is generated for the parameterized part of the query submitted through sp_executesql. Since the plan is not tied to the variable part of the query, the existing execution plan can be reused if this query is resubmitted with a different value for the variable part (d.ProductID=2) as follows:

```
EXEC sp_executesql
N'SELECT * FROM [Order Details] d, Orders o
WHERE d.OrderID=o.OrderID AND d.ProductID=@1'
, N'@1 INT' --Definition of all parameters
, @1=2        --Assignment to all parameters
```

Figure 9-18 shows the output of syscacheobjects.

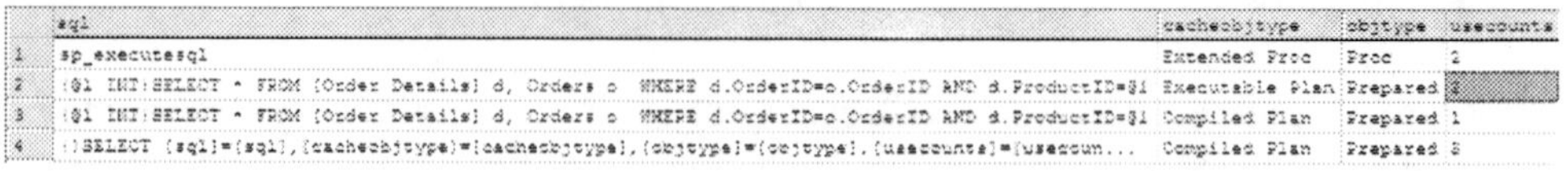

Figure 9-18. *syscacheobjects output showing reuse of the parameterized plan generated using sp_executesql*

From Figure 9-18, you can see that the existing plan is reused (Executable Plan usecounts is 2) when the query is resubmitted with a different variable value. If this query is resubmitted many times with different values for the variable part, the existing execution plan can be reused without regenerating new execution plans.

The query for which the plan is created (the sql column) matches the exact textual string of the parameterized query submitted through sp_executesql. Therefore, if the same query is submitted from different parts of the application, ensure that the same textual string is used at all the places. For example, if the same query is resubmitted with a minor modification in the query string (and in lowercase instead of uppercase letters):

```
EXEC sp_executesql
N'SELECT * FROM [Order Details] d, Orders o
WHERE d.OrderID=o.OrderID and d.ProductID=@1'
, N'@1 INT' --Definition of all parameters
, @1=2        --Assignment to all parameters
```

then the existing plan is not reused, and instead a new plan is created as shown in the syscacheobjects output in Figure 9-19.

sql	cacheobjtype	objtype	usecounts
1	(@1 INT)SELECT * FROM [Order Details] d, Orders o WHERE d.OrderID=o.OrderID and d.ProductID=@1	Executable Plan	Prepared	1
2	(@1 INT)SELECT * FROM [Order Details] d, Orders o WHERE d.OrderID=o.OrderID and d.ProductID=@1	Compiled Plan	Prepared	1
3	sp_executesql	Extended Proc	Proc	3
4	(@1 INT)SELECT * FROM [Order Details] d, Orders o WHERE d.OrderID=o.OrderID AND d.ProductID=@1	Executable Plan	Prepared	2
5	(@1 INT)SELECT * FROM [Order Details] d, Orders o WHERE d.OrderID=o.OrderID AND d.ProductID=@1	Compiled Plan	Prepared	1
6	(-)SELECT [sql]=[sql],[cacheobjtype]=[cacheobjtype],[objtype]=[objtype],[usecounts]=[usecoun...	Compiled Plan	Prepared	4

Figure 9-19. *syscacheobjects output showing sensitivity of the plan generated using sp_executesql*

In general, use sp_executesql to explicitly parameterize queries, to make their execution plans reusable when the queries are resubmitted with different values for the variable parts. This provides the performance benefit of reusable plans without the overhead of managing any persistent object as required for stored procedures. This feature is exposed by both ODBC and OLE DB through SQLExecDirect and ICommandWithParameters, respectively. As .NET developers or users of ADO.NET (ADO 2.7 or higher), you can submit the preceding SELECT statement using ADO Command and Parameters. If you set the ADO Command Prepared property equal to FALSE and use ADO Command ('SELECT * FROM "Order Details" d, Orders o WHERE d.OrderID=o.OrderID and d.ProductID=?') with ADO Parameters, ADO.NET will send the SELECT statement using sp_executesql.

Along with the parameters, sp_executesql sends the entire query string across the network every time the query is re-executed. You can avoid this by using the prepare/execute model of ODBC and OLE DB (or OLE DB .NET).

Prepare/Execute Model

ODBC and OLE DB provide a prepare/execute model to submit queries as a well-defined workload. Like sp_executesql, this model allows the variable parts of the queries to be parameterized explicitly. The prepare phase allows SQL Server to generate the execution plan for the query and return a handle of the execution plan to the application. This execution plan handle is used by the execute phase to execute the query with different parameter values. This model can be used only to submit queries through ODBC or OLE DB, and it can't be used within SQL Server itself—queries within stored procedures can't be executed using this model.

The SQL Server ODBC driver provides the SQLPrepare and SQLExecute APIs to support the prepare/execute model. The SQL Server OLE DB provider exposes this model through the ICommandPrepare interface. Previously, this model introduced the overhead of an additional network round-trip associated with the prepare phase. SQL Server 2000 eliminated this overhead in the ODBC driver and the OLE DB providers distributed with it by piggybacking the prepare phase with the first execute phase. The OLE DB .NET provider of ADO.NET behaves similarly.

■**NOTE** For a detailed description of how to use the prepare/execute model in a database application, please refer to the MSDN article "Preparing SQL Statements" (http://msdn.microsoft.com/library/en-us/architec/8_ar_sa_1a43.asp).

Execution Plan Cache Recommendations

The basic purpose of the plan cache is to improve performance by reusing execution plans. Thus it is important to ensure that your execution plans actually are reusable. Since the plan reusability of ad hoc queries is inefficient, it is generally recommended that you rely on well-defined workload techniques as much as possible. To ensure efficient use of plan cache, follow these recommendations:

- Explicitly parameterize variable parts of a query.

- Use stored procedures to implement business functionality.

- Use sp_executesql to avoid stored procedure maintenance.

- Use the prepare/execute model to avoid resending a query string.

- Avoid ad hoc queries.

- Use sp_executesql over EXECUTE for dynamic queries.

- Parameterize variable parts of queries with care.

- Avoid modifying environment settings between connections.

- Avoid the implicit resolution of objects in queries.

- Avoid the implicit resolution of stored procedure names.

Let's take a closer look at these points.

Explicitly Parameterize Variable Parts of a Query

A query is often run several times, with the only difference between each run being that there are different values for the variable parts. Their plans can be reused, however, if the static and variable parts of the query can be separated. Although SQL Server has an auto-parameterization feature, it has severe limitations. Always perform parameterization explicitly using the standard well-defined workload techniques.

Use Stored Procedures to Implement Business Functionality

If you have explicitly parameterized your query, then placing it in a stored procedure brings the best reusability possible. Since only the parameters need to be sent along with the stored procedure name, network traffic is reduced. Since stored procedures are precompiled, they run faster than other queries. And stored procedures can also maintain a single parameterized plan for the set of queries included within the stored procedure, instead of maintaining a large number of small plans for the individual queries. This prevents the plan cache from being flooded with separate plans for the individual queries.

Use sp_executesql to Avoid Stored Procedure Maintenance

If the object maintenance required for the stored procedures becomes a consideration, then use sp_executesql to submit the queries as well-defined workloads. Unlike the stored procedure model, sp_executesql doesn't create any persistent objects in the database. sp_executesql is suited to execute a singleton query or a small batch query.

The complete business logic implemented in a stored procedure can also be submitted with sp_executesql as a large query string. However, as the complexity of the business logic increases, it becomes difficult to create and maintain a query string for the complete logic.

Use the Prepare/Execute Model to Avoid Resending a Query String

sp_executesql requires the query string to be sent across the network every time the query is re-executed. It also requires the cost of a query string match at the server to identify the corresponding execution plan in the procedure cache. In the case of an ODBC or OLE DB (or OLE DB .NET) application, the prepare/execute model can be used to avoid resending the query string during multiple executions, since only the plan handle and parameters need to be submitted.

In the prepare/execute model, since a plan handle is returned to the application, the plan can be reused by other user connections; it is not limited to the user who created the plan.

Avoid Ad Hoc Queries

Do not design new applications using ad hoc queries! The execution plan created for an ad hoc query cannot be reused when the query is resubmitted with a different value for the variable parts. Even though SQL Server has the auto-parameterization feature to isolate the variable parts of the query, due to the strict conservativeness of SQL Server in auto-parameterization, the feature is limited to simple queries only. For better plan reusability, submit the queries as well-defined workloads.

Use sp_executesql over EXECUTE for Dynamic Queries

SQL query strings generated dynamically within stored procedures or a database application should be executed using sp_executesql instead of the EXECUTE command. The EXECUTE command doesn't allow the variable parts of the query to be explicitly parameterized.

To understand the preceding comparison between sp_executesql and EXECUTE, consider the dynamic SQL query string used to execute the SELECT statement in the adhoc_sproc.sql:

```
DECLARE @n VARCHAR(1)
SET @n = 1
DECLARE @sql VARCHAR(100)
SET @sql = 'SELECT * FROM [Order Details] d, Orders o'
+ ' WHERE d.OrderID=o.OrderID AND d.ProductID=''' + @n + ''''
--Execute the dynamic query using EXECUTE statement
EXECUTE(@sql)
```

The EXECUTE statement submits the query along with the value of d.ProductID as an ad hoc query, and thereby faces the conservativeness of auto-parameterization. For improved plan cache reusability, execute the dynamic SQL string as a parameterized query using sp_executesql:

```
DECLARE @n VARCHAR(1)
SET @n = 1
DECLARE @sql NVARCHAR(100), @paramdef NCHAR(10)
SET @sql = N'SELECT * FROM [Order Details] d, Orders o'
+ ' WHERE d.OrderID=o.OrderID AND d.ProductID=@1'
SET @paramdef = N'@1 VARCHAR(1)'
--Execute the dynamic query using sp_executesql system stored
--procedure
EXECUTE sp_executesql @sql, @paramdef, @1=@n
```

Executing the query as an explicitly parameterized query using sp_executesql generates a parameterized plan for the query, and thereby increases the execution plan reusability.

Parameterize Variable Parts of Queries with Care

Be careful while converting variable parts of a query into parameters. The range of values for some variables may vary so drastically that the execution plan for a certain range of values may not be suitable for the other values. For example, based on the filter criterion value, a query may request either a small number of rows or a large result set. For this query, an index SEEK may be ideal in one case, whereas an index SCAN may be better in the other case. The query requires different plans for the different values of the filter criterion. Do not explicitly parameterize variable parts whose range of values may drastically affect optimization.

To better understand this scenario, consider the following example. The following SELECT statement (care1.sql in the download) uses a different filter criterion value to retrieve a drastically different number of rows:

```
SELECT d.* FROM Orders o, [Order Details] d
  WHERE o.OrderID = d.OrderID
    AND o.OrderID >= 11077 --Last OrderID value
SELECT d.* FROM Orders o, [Order Details] d
  WHERE o.OrderID = d.OrderID
    AND o.OrderID >= 1      --First OrderID value
```

In the first SELECT, the query retrieves a small result set (only 25 rows; around 1% of the total rows) from the Order Details table. In the second SELECT, the query retrieves a large result set (all 2,155 rows; 100% of the total rows) from the Order Details table. Therefore, the optimizer appropriately uses an index SEEK in the first case and an index SCAN in the second case for the Order Details table, as shown in Figure 9-20.

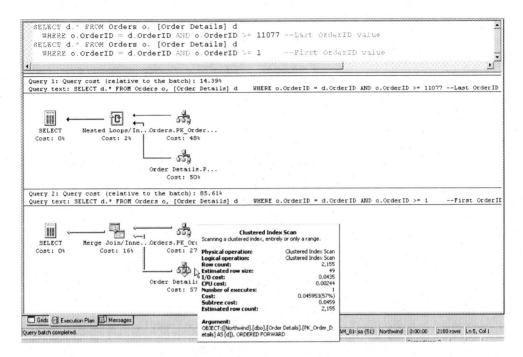

Figure 9-20. *Different execution plans for queries processing different numbers of rows*

You may parameterize this query using sp_executesql (care2.sql in the download):

```
EXEC sp_executesql
  N'SELECT d.* FROM Orders o, [Order Details] d
    WHERE o.OrderID = d.OrderID AND o.OrderID >= @1'
  , N'@1 INT'
  , @1=11077 --Last OrderID value
```

The resultant execution plan shown in Figure 9-21 meets the expectation of having an index SEEK on the Order Details table to retrieve a small result set.

Now if this parameterized query is reused to return a large result set:

```
EXEC sp_executesql
  N'SELECT d.* FROM Orders o, [Order Details] d
    WHERE o.OrderID = d.OrderID AND o.OrderID >= @1'
  , N'@1 INT'
  , @1=1 --First OrderID value
```

the query analyzer finds a cached execution plan and uses it, as shown in Figure 9-22. Unfortunately, this plan uses an index SEEK operation on the Order Details table, which is inappropriate for retrieving a large result set.

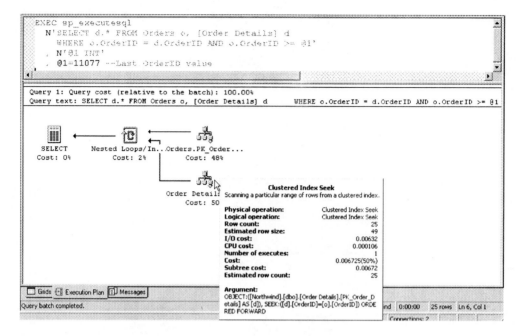

Figure 9-21. *Execution plan for a query processing a small result set*

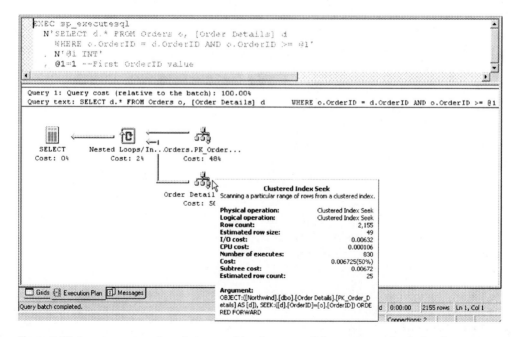

Figure 9-22. *Incorrect execution plan caused by the reuse of the parameterized plan for a query not safe for parameterization*

Since the query requires different plans as the value of the variable part changes, it is unsafe to parameterize this query. Otherwise, create two separate stored procedures to execute these two query types (requiring different execution plans) and execute them appropriately with logic in the application.

Avoid Modifying Environment Settings Between Connections

The execution plan generated for a query depends on the environment settings when the plan is generated. The environment is determined by server settings (sp_configure), database settings (sp_dboption or ALTER DATABASE), and connection settings (SET option). The environment settings in which an execution plan is generated are reflected in the following columns of syscacheobjects: setopts, langid, and dateformat. If the environment settings are modified in between a connection being opened and the queries being resubmitted, then new execution plans are generated for the queries with current environment settings.

To understand how the change of environment settings hurts the reusability of execution plan, consider the following example. Create a small sample table as follows (new_table.sql in the download):

```
IF(SELECT OBJECT_ID('t1')) IS NOT NULL
  DROP TABLE t1
GO
CREATE TABLE t1(c1 INT)
INSERT INTO t1 VALUES(1)
```

With the default environment setting, execute a simple query using sp_executesql:

```
EXECUTE sp_executesql
  N'SELECT * FROM t1 WHERE c1=@1', N'@1 INT', @1=1
```

The output of syscacheobjects2.sql

```
SELECT sql, cacheobjtype, usecounts, setopts, langid, [dateformat]
FROM master.dbo.syscacheobjects
```

with the columns reflecting the environment setting is shown in Figure 9-23.

	sql	cacheobjtype	usecounts	setopts	langid	dateformat
1	sp_executesql	Extended Proc	1	4347	0	1
2	(@1 INT)SELECT * FROM t1 WHERE c1=@1	Executable Plan	1	4347	0	1
3	(@1 INT)SELECT * FROM t1 WHERE c1=@1	Compile	Environment setting when plan was created	4347	0	1
4	()SELECT [sql]=[sql],[cacheobjty...	Compile		4347	0	1

Figure 9-23. *syscacheobjects output showing the environment setting when the plan was created*

By default, the `ANSI_NULLS` environment setting is on. (You can verify this by executing the `DBCC USEROPTIONS` command.) To understand the effect of changing the environment setting on plan reusability, modify the `ANSI_NULLS` setting to `OFF` and re-execute the `SELECT` statement (`ansi2.sql` in the download):

```
SET ANSI_NULLS OFF --Modify environment setting
GO
EXECUTE sp_executesql
  N'SELECT * FROM t1 WHERE c1=@1', N'@1 INT', @1=1
```

The output of `syscacheobjects2.sql` is shown in Figure 9-24.

	sql	cacheobjtype	usecounts	setopts	langid	dateformat
1	sp_executesql	Extended Proc	2	4347	0	1
2	(@1 INT)SELECT * FROM t1 WHERE c1=@1	Executable Plan	1	4315	0	1
3	(@1 INT)SELECT * FROM t1 WHERE c1=@1	Compiled Plan	1	4315	0	1
4	(@1 INT)SELECT * FROM t1 WHERE c1=@1 E	4347	0	1
5	(@1 INT)SELECT * FROM t1 WHERE c1=@1 C	4347	0	1
6	()SELECT [sql]=[sql],[cacheobjty...	Compiled Plan		4315	0	1
7	()SELECT [sql]=[sql],[cacheobjty...	Compiled Plan	2	4347	0	1

> Plan created for the new environment setting

Figure 9-24. *syscacheobjects output showing the new plan created for the new environment setting*

As shown in Figure 9-24, a new execution plan is generated for the same query when it is re-executed under a different environment setting. Therefore, to reuse the execution plans, avoid modifying the environment setting between connections.

Avoid Implicit Resolution of Objects in Queries

SQL Server allows multiple database users to create database objects with the same name under their individual ownership. For example, table t1 can be created by two users (u1 and u2) under their individual ownership. On a production database, the database objects are mostly owned by a special user called dbo (database owner). If user u1 executes the following query:

```
SELECT * FROM t1 WHERE c1 = 1
```

then SQL Server first tries to find whether table t1 exists for user u1. If not, then it tries to find whether table t1 exists for the dbo user. This implicit resolution allows user u1 to create another instance of table t1 under his or her ownership, and access it temporarily (using same application code) without affecting other users.

On a production database, it's generally recommended to have dbo as the owner of all database objects. Thus, using implicit resolution adds the following overheads on a production server:

- It requires more time to identify the objects.

- It decreases the effectiveness of plan cache reusability.

If implicit resolution is used by a query, then the execution plan is generated for the user who executed the query. Consequently, if another user re-executes the query, the existing plan can't be reused by this user. On the other hand, if the owner of the objects referred to in the query is explicitly specified, then the generated execution plan is independent of the user who executes the query, and the plan will be reusable by other users re-executing the query. The user for whom the execution plan is generated is represented in the uid column of syscacheobjects.

To understand the effect of implicit resolution on plan reusability, consider the following example. Use the sample table t1 just created. Create two users, u1 and u2, as follows (users.sql in the code download):

```
--Add user u1
IF(SELECT USER_ID('u1')) IS NOT NULL
BEGIN
  EXEC sp_dropuser 'u1'
  EXEC sp_droplogin 'u1'
END
EXEC sp_addlogin 'u1', '', 'Northwind' --Create login u1
USE Northwind
EXEC sp_adduser 'u1', 'u1' --Add login u1 as user u1 to
                           --Northwind database
GRANT SELECT ON t1 TO u1 --Grant SELECT permission on table
                         --t1 to user u1
GO
--Add user u2
IF(SELECT USER_ID('u2')) IS NOT NULL
BEGIN
  EXEC sp_dropuser 'u2'
  EXEC sp_droplogin 'u2'
END
EXEC sp_addlogin 'u2', '', 'Northwind' --Create login u2
USE Northwind
EXEC sp_adduser 'u2', 'u2' --Add login u2 as user u2 to
                           --Northwind database
GRANT SELECT ON t1 TO u2 --Grant SELECT permission on table
                         --t1 to user u2
GO
```

Execute the following query (using implicit resolution) as user u1:

```
EXECUTE sp_executesql
  N'SELECT * FROM t1 WHERE c1 = @1' --Implicit resolution
                                    --for t1
, N'@1 INT'
, @1=1
```

Figure 9-25 shows the output of `syscacheobjects` using the following `SELECT` statement (`syscacheobjects3.sql`):

```
SELECT sql, cacheobjtype, uid, usecounts
FROM master.dbo.syscacheobjects
```

	sql	cacheobjtype	uid	usecounts
1	SELECT sql, cacheobjtype, uid, usecount...	Compiled Plan	-2	1
2	(@1 INT)SELECT * FROM t1 WHERE c1 = @1	Executable Plan	5	1
3	(@1 INT)SELECT * FROM t1 WHERE c1 = @1	Co~~mpiled P~~	5	1
4	sp_executesql	E~~x~~ Plan for USER_ID=5	1	1
5	()SELECT [sql]=[sql],[cacheobjtype]=[ca...	Co	-2	2

Figure 9-25. *syscacheobjects output showing the plan for USER_ID = 5*

As shown in Figure 9-25, the execution plan is generated for the user who executed the query. You can find the name of the user for a `USER_ID` as follows:

```
SELECT USER_NAME(USER_ID)
```

To understand the reusability of the execution plan, re-execute the same query as user u2. Figure 9-26 shows the output of `syscacheobjects3.sql`.

	sql	cacheobjtype	uid	usecounts
1	SELECT sql, cacheobjtype, uid, usecount...	Compiled Plan	-2	2
2	(@1 INT)SELECT * FROM t1 WHERE c1 = @1	Executable Plan	6	1
3	(@1 INT)SELECT * FROM t1 WHERE c1 = @1	Co~~mpiled Pl~~	6	1
4	(@1 INT)SELECT * FROM t1 WHERE c1 = @1	E~~x~~ Plan for USER_ID=6	5	1
5	(@1 INT)SELECT * FROM t1 WHERE c1 = @1	Co	5	1
6	sp_executesql	Extended Proc	1	2
7	()SELECT [sql]=[sql],[cacheobjtype]=[ca...	Compiled Plan	-2	3

Figure 9-26. *syscacheobjects output showing a separate plan for USER_ID = 6*

From Figure 9-26, you can see that the existing execution plan created for user u1 (or `USER_ID = 5`) is not reused. A new execution plan is generated for user u2 (or `USER_ID = 6`). If this query is re-executed multiple times by different users, then a separate execution plan will be created for the individual users. This impedes execution plan reusability.

To improve the execution plan reusability, don't use implicit resolution. Explicitly specify the owner of the database objects referred to in the query:

```
EXECUTE sp_executesql
  N'SELECT * FROM dbo.t1 WHERE c1 = @1' --Qualify owner of t1
  , N'@1 INT'
  , @1=1
```

On executing this improvised query as user u1 (USER_ID = 5), the execution plan is generated independent of the USER_ID, as shown in Figure 9-27.

	sql	cacheobjtype	uid	usecounts
1	SELECT sql, cacheobjtype, uid, usecount...	Compiled Plan	-2	3
2	(@1 INT)SELECT * FROM t1 WHERE c1 = @1	Executable Plan	6	1
3	(@1 INT)SELECT * FROM t1 WHERE c1 = @1	Compiled Plan	6	1
4	(@1 INT)SELECT * FROM t1 WHERE c1 = @1	Executable Plan	5	1
5	(@1 INT)SELECT * FROM t1 WHERE c1 = @1	Compiled Plan	5	1
6	(@1 INT)SELECT * FROM dbo.t1 WHERE c1 = @1	Executable Plan	-2	1
7	(@1 INT)SELECT * FROM dbo.t1 WHERE c1 = @1	Compiled Plan	-2	1
8	sp_executesql	Ex [Plan for all users]	1	3
9	()SELECT [sql]=[sql],[cacheobjtype]=[ca...	Co	-2	4

Figure 9-27. *syscacheobjects output showing a new plan for all users*

As shown in Figure 9-27, the execution plan generated this time doesn't belong to user u1 (or USER_ID = 5). A uid of -2 in syscacheobjects indicates that *the execution plan can be reused by any user.* To verify the reusability of this execution plan, re-execute the improvised query as user u2.

Figure 9-28 shows the output of syscacheobjects3.sql.

	sql	cacheobjtype	uid	usecounts
1	SELECT sql, cacheobjtype, uid, usecount...	Compiled Plan	-2	4
2	(@1 INT)SELECT * FROM t1 WHERE c1 = @1	Executable Plan	6	1
3	(@1 INT)SELECT * FROM t1 WHERE c1 = @1	Compiled Plan	6	1
4	(@1 INT)SELECT * FROM t1 WHERE c1 = @1	Executable Plan	5	1
5	(@1 INT)SELECT * FROM t1 WHERE c1 = @1	Compiled Plan	5	1
6	(@1 INT)SELECT * FROM dbo.t1 WHERE c1 = @1	Executable Plan	-2	2
7	(@1 INT)SELECT * FROM dbo.t1 WHERE c1 = @1	Compil [Plan reused for the second user]		1
8	sp_executesql	Exten		4
9	()SELECT [sql]=[sql],[cacheobjtype]=[ca...	Compil		5

Figure 9-28. *syscacheobjects output showing reuse of the plan by another user*

You can see that the execution plan generated during the query execution by user u1 is reused when the query is re-executed by user u2.

Avoid Implicit Resolution of Stored Procedure Names

In a production database, the stored procedures are usually owned by dbo. Thus, while executing the stored procedures on a production database, ensure that the stored procedure names are qualified with dbo or the name of the stored-procedure owner. This reduces the number of searches required through the procedure cache when the stored procedures are executed by non-dbo users. To understand this, consider the following example.

Create the following stored procedure (`explicit_sproc.sql` in the download) as user dbo and grant execution permission on the stored procedure to user u1:

```
SETUSER 'dbo'
IF(SELECT OBJECT_ID('p1')) IS NOT NULL
  DROP PROC p1
GO
CREATE PROC p1
@ProductID INT
AS
  SELECT * FROM [Order Details] d, Orders o
  WHERE d.OrderID=o.OrderID AND d.ProductID=@ProductID
GO
GRANT EXECUTE ON p1 TO u1
SETUSER
```

Generate the execution plan by executing the stored procedure as user u1:

```
SETUSER 'u1'
EXEC p1 1
SETUSER
```

As expected, SQL Server finds the existing execution plan in the procedure cache. But it finds the plan in two iterations, as shown in the Profiler trace output in Figure 9-29.

EventClass	TextData	LoginName	SPID
TraceStart			
SP:CacheMiss		u1	52
SP:ExecContextHit		u1	52
SP:Starting	EXEC p1 1	u1	52
SP:StmtCompleted	-- p1 SELECT * FROM [Order Details...	u1	52
SP:Completed	EXEC p1 1	u1	52
TraceStop			

Figure 9-29. *Profiler trace output showing a cache miss for a nonqualified stored procedure execution*

When the stored procedure is executed as user u1, SQL Server first searches through the procedure cache to find whether the execution plan for u1.p1 exists, since the stored procedure name is not qualified as dbo.p1 during execution. It fails to find the plan cache for u1.p1, causing the SP:CacheMiss event.

On failing to find the plan, SQL Server locates the stored procedure dbo.p1 in the system catalog using implicit resolution and makes arrangements to compile the stored procedure. The arrangements include resolving the ObjectID of the stored procedure from the name p1. Using this ObjectID, SQL Server again searches the procedure cache for the existing plan. Since the ObjectID is unique for all users, SQL Server finds the execution plan for dbo.p1, causing the SP:ExecContextHit event.

To avoid the first, unsuccessful search through the procedure cache, qualify the owner as dbo while executing the stored procedure as user u1:

```
SETUSER 'u1'
EXEC dbo.p1 1
SETUSER
```

Figure 9-30 shows the resultant Profiler trace output.

EventClass	TextData	LoginName	SPID
TraceStart			
SP:ExecContextHit		u1	52
SP:Starting	EXEC dbo.p1 1	u1	52
SP:StmtCompleted	-- p1 SELECT * FROM [Order Details...	u1	52
SP:Completed	EXEC dbo.p1 1	u1	52
TraceStop			

Figure 9-30. *Profiler trace output showing an immediate cache hit for an owner-qualified stored-procedure execution*

As you can see, SQL Server finds the existing plan without incurring any cache miss.

Summary

SQL Server's cost-based query optimizer decides upon an effective execution plan not on the exact syntax of the query, but by evaluating the cost of executing the query using different processing strategies. The cost evaluation of using different processing strategies is done in multiple optimization phases to avoid overoptimizing a query. Then, the execution plans are cached to save the cost of execution plan generation when the same queries are re-executed. To improve the reusability of cached plans, SQL Server supports different techniques for execution plan reuse when the queries are rerun with different values for the variable parts.

Using stored procedures is usually the best technique to improve execution plan reusability. SQL Server generates a parameterized execution plan for the stored procedures, so that the existing plan can be reused when the stored procedure is rerun with same or different parameter values. However, if the existing execution plan for a stored procedure is invalidated, the plan can't be reused without a recompilation, decreasing the effectiveness of plan cache reusability.

In the next chapter, I will discuss how to troubleshoot and resolve unnecessary stored procedure plan recompilations.

CHAPTER 10

■■■

Stored Procedure Recompilation

Stored procedures improve the reusability of an execution plan by explicitly converting the variable parts of the queries into parameters. This allows execution plans to be reused when the queries are resubmitted with the same or different values for the variable parts. Since stored procedures are mostly used to implement complex business rules, a typical stored procedure contains a complex set of SQL statements, making the cost of generating the execution plan of a stored procedure a bit costly. Therefore, it is usually beneficial to reuse the existing execution plan of a stored procedure instead of generating a new plan. However, sometimes the existing plan may not be applicable, or it may not provide the best processing strategy during reuse. SQL Server resolves this condition by recompiling the stored procedure to generate a new execution plan.

In this chapter, I cover the following topics:

- The benefits and drawbacks of stored procedure recompilation

- How to identify the stored procedure statements causing recompilation

- How to analyze causes of recompilations

- Ways to avoid recompilations

Benefits and Drawbacks of Recompilation

Recompilation of stored procedures can be both beneficial and harmful. Sometimes, it may be beneficial to consider a new processing strategy for a query instead of reusing the existing plan, especially if the data distribution in the table (or the corresponding statistics) has changed or new indexes are added to the table.

To understand how recompilation of an existing plan can sometimes be beneficial, consider the following example. Say you have a table and a stored procedure based on the table (create_t1_p1.sql in the download):

```
IF(SELECT OBJECT_ID('t1')) IS NOT NULL
  DROP TABLE t1
GO
CREATE TABLE t1(c1 INT, c2 INT, c3 INT)
INSERT INTO t1 VALUES(11, 12, 13)
```

```
CREATE NONCLUSTERED INDEX i1 ON t1(c1)
GO

IF(SELECT OBJECT_ID('p1')) IS NOT NULL
  DROP PROC p1
GO
CREATE PROC p1
AS
  SELECT c1, c2 FROM t1 WHERE c1 = 11
GO
```

With the current indexes, the execution plan for the SELECT statement, which is a part of the stored procedure plan, uses the index i1 on column c1, as shown in Figure 10-1.

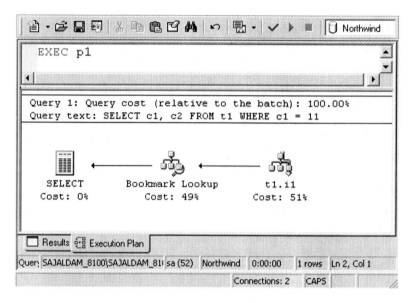

Figure 10-1. *Execution plan for the stored procedure*

This plan is saved in the procedure cache, so that it can be reused when the stored procedure is re-executed. But if a new index is added on the table as follows, then the existing plan won't be the most efficient processing strategy to execute the query:

CREATE NONCLUSTERED INDEX i2 ON t1(c1, c2)

Since index i2 can serve as a covering index for the SELECT statement, the cost of a bookmark lookup can be avoided by using index i2 instead of index i1. SQL Server automatically detects this change, and thereby recompiles the existing plan to consider the benefit of using the new index. This results in a new execution plan for the stored procedure (when executed) as shown in Figure 10-2.

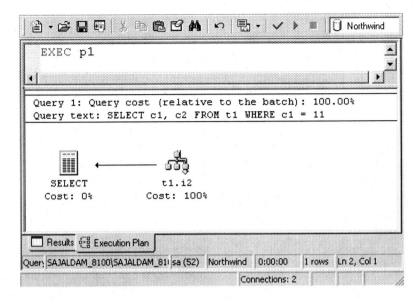

Figure 10-2. *New execution plan for the stored procedure*

In this case, it is beneficial to spend extra CPU cycles to recompile the stored procedure so that you generate a better execution plan.

SQL Server automatically detects the conditions that require recompilation of the existing plan. SQL Server follows certain rules in determining when the existing plan needs to be recompiled. If a specific implementation of a stored procedure falls within the rules of recompilation (execution plan aged out, SET options changed, etc.), then the stored procedure will be recompiled every time it is executed, and SQL Server may not generate a better execution plan. For example, consider the following stored procedure:

```
IF(SELECT OBJECT_ID('t1')) IS NOT NULL
  DROP TABLE t1
GO
CREATE TABLE t1(c1 INT, c2 INT, c3 INT)
GO


IF(SELECT OBJECT_ID('p2')) IS NOT NULL
  DROP PROC p2
GO
CREATE PROC p2
AS
  SELECT * FROM t1
GO
```

The SELECT statement in this stored procedure selects the complete data (all rows and columns) from the table and is therefore best served through a table scan on table t1. As explained in Chapter 4, the processing of the SELECT statement won't benefit a nonclustered index on column c1. Therefore, ideally, creation of the nonclustered index, as follows, before the execution of the stored procedure shouldn't matter:

```
EXEC p2
GO
CREATE NONCLUSTERED INDEX i1 ON t1(c1)
GO
EXEC p2 --After creation of index i1
```

But the stored procedure execution after the index creation faces recompilation, as shown in the corresponding Profiler trace output in Figure 10-3.

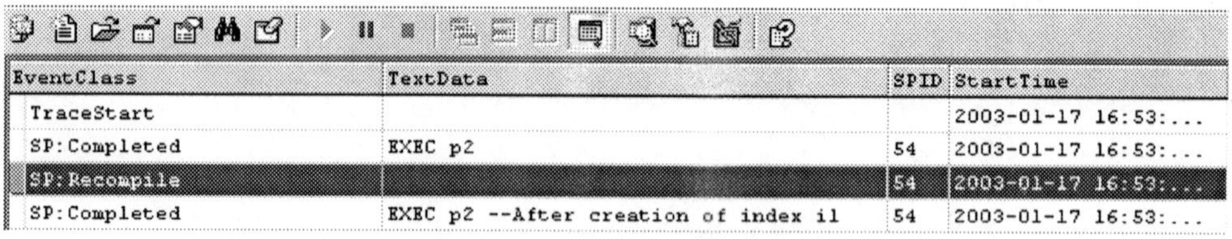

EventClass	TextData	SPID	StartTime
TraceStart			2003-01-17 16:53:...
SP:Completed	EXEC p2	54	2003-01-17 16:53:...
SP:Recompile		54	2003-01-17 16:53:...
SP:Completed	EXEC p2 --After creation of index i1	54	2003-01-17 16:53:...

Figure 10-3. *Nonbeneficial recompilation of the stored procedure*

In this case, the recompilation is of no real benefit to the stored procedure. But unfortunately, it falls within the conditions that cause SQL Server to recompile the stored procedure on every execution. This makes plan caching for the stored procedure ineffective and wastes CPU cycles in regenerating the same plan on every execution. Therefore, it is important to be aware of the conditions that cause recompilation of stored procedures and to make every effort to avoid those conditions when implementing stored procedures. I will discuss these conditions next, after identifying which statements cause SQL Server to recompile the stored procedure in the respective case.

Identifying the Statement Causing Recompilation

When a stored procedure recompiles, it's usually because just one statement in the stored procedure cannot use the existing execution plan, as opposed to the whole stored procedure. Thus, to find the cause of recompilation, it's important to identify the SQL statement that can't reuse the existing plan.

You can use the Profiler tool to track stored procedure recompilation. You can also use Profiler to identify the stored procedure statement that caused the recompilation. The relevant events and data columns you can use are shown in Table 10-1 (sprocTrace.tdf in the download).

Table 10-1. *Events and Data Columns to Analyze Stored Procedure Recompilation*

Events		Data Columns
Event Class	**Event**	
Stored procedures	SP:Completed	EventClass
	SP:Recompile	TextData
	SP:Starting	EventSubClass
	SP:StmtCompleted	SPID
	SP:StmtStarting (Optional)	StartTime

Consider the following simple stored procedure (create_p1.sql in the download):

```
IF(SELECT OBJECT_ID('p1')) IS NOT NULL

  DROP PROC p1
GO
CREATE PROC p1
AS
CREATE TABLE #t1(c1 INT)
SELECT * FROM #t1 --Needs recompilation on 1st execution
GO
```

On executing this stored procedure the first time, you get the following Profiler trace output (see Figure 10-4):

```
EXEC p1
```

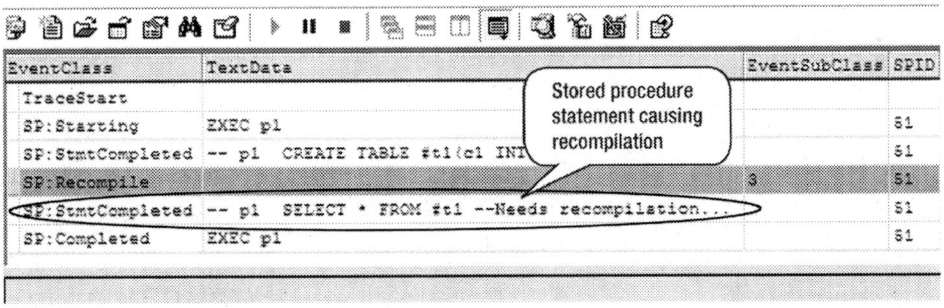

Figure 10-4. *Profiler trace output showing an SP:StmtCompleted event causing recompilation*

In Figure 10-4, you can see that you have a recompilation event (SP:Recompile), indicating that the stored procedure went through recompilation. When a stored procedure is executed for the first time, SQL Server compiles the stored procedure and generates an execution plan, as explained in the previous chapter.

Since execution plans are maintained in volatile memory only, they get dropped when SQL Server is restarted. On the next execution of the stored procedure, after the server restart, SQL Server once again compiles the stored procedure and generates the execution plan. These compilations aren't treated as a stored procedure recompilation, since a plan didn't exist in the cache for reuse. An SP:Recompile event indicates that a plan was already there but couldn't be reused.

Logically, you can deduce that the stored procedure statement (represented by the SP:StmtCompleted event) that immediately follows the recompilation event should be the one that needed a new plan to complete its execution and thus caused the recompilation of the stored procedure.

NOTE I will discuss the significance of the EventSubClass data column later in the chapter.

You can also identify the stored procedure statement causing the recompilation by using the SP:StmtStarting event. The SP:StmtStarting event immediately above the SP:Recompile event indicates the stored procedure statement that caused the recompilation, as shown in Figure 10-5.

NOTE To see the result for yourself, please re-create the stored procedure before re-executing the stored procedure.

EventClass	TextData	EventSubClass	SPID
SP:Starting	EXEC p1		51
SP:StmtStarting	-- p1 CREATE TABLE #t1(c1 INT)		51
SP:StmtCompleted	-- p1 CREATE TABLE #t1(c1 INT)		51
SP:StmtStarting	-- p1 SELECT * FROM #t1 --Needs recompilation...		51
SP:Recompile		3	51
SP:StmtStarting	-- p1 SELECT * FROM #t1 --Needs recompilation...		51
SP:StmtCompleted	-- p1 SELECT * FROM #t1 --Needs recompilation...		51
SP:Completed	EXEC p1		51

Figure 10-5. *Profiler trace output showing an SP:StmtStarting event causing recompilation*

Note that after the stored procedure recompilation, the stored procedure statement that caused the recompilation is started again to execute with the new plan. You may use either the SP:StmtStarting event or the SP:StmtCompleted event to identify the stored procedure statement causing the recompilation; using both the events will duplicate the information.

Analyzing Causes of Recompilation

To improve performance, it is important that you analyze the causes of recompilation. Often, recompilation may not be necessary, and it can be avoided to improve performance. Knowing the different conditions that result in recompilation helps you evaluate the cause of a recompilation and determine how to avoid it. Stored procedure recompilation occurs for the following reasons:

- The schema of regular tables, temporary tables, or views referred to in the stored procedure statement have changed. Schema changes include changes to the metadata of the table or the indexes on the table.

- Bindings (such as defaults/rules) to the columns of regular or temporary tables have changed.

- Statistics on the table indexes or columns have changed.

- An object did not exist when the stored procedure was compiled, but it was created during execution. This is called *deferred object resolution*, which is the cause of the preceding recompilation.

- SET options have changed.

- The execution plan was aged and deallocated.

- An explicit call was made to the sp_recompile system stored procedure.

- There was an explicit use of the RECOMPILE clause.

You can see these changes in Profiler. As of SQL Server 2000 Service Pack 2 (SP2), provisions have been made so that Profiler can indicate the cause of recompilation. The cause is indicated by the EventSubClass data column value for the SP:Recompile event, as shown in Table 10-2.

Table 10-2. *EventSubClass Data Column Reflecting Causes of Recompilation*

EventSubClass	Description
1	Schema or bindings to regular table or view changed
2	Statistics changed
3	Object did not exist in the stored procedure plan, but was created during execution
4	SET options changed
5	Schema or bindings to temporary table changed
6	Schema or bindings of remote rowset changed

Let's look at each of the reasons listed previously for recompilation in more detail and discuss what you can do to avoid them.

Schema or Bindings Changes

When the schema or bindings to a view, regular table, or temporary table change, the existing stored procedure execution plan becomes invalid. The stored procedure must be recompiled before executing any statement that refers to such an object. SQL Server automatically detects this situation and recompiles the stored procedure.

▥NOTE Recompilation due to schema change is presented in the "Benefits and Drawbacks of Recompilation" section.

Statistics Changes

SQL Server keeps track of the number of changes to the table. If the number of changes is more than a threshold value, then SQL Server (by default) automatically updates the statistics when the table is referred to in the stored procedure, as you saw in Chapter 7. When the condition for the automatic update of statistics is detected, SQL Server automatically recompiles the stored procedure, along with the statistics update.

To understand how statistics changes can cause recompilation, consider the following example (stats_changes.sql in the download). The stored procedure is executed the first time with only one row in the table. Before the second execution of the stored procedure, a large number of rows are added to the table.

▥NOTE Please ensure that the AUTO_UPDATE_STATISTICS setting for the database is ON. You can determine the AUTO UPDATE STATISTICS setting by executing the following query: SELECT DATABASEPROPERTYEX('Northwind', 'IsAutoUpdateStatistics').

```
--Create a small table with one row and an index
IF(SELECT OBJECT_ID('t1')) IS NOT NULL
   DROP TABLE t1
GO
CREATE TABLE t1(c1 INT, c2 CHAR(50))
INSERT INTO t1 VALUES(1, '2')
CREATE NONCLUSTERED INDEX i1 ON t1(c1)

--Create a stored procedure referencing the above table
IF(SELECT OBJECT_ID('p1')) IS NOT NULL
   DROP PROC p1
GO
CREATE PROC p1
```

```
AS
SELECT * FROM t1 WHERE c1 = 1
GO


--First execution of stored procedure with 1 row in the table
SET STATISTICS PROFILE ON
GO
EXEC p1 --First execution
GO
SET STATISTICS PROFILE OFF
GO
```

Next, still in stats_changes.sql, you add a number of rows before re-executing the stored procedure:

```
--Add many rows to the table to cause statistics change
SET NOCOUNT ON
DECLARE @n INT
SET @n = 1
WHILE @n <= 1000
BEGIN
  INSERT INTO t1 VALUES(1, @n)
  SET @n = @n + 1
END
GO


--Re-execute the stored procedure with the change in statistics
SET STATISTICS PROFILE ON
GO
EXEC p1 --With change in data distribution
GO
SET STATISTICS PROFILE OFF
GO
```

The first time, SQL Server executes the SELECT statement of the stored procedure using an index seek operation, as shown in Figure 10-6. While re-executing the stored procedure, SQL Server automatically detects that the statistics on the index have changed. This causes a recompilation of the stored procedure, with the optimizer determining a better processing strategy, before executing the SELECT statement within the stored procedure.

■**NOTE** Please ensure that the setting for the graphical execution plan is OFF; otherwise, the output of STATISTICS PROFILE won't display.

---

	c1	c2	
1	1	2	

	Rows	Executes	StmtText	StmtId
1	1	1	SELECT * FROM t1 WHERE c1 = 1	1
2	1	1	|--Bookmark Lookup(BOOKMARK:([Bmk1000]), OBJECT:([Northwind].[dbo].[t1]))	1
3	1	1	|--Index Seek(OBJECT:([Northwind].[dbo].[t1].[i1]), SEEK:([t1].[c1]=1)...	1

	c1	c2	
1	1	2	
2	1	1	
3	1	2	

	Rows	Executes	StmtText	StmtId	NodeId	Pare
1	1001	1	SELECT * FROM t1 WHERE c1 = 1	2	1	0
2	1001	1	|--Table Scan(OBJECT:([Northwind].[dbo].[t1]), WHERE:([t1].[c1]=1))	2	3	1

Figure 10-6. *Effect of statistics change on the execution plan*

Figure 10-7 shows the corresponding Profiler trace output (with the Auto Stats event added).

EventClass	TextData	EventSubClass	SPID
TraceStart			
SP:StmtCompleted	insert [Northwind].[dbo].[t1] select *, ...		51
SP:Starting	EXEC p1 --First execution		
SP:StmtCompleted	-- p1 SELECT * FROM t1 WHERE c1 = 1		
SP:Completed	EXEC p1 --First execution		
SP:Starting	EXEC p1 --With change in data distribution		51
SP:Recompile		2	51
SP:StmtCompleted	SELECT statman([c1],@PSTATMAN) F...		51
SP:StmtCompleted	-- p1 SELECT * FROM t1 WHERE c1 = 1		51
SP:Completed	EXEC p1 --With change in data distribution		51

Recompilation because of statistics change

Figure 10-7. *Effect of statistics change on the stored procedure recompilation*

In Figure 10-7, you can see that to execute the SELECT statement during the second execution of the stored procedure, a recompilation was required. From the value of the EventSubClass (2), you can understand that the recompilation was due to statistics change. As a part of creating the new plan, the statistics are automatically updated, as indicated by the Auto Stats event. You can also verify the automatic update of the statistics using the DBCC SHOW_STATISTICS statement as explained in Chapter 7.

Deferred Object Resolution

Stored procedures often dynamically create and subsequently access database objects. When such a stored procedure is executed for the first time, the first execution plan won't contain the information about the objects to be created during runtime. Thus, in the first execution plan, the processing strategy for those objects is deferred until the runtime of the stored procedure. When a DML statement (within the stored procedure) referring to one of those objects is executed, the stored procedure is recompiled to generate a new plan containing the processing strategy for the object.

Both a regular table and a local temporary table can be created within a stored procedure to hold intermediate result sets. Recompilation of the stored procedure due to deferred object resolution behaves differently for a regular table when compared to a local temporary table, as explained in the following section.

Recompilation Due to a Regular Table

To understand the stored procedure recompilation issue with the creation of a regular table within the stored procedure, consider the following example (regular.sql in the download):

```
IF(SELECT OBJECT_ID('p1')) IS NOT NULL
  DROP PROC p1
GO
CREATE PROC p1
AS
CREATE TABLE p1_t1(c1 INT) --Ensure table doesn't exist
SELECT * FROM p1_t1 --Causes recompilation
DROP TABLE p1_t1
GO

EXEC p1 --First execution
EXEC p1 --Second execution
```

When the stored procedure is executed for the first time, an execution plan is generated before the actual execution of the stored procedure. If the table created within the stored procedure doesn't exist (as expected in the preceding code) before the stored procedure is created, then the plan won't contain the processing strategy for the SELECT statement referring to the table. Thus to execute the SELECT statement, the stored procedure needs to be recompiled, as shown in Figure 10-8.

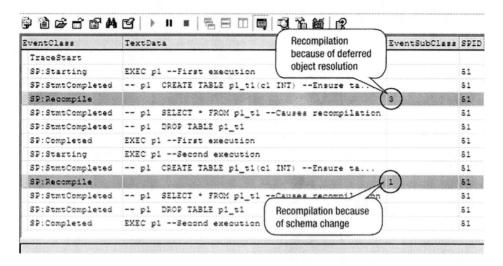

Figure 10-8. *Profiler trace output showing a stored procedure recompilation because of a regular table*

You can see that the stored procedure is recompiled when it's executed the second time. Dropping the table within the stored procedure during the first execution doesn't drop the stored procedure plan saved in the procedure cache. During the subsequent execution of the stored procedure, the existing plan includes the processing strategy for the table. However, due to the re-creation of the table within the stored procedure, SQL Server considers it a change to the table schema. Therefore, SQL Server recompiles the stored procedure before executing the SELECT statement during the subsequent execution of the stored procedure. The value of the EventSubClass for the corresponding SP:Recompile event reflects the cause of the recompilation.

Recompilation Due to a Local Temporary Table

Most of the time in the stored procedure, you create local temporary tables instead of regular tables. To understand how differently the local temporary tables affect stored procedure recompilation, modify the preceding example by just replacing the regular table with a local temporary table:

```
IF(SELECT OBJECT_ID('p1')) IS NOT NULL
  DROP PROC p1
GO
CREATE PROC p1
AS
CREATE TABLE #p1_t1(c1 INT) -- # designates local temp table
SELECT * FROM #p1_t1 --Causes recompilation on 1st execution
DROP TABLE #p1_t1 --Optional
GO

EXEC p1 --First execution
EXEC p1 --Second execution
```

Since a local temporary table is automatically dropped when the execution of a stored procedure finishes, it's not necessary to drop the temporary table explicitly. But, following good programming practice, you can drop the local temporary table as soon as its work is done.

Figure 10-9 shows the Profiler trace output for the preceding example.

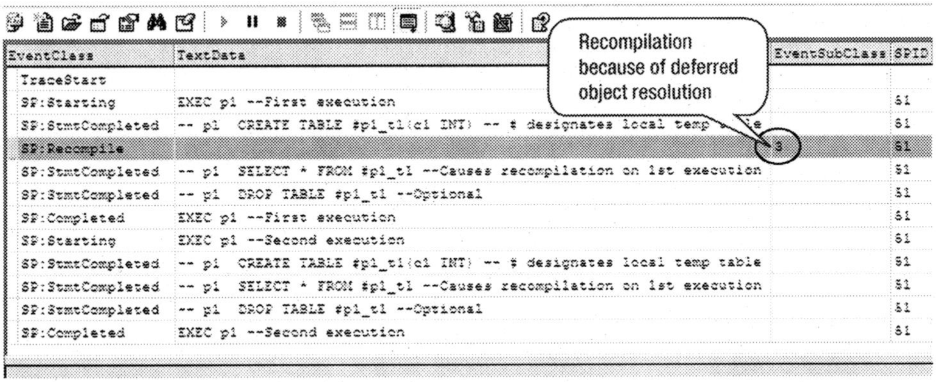

Figure 10-9. *Profiler trace output showing a stored procedure recompilation because of a local-temporary table*

You can see that the stored procedure is recompiled when executed for the first time. The cause of the recompilation, as indicated by the corresponding EventSubClass value, is the same as the cause of the recompilation on a regular table. However, note that when the stored procedure is re-executed, it isn't recompiled, unlike the case with a regular table.

The schema of a local temporary table during subsequent execution of the stored procedure remains exactly the same as during the previous execution. A local temporary table isn't available outside the scope of the stored procedure, so its schema can't be altered in any way between multiple executions. Thus, SQL Server safely reuses the existing plan (based on the previous instance of the local temporary table) during the subsequent execution of the stored procedure, and thereby avoids the recompilation.

■**NOTE** To avoid recompilation, it makes sense to hold the intermediate result sets in the stored procedure using local temporary tables, instead of using regular tables as an alternative.

SET Options Changes

The execution plan of a stored procedure is dependent on the environment settings. If the environment settings are changed within a stored procedure, then SQL Server recompiles the stored procedure on every execution. For example, consider the following code (set.sql in the download):

```
IF(SELECT OBJECT_ID('p1')) IS NOT NULL
  DROP PROC p1
```

```
GO
CREATE PROC p1
AS
SELECT 'a' + null + 'b' --1st
SET CONCAT_NULL_YIELDS_NULL OFF
SELECT 'a' + null + 'b' --2nd
SET ANSI_NULLS OFF
SELECT 'a' + null + 'b' --3rd
GO

EXEC p1 --First execution
EXEC p1 --Second execution
```

Changing the SET options in the stored procedure causes SQL Server to recompile the stored procedure before executing the statement after the SET statement. Thus, this stored procedure is recompiled twice: once before executing the second SELECT statement and once before executing the third SELECT statement. This is shown in the Profiler trace output in Figure 10-10.

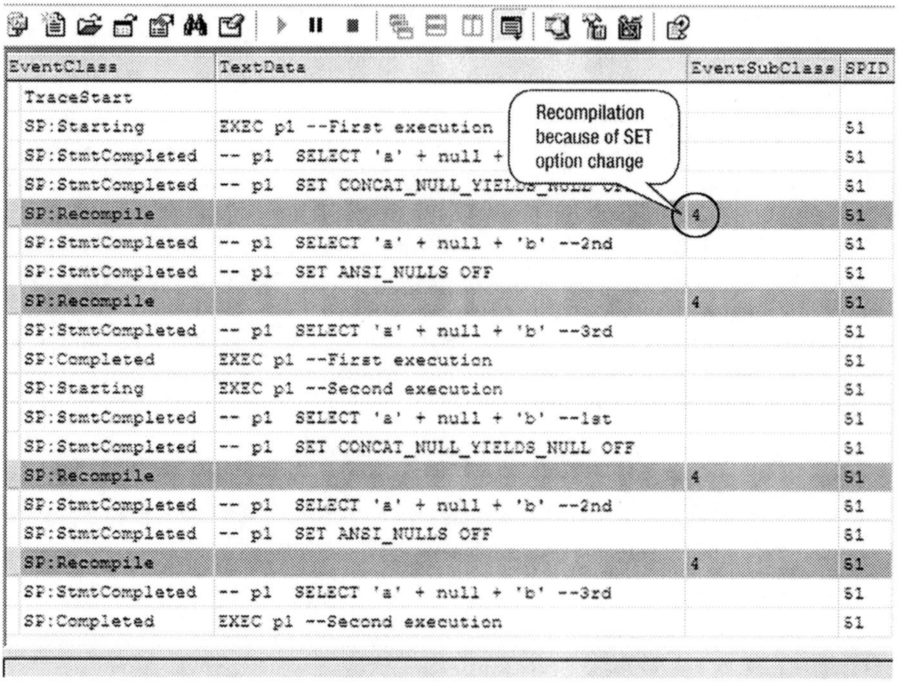

EventClass	TextData	EventSubClass	SPID
TraceStart			
SP:Starting	EXEC p1 --First execution		51
SP:StmtCompleted	-- p1 SELECT 'a' + null +		51
SP:StmtCompleted	-- p1 SET CONCAT_NULL_YIELDS_NULL OF		51
SP:Recompile		4	51
SP:StmtCompleted	-- p1 SELECT 'a' + null + 'b' --2nd		51
SP:StmtCompleted	-- p1 SET ANSI_NULLS OFF		51
SP:Recompile		4	51
SP:StmtCompleted	-- p1 SELECT 'a' + null + 'b' --3rd		51
SP:Completed	EXEC p1 --First execution		51
SP:Starting	EXEC p1 --Second execution		51
SP:StmtCompleted	-- p1 SELECT 'a' + null + 'b' --1st		51
SP:StmtCompleted	-- p1 SET CONCAT_NULL_YIELDS_NULL OFF		51
SP:Recompile		4	51
SP:StmtCompleted	-- p1 SELECT 'a' + null + 'b' --2nd		51
SP:StmtCompleted	-- p1 SET ANSI_NULLS OFF		51
SP:Recompile		4	51
SP:StmtCompleted	-- p1 SELECT 'a' + null + 'b' --3rd		51
SP:Completed	EXEC p1 --Second execution		51

Recompilation because of SET option change

Figure 10-10. *Profiler trace output showing a stored procedure recompilation because of a SET option change*

You can see that the stored procedure is recompiled the same number of times on subsequent execution, too. If this stored procedure is executed multiple times, then it will be recompiled twice on every execution. Since SET NOCOUNT does not change the environment settings unlike the SET statements used to change the ANSI settings as shown previously, SET NOCOUNT does not cause stored procedure recompilation. The use of SET NOCOUNT is explained in detail in Chapter 11.

Execution Plan Aging

SQL Server manages the size of the procedure cache by maintaining the age of the execution plans in the cache, as you saw in Chapter 9. If a stored procedure is not re-executed for a long time, then the age field of the execution plan can come down to 0, and the plan can be removed from the cache due to memory shortage. When this happens and the stored procedure is re-executed, a new plan will be generated and cached in the procedure cache. However, if there is enough memory in the system, unused plans are not removed from the cache until memory pressure increases.

Explicit Call to sp_recompile

SQL Server automatically recompiles stored procedures when the schema or statistics of the underlying objects change. It also provides the sp_recompile system stored procedure to manually mark stored procedures for recompilation. This stored procedure can be called on a table, view, stored procedure, or trigger. If it is called on a stored procedure or a trigger, then the stored procedure or trigger is recompiled the next time it is executed. Calling sp_recompile on a table or a view marks all the stored procedures and triggers that refer to the table/view for recompilation the next time they are executed.

For example, if sp_recompile is called on table t1, all the stored procedures and triggers that refer to table t1 are marked for recompilation, and are recompiled the next time they are executed:

```
sp_recompile 't1'
```

You can use sp_recompile to avoid the reuse of an existing plan by a well-defined workload executed using sp_executesql. As demonstrated in the previous chapter, you should not parameterize the variable parts of a query whose range of values may require different processing strategies for the query. For instance, reconsidering the corresponding example, you know that the second execution of the query reuses the plan generated for the first execution. The example is repeated here for easy reference:

```
DBCC FREEPROCCACHE --Clear the procedure cache
GO
EXEC sp_executesql --First query
  N'SELECT d.* FROM Orders o, [Order Details] d
    WHERE o.OrderID = d.OrderID AND o.OrderID >= @1'
  , N'@1 INT'
  , @1=11077 --Last OrderID value
EXEC sp_executesql --Second query
  N'SELECT d.* FROM Orders o, [Order Details] d
    WHERE o.OrderID = d.OrderID AND o.OrderID >= @1'
  , N'@1 INT'
  , @1=1 --First OrderID value
```

The second execution of the query performs an index seek operation on the [Order Details] table to retrieve all 2,155 rows from the table. As explained in Chapter 4, an index scan operation would have been preferred on the [Order Details] table for the second execution. You can achieve this by executing the sp_recompile system stored procedure on the [Order Details] table as follows:

```
EXEC sp_recompile 'Order Details'
```

Now, if the query with the second parameter value is re-executed, the plan for the query will be recompiled as marked by the preceding sp_recompile statement. This allows SQL Server to generate an optimal plan for the second execution.

Well, there is a slight problem here: you will likely want to re-execute the first statement again. With the plan existing in the cache, SQL Server will reuse the plan (the index scan operation on the [Order Details] table) for the first statement even though an index seek operation (using the index on the filter criterion column [od].[OrderID]) would have been optimal. One way of avoiding this problem can be to create a stored procedure for the query and use a WITH RECOMPILE clause, as explained next.

Explicit Use of the RECOMPILE Clause

SQL Server allows a stored procedure to be explicitly recompiled using the RECOMPILE clause with the CREATE PROCEDURE or EXECUTE statement. These methods decrease the effectiveness of plan reusability, so you should consider them only under the specific circumstances explained in the following sections.

RECOMPILE Clause with the CREATE PROCEDURE Statement

Sometimes the plan requirements of a stored procedure may vary as the parameter values to the stored procedure change. In such a case, reusing the plan with different parameter values may degrade the performance of the stored procedure. You can avoid this by using the RECOMPILE clause with the CREATE PROCEDURE statement. For example, for the query in the preceding section, you can create a stored procedure with the RECOMPILE clause:

```
IF(SELECT OBJECT_ID('p1')) IS NOT NULL
  DROP PROC p1
GO
CREATE PROC p1
@1 INT
WITH RECOMPILE
AS
  SELECT d.* FROM Orders o, [Order Details] d
  WHERE o.OrderID = d.OrderID AND o.OrderID >= @1
GO
```

The RECOMPILE clause prevents the caching of the stored procedure plan. Every time the stored procedure is executed, a new plan will be generated. Therefore, if the stored procedure is executed with the o.OrderID value as 11077 or 1

```
EXEC p1 11077 --o.OrderID >= 11077
EXEC p1 1      --o.OrderID >= 1
```

a new plan will be generated during the individual execution, as shown in Figure 10-11.

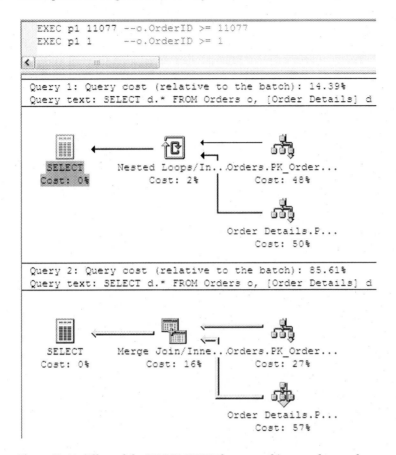

Figure 10-11. *Effect of the RECOMPILE clause used in stored procedure creation*

RECOMPILE Clause with the EXECUTE Statement

As shown previously, specific parameter values in a stored procedure may require a different plan, depending upon the nature of the values. You can take the RECOMPILE clause out of the stored procedure and use it on a case-by-case basis when you execute the stored procedure, as follows:

```
EXEC p1 1 WITH RECOMPILE
```

When the stored procedure is executed with the RECOMPILE clause, a new plan is generated temporarily. The new plan isn't cached, and it doesn't affect the existing plan. When the stored procedure is executed without the RECOMPILE clause, the plan is cached as usual. This provides better reusability of the existing plan cache than using the RECOMPILE clause with the CREATE PROCEDURE statement.

Since the plan for the stored procedure when executed with the RECOMPILE clause is not cached, the plan is regenerated every time the stored procedure is executed with the RECOMPILE clause. However, for better performance, instead of using RECOMPILE, you should consider creating separate stored procedures, one for each set of parameter values that requires a different plan.

Avoiding Recompilations

Sometimes recompilation is beneficial, but at other times it is worth avoiding. If a new index is created on a column referred to in the WHERE clause or the JOIN clause of a query, it makes sense to regenerate the execution plans of stored procedures referring to the table, so they can benefit from using the index. However, if recompilation is deemed detrimental to performance, you can avoid it by following these implementation practices:

- Do not interleave DDL and DML statements.

- Avoid recompilation caused by statistics change:

  - Use the KEEPFIXED PLAN option.

  - Disable the auto update statistics feature on the table.

- Do not refer to temporary tables created outside the stored procedure.

- Use table variables.

- Avoid changing SET options within the stored procedure.

- Isolate the plan for the statement causing recompilation.

Do Not Interleave DDL and DML Statements

In stored procedures, DDL statements are often used to create local temporary tables and to change their schema (including adding indexes). Doing so can affect the validity of the existing plan and can cause recompilation when the stored procedure statements referring to the tables are executed. To understand how the use of DDL statements for local temporary tables can cause repetitive recompilation of the stored procedure, consider the following example (ddl.sql in the download):

```
IF(SELECT OBJECT_ID('p1')) IS NOT NULL
  DROP PROC p1
GO
CREATE PROC p1
AS
CREATE TABLE #t1(c1 INT, c2 INT)
SELECT * FROM #t1 --Needs 1st recompilation
CREATE CLUSTERED INDEX i1 ON #t1(c1)
SELECT * FROM #t1 --Needs 2nd recompilation
```

```
CREATE TABLE #t2(c1 INT)
SELECT * FROM #t2 --Needs 3rd recompilation
GO
```

```
EXEC p1 --First execution
```

The stored procedure has interleaved DDL and DML statements. Figure 10-12 shows the Profiler trace output of the preceding code.

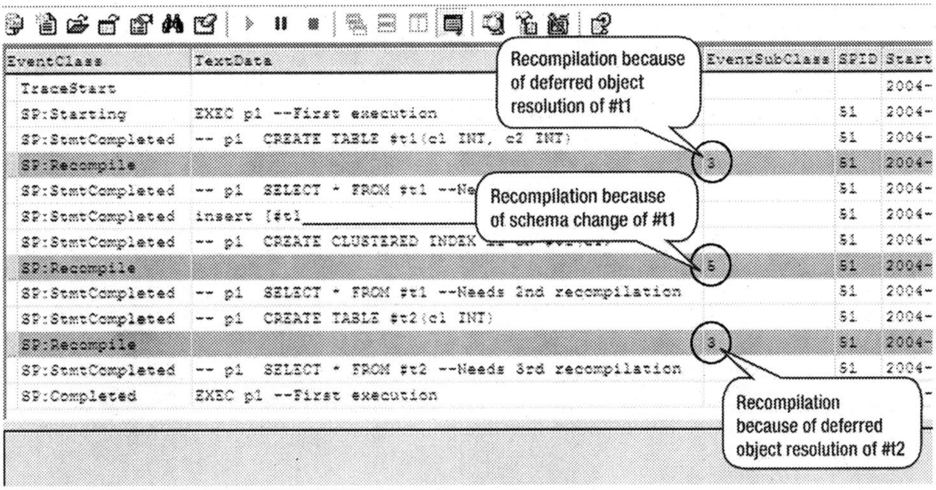

Figure 10-12. *Profiler trace output showing recompilation because of DDL and DML interleaving*

You can see that the stored procedure is recompiled three times:

- The execution plan generated for a stored procedure when it is first executed doesn't contain any information about local temporary tables. Therefore, the first generated plan can never be used to access the temporary table using a DML statement.

- The second recompilation is due to a schema change in the first temporary table (#t1). The creation of the index on #t1 invalidates the existing plan, causing a recompilation when the table is accessed again. If this index had been created before the first recompilation, then the existing plan would have remained valid for the second SELECT statement too. Therefore, this recompilation can be avoided by putting the CREATE INDEX DDL statement above all DML statements referring to the table.

- The third recompilation of the stored procedure generates a plan to include the processing strategy for #t2. The existing plan has no information about #t2 and therefore cannot be used to access #t2 using the third SELECT statement. If the CREATE TABLE DDL statement for #t2 had been placed before all the DML statements that could cause a recompilation, then the first recompilation itself would have included the information on #t2, avoiding the third recompilation.

If this stored procedure is re-executed, then all three recompilations take place again with slightly different causes (see Figure 10-13):

```
EXEC p1 --Second execution
```

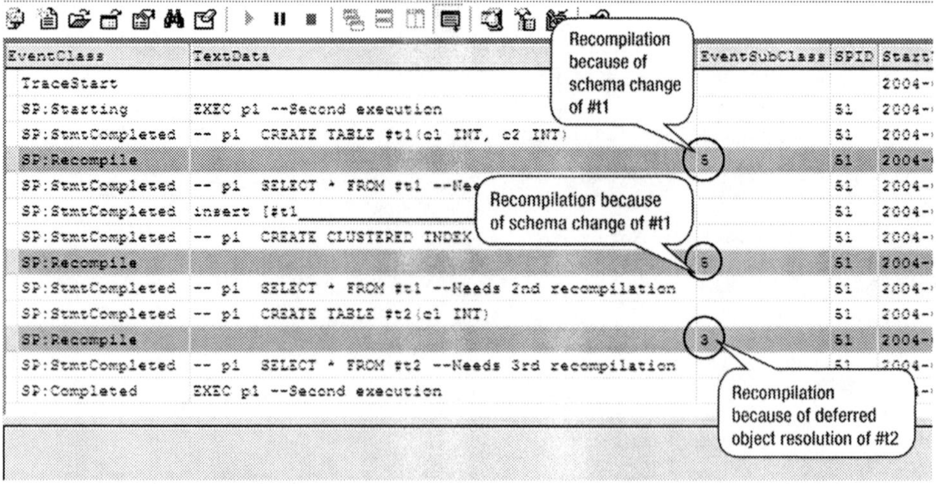

Figure 10-13. *Profiler trace output showing repeated recompilation because of DDL and DML interleaving*

The last plan generated during the first execution of the stored procedure includes the information on #t1 (with an index) and #t2. During this subsequent execution of the stored procedure, #t1 is re-created, and the first SELECT statement attempts to access this table. The current schema of #t1 is different from that in the existing plan generated during the previous execution: currently, the index on #t1 is missing. This causes the first recompilation.

The new plan contains no information about the index and the table #t2 to be created down the line, making this plan exactly the same as the corresponding plan created during the first execution of the stored procedure. Therefore, the second and third recompilations follow just the same process as in the first execution of the stored procedure.

If this stored procedure is executed multiple times, each time it is executed it will be recompiled three times. You can avoid this by having the first recompiled plan include information about all the objects and schema changes before any DML statement tries to access them. This also keeps the plan valid during subsequent executions of the stored procedure, since before the plan is referred to by DML statement, all the objects are restored in the form as available in the existing plan. To confirm this resolution, modify the stored procedure as follows (ddl2.sql in the download):

```
IF(SELECT OBJECT_ID('p1')) IS NOT NULL
  DROP PROC p1
GO
CREATE PROC p1
AS
CREATE TABLE #t1(c1 INT, c2 INT)
CREATE CLUSTERED INDEX i1 ON #t1(c1)
CREATE TABLE #t2(c1 INT)
```

```
--All DML statements below the DDL statements
SELECT * FROM #t1 --1st
SELECT * FROM #t1 --2nd
SELECT * FROM #t2 --3rd
GO

EXEC p1 --First execution
EXEC p1 --Second execution
```

Figure 10-14 shows the subsequent Profiler trace output.

EventClass	TextData	EventSubClass	SPID
TraceStart			
SP:Starting	EXEC p1 --First execution		51
SP:StmtCompleted	-- p1 CREATE TABLE #t1(c1 INT, c2		51
SP:StmtCompleted	insert [#t1		51
SP:StmtCompleted	-- p1 CREATE CLUSTERED INDEX i1 ON		51
SP:StmtCompleted	-- p1 CREATE TABLE #t2(c1 INT) --All DML statements		51
SP:Recompile		3	51
SP:StmtCompleted	-- p1 SELECT * FROM #t1 --1st		51
SP:StmtCompleted	-- p1 SELECT * FROM #t1 --2nd		51
SP:StmtCompleted	-- p1 SELECT * FROM #t2 --3rd		51
SP:Completed	EXEC p1 --First execution		51
SP:Starting	EXEC p1 --Second execution		51
SP:StmtCompleted	-- p1 CREATE TABLE #t1(c1 INT, c2 INT)		51
SP:StmtCompleted	insert [#t1 ...		51
SP:StmtCompleted	-- p1 CREATE CLUSTERED INDEX i1 ON #t1(c1)		51
SP:StmtCompleted	-- p1 CREATE TABLE #t2(c1 INT) --All DML statements...		51
SP:StmtCompleted	-- p1 SELECT * FROM #t1 --1st		51
SP:StmtCompleted	-- p1 SELECT * FROM #t1 --2nd		51
SP:StmtCompleted	-- p1 SELECT * FROM #t2 --3rd		51
SP:Completed	EXEC p1 --Second execution		51

> Recompilation because of deferred object resolution of #t1

Figure 10-14. *Profiler trace output showing a reduction in recompilations by not interleaving DDL and DML statements*

You can see that the stored procedure is recompiled only once during the first execution. As explained previously, the first recompilation of a stored procedure that uses a local temporary table is quite natural, since the temporary table information isn't available when the stored procedure is compiled the first time. Note that the subsequent execution of the stored procedure doesn't face any recompilation. If this stored procedure is executed multiple times, then, except for the first execution, no other subsequent execution faces any recompilation.

Avoid Recompilations Caused by Statistics Change

In the "Analyzing Causes of Recompilation" section, you saw that a change in statistics is one of the causes of recompilation. On a simple table with uniform data distribution, recompilation due to change of statistics may generate a plan identical to the previous plan. In such situations, recompilation is unnecessary and should be avoided.

You have two techniques to avoid recompilations caused by statistics change:

- Use the KEEPFIXED PLAN option.

- Disable the auto update statistics feature on the table.

Use the KEEPFIXED PLAN Option

SQL Server provides a KEEPFIXED PLAN option to avoid recompilations due to statistics change. To understand how you can use KEEPFIXED PLAN, consider stats_changes.sql with an appropriate modification to use the KEEPFIXED PLAN option:

```
--Create a small table with one row and an index
IF(SELECT OBJECT_ID('t1')) IS NOT NULL
  DROP TABLE t1
GO
CREATE TABLE t1(c1 INT, c2 CHAR(50))
INSERT INTO t1 VALUES(1, '2')
CREATE NONCLUSTERED INDEX i1 ON t1(c1)

--Create a stored procedure referencing the above table
IF(SELECT OBJECT_ID('p1')) IS NOT NULL
  DROP PROC p1
GO
CREATE PROC p1
AS
SELECT * FROM t1 WHERE c1 = 1 OPTION(KEEPFIXED PLAN)
GO

--First execution of stored procedure with 1 row in the table
EXEC p1 --First execution

--Add many rows to the table to cause statistics change
DECLARE @n INT
SET @n = 1
WHILE @n <= 1000
BEGIN
  INSERT INTO t1 VALUES(1, @n)
  SET @n = @n + 1
END
GO

--Re-execute the stored procedure with a change in statistics
EXEC p1 --With change in data distribution
```

Figure 10-15 shows the Profiler trace output.

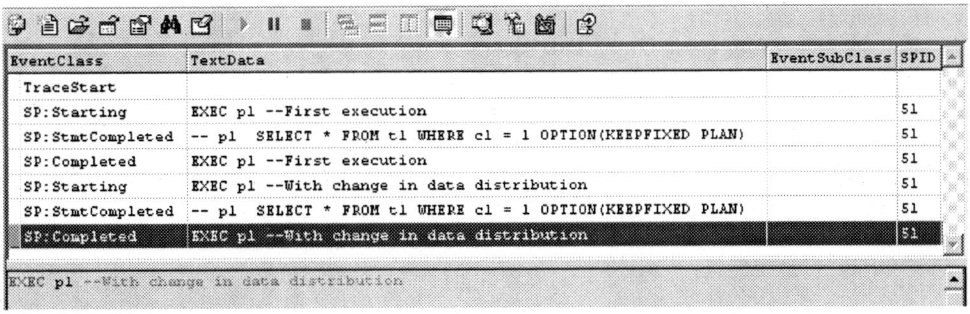

EventClass	TextData	EventSubClass	SPID
TraceStart			
SP:Starting	EXEC p1 --First execution		51
SP:StmtCompleted	-- p1 SELECT * FROM t1 WHERE c1 = 1 OPTION(KEEPFIXED PLAN)		51
SP:Completed	EXEC p1 --First execution		51
SP:Starting	EXEC p1 --With change in data distribution		51
SP:StmtCompleted	-- p1 SELECT * FROM t1 WHERE c1 = 1 OPTION(KEEPFIXED PLAN)		51
SP:Completed	EXEC p1 --With change in data distribution		51

EXEC p1 --With change in data distribution

Figure 10-15. *Profiler trace output showing the role of the KEEPFIXED PLAN option in reducing recompilation*

You can see that, unlike previously, there's no Auto Stats event. Consequently, there's no recompilation. Therefore, by using the KEEPFIXED PLAN option, you can avoid recompilation due to statistics change.

■**NOTE** Before you consider using this option, ensure that any new plans that would have been generated are not superior to the existing plan.

Disable Auto Update Statistics on the Table

Recompilation due to a statistics update can also be avoided by disabling the automatic statistics update on the relevant table. For example, you can disable the auto update statistics feature on table t1 as follows:

```
EXEC sp_autostats 't1', 'OFF'
```

If you disable this feature on the table before inserting the large number of rows that causes statistics change, then you can avoid the recompilation due to statistics change.

However, be cautious with this technique, since outdated statistics can adversely affect the effectiveness of the cost-based optimizer, as discussed in Chapter 7. Also, as explained in Chapter 7, if you disable the automatic update of statistics, you should have a SQL job to update the statistics regularly.

Do Not Refer to a Temporary Table Created Outside the Stored Procedure

To avoid recompilation, ensure that all the local temporary tables referred to in a stored procedure are created within the same stored procedure. If a local temporary table referred to in a called stored procedure is created in the caller stored procedure, then every time a DML statement refers to the temporary table in the called stored procedure, the called stored procedure is recompiled. To see this in action, consider the following parent and child stored procedures (parent_child.sql in the download):

```
--Parent stored procedure
IF(SELECT OBJECT_ID('pParent')) IS NOT NULL
  DROP PROC pParent
GO
CREATE PROC pParent
AS
CREATE TABLE #t1(c1 INT)
EXEC pChild
GO

--Child stored procedure
IF(SELECT OBJECT_ID('pChild')) IS NOT NULL
  DROP PROC pChild
GO
CREATE PROC pChild
AS
SELECT * FROM #t1 --Causes recompilation
GO

--Execute parent stored procedure multiple times
EXEC pParent --1st execution
EXEC pParent --2nd execution
EXEC pParent --3rd execution
```

When the stored procedure pParent is executed for the first time, the temporary table is created and then the nested stored procedure pChild is executed. On this first execution of the pChild stored procedure, the execution plan for the pChild procedure is generated. Since the temporary table is created before the execution plan of the pChild stored procedure is generated, the first-time execution plan of the pChild stored procedure uses the schema of the temporary table, making the execution plan a fully usable execution plan. Therefore, the first execution of the pChild stored procedure doesn't undergo recompilation, as you can see in the corresponding Profiler trace output in Figure 10-16.

However, you can see that the pChild stored procedure is recompiled when it is executed the second and the third time, or during every subsequent execution. Although the schema of the temporary table during subsequent execution of the pChild stored procedure remains exactly the same, the temporary table is available outside the scope of the pChild stored procedure, making it possible to alter the schema of the temporary table between multiple executions of the pChild stored procedure, if called so from the pParent stored procedure. Therefore, SQL Server recompiles the pChild stored procedure before executing the SELECT statement during the subsequent executions of the pChild stored procedure. The value of EventSubClass for the corresponding SP:Recompile event reflects the cause of the recompilation.

To avoid this recompilation, create the temporary table in the same stored procedure where the temporary table is referred to by the DML statements.

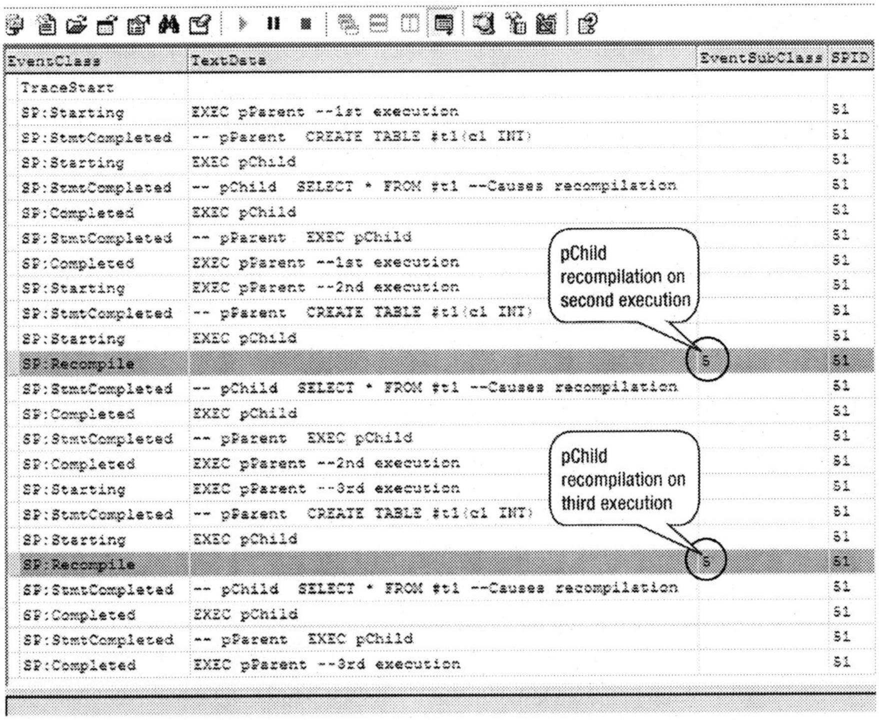

Figure 10-16. *Profiler trace output showing recompilation because of referencing an external temporary table*

Use Table Variables

One of the variable types supported by SQL Server 2000 is the table variable. You can create the table variable data type like other data types, using the DECLARE statement. It behaves like a local variable, and you can use it inside a stored procedure to hold intermediate result sets, as you do using a temporary table.

You can avoid the recompilations caused by a temporary table if you use a table variable. Since the table variable is not saved in the database as a database object, the different recompilation issues associated with temporary tables are not applicable to it. For instance, consider create_p1.sql used in the section "Identifying the Statement Causing Recompilation." It is repeated here for your reference:

```
IF(SELECT OBJECT_ID('p1')) IS NOT NULL
  DROP PROC p1
GO
CREATE PROC p1
AS
CREATE TABLE #t1(c1 INT)
SELECT * FROM #t1 --Needs recompilation on 1st execution
GO

EXEC p1 --First execution
```

Due to deferred object resolution, the stored procedure is recompiled during the first execution. You can avoid this recompilation caused by the temporary table by using the table variable as follows:

```
IF(SELECT OBJECT_ID('p1')) IS NOT NULL
  DROP PROC p1
GO
CREATE PROC p1
AS
DECLARE @t1 TABLE(c1 INT)
SELECT * FROM @t1 --Recompilation not needed
GO


EXEC p1 --First execution
```

Figure 10-17 shows the Profiler trace output for the first execution of the stored procedure. The recompilation caused by the temporary table has been avoided by using the table variable.

EventClass	TextData	EventSubClass	SPID
TraceStart			
SP:Starting	EXEC p1 --First execution		51
SP:StmtCompleted	-- p1 SELECT * FROM @t1 --Recompila...		51
SP:Completed	EXEC p1 --First execution		51

EXEC p1 --First execution

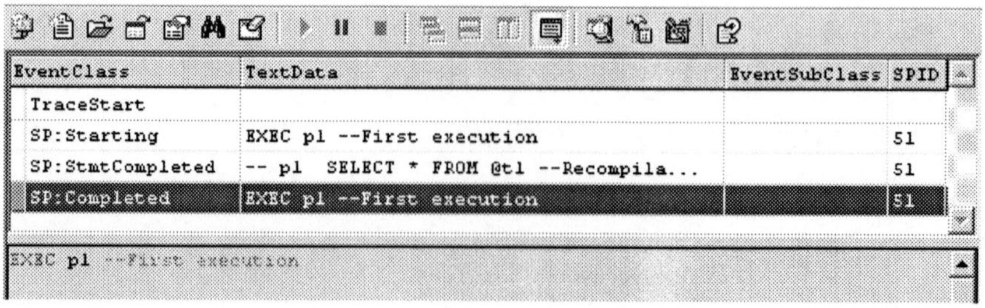

Figure 10-17. *Profiler trace output showing the role of a table variable in resolving recompilation*

Additional benefits of using the table variables are as follows:

- *No transaction log overhead*: No transaction log activities are performed for table variables, whereas they are for both regular and temporary tables.

- *No lock overhead*: Since table variables are treated like local variables (not database objects), the locking overhead associated with regular tables and temporary tables does not exist.

- *No rollback overhead*: Since no transaction log activities are performed for table variables, no rollback overhead is applicable for table variables. For example, consider the following code (rollback.sql in the download):

```
DECLARE @t1 TABLE(c1 INT)
INSERT INTO @t1 VALUES(1)
BEGIN TRAN
  INSERT INTO @t1 VALUES(2)
ROLLBACK
SELECT * FROM @t1 --Returns 2 rows
```

The ROLLBACK statement won't roll back the second row insertion into the table variable.

However, table variables have their limitations. The main ones are as follows:

- No DDL statement can be executed on the table variable once it is created, which means no indexes or constraints can be added to the table variable later. Constraints can be specified only as a part of the table variable's DECLARE statement. Therefore, only one index can be created on a table variable, using the PRIMARY KEY or the UNIQUE constraint.

- The following statements are not supported on the table variables:

  - INSERT INTO TableVariable EXEC StoredProcedure

  - SELECT SelectList INTO TableVariable FROM Table

  - SET TableVariable = Value

Avoid Changing SET Options Within a Stored Procedure

It is generally recommended that you not change the environment settings within a stored procedure, and thus avoid recompilation due to changing the SET options. For ANSI compatibility, it is recommended that you keep the following SET options ON:

- ARITHABORT

- CONCAT_NULL_YIELDS_NULL

- QUOTED_IDENTIFIER

- ANSI_NULLS

- ANSI_PADDING

- ANSI_WARNINGS

NUMERIC_ROUNDABORT should be OFF.

Although the following approach is not recommended, you can avoid recompilation caused by some of these SET options changes by resetting the options for the connection as shown in the following modifications to set.sql:

```
IF(SELECT OBJECT_ID('p1')) IS NOT NULL
  DROP PROC p1
GO
CREATE PROC p1
AS
SELECT 'a' + null + 'b' --1st
SET CONCAT_NULL_YIELDS_NULL OFF
SELECT 'a' + null + 'b' --2nd
SET ANSI_NULLS OFF
SELECT 'a' + null + 'b' --3rd
GO


SET CONCAT_NULL_YIELDS_NULL OFF
```

```
SET ANSI_NULLS OFF
EXEC p1
SET CONCAT_NULL_YIELDS_NULL ON --Reset to default
SET ANSI_NULLS ON                --Reset to default
```

Figure 10-18 shows the Profiler trace output.

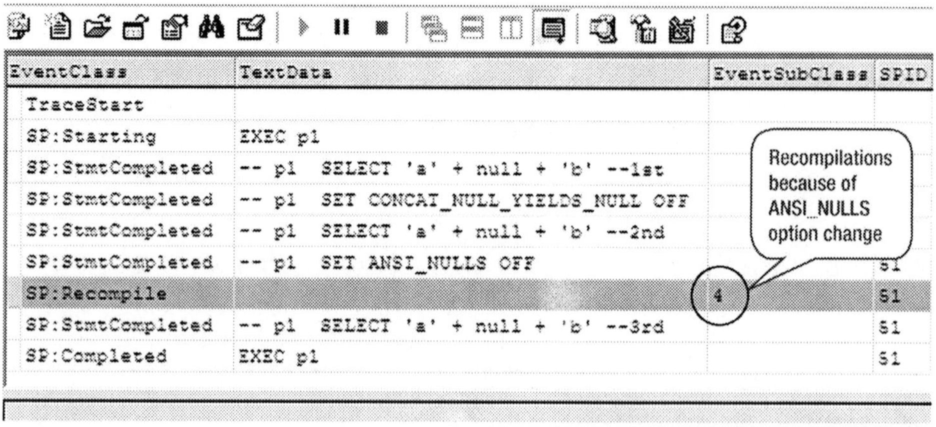

Figure 10-18. *Profiler trace output showing effect of the ANSI SET options on stored procedure recompilation*

You can see that the stored procedure faced fewer recompilations when compared to the original set.sql code. Unlike previously, the recompilation due to SET CONCAT_NULL_YIELDS_NULL OFF is avoided. However, SET ANSI_NULLS OFF still caused a recompilation.

Out of the SET options listed previously, the ANSI_NULLS and QUOTED_IDENTIFIER options are saved as a part of the stored procedure when it is created. Therefore, setting these options in the connection outside the stored procedure won't affect any recompilation issues; only re-creating the stored procedure can change these settings.

Isolate the Plan for the Statement Causing Recompilation

Sometimes it becomes too difficult to avoid recompilation. In such cases, you can identify the statement causing the recompilation, and then execute the statement using

- A sub-stored procedure

- The sp_executesql system stored procedure

- The EXECUTE statement

By executing the statement using one of these methods, you can isolate the plan of the statement causing recompilation from the plan of the stored procedure.

Sub-Stored Procedure

Placing the offending statement in a sub-stored procedure doesn't really reduce the number of recompilations, but it does avoid recompilation of the main stored procedure. Since the overhead of recompilation is proportional to the complexity of the stored procedure, you can reduce the overall cost of recompilation by using a sub-stored procedure.

sp_executesql or EXECUTE

You can also isolate the statement causing recompilation from the plan of the stored procedure by executing it using the sp_executesql or EXECUTE method. For example, consider ddl.sql again:

```
IF(SELECT OBJECT_ID('p1')) IS NOT NULL
  DROP PROC p1
GO
CREATE PROC p1
AS
CREATE TABLE #t1(c1 INT, c2 INT)
SELECT * FROM #t1 --Needs 1st recompilation
CREATE CLUSTERED INDEX i1 ON #t1(c1)
SELECT * FROM #t1 --Needs 2nd recompilation
CREATE TABLE #t2(c1 INT)
SELECT * FROM #t2 --Needs 3rd recompilation
GO

EXEC p1
```

As you saw earlier, this stored procedure is recompiled three times on every execution. You know that you can avoid these recompilations by not interleaving the DDL and DML statements as suggested previously. However, if it becomes too difficult to avoid these recompilations, you can execute the DML statements using the sp_executesql system stored procedure as follows:

```
IF(SELECT OBJECT_ID('p1')) IS NOT NULL
  DROP PROC p1
GO
CREATE PROC p1
AS
CREATE TABLE #t1(c1 INT, c2 INT)
EXEC sp_executesql N'SELECT * FROM #t1' --Avoid 1st recompilation
CREATE CLUSTERED INDEX i1 ON #t1(c1)
EXEC sp_executesql N'SELECT * FROM #t1' --Avoid 2nd recompilation
CREATE TABLE #t2(c1 INT)
EXEC sp_executesql N'SELECT * FROM #t2' --Avoid 3rd recompilation
GO
EXEC p1
```

Figure 10-19 shows the resultant Profiler trace output. You can see that all three recompilations of the stored procedure are avoided by using the sp_executesql method.

EventClass	TextData	EventSubClass	SPID
TraceStart			
SP:Starting	EXEC p1		51
SP:StmtCompleted	-- p1 CREATE TABLE #t1(c1 INT, c2 INT)		51
SP:StmtCompleted	SELECT * FROM #t1		51
SP:StmtCompleted	-- p1 EXEC sp_executesql N'SELECT * ...		51
SP:StmtCompleted	-- p1 CREATE CLUSTERED INDEX i1 ON #...		51
SP:StmtCompleted	SELECT * FROM #t1		51
SP:StmtCompleted	-- p1 EXEC sp_executesql N'SELECT * ...		51
SP:StmtCompleted	-- p1 CREATE TABLE #t2(c1 INT)		51
SP:StmtCompleted	SELECT * FROM #t2		51
SP:StmtCompleted	-- p1 EXEC sp_executesql N'SELECT * ...		51
SP:Completed	EXEC p1		51

EXEC p1

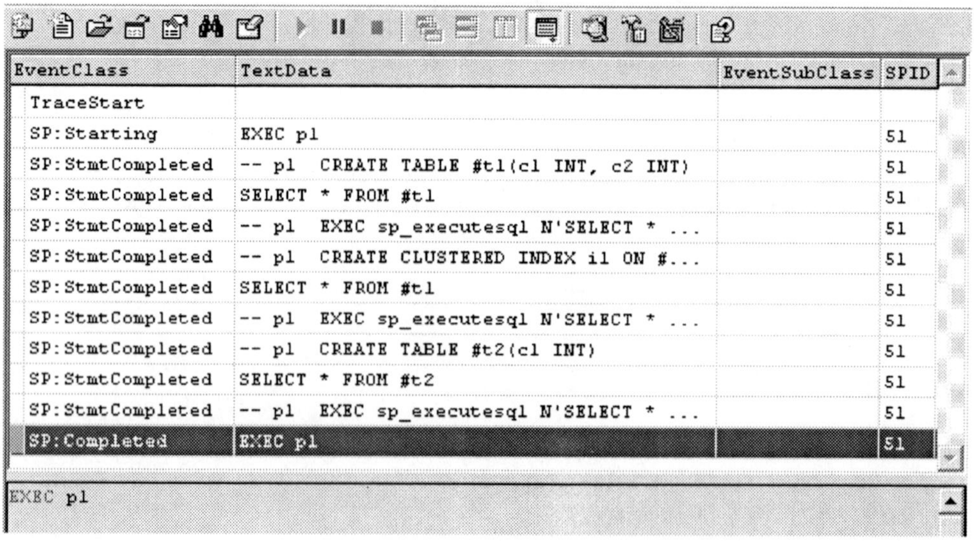

Figure 10-19. *Profiler trace output showing the role of sp_executesql in reducing recompilation*

In this case, you can also use the EXECUTE statement in place of sp_executesql to avoid the recompilations of the stored procedure:

```
IF(SELECT OBJECT_ID('p1')) IS NOT NULL
  DROP PROC p1
GO
CREATE PROC p1
AS
CREATE TABLE #t1(c1 INT, c2 INT)
EXECUTE('SELECT * FROM #t1') --Avoid 1st recompilation
CREATE CLUSTERED INDEX i1 ON #t1(c1)
EXECUTE('SELECT * FROM #t1') --Avoid 2nd recompilation
CREATE TABLE #t2(c1 INT)
EXECUTE('SELECT * FROM #t2') --Avoid 3rd recompilation
GO

EXEC p1
```

In either case, the plan of the statement executed using sp_executesql/EXECUTE is isolated from the plan of the stored procedure. To improve the plan reusability for the statement, use the sp_executesql method over the EXECUTE method, since sp_executesql allows explicit parameterization of the variable parts of the query, as explained in the previous chapter.

Summary

As you learned in this chapter, stored procedure recompilation can both benefit and hurt performance. Recompilations that generate better plans improve the performance of the stored procedure. However, recompilations that regenerate the same plan consume extra CPU cycles without any improvement in processing strategy. Therefore, you should look closely at recompilations to determine their usefulness. You can use Profiler to identify which stored procedure statement caused the recompilation, and you can determine the cause from the EventSubClass data column value (in Profiler), available in SQL Server 2000 SP2 onward. Once you determine the cause of the recompilation, you can apply different techniques to avoid the unnecessary recompilations.

Up until now, you have seen how to benefit from proper indexing and plan caching. However, the performance benefit of these techniques depends on the way the queries are designed. The cost-based optimizer of SQL Server takes care of many of the query design issues. However, you should adopt a number of best practices while designing queries. In the next chapter, I will cover some of the common query design issues that affect performance.

CHAPTER 11

■■■

Query Design Analysis

A database schema may include a number of performance-enhancement features such as indexes, statistics, and stored procedures. None of these features guarantees good performance if your queries are written badly in the first place; the SQL queries constituting requests to the database may not be able to use the available indexes effectively. Furthermore, the structure of the SQL queries may add avoidable overhead to query cost. To improve the performance of a database application, it is important to understand the cost comparison among different ways of writing queries.

In this chapter, I cover the following topics:

- Aspects of query design that affect performance

- How query designs use indexes effectively

- The role of optimizer hints on query performance

- The role of database constraints on query performance

- Query designs that are less resource-intensive

- Query designs that use the procedure cache effectively

- Query designs that reduce network overhead

- Techniques to reduce the transaction cost of a query

Query Design Recommendations

When you need to run a query, you can often use many different approaches to get the same result. In many cases, the optimizer generates the same plan, irrespective of the structure of the query. However, there are situations in which the query structure won't allow the optimizer to select the best possible processing strategy. It is important that you know when this happens and what you can do to avoid it.

In general, keep the following recommendations in mind to ensure the best performance:

- Operate on small result sets.

- Use indexes effectively.

- Avoid optimizer hints.

- Use domain and referential integrity.

- Avoid resource-intensive queries.

- Reduce the number of network round-trips.

- Reduce the transaction cost.

Careful testing is essential to identify the query form that provides the best performance in a specific database environment. You should be conversant with writing and comparing different SQL query forms, to evaluate the query form that provides the best performance in a given environment.

Operate on Small Result Sets

To improve the performance of a query, limit the amount of data it operates on, including both columns and rows. Operating on small result sets reduces the amount of resources consumed by a query and increases the effectiveness of indexes. Two of the rules you should follow to limit the dataset's size are as follows:

- Limit the number of columns in select_list.

- Use highly selective WHERE clauses.

I discuss these rules further in the sections that follow.

Limit the Number of Columns in select_list

Use a minimum set of columns in the select_list of a SELECT statement. Do not use columns that are not required in the output result set. For instance, do not use SELECT * to return all columns, unless all columns are required by the application. SELECT * statements render covered indexes ineffective, since it is impractical to include all columns in an index. For example, consider the following query (against the Northwind database):

```
SELECT ProductID, SupplierID
FROM Products
WHERE SupplierID = 1
```

A covering index on the SupplierID and ProductID columns serves the query quickly through the index itself, without accessing the base table. If you have STATISTICS IO switched on, you get the following number of logical reads and the corresponding execution plan (shown in Figure 11-1):

```
Table 'Products'. Scan count 1, logical reads 1
```

Figure 11-1. *Execution plan showing the benefit of referring to a limited number of columns*

If this query is modified to include all columns in the `select_list` as follows, then the previous covering index becomes ineffective, as all the columns required by this query are not included in that index:

```
SELECT *
FROM Products
WHERE SupplierID = 1
```

Subsequently, the base table (or the clustered index) containing all the columns has to be accessed as shown next (see Figure 11-2). The number of logical reads has increased:

```
Table 'Products'. Scan count 1, logical reads 7
```

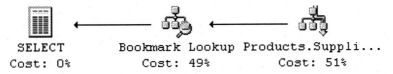

Figure 11-2. *Execution plan showing the added cost of referring to too many columns*

As shown in Figure 11-2, the fewer the columns in the `select_list`, the better the query performance. Selecting too many columns also increases data transfer across the network, further degrading performance.

Use Highly Selective WHERE Clauses

As explained in Chapter 4, the selectivity of a column referred to in the `WHERE` clause governs the use of a nonclustered index on the column. A request for a large number of rows from a table can't benefit from using a nonclustered index due to the overhead cost of the bookmark lookup operation associated with nonclustered indexes. To keep the cost of using nonclustered indexes low, the columns referred to in the `WHERE` clause must be highly selective.

Most of the time, an end user concentrates on a limited number of rows at a time. Therefore, design database applications to request data incrementally as the user navigates through the data. For applications that rely on a large amount of data for data analysis or reporting, consider using data analysis solutions such as Online Analytical Processing (OLAP).

Use Indexes Effectively

It is extremely important to have effective indexes on database tables to improve performance. However, it is equally important to ensure that the queries are designed properly to use these indexes effectively. Some of the query design rules you should follow to improve the use of indexes are as follows:

- Avoid nonindexable search conditions.

- Avoid arithmetic operators on the WHERE clause column.

- Avoid functions on the WHERE clause column.

I cover each of these rules in detail in the following sections.

Avoid Nonindexable Search Conditions

The optimizer's ability to benefit from an index depends on the selectivity of the search condition, which in turn depends on the selectivity of the column(s) referred to in the WHERE clause. The search condition used on the column(s) in the WHERE clause determines whether or not an index operation on the column can be performed.

The inclusion search conditions listed in Table 11-1 generally allow the optimizer to use a nonclustered index on the column(s) referred to in the WHERE clause. The inclusion search conditions generally allow SQL Server to seek to a row in the index and retrieve the row (or the adjacent range of rows until the search condition remains true).

On the other hand, the exclusion search conditions listed in Table 11-1 generally prevent the optimizer from using a nonclustered index on the column(s) referred to in the WHERE clause. The exclusion search conditions generally don't allow SQL Server to perform index seek operations as supported by the inclusion search conditions. For example, the != exclusion condition requires scanning all the rows to identify the matching rows.

Table 11-1. *Common Indexable and Nonindexable Search Conditions*

Type	Search Conditions
Indexable	Inclusion conditions =, >, >=, <, <=, and BETWEEN, and some LIKE conditions such as LIKE '<literal>%'
Nonindexable	Exclusion conditions <>, !=, !>, !<, NOT EXISTS, NOT IN, and NOT LIKE IN, OR, and some LIKE conditions such as LIKE '%<literal>'

Try to implement workarounds for these nonindexable search conditions to improve performance. In some cases, it may be possible to rewrite a query to avoid a nonindexable search condition. For example, consider replacing an IN/OR search condition with a BETWEEN condition, as described in the following section.

BETWEEN vs. IN/OR

Consider the following query, which uses the search condition IN:

```
SELECT * FROM [Order Details]
WHERE OrderID IN (10300, 10301, 10302, 10303)
```

The nonindexable search condition in this query can be replaced with a BETWEEN clause as follows:

```
SELECT * FROM [Order Details]
WHERE OrderID BETWEEN 10300 AND 10303
```

On the face of it, the execution plan of both the queries appears to be the same as shown in the execution plan in Figure 11-3.

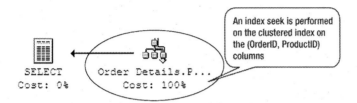

Figure 11-3. *Execution plan for a simple SELECT statement using a BETWEEN clause*

However, taking a closer look at execution plans reveals the difference in their data-retrieval mechanism, as shown in Figure 11-4. The left box is the IN condition, and the right box is the BETWEEN condition.

Clustered Index Seek			**Clustered Index Seek**	
Scanning a particular range of rows from a clustered index.			Scanning a particular range of rows from a clustered index.	
Physical operation:	Clustered Index Seek		**Physical operation:**	Clustered Index Seek
Logical operation:	Clustered Index Seek		**Logical operation:**	Clustered Index Seek
Row count:	10		**Row count:**	10
Estimated row size:	45		**Estimated row size:**	45
I/O cost:	0.00632		**I/O cost:**	0.00632
CPU cost:	0.000089		**CPU cost:**	0.000088
Number of executes:	1		**Number of executes:**	1
Cost:	0.006418(100%)		**Cost:**	0.006416(100%)
Subtree cost:	0.00641		**Subtree cost:**	0.00641
Estimated row count:	9		**Estimated row count:**	8
Argument:			**Argument:**	
OBJECT:([Northwind].[dbo].[Order Details].[PK_Order_D etails]), SEEK:([Order Details].[OrderID]=10300 OR [Ord er Details].[OrderID]=10301 OR [Order Details].[OrderID]=10302 OR [Order Details].[OrderID]=10303) ORDERED FORWARD			OBJECT:([Northwind].[dbo].[Order Details].[PK_Order_D etails]), SEEK:([Order Details].[OrderID] >= Convert([@1]) AND [Order Details].[OrderID] <= Convert([@2])) ORD ERED FORWARD	

Figure 11-4. *Execution plan details for an IN condition (left) and a BETWEEN condition (right)*

As shown in Figure 11-4, SQL Server resolved the IN condition containing four values into four OR conditions. Accordingly, the clustered index (PK_Order_Details) is accessed four times (Scan count 4) to retrieve rows for the four OR conditions as shown in the following corresponding STATISTICS IO output. On the other hand, the BETWEEN condition is resolved into a pair of >= and <= conditions, as shown in Figure 11-4. SQL Server accesses the clustered index only once (Scan count 1) from the first matching row until the match condition is true, as shown in the following corresponding STATISTICS IO output.

- With the IN condition:

      Table 'Order Details'. Scan count 4, logical reads **8**

- With the BETWEEN condition:

      Table 'Order Details'. Scan count 1, logical reads **2**

Replacing the search condition IN with BETWEEN decreases the number of logical reads for this query from 8 to 2. As just shown, although both queries use a clustered index seek on OrderID, the optimizer locates the range of rows much faster with the BETWEEN clause than with the IN clause. The same thing happens when you look at the BETWEEN condition and the OR clause. Therefore, if there is a choice between using IN/OR and the BETWEEN search condition, always choose the BETWEEN condition, as it is generally much more efficient than the IN/OR condition. In fact, you should go one step further and use the combination of >= and <= instead of the BETWEEN clause, as explained in Chapter 9.

Not every WHERE clause that uses exclusion search conditions prevents the optimizer from using the index on the column referred to in the search condition. In many cases, the SQL Server 2000 optimizer does a wonderful job of converting the exclusion search condition to an indexable search condition. To understand this, consider the following two search conditions, which I discuss in the sections that follow:

- The LIKE condition

- The !< condition versus the >= condition

LIKE Condition

While using the LIKE search condition, try to use one or more leading characters in the WHERE clause if possible. Using leading characters in the LIKE clause allows the optimizer to convert the LIKE condition to an indexable search condition. The greater the number of leading characters in the LIKE condition, the better the optimizer is able to determine an effective index. Be aware that using a wildcard character as the leading character in the LIKE condition *prevents* the optimizer from performing a SEEK (or a narrow-range scan) on the index; it relies on scanning the complete table instead.

To understand this ability of the SQL Server 2000 optimizer, consider the following SELECT statement that uses the LIKE condition with a leading character:

```
SELECT * FROM Products
WHERE ProductName LIKE 'S%'
```

The SQL Server 2000 optimizer does this conversion automatically, as shown in Figure 11-5.

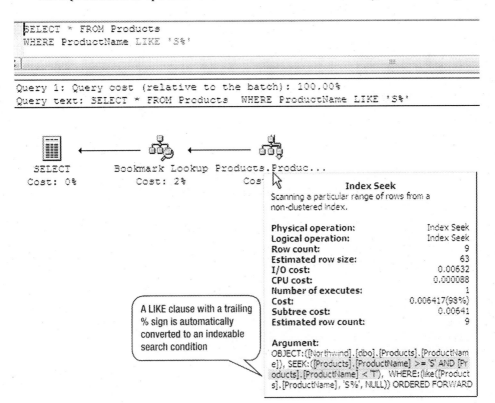

```
SELECT * FROM Products
WHERE ProductName LIKE 'S%'
```

Query 1: Query cost (relative to the batch): 100.00%
Query text: SELECT * FROM Products WHERE ProductName LIKE 'S%'

SELECT   Bookmark Lookup Products.Produc...
Cost: 0%   Cost: 2%   Cos

A LIKE clause with a trailing % sign is automatically converted to an indexable search condition

Index Seek
Scanning a particular range of rows from a non-clustered index.

Physical operation:	Index Seek
Logical operation:	Index Seek
Row count:	9
Estimated row size:	63
I/O cost:	0.00632
CPU cost:	0.000088
Number of executes:	1
Cost:	0.006417(98%)
Subtree cost:	0.00641
Estimated row count:	9

Argument:
OBJECT:([Northwind].[dbo].[Products].[ProductName]), SEEK:([Products].[ProductName] >= 'S' AND [Products].[ProductName] < 'T'), WHERE:(like([Products].[ProductName], 'S%', NULL)) ORDERED FORWARD

Figure 11-5. *Execution plan showing automatic conversion of a LIKE clause with a trailing % sign to an indexable search condition*

As you can see, the optimizer automatically converts the LIKE condition to an equivalent pair of >= and < conditions. You can therefore rewrite this SELECT statement to replace the LIKE condition with an indexable search condition as follows:

```
SELECT * FROM Products
WHERE ProductName >= 'S' AND ProductName < 'T'
```

Note that in both cases, the number of logical reads for the query with the LIKE condition and the manually converted indexable search condition is the same. Thus, if you include leading characters in the LIKE clause, the SQL Server 2000 optimizer optimizes the search condition to allow the use of indexes on the column.

With SQL Server 7.0, you should always redesign this SELECT statement to manually replace the LIKE condition with a pair of >= and < search conditions. The SELECT statement with a LIKE condition uses a greater number of logical reads, as indicated in the following STATISTICS IO outputs.

- With the LIKE condition:

```
Table 'Products'. Scan count 1, logical reads 24
```

- With a pair of >= and < conditions:

```
Table 'Products'. Scan count 1, logical reads 19
```

!< Condition vs. >= Condition

Even though both the !< and >= search conditions retrieve the same result set, they may perform different operations internally. The >= comparison operator allows the optimizer to use an index on the column referred to in the search argument, as the = part of the operator allows the optimizer to seek to a starting point in the index and access all the index rows from there onward. On the other hand, the !< operator doesn't have an = element and needs to access the column value for every row.

Or does it? As explained in Chapter 9, the SQL Server 2000 (and SQL Server 7.0) optimizer performs syntax-based optimization, before executing a query, to improve performance. This allows SQL Server to take care of the performance concern with the !< operator by converting it to >=, as shown in the execution plan in Figure 11-6 for the two following SELECT statements:

```
SELECT * FROM Orders WHERE OrderID >= 11077
SELECT * FROM Orders WHERE OrderID !< 11077
```

As you can see, the optimizer often provides you with the flexibility of writing queries in the preferred T-SQL syntax without sacrificing performance.

Although the SQL Server optimizer can automatically optimize query syntax to improve performance in many cases, you should not rely on it to do so. It is a good practice to write efficient queries in the first place.

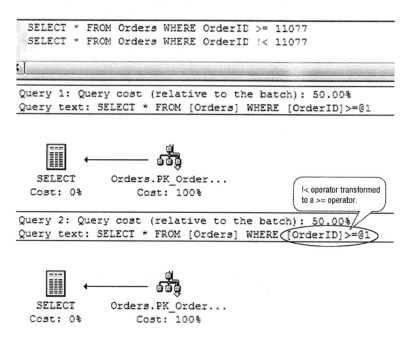

Figure 11-6. *Execution plan showing automatic transformation of a nonindexable !< operator to an indexable >= operator*

Avoid Arithmetic Operators on the WHERE Clause Column

Using an arithmetic operator on a column in the WHERE clause prevents the optimizer from using the index on the column. For example, consider the following SELECT statement:

```
SELECT * FROM Orders WHERE OrderID*2 = 22000
```

A multiplication operator, *, has been applied on the column in the WHERE clause. You can avoid this on the column by rewriting the SELECT statement as follows:

```
SELECT * FROM Orders WHERE OrderID = 22000/2
```

The table has a clustered index on the OrderID column. As explained in Chapter 4, an index seek operation on this index will be suitable for this query since it returns only one row. Even though both queries return the same result set, the use of the multiplication operator on the OrderID column in the first query prevents the optimizer from using the index on the column, as you can see in Figure 11-7.

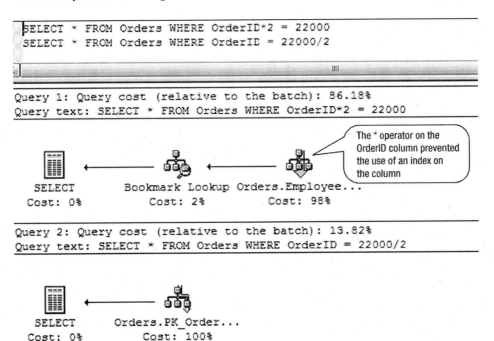

Figure 11-7. *Execution plan showing the detrimental effect of an arithmetic operator on a WHERE clause column*

Their corresponding STATISTICS IO outputs are as follows.

- With the * operator on the OrderID column:

  Table 'Orders'. Scan count 1, logical reads 5

- With no operator on the OrderID column:

  Table 'Orders'. Scan count 1, logical reads 2

Therefore, to use the indexes effectively and improve query performance, avoid using arithmetic operators on column(s) in the WHERE clause.

▓**NOTE** For small result sets, even though an index seek is usually a better data-retrieval strategy than a table scan (or a complete clustered index scan), for very small tables (in which all data rows fit on one page) a table scan can be cheaper. This is explained in more detail in Chapter 4.

Avoid Functions on the WHERE Clause Column

In a similar way to arithmetic operators, functions on WHERE clause columns also hurt query performance, and for similar reasons. Try to avoid using functions on WHERE clause columns, as shown in the following two examples:

- SUBSTRING versus LIKE

- Date part comparison

SUBSTRING vs. LIKE

In the following SELECT statement (substring.sql in the download), using the SUBSTRING function prevents the use of the index on the ShipPostalCode column:

```
SELECT * FROM Orders --Get orders booked by specific customers
WHERE SUBSTRING(ShipPostalCode,1,1) = 'V'
```

Figure 11-8 illustrates this.

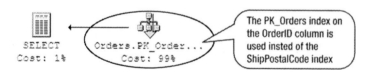

Figure 11-8. *Execution plan showing the detrimental effect of using the SUBSTRING function on a WHERE clause column*

The corresponding STATISTICS IO output is

```
Table 'Orders'. Scan count 1, logical reads 21
```

As you can see, using the SUBSTRING function prevented the optimizer from using the index on the ShipPostalCode column. This function on the column made the optimizer use a clustered index scan. In the absence of the clustered index on the OrderID column, a table scan would have been performed.

You can redesign this SELECT statement to avoid the function on the column as follows:

```
SELECT * FROM Orders --Get orders booked by specific customers
WHERE ShipPostalCode LIKE 'V%'
```

or

```
SELECT * FROM Orders --Get orders booked by specific customers
WHERE ShipPostalCode >= 'V' AND ShipPostalCode < 'W'
```

Either query allows the optimizer to choose the index on the ShipPostalCode column, as shown in Figure 11-9.

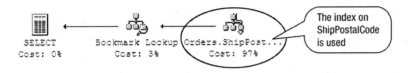

Figure 11-9. *Execution plan showing the benefit of not using the SUBSTRING function on a WHERE clause column*

The corresponding STATISTICS IO output is

```
Table 'Orders'. Scan count 1, logical reads 8
```

Date Part Comparison

SQL Server doesn't have a separate data type for dates. DATETIME stores both the date and time together, but sometimes you only want the date, which usually means you have to apply a conversion function to extract the date part from the DATETIME data type. Doing this prevents the optimizer from choosing the index on the column, as shown in the following example.

Create a sample table with a DATETIME column as follows (create_datetime.sql in the download):

```
IF(SELECT OBJECT_ID('t1')) IS NOT NULL
  DROP TABLE t1
GO
CREATE TABLE t1(c1 INT, c2 DATETIME, c3 CHAR(40))
CREATE INDEX i1 ON t1(c2)
DECLARE @c2 DATETIME
SET @c2 = '2000-01-01 08:00:00'
WHILE DATEPART(YEAR, @c2) < '2003'
BEGIN
  INSERT INTO t1 VALUES(1, @c2, 'c3')
  SELECT @c2 = DATEADD(DAY, 1, @c2)
END
```

To retrieve all rows with c2 = "2002-01-30", you can execute the following SELECT statement (datetime.sql):

```
SELECT * FROM t1 --Get rows with c2='2002-01-30'
WHERE CONVERT(CHAR(10),c2,120) = '2002-01-30'
```

Using the CONVERT function on column c2 prevents the optimizer from considering index i1 on the column and instead causes a table scan, as shown in Figure 11-10.

SELECT   Table Scan
Cost: 1%   Cost: 99%

Figure 11-10. *Execution plan showing the detrimental effect of using the CONVERT function on a WHERE clause column*

This is the output of SET STATISTICS IO:

Table 't1'. Scan count 1, logical reads 9

The date part comparison can be done without applying the function on the DATETIME column:

```
SELECT * FROM t1 --Get rows with c2='2002-01-30'
WHERE c2 >= '2002-01-30' AND c2 < '2002-01-31'
```

This allows the optimizer to consider index i1 on the DATETIME column, as shown in Figure 11-11.

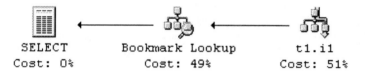

SELECT   Bookmark Lookup   t1.i1
Cost: 0%   Cost: 49%   Cost: 51%

Figure 11-11. *Execution plan showing the benefit of not using the CONVERT function on a WHERE clause column*

This is the output of SET STATISTICS IO:

Table 't1'. Scan count 1, logical reads **3**

Therefore, to allow the optimizer to consider an index on a column referred to in the WHERE clause, always avoid using a function on the indexed column. This increases the effectiveness of indexes, which improves query performance.

Avoid Optimizer Hints

SQL Server's cost-based optimizer dynamically determines the processing strategy for a query, based on the current table/index structure and data. This dynamic behavior can be overridden using optimizer hints, taking some of the decisions away from the optimizer by instructing it to use a certain processing strategy. This makes the optimizer behavior static and doesn't allow it to dynamically update the processing strategy as the table/index structure or data changes.

Since it is usually difficult to outsmart a cost-based optimizer, the usual recommendation is to avoid optimizer hints. Generally, it is beneficial to let the optimizer determine a cost-effective processing strategy based on the data distribution statistics, indexes, and other factors. Forcing the optimizer (with optimizer hints) to use a specific processing strategy hurts performance more often than not, as shown in the following examples for these hints:

- JOIN hint

- INDEX hint

- FORCEPLAN hint

JOIN Hint

As explained in Chapter 3, the optimizer dynamically determines a cost-effective JOIN strategy between two datasets, based on the table/index structure and data. Table 11-2 presents a summary of the JOIN types supported by SQL Server 2000 (and SQL Server 7.0) for easy reference.

Table 11-2. *JOIN Types Supported by SQL Server 2000*

JOIN Type	Index on Joining Columns	Usual Size of Joining Tables	Presorted	JOIN Clause
Nested Loop	Inner table: Must Outer table: Preferable	Small	Optional	All
Merge	Both tables: Must Optimal condition: Clustered or covering index on both	Large	Yes	=
Hash	Inner table: Not indexed Outer table: Optional	Any Optimal condition: Small outer table, large inner table	No	=

▓**NOTE** The outer table is usually the smaller of the two joining tables.

You can instruct SQL Server to use a specific JOIN type by using the JOIN hints in Table 11-3.

Table 11-3. *JOIN Hints*

JOIN Type	JOIN Hint
Nested loop	LOOP JOIN
Merge	MERGE JOIN
Hash	HASH JOIN

To understand how use of JOIN hints can affect performance, consider the following SELECT statement (join.sql in the download):

```
SELECT * FROM [Order Details] od JOIN Orders o
  ON od.Orderid = o.Orderid
  WHERE o.ShipCountry = 'Spain'
```

Figure 11-12 shows the execution plan.

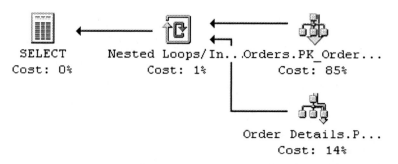

Figure 11-12. *Execution plan showing a simple join between two tables*

As you can see, SQL Server dynamically decided to use a LOOP JOIN as the JOIN strategy. As demonstrated in Chapter 3, for simple queries affecting a small result set, the LOOP JOIN generally provides better performance than a HASH JOIN or MERGE JOIN. Observing the fact that the optimizer uses the LOOP JOIN for this query, you may feel comfortable specifying this JOIN hint in the query as follows:

```
SELECT * FROM [Order Details] od INNER LOOP JOIN Orders o
  ON od.Orderid = o.Orderid
  WHERE o.ShipCountry = 'Spain'
```

Note that the INNER clause in the preceding JOIN hint is a JOIN operator, not a JOIN hint, but it is required to specify the JOIN hints.

If you run these two queries together, note the relative cost of each query, as shown in Figure 11-13.

Their corresponding STATISTICS IO outputs are as follows.

- With no JOIN hint:

  ```
  Table 'Order Details'. Scan count 23, logical reads 46
  Table 'Orders'. Scan count 1, logical reads 21
  ```

- With a JOIN hint:

  ```
  Table 'Orders'. Scan count 2155, logical reads 4504
  Table 'Order Details'. Scan count 1, logical reads 10
  ```

You can see that the query with the JOIN hint costs much more than the query without the hint, even though both use the same JOIN strategy.

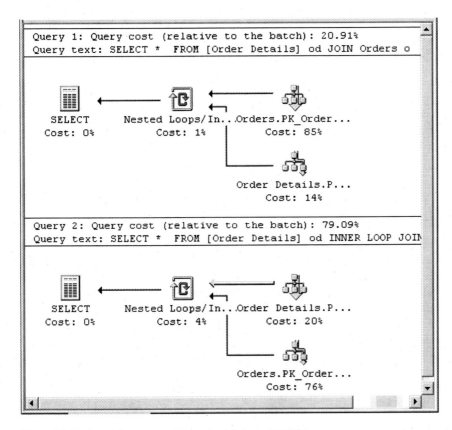

```
Query 1: Query cost (relative to the batch): 20.91%
Query text: SELECT *  FROM [Order Details] od JOIN Orders o



    SELECT          Nested Loops/In...Orders.PK_Order...
    Cost: 0%            Cost: 1%         Cost: 85%


                                    Order Details.P...
                                        Cost: 14%

Query 2: Query cost (relative to the batch): 79.09%
Query text: SELECT *  FROM [Order Details] od INNER LOOP JOIN



    SELECT          Nested Loops/In...Order Details.P...
    Cost: 0%            Cost: 4%         Cost: 20%


                                    Orders.PK_Order...
                                        Cost: 76%
```

Figure 11-13. *Cost of a query with and without a JOIN hint*

Note one of the major differences in the execution plan of the second query: the Order Details table is used as the outer table in the LOOP JOIN. Using the JOIN hint forced the optimizer to behave statically and use the first table mentioned in the FROM list as the outer table. However, using the [Orders] table as the outer table is optimal in this case, since the filter criterion on the [Orders] table reduces the number of matching rows from the [Orders] table to 23. Consequently, the [Order Details] table needs to be accessed only 23 times, as shown in the previous corresponding STATISTICS IO output (Scan count 23).

However, using the [Order Details] table as the outer table doesn't reduce the number of matching rows from the [Order Details] table, since the filter criterion column (ShipCountry) isn't present in this table. Consequently, all the 2,155 rows are retrieved from the [Order Details] table, and the [Orders] table is accessed 2,155 times, as shown in the corresponding STATISTICS IO output (Scan count 2155).

For each access of the [Orders] table, even if the number of matching rows on the OrderID column (od.Orderid = o.Orderid) between the two tables would have been just one row, the number of logical reads required on the [Orders] table would have been 2,155. This significantly increases the number of logical reads on the [Orders] table, as shown previously (logical reads 4504). Therefore, overriding the joining strategy of the optimizer using a JOIN hint prevented it from determining the correct joining order of the tables for better performance.

`JOIN` hints force the optimizer to ignore its own optimization strategy and use instead the strategy specified by the query. `JOIN` hints generally hurt query performance because of the following factors:

- Hints prevent auto-parameterization.

- Query plan caching is rendered less effective.

- The optimizer is prevented from dynamically deciding the joining order of the tables.

Therefore, it makes sense to not use the `JOIN` hint, but instead let the optimizer dynamically determine a cost-effective processing strategy.

INDEX Hints

As mentioned earlier, using an arithmetic operator on a `WHERE` clause column prevents the optimizer from choosing the index on the column. To improve performance, you can rewrite the query without using the arithmetic operator on the `WHERE` clause, as shown in the corresponding example. Alternatively, you may even think of forcing the optimizer to use the index on the column with an `INDEX` hint (a type of optimizer hint). However, most of the time, it is better to avoid the `INDEX` hint and let the optimizer behave dynamically.

To understand the effect of an `INDEX` hint on query performance, consider the example presented in the "Avoid Arithmetic Operators on the WHERE Clause Column" section. The multiplication operator on the `OrderID` column prevented the optimizer from choosing the index on the column. You can use an `INDEX` hint to force the optimizer to use the index on the `OrderID` column as follows:

```
SELECT * FROM Orders WITH(INDEX(PK_Orders)) WHERE OrderID*2 = 22000
```

Note the relative cost of using the `INDEX` hint in comparison to not using the `INDEX` hint, as shown in Figure 11-14.

Also, note the difference in the number of logical reads shown in the following `STATISTICS IO` outputs.

- No hint (with the arithmetic operator on the `WHERE` clause column):

  ```
  Table 'Orders'. Scan count 1, logical reads 5
  ```

- No hint (without the arithmetic operator on the `WHERE` clause column):

  ```
  Table 'Orders'. Scan count 1, logical reads 2
  ```

- `INDEX` hint:

  ```
  Table 'Orders'. Scan count 1, logical reads 21
  ```

```
Query 1: Query cost (relative to the batch): 38.63%
Query text: SELECT * FROM Orders WHERE OrderID*2 = 22000
```

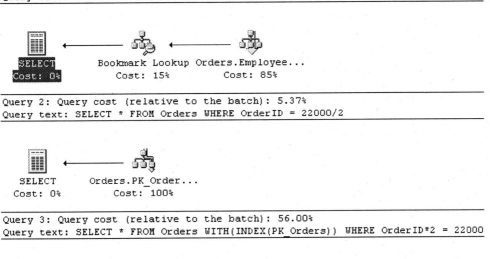

```
Query 2: Query cost (relative to the batch): 5.37%
Query text: SELECT * FROM Orders WHERE OrderID = 22000/2
```

```
Query 3: Query cost (relative to the batch): 56.00%
Query text: SELECT * FROM Orders WITH(INDEX(PK_Orders)) WHERE OrderID*2 = 22000
```

SELECT   Orders.PK_Order...
Cost: 0%   Cost: 100%

Figure 11-14. *Cost of a query with and without an INDEX hint*

From the relative cost of execution plans and number of logical reads, it is evident that the query with the INDEX hint actually impaired the query performance. Even though it allowed the optimizer to use the index on the OrderID column, it did not allow the optimizer to determine the proper index-access mechanism. Consequently, the optimizer used the index scan to access just one row. In comparison, avoiding the arithmetic operator on the WHERE clause column and not using the INDEX hint allowed the optimizer not only to use the index on the OrderID column, but also to determine the proper index access mechanism: index seek.

Therefore, in general, let the optimizer choose the best indexing strategy for the query, and don't override the optimizer behavior using an INDEX hint. Also, not using INDEX hints allows the optimizer to decide the best indexing strategy dynamically as the data changes over time.

FORCEPLAN Hints

As its name signifies, FORCEPLAN forces the optimizer to process a JOIN in the same order as the order of tables referred to in the FROM clause. It helps a query developer experiment with a processing strategy, if needed. However, avoid this query hint in production code, as it forces the optimizer to ignore its optimization techniques and follow the query syntax statically.

In general, it is advisable to avoid all optimizer hints. If you find through testing that an optimizer hint is useful in a particular situation, then perform the following actions before finalizing the use of the particular hint:

- Update statistics on all tables and indexes referred to in the query.

- Identify and create missing indexes and statistics, if any.

- Analyze and update existing indexes, if you find they're inappropriate for the query.

- Rewrite the query to avoid nonindexable search conditions, if any.

- Defragment all tables and indexes referred to in the query.

- Recompile the stored procedure, if the problematic query is within a stored procedure.

If the performance of the query still doesn't improve, then you may use the optimizer hint as a performance-enhancement solution. But please keep track of this optimizer hint to ensure that the query performance isn't impaired by the hint as the structure and size of the data change over time.

Use Domain and Referential Integrity

Domain and referential integrity help define and enforce valid values for a column, maintaining the integrity of the database. This is done through column/table constraints.

Since data access is usually one of the most costly operations in a query execution, avoiding redundant data access helps the optimizer reduce the query execution time. Domain and referential integrity help the SQL Server 2000 optimizer analyze valid data values without physically accessing the data, reducing query time.

To understand how this happens, consider the following examples:

- The NOT NULL constraint

- Declarative referential integrity (DRI)

NOT NULL Constraint

The NOT NULL column constraint is used to implement domain integrity by defining the fact that a NULL value cannot be entered in a particular column. SQL Server automatically enforces this fact at runtime to maintain the domain integrity for that column. Also, defining the NOT NULL column constraint helps the optimizer generate an efficient processing strategy when the ISNULL function is used on that column in a query.

To understand the performance benefit of the NOT NULL column constraint, consider the following example. Create a sample table (create_notnull.sql in the download) as follows:

```
IF(SELECT OBJECT_ID('t1')) IS NOT NULL
   DROP TABLE t1
GO
CREATE TABLE t1(c1 INT, c2 INT)
CREATE INDEX i1 ON t1(c1)
INSERT INTO t1 VALUES(11, 12)
```

Consider the following two SELECT statements:

```
SELECT * FROM t1 WHERE c1 = 11
SELECT * FROM t1 WHERE ISNULL(c1, 11) = 11
```

Both SELECT statements return the same result set, but they use different execution plans, as you can see in Figure 11-15.

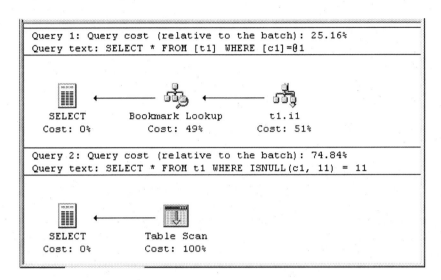

Figure 11-15. *Effect of the ISNULL function when a NOT NULL column constraint is not used*

Since the column c1 can contain NULL, the second query with the ISNULL function can return a different result set from the first query. Using the ISNULL function on column c1 prevented the optimizer from using the index on column c1. Thus, the optimizer could not use the index on column c1 to verify whether or not a particular row value in column c1 contained NULL. Consequently, the optimizer performed a table scan to verify the NULL values for the column, as requested by the ISNULL function in the second query.

The optimizer can be assured of the fact that column c1 cannot contain NULL by defining a NOT NULL column constraint on the column. This will allow the optimizer to use the index on column c1, since the NOT NULL domain integrity constraint assures that NULL values for the column data need not be verified at runtime. To understand the effect of the NOT NULL constraint on query performance, modify create_notnull.sql as follows:

```
IF(SELECT OBJECT_ID('t1')) IS NOT NULL
  DROP TABLE t1
GO
CREATE TABLE t1(c1 INT NOT NULL, c2 INT)
CREATE INDEX i1 ON t1(c1)
INSERT INTO t1 VALUES(11, 12)
```

Figure 11-16 shows the resultant execution plan for the two SELECT statements.

```
Query 1: Query cost (relative to the batch): 50.00%
Query text: SELECT * FROM [t1] WHERE [c1]=@1
```

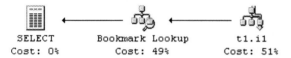

```
    SELECT        Bookmark Lookup        t1.i1
   Cost: 0%          Cost: 49%          Cost: 51%
```

```
Query 2: Query cost (relative to the batch): 50.00%
Query text: SELECT * FROM t1 WHERE ISNULL(c1, 11) = 11
```

```
    SELECT        Bookmark Lookup        t1.i1
   Cost: 0%          Cost: 49%          Cost: 51%
```

Figure 11-16. *Effect of the ISNULL function when a NOT NULL column constraint is used*

As shown in Figure 11-16, the optimizer generated the same execution plan for both
SELECT statements. Since c1 is NOT NULL, the ISNULL function always returns FALSE. With the
NOT NULL column constraint defined, the optimizer can use the index on column c1 and be
assured of the fact that there are no NULL values for that column in the base table. This feature
is an enhancement of SQL Server 2000 over SQL Server 7.0.

Declarative Referential Integrity

Declarative referential integrity (DRI) is used to define referential integrity between a parent
and a child table. It ensures that a record in the child table exists only if the corresponding
record in the parent table exists. The only exception to this rule is that the child table can
contain a NULL value for the identifier that links the rows of the child table to the rows of the
parent table. For all other values of the identifier in the child, a corresponding value must exist
in the parent table. In SQL Server, DRI is implemented using a PRIMARY KEY constraint on the
parent table and a FOREIGN KEY constraint on the child table.

With DRI established between two tables, and the foreign key columns of the child table
set to NOT NULL, the SQL Server 2000 optimizer is assured that for every record in the child
table, the parent table has a corresponding record. Sometimes this can help the SQL Server
2000 optimizer improve performance, as accessing the parent table is not necessary to verify
the existence of a parent record for a corresponding child record.

To understand the performance benefit of implementing declarative referential integrity,
let's consider an example. Create a parent and a child table as follows (create_dri.sql in the
download):

```
--Create parent table
IF(SELECT OBJECT_ID('Prod')) IS NOT NULL
  DROP TABLE Prod
GO
SELECT * INTO Prod FROM Products
ALTER TABLE Prod
  ADD CONSTRAINT pk_ProdID PRIMARY KEY (ProductID)
```

```
--Create child table
IF(SELECT OBJECT_ID('od')) IS NOT NULL
  DROP TABLE od
GO
SELECT * INTO od FROM [Order Details]
ALTER TABLE od
  ADD CONSTRAINT pk_OrdID_ProdID PRIMARY KEY (OrderID,ProductID)
```

▓**NOTE** There is no referential integrity yet between the parent and child tables.

Consider the following SELECT statement (prod.sql in the download):

```
SELECT Prod.ProductID, od.OrderID, od.UnitPrice, od.Quantity
  FROM Prod, od
  WHERE Prod.ProductID = od.ProductID AND od.OrderID = 10300
```

Note that the SELECT statement fetches the value of the ProductID column from the parent table (Prod). If the nature of the data requires that for every product (identified by ProductID) in the child table (od) the parent table (Prod) contains a corresponding product, then the preceding SELECT statement can be rewritten as follows (prod.sql in the download):

```
SELECT od.ProductID, od.OrderID, od.UnitPrice, od.Quantity
  FROM Prod, od
  WHERE Prod.ProductID = od.ProductID AND od.OrderID = 10300
```

Both SELECT statements should return the same result set. Even the optimizer generates the same execution plan for both the SELECT statements, as shown in Figure 11-17.

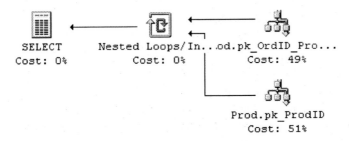

```
SELECT          Nested Loops/In...od.pk_OrdID_Pro...
Cost: 0%           Cost: 0%          Cost: 49%

                                    Prod.pk_ProdID
                                     Cost: 51%
```

Figure 11-17. *Execution plan when DRI is not defined between the two tables*

To understand how declarative referential integrity can affect query performance, add a FOREIGN KEY to the child table (add_fk.sql in the download):

```
ALTER TABLE od
  ADD CONSTRAINT fk_ProdID FOREIGN KEY (ProductID)
    REFERENCES Prod(ProductID)
```

■NOTE There is now referential integrity between the parent and child tables.

Figure 11-18 shows the resultant execution plans for the two SELECT statements.

```
Query 1: Query cost (relative to the batch): 67.07%
Query text: SELECT Prod.ProductID, od.OrderID, od.UnitPrice,
```

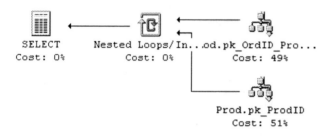

```
   SELECT        Nested Loops/In...od.pk_OrdID_Pro...
   Cost: 0%           Cost: 0%            Cost: 49%

                                     Prod.pk_ProdID
                                       Cost: 51%
```

```
Query 2: Query cost (relative to the batch): 32.93%
Query text: SELECT od.ProductID, od.OrderID, od.UnitPrice, od
```

```
   SELECT        od.pk_OrdID_Pro...
   Cost: 0%          Cost: 100%
```

Figure 11-18. *Execution plans showing the benefit of defining DRI between the two tables*

As you can see, the execution plan of the second SELECT statement is highly optimized: the Prod table is not accessed. With the declarative referential integrity in place (and od.ProductID set to NOT NULL), the optimizer is assured that for every record in the child table (od), the parent table (Prod) contains a corresponding record. Therefore, the JOIN clause (Prod.ProductID = od.ProductID) between the parent and child tables is redundant in the second SELECT statement, with no other data requested from the parent table. This feature is another enhancement of SQL Server 2000's optimizer over SQL Server 7.0's optimizer.

You probably already knew that domain and referential integrity are a Good Thing, but you can see that they not only ensure data integrity, but also improve performance. As just illustrated, domain and referential integrity provide more choices to the optimizer to generate cost-effective execution plans and improve performance.

To achieve the performance benefit of DRI, as mentioned previously, the foreign key columns in the child table should be NOT NULL. Otherwise, there can be rows (with foreign key column values as NULL) in the child table with no representation in the parent table. That won't prevent the optimizer from accessing the primary table (Prod) in the previous query. By default—that is, if the NOT NULL attribute isn't mentioned for a column—the column can have NULL values. Considering the benefit of the NOT NULL attribute and the other benefits explained in this section, always mark the attribute of a column as NOT NULL if NULL isn't a valid value for that column.

Avoid Resource-Intensive Queries

Many database functionalities can be implemented using a variety of query techniques. The approach you should take is to use query techniques that are very resource-friendly. A few techniques you can use to reduce the footprint of a query are as follows:

- Avoid implicit data type conversion.

- Use EXISTS over COUNT(*) to verify data existence.

- Optimize the row count technique.

- Use UNION ALL over UNION.

- Use an additional JOIN clause over UNION.

- Use indexes for aggregate and sort operations.

- Avoid redundant WHERE clause conditions.

- Use JOIN operations rather than subqueries.

- Avoid local variables in a batch query.

- Be careful naming stored procedures.

I cover these points in more detail in the next sections.

Avoid Implicit Data Type Conversion

SQL Server allows a value/constant with different but compatible data types to be compared with a column's data. SQL Server automatically converts the data from one data type to another. This process is called *implicit data type conversion*. Although useful, implicit conversion adds an overhead to the query optimizer. To improve performance, use a variable/constant with the same data type as that of the column to which it is compared.

To understand how implicit data type conversion affects performance, consider the following example (conversion.sql in the download):

```
DECLARE @int INT, @float FLOAT
SET @int = 10
SET @float = 10
SELECT * FROM Products WHERE SupplierID = @int --INT data type
SELECT * FROM Products WHERE SupplierID = @float --FLOAT data type
```

Both queries return the same result set. As you can see, both queries are identical except for the data type of the variable equated to the SupplierID column. Since this column is INT, the first query doesn't require an implicit data type conversion. The second query uses a different data type from that of the SupplierID column, requiring an implicit data type conversion and thereby adding an overhead to the query performance. Figure 11-19 shows the execution plans for both queries.

```
Query 1: Query cost (relative to the batch): 49.97%
Query text: SELECT * FROM [Products] WHERE [SupplierID]=@1
```

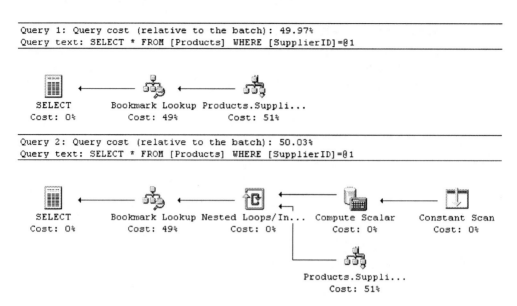

```
Query 2: Query cost (relative to the batch): 50.03%
Query text: SELECT * FROM [Products] WHERE [SupplierID]=@1
```

Figure 11-19. *Cost of a query with and without implicit data type conversion*

The complexity of the implicit data type conversion depends on the precedence of the data types involved in the comparison. The data type precedence rules of SQL Server specify which data type is converted to the other. Usually, the data type of lower precedence is converted to the data type of higher precedence. For example, the TINYINT data type has a lower precedence than the INT data type. For a complete list of data type precedence in SQL Server 2000, please refer to the MSDN article "Data Type Precedence" (http://msdn.microsoft.com/library/en-us/tsqlref/ts_da-db_2js5.asp).

When SQL Server compares a column value with a certain data type and a variable (or constant) with a different data type, the data type of the variable (or constant) is always converted to the data type of the column. This is done because the column value is accessed based on the implicit conversion value of the variable (or constant). Therefore, in such cases, the implicit conversion is always applied on the variable (or constant).

For instance, in the preceding example (where the column of INT data type is compared with the variable of FLOAT data type), even though the INT data type has a lower precedence than the FLOAT data type, the FLOAT data type is implicitly converted into the INT data type. The conversion of the data types in reverse order to that of the data type precedence rule complicates the implicit conversion of the variable value, as shown in the corresponding execution plan. Figure 11-20 shows that if the INT column is compared with a TINYINT variable, which is of lower precedence than INT, then SQL Server performs the implicit conversion without the additional steps of "Constant Scan" and "Compute Scalar" (tiny_int.sql):

```
DECLARE @tinyint TINYINT
SET @tinyint = 10
SELECT * FROM Products WHERE SupplierID = @tinyint
```

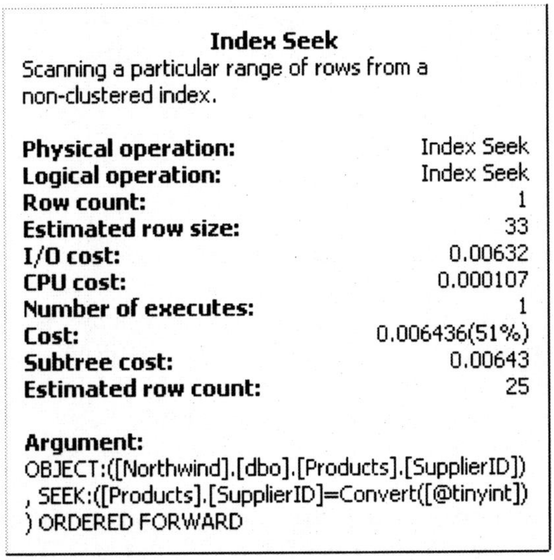

```
                    Index Seek
Scanning a particular range of rows from a
non-clustered index.

Physical operation:              Index Seek
Logical operation:               Index Seek
Row count:                                1
Estimated row size:                      33
I/O cost:                           0.00632
CPU cost:                          0.000107
Number of executes:                       1
Cost:                       0.006436(51%)
Subtree cost:                       0.00643
Estimated row count:                     25

Argument:
OBJECT:([Northwind].[dbo].[Products].[SupplierID])
, SEEK:([Products].[SupplierID]=Convert([@tinyint])
) ORDERED FORWARD
```

Figure 11-20. *Execution plan detail showing implicit data type conversion*

If the two expressions being compared are from two different tables, then to optimize performance, SQL Server can access them in any order, unlike when one of them is a variable or constant. This allows SQL Server to access columns with a higher precedence data type later so that a simple implicit conversion (without the additional steps of "Constant Scan" and "Compute Scalar") can be performed on the lower precedence data type.

To understand this feature of SQL Server, consider the following example that compares two columns with different data types. Create two test tables (data_type.sql):

```
--Create test table 1
IF(SELECT OBJECT_ID('t1')) IS NOT NULL
  DROP TABLE t1
GO
CREATE TABLE t1(c_tinyint TINYINT, c_int INT, c_bigint BIGINT)
CREATE INDEX i_int ON t1(c_int)
INSERT INTO t1 VALUES(1, 1, 1)
GO
--Create test table 2
IF(SELECT OBJECT_ID('t2')) IS NOT NULL
  DROP TABLE t2
GO
CREATE TABLE t2(c_tinyint TINYINT, c_int INT, c_bigint BIGINT)
CREATE INDEX i_tinyint ON t2(c_tinyint)
CREATE INDEX i_bigint ON t2(c_bigint)
INSERT INTO t2 VALUES(1, 1, 1)
```

Execute the following two SELECT statements (compare_data_types.sql in the download). The first SELECT statement compares the INT and TINYINT data types. The second SELECT statement compares the INT and BIGINT data types.

```
SELECT * FROM t1, t2 WHERE t1.c_int = t2.c_tinyint
SELECT * FROM t1, t2 WHERE t1.c_int = t2.c_bigint
```

Figure 11-21 shows the execution plans.

As shown in Figure 11-21, during the comparison between INT and TINYINT, SQL Server accessed the index on the column (t1.i_int) of the higher precedence data type (INT) later (as it is in the inner table). It allowed a simple implicit conversion of the TINYINT column value before comparing its value with that of the INT column. Similarly, during the comparison between INT and BIGINT, SQL Server accessed the index on the column (t2.i_bigint) of the higher precedence data type (BIGINT) later for a simple implicit conversion of the INT data type value to BIGINT. In either case, note that applying implicit conversion on the column's data type prevented the use of the index on the column.

As you can see, implicit data type conversion adds an overhead to the query performance. Therefore, to improve performance, always use the same data type for both expressions.

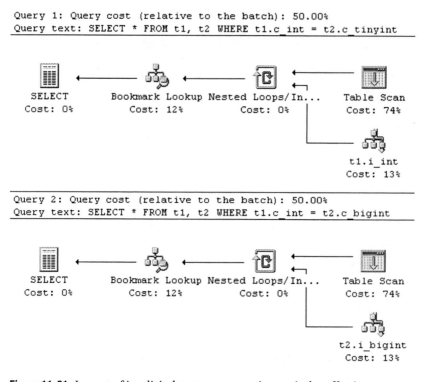

Figure 11-21. *Impact of implicit data type conversion on index effectiveness*

Use EXISTS over COUNT(*) to Verify Data Existence

A common database requirement is to verify whether or not a set of data exists. Generally, you'll implement this using a batch of SQL queries, as follows (count.sql in the download):

```
DECLARE @n INT
SELECT @n = COUNT(*) FROM [Order Details] WHERE Quantity = 1
IF @n > 0
  PRINT 'Record Exists'
```

Using COUNT(*) to verify the existence of data is highly resource-intensive, as COUNT(*) has to scan all the rows in a table. EXISTS merely has to scan and stop at the first record that matches the EXISTS criterion. To improve performance, use EXISTS instead of the COUNT(*) approach:

```
IF EXISTS(SELECT * FROM [Order Details] WHERE Quantity = 1)
  PRINT 'Record Exists'
```

The performance benefit of the EXISTS technique over the COUNT(*) technique can be compared using the STATISTICS IO output, as you can see from the output of running these queries:

```
Table 'Order Details'. Scan count 1, logical reads 7, physical reads 1,
 read-ahead reads 6.
Record Exists

(1 row(s) affected)

Table 'Order Details'. Scan count 1, logical reads 2, physical reads 0,
 read-ahead reads 0.
Record Exists
```

As you can see, the EXISTS technique used only two logical reads compared to the seven used by the COUNT(*) technique. Therefore, to determine whether data exists or not, use the EXISTS technique.

Optimize the Row Count Technique

Usually, COUNT(*) is the appropriate technique to count the number of rows in a table. In some cases, you may use COUNT(<Column Name>) to count the number of rows for a particular column. To compare the performance between using COUNT(*) and COUNT(<Column Name>), consider the following sample table (rowcount.sql in the download):

```
IF(SELECT OBJECT_ID('Hotel')) IS NOT NULL
  DROP TABLE Hotel
GO
CREATE TABLE Hotel(RoomID INT IDENTITY, RoomNumber INT, Location CHAR(100))
DECLARE @n INT
SET @n = 1
WHILE @n <= 5000
BEGIN
```

```
    INSERT INTO Hotel (RoomNumber, Location) VALUES(@n,'1st Floor')
    SET @n = @n + 1
END
CREATE INDEX i_RoomID ON Hotel(RoomID)
```

You can find out the number of rooms in the hotel by executing the following SELECT statement:

```
SELECT COUNT(RoomNumber) FROM Hotel --Number of rooms
```

This SELECT statement indicates that you want to find out the number of RoomNumbers in the Hotel table. You can fulfill the same requirement using this SELECT statement:

```
SELECT COUNT(*) FROM Hotel --Number of rows
```

Both SELECT statements return the same result. The first requires an index on the RoomNumber column. However, as this is missing, the optimizer resorts to a table scan. In the second SELECT statement using COUNT(*), the optimizer is able to use the index on i_RoomID, as you can see in Figure 11-22.

```
Query 1: Query cost (relative to the batch): 66.35%
Query text: SELECT COUNT(RoomNumber) FROM Hotel --Number of rooms
```

SELECT	Compute Scalar	Stream Aggregat...	Table Scan
Cost: 0%	Cost: 0%	Cost: 1%	Cost: 99%

```
Query 2: Query cost (relative to the batch): 33.65%
Query text: SELECT COUNT(*) FROM Hotel --Number of rows
```

SELECT	Compute Scalar	Stream Aggregat...	Hotel.i_RoomID
Cost: 0%	Cost: 0%	Cost: 1%	Cost: 99%

Figure 11-22. *Cost of a query with and without the COUNT function on a specific column*

You can see that using COUNT(*) over COUNT(<Column Name>) allows the optimizer to choose the best available index on the table, thereby ensuring the best performance if the indexes are modified later.

Another performance enhancement may be applicable in a few selective cases. Considering the fact that the RoomID column is an identity column with contiguous values starting from 1, and rooms (or rows) are not deleted (which creates empty spots in the identity column values), you can find the number of rooms in the hotel in two other ways:

```
SELECT MAX(RoomID) FROM Hotel
SELECT TOP 1 RoomID FROM Hotel ORDER BY RoomID DESC
```

Figure 11-23 shows that these techniques are much more efficient than the COUNT(*) approach.

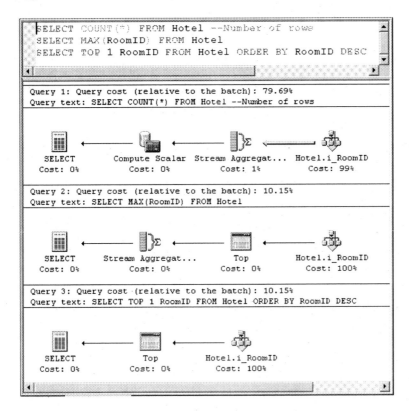

Figure 11-23. *Cost comparison among queries with different ways of determining the number of items in a list*

Therefore, use COUNT(*) instead of COUNT(<Column Name>) to let the optimizer choose the best index around. Also, if the data set permits, consider the last two variations of the SELECT statement (MAX and TOP 1) to improve performance.

Use UNION ALL over UNION

You can concatenate the result set of multiple SELECT statements using the UNION clause as follows:

```
SELECT * FROM Products WHERE SupplierID = 1
UNION
SELECT * FROM Products WHERE SupplierID = 2
```

The UNION clause processes the result set from the two SELECT statements, removing duplicates from the final result set. If the result sets of the SELECT statements participating in the UNION clause are exclusive to each other, or you are allowed to have duplicate rows in the final result set, then use UNION ALL instead of UNION. This avoids the overhead of detecting and removing any duplicates, improving performance as shown in Figure 11-24.

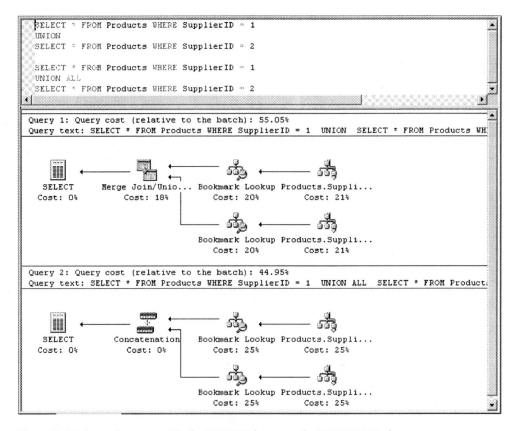

Figure 11-24. *Cost of a query with the UNION clause vs. the UNION ALL clause*

As you can see, in the first case (using UNION) the optimizer used a merge JOIN to process the duplicates while concatenating the result set of the two SELECT statements. Since the result sets are exclusive to each other, you can use UNION ALL instead of the UNION clause. Using the UNION ALL clause avoids the overhead of detecting duplicates, and thereby improves performance.

Use an Additional JOIN Clause over UNION

The UNION or UNION ALL clause executes the constituent queries independently and concatenates the result sets of the queries to generate the final result. It doesn't allow the optimizer to optimize a constituent query by taking into consideration the WHERE clause and the JOIN criteria of the other constituent queries: all the queries are optimized independently.

Many of the queries written using UNION or UNION ALL can be rewritten using an additional JOIN condition in the WHERE clause. This allows the optimizer to consider all the WHERE clause and JOIN conditions together while optimizing the consolidated query. Consequently, most often, the cost of the consolidate query will be cheaper than the total cost of the constituent queries executed using UNION or UNION ALL.

To consider the performance benefit of using an additional JOIN clause in the WHERE condition over the UNION clause, consider the following example:

```
SELECT * FROM [Order Details]
WHERE OrderID = (SELECT MIN(OrderID) from Orders)
UNION ALL
SELECT * FROM [Order Details]
WHERE ProductID = (SELECT MIN(ProductID) from Products)
```

You can rewrite this query as a single consolidated query by using additional JOIN clause in the WHERE condition of the first constituent SELECT statement as follows:

```
SELECT * FROM [Order Details]
WHERE OrderID = (SELECT MIN(OrderID) from Orders)
  OR ProductID = (SELECT MIN(ProductID) from Products)
```

The STATISTICS IO outputs for the two query forms are as follows.

- With UNION ALL:

  ```
  Table 'Order Details'. Scan count 2, logical reads 80
  Table 'Products'. Scan count 1, logical reads 2
  Table 'Orders'. Scan count 1, logical reads 2,
  ```

- With an additional JOIN clause:

  ```
  Table 'Products'. Scan count 1, logical reads 2
  Table 'Order Details'. Scan count 1, logical reads 10
  Table 'Orders'. Scan count 1, logical reads 2
  ```

From the STATISTICS IO outputs, you can see that the query rewritten using the additional JOIN clause required fewer logical reads than required by the query written using UNION ALL.

Use Indexes for Aggregate and Sort Conditions

Generally, aggregate functions such as MIN and MAX benefit from indexes on the corresponding column. Without any index on the column, the optimizer has to scan the base table (or the clustered index), retrieve all the rows, and perform a stream aggregate on the group (containing all rows) to identify the MIN/MAX value, as shown in the following example:

```
IF(SELECT OBJECT_ID('od')) IS NOT NULL
  DROP TABLE od
GO
SELECT * INTO od FROM [Order Details]
--Find the minimum UnitPrice
SELECT MIN(UnitPrice) FROM od
```

The STATISTICS IO output of the SELECT statement using the MIN aggregate function is as follows:

```
Table 'od'. Scan count 1, logical reads 10
```

As shown in the STATISTICS IO output, the query performed ten logical reads just to retrieve the row containing the minimum value for the UnitPrice column. If you create an index on the UnitPrice column, then the UnitPrice values will be presorted by the index in the leaf pages:

```
CREATE INDEX UnitPrice ON od(UnitPrice ASC) --Default sort order is
                                            --ascending
```

The index on the UnitPrice column improves the performance of the MIN aggregate function significantly. The optimizer can retrieve the minimum UnitPrice value by seeking to the topmost row in the index. This reduces the number of logical reads for the query, as shown in the corresponding STATISTICS IO output:

```
Table 'od'. Scan count 1, logical reads 2
```

Similarly, creating an index on the columns referred to in an ORDER BY clause helps the optimizer organize the result set fast because the column values are prearranged in the index. The internal implementation of the GROUP BY clause also sorts the column values first because sorted column values allow the adjacent matching values to be grouped quickly. Therefore, like the ORDER BY clause, the GROUP BY clause also benefits from having the values of the columns referred to in the GROUP BY clause sorted in advance.

Avoid Redundant WHERE Clause Conditions

Sometimes we all accidentally add redundant WHERE clause conditions in a query. This adds overhead to the optimizer. For example, consider the following query:

```
SELECT * FROM Products
WHERE (ProductID = 1 AND SupplierID = 1)
   OR ProductID = 1
```

The filter criterion before the OR clause is truly redundant, as the criterion after it (ProductID = 1) refers to a broader part of the data. This kind of redundant filter criterion is not uncommon to find in queries using the OR clause to apply a collection of filter criteria.

This type of query creates extra work for the query optimizer. In the preceding example, SQL Server 7.0 does exactly what you have asked it to do: it evaluates both filter criteria (even though the first filter criterion is redundant) and subsequently removes the repeated rows produced by the two overlapping filter criteria. This is depicted in the execution plan in Figure 11-25.

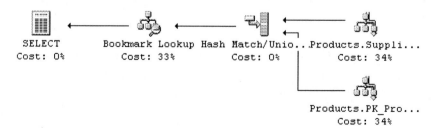

Figure 11-25. *Execution plan in SQL Server 7.0 with redundant WHERE clause conditions*

With its more advanced optimization features, SQL Server 2000 optimizes this query and generates a better execution plan—the same as you would get without the redundant filter criterion (see Figure 11-26).

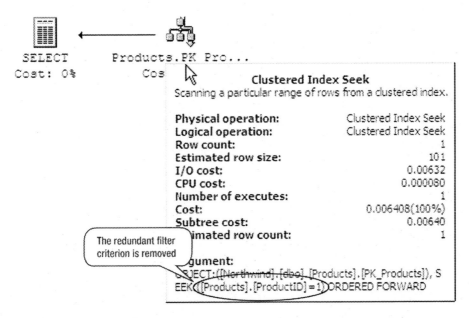

Figure 11-26. *Execution plan in SQL Server 2000 with the automatic removal of the redundant filter criterion*

Even though SQL Server 2000 does a great job removing the redundant OR conditions, it remains a good practice to write optimized queries in the first place.

Use of JOIN Operations vs. Subqueries

Many SQL queries include subqueries that can be written as JOINs. If you have a choice between using a subquery and a JOIN to implement the same functionality, generally the JOIN provides better performance, although this is not always the case. Therefore, it is worth testing both variations of the query before selecting one.

Consider the following subquery (sub.sql in the download) to understand how the SQL Server optimizer manages a subquery. Create two test tables:

```
DROP TABLE od
SELECT * INTO od FROM [Order Details]
CREATE CLUSTERED INDEX ProdID ON od(ProductID)
DROP TABLE Prod
SELECT * INTO Prod FROM Products
CREATE NONCLUSTERED INDEX SuppID ON Prod(SupplierID)
```

Suppose you want detailed order information for the products supplied by the SupplierID 10. You can obtain this information using a subquery as follows:

```
SELECT od.* FROM od
WHERE od.ProductID IN (SELECT p.ProductID FROM Prod p
                        WHERE p.SupplierID = 10)
```

In general, the inner query should be executed first to obtain the list of ProductIDs supplied by the supplier with SupplierID = 10. The outer query can be executed against the output of the inner query to obtain the order details for such products from od table.

You can rewrite this query using a JOIN:

```
SELECT od.* FROM od, Prod p
WHERE od.ProductID = p.ProductID
      AND p.SupplierID = 10
```

Figure 11-27 shows the execution plans of these two query forms.

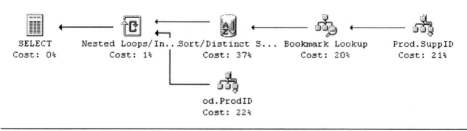

```
Query 1: Query cost (relative to the batch): 61.17%
Query text: SELECT od.* FROM od  WHERE od.ProductID IN (SELECT p.ProductID FROM Prod p
```

```
SELECT          Nested Loops/In...Sort/Distinct S... Bookmark Lookup    Prod.SuppID
Cost: 0%          Cost: 1%          Cost: 37%          Cost: 20%         Cost: 21%

                                    od.ProdID
                                    Cost: 22%
```

```
Query 2: Query cost (relative to the batch): 38.83%
Query text: SELECT od.* FROM od, Prod p  WHERE od.ProductID = p.ProductID          AND p
```

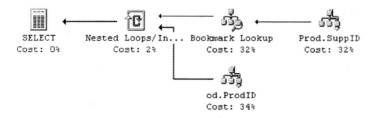

```
SELECT          Nested Loops/In...  Bookmark Lookup    Prod.SuppID
Cost: 0%          Cost: 2%          Cost: 32%          Cost: 32%

                                    od.ProdID
                                    Cost: 34%
```

Figure 11-27. *Cost of a query written using a JOIN operation versus a subquery*

As shown in Figure 11-27, the execution plan of the subquery has an additional processing step to sort the result set from the Prod table. This makes the processing cost of the subquery form (61.17%) higher than that of the JOIN form (38.83%). The subquery uses the "Sort" step to optimize the number of accesses to the inner table (od). For instance, suppose the result set returned by the subquery contains the following ProductIDs: {1, 2, 1}. Then the search on the od table can be considered as three OR conditions:

```
ProductID = 1 OR ProductID = 2 OR ProductID = 1
```

Since the first and the third `OR` conditions are the same (`ProductID = 1`), the optimizer eliminates the repeat `OR` condition by using the "Sort" step. The optimizer sorts the result set from the subquery and chooses only one out of the two adjacent identical `ProductID` values. This additional "Sort" step increases the amount of processing required for the subquery form compared to that of the `JOIN` form.

For additional information, this query can also be written in two other forms as follows (`sub2.sql`):

```
SELECT od.* --Correlated subquery
FROM [Order Details] od
WHERE EXISTS (SELECT p.ProductID FROM Products p
            WHERE p.SupplierID = 10
              AND p.ProductID = od.ProductID)


SELECT od.*
FROM [Order Details] od, (SELECT ProductID FROM Products
                    WHERE SupplierID = 10) p
WHERE od.ProductID = p.ProductID
```

Is there anything you can do to avoid the extra processing performed in the subquery form? From the preceding explanation, you understand the cause of the additional processing required for the subquery form—that is, to remove the duplicates from the input to the `IN` operation. If you know that the table (`Prod`) used in the subquery can't contain duplicates for the column (`ProductID`) returned to the `IN` operation, then you can pass this information to the optimizer in advance by marking the column attribute `UNIQUE`:

```
CREATE UNIQUE NONCLUSTERED INDEX ProdID ON Prod(ProductID)
```

Figure 11-28 shows the resultant execution plan of the subquery form.

```
Query 1: Query cost (relative to the batch): 100.00%
Query text: SELECT od.* FROM od  WHERE od.ProductID IN (SELECT p.
```

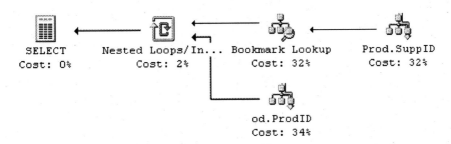

Figure 11-28. *Optimized execution plan for the query written using a subquery*

The `UNIQUE` constraint on the `Prod.ProductID` column assures the optimizer that there are no duplicates in the result set returned by the subquery. This eliminates the "Sort" step and generates an execution plan exactly the same as that of the `JOIN` form.

In the preceding example, the step of removing duplicates by the subquery form (without the unique index on Prod.ProductID) added overhead to the query processing and made the subquery form relatively costly. But in some cases, removal of the duplicates by the subquery may be highly desirable.

To understand the benefit of the additional processing performed by the subquery form, consider the following example. Modify the two test tables a little bit by re-creating them as follows (sub3.sql):

```
DROP TABLE od
SELECT * INTO od FROM [Order Details]
DROP TABLE Prod
SELECT * INTO Prod FROM Products
CREATE CLUSTERED INDEX ProdID ON Prod(ProductID)
```

Suppose you want detailed information of all the products that are sold in pairs. You can obtain this information by executing the following subquery:

```
SELECT p.* FROM Prod p
WHERE p.ProductID IN (SELECT od.ProductID FROM od
                      WHERE od.Quantity = 2)
```

Figure 11-29 shows the execution plan of this subquery.

```
Query 1: Query cost (relative to the batch): 100.00%
Query text: SELECT p.* FROM Prod p  WHERE p.ProductID IN (SELECT o
```

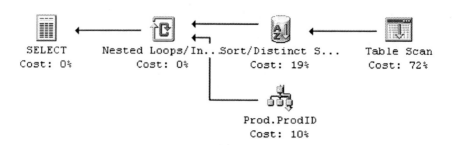

Figure 11-29. *Execution plan for a query that benefits from a subquery*

The "Sort" step in the execution plan removes the duplicate ProductIDs from the result set returned by the subquery, and thereby feeds unique ProductIDs to the IN condition. Consequently, the query retrieves the product information from the Prod table for every matching ProductID only once. If this subquery form of the query is converted into the JOIN form as follows, then you will have some product information returned more than once for the repeat instances (or rows) of ProductIDs from the od table with od.Quantity = 2:

```
SELECT p.* FROM Prod p, od
WHERE p.ProductID = od.ProductID
  AND od.Quantity = 2
```

Consequently, the JOIN form returns 52 rows compared to the 40 distinct pieces of product information (or rows) returned by the subquery form. You can eliminate the nonunique product information returned by the JOIN form from the final result set by using the DISTINCT clause:

```
SELECT DISTINCT p.* FROM Prod p, od
WHERE p.ProductID = od.ProductID
  AND od.Quantity = 2
```

But the JOIN form still accesses the Prod table more times than the subquery form. The DISTINCT clause is applied on the final result set, not before SQL Server accesses the Prod table. Consequently, the JOIN form requires more logical reads compared to the subquery form, as shown in the following STATISTICS IO outputs.

- With the subquery form:

  ```
  Table 'Prod'. Scan count 40, logical reads 82
  Table 'od'. Scan count 1, logical reads 10
  ```

- With the JOIN form (including the DISTINCT clause):

  ```
  Table 'Prod'. Scan count 52, logical reads 106
  Table 'od'. Scan count 1, logical reads 10
  ```

As demonstrated in the first example, the JOIN form fared better than the subquery form, even without the unique index on the Prod.ProductID column. In the second example, the subquery form obtained the product information with fewer logical reads than the JOIN form. Therefore, it is generally advisable to verify which query form performs better for a particular database requirement, and implement the form that provides the better performance. In general, if you do not need the DISTINCT clause in the JOIN form, then the JOIN form usually fares better than the subquery form.

Avoid Local Variables in a Batch Query

Often, multiple queries are submitted together as a batch, avoiding multiple network round-trips. It's common to use local variables in a query batch to pass a value between the individual queries. However, using local variables in the WHERE clause of a query in a batch doesn't allow the optimizer to generate an efficient execution plan.

To understand how the use of a local variable in the WHERE clause of a query in a batch can affect performance, consider the following batch query (batch.sql):

```
DECLARE @id INT
SET @id = 1
SELECT od.* --Retrieve all rows from [Order Details]
  FROM [Order Details] od, Orders o
  WHERE od.OrderID = o.OrderID
    AND o.OrderID >= @id --@id=1
```

The execution plan of this SELECT statement is shown in Figure 11-30.

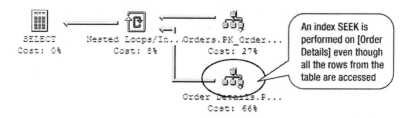

Figure 11-30. *Execution plan showing the effect of a local variable in a batch query*

As you can see, an index seek operation is performed to access the rows from the Order Details table. Since all rows of the table are accessed, an index scan operation would have been preferable for better performance. The index seek operation causes a large number of logical reads, as shown in the following STATISTICS IO output:

```
Table 'Order Details'. Scan count 830, logical reads 1672
Table 'Orders'. Scan count 1, logical reads 21
```

If the SELECT statement is executed without using the local variable, by replacing the local variable value with an appropriate constant value, the optimizer uses the best processing strategy:

```
SELECT od.* --Retrieve all rows from [Order Details]
  FROM [Order Details] od, Orders o
  WHERE od.OrderID = o.OrderID
    AND o.OrderID >= 1 --@id=1
```

Figure 11-31 shows the result.

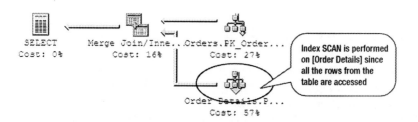

Figure 11-31. *Execution plan for the query when the local variable is not used*

An index scan is the preferred method of data access when a query accesses a large number of rows. This reduces the number of logical reads significantly, as shown in the corresponding STATISTICS IO output:

```
Table 'Order Details'. Scan count 1, logical reads 10
Table 'Orders'. Scan count 1, logical reads 21
```

Based on these facts, you may assume that the execution plan of the first query will be relatively costly compared to the second query. But the reality is quite different, as shown in the execution plan cost comparison in Figure 11-32.

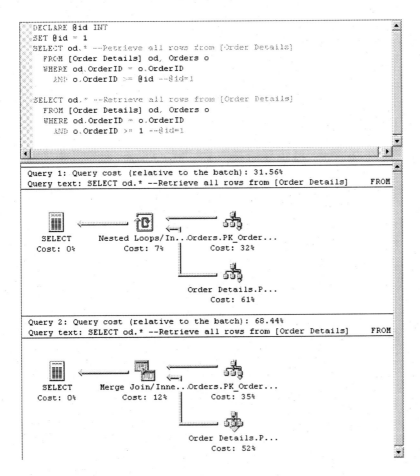

```
DECLARE @id INT
SET @id = 1
SELECT od.* --Retrieve all rows from [Order Details]
  FROM [Order Details] od, Orders o
  WHERE od.OrderID = o.OrderID
    AND o.OrderID >= @id --@id=1

SELECT od.* --Retrieve all rows from [Order Details]
  FROM [Order Details] od, Orders o
  WHERE od.OrderID = o.OrderID
    AND o.OrderID >= 1 --@id=1
```

```
Query 1: Query cost (relative to the batch): 31.56%
Query text: SELECT od.* --Retrieve all rows from [Order Details]    FROM
```

```
SELECT          Nested Loops/In...  Orders.PK_Order...
Cost: 0%        Cost: 7%            Cost: 32%

                                    Order Details.P...
                                    Cost: 61%
```

```
Query 2: Query cost (relative to the batch): 68.44%
Query text: SELECT od.* --Retrieve all rows from [Order Details]    FROM
```

```
SELECT          Merge Join/Inne...  Orders.PK_Order...
Cost: 0%        Cost: 12%           Cost: 35%

                                    Order Details.P...
                                    Cost: 52%
```

Figure 11-32. *Relative cost of the query with and without the use of a local variable*

From the relative cost of the two execution plans, it appears that the second query isn't cheaper than the first query (even though it used the correct indexing strategy for the [Order Details] table). However, from the STATISTICS IO comparison, it appears that the second query should be cheaper than the first query. Which one should you believe: the comparison of STATISTIC IO or the relative cost of execution plan? What's the source of this anomaly?

The execution plan is generated based on the optimizer's estimation of the number of rows affected for each execution step. So, if the estimation for the first query were correct, then its STATISTICS IO wouldn't have been so high (1,672 logical reads for the [Order Details] table) compared to that of the second query (10 logical reads for the [Order Details] table). Let's compare the estimated number of rows with the actual number of rows returned for the individual execution steps of the two queries using STATISTICS PROFILE:

```
SET STATISTICS PROFILE ON
GO
DECLARE @id INT
SET @id = 1
SELECT od.* --Retrieve all rows from [Order Details]
```

```
    FROM [Order Details] od, Orders o
    WHERE od.OrderID = o.OrderID
      AND o.OrderID >= @id --@id=1
GO
SELECT od.* --Retrieve all rows from [Order Details]
    FROM [Order Details] od, Orders o
    WHERE od.OrderID = o.OrderID
      AND o.OrderID >= 1 --@id=1
GO
SET STATISTICS PROFILE OFF
```

> **NOTE** To get the output of STATISTICS PROFILE, turn the Show Execution Plan option off.

Figure 11-33 shows the STATISTICS PROFILE output for the query with a local variable in the WHERE clause.

	Rows	Executes	StmtText	S	N	P	P	L	A	D	EstimateRows
1	2155	1	SELECT od.* --Retrieve all rows fro...	1	1	0	.	.	.	.	758.28821
2	2155	1	|--Nested Loops(Inner Join, OUTER...	1	3	1	.	.	.	.	758.28821
3	830	1	|--Clustered Index Seek(OBJE...	1	5	3	.	.	.	.	249.00002
4	2155	830	|--Clustered Index Seek(OBJE...	1	6	3	.	.	.	.	3.0453341

Figure 11-33. *Estimated versus real cost for the query with a local variable*

Figure 11-34 shows the STATISTICS PROFILE output for the query with a constant in the WHERE clause.

	Rows	Executes	StmtText	S	N	P	P	L	A	D	EstimateRows
1	2155	1	SELECT od.* --Retrieve all rows fro...	2	1	0	.	.	.	.	2145.1421
2	2155	1	|--Merge Join(Inner Join, MERGE:(...	2	3	1	.	.	.	.	2145.1421
3	830	1	|--Clustered Index Seek(OBJE...	2	4	3	.	.	.	.	828.95526
4	2155	1	|--Clustered Index Scan(OBJE...	2	5	3	.	.	.	.	2155.0

Figure 11-34. *Estimated versus real cost for the query without a local variable*

As explained in Chapter 7, the actual number of rows affected by an individual execution step is the product of Rows and Executes. The estimated rows and the actual rows for the two queries are summarized in Table 11-4.

Table 11-4. *Estimated vs. Real Cost for the Query with and Without a Local Variable*

Query Type	Step #	Estimated Rows	Actual Rows Returned
With a local variable in the WHERE clause	1	758	2,155
	2	758	2,155
	3	249	830
	4	3	1,788,650
With a constant in the WHERE clause	1	2,145	2,155
	2	2,145	2,155
	3	830	830
	4	2,155	2,155

From Table 11-4, you can see that the estimated rows for the execution steps of the first query (using a local variable in the WHERE clause) is way off the actual number of rows returned by the steps. Consequently, the execution plan cost for the first query, which is based on the estimated rows, is quite misleading. The incorrect estimation (for step 4, the estimated rows is 3 and the actual rows is 1,788,650) also misguided the optimizer to use an index seek to access rows from the [Order Details] table. For the second query (using a constant in the WHERE clause), however, the estimated rows and actual rows returned are very close.

The accurate estimation (for step 4, the estimated rows is 2,155 and the actual rows is 2,155) caused the optimizer to perform an index scan on the [Order Details] table.

■**NOTE** You can also obtain the actual rows returned by the individual steps from the graphical execution plan by moving your mouse pointer over the connector going out of the step.

Anytime you find such an anomaly between the relative execution plan cost and the STATISTICS IO output for the queries under analysis, you should verify the basis of the estimation. If the underlying facts (estimated rows) of the execution plan itself are wrong, then it is quite likely that the cost represented in the execution plan will also be wrong. But since the output of STATISTICS IO shows the actual number of logical reads performed by the query without being affected by the initial estimation, you can fall back on the STATISTICS IO output.

Now let's get back to the actual performance issue associated with using local variables in the WHERE clause. As shown in the preceding example, using the local variable as the filter criterion in the WHERE clause of a batch query doesn't allow the optimizer to determine the right indexing strategy. This happens because, during the optimization of the queries in the batch, the optimizer doesn't know the value of the variable used in the WHERE clause and can't determine the right access strategy—it knows the value of the variable only during execution.

To avoid this performance problem, use one of the following approaches:

- Do not use a local variable as a filter criterion in a batch.

- Create a stored procedure for the batch and execute it as follows (`batch_sproc.sql`):

```
IF(SELECT OBJECT_ID('p1')) IS NOT NULL
    DROP PROC p1
GO
CREATE PROC p1
@id INT
AS
SELECT od.* --Retrieve all rows from [Order Details]
    FROM [Order Details] od, Orders o
    WHERE od.OrderID = o.OrderID
        AND o.OrderID >= @id --@id=1
GO
EXEC p1 1 --@id=1
```

The optimizer generates the same execution plan as the query that does not use a local variable for the ideal case. Correspondingly, the logical reads are also reduced. In the case of a stored procedure, the optimizer generates the execution plan during the first execution of the stored procedure and uses the parameter value supplied to determine the right processing strategy.

Be Careful Naming Stored Procedures

The name of a stored procedure does matter. The following aspects are important for the stored procedure name:

- Do not prefix a stored procedure name with `sp_`.

- Execute the stored procedure in the correct case.

Do Not Prefix a Stored Procedure Name with sp_

Developers often prefix their stored procedures with `sp_`, so that they can easily identify the stored procedures. However, SQL Server assumes that any stored procedure with this prefix is probably a system stored procedure, whose home is in the `master` database. When a stored procedure with an `sp_` prefix is submitted for execution, SQL Server looks for the stored procedure in the following places in the following order:

- In the `master` database

- In the current database based on any qualifiers provided (database name or owner)

- In the current database using `dbo` as the owner, if an owner is not specified

Therefore, although the user-created stored procedure prefixed with sp_ exists in the current database, the master database is checked first. This happens even when the stored procedure is qualified with the database name. Do not use the sp_ prefix unless, of course, you want to create a new stored procedure in the master database.

To understand the effect of prefixing sp_ to a stored procedure name, consider the following stored procedure (sp_dont.sql in the download):

```
USE Northwind
GO
IF(SELECT OBJECT_ID('sp_p1')) IS NOT NULL
  DROP PROC [sp_p1]
GO
CREATE PROC [sp_p1]
AS
  PRINT 'Done!'
GO

EXEC Northwind.dbo.[sp_p1] --Add plan of sp_p1 to procedure cache
EXEC Northwind.dbo.[sp_p1] --Use the above cached plan of sp_p1
```

The first execution of the stored procedure adds the execution plan of the stored procedure to the procedure cache. A subsequent execution of the stored procedure reuses the existing plan from the procedure cache unless a recompilation of the plan is required (the causes of stored procedure recompilation are explained in Chapter 10). Therefore, the second execution of the stored procedure sp_p1 shown in Figure 11-35 should find a plan in the procedure cache. This is indicated by a SP:CacheHit event in the corresponding Profiler trace output.

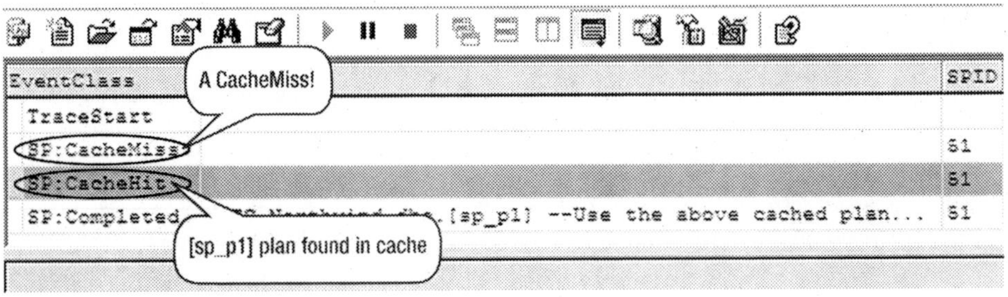

Figure 11-35. *Profile trace output showing the effect of the sp_ prefix on a stored procedure name*

Note that an SP:CacheMiss event is fired before SQL Server tries to locate the plan for the stored procedure in the procedure cache. The SP:CacheMiss event is caused by SQL Server looking in the master database for the stored procedure, even though the execution of the stored procedure is properly qualified with the user database name.

This aspect of the sp_ prefix becomes more interesting when you create a stored procedure with the name of an existing system stored procedure (sp_addlogin.sql in the download):

```
USE Northwind
GO
CREATE PROC [sp_addlogin]
@param1 CHAR(10)
AS
  PRINT '@param1 = ' + @param1
GO
```

```
EXEC Northwind.dbo.[sp_addlogin] 'Northwind'
```

The execution of this user-defined stored procedure causes the execution of the system stored procedure sp_addlogin from the master database instead, as you can see in Figure 11-36.

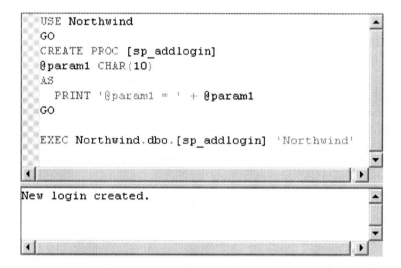

Figure 11-36. *Execution result for stored procedure showing the effect of the sp_ prefix on a stored procedure name*

Unfortunately, it is not possible to execute this user-defined stored procedure.

▓**TIP** As a side note, please don't try to execute the DROP PROCEDURE statement on this stored procedure twice. On the second execution, the system stored procedure will be dropped from the master database. To share a secret, this caused me a lot of problems.

You can see now why you should not prefix a user-defined stored procedure's name with sp_. Use some other naming convention—even if it's just sp or usp_.

Execute the Stored Procedure in the Correct Case

A case-insensitive installation of SQL Server allows you to execute a stored procedure with a different case for the name from that used when the stored procedure was created. However, to keep the cost of stored procedure execution low, execute stored procedures with exact case.

To illustrate this, consider the following stored procedure (StoredProcedure1.sql in the download):

```
IF(SELECT OBJECT_ID('StoredProcedure1')) IS NOT NULL
  DROP PROC StoredProcedure1
GO
CREATE PROC StoredProcedure1
AS
  PRINT 'Done!'
GO
EXEC StoredProcedure1
```

Once the initial overhead cost associated with the first execution of the stored procedure is taken care of, execute the stored procedure with a different name case, as follows:

```
EXEC StoredProcedure1 --Case of the name matches
GO
EXEC STOREDPROCEDURE1 --Case doesn't match
GO
```

The stored procedure execution with a different case for the stored procedure name uses a larger number of reads compared to the execution of the stored procedure with the same case for the name as when it was created. This is shown in the Profiler trace output in Figure 11-37.

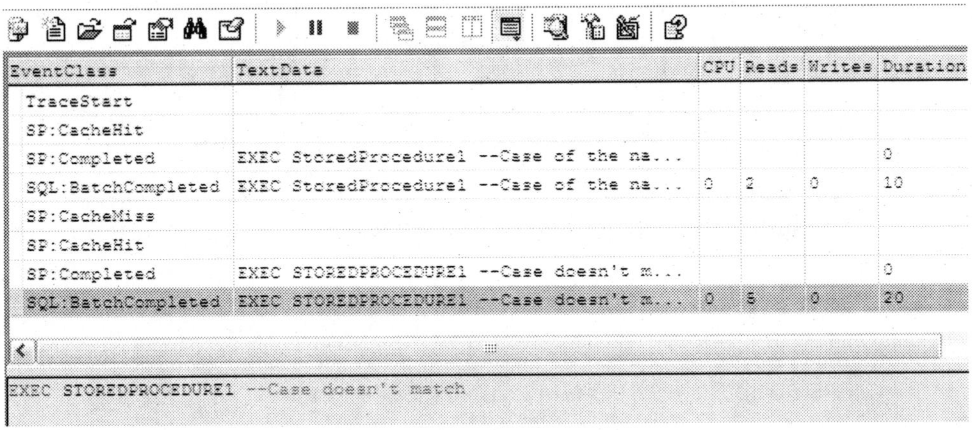

EventClass	TextData	CPU	Reads	Writes	Duration
TraceStart					
SP:CacheHit					
SP:Completed	EXEC StoredProcedure1 --Case of the na...				0
SQL:BatchCompleted	EXEC StoredProcedure1 --Case of the na...	0	2	0	10
SP:CacheMiss					
SP:CacheHit					
SP:Completed	EXEC STOREDPROCEDURE1 --Case doesn't m...				0
SQL:BatchCompleted	EXEC STOREDPROCEDURE1 --Case doesn't m...	0	5	0	20

EXEC STOREDPROCEDURE1 --Case doesn't match

Figure 11-37. *Profiler trace output showing the effect of improper casing of a stored procedure name*

The case mismatch in the second instance not only caused a redundant cache miss (SP:CacheMiss), but also increased the number of reads for the stored procedure execution compared to the first instance when the case matched. When the stored procedure STORED-PROCEDURE1 executed, SQL Server failed to find any cache entry for the exact case of the name, causing an SP:CacheMiss event. On not finding a cached plan, SQL Server makes arrangements to compile the stored procedure, including resolving the ObjectID of the stored procedure from the name STOREDPROCEDURE1. Using this ObjectID, SQL Server again searched the procedure cache for the existing plan. Since the ObjectID is unique for all users, SQL Server found the execution plan for STOREDPROCEDURE1, causing the SP:CacheHit event.

As you can see, executing the stored procedure with a different case for the name adds a cost overhead, because SQL Server has to correctly identify and execute the stored procedure. Therefore, always use the same case for the name as that used during the stored procedure creation, even on a case-insensitive installation.

Reduce the Number of Network Round-trips

Database applications often execute multiple queries to implement a database operation. Besides optimizing the performance of the individual query, it is important that you optimize the performance of the batch. To reduce the overhead of multiple network round-trips, consider the following techniques:

- Execute multiple queries together.

- Use SET NOCOUNT.

Let's look at these techniques in a little more depth.

Execute Multiple Queries Together

It is preferable to submit all the queries of a set together as a batch or a stored procedure. Besides reducing the network round-trips between the database application and the server, stored procedures also provide multiple performance and administrative benefits, as described in Chapter 9.

Use SET NOCOUNT

There is one more factor that you should consider when executing a batch or a stored procedure. After every query in the batch or the stored procedure is executed, the server reports the number of rows affected:

```
(<Number> row(s) affected)
```

This information is returned to the database application and adds to the network overhead. Use the T-SQL statement SET NOCOUNT to avoid this overhead:

```
SET NOCOUNT ON
<SQL queries>
SET NOCOUNT OFF
```

Note that the SET NOCOUNT statement doesn't cause any recompilation issue with stored procedures, unlike some SET statements as explained in Chapter 10.

Reduce the Transaction Cost

Every action query in SQL Server is performed as an *atomic* action, so that the state of a database table moves from one *consistent* state to another. SQL Server does this automatically and it cannot be disabled. If the transition from one consistent state to another requires multiple database queries, then atomicity across the multiple queries should be maintained using explicitly defined database transactions. The old and new state of every atomic action is maintained in the transaction log (on the disk) to ensure *durability*, which guarantees that the outcome of an atomic action won't be lost once it completes successfully. An atomic action during its execution is *isolated* from other database actions using database locks.

Based on the characteristics of a transaction, here are two broad recommendations to reduce the cost of the transaction:

- Reduce logging overhead.

- Reduce lock overhead.

Reduce Logging Overhead

A database query may consist of multiple action queries. If atomicity is maintained for each action query separately, then too many disk writes are performed on the transaction log disk to maintain the durability of each atomic action. Since disk activity is extremely slow compared to memory or CPU activity, the excessive disk activities increase the execution time of the database functionality. For example, consider the following batch query (logging.sql in the download):

```
--Create a test table
IF(SELECT OBJECT_ID('t1')) IS NOT NULL
  DROP TABLE t1
GO
CREATE TABLE t1(c1 TINYINT)
GO
--Insert 10000 rows
DECLARE @Count INT
SET @Count = 1
WHILE @Count <= 10000
BEGIN
  INSERT INTO t1 VALUES(@Count%256)
  SET @Count = @Count + 1
END
```

Since every execution of the INSERT statement is atomic in itself, SQL Server will write to the transaction log for every execution of the INSERT statement.

An easy way to reduce the number of log disk writes is to include the action queries within an explicit transaction:

```
--Insert 10000 rows
DECLARE @Count INT
SET @Count = 1
BEGIN TRANSACTION
  WHILE @Count <= 10000
  BEGIN
    INSERT INTO t1 VALUES(@Count%256)
    SET @Count = @Count + 1
  END
COMMIT
```

The defined transaction scope (between the BEGIN TRANSACTION and COMMIT pair of commands) expands the scope of atomicity to the multiple INSERT statements included within the transaction. This decreases the number of log disk writes and improves the performance of the database functionality.

One area of caution, however, is that by including too many action queries within a transaction, the duration of the transaction is increased. During that time, all other queries trying to access the resources referred to in the transaction are blocked. You will see how to juggle these requirements later, in Chapter 17.

Reduce Lock Overhead

By default, all four SQL statements (SELECT, INSERT, UPDATE, and DELETE) use database locks to isolate their work from that of other SQL statements. This lock management adds a performance overhead to the query. The performance of a query can be improved by requesting fewer locks.

By default, SQL Server can provide row-level lock. For a query working on a large number of rows, requesting a row lock on the individual row adds a significant overhead to the lock-management process. This lock overhead can be reduced by decreasing the lock granularity, say to the page level or table level. SQL Server performs the lock escalation dynamically by taking into consideration the lock overheads. Therefore, generally, it is not necessary to manually escalate the lock level. But, if required, the concurrency of a query can be controlled programmatically using lock hints as follows:

```
SELECT * FROM <TableName> WITH(PAGLOCK) --Use page level lock
```

Similarly, by default, SQL Server uses locks for SELECT statements besides those for INSERT, UPDATE, and DELETE statements. This allows the SELECT statements to read data that isn't being modified. In some cases, the data may be quite static, and it doesn't go through much modification. In such cases, you can reduce the lock overhead of the SELECT statements in one of the following ways:

- Mark the database as READ_ONLY:

```
ALTER DATABASE <DatabaseName> SET READ_ONLY
```

This allows users to retrieve data from the database, but it prevents them from modifying the data. The setting takes effect immediately. If occasional modifications to the database are required, then it may be temporarily converted to READ_WRITE mode:

```
ALTER DATABASE <DatabaseName> SET READ_WRITE
<Database modifications>
ALTER DATABASE <DatabaseName> SET READ_ONLY
```

- Place the specific tables on a filegroup and mark the filegroup as READONLY:

```
--Add a new filegroup with a file to the database
ALTER DATABASE Northwind
   ADD FILEGROUP ReadOnlyFileGroup
ALTER DATABASE Northwind
   ADD FILE(NAME=ReadOnlyFile, FILENAME='C:\NW_1.ndf')
   TO FILEGROUP ReadOnlyFileGroup

--Create specific table(s) on the new filegroup
CREATE TABLE T1(C1 INT, C2 INT) ON ReadOnlyFileGroup
CREATE CLUSTERED INDEX I1 ON T1(C1)
INSERT INTO T1 VALUES(1, 1)
--Or move existing table(s) to the new filegroup
CREATE CLUSTERED INDEX I1 ON T1(C1)
   WITH DROP_EXISTING ON ReadOnlyFileGroup

--Set the filegroup property to READONLY
ALTER DATABASE Northwind
   MODIFY FILEGROUP ReadOnlyFileGroup READONLY
```

This allows you to limit the data access to only the tables residing on the specific filegroup to READONLY, but keep the data access to tables on other filegroups as READWRITE. This filegroup setting takes effect immediately. If occasional modifications to the specific tables are required, then the property of the corresponding filegroup may be temporarily converted to READWRITE mode:

```
ALTER DATABASE Northwind
   MODIFY FILEGROUP ReadOnlyFileGroup READWRITE
<Database modifications>
ALTER DATABASE Northwind
   MODIFY FILEGROUP ReadOnlyFileGroup READONLY
```

- Prevent SELECT statements from requesting any lock:

`SELECT * FROM <TableName> WITH(NOLOCK)`

This prevents the SELECT statement from requesting any lock, and it is applicable to SELECT statements only. Although the NOLOCK hint cannot be used directly on the tables referred to in the action queries (INSERT, UPDATE, and DELETE), it may be used on the data retrieval part of the action queries, as shown below:

```
DELETE [Order Details]
FROM [Order Details] od WITH(NOLOCK)
JOIN [Products] p WITH(NOLOCK)
 ON od.ProductID = p.ProductID
 AND p.ProductID = 0
```

I discuss the different types of lock requests and how to manage lock overhead in the next chapter.

Summary

As discussed in this chapter, to improve the performance of a database application, it is important to ensure that SQL queries are designed properly to benefit from performance-enhancement techniques such as indexes, stored procedures, database constraints, and so on. Ensure that queries are resource-friendly, and don't prevent the use of indexes. Even though, in many cases, the optimizer has the ability to generate cost-effective execution plans, irrespective of query structure, it is still a good practice to design the queries properly in the first place.

Even after you design individual queries for great performance, the overall performance of a database application may not be satisfactory. It is important not only to improve the performance of individual queries, but also to ensure that they work well with other queries without causing serious blocking issues. In the next chapter you will look into the different blocking aspects of a database application.

■■■

CHAPTER 12

Blocking Analysis

You would ideally like your database application to scale linearly with the number of database users. However, it is very common to find that performance degrades as the number of users increases, since they tend to block each other. In fact, database blocking is usually the biggest enemy of scalability for database applications.

In this chapter, I cover the following topics:

- The fundamentals of blocking in SQL Server

- The ACID properties of a transactional database

- Database lock granularity, escalation, modes, and compatibility

- ANSI isolation levels

- The effect of indexes on locking

- The information necessary to analyze blocking

- A SQL script to collect blocking information

- Resolutions and recommendations to avoid blocking

- Techniques to automate the blocking detection and information collection processes

Blocking Fundamentals

In an ideal world, every SQL query would be able to execute concurrently, without any blocking by other queries. However, in the real world, queries *do* block each other, similar to the way a car crossing through a green traffic-signal at a road intersection blocks other cars waiting to cross the intersection. In SQL Server, this traffic management takes the form of the *lock manager*, which controls concurrent access to a database resource to maintain data consistency. The concurrent access to a database resource is controlled across multiple database connections.

In SQL Server, a database connection is identified by a system process ID (SPID). Connections may be from one or many applications; as far as SQL Server is concerned, every connection is treated as a separate SPID. Blocking between two SPIDs accessing the same piece of data at the same time is a natural phenomenon in SQL Server. Whenever two SPIDs try to access a common database resource in conflicting ways, the lock manager ensures that the second SPID waits until the first SPID completes its work. For example, a SPID might be modifying a table record, while another SPID tries to delete the record. Since these two data access requests are incompatible, the second SPID will be blocked until the first SPID completes its task.

On the other hand, if the two SPIDs try to read a table concurrently, both SPIDs are allowed to execute without blocking, since these data accesses are compatible with each other.

Usually, the effect of blocking on a SPID is quite small and doesn't affect its performance noticeably. At times, however, due to poor query and/or transaction design (or maybe bad luck), blocking can affect query performance significantly. In a database application, every effort should be made to minimize blocking, and thereby increase the number of concurrent users that can use the database.

Understanding Blocking

In SQL Server, a database query can execute as a logical unit of work in itself, or it can participate in a bigger logical unit of work. A bigger logical unit of work can be defined using the BEGIN TRANSACTION statement along with COMMIT and/or ROLLBACK statements. Every logical unit of work must conform to a set of four properties called *ACID* properties:

- Atomicity

- Consistency

- Isolation

- Durability

I cover these properties in the sections that follow, as understanding how transactions work is fundamental to understanding blocking.

Atomicity

A logical unit of work must be *atomic*. That is, either all the actions of the logical unit of work are completed or no effect is retained. To understand the atomicity of a logical unit of work, consider the following example (atomicity.sql in the download):

```
--Create a test table
IF(SELECT OBJECT_ID('t1')) IS NOT NULL
  DROP TABLE t1
GO
CREATE TABLE t1 (c1 INT CONSTRAINT chk_c1 CHECK(c1 = 1))
GO


--All ProductIDs are added into t1 as a logical unit of work
INSERT INTO t1
  SELECT ProductID FROM Northwind..Products
GO
SELECT * FROM t1 --Returns 0 rows
```

SQL Server treats the preceding INSERT statement as a logical unit of work. The CHECK constraint on column c1 of table t1 allows only the value 1. Although the ProductID column in the Products table starts with the value 1, it also contains other values. For this reason, the INSERT statement won't add any records at all to the table t1, and an error due to the CHECK constraint is raised. This atomicity is automatically ensured by SQL Server.

So far, so good. But in case of a bigger logical unit of work, you should be aware of an interesting behavior of SQL Server. Imagine that the previous insert task consists of multiple INSERT statements. These can be combined together to form a bigger logical unit of work as follows (logical.sql in the download):

```
BEGIN TRAN --Start: Logical unit of work
  --First:
  INSERT INTO t1
    SELECT ProductID FROM Northwind..Products
  --Second:
  INSERT INTO t1 VALUES(1)
COMMIT --End: Logical unit of work
GO
```

With table t1 already created in atomicity.sql, the BEGIN TRAN and COMMIT pair of statements defines a logical unit of work, suggesting that all the statements within the transaction should be atomic in nature. However, the default behavior of SQL Server doesn't ensure that the failure of one of the statements within a user-defined transaction scope will undo the effect of the prior statement(s). In the preceding transaction, the first INSERT statement will fail as explained earlier, whereas the second INSERT is perfectly fine. The default behavior of SQL Server allows the second INSERT statement to execute, even though the first INSERT statement fails. A SELECT statement, as shown in the following code, will return the row inserted by the second INSERT statement:

```
SELECT * FROM t1 --Returns a row with t1.c1 = 1
```

The atomicity of a user-defined transaction can be ensured in the following two ways:

- SET XACT_ABORT ON

- Explicit rollback

Let's look at these quickly.

SET XACT_ABORT ON

You can modify the atomicity of the insert task in the preceding section using the SET XACT_ABORT ON statement:

```
SET XACT_ABORT ON
GO
BEGIN TRAN --Start: Logical unit of work
  --First:
  INSERT INTO t1 SELECT ProductID FROM Northwind..Products
  --Second:
```

```
    INSERT INTO t1 VALUES(1)
COMMIT --End: Logical unit of work
GO
SET XACT_ABORT OFF
GO
```

The SET XACT_ABORT statement specifies whether SQL Server should automatically roll back and abort an entire transaction when a statement within the transaction fails. The failure of the first INSERT statement will automatically suspend the entire transaction, and thus the second INSERT statement will not be executed. The effect of SET XACT_ABORT is at the connection level, and it remains applicable until it is reconfigured or the connection is closed. By default, SET XACT_ABORT is OFF.

Explicit Rollback

You can also manage the atomicity of a user-defined transaction by checking the value of the @@ERROR system function after every SQL statement that can raise an error. @@ERROR returns 0 if the statement above it is executed successfully; otherwise, it returns a nonzero value indicating the cause of the error. If @@ERROR returns a nonzero value, then the entire work of a user-defined transaction can be rolled back and further statements can be prevented from execution, as follows (rollback.sql in the download):

```
BEGIN TRAN --Start: Logical unit of work
  --First:
  INSERT INTO t1 SELECT ProductID FROM Northwind..Products
  IF @@ERROR <> 0
  BEGIN
    ROLLBACK --Optional, since there is nothing to undo
    RETURN --Prevent any further execution
  END
  --Second:
  INSERT INTO t1 VALUES(1)
  IF @@ERROR <> 0
  BEGIN
    ROLLBACK --Roll back the effect of first INSERT
    RETURN --Prevent any further execution
  END
COMMIT --End: Logical unit of work
GO
```

The ROLLBACK statement rolls back all the actions performed in the transaction until that point. This statement does not prevent the execution of the next statement within the transaction. Therefore, a RETURN statement (or branching using an ELSE statement) is required to prevent the execution of further statements once an error is detected. For a detailed description of how to implement error handling in SQL Server–based applications, please refer to the MSDN Library article titled "Error Handling" (http://msdn.microsoft.com/library/en-us/acdata/ac_8_con_05_6zw8.asp).

Since the atomicity property requires that either all the actions of a logical unit of work are completed or no effects are retained, SQL Server *isolates* the work of a transaction from that of others by granting it exclusive rights on the affected resources so that the transaction can safely roll back the effect of all its actions, if required. The exclusive rights granted to a transaction on the affected resources block all other transactions (or database requests) trying to access those resources during that time period. Therefore, although atomicity is required to maintain the integrity of data, it introduces the undesirable side effect of blocking.

Consistency

A logical unit of work should cause the state of the database to travel from one *consistent* state to another. At the end of a transaction, the state of the database should be fully consistent. SQL Server always ensures that the internal state of the databases is correct and valid by automatically applying all the constraints of the affected database resources as a part of the transaction. SQL Server ensures that the state of internal structures, such as data and index layout, are correct after the transaction. For instance, when the data of a table is modified, SQL Server automatically identifies all the indexes, constraints, and other dependent objects on the table, and applies the necessary modifications to all the dependent database objects as a part of the transaction.

The logical consistency of the data required by the business rules should be ensured by a database developer. A business rule may require changes to be applied on multiple tables. The database developer should accordingly define a logical unit of work to ensure that all the criteria of the business rules are taken care of. SQL Server provides different transaction management features that the database developer can use to ensure the logical consistency of the data.

As just explained, maintaining a consistent logical state requires the use of transactions to define the logical unit of work as per the business rules. Also, to maintain a consistent physical state, SQL Server identifies and works on the dependent database objects as a part of the logical unit of work. The atomicity characteristic of the logical unit of work blocks all other transactions (or database requests) trying to access the affected object(s) during that time period. Therefore, even though consistency is required to maintain a valid logical and physical state of the database, it also introduces the undesirable side effect of blocking.

Isolation

In a multiuser environment, more than one transaction can be executed simultaneously. These concurrent transactions should be isolated from one another so that the intermediate changes made by one transaction don't affect the data consistency of other transactions. The degree of *isolation* required by a transaction can vary. SQL Server provides different transaction isolation features to implement the degree of isolation required by a transaction.

▓**NOTE** Transaction isolation levels are explained later in the chapter in the "Isolation Levels" section.

The isolation requirements of a transaction operating on a database resource can block other transactions trying to access the resource. In a multiuser database environment, multiple transactions are usually executed simultaneously. It is imperative that the data modifications made by an ongoing transaction be protected from the modifications made by other transactions. For instance, suppose a transaction is in the middle of modifying a few rows in a table. During that period, to maintain database consistency, you must ensure that other transactions do not modify or delete the same rows. SQL Server logically isolates the activities of a transaction from that of others, allowing multiple transactions to execute simultaneously without corrupting one another's work, by blocking them appropriately.

Excessive blocking caused by isolation can adversely affect the scalability of a database application. A transaction may inadvertently block other transactions for a long period of time, thereby hurting database concurrency. Since SQL Server manages isolation using locks, it is important to understand the locking architecture of SQL Server. This helps you analyze a blocking scenario and implement resolutions.

▓**NOTE** The fundamentals of database locks are explained later in the chapter in the "Blocking Analysis" section.

Durability

Once a transaction is completed, the changes made by the transaction should be *durable*. Even if the electrical power to the machine is tripped off immediately after the transaction is completed, the effect of all actions within the transaction should be retained. SQL Server ensures durability by keeping track of all pre- and post-images of the data under modification in a transaction log as the changes are made. Immediately after the completion of a transaction, even if SQL Server, the operating system, or the hardware fails (excluding the log disk), SQL Server ensures that all the changes made by the transaction are retained. During restart, SQL Server runs its database recovery feature, which identifies the pending changes from the transaction log for completed transactions and applies them on the database resources. This database feature is called *roll forward*.

The recovery interval period depends on the number of pending changes that need to be applied to the database resources during restart. To reduce the recovery interval period, SQL Server intermittently applies the intermediate changes made by the running transactions as configured by the recovery interval option. The recovery interval option can be configured using the sp_configure statement. The process of intermittently applying the intermediate changes is referred to as the *checkpoint* process. During restart, the recovery process identifies all uncommitted changes and removes them from the database resources by using the pre-images of the data from the transaction log.

The durability property isn't a direct cause of blocking since it doesn't require the actions of a transaction to be isolated from those of others. But in an indirect way, it increases the duration of the blocking. Since the durability property requires saving the pre- and post-images of the data under modification to the transaction log on disk, it increases the duration of the transaction and blocking.

▓**NOTE** Out of the four ACID properties, the isolation property, which is also used to ensure atomicity and consistency, is the main cause of blocking in a SQL Server database. In SQL Server, isolation is implemented using database locks, as explained in the following section.

Database Locks

When a SPID executes a query, SQL Server determines the database resources that need to be accessed and, if required, the lock manager grants database locks to the SPID. The query is blocked if another SPID has already been granted the locks; however, to provide both transaction isolation and concurrency, SQL Server uses different lock granularities and modes, as explained in the sections that follow.

Lock Granularity

SQL Server databases are maintained as files on the physical disk. In the case of a nondatabase file such as an Excel file, the file may only be written to by one user at a time. Any attempt to write to the file by other users fails. However, unlike the limited concurrency on a nondatabase file, SQL Server allows multiple users to modify (or access) contents simultaneously, as long as they don't affect one another's data consistency. This decreases blocking and improves concurrency among the transactions.

To improve concurrency, SQL Server implements lock granularities at the following resource levels:

- Row (RID)

- Key (KEY)

- Page (PAG)

- Extent (EXT)

- Table (TAB)

- Database (DB)

Let's take a look at these lock levels in more detail.

Row-Level Lock

This lock is maintained on a single row within a table and is the lowest level of lock on a database table. When a query modifies a row in a table, an RID lock is granted to the query on the row. For example, consider the transaction on the following test table (rowlock.sql):

```
--Create a test table
IF(SELECT OBJECT_ID('t1')) IS NOT NULL
  DROP TABLE t1
GO
CREATE TABLE t1 (c1 INT)
INSERT INTO t1 VALUES(1)
GO

BEGIN TRAN
  DELETE t1 WHERE c1 = 1
  EXEC sp_lock --Display locks held by the DELETE statement
ROLLBACK
```

The system stored procedure sp_lock can be used to display the lock status. The output of sp_lock in Figure 12-1 shows that the DELETE statement acquired an RID lock on the row to be deleted.

spid	dbid	ObjId	IndId	Type	Resource	Mode	Status
61	13	0	0	DB		S	GRANT
61	13	946102411	0	PAG	1:242	IX	GRANT
61	13	946102411	0	RID	1:242:0	X	GRANT
61	13	946102411	0	TAB		IX	GRANT

Figure 12-1. *sp_lock output showing the row-level lock granted to the DELETE statement*

■**NOTE** I explain lock modes later in the chapter in the "Lock Modes" section.

Granting an RID lock to the DELETE statement prevents other transactions from accessing the row.

The resource locked by the RID lock can be represented in the following format:

```
DatabaseID:FileID:PageID:Slot(row)
```

In the sp_lock output in Figure 12-1, the DatabaseID is displayed separately under the dbid column. The Resource column value for the RID type represents the remaining part of the RID resource as 1:242:0. In this case, a FileID of 1 is the primary data file, a PageID of 242 is a page belonging to table t1 identified by the ObjId column, and a slot (row) of 0 represents the row position within the page. You can obtain the table name and the database name by executing the following SQL statements:

```
SELECT OBJECT_NAME(946102411)
SELECT DB_NAME(13)
```

The row-level lock provides a very high concurrency, since blocking is restricted to the row under effect.

Key-Level Lock

This is a row lock within an index, and it is identified as a KEY lock. As you know, for a table with a clustered index, the data pages of the table and the leaf pages of the clustered index are the same. Since both the rows are the same for a table with a clustered index, only a KEY lock is acquired on the clustered index row while accessing the row from the table (or the clustered index). For example, consider having a clustered index on the table t1:

```
CREATE CLUSTERED INDEX i1 ON t1(c1)
```

If you now rerun

```
BEGIN TRAN
  DELETE t1 WHERE c1 = 1
  EXEC sp_lock --Display locks held by the DELETE statement
ROLLBACK
```

the corresponding sp_lock output shows a KEY lock instead of the RID lock, as you can see in Figure 12-2.

spid	dbid	ObjId	IndId	Type	Resource	Mode	Status
61	13	0	0	DB		S	GRANT
61	13	962102468	1	PAG	1:244	IX	GRANT
61	13	962102468	0	TAB		IX	GRANT
61	13	962102468	1	KEY	(01005221bd04)	X	GRANT

Figure 12-2. *sp_lock output showing the key-level lock granted to the DELETE statement*

The resource locked by the KEY lock can be represented in the following format:

```
DatabaseID:ObjectID:IndexID (Hash value for index key)
```

From the output of sp_lock shown in Figure 12-2, the resource acquired by the KEY lock can be represented as 13:946102411:1 (01005221bd04). In this case, the IndId of 1 is the clustered index on table t1.

■NOTE Different values for the IndId column and how to determine the corresponding index name are explained later in the "Effect of Indexes on Locking" section.

Like the row-level lock, the key-level lock provides a very high concurrency.

Page-Level Lock

This is maintained on a single page within a table or an index, and is identified as a PAG lock. When a query requests multiple rows within a page, the consistency of all the requested rows can be maintained by acquiring either RID/KEY locks on the individual rows or a PAG lock on the entire page. From the query plan, the lock manager determines the resource pressure of acquiring multiple RID/KEY locks and, if the pressure is found to be high, the lock manager requests a PAG lock instead.

The resource locked by the PAG lock can be represented in the following format:

DatabaseID:FileID:PageID

The page-level lock increases performance of an individual query by reducing its locking overhead, but it hurts concurrency of the database by blocking access to all rows in the page.

Extent-Level Lock

This is maintained on an extent (a group of eight contiguous data or index pages) and is identified as an EXT lock. This lock is used, for example, when a DBCC DBREINDEX command is executed on a table, and the pages of the table may be moved from an existing extent to a new extent. During this period, the integrity of the extents is protected using EXT locks.

Table-Level Lock

This is the highest level of lock on a table, and it is identified as a TAB lock. A table-level lock on a table reserves access to the complete table and all its indexes.

When a query is executed, the lock manager automatically determines the locking overhead of acquiring multiple locks at the lower levels. If the resource pressure of acquiring locks at the row level or the page level is determined to be high, then the lock manager directly acquires a table-level lock for the query.

The resource locked by the TAB lock can be represented in the following format:

DatabaseID:ObjectID

A table-level lock requires the least overhead compared to the other locks, and thus improves performance of the individual query. On the other hand, since the table-level lock blocks all write requests on the entire table (including indexes), it can significantly hurt database concurrency.

Database-Level Lock

This is maintained on a database, and is identified as a DB lock. When an application makes a database connection, the lock manager assigns a database-level shared lock to the corresponding SPID. This prevents a user from accidentally dropping or restoring the database while other users are connected to it.

SQL Server ensures that the locks requested at one level respect the locks granted at other levels. For instance, while a user acquires a row-level lock on a table row, another user can't acquire a lock at any other level that may affect the integrity of the row. The second user may acquire a row-level lock on other rows or a page-level lock on other pages, but an incompatible page or table-level lock containing the row won't be granted to other users.

The level at which locks should be applied need not be specified by a user or database administrator; the lock manager determines that automatically. It generally prefers row-level and key-level locks while accessing a small number of rows, to aid concurrency. However, if the locking overhead of multiple low-level locks turns out to be very high, the lock manager automatically selects an appropriate higher-level lock.

Sometimes an application feature may benefit from using a specific lock level for a table referred to in a query. For instance, if an administrative query is executed during nonpeak hours, then a table-level lock may not affect concurrency much, but it can reduce the locking overhead of the query and thereby improve its performance. In such cases, a query developer may override the lock manager's lock level selection for a table referred to in the query using locking hints:

```
SELECT * FROM <TableName> WITH(TABLOCK)
```

Lock Escalation

When a query is executed, SQL Server determines the required lock level for the database objects referred to in the query and starts executing the query after acquiring the required locks. During the query execution, the lock manager keeps track of the number of locks requested by the query to determine the need to escalate the lock level from the current level to a higher level.

The lock escalation threshold is dynamically determined by SQL Server during the course of a transaction. Row locks and page locks are automatically escalated to a table lock when a transaction exceeds its threshold. After the lock level is escalated to a table-level lock, all the lower-level locks on the table are automatically released. This dynamic lock escalation feature of the lock manager optimizes the locking overhead of a query.

Lock Modes

The degree of isolation required by different transactions may vary. For instance, consistency of data is not affected if two transactions read the data simultaneously, but the consistency is affected if two transactions are allowed to modify the data simultaneously. Depending on the type of access requested, SQL Server uses different lock modes while locking resources:

- Shared (S)

- Update (U)

- Exclusive (X)

- Intent:

  - Intent Shared (IS)

  - Intent Exclusive (IX)

- Schema:

  - Schema Modification (Sch-M)

  - Schema Stability (Sch-S)

Shared (S) Mode

This mode is used for read-only queries, such as a SELECT statement. It doesn't prevent other read-only queries from accessing the data simultaneously, since the integrity of the data isn't compromised by the concurrent reads. But the concurrent action queries on the data are prevented to maintain data integrity. The (S) lock is held on the data until the data is read. By default, the (S) lock acquired by a SELECT statement is released immediately after the data is read. For example, consider the following transaction:

```
BEGIN TRAN
  SELECT * FROM Products WHERE ProductID = 1
  --Other queries
COMMIT
```

The (S) lock acquired by the SELECT statement is not held until the end of the transaction. The (S) lock is released immediately after the data is read by the SELECT statement. This behavior of the (S) lock can be altered using a higher isolation level or a lock hint.

Update (U) Mode

This mode may be considered similar to the (S) lock but with an objective to modify the data as a part of the same query. Unlike the (S) lock, the (U) lock indicates that the data is read for modification. Since the data is read with an objective to modify it, more than one (U) lock is not allowed on the data simultaneously in order to maintain data integrity, but concurrent (S) locks on the data are allowed. The (U) lock is associated with an UPDATE statement.

The action of an UPDATE statement actually involves two intermediate steps:

- Read the data to be modified.

- Modify the data.

Different lock modes are used in the two intermediate steps to maximize concurrency. Instead of acquiring an exclusive right while reading the data, the first step acquires a (U) lock on the data. In the second step, the (U) lock is converted to an exclusive lock for modification. If no modification is required, then the (U) lock is released; in other words, it's not held until the end of the transaction. Consider the following example, which demonstrates the locking behavior of the UPDATE statement (create_t1.sql in the download):

```
--Create a test table
IF(SELECT OBJECT_ID('t1')) IS NOT NULL
  DROP TABLE t1
GO
CREATE TABLE t1 (c1 INT, c2 DATETIME)
INSERT INTO t1 VALUES(1, GETDATE())
GO
```

Consider the following UPDATE statement (update1.sql in the download):

```
BEGIN TRANSACTION Tx1
  UPDATE t1 SET c2 = GETDATE() WHERE c1 = 1
  EXEC sp_lock --Lock status after second step of UPDATE
COMMIT
```

To understand the locking behavior of the intermediate steps of the UPDATE statement, you need to obtain an sp_lock output at the end of each step. You can obtain the lock status after each step of the UPDATE statement by following these steps:

1. Block the second step of the UPDATE statement by first executing a transaction from another connection (update2.sql in the download):

   ```
   --Execute from second connection
   BEGIN TRANSACTION Tx2
     --Retain a (S) lock on the resource
     SELECT * FROM t1 WITH(REPEATABLEREAD) WHERE c1 = 1
     --Allow sp_lock to be executed before second step of
     -- UPDATE statement is executed by transaction Tx1
     WAITFOR DELAY '00:00:10'
   COMMIT
   ```

   The REPEATABLEREAD locking hint allows the SELECT statement to retain the (S) lock on the resource.

2. While the transaction Tx2 is executing, execute the UPDATE transaction (update1.sql) from the first connection.

3. While the UPDATE statement is blocked, execute sp_lock from a third connection as follows:

   ```
   EXEC sp_lock --Lock status after first step of UPDATE
   ```

   The output of sp_lock will provide the lock status after the first step of the UPDATE statement since the lock conversion to an exclusive (X) lock by the UPDATE statement is blocked by the SELECT statement.

4. The lock status after the second step of the UPDATE statement will be provided by the sp_lock statement in the UPDATE transaction.

The lock status provided by sp_lock after the individual steps of the UPDATE statement is as follows:

- The lock status after step 1 of the UPDATE statement (obtained from the output of sp_lock executed on the third connection as explained previously) is shown in Figure 12-3.

spid	dbid	ObjId	IndId	Type	Resource	Mode	Status
51	6	0	0	DB		S	GRANT
51	6	158623608	0	PAG	1:325	IX	GRANT
51	6	158623608	0	RID	1:325:0	U	GRANT
51	6	158623608	0	PID	1:325:0	X	CNVT
51	6	158623608	0	TAB		IX	GRANT

Figure 12-3. *sp_lock output showing the lock conversion state of an UPDATE statement*

▓**NOTE** The output of sp_lock is filtered on the SPID of the connection executing the UPDATE statement and the OBJECT_ID for table t1. The order of these rows is not that important.

- The lock status after step 2 of the UPDATE statement is shown in Figure 12-4.

spid	dbid	ObjId	IndId	Type	Resource	Mode	Status
51	6	0	0	DB		S	GRANT
51	6	158623608	0	PAG	1:325	IX	GRANT
51	6	158623608	0	RID	1:325:0	X	GRANT
51	6	158623608	0	TAB		IX	GRANT

Figure 12-4. *sp_lock output showing the final lock status held by the UPDATE statement*

▓**NOTE** The output of sp_lock is filtered on the SPID of the connection executing the UPDATE statement and the OBJECT_ID for table t1. The order of these rows is not that important. The sp_lock outputs have been trimmed for brevity.

From the sp_lock output after the first step of the UPDATE statement, you can note the following:

- A (U) lock is granted to the SPID on the data row.

- A conversion to an (X) lock on the data row is requested.

From the output of sp_lock after the second step of the UPDATE statement, you can see that the UPDATE statement holds only an (X) lock on the data row. Essentially, the (U) lock on the data row is converted to an (X) lock.

By not acquiring an exclusive lock at the first step, an UPDATE statement allows other transactions to read the data using the SELECT statement during that period, since (U) and (S) locks are compatible with each other. This increases database concurrency.

▓**NOTE** I discuss lock compatibility among different lock modes later in this chapter.

You may be curious to learn why a (U) lock is used instead of an (S) lock in the first step of the UPDATE statement. To understand the drawback of using an (S) lock instead of a (U) lock in the first step of the UPDATE statement, let's break the UPDATE statement into the following two steps:

- Read the data to be modified using an (S) lock instead of a (U) lock.

- Modify the data by acquiring an (X) lock.

Consider the following code (split_update.sql in the download):

```
BEGIN TRAN
  --1. Read data to be modified using (S)lock instead of (U)lock.
  --   Retain the (S)lock using REPEATABLEREAD locking hint,
  --   since the original (U)lock is retained until the conversion
  --   to (X)lock.
  SELECT * FROM t1 WITH(REPEATABLEREAD) WHERE c1 = 1

  --Allow another equivalent update action to start concurrently
  WAITFOR DELAY '00:00:10'

  --2. Modify the data by acquiring (X)lock
  UPDATE t1 WITH(XLOCK) SET c2 = GETDATE() WHERE c1 = 1
COMMIT
```

If this transaction is executed from two connections simultaneously, then it causes a deadlock as follows:

```
Server: Msg 1205, Level 13, State 50, Line 8
Transaction (Process ID 52) was deadlocked on lock resources with another process
 and has been chosen as the deadlock victim. Rerun the transaction.
```

Both transactions read the data to be modified using an (S) lock and then request an (X) lock for modification. When the first transaction attempts the conversion to the (X) lock, it is blocked by the (S) lock held by the second transaction. Similarly, when the second transaction attempts the conversion from (S) to (X) lock, it is blocked by the (S) lock held by the first transaction, which in turn is blocked by the second transaction. This causes a circular block and therefore a deadlock.

To avoid this typical deadlock, the UPDATE statement uses a (U) lock instead of an (S) lock at its first intermediate step. Unlike an (S) lock, a (U) lock doesn't allow another (U) lock on the same resource simultaneously. This forces the second concurrent UPDATE statement to wait until the first UPDATE statement completes.

Exclusive (X) Mode

This lock provides an exclusive right on a database resource for modification by action queries such as INSERT, UPDATE, and DELETE. It prevents other concurrent transactions from accessing the resource under modification. Both the INSERT and DELETE statements acquire (X) locks at the very beginning of their execution. As explained earlier, the UPDATE statement converts to the (X) lock after the data to be modified is read. The (X) locks granted in a transaction are held until the end of the transaction.

The (X) lock serves two purposes:

- It prevents other transactions from accessing the resource under modification so that they see a value either before or after the modification, not a value undergoing modification.

- It allows the transaction modifying the resource to safely roll back to the original value before modification, if needed, since no other transaction is allowed to modify the resource simultaneously.

Intent Shared (IS) and Intent Exclusive (IX) Modes

These are two intent locks that indicate the query intends to grab a corresponding (S) or (X) lock at a lower lock level. For example, consider the following transaction on the test table (isix.sql in the download):

```
IF(SELECT OBJECT_ID('t1')) IS NOT NULL
  DROP TABLE t1
GO
CREATE TABLE t1 (c1 INT)
INSERT INTO t1 VALUES(1)
GO


BEGIN TRAN
  DELETE t1 WHERE c1 = 1 --Delete a row
  EXEC sp_lock --Display locks held by the DELETE statement
ROLLBACK
```

Figure 12-5 shows the output of sp_lock.

spid	dbid	ObjId	IndId	Type	Resource	Mode	Status
51	6	0	0	DB		S	GRANT
51	6	174623665	0	PAG	1:325	IX	GRANT
51	6	174623665	0	RID	1:325:0	X	GRANT
51	6	174623665	0	TAB		IX	GRANT

Figure 12-5. *sp_lock output showing the intent locks granted at higher levels*

The (IX) lock at the table level (TAB) indicates that the DELETE statement intends to acquire an (X) lock at a page level, row level, or key level. Similarly, the (IX) lock at the page level (PAG) indicates that the query intends to acquire an (X) lock on a row in the page. The (IX) locks at the higher levels prevent another transaction from acquiring an incompatible lock on the table or on the page containing the row.

Flagging the intent lock [(IS) or (IX)] at a corresponding higher level by a transaction, while holding the lock at a lower level, prevents other transactions from acquiring an incompatible lock at the higher level. If the intent locks were not used, then a transaction trying to acquire a lock at a higher level would have to scan through the lower levels to detect the presence of lower-level locks. As the intent lock at the higher levels indicates the presence of a lower-level lock, the locking overhead of acquiring a lock at a higher level is optimized. The intent locks granted to a transaction are held until the end of the transaction.

Furthermore, there can be combination of locks requested (or acquired) at a certain level and the intention of having lock(s) at a lower level. For example, a query may acquire an (S) lock at the table level, and intend (I) to grab an exclusive lock (X) at a lower level. This means that the lock at the table level will be represented as (SIX). Similarly, there can be (SIU) and (UIX) lock combinations indicating that an (S) or a (U) lock is acquired at the corresponding level and (U) or (X) lock(s) are intended at a lower level.

Schema Modification (Sch-M) and Schema Stability (Sch-S) Modes

These locks are acquired on a table by SQL statements that depend on the schema of the table. A DDL statement, working on the schema of a table, acquires an (Sch-M) lock on the table and prevents other transactions from accessing the table. An (Sch-S) lock is acquired for database activities that depend on the table schema but does not modify the schema, such as a query compilation. It prevents an (Sch-M) lock on the table, but it allows other locks to be granted on the table.

Since, on a production database, schema modifications are infrequent, (Sch-M) locks don't usually become a blocking issue. And because (Sch-S) locks don't block other locks except (Sch-M) locks, concurrency is generally not affected by (Sch-S) locks either.

Lock Compatibility

SQL Server provides isolation to a transaction by preventing other transactions from accessing the same resource in an incompatible way. However, if a transaction attempts a compatible task on the same resource then, to increase concurrency, it won't be blocked by the first transaction. SQL Server ensures this kind of selective blocking by preventing a transaction from acquiring an incompatible lock on a resource held by another transaction. For example, an (S) lock acquired on a resource by a transaction allows other transactions to acquire an (S) lock on the same resource. However, an (Sch-M) lock on a resource by a transaction prevents other transactions from acquiring any lock on that resource.

Table 12-1 lists the compatibility among different lock modes.

Table 12-1. *Compatibility of Locks*

Lock Requested	Lock Granted on the Resource						
	IS	S	U	IX	X	Sch-S	Sch-M
Intent Shared (IS)	Yes	Yes	Yes	Yes		Yes	
Shared (S)	Yes	Yes	Yes			Yes	
Update (U)	Yes	Yes				Yes	
Intent Exclusive (IX)	Yes			Yes		Yes	
Exclusive (X)						Yes	
Schema Stability (Sch-S)	Yes	Yes	Yes	Yes	Yes	Yes	
Schema Modification (Sch-M)							

"Yes" means the lock modes are compatible and can be acquired simultaneously.

Isolation Levels

The lock modes explained in the previous section help a transaction protect its data consistency from other concurrent transactions. The degree of data protection or isolation a transaction gets depends not only on the lock modes, but also on the isolation level of the transaction. This level influences the behavior of the lock modes. For example, by default, an (S) lock is released immediately after the data is read; it isn't held until the end of the transaction. This behavior may not be suitable for some application functionality. In such cases, you can configure the isolation level of the transaction to achieve the desired degree of isolation.

SQL Server implements all four isolation levels defined by ANSI:

- Read uncommitted

- Read committed

- Repeatable read

- Serializable

The isolation levels are listed in increasing order of degree of isolation. You can configure them at either connection or query level by using the SET TRANSACTION ISOLATION LEVEL statement or the locking hints, respectively. The isolation level configuration at the connection level remains effective until the isolation level is reconfigured using the SET statement or until the connection is closed. The four isolation levels are explained in the sections that follow.

Read Uncommitted

This is the lowest of the four isolation levels, and it allows SELECT statements to read data without requesting an (S) lock. Since an (S) lock is not requested by a SELECT statement, it neither blocks nor is blocked by the (X) lock. It allows a SELECT statement to read data while the data is under modification. This kind of data read is called a *dirty read*. For an application in which the amount of data modification is minimal and makes a negligible impact on the accuracy of the data read by the SELECT statement, you may use this isolation level to avoid blocking the SELECT statement by a data modification activity.

You can use the following SET statement to configure the isolation level of a database connection to the read uncommitted isolation level:

```
SET TRANSACTION ISOLATION LEVEL READ UNCOMMITTED
```

You can also achieve this degree of isolation on a query basis using the NOLOCK locking hint:

```
SELECT * FROM Products WITH(NOLOCK)
```

The effect of the locking hint remains applicable for the query and doesn't change the isolation level of the connection.

The read uncommitted isolation level avoids the blocking caused by a SELECT statement, but you should not use it if the transaction depends on the accuracy of the data read by the SELECT statement, or the transaction cannot withstand a concurrent change of data by another transaction.

Read Committed

This isolation level prevents the dirty read caused by the read uncommitted isolation level. This means that (S) locks are requested by the SELECT statements at this isolation level. This is the default isolation level of SQL Server. If needed, you can change the isolation level of a connection to read committed by using the following SET statement:

```
SET TRANSACTION ISOLATION LEVEL READ COMMITTED
```

The read committed isolation level is good for most cases, but since the (S) lock acquired by the SELECT statement isn't held until the end of the transaction, it can cause nonrepeatable read or phantom read issues, as explained in the sections that follow.

Repeatable Read

The repeatable read isolation level allows a SELECT statement to retain its (S) lock until the end of the transaction, thereby preventing other transactions from modifying the data during that time. Database functionality may implement a logical decision inside a transaction based on the data read by a SELECT statement within the transaction. If the outcome of the decision is dependent on the data read by the SELECT statement, then you should consider preventing modification of the data by other concurrent transactions. For example, consider the following two transactions:

- Normalize the price for ProductID = 1: For ProductID = 1, if Price > 10, decrease the price by 10.

- Apply a discount: For Products with Price > 10, apply a discount of 40%.

Considering the following test table (repeatable.sql in the download):

```
IF(SELECT OBJECT_ID('MyProducts')) IS NOT NULL
  DROP TABLE MyProducts
GO
CREATE TABLE MyProducts(ProductID INT, Price MONEY)
INSERT INTO MyProducts VALUES(1, 15.0)
```

you may write the two transactions like this (repeatable_trans.sql):

```
--Transaction 1 from Connection 1
DECLARE @Price INT
BEGIN TRAN NormailizePrice
  SELECT @Price = Price FROM MyProducts
    WHERE ProductID = 1
  /*Allow transaction 2 to execute*/ WAITFOR DELAY '00:00:10'
  IF @Price > 10
    UPDATE MyProducts SET Price = Price - 10 WHERE ProductID = 1
COMMIT
GO

--Transaction 2 from Connection 2
BEGIN TRAN ApplyDiscount
  UPDATE MyProducts
    SET Price = Price * 0.6 --Discount = 40%
    WHERE Price > 10
COMMIT
```

On the surface, the preceding transactions may look good, and yes, they do work in a single-user environment. But in a multiuser environment where multiple transactions can be executed concurrently, you have a problem here!

To figure out the problem, let's execute the two transactions from different connections in the following order:

- Start transaction 1 first.

- Start transaction 2 within 10 seconds of the start of transaction 1.

As you may have guessed, at the end of the transactions, the new price of the product (with ProductID = 1) will be –1.0. Ouch—it appears that you're ready to go out of business!

The problem occurs because transaction 2 is allowed to modify the data while transaction 1 has finished reading the data and is about to make a decision on it. Transaction 1 requires a higher degree of isolation than that provided by the default isolation level (read committed). As a solution, you want to prevent transaction 2 from modifying the data while transaction 1 is working on it. In other words, provide transaction 1 with the ability to read the data again later in the transaction without being modified by others. This feature is called *repeatable read*. Considering the context, the implementation of the solution is probably obvious. After re-creating the table, you can write this:

```
SET TRANSACTION ISOLATION LEVEL REPEATABLE READ
GO
--Transaction 1 from Connection 1
DECLARE @Price INT
BEGIN TRAN NormailizePrice
  SELECT @Price = Price FROM MyProducts
    WHERE ProductID = 1
  /*Allow transaction 2 to execute*/ WAITFOR DELAY '00:00:10'
```

```
   IF @Price > 10
      UPDATE MyProducts SET Price = Price - 10 WHERE ProductID = 1
COMMIT
GO
SET TRANSACTION ISOLATION LEVEL READ COMMITTED --Back to default
GO
```

Increasing the isolation level of transaction 1 to repeatable read will prevent transaction 2 from modifying the data during the execution of transaction 1. Consequently, you won't have an inconsistency in the price of the product. Since the intention isn't to release the (S) lock acquired by the SELECT statement until the end of the transaction, the effect of setting the isolation level to repeatable read can also be implemented at the query level using the lock hint:

```
--Transaction 1 from Connection 1
DECLARE @Price INT
BEGIN TRAN NormailizePrice
   SELECT @Price = Price FROM MyProducts WITH(REPEATABLEREAD)
      WHERE ProductID = 1
   /*Allow transaction 2 to execute*/ WAITFOR DELAY '00:00:10'
   IF @Price > 10
      UPDATE MyProducts SET Price = Price - 10 WHERE ProductID = 1
COMMIT
GO
```

This solution prevents the data inconsistency of MyProduct.Price, but it introduces another problem to this scenario. On observing the result of transaction 2, you realize that it faced a deadlock. Therefore, although the preceding solution prevented the data inconsistency, it is not a complete solution. Looking closely at the effect of the repeatable read isolation level on the transactions, you see that it introduced the typical deadlock issue avoided by the internal implementation of an UPDATE statement, as explained previously. The SELECT statement acquired and retained an (S) lock instead of a (U) lock, even though it intended to modify the data later within the transaction. The (S) lock allowed transaction 2 to acquire a (U) lock, but it blocked the (U) lock's conversion to an (X) lock. The attempt of transaction 1 to acquire a (U) lock on the data at a later stage caused a circular blocking, resulting in a deadlock.

To prevent the deadlock and still avoid data corruption, you can use an equivalent strategy as adopted by the internal implementation of the UPDATE statement. Thus, instead of requesting an (S) lock, transaction 1 can request a (U) lock using an UPDLOCK locking hint when executing the SELECT statement:

```
--Transaction 1 from Connection 1
DECLARE @Price INT
BEGIN TRAN NormailizePrice
   SELECT @Price = Price FROM MyProducts WITH(UPDLOCK)
      WHERE ProductID = 1
   /*Allow transaction 2 to execute*/ WAITFOR DELAY '00:00:10'
   IF @Price > 10
      UPDATE MyProducts SET Price = Price - 10 WHERE ProductID = 1
COMMIT
GO
```

This solution prevents both data inconsistency and the possibility of the deadlock. If the increase of the isolation level to repeatable read had not introduced the typical deadlock, then it would have done the job. Since there is a chance of a deadlock occurring due to the retention of an (S) lock until the end of a transaction, it is usually preferable to grab a (U) lock instead of holding the (S) lock, as just illustrated.

Serializable

This is the highest of the four isolation levels. Instead of acquiring a lock only on the row to be accessed, the serializable isolation level acquires a range lock on the row and the next row in the order of the dataset requested. For instance, a SELECT statement executed at the serializable isolation level acquires a (RangeS-S) lock on the row to be accessed and the next row in the order. This prevents the addition of rows by other transactions in the dataset operated on by the first transaction, and it protects the first transaction from finding new rows in its dataset within its transaction scope. Finding new rows in a dataset within a transaction is also called a *phantom read*.

To understand the need for a serializable isolation level, let's consider an example. Suppose a group (with GroupID = 10) in a company has a fund of $100 to be distributed among the employees in the group as bonus. The fund balance after the bonus payment should be $0. Consider the following test table (serializable.sql in the download):

```
IF(SELECT OBJECT_ID('MyEmployees')) IS NOT NULL
  DROP TABLE MyEmployees
GO
CREATE TABLE MyEmployees(EmployeeID INT, GroupID INT, Salary MONEY)
CREATE CLUSTERED INDEX i1 ON MyEmployees(GroupID)
INSERT INTO MyEmployees VALUES(1, 10, 1000) --Employee 1 in group 10
INSERT INTO MyEmployees VALUES(2, 10, 1000) --Employee 2 in group 10
--Employee 3 & 4 in different groups
INSERT INTO MyEmployees VALUES(3, 20, 1000)
INSERT INTO MyEmployees VALUES(4, 9, 1000)
```

The preceding business functionality may be implemented as follows (bonus.sql in the download):

```
DECLARE @Fund MONEY, @Bonus MONEY, @NumberOfEmployees INT
SET @Fund = 100
BEGIN TRAN PayBonus
  SELECT @NumberOfEmployees = COUNT(*)
    FROM MyEmployees WHERE GroupID = 10
  /*Allow transaction 2 to execute*/ WAITFOR DELAY '00:00:10'
  IF @NumberOfEmployees > 0
  BEGIN
    SET @Bonus = @Fund / @NumberOfEmployees
    UPDATE MyEmployees
      SET Salary = Salary + @Bonus
      WHERE GroupID = 10
    PRINT 'Fund balance =
          ' + CAST((@Fund-(@@ROWCOUNT*@Bonus))
          AS VARCHAR(6)) + ' $'
```

```
  END
COMMIT
GO
```

The PayBonus transaction works well in a single-user environment. However, in a multi-user environment, there is a problem.

Consider another transaction that adds a new employee to GroupID = 10 as follows (new_employee.sql in the download) and is executed concurrently (immediately after the start of the PayBonus transaction) from a second connection:

```
--Transaction 2 from Connection 2
BEGIN TRAN NewEmployee
  INSERT INTO MyEmployees VALUES(5, 10, 1000)
COMMIT
```

The fund balance after the PayBonus transaction will be –$50! Although the new employee may like it, the group fund will be in the red. This causes an inconsistency in the logical state of the data.

To prevent this data inconsistency, the addition of the new employee to the group (or dataset) under operation should be blocked. None of the three isolation levels discussed so far can prevent this inconsistency, since the transaction has to be protected not only on the existing data, but also from the entry of new data in the dataset. The serializable isolation level can provide this kind of isolation by acquiring a range lock on the affected row and the next row in the order determined by the i1 index on the GroupID column. Thus, the data inconsistency of the PayBonus transaction can be prevented by setting the transaction isolation level to serializable.

Remember to re-create the table first:

```
SET TRANSACTION ISOLATION LEVEL SERIALIZABLE
GO
DECLARE @Fund MONEY, @Bonus MONEY, @NumberOfEmployees INT
SET @Fund = 100
BEGIN TRAN PayBonus
  SELECT @NumberOfEmployees = COUNT(*)
    FROM MyEmployees WHERE GroupID = 10
  /*Allow transaction 2 to execute*/ WAITFOR DELAY '00:00:10'
  IF @NumberOfEmployees > 0
  BEGIN
    SET @Bonus = @Fund / @NumberOfEmployees
    UPDATE MyEmployees
      SET Salary = Salary + @Bonus
      WHERE GroupID = 10
    PRINT 'Fund balance = ' + CAST((@Fund-(@@ROWCOUNT*@Bonus))
    AS VARCHAR(6)) + ' $'
  END
COMMIT
GO
SET TRANSACTION ISOLATION LEVEL READ COMMITTED --Back to default
GO
```

The effect of the serializable isolation level can also be achieved at the query level by using the HOLDLOCK locking hint on the SELECT statement, as shown here:

```
DECLARE @Fund MONEY, @Bonus MONEY, @NumberOfEmployees INT
SET @Fund = 100
BEGIN TRAN PayBonus
  SELECT @NumberOfEmployees = COUNT(*)
    FROM MyEmployees WITH(HOLDLOCK) WHERE GroupID = 10
  /*Allow transaction 2 to execute*/ WAITFOR DELAY '00:00:10'
  IF @NumberOfEmployees > 0
  BEGIN
    SET @Bonus = @Fund / @NumberOfEmployees
    UPDATE MyEmployees
      SET Salary = Salary + @Bonus
      WHERE GroupID = 10
    PRINT 'Fund balance = ' + CAST((@Fund-(@@ROWCOUNT*@Bonus))
    AS VARCHAR(6)) + ' $'
  END
COMMIT
GO
```

The range locks acquired by the PayBonus transaction can be observed by executing sp_lock from another connection while the PayBonus transaction is executing, as shown in Figure 12-6.

	spid	dbid	ObjId	IndId	Type	Resource	Mode	Status
1	52	1	107863451	1	KEY	(1400a039bdac)	RangeS-S	GRANT
2	52	1	107863451	0	TAB		IS	GRANT
3	52	1	107863451	1	KEY	(0b003b5ba1b3)	RangeS-S	GRANT
4	52	1	107863451	1	PAG	1:1797	IS	GRANT
5	52	1	107863451	1	KEY	(0a0043106d73)	RangeS-S	GRANT
6	53	1	85575343	0	TAB		IS	GRANT

Figure 12-6. *sp_lock output showing range locks granted to the serializable transaction*

NOTE The output of sp_lock has been trimmed for brevity.

The output of sp_lock shows that shared-range (RangeS-S) locks are acquired on three index rows: the first employee in GroupID = 10, the second employee in GroupID = 10, and the third employee in GroupID = 20. These range locks prevent the entry of any new employee in GroupID = 10.

The range locks just shown introduce a few interesting side effects:

- No new employee with a GroupID between 10 and 20 can be added during this period. For instance, an attempt to add a new employee with a GroupID of 15 will be blocked by the PayBonus transaction:

```
--Transaction 2 from Connection 2
BEGIN TRAN NewEmployee
  INSERT INTO MyEmployees VALUES(6, 15, 1000)
COMMIT
```

- If the dataset of the PayBonus transaction turns out to be the last set in the existing data ordered by the index, then the range lock required on the row, after the last one in the dataset, is acquired on the last possible data value in the table.

To understand this behavior, let's delete the employees with a GroupID > 10 to make the GroupID = 10 dataset the last dataset in the clustered index (or table):

```
DELETE MyEmployees WHERE GroupID > 10
```

Run the updated bonus.sql and new_employee.sql again. The resultant output of sp_lock for the PayBonus transaction is shown in Figure 12-7.

spid	dbid	ObjId	IndId	Type	Resource	Mode	Status
52	1	107863451	0	TAB		IS	GRANT
52	1	107863451	1	KEY	(0b003b5ba1b3)	RangeS-S	GRANT
52	1	107863451	1	PAG	1:1797	IS	GRANT
52	1	107863451	1	KEY	(ffffffffffff)	RangeS-S	GRANT
52	1	107863451	1	KEY	(0a0043106d73)	RangeS-S	GRANT

Figure 12-7. *sp_lock output showing extended range locks granted to the serializable transaction*

■**NOTE** The output of sp_lock has been trimmed for brevity.

The range lock on the last possible row (KEY = ffffffffffff) in the clustered index as shown in Figure 12-7 will block the addition of employees with all GroupIDs greater than or equal to 10. For example, an attempt to add a new employee with GroupID = 999 will be blocked by the PayBonus transaction:

```
--Transaction 2 from Connection 2
BEGIN TRAN NewEmployee
  INSERT INTO MyEmployees VALUES(7, 999, 1000)
COMMIT
```

Guess what will happen if the table doesn't have an index on the GroupID column (i.e., the column in the WHERE clause)? While you're thinking (probably!), I'll re-create the table with the clustered index on a different column:

```
IF(SELECT OBJECT_ID('MyEmployees')) IS NOT NULL
  DROP TABLE MyEmployees
GO
CREATE TABLE MyEmployees(EmployeeID INT, GroupID INT, Salary MONEY)
CREATE CLUSTERED INDEX i1 ON MyEmployees(EmployeeID)
INSERT INTO MyEmployees VALUES(1, 10, 1000) --Employee 1 in group 10
INSERT INTO MyEmployees VALUES(2, 10, 1000) --Employee 2 in group 10
--Employee 3 & 4 in different groups
INSERT INTO MyEmployees VALUES(3, 20, 1000)
INSERT INTO MyEmployees VALUES(4, 9, 1000)
GO
```

Rerun the updated bonus.sql and new_employee.sql. The resultant output of sp_lock for the PayBonus transaction is shown in Figure 12-8.

	spid	dbid	ObjId	IndId	Type	Resource	Mode	Status
1	51	6	0	0	DB		S	GRANT
2	51	6	1858105660	1	PAG	1:347	IS	GRANT
3	51	6	1858105660	1	KEY	(0200825b1d43)	RangeS-S	GRANT
4	51	6	1858105660	1	KEY	(040022ae5dcc)	RangeS-S	GRANT
5	51	6	1858105660	1	KEY	(01005221bd04)	RangeS-S	GRANT
6	51	6	1858105660	1	KEY	(030032727d7e)	RangeS-S	GRANT
7	51	6	1858105660	0	TAB		IS	GRANT
8	51	6	1858105660	1	KEY	(ffffffffffff)	RangeS-S	GRANT

Figure 12-8. *sp_lock output showing range locks granted to the serializable transaction with no index on the WHERE clause column*

NOTE The output of sp_lock has been trimmed for brevity.

Once again, the range lock on the last possible row (KEY = ffffffffffff) in the new clustered index, as shown in Figure 12-8, will block the addition of any new row to table. I will discuss the reason behind this extensive locking later in the chapter in the "Effect of Indexes on the Serializable Isolation Level" section.

As you've seen, the serializable isolation level not only holds the share locks until the end of the transaction like the repeatable read isolation level, but also prevents any new row in the dataset (or more) by holding range locks. Because this increased blocking can hurt database concurrency, you should avoid the serializable isolation level.

Effect of Indexes on Locking

Indexes affect the locking behavior on a table. On a table with no indexes, the lock granularities are RID, PAG (on the page containing the RID), and TAB. Adding indexes to the table affects the resources to be locked. For example, consider the following test table with no indexes (create_t1_2.sql in the download):

```
IF(SELECT OBJECT_ID('t1')) IS NOT NULL
   DROP TABLE t1
GO
CREATE TABLE t1(c1 INT, c2 DATETIME)
INSERT INTO t1 VALUES(1, GETDATE())
```

Observe the locking behavior on the table for the transaction (indexlock.sql in the download):

```
BEGIN TRAN LockBehavior
  UPDATE t1 WITH(REPEATABLEREAD) --Hold all acquired locks
    SET c2 = GETDATE()
    WHERE c1 = 1
  --Observe lock behavior using sp_lock from another connection
  WAITFOR DELAY '00:00:10'
COMMIT
```

Figure 12-9 shows the output of sp_lock applicable to the test table.

spid	dbid	ObjId	IndId	Type	Resource	Mode	Status
51	6	350624292	0	PAG	1:325	IX	GRANT
51	6	350624292	0	RID	1:325:0	X	GRANT
51	6	350624292	0	TAB		IX	GRANT

Figure 12-9. *sp_lock output showing the locks granted on a table with no index*

■**NOTE** Lock entries on other resources have been removed for brevity.

The following locks are acquired by the transaction:

- An (IX) lock on the table

- An (IX) lock on the page containing the data row

- An (X) lock on the data row within the table

The IndId column value in the sp_lock output indicates whether the lock is on the table or on one of its indexes:

- IndId = 0: Lock on the table.

- IndId = 1: Lock on the clustered index.

- IndId >= 2 and < 255: Lock on the nonclustered index. You can obtain the specific nonclustered index on which the lock is acquired from the sysindexes system table as follows:

```
SELECT name FROM sysindexes
WHERE id = <ObjID from sp_lock output>
    AND indid = <IndID from sp_lock output>
```

The effect of the index on the locking behavior of the table varies with the type of index on the WHERE clause column. The difference arises from the fact that the leaf pages of the nonclustered and clustered indexes have a different relationship with the data pages of the table. Let's look into the effect of these indexes on the locking behavior of the table.

Effect of a Nonclustered Index

As the leaf pages of the nonclustered index are separate from the data pages of the table, the resources associated with the nonclustered index are also protected from corruption. SQL Server automatically ensures this. To see this in action, create a nonclustered index on the test table:

CREATE NONCLUSTERED INDEX i1 ON t1(c1)

On running the LockBehavior transaction (indexlock.sql) again, and executing sp_lock from a separate connection, you get the result shown in Figure 12-10.

	spid	dbid	ObjId	IndId	Type	Resource	Mode	Status
1	52	1	139863565	2	KEY	(a000d78a9e58)	U	GRANT
2	52	1	139863565	0	PAG	1:1950	IX	GRANT
3	52	1	139863565	0	RID	1:1950:0	X	GRANT
4	52	1	139863565	2	PAG	1:1960	IU	GRANT
5	52	1	139863565	0	TAB		IX	GRANT

Figure 12-10. *sp_lock output showing the effect of a nonclustered index on locking behavior*

NOTE Lock entries on other resources have been removed for brevity.

The following locks are acquired by the transaction:

- An (IU) lock on the page containing the nonclustered index row, (IndId = 2)

- A (U) lock on the nonclustered index row within the index page, (IndId = 2)

- An (IX) lock on the table, (IndId = 0)

- An (IX) lock on the page containing the data row, (IndId = 0)

- An (X) lock on the data row within the data page, (IndId = 0)

Note that only the row-level and page-level locks are directly associated with the nonclustered index. The next higher level of lock granularity for the nonclustered index is the table-level lock on the corresponding table.

Thus, nonclustered indexes introduce an additional locking overhead on the table. You can avoid the locking overhead on the index by using the sp_indexoption system stored procedure (indexoption.sql in the download):

```
--Avoid KEY lock on the index rows
EXEC sp_indexoption 't1.i1', ALLOWROWLOCKS, FALSE
--Avoid PAG lock on index pages
EXEC sp_indexoption 't1.i1', ALLOWPAGELOCKS, FALSE
BEGIN TRAN LockBehavior
  UPDATE t1 WITH(REPEATABLEREAD)
    SET c2 = GETDATE()
    WHERE c1 = 1
  --Observe lock behavior using sp_lock from another connection
  WAITFOR DELAY '00:00:10'
COMMIT
EXEC sp_indexoption 't1.i1', ALLOWROWLOCKS, TRUE
EXEC sp_indexoption 't1.i1', ALLOWPAGELOCKS, TRUE
```

You can use the sp_indexoption system stored procedure to enable/disable the KEY locks and PAG locks on the index. Disabling just the KEY lock causes the lowest lock granularity on the index to be the PAG lock. Configuration of lock granularity on the index remains effective until it is reconfigured.

Figure 12-11 displays the output of sp_lock executed from a separate connection.

	spid	dbid	ObjId	IndId	Type	Resource	Mode	Status
1	55	1	139863565	0	TAB		X	GRANT

Figure 12-11. *sp_lock output showing the effect of sp_indexoption on lock granularity*

▓**NOTE** Lock entries on other resources have been removed for brevity.

The only lock acquired by the transaction on the test table is an (X) lock on the table (IndId = 0).

You can see from the new locking behavior that disabling both the KEY lock and the PAG lock on the index using the sp_indexoption escalates lock granularity to the table level. This will block every concurrent access to the table or to the indexes on the table, and consequently it can hurt the database concurrency very seriously. However, if a nonclustered index becomes a point of contention in a blocking scenario, then it may be beneficial to disable the PAG locks on the index, thereby allowing only KEY locks on the index.

Effect of a Clustered Index

Since for a clustered index the leaf pages of the index and the data pages of the table are the same, the clustered index can be used to avoid the overhead of locking additional pages (leaf pages) and rows introduced by a nonclustered index. To understand the locking overhead associated with a clustered index, convert the preceding nonclustered index to a clustered index:

```
CREATE CLUSTERED INDEX i1 ON t1(c1) WITH DROP_EXISTING
```

If you run indexlock.sql again and execute sp_lock in a different connection, you should see the resultant output for the LockBehavior transaction on t1 in Figure 12-12.

	spid	dbid	ObjId	IndId	Type	Resource	Mode	Status
1	52	20	2073058421	1	PAG	1:79	IX	GRANT
2	52	20	2073058421	1	KEY	(01005221bd04)	X	GRANT
3	52	20	2073058421	0	TAB		IX	GRANT

Figure 12-12. *sp_lock output showing the effect of a clustered index on locking behavior*

▓**NOTE** Lock entries on other resources have been removed for brevity.

The following locks are acquired by the transaction:

- An (IX) lock on the table, (IndId = 0)

- An (IX) lock on the page containing the clustered index row, (IndId = 1)

- An (X) lock on the clustered index row within the table (or clustered index), (IndId = 1)

The locks on the clustered index row and the leaf page are actually the locks on the data row and data page too, since the data pages and the leaf pages are the same. Thus, the clustered index reduced the locking overhead on the table compared to the nonclustered index.

Reduced locking overhead of a clustered index is another benefit of using a clustered index over a nonclustered index.

Effect of Indexes on the Serializable Isolation Level

Indexes play a significant role in determining the amount of blocking caused by the serializable isolation level. The availability of an index on the WHERE clause column (that causes the dataset to be locked) allows SQL Server to determine the order of the rows to be locked. For instance, consider the example used in the section on the serializable isolation level. The SELECT statement uses a GroupID filter column to form its dataset, like so:

```
...
SELECT @NumberOfEmployees = COUNT(*)
  FROM MyEmployees WITH(HOLDLOCK) WHERE GroupID = 10
...
```

A clustered index is available on the GroupID column, allowing SQL Server to acquire a (RangeS-S) lock on the row to be accessed and the next row in the correct order.

If the index on the GroupID column is removed, then SQL Server cannot determine the rows on which the range locks should be acquired, since the order of the rows is no longer guaranteed. Consequently, the SELECT statement acquires an (S) lock at the table level instead of acquiring lower granularity locks at the row level, as shown in Figure 12-13.

	spid	dbid	ObjId	IndId	Type	Resource	Mode	Status
1	51	20	21575115	0	TAB		S	GRANT

Figure 12-13. *sp_lock output showing the locks granted to a SELECT statement with no index on the WHERE clause column*

NOTE The output of sp_lock has been trimmed for brevity.

By failing to have an index on the filter column, you significantly increase the degree of blocking caused by the serializable isolation level. This is another good reason to have an index on the WHERE clause columns.

Blocking Analysis

Although blocking is necessary to isolate a transaction from other concurrent transactions, sometimes it may rise to unprecedented levels, adversely affecting database concurrency. In the simplest blocking scenario, the lock acquired by a SPID on a resource blocks another SPID requesting an incompatible lock on the resource. To improve concurrency, it is important to analyze the cause of blocking and apply the appropriate resolution.

In a blocking scenario, you need the following information to have a clear understanding of the cause of the blocking:

- *The connection information of the blocking and blocked SPIDs*: You can obtain this information from the sysprocesses system table and the sp_who2 system stored procedure.

- *The lock information of the blocking and blocked SPIDs*: You can obtain this information from the `syslockinfo` system table and the `sp_lock` system stored procedure.

- *The SQL statements last executed by the blocking and blocked SPIDs*: You can use the `DBCC INPUTBUFFER` statement or SQL Profiler to obtain this information.

You can also obtain the following information from the SQL Server Enterprise Manager under <*ServerName*> ➤ Management ➤ Current Activity:

- *Process Info*: Provides connection information of all SPIDs. Additionally, the properties of a SPID provide the last batch of SQL statements executed by the SPID.

- *Locks/ProcessID*: Provides a list of SPIDs for the open connections and the locks held by those SPIDs.

- *Locks/Object*: Provides a list of database objects accessed by the user SPIDs and the locks held on those objects.

The current activity information provided by Enterprise Manager is not dynamically updated as the status of current activities changes. During a blocking scenario, it is generally recommended to obtain the blocking information using SQL statements instead of using Enterprise Manager, as Enterprise Manager may itself block on `tempdb` while trying to present the current activity information.

To simplify the process of collecting the blocking information, a SQL Server administrator can use SQL scripts to provide the relevant information listed here.

Blocker Script

The following Microsoft Knowledge Base articles provide SQL scripts to collect the blocking information:

- Q251004, "How to Monitor SQL Server 7.0 Blocking":
  `http://support.microsoft.com/default.aspx?scid=kb;en-us;Q251004`

- Q271509, "How to Monitor SQL Server 2000 Blocking":
  `http://support.microsoft.com/default.aspx?scid=kb;en-us;Q271509`

These scripts (generally referred as *blocker scripts*) provide most of the relevant information to analyze a blocking scenario in detail. When database blocking occurs, the stored procedure created by the blocker script may be executed, as explained in the corresponding Microsoft Knowledge Base article.

To understand how to analyze a blocking scenario and the relevant information provided by the blocker script, consider the following example (blocker.sql in the download). First, create a test table:

```
IF(SELECT OBJECT_ID('t1')) IS NOT NULL
  DROP TABLE t1
GO
CREATE TABLE t1 (c1 INT, c2 INT, c3 DATETIME)
INSERT INTO t1 VALUES(11, 12, GETDATE())
INSERT INTO t1 VALUES(21, 22, GETDATE())
```

Now, open three connections, and run the following three queries concurrently. Execute the code in Listing 12-1 first.

Listing 12-1. *Connection 1*

```
BEGIN TRAN User1
  UPDATE t1 SET c3 = GETDATE()
  /*Do something useful*/ WAITFOR DELAY '00:00:20'
COMMIT
```

Execute Listing 12-2 while the User1 transaction is executing.

Listing 12-2. *Connection 2*

```
BEGIN TRAN User2
  SELECT c2 FROM t1 WHERE c1 = 11
COMMIT
```

Execute the blocker script in Listing 12-3 in a loop.

Listing 12-3. *Connection 3*

```
WHILE 1=1 --Stop the execution when the diagnostic-data collection is over
BEGIN
    -- EXEC master.dbo.sp_blocker_pss80
    -- Or for fast mode
    EXEC master.dbo.sp_blocker_pss80 @fast=1
    -- Or for latch mode
    -- EXEC master.dbo.sp_blocker_pss80 @latch=1
    WAITFOR DELAY '00:00:15'
END
```

▓**TIP** For ease of viewing of the results of this script, run Query Analyzer in Results in Text mode.

This creates a simple blocking scenario where the User1 transaction blocks the User2 transaction.

The output of the blocker script provides the following information:

- Connection information for SPIDs

- SPID(s) at the head of blocking chain(s)

- Lock information for SPIDs

- SQL statements executed by blocking and blocked SPIDs

- Process Status Structure (PSS) for SPID(s) at the head of blocking chain(s)

Let's look at examples of each of these.

Connection Information for SPIDs

The SYSPROCESSES section, which is the output of the sysprocesses system table, provides connection information of the blocking and the blocked SPIDs. You can obtain this by running the blocker script with the @fast parameter setting. Running the script without the @fast parameter setting provides the process information for all the existing database connections. For a list of all the columns in the sysprocesses system table and their description, refer to the MSDN Library article "sysprocesses" (http://msdn.microsoft.com/library/en-us/tsqlref/ts_sys-p_3kmr.asp).

To understand the activities of the SPIDs, look at the status, blocked, open_tran, waitresource, waittype, waittime, and lastwaittype columns, as shown in the excerpt of the SYSPROCESSES section of the output shown in Figure 12-14.

```
SYSPROCESSES  DOPEY\DOPEY  134218262
spid   status                            blocked open_tran waitresource      waittype waittime   cmd               lastwaittype
------ --------------------------------- ------- --------- ----------------- -------- ---------- ----------------- ------------
57     sleeping                          0       1                           0x020B   15953      WAITFOR           WAITFOR
63     sleeping                          57      1         RID: 20:1:78:0    0x0003   14961      SELECT            LCK_M_S
```

Figure 12-14. *SYSPROCESSES section from the blocker script output*

The status of a blocking SPID with open_tran >= 1 should not be sleeping. Otherwise, this is an indication of a potential blocking issue. If the waittype is 0x0000, then the SPID is not waiting on any resource, and the lastwaittype column indicates the last wait type for the SPID. If the waittype is nonzero, then the SPID is waiting on a resource represented by the waitresource column, and the lastwaittype indicates the name of the current wait type.

For a detailed description of the waittype and lastwaittype columns, please refer to the Microsoft Knowledge Base article Q244455 titled "INF: Definition of Sysprocesses Waittype and Lastwaittype Fields for SQL Server 7.0" (http://support.microsoft.com/default.aspx?scid=kb;en-us;Q244455).

If the waittime of a blocked SPID decreases compared to its value in the previous iteration of the blocker script output, this indicates that the SPID is blocked on a new resource. You can verify this by comparing the waitresource between the two outputs. (Most of the resources identified by the waitresource column are explained in the preceding section on lock granularity.) The waitresource value COMPILE (the format is DatabaseID:ObjectID) indicates that the SPID is waiting to compile a plan for the stored procedure identified by the ObjectID.

The SYSPROCESSES section shown previously provides the following information:

- SPID 63 is blocked on SPID 57 on a data row.

- The contended data row is identified by an RID, 20:1:78:0, which can be translated into DatabaseID:FileID:PageID:Slot(row). In this case, a DatabaseID of 20 is my test database, a FileID of 1 is the primary data file, a PageID of 78 is a page belonging to table t1, and a slot(row) of 0 indicates the row position within the page. You can obtain the database name by executing the following SQL statement:

```
SELECT DB_NAME(20)
```

You can obtain the table to which the `PageID` belongs by following these steps:

1. Execute the following SQL statements:

   ```
   DBCC TRACEON(3604)
   DBCC PAGE(20,1,78)
   ```

2. From the output of the `DBCC PAGE`, get the value of `m_objId`.

3. Use the `OBJECT_NAME` system function, supplying the value of `m_objId`:

   ```
   SELECT OBJECT_NAME(37575172)
   ```

   The `DBCC PAGE` command is explained in Chapter 14.

   - The `waittype` for SPID 57 is nonzero, which means the execution of the SPID is suspended until the event, as indicated by the `lastwaittype` column value (`WAITFOR`), completes. Similarly, the `waittype` for SPID 63 is also nonzero, which means the execution of the SPID is also suspended until the event, as indicated by the corresponding `lastwaittype` column value (`LCK_M_S`; in other words, *Lock Mode Share*) succeeds.

From the preceding information, you can tell that that SPID 63 is blocked on SPID 57 on a data row (`RID = 20:1:78:0`) for (S) lock. The blocking SPID 57 is sleeping (with an open transaction) on a wait initiated by a `WAITFOR` command, and it is not blocked by anyone.

The `cpu`, `physical_io`, and `memusage` columns in the `SYSPROCESSES` output provide the resources used by the SPID until that time. The `hostname`, `hostprocess`, `program_name`, `nt_domain`, and `nt_username` columns help identify the database application owning the connection.

SPID(s) at the Head of Blocking Chain(s)

In a complex blocking scenario, a blocking SPID may be blocked by another blocking SPID. This chain of blocking will have a SPID at the head of the blocking chain with nothing blocking it. A complex blocking scenario may have multiple blocking chains, leading to multiple blocking heads. Identifying and resolving a blocking head will clear the set of SPIDs directly or indirectly blocked on the SPID at the head.

Figure 12-15 shows the output of the blocker script for this example.

```
SPIDs at the head of blocking chains
spid
------
57
```

Figure 12-15. *Blocker script output showing the head of the blocking chain*

This indicates that SPID 57 is directly or indirectly blocking all other blocked SPIDs (in this case, SPID 63).

You can even determine the head of the blocking chain by analyzing the output of the SYSPROCESSES section. For a blocked SPID, the blocked column indicates the blocking SPID. By following the blocked column value for the blocking SPID, you can determine the SPID on which the blocking SPID might have been blocked. You can continue this process until you reach a blocking SPID with a blocked column value of 0. This blocking SPID will be the head of the blocking chain. *Remember that in a complex blocking scenario, there can be more than one head.*

Lock Information for SPIDs

The SYSLOCKINFO section, which is the output of the syslockinfo system table, provides locking information for the blocking and blocked SPIDs. You can obtain locking information for all the SPIDs by executing the blocker script without the @fast parameter setting. The output of this section is a superset of the output of the sp_lock system stored procedure.

For a blocked SPID, the value of the Status column will be WAIT. The resource on which the blocked SPID waits can be identified from the Type and Resource columns. The blocking SPID will be the one that has been granted this resource. The Mode column indicates the lock type held by the blocking SPID and the lock type requested by the blocked SPID.

Figure 12-16 shows an excerpt of the SYSLOCKINFO section output of the blocker script result for the example.

```
SYSLOCKINFO
spid    ecid    dbid    ObjId         IndId    Type   Resource            Mode           Status  TransID
------  ------  ------  -----------   ------   ----   ------------------  ------------   ------  --------
63      0       20      0             0        DB                         S              GRANT   0
57      0       20      0             0        DB                         S              GRANT   0
57      0       20      37575172      0        RID    1:78:0              X              GRANT   6382726
63      0       20      37575172      0        RID    1:78:0              S              WAIT    6382779
57      0       20      37575172      0        RID    1:78:1              X              GRANT   6382726
63      0       20      37575172      0        PAG    1:78                IS             GRANT   6382779
57      0       20      37575172      0        PAG    1:78                IX             GRANT   6382726
63      0       20      37575172      0        TAB                        IS             GRANT   6382779
57      0       20      37575172      0        TAB                        IX             GRANT   6382726
```

Figure 12-16. *SYSLOCKINFO section from the blocker script output*

This output provides the following information:

- SPID 63 is waiting to acquire a (S) lock on a data row.

- The contended data row belongs to table t1 (ObjId = 37575172) in my test database (dbid = 20).

- The contended data row is identified as 1:78:0, which can be translated into FileID:PageID:Slot(row). In this case, the FileID of 1 is the primary data file, the PageID of 78 is a page belonging to the table t1, and the slot(row) of 0 indicates the row position, in this case the first row within the page.

- SPID 57 is holding an (X) lock on the contented data row.

From this information, you can infer that the blocked SPID 63 requested an (S) lock on a data row in the `Northwind..t1` table and is waiting on SPID 57. The blocking SPID 57 is holding an (X) lock on the contended row and is not blocked by anyone.

SQL Statements Executed by Blocking and Blocked SPIDs

Knowing the SQL statements executed by the blocking and the blocked SPIDs always helps. You can use the DBCC INPUTBUFFER command or the SQL Profiler tool to determine the SQL statement last executed by a SPID.

The DBCC INPUTBUFFER section of the blocker script result provides the information shown in Figures 12-17 and 12-18 for the example.

```
DBCC INPUTBUFFER FOR SPID 57
EventType        Parameters EventInfo
-------------- ---------- -------------------------
Language Event 0           BEGIN TRAN User1
  UPDATE t1 SET c3 = GETDATE()
  /*Do something useful*/ WAITFOR DELAY '00:00:20'
COMMIT
```

Figure 12-17. *Blocker script output showing the SQL statement executed by a blocker/blocking SPID*

```
DBCC INPUTBUFFER FOR SPID 63
EventType        Parameters EventInfo
-------------- ---------- -----------------
Language Event 0           BEGIN TRAN User2
  SELECT c2 FROM t1 WHERE c1 = 11
COMMIT
```

Figure 12-18. *Blocker script output showing the SQL statement executed by another blocker/blocking SPID*

From the preceding SQL statements, you can infer that SPID 63 requires an (S) lock on a row that is under modification (the lock mode is (X) lock) by SPID 57. Since the (S) lock is incompatible with the (X) lock, SPID 63 (which is executed later) is blocked by SPID 57. The connection information and the lock information for these SPIDs further explain this blocking scenario.

Because the output of the blocker script is generated in multiple steps, it is possible that a SPID may appear as the head of a blocking chain, but by the time the DBCC INPUTBUFFER statement is executed, it is no longer blocking and the INPUTBUFFER is not captured. This indicates that the blocking is resolved and may no longer be a problem.

PSS for SPID(s) at the Head of Blocking Chain(s)

This section provides the Process Status Structure (PSS) for the SPIDs at the head of the blocking chains. One of the most useful pieces of information in this section is the ec_stat field. Table 12-2 shows the common values for this field.

Table 12-2. *Common Values for ec_stat*

Value	Description
0x0	Normal state.
0x2	Process should end. This indicates that the SPID should be terminated.
0x40	Process received the attention signal from a client due to query timeout or cancel. This indicates that the currently active query is being terminated, but not the entire SPID as with 0x2.
0x80	Process is involved in a multidatabase transaction.
0x200	Process is performing a server-to-server remote procedure call.
0x400	User is performing a query with the NOLOCK hint.
0x800	Process is in rollback and cannot be chosen as a deadlock victim.
0x2000	Process is currently being killed.

The stored procedure created by the blocker script has a code section that can be modified to prevent the PSS output when the blocker script is executed in the fast mode.

Profiler Trace

The blocking caused by a SPID is generally an artifact of a resource-intensive operation by the SPID. In a database application with poor performance, it is generally preferable to first identify the costly or resource-intensive queries using the Profiler tool, as explained in Chapter 3. The optimization of the costly queries may resolve many of the blocking issues in the database. Once the costly queries are optimized, then the blocker script may be used to diagnose the cause of remaining blocking issues.

You can also use the Profiler trace output to detect possible blocking faced by a SPID, by comparing the value of the CPU and Duration columns for long-running queries. A long-running query (with a high Duration column value) with very low CPU (one-tenth or less of the Duration column value) indicates that the query took a long time outside the CPU. If the corresponding Read/Write column values are not high, then the most likely explanation is that the SPID was blocked by another SPID.

Even when diagnosing the blocking issues with the blocker script, it is generally useful to capture the SQL queries executed on the database. The output of the DBCC INPUTBUFFER captured by the blocker script provides the last SQL statement executed by the blocking and the blocked SPIDs. In many cases, the blocking might have been caused by a SQL statement executed earlier (not the last executed SQL statement) by the blocking SPID. You can use the Profiler trace output to analyze all the SQL statements executed by the blocking SPID. To capture the SQL queries, use SQL Profiler as explained in the Chapter 3 and, to minimize the overhead of SQL tracing, use the stored procedure technique as explained in the section "Capturing a Trace Using Stored Procedures."

Blocking Resolutions

Once you've analyzed the cause of a block, the next step is to determine any possible resolutions. A few techniques you can use to do this are as follows:

- Optimize the queries executed by blocking and blocked SPIDs.

- Decrease the isolation level.

- Partition the contended data.

- Use a covering index on the contended data.

NOTE A detailed list of recommendations to avoid blocking appears later in the chapter in the section "Recommendations to Reduce Blocking."

To understand these resolution techniques, let's apply them in turn to the preceding blocking scenario.

Optimize the Queries

Optimizing the queries executed by the blocking and blocked SPIDs help reduce the blocking duration. In the blocking scenario, the queries executed by the SPIDs participating in the blocking are as follows:

- Blocking SPID

```
BEGIN TRAN User1
  UPDATE t1 SET c3 = GETDATE()
  /*Do something useful*/ WAITFOR DELAY '00:00:20'
COMMIT
```

- Blocked SPID

```
BEGIN TRAN User2
  SELECT c2 FROM t1 WHERE c1 = 11
COMMIT
```

Let's analyze the individual SQL statements executed by the blocking and blocked SPIDs to optimize their performance:

- The UPDATE statement of the blocking SPID accesses the data without a WHERE clause. This makes the query inherently costly on a large table. If possible, break the action of the UPDATE statement into multiple batches using appropriate WHERE clauses. If the individual UPDATE statements of the batch are executed in separate transactions, then fewer locks will be held on the resource within one transaction, and for shorter time periods.

- The SELECT statement executed by the blocked SPID has a WHERE clause on column c1. From the index structure on the test table, you can see that there is no index on this column. To optimize the SELECT statement, you should create a clustered index on column c1:

```
CREATE CLUSTERED INDEX i1 ON t1(c1)
```

▓**NOTE** Since the table fits within one page, adding the clustered index won't make much difference to the query performance. However, as the number of rows in the table increases, the beneficial effect of the index will become more pronounced.

Optimizing the queries reduces the duration for which the locks are held by the SPIDs. The query optimization reduces the impact of blocking; it doesn't prevent the blocking completely. However, as long as the optimized queries execute within acceptable performance limits, a small amount of blocking may be neglected.

Decrease the Isolation Level

Another approach to resolve blocking can be to use a lower isolation level, if possible. The SELECT statement of the User2 transaction gets blocked while requesting an (S) lock on the data row. The isolation level of this transaction can be decreased to read uncommitted, so that the (S) lock is not requested by the SELECT statement. The read uncommitted isolation level can be configured for the connection using the SET statement:

```
SET TRANSACTION ISOLATION LEVEL READ UNCOMMITTED
GO
BEGIN TRAN User2
  SELECT c2 FROM t1 WHERE c1 = 11
COMMIT
GO
SET TRANSACTION ISOLATION LEVEL READ COMMITTED --Back to default
GO
```

The read uncommitted isolation level can also be configured for the SELECT statement at a query level by using the NOLOCK locking hint:

```
BEGIN TRAN User2
  SELECT c2 FROM t1 WITH(NOLOCK) WHERE c1 = 11
COMMIT
```

The read uncommitted isolation level avoids the blocking faced by the User2 transaction.

Every transaction may not be able to withstand the dirty data returned by the SELECT statements at the read uncommitted isolation level. Therefore, this resolution technique can be applied only to a limited number of blocking scenarios.

Partition the Contended Data

If the columns of the tables used by the transactions are independent, then you can vertically split the contended table into two parts with a one-to-one relationship between the two parts. This allows the transactions to execute concurrently on their individual resources, without blocking each other. For instance, in the preceding blocking scenario, the two parts of the table can be

```
CREATE TABLE t1(c1 INT, c2 INT, clink INT UNIQUE)
CREATE TABLE t1_part(clink INT REFERENCES t1(clink), c3 DATETIME)
```

creating two tables like so:

Table t1		
c1	c2	clink

Table t1_part	
clink (from t1)	c3

As long as proper integrity is maintained between the parts of the table, the two parts jointly represent the original dataset. The modified UPDATE statement on the t1_part table and the original SELECT statement will be able to execute concurrently with this vertical partitioning configuration.

The vertical partitioning technique may also be used to partition less frequently used columns into a separate table. This narrows down the width of the remaining table, accommodating more rows in a page. The frequently executed queries accessing the remaining columns can benefit from the compressed pages, and thus perform better.

Vertical partitioning of the table does add some overhead to maintain integrity between the parts of the table. However, if done properly, it can improve both performance and concurrency.

Covering Index on Contended Data

In a blocking scenario, you should analyze whether the query of the blocking or the blocked SPID can be fully satisfied using a covering index. If the query of one of the SPIDs can be satisfied using a covering index, then it will prevent the SPID from requesting locks on the contended resource. Also, if the other SPID doesn't need a lock on the covering index (to maintain data integrity), then both SPIDs will be able to execute concurrently without blocking each other.

For instance, in the preceding blocking scenario, the SELECT statement by the blocked SPID can be fully satisfied by a covering index on columns c1 and c2:

```
CREATE NONCLUSTERED INDEX iAvoidBlocking ON t1(c1, c2)
```

The transaction of the blocking SPID need not acquire a lock on the covering index since it accesses only column c3 of the table. The covering index will allow the SELECT statement to get the values for columns c1 and c2 without accessing the base table. Thus, the SELECT statement of the blocked SPID can acquire an (S) lock on the covering-index row without being blocked by the (X) lock on the data row acquired by the blocking SPID. This allows both transactions to execute concurrently without any blocking.

Consider a covering index as a mechanism to "duplicate" a part of the table data whose consistency is automatically maintained by SQL Server. This covering index, if mostly read-only, can allow some transactions to be served from the "duplicate" data while the base table (and other indexes) can continue to serve other transactions.

Recommendations to Reduce Blocking

Single-user performance and the ability to scale with multiple users are both important for a database application. In a multiuser environment, it is important to ensure that the database operations don't hold database resources for a long time. This allows the database to support a large number of operations (or database users) concurrently without much performance degradation. The following is a list of tips to reduce/avoid database blocking:

- Keep transactions short.

  - Perform the minimum steps/logic within a transaction.

  - Do not perform costly external activity within a transaction, such as sending an acknowledgment e-mail or performing activities driven by the end user.

- Optimize queries using indexes.

  - Create an index on WHERE clause column(s).

  - Avoid a clustered index on frequently updated columns. Updates to clustered index key columns require locks on the clustered index and all nonclustered indexes (since their row locator contains the clustered index key).

  - Consider using a covering index to serve the blocked SELECT statements.

- Consider vertically partitioning a contended table.

- Use query timeouts to control runaway queries.

- Avoid losing control over the scope of the transactions due to poor error-handling routines or application logic.

  - Use SET XACT_ABORT ON to avoid a transaction being left open on an error condition within the transaction.

  - Execute the following SQL statement from a client error-handler after executing a SQL batch or stored procedure containing a transaction:

    ```
    IF @@TRANCOUNT > 0 ROLLBACK
    ```

- Use MDAC 2.6 or later. In the corresponding ODBC driver and OLE DB provider, a pooled connection is reset before being used for a new connection request. This aborts any uncommitted transaction left behind by the previous user of the connection.

- Use the lowest isolation level required.

   - Use the default isolation level (read committed).

   - Consider avoiding lock requests by SELECT statements by using the NOLOCK locking hint in the SELECT statement, if possible.

Automation to Detect and Collect Blocking Information

You can automate the process of detecting a blocking condition and collecting the relevant information using SQL Server Agent. SQL Server provides Performance Monitor counters shown in Table 12-3, to track the amount of wait time.

Table 12-3. *Performance Monitor Counters*

Object	Counter	Instance	Description
SQLServer:Locks (For SQL Server named instance: MSSQL$<InstanceName>:Locks)	Average Wait Time (ms)	_Total	The average amount of wait time for each lock request that resulted in a wait
	Lock Wait Time (ms)	_Total	Total wait time for locks in the last second

You can create a combination of the SQL Server alerts and jobs to automate the following process:

1. Determine when the average amount of wait time exceeds an acceptable amount of blocking using the Average Wait Time (ms) counter. Based on your preferences, you may use the Lock Wait Time (ms) counter instead.

2. When the average wait time exceeds the limit, notify the SQL Server DBA of the blocking situation through e-mail and/or pager.

3. Automatically collect the blocking information using the blocker script for a certain period of time.

Let's see how to do this. First, create the SQL Server job, Blocking Analysis, so that it can be used by the SQL Server alert created later. You can create this SQL Server job from SQL Server Enterprise Manager to collect blocking information by following these steps:

1. Create a file named C:\BlockerScript.sql to trace the SQL queries and to capture the blocking information for 10 minutes using a SQL batch:

```
--Collect blocking information for 10 minutes
SET XACT_ABORT ON
DECLARE @MonitoringPeriod TINYINT
SET @MonitoringPeriod = 10 --Minutes


/*************************/
/* Start SQL tracing      */
/*************************/

-- Create a Queue
declare @rc int
declare @TraceID int
declare @maxfilesize bigint
set @maxfilesize = 500

DECLARE @TRACE_FILE_ROLLOVER INT
DECLARE @BlockingTrace NCHAR(35)
SET @TRACE_FILE_ROLLOVER = 2
SET @BlockingTrace = 'BlockingTrace' + CONVERT(NCHAR(32),GETDATE(),120)
SET @BlockingTrace = 'C:\' + REPLACE(@BlockingTrace,':','_')
exec @rc = sp_trace_create @TraceID output,
  @TRACE_FILE_ROLLOVER, @BlockingTrace, @maxfilesize, NULL
if (@rc != 0) goto error

-- Set the events
declare @on bit
set @on = 1
exec sp_trace_setevent @TraceID, 10, 1, @on --RPC:Completed, TextData
exec sp_trace_setevent @TraceID, 10, 2, @on --RPC:Completed, BinaryData
exec sp_trace_setevent @TraceID, 10, 3, @on --RPC:Completed, DatabaseID
exec sp_trace_setevent @TraceID, 10, 4, @on --RPC:Completed
                                      --, TransactionID
exec sp_trace_setevent @TraceID, 10, 12, @on --RPC:Completed, SPID
exec sp_trace_setevent @TraceID, 10, 13, @on --RPC:Completed, Duration
exec sp_trace_setevent @TraceID, 10, 14, @on --RPC:Completed, StartTime
exec sp_trace_setevent @TraceID, 10, 15, @on --RPC:Completed, EndTime
exec sp_trace_setevent @TraceID, 10, 16, @on --RPC:Completed, Reads
exec sp_trace_setevent @TraceID, 10, 17, @on --RPC:Completed, Writes
exec sp_trace_setevent @TraceID, 10, 18, @on --RPC:Completed, CPU
exec sp_trace_setevent @TraceID, 10, 21, @on --RPC:Completed
                                      --, EventSubClass
```

```
exec sp_trace_setevent @TraceID, 10, 25, @on --RPC:Completed
                                        --, IntegerData
exec sp_trace_setevent @TraceID, 10, 31, @on --RPC:Completed, Error
exec sp_trace_setevent @TraceID, 12, 1, @on --SQL:BatchCompleted
                                        --, TextData
exec sp_trace_setevent @TraceID, 12, 2, @on --SQL:BatchCompleted
                                        --, BinaryData
exec sp_trace_setevent @TraceID, 12, 3, @on --SQL:BatchCompleted
                                        --, DatabaseID
exec sp_trace_setevent @TraceID, 12, 4, @on --SQL:BatchCompleted,
TransactionID
exec sp_trace_setevent @TraceID, 12, 12, @on --SQL:BatchCompleted, SPID
exec sp_trace_setevent @TraceID, 12, 13, @on --SQL:BatchCompleted
                                        --, Duration
exec sp_trace_setevent @TraceID, 12, 14, @on --SQL:BatchCompleted
                                        --, StartTime
exec sp_trace_setevent @TraceID, 12, 15, @on --SQL:BatchCompleted
                                        --, EndTime
exec sp_trace_setevent @TraceID, 12, 16, @on --SQL:BatchCompleted, Reads
exec sp_trace_setevent @TraceID, 12, 17, @on --SQL:BatchCompleted
                                        --, Writes
exec sp_trace_setevent @TraceID, 12, 18, @on --SQL:BatchCompleted, CPU
exec sp_trace_setevent @TraceID, 12, 21, @on --SQL:BatchCompleted
                                        --, EventSubClass
exec sp_trace_setevent @TraceID, 12, 25, @on --SQL:BatchCompleted
                                        --, IntegerData
exec sp_trace_setevent @TraceID, 12, 31, @on --SQL:BatchCompleted, Error
exec sp_trace_setevent @TraceID, 14, 1, @on --Login, TextData
exec sp_trace_setevent @TraceID, 14, 2, @on --Login, BinaryData
exec sp_trace_setevent @TraceID, 14, 3, @on --Login, DatabaseID
exec sp_trace_setevent @TraceID, 14, 4, @on --Login, TransactionID
exec sp_trace_setevent @TraceID, 14, 12, @on --Login, SPID
exec sp_trace_setevent @TraceID, 14, 13, @on --Login, Duration
exec sp_trace_setevent @TraceID, 14, 14, @on --Login, StartTime
exec sp_trace_setevent @TraceID, 14, 15, @on --Login, EndTime
exec sp_trace_setevent @TraceID, 14, 16, @on --Login, Reads
exec sp_trace_setevent @TraceID, 14, 17, @on --Login, Writes
exec sp_trace_setevent @TraceID, 14, 18, @on --Login, CPU
exec sp_trace_setevent @TraceID, 14, 21, @on --Login, EventSubClass
exec sp_trace_setevent @TraceID, 14, 25, @on --Login, IntegerData
exec sp_trace_setevent @TraceID, 14, 31, @on --Login, Error
exec sp_trace_setevent @TraceID, 15, 1, @on --Logout, TextData
exec sp_trace_setevent @TraceID, 15, 2, @on --Logout, BinaryData
exec sp_trace_setevent @TraceID, 15, 3, @on --Logout, DatabaseID
exec sp_trace_setevent @TraceID, 15, 4, @on --Logout, TransactionID
exec sp_trace_setevent @TraceID, 15, 12, @on --Logout, SPID
exec sp_trace_setevent @TraceID, 15, 13, @on --Logout, Duration
```

```
    exec sp_trace_setevent @TraceID, 15, 14, @on --Logout, StartTime
    exec sp_trace_setevent @TraceID, 15, 15, @on --Logout, EndTime
    exec sp_trace_setevent @TraceID, 15, 16, @on --Logout, Reads
    exec sp_trace_setevent @TraceID, 15, 17, @on --Logout, Writes
    exec sp_trace_setevent @TraceID, 15, 18, @on --Logout, CPU
    exec sp_trace_setevent @TraceID, 15, 21, @on --Logout, EventSubClass
    exec sp_trace_setevent @TraceID, 15, 25, @on --Logout, IntegerData
    exec sp_trace_setevent @TraceID, 15, 31, @on --Logout, Error
    exec sp_trace_setevent @TraceID, 16, 1, @on --Attention, TextData
    exec sp_trace_setevent @TraceID, 16, 2, @on --Attention, BinaryData
    exec sp_trace_setevent @TraceID, 16, 3, @on --Attention, DatabaseID
    exec sp_trace_setevent @TraceID, 16, 4, @on --Attention, TransactionID
    exec sp_trace_setevent @TraceID, 16, 12, @on --Attention, SPID
    exec sp_trace_setevent @TraceID, 16, 13, @on --Attention, Duration
    exec sp_trace_setevent @TraceID, 16, 14, @on --Attention, StartTime
    exec sp_trace_setevent @TraceID, 16, 15, @on --Attention, EndTime
    exec sp_trace_setevent @TraceID, 16, 16, @on --Attention, Reads
    exec sp_trace_setevent @TraceID, 16, 17, @on --Attention, Writes
    exec sp_trace_setevent @TraceID, 16, 18, @on --Attention, CPU
    exec sp_trace_setevent @TraceID, 16, 21, @on --Attention, EventSubClass
    exec sp_trace_setevent @TraceID, 16, 25, @on --Attention, IntegerData
    exec sp_trace_setevent @TraceID, 16, 31, @on --Attention, Error
    exec sp_trace_setevent @TraceID, 25, 1, @on --Lock:Deadlock, TextData
    exec sp_trace_setevent @TraceID, 25, 2, @on --Lock:Deadlock, BinaryData
    exec sp_trace_setevent @TraceID, 25, 3, @on --Lock:Deadlock, DatabaseID
    exec sp_trace_setevent @TraceID, 25, 4, @on --Lock:Deadlock
                                        --, TransactionID
    exec sp_trace_setevent @TraceID, 25, 12, @on --Lock:Deadlock, SPID
    exec sp_trace_setevent @TraceID, 25, 13, @on --Lock:Deadlock, Duration
    exec sp_trace_setevent @TraceID, 25, 14, @on --Lock:Deadlock, StartTime
    exec sp_trace_setevent @TraceID, 25, 15, @on --Lock:Deadlock, EndTime
    exec sp_trace_setevent @TraceID, 25, 16, @on --Lock:Deadlock, Reads
    exec sp_trace_setevent @TraceID, 25, 17, @on --Lock:Deadlock, Writes
    exec sp_trace_setevent @TraceID, 25, 18, @on --Lock:Deadlock, CPU
    exec sp_trace_setevent @TraceID, 25, 21, @on --Lock:Deadlock
                                        --, EventSubClass
    exec sp_trace_setevent @TraceID, 25, 25, @on --Lock:Deadlock
                                        --, IntegerData
    exec sp_trace_setevent @TraceID, 25, 31, @on --Lock:Deadlock, Error
    exec sp_trace_setevent @TraceID, 27, 1, @on --Lock:Timeout, TextData
    exec sp_trace_setevent @TraceID, 27, 2, @on --Lock:Timeout, BinaryData
    exec sp_trace_setevent @TraceID, 27, 3, @on --Lock:Timeout, DatabaseID
    exec sp_trace_setevent @TraceID, 27, 4, @on --Lock:Timeout
                                        --, TransactionID
    exec sp_trace_setevent @TraceID, 27, 12, @on --Lock:Timeout, SPID
    exec sp_trace_setevent @TraceID, 27, 13, @on --Lock:Timeout, Duration
    exec sp_trace_setevent @TraceID, 27, 14, @on --Lock:Timeout, StartTime
```

```
exec sp_trace_setevent @TraceID, 27, 15, @on --Lock:Timeout, EndTime
exec sp_trace_setevent @TraceID, 27, 16, @on --Lock:Timeout, Reads
exec sp_trace_setevent @TraceID, 27, 17, @on --Lock:Timeout, Writes
exec sp_trace_setevent @TraceID, 27, 18, @on --Lock:Timeout, CPU
exec sp_trace_setevent @TraceID, 27, 21, @on --Lock:Timeout
                                        --, EventSubClass
exec sp_trace_setevent @TraceID, 27, 25, @on --Lock:Timeout, IntegerData
exec sp_trace_setevent @TraceID, 27, 31, @on --Lock:Timeout, Error
exec sp_trace_setevent @TraceID, 33, 1, @on --Exception, TextData
exec sp_trace_setevent @TraceID, 33, 2, @on --Exception, BinaryData
exec sp_trace_setevent @TraceID, 33, 3, @on --Exception, DatabaseID
exec sp_trace_setevent @TraceID, 33, 4, @on --Exception, TransactionID
exec sp_trace_setevent @TraceID, 33, 12, @on --Exception, SPID
exec sp_trace_setevent @TraceID, 33, 13, @on --Exception, Duration
exec sp_trace_setevent @TraceID, 33, 14, @on --Exception, StartTime
exec sp_trace_setevent @TraceID, 33, 15, @on --Exception, EndTime
exec sp_trace_setevent @TraceID, 33, 16, @on --Exception, Reads
exec sp_trace_setevent @TraceID, 33, 17, @on --Exception, Writes
exec sp_trace_setevent @TraceID, 33, 18, @on --Exception, CPU
exec sp_trace_setevent @TraceID, 33, 21, @on --Exception, EventSubClass
exec sp_trace_setevent @TraceID, 33, 25, @on --Exception, IntegerData
exec sp_trace_setevent @TraceID, 33, 31, @on --Exception, Error
exec sp_trace_setevent @TraceID, 37, 1, @on --SP:Recompile, TextData
exec sp_trace_setevent @TraceID, 37, 2, @on --SP:Recompile, BinaryData
exec sp_trace_setevent @TraceID, 37, 3, @on --SP:Recompile, DatabaseID
exec sp_trace_setevent @TraceID, 37, 4, @on --SP:Recompile
                                        --, TransactionID
exec sp_trace_setevent @TraceID, 37, 12, @on --SP:Recompile, SPID
exec sp_trace_setevent @TraceID, 37, 13, @on --SP:Recompile, Duration
exec sp_trace_setevent @TraceID, 37, 14, @on --SP:Recompile, StartTime
exec sp_trace_setevent @TraceID, 37, 15, @on --SP:Recompile, EndTime
exec sp_trace_setevent @TraceID, 37, 16, @on --SP:Recompile, Reads
exec sp_trace_setevent @TraceID, 37, 17, @on --SP:Recompile, Writes
exec sp_trace_setevent @TraceID, 37, 18, @on --SP:Recompile, CPU
exec sp_trace_setevent @TraceID, 37, 21, @on --SP:Recompile
                                        --, EventSubClass
exec sp_trace_setevent @TraceID, 37, 25, @on --SP:Recompile, IntegerData
exec sp_trace_setevent @TraceID, 37, 31, @on --SP:Recompile, Error
exec sp_trace_setevent @TraceID, 41, 1, @on --SQL:StmtCompleted
                                        --, TextData
exec sp_trace_setevent @TraceID, 41, 2, @on --SQL:StmtCompleted
                                        --, BinaryData
exec sp_trace_setevent @TraceID, 41, 3, @on --SQL:StmtCompleted
                                        --, DatabaseID
exec sp_trace_setevent @TraceID, 41, 4, @on --SQL:StmtCompleted
                                        --, TransactionID
exec sp_trace_setevent @TraceID, 41, 12, @on --SQL:StmtCompleted, SPID
```

```
        exec sp_trace_setevent @TraceID, 41, 13, @on --SQL:StmtCompleted
                                            --, Duration
        exec sp_trace_setevent @TraceID, 41, 14, @on --SQL:StmtCompleted
                                            --, StartTime
        exec sp_trace_setevent @TraceID, 41, 15, @on --SQL:StmtCompleted
                                            --, EndTime
        exec sp_trace_setevent @TraceID, 41, 16, @on --SQL:StmtCompleted, Reads
        exec sp_trace_setevent @TraceID, 41, 17, @on --SQL:StmtCompleted, Writes
        exec sp_trace_setevent @TraceID, 41, 18, @on --SQL:StmtCompleted, CPU
        exec sp_trace_setevent @TraceID, 41, 21, @on --SQL:StmtCompleted
                                            --, EventSubClass
        exec sp_trace_setevent @TraceID, 41, 25, @on --SQL:StmtCompleted
                                            --, IntegerData
        exec sp_trace_setevent @TraceID, 41, 31, @on --SQL:StmtCompleted, Error
        exec sp_trace_setevent @TraceID, 43, 1, @on --SP:Completed, TextData
        exec sp_trace_setevent @TraceID, 43, 2, @on --SP:Completed, BinaryData
        exec sp_trace_setevent @TraceID, 43, 3, @on --SP:Completed, DatabaseID
        exec sp_trace_setevent @TraceID, 43, 4, @on --SP:Completed
                                            --, TransactionID
        exec sp_trace_setevent @TraceID, 43, 12, @on --SP:Completed, SPID
        exec sp_trace_setevent @TraceID, 43, 13, @on --SP:Completed, Duration
        exec sp_trace_setevent @TraceID, 43, 14, @on --SP:Completed, StartTime
        exec sp_trace_setevent @TraceID, 43, 15, @on --SP:Completed, EndTime
        exec sp_trace_setevent @TraceID, 43, 16, @on --SP:Completed, Reads
        exec sp_trace_setevent @TraceID, 43, 17, @on --SP:Completed, Writes
        exec sp_trace_setevent @TraceID, 43, 18, @on --SP:Completed, CPU
        exec sp_trace_setevent @TraceID, 43, 21, @on --SP:Completed
                                            --, EventSubClass
        exec sp_trace_setevent @TraceID, 43, 25, @on --SP:Completed, IntegerData
        exec sp_trace_setevent @TraceID, 43, 31, @on --SP:Completed, Error
        exec sp_trace_setevent @TraceID, 45, 1, @on --SP:StmtCompleted, TextData
        exec sp_trace_setevent @TraceID, 45, 2, @on --SP:StmtCompleted
                                            --, BinaryData
        exec sp_trace_setevent @TraceID, 45, 3, @on --SP:StmtCompleted
                                            --, DatabaseID
        exec sp_trace_setevent @TraceID, 45, 4, @on --SP:StmtCompleted
                                            --, TransactionID
        exec sp_trace_setevent @TraceID, 45, 12, @on --SP:StmtCompleted, SPID
        exec sp_trace_setevent @TraceID, 45, 13, @on --SP:StmtCompleted
                                            --, Duration
        exec sp_trace_setevent @TraceID, 45, 14, @on --SP:StmtCompleted
                                            --, StartTime
        exec sp_trace_setevent @TraceID, 45, 15, @on --SP:StmtCompleted, EndTime
        exec sp_trace_setevent @TraceID, 45, 16, @on --SP:StmtCompleted, Reads
        exec sp_trace_setevent @TraceID, 45, 17, @on --SP:StmtCompleted, Writes
        exec sp_trace_setevent @TraceID, 45, 18, @on --SP:StmtCompleted, CPU
        exec sp_trace_setevent @TraceID, 45, 21, @on --SP:StmtCompleted
```

```
                                           --, EventSubClass
exec sp_trace_setevent @TraceID, 45, 25, @on --SP:StmtCompleted
                                           --, IntegerData
exec sp_trace_setevent @TraceID, 45, 31, @on --SP:StmtCompleted, Error
exec sp_trace_setevent @TraceID, 50, 1, @on --SQL Transaction, TextData
exec sp_trace_setevent @TraceID, 50, 2, @on --SQL Transaction
                                           --, BinaryData
exec sp_trace_setevent @TraceID, 50, 3, @on --SQL Transaction
                                           --, DatabaseID
exec sp_trace_setevent @TraceID, 50, 4, @on --SQL Transaction
                                           --, TransactionID
exec sp_trace_setevent @TraceID, 50, 12, @on --SQL Transaction, SPID
exec sp_trace_setevent @TraceID, 50, 13, @on --SQL Transaction, Duration
exec sp_trace_setevent @TraceID, 50, 14, @on --SQL Transaction
                                           --, StartTime
exec sp_trace_setevent @TraceID, 50, 15, @on --SQL Transaction, EndTime
exec sp_trace_setevent @TraceID, 50, 16, @on --SQL Transaction, Reads
exec sp_trace_setevent @TraceID, 50, 17, @on --SQL Transaction, Writes
exec sp_trace_setevent @TraceID, 50, 18, @on --SQL Transaction, CPU
exec sp_trace_setevent @TraceID, 50, 21, @on --SQL Transaction
                                           --, EventSubClass
exec sp_trace_setevent @TraceID, 50, 25, @on --SQL Transaction
                                           --, IntegerData
exec sp_trace_setevent @TraceID, 50, 31, @on --SQL Transaction, Error
exec sp_trace_setevent @TraceID, 55, 1, @on --Hash Warning, TextData
exec sp_trace_setevent @TraceID, 55, 2, @on --Hash Warning, BinaryData
exec sp_trace_setevent @TraceID, 55, 3, @on --Hash Warning, DatabaseID
exec sp_trace_setevent @TraceID, 55, 4, @on --Hash Warning
                                           --, TransactionID
exec sp_trace_setevent @TraceID, 55, 12, @on --Hash Warning, SPID
exec sp_trace_setevent @TraceID, 55, 13, @on --Hash Warning, Duration
exec sp_trace_setevent @TraceID, 55, 14, @on --Hash Warning, StartTime
exec sp_trace_setevent @TraceID, 55, 15, @on --Hash Warning, EndTime
exec sp_trace_setevent @TraceID, 55, 16, @on --Hash Warning, Reads
exec sp_trace_setevent @TraceID, 55, 17, @on --Hash Warning, Writes
exec sp_trace_setevent @TraceID, 55, 18, @on --Hash Warning, CPU
exec sp_trace_setevent @TraceID, 55, 21, @on --Hash Warning
                                           --, EventSubClass
exec sp_trace_setevent @TraceID, 55, 25, @on --Hash Warning, IntegerData
exec sp_trace_setevent @TraceID, 55, 31, @on --Hash Warning, Error
exec sp_trace_setevent @TraceID, 59, 1, @on --Lock:Deadlock Chain
                                           --, TextData
exec sp_trace_setevent @TraceID, 59, 2, @on --Lock:Deadlock Chain
                                           --, BinaryData
exec sp_trace_setevent @TraceID, 59, 3, @on --Lock:Deadlock Chain
                                           --, DatabaseID
```

```
exec sp_trace_setevent @TraceID, 59, 4, @on --Lock:Deadlock Chain
                                       --, TransactionID
exec sp_trace_setevent @TraceID, 59, 12, @on --Lock:Deadlock Chain, SPID
exec sp_trace_setevent @TraceID, 59, 13, @on --Lock:Deadlock Chain
                                        --, Duration
exec sp_trace_setevent @TraceID, 59, 14, @on --Lock:Deadlock Chain
                                        --, StartTime
exec sp_trace_setevent @TraceID, 59, 15, @on --Lock:Deadlock Chain
                                        --, EndTime
exec sp_trace_setevent @TraceID, 59, 16, @on --Lock:Deadlock Chain
                                        --, Reads
exec sp_trace_setevent @TraceID, 59, 17, @on --Lock:Deadlock Chain
                                        --, Writes
exec sp_trace_setevent @TraceID, 59, 18, @on --Lock:Deadlock Chain, CPU
exec sp_trace_setevent @TraceID, 59, 21, @on --Lock:Deadlock Chain
                                        --, EventSubClass
exec sp_trace_setevent @TraceID, 59, 25, @on --Lock:Deadlock Chain
                                        --, IntegerData
exec sp_trace_setevent @TraceID, 59, 31, @on --Lock:Deadlock Chain
                                        --, Error
exec sp_trace_setevent @TraceID, 67, 1, @on --Execution Warnings
                                       --, TextData
exec sp_trace_setevent @TraceID, 67, 2, @on --Execution Warnings
                                       --, BinaryData
exec sp_trace_setevent @TraceID, 67, 3, @on --Execution Warnings
                                       --, DatabaseID
exec sp_trace_setevent @TraceID, 67, 4, @on --Execution Warnings
                                       --, TransactionID
exec sp_trace_setevent @TraceID, 67, 12, @on --Execution Warnings, SPID
exec sp_trace_setevent @TraceID, 67, 13, @on --Execution Warnings
                                        --, Duration
exec sp_trace_setevent @TraceID, 67, 14, @on --Execution Warnings
                                        --, StartTime
exec sp_trace_setevent @TraceID, 67, 15, @on --Execution Warnings
                                        --, EndTime
exec sp_trace_setevent @TraceID, 67, 16, @on --Execution Warnings, Reads
exec sp_trace_setevent @TraceID, 67, 17, @on --Execution Warnings
                                        --, Writes
exec sp_trace_setevent @TraceID, 67, 18, @on --Execution Warnings, CPU
exec sp_trace_setevent @TraceID, 67, 21, @on --Execution Warnings
                                        --, EventSubClass
exec sp_trace_setevent @TraceID, 67, 25, @on --Execution Warnings
                                        --, IntegerData
exec sp_trace_setevent @TraceID, 67, 31, @on --Execution Warnings, Error
exec sp_trace_setevent @TraceID, 69, 1, @on --Sort Warnings, TextData
exec sp_trace_setevent @TraceID, 69, 2, @on --Sort Warnings, BinaryData
exec sp_trace_setevent @TraceID, 69, 3, @on --Sort Warnings, DatabaseID
```

```
exec sp_trace_setevent @TraceID, 69, 4, @on --Sort Warnings
                                    --, TransactionID
exec sp_trace_setevent @TraceID, 69, 12, @on --Sort Warnings, SPID
exec sp_trace_setevent @TraceID, 69, 13, @on --Sort Warnings, Duration
exec sp_trace_setevent @TraceID, 69, 14, @on --Sort Warnings, StartTime
exec sp_trace_setevent @TraceID, 69, 15, @on --Sort Warnings, EndTime
exec sp_trace_setevent @TraceID, 69, 16, @on --Sort Warnings, Reads
exec sp_trace_setevent @TraceID, 69, 17, @on --Sort Warnings, Writes
exec sp_trace_setevent @TraceID, 69, 18, @on --Sort Warnings, CPU
exec sp_trace_setevent @TraceID, 69, 21, @on --Sort Warnings
                                    --, EventSubClass
exec sp_trace_setevent @TraceID, 69, 25, @on --Sort Warnings
                                    --, IntegerData
exec sp_trace_setevent @TraceID, 69, 31, @on --Sort Warnings, Error
exec sp_trace_setevent @TraceID, 76, 1, @on --CursorImplicitConversion
                                    --, TextData
exec sp_trace_setevent @TraceID, 76, 2, @on --CursorImplicitConversion
                                    --, BinaryData
exec sp_trace_setevent @TraceID, 76, 3, @on --CursorImplicitConversion
                                    --, DatabaseID
exec sp_trace_setevent @TraceID, 76, 4, @on --CursorImplicitConversion
                                    -- , TransactionID
exec sp_trace_setevent @TraceID, 76, 12, @on --CursorImplicitConversion
                                    --, SPID
exec sp_trace_setevent @TraceID, 76, 13, @on --CursorImplicitConversion
                                    --, Duration
exec sp_trace_setevent @TraceID, 76, 14, @on --CursorImplicitConversion
                                    --, StartTime
exec sp_trace_setevent @TraceID, 76, 15, @on --CursorImplicitConversion
                                    --, EndTime
exec sp_trace_setevent @TraceID, 76, 16, @on --CursorImplicitConversion
                                    --, Reads
exec sp_trace_setevent @TraceID, 76, 17, @on --CursorImplicitConversion
                                    --, Writes
exec sp_trace_setevent @TraceID, 76, 18, @on --CursorImplicitConversion
                                    --, CPU
exec sp_trace_setevent @TraceID, 76, 21, @on --CursorImplicitConversion
                                    --, EventSubClass
exec sp_trace_setevent @TraceID, 76, 25, @on --CursorImplicitConversion
                                    -- , IntegerData
exec sp_trace_setevent @TraceID, 76, 31, @on --CursorImplicitConversion
                                    --, Error
exec sp_trace_setevent @TraceID, 79, 1, @on --Missing Column Statistics
                                    --, TextData
exec sp_trace_setevent @TraceID, 79, 2, @on --Missing Column Statistics
                                    --, BinaryData
```

```
exec sp_trace_setevent @TraceID, 79, 3, @on --Missing Column Statistics
                                      --, DatabaseID
exec sp_trace_setevent @TraceID, 79, 4, @on --Missing Column Statistics
                                      --, TransactionID
exec sp_trace_setevent @TraceID, 79, 12, @on --Missing Column Statistics
                                      --, SPID
exec sp_trace_setevent @TraceID, 79, 13, @on --Missing Column Statistics
                                      --, Duration
exec sp_trace_setevent @TraceID, 79, 14, @on --Missing Column Statistics
                                      --, StartTime
exec sp_trace_setevent @TraceID, 79, 15, @on --Missing Column Statistics
                                      --, EndTime
exec sp_trace_setevent @TraceID, 79, 16, @on --Missing Column Statistics
                                      --, Reads
exec sp_trace_setevent @TraceID, 79, 17, @on --Missing Column Statistics
                                      --, Writes
exec sp_trace_setevent @TraceID, 79, 18, @on --Missing Column Statistics
                                      --, CPU
exec sp_trace_setevent @TraceID, 79, 21, @on --Missing Column Statistics
                                      --, EventSubClass
exec sp_trace_setevent @TraceID, 79, 25, @on --Missing Column Statistics
                                      --, IntegerData
exec sp_trace_setevent @TraceID, 79, 31, @on --Missing Column Statistics
                                      --, Error
exec sp_trace_setevent @TraceID, 80, 1, @on --Missing Join Predicate
                                      --, TextData
exec sp_trace_setevent @TraceID, 80, 2, @on --Missing Join Predicate
                                      --, BinaryData
exec sp_trace_setevent @TraceID, 80, 3, @on --Missing Join Predicate
                                      --, DatabaseID
exec sp_trace_setevent @TraceID, 80, 4, @on --Missing Join Predicate
                                      --, TransactionID
exec sp_trace_setevent @TraceID, 80, 12, @on --Missing Join Predicate
                                      --, SPID
exec sp_trace_setevent @TraceID, 80, 13, @on --Missing Join Predicate
                                      --, Duration
exec sp_trace_setevent @TraceID, 80, 14, @on --Missing Join Predicate
                                      --, StartTime
exec sp_trace_setevent @TraceID, 80, 15, @on --Missing Join Predicate
                                      --, EndTime
exec sp_trace_setevent @TraceID, 80, 16, @on --Missing Join Predicate
                                      --, Reads
exec sp_trace_setevent @TraceID, 80, 17, @on --Missing Join Predicate
                                      --, Writes
exec sp_trace_setevent @TraceID, 80, 18, @on --Missing Join Predicate
                                      --, CPU
exec sp_trace_setevent @TraceID, 80, 21, @on --Missing Join Predicate
                                      --, EventSubClass
```

```
exec sp_trace_setevent @TraceID, 80, 25, @on --Missing Join Predicate
                                       --, IntegerData
exec sp_trace_setevent @TraceID, 80, 31, @on --Missing Join Predicate
                                       --, Error


-- Set the Filters
declare @intfilter int
declare @bigintfilter bigint

exec sp_trace_setfilter @TraceID, 10, 0, 7, N'SQL Profiler'
set @intfilter = @@SPID --Exclude its own SPID
exec sp_trace_setfilter @TraceID, 12, 0, 1, @intfilter

-- Set the trace status to start
exec sp_trace_setstatus @TraceID, 1

-- display name of the trace file and trace id for future references
Print 'Trace file = ''' + @BlockingTrace + '.trc'''
Print 'TraceID = ' + CAST(@TraceID AS VARCHAR(3)) + CHAR(10)
goto finish

error:
select ErrorCode=@rc

finish:

/*************************/
/* Start blocker script   */
/*************************/
DECLARE @StartTime DATETIME
SET @StartTime = GETDATE()
WHILE DATEDIFF(mi, @StartTime, GETDATE()) <= @MonitoringPeriod
BEGIN
   EXEC master.dbo.sp_blocker_pss80 @fast=1
   WAITFOR DELAY '00:00:15'
END

/************************/
/* Stop SQL tracing       */
/************************/
EXEC sp_trace_setstatus @TraceID, 0
EXEC sp_trace_setstatus @TraceID, 2

SET XACT_ABORT OFF
GO
```

2. Select *<ServerName>* ➤ Management ➤ SQL Server Agent ➤ Jobs ➤ New Job.

3. On the General tab of the New Job Properties dialog box, enter the job name and other details, as shown in Figure 12-19.

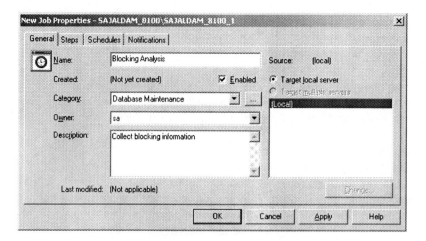

Figure 12-19. *Entering the job name and other details*

4. On the Steps tab, click New and enter the command to run the blocker script from a Windows command prompt, as shown in Figure 12-20.

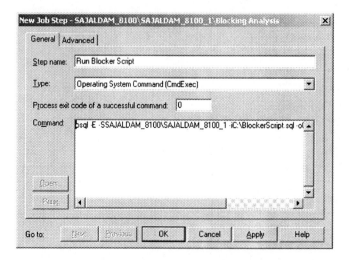

Figure 12-20. *Entering the command to run the blocker script*

You can use the command

```
osql -E -S<ServerName> -iC:\BlockerScript.sql -oC:\BlockerScript.out ↵
 -w2000 -n
```

The output of the blocker script is saved in the file C:\BlockerScript.out.

5. Return to the New Job Properties dialog box by clicking OK.

6. Click OK to create the SQL Server job. The SQL Server job will be created with an enabled and runnable state to collect blocking information for 10 minutes using the blocker script.

You can create a SQL Server alert to automate the following tasks:

• Monitor the `Average Wait Time (ms)` counter value.

• Inform the DBA whenever the counter value exceeds 15 seconds.

• Execute the Blocking Analysis job to collect blocking information for 10 minutes.

You can create the SQL Server alert from SQL Server Enterprise Manager by following these steps:

1. In Enterprise Manager, select <*ServerName*> ➤ Management ➤ SQL Server Agent ➤ Alerts ➤ New Alert.

2. On the General tab of the New Alert Properties dialog box, enter the alert name and other details as shown in Figure 12-21.

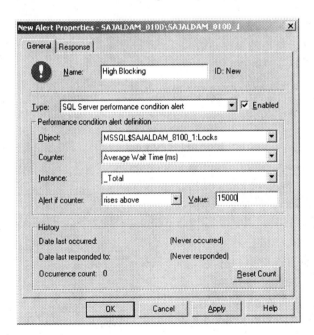

Figure 12-21. *Entering the alert name and other details*

3. On the Response tab, click New Operator and enter the operator details as shown in Figure 12-22.

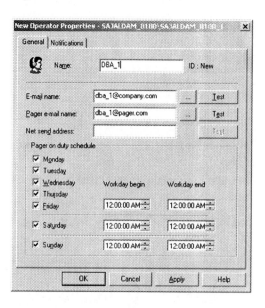

Figure 12-22. *Entering the operator details*

4. Return to the New Alert Properties dialog box by clicking OK.

5. On the Response tab, enter the remaining information shown in Figure 12-23.

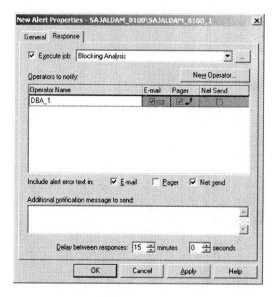

Figure 12-23. *Entering the actions to be performed when the alert is triggered*

The Blocking Analysis job is selected to automatically collect the blocking information.

6. Once you've finished entering all the information, click OK to create the SQL Server alert. The SQL Server alert will be created in the enabled state to perform the intended tasks.

7. Ensure that the SQL Server Agent is running.

The SQL Server alert and the job together will automate the blocking detection and the information collection process. This automatic collection of the blocking information will ensure that a good amount of the blocking information will be available whenever the system gets into a massive blocking state.

Summary

Even though blocking is inevitable, and is in fact essential to maintain isolation among transactions, it can sometimes adversely affect database concurrency. In a multiuser database application, you must minimize blocking among concurrent transactions.

SQL Server provides different techniques to avoid/reduce blocking, and a database application should take advantage of these techniques to scale linearly as the number of database users increases. When an application faces a high degree of blocking, you can collect the relevant blocking information using a blocker script to understand the root cause of the blocking, and accordingly use an appropriate technique to either avoid or reduce blocking.

Blocking can not only hurt concurrency, but also cause an abrupt termination of a database request in the case of circular blocking. I will cover circular blocking, or deadlocks, in the next chapter.

Deadlock Analysis

When a deadlock occurs between two or more transactions, SQL Server terminates one of the transactions and returns an error to the corresponding application. This leaves the application with only one option: resubmit the transaction (or maybe say a big sorry to the end user). To successfully complete a transaction and avoid the sorry part, it is important to understand the cause of a deadlock and the ways to handle a deadlock.

In this chapter, I cover the following topics:

- Deadlock fundamentals

- How to handle a deadlock condition

- Ways to analyze the cause of a deadlock

- Techniques to resolve a deadlock

Deadlock Fundamentals

A *deadlock* is a special blocking scenario, in which two SPIDs get blocked by each other. Each SPID, while holding its own resources, attempts to access a resource that is locked by the other SPID. This will lead to a circular blocking scenario, as illustrated in Figure 13-1.

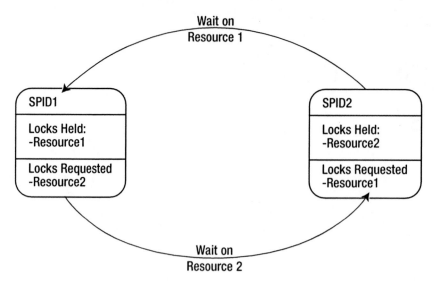

Figure 13-1. *Circular blocking scenario*

This is an especially nasty type of blocking, because a deadlock cannot resolve on its own, even if given an unlimited period of time. A deadlock requires an external input to break the circular blocking.

SQL Server has a deadlock detection routine, called *lock monitor*, that regularly checks for the presence of deadlocks in SQL Server. Once a deadlock condition is detected, SQL Server victimizes one of the SPIDs participating in the deadlock to break the circular blocking. This process involves withdrawing all the resources held by the SPID. SQL Server does so by rolling back the uncommitted transaction of the victimized SPID.

Choosing the Deadlock Victim

SQL Server determines the SPID to be victimized by evaluating the cost of undoing the transaction of the participating SPIDs, and it selects the one with the least cost. You can control the SPID to be victimized by setting the deadlock priority of its connection to LOW:

```
SET DEADLOCK_PRIORITY LOW
```

This steers SQL Server toward victimizing this particular SPID in the event of a deadlock. The deadlock priority of the connection can be reset to its normal value by executing the following SET statement:

```
SET DEADLOCK_PRIORITY NORMAL
```

The SET statement only allows you to mark a SPID as a preferred deadlock victim or set the SPID's deadlock priority back to NORMAL. It doesn't allow you to mark the SPID as not to be victimized or HIGH deadlock priority.

Handling Deadlocks

When SQL Server victimizes a SPID, it returns the error number 1205 to the application owning the SPID. Since SQL Server ensures the consistency of the database by automatically rolling back the transaction of the victimized SPID, the SPID is assured that it is back to the same state it was in before the start of its transaction. Typically, if an error occurs, an application should check the error number (@@ERROR) to determine whether or not it is victimized due to a deadlock. On determining a deadlock situation, the application may try to re-execute its transaction automatically a limited number of times, before passing the error message to the end user.

Determining the error number as 1205 and automatically re-executing the failed transaction improves the user's experience with the application. Additionally, it is preferable to analyze the cause of the deadlock and resolve it, if possible.

Deadlock Analysis

You can sometimes prevent a deadlock from happening by analyzing the causes. You need the following information to do this:

- The SPIDs participating in the deadlock

- The resources involved in the deadlock

- The queries executed by the SPIDs

Collecting Deadlock Information

You can collect the deadlock information using the Profiler tool or the DBCC trace flag 1204. DBCC trace flags are used to customize certain SQL Server behavior such as, in this case, generating the deadlock information. Profiler provides information on basic deadlock detection. It has the following two events to provide the deadlock information:

- Locks\Lock:Deadlock

- Locks\Lock:Deadlock Chain

The DBCC trace flag 1204 provides detailed deadlock information that helps you analyze the cause of a deadlock. It can be used along with the DBCC trace flag 3605 to collect the deadlock information in the SQL Server error log file, as follows (dbcc_deadlocktrace.sql in the download):

```
DBCC TRACEON(-1, 1204) --Deadlock information
DBCC TRACEON(-1, 3605) --Redirect DBCC output to error log
```

▒**NOTE** The -1 parameter sets the trace flag at the serverwide level.

The DBCC TRACEON statement is used to turn on (or enable) DBCC trace flags. A trace flag remains enabled until it is disabled using the DBCC TRACEOFF statement. The status of a trace flag can be determined using the DBCC TRACESTATUS statement. The DBCC trace flags can also be turned on as startup parameters from SQL Server Enterprise Manager by following these steps:

1. Open the Properties dialog box of the SQL Server.

2. On the General tab of the Properties dialog box, click Startup Parameters, as shown in Figure 13-2.

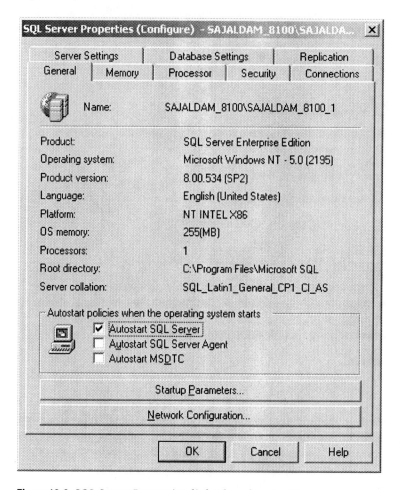

Figure 13-2. *SQL Server Properties dialog box showing the server's generic properties*

3. Type **/T1204** in the Parameter text box and click Add to add trace flag 1204, as shown in Figure 13-3.

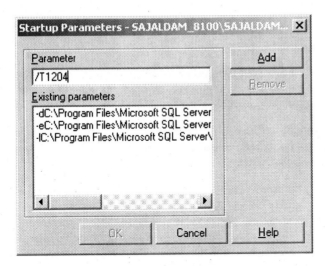

Figure 13-3. *SQL Server Startup Parameters settings*

4. Add trace flag 3605 using the parameter **/T3605**.

5. Click the OK button to close all the dialog boxes.

These trace flag settings will be in effect after you restart SQL Server.

Analyzing the Deadlock

To analyze the cause of a deadlock, let's consider an interesting little example (create_trig.sql in the download). This example shows not only how to analyze a deadlock scenario, but also the role of indexes in causing a deadlock.

```
--Create a test table
IF(SELECT OBJECT_ID('t1')) IS NOT NULL
  DROP TABLE t1
GO
CREATE TABLE t1(c1 INT, c2 INT, Data CHAR(1), Modifier CHAR(10))
CREATE INDEX i_c1 ON t1(c1)
INSERT INTO t1 VALUES(11, 12, '', '')
GO
--Create an update trigger to update the row again with user_name
CREATE TRIGGER trig1 ON t1
FOR UPDATE
AS
BEGIN
  /*Allow another UPDATE concurrently*/ WAITFOR DELAY '00:00:10'
  UPDATE t1
```

```
      SET t1.Modifier = USER_NAME()
      FROM t1, inserted
      WHERE t1.c1 = inserted.c1
END
```

There are a few things about this script to note:

- The UPDATE trigger trig1 is a postexecution trigger that will be executed automatically when an UPDATE statement is executed on the table. The execution of the trigger will follow the action of the UPDATE statement.

- The SQL statements executed within the trigger become part of the ongoing transaction. Therefore, if a ROLLBACK statement is executed within the trigger, the action of the UPDATE statement that initiated the trigger will also be undone.

- The table named inserted referred to in the UPDATE trigger is a system table that is available within the scope of INSERT and UPDATE triggers. SQL Server creates this system table dynamically based on the structure of the table on which the trigger is created to track data modifications. For an INSERT statement, the inserted table contains the new rows added to the table. For an UPDATE statement, the rows of the inserted table contain the new data values set by the UPDATE statement. This system table is local within the scope of the trigger. Therefore, two UPDATE statements executed concurrently will have their own inserted table. SQL Server similarly provides a deleted system table to track the deleted data within DELETE and UPDATE triggers.

Run create_trig1.sql. Now, execute the following UPDATE statement (deadupdate.sql) from two connections simultaneously:

```
UPDATE t1
SET t1.Data = 'a'
WHERE t1.c1 = 11
```

Ideally, you expect the first connection to enter the UPDATE trigger and sleep for 10 seconds. Meanwhile, the second connection trying to execute the UPDATE statement should wait for the first connection to finish, and then proceed with its own work.

But, unfortunately, the second connection faces a deadlock:

```
Server: Msg 1205, Level 13, State 3, Line 1
Transaction (Process ID 53) was deadlocked on lock resources with another process
 and has been chosen as the deadlock victim. Rerun the transaction.
```

Any idea what's wrong here?

Let's analyze the deadlock by collecting the deadlock information using the DBCC trace flag 1204. If you followed the steps in the "Collecting Deadlock Information" section, you can rerun deadupdate.sql to get the following error log file output:

```
2002-09-28 21:06:21.58 spid4
Deadlock encountered .... Printing deadlock information
2002-09-28 21:06:21.59 spid4
2002-09-28 21:06:21.59 spid4     Wait-for graph
2002-09-28 21:06:21.59 spid4
```

```
2002-09-28 21:06:21.59 spid4        Node:1
2002-09-28 21:06:21.59 spid4        KEY: 6:878626173:2 (89000e7526dc) CleanCnt:1
 Mode: U Flags: 0x0
2002-09-28 21:06:21.59 spid4        Grant List::
2002-09-28 21:06:21.59 spid4          Owner:0x193e1400 Mode: U        Flg:0x0 Ref:1
 Life:00000000 SPID:53 ECID:0
2002-09-28 21:06:21.59 spid4        SPID: 53 ECID: 0 Statement Type:
 UPDATE Line #: 1
2002-09-28 21:06:21.65 spid4        Input Buf: Language Event: UPDATE t1
SET t1.Data = 'a'
WHERE t1.c1 = 11


2002-09-28 21:06:21.68 spid4        Requested By:
2002-09-28 21:06:21.68 spid4          ResType:LockOwner Stype:'OR' Mode: U SPID:52
 ECID:0 Ec:(0x19901528) Value:0x193dd400 Cost:(0/E4)
2002-09-28 21:06:21.68 spid4
2002-09-28 21:06:21.68 spid4        Node:2
2002-09-28 21:06:21.68 spid4        RID: 6:1:381:0              CleanCnt:1 Mode:
 X Flags: 0x2
2002-09-28 21:06:21.68 spid4        Grant List::
2002-09-28 21:06:21.68 spid4          Owner:0x193e1340 Mode: X        Flg:0x0 Ref:0
 Life:02000000 SPID:52 ECID:0
2002-09-28 21:06:21.68 spid4        SPID: 52 ECID: 0 Statement Type:
 UPDATE Line #: 7
2002-09-28 21:06:21.68 spid4        Input Buf: Language Event: UPDATE t1
SET t1.Data = 'a'
WHERE t1.c1 = 11


2002-09-28 21:06:21.68 spid4        Requested By:
2002-09-28 21:06:21.68 spid4          ResType:LockOwner Stype:'OR' Mode: U SPID:53
 ECID:0 Ec:(0x19cc7528) Value:0x193e13a0 Cost:(0/0)
2002-09-28 21:06:21.68 spid4        Victim Resource Owner:
2002-09-28 21:06:21.68 spid4          ResType:LockOwner Stype:'OR' Mode: U SPID:53
 ECID:0 Ec:(0x19cc7528) Value:0x193e13a0 Cost:(0/0)
```

Each node section in the deadlock information represents a resource involved in the deadlock, and it includes a list of SPIDs that have access to it and the SPIDs waiting for it. The last section on Victim Resource Owner indicates the victimized SPID. The deadlock information includes the following additional information:

- ECID: Represents the thread of a SPID in the case of parallel processes. ECID 0 represents the main thread.

- Input Buf: Provides all statements in the current batch executed by the SPID.

- Line #: Provides the SQL statement number in the current batch that was executed when the deadlock occurred.

From the Input Buf and Line # entries in the deadlock information, you can infer the following:

- SPID 53

  - SQL batch executed

    ```
    UPDATE t1
    SET t1.Data = 'a'
    WHERE t1.c1 = 11
    ```

  - SQL statement number within the batch: 1

- SPID 52

  - SQL batch executed

    ```
    UPDATE t1
    SET t1.Data = 'a'
    WHERE t1.c1 = 11
    ```

  - SQL statement number within the batch: 7. Since the current batch seems to have only one SQL statement, Line #: 7 indicates that a SQL statement within the associated UPDATE trigger was executed.

The preceding deadlock information can be represented in a graphical form, as shown in Figure 13-4.

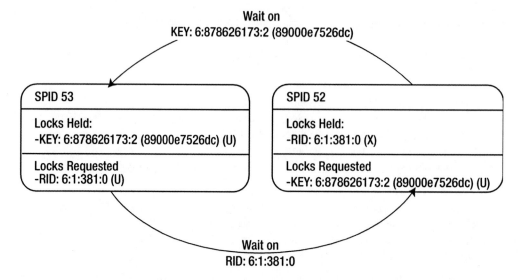

Figure 13-4. *Deadlock graph showing circular blocking between the participating SPIDs*

For ease of understanding, the representation of the circular blocking can be simplified as shown in Figure 13-5.

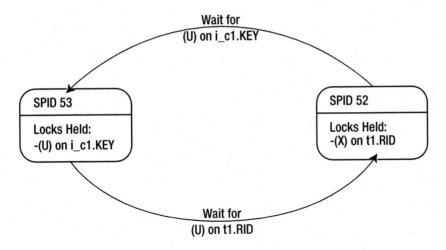

Figure 13-5. *A simplified representation of the deadlock graph*

From the preceding information, you can make following conclusions.

- SPID 52 executed the following UPDATE statement:

```
UPDATE t1
SET t1.Data = 'a'
WHERE t1.c1 = 11
```

It updated the row by acquiring an (X) lock on the corresponding RID.

- SPID 53 executed the following UPDATE statement:

```
UPDATE t1
SET t1.Data = 'a'
WHERE t1.c1 = 11
```

It acquired a (U) lock on an index row. As explained in the previous chapter, the IndId 2 in the resource format of the KEY (6:878626173:2) indicates that the index involved is a nonclustered index. Also, from the resource representation of the KEY (6:878626173:2 [89000e7526dc]), as shown previously, and the format of the KEY lock (DatabaseID:ObjectID:IndexID [hash value for index key]), as mentioned in the previous chapter, you can determine the name of the database, the table, and the index as follows:

```
SELECT DB_NAME(6) --Database name: northwind
SELECT OBJECT_NAME(878626173) --Table name: t1
SELECT name FROM sysindexes --Index name: i_c1
WHERE id = 878626173
  AND indid = 2
```

Note that the index i_c1 on the WHERE clause of column c1 caused SPID 53 to hit the index row first.

■**NOTE** SPID 52 also acquired a (U) lock on the index row while executing the UPDATE statement outside the trigger. However, this lock was released since SPID 52 made no modification to the indexed column.

- SPID 53 requested a (U) lock on the data row within table t1. Since this RID resource is held by SPID 52 in (X) mode, the (U) lock request by SPID 53 is blocked on this resource.

- Note that SPID 53 has not updated the row, as it has not received an (X) lock on the corresponding RID. It was in the process of navigating from the index row to the corresponding data row.

- SPID 52 executed the statement within the UPDATE trigger. While doing so, it requested a (U) lock on the index row within the i_c1 index. Since this KEY resource is held by SPID 53 in (U) mode, the (U) lock requested by SPID 52 is blocked on this resource.

- The circular blocking of SPIDs 52 and 53 on each other caused the deadlock.

- SQL Server victimized SPID 53 since it performed the least amount of transaction log activity compared to SPID 52. SPID 52 completed the data modifications for the main UPDATE statement.

The obvious question at this stage is, can you avoid this deadlock? If the answer is yes, then how?

Deadlock Resolutions

The resolutions applicable to a deadlock scenario depend upon the nature of the deadlock. The following list contains some of the techniques you may use to resolve a deadlock:

- Ensure that transactions always access resources in the same chronological order.

- Serialize access to resources.

- Decrease the number of resources accessed.

- Minimize lock contention.

Access Resources in the Same Chronological Order

One of the most commonly adopted techniques in resolving a deadlock is to ensure that every transaction accesses the resources in the same chronological order. For instance, suppose that two transactions need to access two resources. If each transaction accesses the resources in the same chronological order, then the first transaction will successfully acquire locks on the resources without being blocked by the second transaction. The second transaction will be blocked by the first while trying to acquire a lock on the first resource. This will cause a typical blocking scenario without leading to a circular blocking.

If the resources are not accessed in the same chronological order, as follows, this can cause a circular blocking between the two transactions:

- Transaction1:

  - Access Resource1

  - Access Resource2

- Transaction 2:

  - Access Resource2

  - Access Resource1

In the current deadlock scenario, the following resources are involved in the deadlock:

- Resource1: KEY: 6:878626173:2 (89000e7526dc): This is the index row within index i_c1 on table t1.

- Resource2: RID: 6:1:381:0: This is the data row within table t1.

Both SPIDs access the resources in the same chronological order: Resource1 (i.e., the nonclustered index key) first, Resource2 (i.e., the data row in the table) next, and then within the trigger once again, Resource 1 first and Resource 2 next.

This resolution technique is already in place in the current deadlock scenario. Unfortunately, you still got a deadlock since SPID 52 tried to access the KEY resource again within its transaction, without retaining the (U) lock initially acquired on the KEY (while navigating from the index row to the data row). Failing to hold the (U) lock on the KEY enabled SPID 53 to acquire a (U) lock on the KEY, which ultimately led to the circular blocking.

Serialize Access to Resources

Another technique for resolving deadlocks is to serialize access to the resources involved in the deadlock. Ensure that no two transactions can simultaneously acquire a lock on a resource involved in the deadlock. This will serialize the lock requests of the transaction executed later. Depending on the deadlock scenario, the access to the resources can be serialized in the following ways:

- Increase the isolation level.

- Use locking hints.

- Increase lock granularity.

Increase the Isolation Level

Depending on the deadlock scenario, the REPEATABLE READ or SERIALIZABLE isolation level can be used to resolve a deadlock. Both the REPEATABLE READ and SERIALIZABLE isolation levels allow a SPID to hold locks until the end of its transaction. The SERIALIZABLE isolation level provides additional protection against phantom reads, as explained in Chapter 12.

In the current deadlock scenario, the isolation level of the SPIDs can be increased to the SERIALIZABLE isolation level by executing the UPDATE query within SET statements:

```
SET TRANSACTION ISOLATION LEVEL SERIALIZABLE
GO
UPDATE t1
SET t1.Data = 'a'
WHERE t1.c1 = 11
GO
SET TRANSACTION ISOLATION LEVEL READ COMMITTED --Back to default
GO
```

Using the SERIALIZABLE isolation level allows SPID 52 to hold the (U) lock on the index row until the end of its transaction. SPID 52 acquired this lock while executing the UPDATE statement outside the UPDATE trigger. Consequently, SPID 53, while requesting a (U) lock on the index row, will be blocked by SPID 52, since two (U) locks are incompatible. SPID 52 will be able to acquire all the locks required to execute the UPDATE statement within the trigger. This will prevent circular blocking and thereby resolve the deadlock.

Be aware that increasing the isolation level to REPEATABLE READ or SERIALIZABLE doesn't always resolve a deadlock scenario. For example, consider the following transaction executed on the current test table (trans.sql in the download):

```
BEGIN TRAN IsolationIncreaseDoNotWork
  SELECT * FROM t1
    WHERE t1.c1 = 11
  /*Allow concurrent transactions*/ WAITFOR DELAY '00:00:10'
  UPDATE t1
    SET t1.Data = 'a'
    WHERE t1.c1 = 11
COMMIT
```

Executing this transaction concurrently by two SPIDs causes a deadlock similar to the current deadlock scenario. The isolation level of this transaction can be increased to SERIALIZABLE:

```
SET TRANSACTION ISOLATION LEVEL SERIALIZABLE
GO
BEGIN TRAN IsolationIncreaseDoNotWork
  SELECT * FROM t1
    WHERE t1.c1 = 11
  /*Allow concurrent transactions*/ WAITFOR DELAY '00:00:10'
  UPDATE t1
    SET t1.Data = 'a'
    WHERE t1.c1 = 11
COMMIT
GO
SET TRANSACTION ISOLATION LEVEL READ COMMITTED --Back to default
GO
```

Increasing the isolation level of this transaction to SERIALIZABLE (or REPEATABLE READ) will not resolve the deadlock:

- The increase of the isolation level will not prevent the second SPID from acquiring (and holding) an (S) lock on the index row and the data row.

- The (S) lock on the data row held by the second SPID will allow the first SPID to later acquire a (U) lock on the data row, but it will block the first SPID from converting the (U) lock to an (X) lock as required by the UPDATE statement.

- Later, when the second SPID will execute its UPDATE statement, it will be blocked by the (U) lock held by the first SPID on the data row.

- The resultant circular blocking will cause a deadlock.

This deadlock can be resolved using the UPDLOCK locking hint, as explained in the following resolution technique.

Therefore, be careful if you're trying to resolve a deadlock by using higher isolation levels. Although it may work in many cases, sometimes it doesn't, as demonstrated in the previous named transaction (IsolationIncreaseDoNotWork) example, because holding an (S) lock by one transaction doesn't serialize the (S) lock request by another transaction. Although allowing read access to two transactions simultaneously is good for concurrency, it may lead to the typical deadlock avoided by the internal implementation of the UPDATE statement, as explained in Chapter 12.

There is another major concern with increasing the isolation level: allowing a transaction to hold every lock until the end of the transaction can increase blocking. Further, the SERIAL-IZABLE isolation level causes more bottlenecks than the REPEATABLE READ isolation level, as explained in the previous chapter. Therefore, please be careful when using the higher isolation levels. Instead of increasing the isolation level of the complete transaction, increase the isolation level of only the resources participating in the deadlock using locking hints, as explained in the following section.

Use Locking Hints

The current deadlock caused by the concurrent execution of the UPDATE statement by SPIDs 52 and 53 can also be resolved using the following locking hints:

- REPEATABLEREAD

- HOLDLOCK

- UPDLOCK

A locking hint can be applied on an individual table referred to in a query.

The REPEATABLEREAD locking hint simulates the REPEATABLE READ isolation level. Similarly, the HOLDLOCK locking hint simulates the SERIALIZABLE isolation level. They can be applied on the table t1 referred to in the UPDATE statement as follows:

```
UPDATE t1 WITH(REPEATABLEREAD) --or WITH(HOLDLOCK)
SET t1.Data = 'a'
WHERE t1.c1 = 11
```

Both the REPEATABLEREAD and the HOLDLOCK locking hints will allow SPID 52 to retain the (U) lock on the index row initially acquired by it outside the trigger. This will block the (U) lock request by SPID 53 on the index row, preventing the circular blocking.

As mentioned earlier, the current deadlock can also be resolved using the UPDLOCK locking hint:

```
UPDATE t1 WITH(UPDLOCK)
SET t1.Data = 'a'
WHERE t1.c1 = 11
```

In the case of an UPDATE statement, the UPDLOCK locking hint works exactly the same as the REPEATABLEREAD locking hint. However, in the case of a SELECT statement, the UPDLOCK locking hint allows the SELECT statement to hold a (U) lock, unlike the REPEATABLEREAD locking hint, which holds an (S) lock. Holding a (U) lock allows the UPDLOCK locking hint to resolve the deadlock caused by the concurrent execution of the IsolationIncreaseDoNotWork transaction as well, since it serializes the (U) lock request of the second transaction.

Generally, it is preferable to use the UPDLOCK locking hint over the REPEATABLEREAD and HOLDLOCK locking hints, since this prevents the possibility of the typical deadlock avoided by the internal implementation of the UPDATE statement, as explained in Chapter 12. This works because the UPDLOCK locking hint serializes the lock requests by other transactions on a resource by holding a (U) lock on the resource irrespective of whether it is used for a SELECT statement or an UPDATE statement.

Increase Lock Granularity

Sometimes the SPIDs participating in the deadlock form a circular blocking while contending for resources associated with the same table. Each SPID may hold a lock on a data row, data page, index row, or index page, and then request an incompatible lock on the resource held by the other SPID. This type of circular blocking or deadlock can be resolved by increasing the lock granularity of the SPIDs. It will serialize the lock request of the second SPID on the lock held by the first SPID until the first SPID finishes.

In the current deadlock scenario, note that the resources (RID and KEY) disputed by SPIDs 52 and 53 are associated with the same table, t1. The KEY resource represents an index row within the index i_c1, which is associated with the table t1. The RID resource represents a data row within the table t1.

To support concurrency, SQL Server allowed SPIDs 52 and 53 to attain RID and KEY locks on table t1 simultaneously. These two resources (RID and KEY) have a common lock granularity at the table level. Changing the lock granularity of the UPDATE statement to table level will allow only one SPID to acquire the locks, and consequently the lock request by the second SPID will be blocked. Serialization of the second SPID's lock request will prevent the circular blocking or the deadlock. You can use the following techniques to increase the lock granularity level to table level:

- The TABLOCK locking hint

- The sp_indexoption system stored procedure

Be careful when increasing the lock granularity to table level, because it increases blocking, as explained in Chapter 12. It blocks all write requests on the entire table (including all indexes on the table), which can hurt database concurrency significantly.

TABLOCK Locking Hint

The TABLOCK locking hint can be used on table t1 in the UPDATE statement to increase the lock granularity to table level as follows:

```
UPDATE t1 WITH(TABLOCK)
SET t1.Data = 'a'
WHERE t1.c1 = 11
```

sp_indexoption System Stored Procedure

The lock granularity can also be increased to table level by using the sp_indexoption system stored procedure. Setting both ALLOWROWLOCKS and ALLOWPAGELOCKS to FALSE, as follows, will increase the lock granularity to table level (indexoption.sql in the download) because the next higher level of lock granularity for an index is the table-level lock on the corresponding table:

```
--Avoid KEY lock on the index row
EXEC sp_indexoption 't1.i_c1', ALLOWROWLOCKS, FALSE
--Avoid PAG lock on index page
EXEC sp_indexoption 't1.i_c1', ALLOWPAGELOCKS, FALSE
UPDATE t1
SET t1.Data = 'a'
WHERE t1.c1 = 11
EXEC sp_indexoption 't1.i_c1', ALLOWROWLOCKS, TRUE
EXEC sp_indexoption 't1.i_c1', ALLOWPAGELOCKS, TRUE
```

Both the TABLOCK locking hint and the sp_indexoption system stored procedure avoid the current deadlock by serializing the lock requests of the two SPIDs. This technique prevents the deadlock at the cost of concurrency, as mentioned earlier in the section. Due to the major impact on concurrency, avoid using the table-level lock.

Decrease the Number of Resources Accessed

A deadlock involves at least two resources. A SPID holds the first resource and then requests the second resource. The other SPID holds the second resource and requests the first resource. If you can prevent the SPIDs (or at least one of them) from accessing one of the resources involved in the deadlock, then the deadlock can be prevented. You can achieve this by redesigning the application: a solution highly resisted by developers at a late stage of the project. However, you can consider using the following features of SQL Server without changing the application design:

- Convert a nonclustered index to a clustered index.

- Use a covering index for a SELECT statement.

Convert a Nonclustered Index to a Clustered Index

As you know, the leaf pages of a nonclustered index are separate from the data pages of the table. Therefore, a nonclustered index takes two locks: one for the base table and one for the nonclustered index. However, in the case of a clustered index, the leaf pages of the index and the data pages of the table are the same; it requires one lock, and that one lock protects both the clustered index and the table, since the leaf pages and the data pages are the same. This decreases the number of resources to be accessed by the same query, compared to a nonclustered index.

In the current deadlock scenario, you can see that separate locks are required on the index row and the data row to maintain their consistency. In this case, you can decrease the number of resources to be accessed by converting the nonclustered index to a clustered index as follows:

```
CREATE CLUSTERED INDEX i_c1 ON t1(c1) WITH DROP_EXISTING
```

Converting the nonclustered index to a clustered index avoids the current deadlock, since both SPIDs will be essentially working on the same resource. There won't be any separate KEY and RID resources to be locked.

■**NOTE** To continue with the other deadlock resolution techniques, you will convert the clustered index back to nonclustered index:

```
DROP INDEX t1.i_c1
CREATE INDEX i_c1 ON t1(c1)
```

Use a Covering Index for a SELECT Statement

You can also use a covering index to decrease the number of resources accessed by a SELECT statement. Since a SELECT statement can get everything from the covering index itself, it doesn't need to access the base table. Otherwise, the SELECT statement needs to access both the index and the base table to retrieve all the required column values. Using a covering index stops the SELECT statement from accessing the base table, leaving the base table free to be locked by another SPID.

For example, consider the following two transactions (trans1_2.sql in the download) executed on the current test table. Here is the transaction from the first connection, which is executed first:

```
BEGIN TRAN Tx1
  UPDATE t1
    SET t1.Data = 'a'
    WHERE t1.c1 = 11
  /*Allow concurrent transactions*/ WAITFOR DELAY '00:00:10'
  DELETE t1
    WHERE t1.c1 = 11
COMMIT
GO
```

Here is the transaction from the second connection, which is executed within 10 seconds of the execution of Tx1:

```
BEGIN TRAN Tx2
  SELECT c1, c2 FROM t1
    WHERE t1.c1 = 11
COMMIT
```

The second transaction (Tx2) faces a deadlock due to the formation of circular blocking, as shown in Figure 13-6.

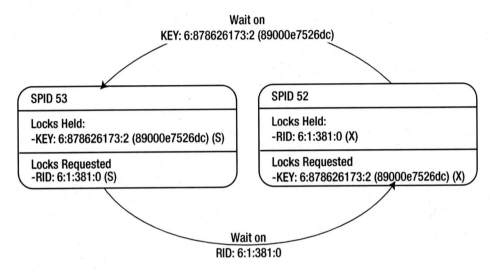

Figure 13-6. *Deadlock graph showing circular blocking between the two SPIDs*

For ease of understanding, you can simplify the representation of the circular blocking as shown in Figure 13-7.

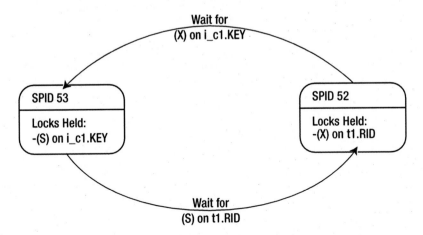

Figure 13-7. *A simplified representation of the deadlock graph*

You can avoid the (S) lock requested by the SELECT statement on the data row (RID: 6:1:381:0) by creating a covering index on columns c1 and c2:

```
CREATE INDEX i_covering ON t1(c1, c2)
```

This prevents SPID 53 from requesting locks on two resources, since all the column values requested by SPID 53 are fully satisfied from the covering index. This avoids the formation of the circular blocking.

■**NOTE** To continue with the other deadlock resolution techniques, drop the covering index and replace the deleted row:

```
DROP INDEX t1.i_covering
INSERT INTO t1 VALUES(11, 12, '', '')
```

Minimize Lock Contention

You can also resolve a deadlock by avoiding the lock request on one of the contended resources. You can do this when the resource is accessed only for reading data. Modifying a resource will always acquire an (X) lock on the resource to maintain the consistency of the resource so, in a deadlock situation, identify the resource accesses that are read-only and try to avoid their corresponding lock requests by using the dirty read feature, if possible. You can use the following techniques to avoid the lock request on a contended resource:

- Decrease the isolation level.

- Use locking hints.

Decrease the Isolation Level

Sometimes the (S) lock requested by a SELECT statement contributes to the formation of circular blocking. You can avoid this type of circular blocking by reducing the isolation level of the transaction containing the SELECT statement to READ UNCOMMITTED. It will allow the SELECT statement to read the data without requesting an (S) lock, and thereby avoid the circular blocking.

For example, consider the two transactions in trans1_2.sql. You know that without a covering index for the SELECT statement, the second transaction (Tx2) faces a deadlock due to the formation of circular blocking. You can see from Figure 13-6 that SPID 53 needs only (S) locks. In this case, you can avoid circular blocking by decreasing the isolation level of SPID 53's connection to READ UNCOMMITTED as follows:

```
SET TRANSACTION ISOLATION LEVEL READ UNCOMMITTED
GO
BEGIN TRAN
  SELECT c1,c2 FROM t1
    WHERE t1.c1 = 11
COMMIT
```

```
GO
SET TRANSACTION ISOLATION LEVEL READ COMMITTED --Back to default
GO
```

Avoiding the (S) locks of SPID 53 will prevent the deadlock.

Use Locking Hints

You can also resolve the deadlock presented in the preceding technique using the following locking hints:

- NOLOCK

- READUNCOMMITTED

You can use these locking hints on table t1 in the SELECT statement as follows:

```
BEGIN TRAN
  SELECT * FROM t1 WITH(NOLOCK) --or WITH(READUNCOMMITTED)
    WHERE t1.c1 = 11
COMMIT
```

Like the READ UNCOMMITTED isolation level, the NOLOCK or READUNCOMMITTED locking hint will avoid the (S) locks requested by SPID 53, thereby preventing the formation of circular blocking.

The effect of the locking hint is at a query level and is limited to the table (and its indexes) on which it is applied. The NOLOCK and READUNCOMMITTED locking hints are allowed only in SELECT statements and the data selection part of the INSERT, DELETE, and UPDATE statements, as follows (create t2 in the same way you created t1 at the beginning of the chapter, or use create_t2.sql from the download):

```
INSERT INTO t2              --Dirty read NOT allowed
SELECT * FROM t1 WITH(NOLOCK) --Dirty read applicable for data selection only

UPDATE t2                 --Dirty read NOT allowed
  SET t2.data = ''
  FROM t2 INNER JOIN
      t1 WITH(NOLOCK)  --Dirty read applicable for data selection only
  ON t2.c1 = t1.c1

DELETE t2                 --Dirty read NOT allowed
  FROM t2 INNER JOIN
      t1 WITH(NOLOCK)  --Dirty read applicable for data selection only
  ON t2.c1 = t1.c1
```

The resolution techniques of minimizing lock contention introduce the side effect of a dirty read, which may not be acceptable in every transaction. Therefore, use these resolution techniques only in situations in which a dirty read is acceptable.

Summary

As you learned in this chapter, a deadlock is the result of circular blocking and is reported to an application with the error number 1205. You can analyze the cause of a deadlock by collecting the deadlock information using the trace flag 1204.

You have a number of techniques to resolve a deadlock; which technique is applicable depends upon the type of the queries executed by the participating SPIDs, the locks held and requested on the involved resources, and the business rules governing the degree of isolation required. Generally, you can resolve a deadlock by reconfiguring the indexes and the transaction isolation levels. However, at times you may need to redesign the application or automatically re-execute the transaction on a deadlock.

In the next chapter, I cover the performance aspects of cursors and how to optimize the cost overhead of using cursors.

CHAPTER 14

Cursor Cost Analysis

It is very common to find database applications that use cursors to process one row at a time. As data manipulation through a cursor in SQL Server incurs additional overhead, database applications should either avoid using a cursor or use a cursor with the least cost.

In this chapter, I cover the following topics:

- The fundamentals of cursors

- A cost analysis of different characteristics of cursors

- The benefits of a default result set over cursors

- Recommendations to minimize the cost overhead of cursors

Cursor Fundamentals

When a query is executed by an application, SQL Server returns a set of data consisting of rows. Generally, applications can't process multiple rows together, so instead they process one row at a time by walking through the result set returned by SQL Server. This functionality is provided by a *cursor*, which is a mechanism to work with one row at a time out of a multirow result set.

Cursor processing usually involves the following steps:

1. Declare the cursor to associate it with a SELECT statement and define the characteristics of the cursor.

2. Open the cursor to access the result set returned by the SELECT statement.

3. Retrieve a row from the cursor. Optionally, modify the row through the cursor.

4. Once all the rows in the result set are processed, close the cursor and release the resources assigned to the cursor.

Cursors can be created using T-SQL statements or the data access layers (ADO, OLE DB, and ODBC) used to connect to SQL Server. Cursors created using data access layers are commonly referred to as *database API* cursors. You can write a T-SQL cursor processing for a test table, t1, as follows (cursor.sql in the download):

```
--Create a test table
IF(SELECT OBJECT_ID('t1')) IS NOT NULL
  DROP TABLE t1
GO
CREATE TABLE t1(c1 INT, c2 VARCHAR(10))
INSERT INTO t1 (c1, c2) VALUES(1, '1')
INSERT INTO t1 (c1, c2) VALUES(1, '2')

--Associate a SELECT statement to a cursor and define the
--cursor's characteristics
DECLARE cursor_t1 CURSOR /*<cursor characteristics>*/ FOR
  SELECT * FROM t1 WHERE c1 = 1
--Open the cursor to access the result set returned by the
--SELECT statement
OPEN cursor_t1
--Retrieve one row at a time from the result set returned by
--the SELECT statement
DECLARE @c1 INT, @c2 VARCHAR(10)
FETCH NEXT FROM cursor_t1 INTO @c1, @c2
WHILE @@FETCH_STATUS = 0
BEGIN
  PRINT 'c2 = ' + @c2
  --Optionally, modify the row through the cursor
  UPDATE t1
    SET c2 = c2 + '1'
    WHERE CURRENT OF cursor_t1
  FETCH NEXT FROM cursor_t1 INTO @c1, @c2
END
--Close the cursor and release all resources assigned to the
--cursor
CLOSE cursor_t1
DEALLOCATE cursor_t1
```

The overhead of the cursor depends on the cursor characteristics. The characteristics of the cursors provided by SQL Server and the data access layers can be broadly classified into three categories:

- *Cursor location*: Defines the location of the cursor creation

- *Cursor concurrency*: Defines the degree of isolation and synchronization of a cursor with the underlying content

- *Cursor type*: Defines the specific characteristics of a cursor

Before looking at the costs of cursors, I'll take a few pages to introduce the various characteristics of cursors.

Cursor Location

Based on the location of a cursor creation, cursors can be classified into two categories:

- Client-side cursor
- Server-side cursor

The T-SQL cursors are always created on SQL Server. However, the database API cursors can be created on either the client side or the server side.

Client-Side Cursor

As its name signifies, a *client-side cursor* is created on the machine running the application. It has the following characteristics:

- It is created on the client machine.
- The cursor metadata is maintained on the client machine.
- It is created using the data access layers.
- It works against most of the data access layers (OLE DB providers and ODBC drivers).
- It can be a forward-only or a static cursor.

▓**NOTE** Cursor types, including forward-only and static cursor types, are described later in the chapter in the "Cursor Types" section.

Server-Side Cursor

A *server-side cursor* is created on the SQL Server machine. It has the following characteristics:

- It is created on the server machine.
- The cursor metadata is maintained on the server machine.
- It is created using either data access layers or T-SQL statements.
- A server-side cursor created using T-SQL statements is tightly integrated with SQL Server.
- It can be any type of cursor. (Note: Cursor type is explained later in the chapter.)

■NOTE The cost comparison between client-side and server-side cursors is covered later in the chapter in the "Cost Comparison on Cursor Type" section.

Cursor Concurrency

Depending on the required degree of isolation and synchronization with the underlying content, cursors can be classified into the following concurrency models:

- *Read-only*: A nonupdateable cursor

- *Optimistic*: An updateable cursor that uses the optimistic concurrency model (no locks retained on the underlying data rows)

- *Scroll locks*: An updateable cursor that holds a lock on any data row to be updated

Read-Only

A read-only cursor is nonupdateable; no locks are held on the base table(s). While fetching a cursor row, whether an (S) lock will be acquired on the underlying row or not depends upon the isolation level of the connection and the locking hint used in the SELECT statement for the cursor. However, once the row is fetched, by default the locks are released.

The following T-SQL statement creates a read-only T-SQL cursor:

```
DECLARE cursor_t1 CURSOR READ_ONLY FOR
    SELECT * FROM t1 WHERE c1 = 1
```

Optimistic

The optimistic concurrency model makes a cursor updateable. No locks are held on the underlying data. The factors governing whether or not an (S) lock will be acquired on the underlying row are the same as for a read-only cursor.

The optimistic concurrency model uses row versioning to determine whether a row has been modified since it was read into the cursor instead of locking the row while it is read into the cursor. Version-based optimistic concurrency requires a TIMESTAMP column in the underlying user table on which the cursor is created. The TIMESTAMP data type is a binary number that indicates the relative sequence of modifications on a row. Each time a row with a TIMESTAMP column is modified, SQL Server stores the current value of the global TIMESTAMP value, @@DBTS, in the TIMESTAMP column and then increments the @@DBTS value.

Before applying a modification through the optimistic cursor, SQL Server determines whether the current TIMESTAMP column value for the row matches the TIMESTAMP column value for the row when it was read into the cursor. The underlying row is modified only if the TIMESTAMP values match, indicating that the row hasn't been modified by another user in the meantime. Otherwise, an error is raised. In case of an error, first refresh the cursor with the updated data.

If the underlying table doesn't contain a TIMESTAMP column, then the cursor defaults to value-based optimistic concurrency, which requires matching the current value of the row with the value when the row was read into the cursor. The version-based concurrency control is more efficient than the value-based concurrency control since it requires less processing to determine modification of the underlying row. Therefore, for the best performance of a cursor with the optimistic concurrency model, ensure that the underlying table has a TIMESTAMP column.

The following T-SQL statement creates an optimistic T-SQL cursor:

```
DECLARE cursor_t1 CURSOR OPTIMISTIC FOR
    SELECT * FROM t1 WHERE c1 = 1
```

Scroll Locks

A cursor with scroll locks concurrency holds a (U) lock on the underlying row until another cursor row is fetched or the cursor is closed. This prevents other users from modifying the underlying row when the cursor fetches it. The scroll locks concurrency model makes the cursor updateable.

The following T-SQL statement creates a T-SQL cursor with the scroll locks concurrency model:

```
DECLARE cursor_t1 CURSOR SCROLL_LOCKS FOR
    SELECT * FROM t1 WHERE c1 = 1
```

Since locks are held on the underlying rows (until another cursor row is fetched or the cursor is closed), it blocks all the other users trying to modify the row during that period. This hurts database concurrency.

Cursor Types

Cursors can be classified into the following four types:

- Forward-only cursor

- Static cursor

- Keyset-driven cursor

- Dynamic cursor

Let's take a closer look at these four types in the sections that follow.

Forward-Only Cursor

These are the characteristics of a forward-only cursor:

- It operates directly on the base table(s).

- Rows from the underlying table(s) are usually not retrieved until the cursor rows are fetched using the cursor FETCH operation. However, the database API forward-only cursor type, with the following additional characteristics, retrieves all the rows from the underlying table first:

  - Client-side cursor location

  - Server-side cursor location and read-only cursor concurrency

- It only supports forward scrolling (FETCH NEXT) through the cursor.

- It allows all changes (INSERT, UPDATE, and DELETE) through the cursor. Also, the cursor reflects all changes made to the underlying table(s).

The forward-only characteristic is implemented differently by the database API cursors and the T-SQL cursor. The data access layers implement the forward-only cursor characteristic as one of the four previously listed cursor types. But the T-SQL cursor doesn't implement the forward-only cursor characteristic as a cursor type; rather, it implements it as a property that defines the scrollable behavior of the cursor. Thus, for a T-SQL cursor, the forward-only characteristic can be used to define the scrollable behavior of one of the remaining three cursor types.

A forward-only cursor with a read-only property is also called a *fast forward–only* cursor. The T-SQL syntax provides a specific cursor type option, FAST_FORWARD, to create a fast forward–only cursor. The following T-SQL statement creates a fast forward–only T-SQL cursor:

```
DECLARE cursor_t1 CURSOR FAST_FORWARD FOR
  SELECT * FROM t1 WHERE c1 = 1
```

The FAST_FORWARD property specifies a forward-only, read-only cursor with performance optimizations enabled. You can create the server-side cursor with the FAST_FORWARD property using the data access layers, as explained in the MSDN article titled "How to obtain a FAST_FORWARD cursor" (http://msdn.microsoft.com/library/en-us/howtosql/ht_olehowt1_404y.asp).

▓NOTE The client-side, fast forward–only cursor is explained later in this chapter in the "Default Result Set" section.

Static Cursor

These are the characteristics of a static cursor:

- It creates a snapshot of cursor results in the `tempdb` database when the cursor is opened. Thereafter, it operates on the snapshot in the `tempdb` database.

- Data is retrieved from the underlying table(s) when the cursor is opened.

- It supports all scrolling options: `FETCH FIRST`, `FETCH NEXT`, `FETCH PRIOR`, `FETCH LAST`, `FETCH ABSOLUTE n`, and `FETCH RELATIVE n`.

- Static cursors are always read-only; data modifications are not allowed through static cursors. Also, changes (`INSERT`, `UPDATE`, and `DELETE`) made to the underlying table(s) are not reflected in the cursor.

The following T-SQL statement creates a static T-SQL cursor:

```
DECLARE cursor_t1 CURSOR STATIC FOR
  SELECT * FROM t1 WHERE c1 = 1
```

Keyset-Driven Cursor

These are the characteristics of a keyset-driven cursor:

- It is controlled by a set of unique identifiers (or keys) known as a *keyset*. The keyset is built from a set of columns that uniquely identify the rows in the result set.

- It creates the keyset of rows in the `tempdb` database when the cursor is opened.

- Membership of rows in the cursor is limited to the keyset of rows created in the `tempdb` database when the cursor is opened.

- On fetching a cursor row, it first looks at the keyset of rows in `tempdb`, and then it navigates to the corresponding data row in the underlying table(s) to retrieve the remaining columns.

- It supports all scrolling options.

- It allows all changes through the cursor. An `INSERT` performed outside the cursor is not reflected in the cursor, since the membership of rows in the cursor is limited to the keyset of rows created in the `tempdb` database on opening the cursor. An `INSERT` through the cursor appears at the end of the cursor. A `DELETE` performed on the underlying table(s) is notified as an error when the cursor navigation reaches the deleted row. An `UPDATE` on the nonkeyset columns of the underlying table(s) is reflected in the cursor. An `UPDATE` on the keyset column(s) is treated like a delete of an old key value and the insert of a new key value. If a change disqualifies a row for membership or affects the order of a row, the row does not disappear or move unless the cursor is closed and reopened.

The following T-SQL statement creates a keyset-driven T-SQL cursor:

```
DECLARE cursor_t1 CURSOR KEYSET FOR
  SELECT * FROM t1 WHERE c1 = 1
```

Dynamic Cursor

These are the characteristics of a dynamic cursor:

- It operates directly on the base table(s).

- Membership of rows in the cursor is not fixed, since it operates directly on the base table(s).

- Like the forward-only cursor, rows from the underlying table(s) are not retrieved until the cursor rows are fetched using a cursor FETCH operation.

- It supports all scrolling options except FETCH ABSOLUTE n, since the membership of rows in the cursor is not fixed.

- It allows all changes through the cursor. Also, all changes made to the underlying table(s) are reflected in the cursor.

- It doesn't support all properties and methods implemented by the database API cursors. Properties such as AbsolutePosition, Bookmark, and RecordCount, and methods such as clone and Resync, are not supported by dynamic cursors, but are supported by keyset-driven cursors.

The following T-SQL statement creates a dynamic T-SQL cursor:

```
DECLARE cursor_t1 CURSOR DYNAMIC FOR
  SELECT * FROM t1 WHERE c1 = 1
```

Cursor Cost Comparison

Now that you've seen the different cursor flavors, let's look at their costs. You should always use the lightest weight cursor that meets the requirements of your application. The cost comparisons among the different characteristics of the cursors are detailed next.

Cost Comparison on Cursor Location

The client-side and server-side cursors have their own cost benefits and overheads, as explained in the sections that follow.

Client-Side Cursor

The client-side cursor has the following cost benefits compared to the server-side cursor:

- *Higher scalability:* Since the cursor metadata is maintained on the individual client machines connected to the server, the overhead of maintaining the cursor metadata is taken up by the client machines. Consequently, the ability to serve a larger number of users is not limited by the server resources.

- *Fewer network round-trips*: Since the result set returned by the SELECT statement is passed to the client where the cursor is maintained, extra network round-trips to the server are not required while retrieving rows from the cursor.

- *Faster scrolling*: Since the cursor is maintained locally on the client machine, it's faster to walk through the rows of the cursor.

- *Highly portable*: Since the cursor is implemented using data access layers, it works across a large range of databases: SQL Server, Oracle, Sybase, and so forth.

The client-side cursor has the following cost overheads or drawbacks:

- *Higher pressure on client resources*: Since the cursor is managed at the client side, it increases pressure on the client resources. But it may not be all that bad, considering that most of the time the client applications are web applications and scaling out web applications (or web servers) is quite easy using standard load-balancing solutions. On the other hand, scaling out a transactional SQL Server database is still an art!

- *Support for limited cursor types*: Dynamic and keyset-driven cursors are not supported.

- *Only one active cursor-based statement on one connection*: As many rows of the result set as the client network can buffer are arranged in the form of network packets and sent to the client application. Therefore, until all the cursors rows are fetched by the application, the database connection remains busy, pushing the rows to the client. During this period, the connection cannot be used by other cursor-based statements.

Server-Side Cursor

The server-side cursor has the following cost benefits:

- *Multiple active cursor-based statements on one connection*: While using server-side cursors, no results are left outstanding on the connection between the cursor operations. This frees the connection, allowing the use of multiple cursor-based statements on one connection at the same time. In the case of client-side cursors, as explained previously, the connection remains busy until all the cursor rows are fetched by the application, and therefore cannot be used simultaneously by multiple cursor-based statements.

- *Row processing near the data*: If the row processing involves joining with other tables and a considerable amount of set operations, then it is advantageous to perform the row processing near the data using a server-side cursor.

- *Less pressure on client resources*: It reduces pressure on the client resources. But this may not be that desirable, because if the server resources are maxed out (instead of the client resources), then it will require scaling out the database, which is a difficult proposition.

- *Support for all cursor types.*

The server-side cursor has the following cost overheads or disadvantages:

- *Lower scalability*: It makes the server less scalable since server resources are consumed to manage the cursor.

- *More network round-trips*: It increases network round-trips, if the cursor row processing is done in the client application. The number of network round-trips can be optimized by processing the cursor rows in the stored procedure or by using the cache size feature of data access layer.

- *Less portable*: Server-side cursors implemented using T-SQL cursors are not readily portable to other databases because the syntax of the database code managing the cursor is different across databases.

Cost Comparison on Cursor Concurrency

As expected, cursors with a higher concurrency model create the least amount of blocking in the database and support higher scalability, as explained in the following sections.

Read-Only

The read-only concurrency model provides the following cost benefits:

- *Lowest locking overhead*: The read-only concurrency model introduces the least locking and synchronization overhead on the database. Since (S) locks are not held on the underlying row after a cursor row is fetched, other users are not blocked from accessing the row. Furthermore, the (S) lock acquired on the underlying row while fetching the cursor row can be avoided by using the NOLOCK locking hint in the SELECT statement of the cursor.

- *Highest concurrency*: Since locks are not held on the underlying rows, the read-only cursor doesn't block other users from accessing the underlying table(s).

The main drawback of the read-only cursor is as follows:

- *Nonupdateable*: The content of underlying table(s) cannot be modified through the cursor.

Optimistic

The optimistic concurrency model provides the following benefits:

- *Low locking overhead*: Similar to the read-only model, the optimistic concurrency model doesn't hold an (S) lock on the cursor row after the row is fetched. To further improve concurrency, the NOLOCK locking hint can also be used, as in the case of the read-only concurrency model. Modification through the cursor to an underlying row requires exclusive rights on the row as required by an action query.

- *High concurrency*: Since locks aren't held on the underlying rows, the cursor doesn't block other users from accessing the underlying table(s). But the modification through the cursor to an underlying row will block other users from accessing the row during the modification.

The following are the cost overheads of the optimistic concurrency model:

- *Row versioning*: Since the optimistic concurrency model allows the cursor to be updateable, an additional cost is incurred to ensure that the current underlying row is first compared (using either version-based or value-based concurrency control) with the original cursor row fetched, before applying a modification through the cursor. This prevents the modification through the cursor from accidentally overwriting the modification made by another user after the cursor row is fetched.

- *Concurrency control without a TIMESTAMP column*: As explained previously, a TIMESTAMP column in the underlying table allows the cursor to perform an efficient version-based concurrency control. In case the underlying table doesn't contain a TIMESTAMP column, the cursor resorts to value-based concurrency control, which requires matching the current value of the row to the value when the row was read into the cursor. This increases the cost of the concurrency control.

Scroll Locks

The major benefit of the scroll locks concurrency model is as follows:

- *Simple concurrency control*: By locking the underlying row corresponding to the last fetched row from the cursor, the cursor assures that the underlying row can't be modified by another user. It eliminates the versioning overhead of optimistic locking. Also, since the row cannot be modified by another user, the application is relieved from checking for a row-mismatch error.

The scroll locks concurrency model incurs the following cost overheads:

- *Highest locking overhead*: The scroll locks concurrency model introduces a pessimistic locking characteristic. A (U) lock is held on the last cursor row fetched, until another cursor row is fetched or the cursor is closed.

- *Lowest concurrency*: Since a (U) lock is held on the underlying row, all other users requesting a (U) or (X) lock on the underlying row will be blocked. This can significantly hurt concurrency. Therefore, please avoid using this cursor concurrency model unless absolutely necessary.

Cost Comparison on Cursor Type

The basic four cursor types mentioned in the "Cursor Fundamentals" section earlier in the chapter each incur a different cost overhead on the server. Choosing an incorrect cursor type can hurt database performance. Besides the four basic cursor types, a fast forward–only cursor, a variation of the forward-only cursor, is provided to enhance performance. The cost overhead of these cursors types is explained in the sections that follow.

Forward-Only Cursor

These are the cost benefits of the forward-only cursor:

- *Lower cursor open cost than static and keyset-driven cursors*: Since the cursor rows are not retrieved from the underlying table(s) and are not copied into the `tempdb` database during cursor open, the forward-only T-SQL cursor opens very quickly. Similarly, the forward-only, server-side API cursors with optimistic/scroll locks concurrency also open quickly since they do not retrieve the rows during cursor open.

- *Lower scroll overhead*: Since only FETCH NEXT can be performed on this cursor type, it requires a lower overhead to support different scroll operations.

- *Lower impact on the `tempdb` database than static and keyset-driven cursors*: Since the forward-only T-SQL cursor doesn't copy the rows from the underlying table(s) into the `tempdb` database, no additional pressure is created on the database.

The forward-only cursor type has the following drawbacks:

- *Lower concurrency*: Every time a cursor row is fetched, the corresponding underlying row is accessed with a lock request depending on the cursor concurrency model. It can block other users from accessing the resource.

- *No backward scrolling*: Applications requiring two-way scrolling can't use this cursor type. But if the applications are designed properly, then it isn't difficult to live without backward scrolling.

Fast Forward–Only Cursor

The fast forward–only cursor is the fastest cursor type. This forward-only and read-only cursor is specially optimized for performance. Because of this, you should always prefer it to the other SQL Server cursor types.

Furthermore, the data access layer provides a fast forward–only cursor on the client side, making the cursor overhead almost disappear by using a default result set.

NOTE The default result set is explained later in the chapter in the section "Default Result Set."

Static Cursor

These are the cost benefits of the static cursor:

- *Lower fetch cost than other cursor types*: Since a snapshot is created in the `tempdb` database from the underlying rows on opening the cursor, the cursor row fetch is targeted to the snapshot instead of the underlying rows. This avoids the lock overhead that would otherwise be required to fetch the cursor rows.

- *No blocking on underlying rows*: Since the snapshot is created in the `tempdb` database, other users trying to access the underlying rows are not blocked.

On the downside, the static cursor has the following cost overheads:

- *Higher open cost than other cursor types*: The cursor open operation of the static cursor is slower than that of other cursor types, since all the rows of the result set have to be retrieved from the underlying table(s) and the snapshot has to be created in the tempdb database during the cursor open.

- *Higher impact on tempdb than other cursor types*: There can be significant impact on server resources for creating, populating, and cleaning up the snapshot in the tempdb database.

Keyset-Driven Cursor

These are the cost benefits of the keyset-driven cursor:

- *Lower open cost than the static cursor*: Since only the keyset, not the complete snapshot, is created in the tempdb database, the keyset-driven cursor opens faster than the static cursor. SQL Server populates the keyset of a large keyset-driven cursor asynchronously, which shortens the time between when the cursor is opened and the first cursor row is fetched.

- *Lower impact on tempdb than that with the static cursor.*

The cost overheads of keyset-driven cursor are as follows:

- *Higher open cost than forward-only and dynamic cursors*: Populating the keyset in the tempdb database makes the cursor open operation of the keyset-driven cursor costlier than that of forward-only (with exceptions as mentioned in the previous forward-only cursor section) and dynamic cursors.

- *Higher fetch cost than other cursor types*: For every cursor row fetch, the key in the keyset has to be accessed first, and then the corresponding underlying row in the user database can be accessed. Accessing both the tempdb and the user database for every cursor row fetch makes the fetch operation costlier than that of other cursor types.

- *Higher impact on tempdb than forward-only and dynamic cursors*: Creating, populating, and cleaning up the keyset in tempdb impacts server resources.

- *Higher lock overhead and blocking than the static cursor*: Since row fetch from the cursor retrieves rows from the underlying table, it acquires an (S) lock on the underlying row (unless the NOLOCK locking hint is used) during the row fetch operation.

Dynamic Cursor

The dynamic cursor has the following cost benefits:

- *Lower open cost than static and keyset-driven cursors*: Since the cursor is opened directly on the underlying rows without copying anything to the tempdb database, the dynamic cursor opens faster than the static and keyset-driven cursors.

- *Lower impact on tempdb than static and keyset-driven cursors.*

The dynamic cursor has the following cost overhead:

- *Higher lock overhead and blocking than the static cursor*: Every cursor row fetch in a dynamic cursor requeries the underlying table(s) involved in the SELECT statement of the cursor. The dynamic fetches are generally expensive, since the original select condition might have to be reapplied.

Default Result Set

The default cursor type for the data access layers (ADO, OLE DB, and ODBC) is forward-only and read-only. The default cursor type created by the data access layers isn't a true cursor, but a stream of data from the server to the client, generally referred to as the *default result set* or fast forward–only cursor (created by the data access layer). In ADO.NET, the DataReader control has the forward-only and read-only properties, and can be considered as the default result set in the ADO.NET environment. SQL Server uses this type of result set processing under the following conditions:

- The application, using the data access layers (ADO, OLE DB, ODBC), leaves all the cursor characteristics at the default settings, which requests a forward-only and read-only cursor.

- The application executes a SELECT statement instead of executing a DECLARE CURSOR statement.

■**NOTE** As SQL Server is designed to work with sets of data, not to walk through records one by one, the default result set is always faster than any other type of cursor.

The only request sent from the client to SQL Server is the SQL statement associated with the default cursor. SQL Server executes the query, organizes the rows of the result set in network packets (filling the packets as best as possible), and then sends the packets to the client. These network packets are cached in the network buffers of the client. SQL Server sends as many rows of the result set to the client as the client-network buffers can cache. As the client application requests one row at a time, the data access layer on the client machine pulls the row from the client-network buffers and transfers it to the client application.

The following sections outline the benefits and drawbacks of the default result set.

Benefits

The default result set is generally the best and most efficient way of returning rows from SQL Server for the following reasons:

- *Minimum network round-trips between the client and SQL Server*: Since the result set returned by SQL Server is cached in the client-network buffers, the client doesn't have to make a request across the network to get the individual rows. SQL Server puts most of the rows that it can in the network buffer, and sends to the client as much as the client-network buffer can cache.

- *Minimum server overhead*: Since SQL Server doesn't have to store data on the server, this reduces server resource utilization.

Autoclose and Autofetch

The ODBC driver for SQL Server 2000 (also SQL Server 7.0) provides an additional performance characteristic with the default result set: SQL Server automatically closes the cursor when the end of the cursor is detected. The application using the ODBC driver must still call SQLCloseCursor or SQLFreeStmt(SQL_CLOSE), but the driver does not have to send the close request to SQL Server, which saves a round-trip across the network to SQL Server.

To have the *autoclose* option, an ODBC application must request the default result set (or read-only plus forward-only cursor) using the driver-specific statement attribute SQL_SOPT_SS_CURSOR_OPTIONS set to SQL_CO_FFO_AF. It also returns the rows comprising the first rowset to the bound application variables as part of the cursor open, saving another round-trip across the network to the server. This feature is generally referred to as *autofetch*.

The default result set is definitely recommended when the complete result set returned by SQL Server is consumed immediately.

Drawbacks

The use of the default result set requires some special conditions for maximum performance:

- *Doesn't support all properties and methods*: Properties such as AbsolutePosition, Bookmark, and RecordCount, and methods such as Clone, MoveLast, MovePrevious, and Resync are not supported.

- *Only one active statement per connection*: The major consideration with the default result set is that there can be only one active statement on the connection at a time. The client application can't execute another statement on the connection until all rows of the result set are consumed or a cancel is issued.

  That said, if the result set is small enough to be cached by the client-network buffer, then the client network can cache all the rows from the server during the cursor open itself, thereby freeing the database connection immediately.

- *Locks may be held on the underlying resource*: SQL Server sends as many rows of the result set to the client as the client-network buffers can cache. If the size of the result set is large, then the client-network buffers may not be able to receive all the rows. SQL Server then holds a lock on the next page of the underlying table(s), which has not been sent to the client.

To demonstrate these concepts, consider the following test table (create_t1.sql in the download):

```
USE Northwind
GO
IF(SELECT OBJECT_ID('t1')) IS NOT NULL
  DROP TABLE t1
GO
```

```
CREATE TABLE t1(c1 INT, c2 CHAR(996))
CREATE CLUSTERED INDEX i1 ON t1(c1)
INSERT INTO t1 VALUES(1,'1')
INSERT INTO t1 VALUES(2,'2')
GO
```

Consider a web page accessing the rows of the test table using ADO with OLE DB, and the default cursor type for the database API cursor (ADODB.Recordset object) as follows (default_cursor.asp in the download):

```
<%@ LANGUAGE="VBSCRIPT" %>
<%
Dim strConn, Conn, Rs
Set Conn = CreateObject("ADODB.Connection")
strConn = "Provider=SQLOLEDB;" _
          & "Data Source=<Server Name>;" _
          & "Initial Catalog=Northwind;" _
          & "User ID=<User ID>; Password=<Password>;"
Conn.Open strConn
Set Rs = CreateObject("ADODB.Recordset")
'Declare & open a database API cursor with default settings
' (forward-only, read-only are the default settings)
Rs.Open "SELECT * FROM t1", Conn
'Consume the rows in the cursor one row at a time
While Not Rs.EOF
  'Fetch a row from the cursor
  Response.Write "c1 = " & Rs.Fields("c1").Value & "<BR>"
  Rs.MoveNext
Wend
'Close the cursor and release all resources assigned to the
'cursor
Rs.Close
Set Rs = Nothing
Conn.Close
Set Conn = Nothing
%>
```

Note that the table has two rows with the size of each row equal to 1,000 bytes (= 4 bytes for INT + 996 bytes for CHAR(996)) without considering the internal overheads. Therefore, the size of the complete result set returned by the SELECT statement is approximately 2,000 bytes (= 2 × 1,000 bytes).

You can execute the code of the preceding web page step by step using Microsoft Visual Studio .NET. On execution of the cursor open (Rs.Open) statement, a default result set is created on the client machine running the code. The default result set holds as many rows as the client-network buffer can cache.

Since the size of the result set is small enough to be cached by the client-network buffer, all the cursor rows are cached on the client machine during the cursor open statement itself, without retaining any lock on table t1. You can verify the lock status for the connection using the sp_lock system stored procedure. During the complete cursor operation, the only request from the client to SQL Server is the SELECT statement associated to the cursor, as shown in the Profiler output in Figure 14-1.

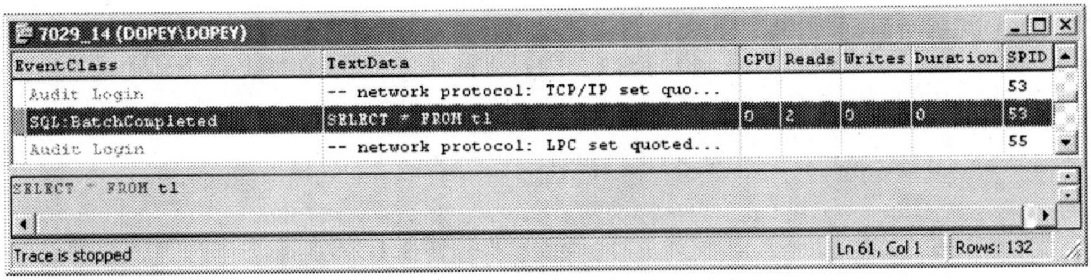

Figure 14-1. *Profiler trace output showing database requests made by the default result set*

To find out the effect of a large result set on the default result set processing, let's add some more rows to the test table (addrows.sql in the download):

```
--Add 98 rows to the test table
DECLARE @n INT
SET @n = 3
WHILE @n <= 100
BEGIN
  INSERT INTO t1 VALUES(@n, @n)
  SET @n = @n + 1
END
GO
```

This increases the size of the result set returned by the SELECT statement to approximately 100,000 bytes (= 100 × 1000 bytes) without considering the internal overheads. Depending on the size of the client-network buffer, only a part of the result set can be cached. On execution of the Rs.Open statement, the default result set on the client machine will get a part of the result set, with SQL Server waiting on the other end of the network to send the remaining rows.

On my machine, during this period, the locks shown in Figure 14-2 are held on the underlying table t1 as obtained from the output of sp_lock.

6	55	6	1198627313	1	PAG	1:1608	IS	GRANT
7	55	6	1198627313	0	TAB		IS	GRANT

Figure 14-2. *sp_lock output showing the locks held by the default result set while processing the large result set*

The (IS) locks on the page and the table will block other users trying to acquire an (X) lock. To minimize the blocking issue, follow these recommendations:

- Process all rows of the default result set immediately.

- Keep the result set small. As demonstrated in the example, if the size of the result set is small, then the default result set will be able to read all the rows during the cursor open operation itself.

If you are curious to know the rows included in the page resource (6:1:1608) indicated in the preceding sp_lock output, you can use the DBCC PAGE statement to find out:

```
DBCC PAGE(6, 1, 1608, 3)
```

The output of the DBCC PAGE statement indicates that the rows $c_1 = 65$ to 72 are on the page (6:1:1608). The general format of the DBCC PAGE statement is as follows:

```
DBCC PAGE(<DatabaseID | DatabaseName>, <FileID>, <PageID>[, OutputFlag])
```

Table 14-1 shows the OutputFlag values.

Table 14-1. *OutputFlag Values for the DBCC PAGE Command*

Value	Description
1	Show buffer and page headers, memory value of each row (or slot), and row offset table
2	Show buffer and page headers, memory value of the whole page, and row offset table
3	Show buffer and page headers, memory value of each row (or slot), with column values listed separately

Analyzing SQL Server Overhead with Cursors

While implementing a cursor-centric functionality in an application, you have two choices. You may use either a T-SQL cursor or a database API cursor. Because of the differences between the internal implementation of a T-SQL cursor and a database API cursor, the load created by these cursors on SQL Server is different. The impact of these cursors on the database also depends on the different characteristics of the cursors, such as location, concurrency, and type. You can use the SQL Profiler tool to analyze the load generated by the T-SQL and database API cursors using the events and data columns listed in Table 14-2.

Table 14-2. *Events and Data Columns to Analyze SQL Server Overhead with Cursors*

Events		Data Column
Event Class	**Event**	
Cursors	All events	EventClass
Security audit	Audit Login	TextData
	Audit Logout	CPU
Stored procedures	RPC:Completed	Reads
	SP:StmtCompleted	Writes
T-SQL	SQL:BatchCompleted	Duration
		SPID
		StartTime

Even the optimization options for these cursors are different. Let's analyze the overhead of these cursors one by one.

Analyzing SQL Server Overhead with T-SQL Cursors

The T-SQL cursors implemented using T-SQL statements are always executed on SQL Server, since they need the SQL Server engine to process their T-SQL statements. You may use a combination of the cursor characteristics explained previously to reduce the overhead of these cursors. As mentioned earlier, the most lightweight T-SQL cursor is the one created with the default settings, also referred to as a fast forward–only cursor. But even so, the T-SQL statements used to implement the cursor operations have to be processed by SQL Server. The complete load of the cursor is supported by SQL Server without any help from the client machine. To analyze the overhead of T-SQL cursors on SQL Server, consider the following example.

Suppose an application requirement consists of the following functionalities:

- Identify all products (from the Northwind.Products table) that have been discarded.

- For each discarded product, determine the money lost, where

    Money lost per product = Units in stock × Unit price of the product

- Calculate the total loss.

- Based on the total loss, determine the business status.

The "For each" phrase in the second point suggests that these application requirements probably deserve a cursor. You can implement this application requirement using a T-SQL cursor as follows (app_requirements.sql in the download):

```
IF(SELECT OBJECT_ID('spTotalLoss_CursorBased')) IS NOT NULL
   DROP PROC spTotalLoss_CursorBased
GO
CREATE PROC spTotalLoss_CursorBased
AS
--Declare a T-SQL cursor with default settings, i.e. fast
--forward-only to retrieve products that have been discarded
DECLARE DiscardedProducts CURSOR FOR
   SELECT UnitsInStock, UnitPrice
   FROM Products
   WHERE Discontinued = 1

--Open the cursor to process one product at a time
OPEN DiscardedProducts

DECLARE @MoneyLostPerProduct MONEY, @TotalLoss MONEY
SET @MoneyLostPerProduct = 0
SET @TotalLoss = 0

--Calculate money lost per product by processing one product
--at a time
```

```
DECLARE @UnitsInStock SMALLINT, @UnitPrice MONEY
FETCH NEXT FROM DiscardedProducts INTO @UnitsInStock, @UnitPrice
WHILE @@FETCH_STATUS = 0
BEGIN
  SET @MoneyLostPerProduct = @UnitsInStock * @UnitPrice
  --Calculate total loss
  SET @TotalLoss = @TotalLoss + @MoneyLostPerProduct
  FETCH NEXT FROM DiscardedProducts INTO @UnitsInStock, @UnitPrice
END

--Determine status
IF(@TotalLoss > 5000)
  SELECT 'We are bankrupt!' AS Status
ELSE
  SELECT 'We are safe!' AS Status

--Close the cursor and release all resources assigned to the cursor
CLOSE DiscardedProducts
DEALLOCATE DiscardedProducts
GO
```

The stored procedure can be executed as follows:

```
EXEC spTotalLoss_CursorBased
```

Figure 14-3 shows the Profiler trace output for this stored procedure.

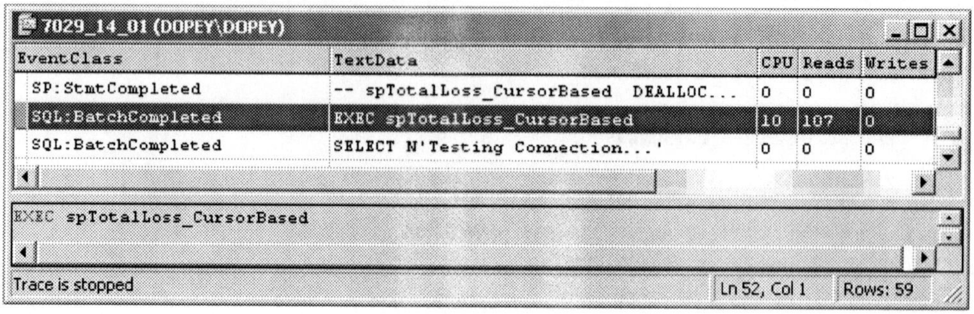

Figure 14-3. *Profiler trace output showing the total cost of the data processing using a T-SQL–based cursor*

As you can see in Figure 14-3, lots of statements are executed on SQL Server. Essentially all the SQL statements within the stored procedure are executed on SQL Server, with the statements within the WHILE loop executed several times (one for each row returned by the cursor's SELECT statement).

The total number of logical reads performed by the stored procedure is 107 (indicated by the last SQL:BatchCompleted event). Well, is it high or low? Considering the fact that the Products table has only one page, it's surely not low. You can determine the number of pages allocated to the Products table using DBCC SHOWCONTIG statement:

```
DBCC SHOWCONTIG(Products)
```

▓**NOTE** The DBCC SHOWCONTIG statement is explained in detail in Chapter 8.

For a little comfort, the second execution of the stored procedure brings down the total number of logical reads to 104, since it finds the execution plan available in the plan cache. Nonetheless, 104 logical reads to process a table with only one page is quite high.

In most cases, the cursor operations can be avoided by rewriting the functionality using SQL queries. The only problem is that the resultant SQL query is generally not a simple one. For example, you can rewrite the preceding stored procedure using SQL queries (instead of the cursor operations) as follows (no_cursor.sql in the download):

```
IF(SELECT OBJECT_ID('spTotalLoss')) IS NOT NULL
  DROP PROC spTotalLoss
GO
CREATE PROC spTotalLoss
AS
SELECT
  CASE --Determine status based on below computation
    WHEN SUM(MoneyLostPerProduct) > 5000 THEN 'We are bankrupt!'
    ELSE 'We are safe!'
  END AS Status
FROM (--Calculate total money lost for all discarded products
      SELECT SUM(UnitsInStock*UnitPrice) AS MoneyLostPerProduct
      FROM Products
      WHERE Discontinued = 1
      GROUP BY ProductID) DiscardedProducts
GO
```

In this stored procedure, the aggregation functions of SQL Server are used to compute the money lost per product and the total loss. The CASE statement is used to determine the business status based on the total loss incurred. The stored procedure can be executed as follows:

```
EXEC spTotalLoss --1st execution
GO
EXEC spTotalLoss --2nd execution to take advantage of plan caching
```

Figure 14-4 shows the corresponding Profiler trace output.

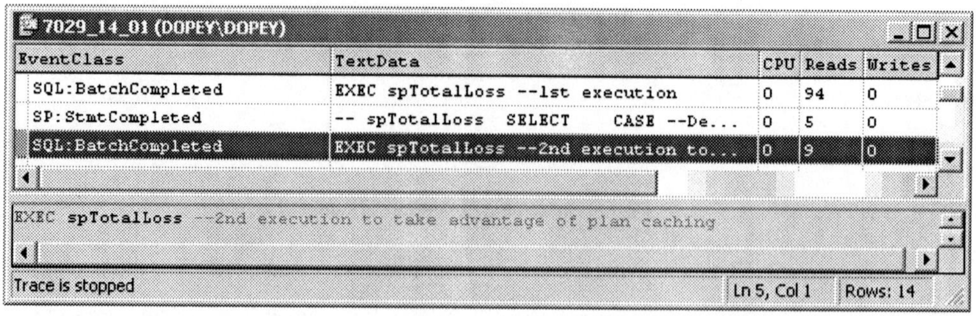

Figure 14-4. *Profiler trace output showing the total cost of the data processing using an equivalent SELECT statement*

From Figure 14-4, you can see that the second execution of the stored procedure, which reuses the existing plan, uses a total of nine logical reads. The use of SQL queries instead of the cursor operations reduced the number of logical reads from 107 to 9.

Therefore, for better performance, it is always recommended that you use SQL queries instead of T-SQL cursors.

Analyzing SQL Server Overhead with API Cursors

SQL Server DBAs should always try to avoid cursors, keeping in mind that SQL Server is designed to work with sets of data, not to walk through records one by one. To improve database performance, as a matter of practice, you use the set-based operations to avoid the burden of row-by-row processing on SQL Server.

Unfortunately, the different languages used to implement the client portion of the application that consumes the data from SQL Server don't have the ability to perform set-based operations. The only option a client application has while processing a group of rows is to walk through the rows one at a time.

Therefore, it's important even for SQL Server DBAs to know how to analyze the cost of the database API cursors and minimize their cost overhead on SQL Server. So, let's roll up our sleeves and develop some understanding of the client application world that uses the result set returned by SQL Server, because ultimately it affects SQL Server performance.

As different cursor characteristics contribute to different amounts of load on SQL Server, it is always recommended that you use API cursors with the lowest cost. This often requires an analysis of the cursor type created by a database application. The database application uses a data access layer to connect to the database, and it opens a cursor to walk through the rows in the result set one at a time. The load generated by the cursor on SQL Server can be observed using the Profiler tool.

Let's see how to analyze and optimize API cursor cost with the help of an example. Suppose you want the following functionalities in the database application:

- Display information of all shippers from the Northwind database in a web page.

- Display the last shipper's company name for modification.

- Modify the last shipper's company name.

You can implement the preceding functionality using an ASP page (analysis.asp in the download) with the following cursor characteristics, shown in the following code:

- ADO with the OLE DB provider for SQL Server.

- Dynamic cursor to allow modification to the last shipper's company name. Note that the Open method of the ADODB.Recordset object creates the cursor.

- Optimistic cursor concurrency model to allow update through the cursor.

```
<%@ LANGUAGE="VBSCRIPT" %>
<HTML>
<HEAD><TITLE>Efficient use of Cursors</TITLE></HEAD>
<BODY>
<%
'Cursor constants
Const adOpenDynamic = 2
Const adLockOptimistic = 3

'Cursor open
Dim Conn, Rs, strConn
strConn = "Provider=SQLOLEDB;" _
          & "Data Source=<Server Name>;" _
          & "Initial Catalog=Northwind;" _
          & "User ID=<User ID>; Password=<Password>;"
Set Conn = Server.CreateObject("ADODB.Connection")
Conn.Open strConn
Set Rs = Server.CreateObject("ADODB.Recordset")
'Declare and open an API cursor to retrieve shippers
'information
Rs.Open "SELECT * FROM Shippers", Conn, adOpenDynamic, adLockOptimistic
%>

<!--Display information of all Shippers-->
<TABLE BORDER="1">
  <TR><TH>Shipper ID</TH><TH>Company Name</TH></TR>
  <%Do While Not Rs.EOF%>
  <!--Display information of a shipper by processing one row
  at a time-->
  <TR><TD><%=Rs("ShipperID")%></TD><TD><%=Rs("CompanyName")%></TD></TR>
  <%
  Rs.MoveNext
  Loop
  %>
</TABLE>

<!--Display Company Name of last Shipper-->
<BR>Company name of the last shipper is
<%Rs.MovePrevious%>
<INPUT TYPE=TEXT VALUE="<%=Rs("CompanyName")%>" SIZE=40>
```

```
<%
'Update the last shipper's company name
'Modify the row through the cursor
Rs("CompanyName") = left(Rs("CompanyName"),16) & CStr(now)
Rs.update

'Close the cursor and release all resources assigned to the
'cursor
Rs.close
Set Rs = Nothing
Conn.close
Set Conn = Nothing
%>
</BODY>
</HTML>
```

TIP Any ASP expert will recommend that all the server-side scripting (included within <% %>) should be written within a single server-side scripting group—in other words, within one set of <% and %> tags. This will reduce the number of interactions between the ASP engine and the script engine. It is different in the code in this section for code readability purposes.

The preceding code will deliberately produce bad performance, and you can see the cursor activities on SQL Server in the Profiler trace output shown in Figure 14-5.

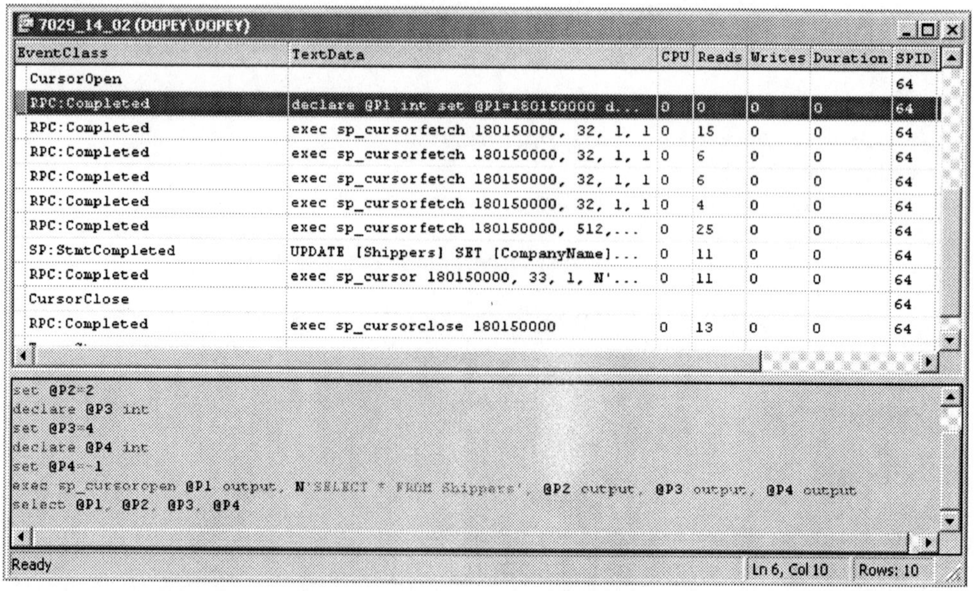

EventClass	TextData	CPU	Reads	Writes	Duration	SPID
CursorOpen						64
RPC:Completed	declare @P1 int set @P1=180150000 d...	0	0	0	0	64
RPC:Completed	exec sp_cursorfetch 180150000, 32, 1, 1	0	15	0	0	64
RPC:Completed	exec sp_cursorfetch 180150000, 32, 1, 1	0	6	0	0	64
RPC:Completed	exec sp_cursorfetch 180150000, 32, 1, 1	0	6	0	0	64
RPC:Completed	exec sp_cursorfetch 180150000, 32, 1, 1	0	4	0	0	64
RPC:Completed	exec sp_cursorfetch 180150000, 512,...	0	25	0	0	64
SP:StmtCompleted	UPDATE [Shippers] SET [CompanyName]...	0	11	0	0	64
RPC:Completed	exec sp_cursor 180150000, 33, 1, N'...	0	11	0	0	64
CursorClose						64
RPC:Completed	exec sp_cursorclose 180150000	0	13	0	0	64

```
set @P2=2
declare @P3 int
set @P3=4
declare @P4 int
set @P4=-1
exec sp_cursoropen @P1 output, N'SELECT * FROM Shippers', @P2 output, @P3 output, @P4 output
select @P1, @P2, @P3, @P4
```

Ready   Ln 6, Col 10   Rows: 10

Figure 14-5. *Profile trace output showing database requests made by the API cursor*

As shown in Figure 14-5, the database API cursor uses special system stored procedures to perform cursor operations on the server. They can be mapped to the T-SQL cursor statements as shown in Table 14-3.

Table 14-3. *Mapping Between T-SQL Cursor and API Cursor Operations*

T-SQL Cursor Statement	System Stored Procedure for API Cursors
DECLARE/OPEN	sp_cursoropen
FETCH	sp_cursorfetch
UPDATE/DELETE with WHERE CURRENT OF	sp_cursor
CLOSE/DEALLOCATE	sp_cursorclose

These stored procedures are server extended stored procedures and are intended only for the internal use of the database API cursors. For a complete list of extended stored procedures, execute this SQL statement:

EXEC sp_helpextendedproc

The full potential of these system stored procedures is available to the database applications through the database API cursors. Direct use of these stored procedures by client applications is not supported.

You can see that a cursor was opened at the server, as indicated by the CursorOpen event (or the sp_cursoropen system stored procedure). The rows from the cursor were fetched using the system stored procedure sp_cursorfetch. The modification to the last shipper's company name was performed through the system stored procedure sp_cursor. Finally, the cursor was closed as indicated by the CursorClose event (or the sp_cursorclose system stored procedure). All in all, a large number of activities was performed on SQL Server with the following cost considerations:

- The large number of activities on SQL Server impacts the server resources.

- A separate round-trip for every cursor row fetch hurts the application performance.

The sp_cursorfetch stored procedure has been executed five times: three times to fetch three rows from the Shippers table, one time at the end of processing all cursor rows, and one time to scroll backward (using the Rs.MovePrevious statement). The multiple round-trips to the server to fetch the three rows from the underlying table (Shippers) can be reduced using the CacheSize property of ADO. The default value of the CacheSize property is 1, which means only one row is fetched by the sp_cursorfetch stored procedure.

You can increase the CacheSize property to fetch multiple rows with one execution of the sp_cursorfetch stored procedure:

```
...
'Declare and open an API cursor to retrieve shippers
'information
Rs.CacheSize = 3 'Increase CacheSize to fetch the 3 cursor
                 'rows in one round-trip
Rs.Open "SELECT * FROM Shippers", Conn, adOpenDynamic, adLockOptimistic
...
```

Figure 14-6 shows the resultant Profiler trace output.

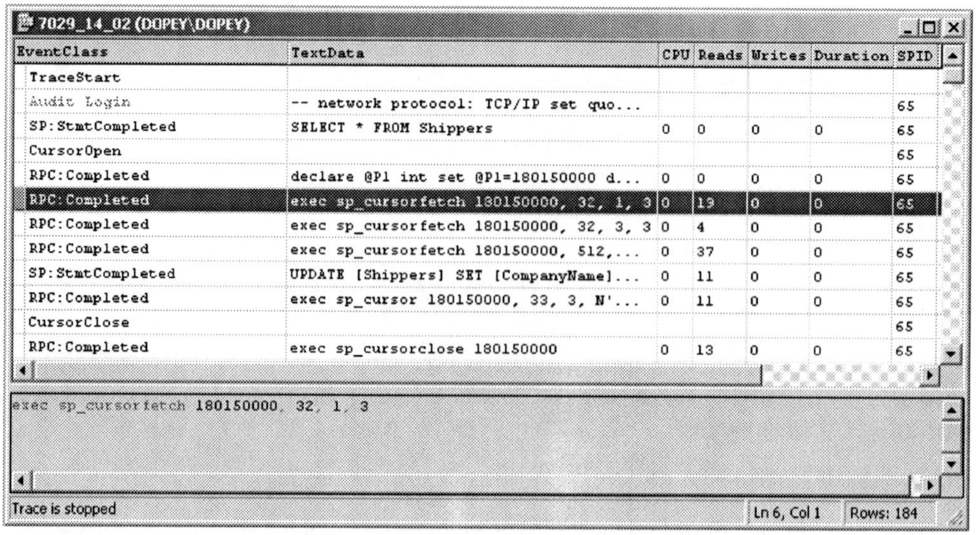

Figure 14-6. *Profiler trace output showing a reduced number of database requests with increased cache size*

The first execution of the sp_cursorfetch stored procedure retrieved all three cursor rows in one round-trip. As mentioned previously, the remaining two executions of the sp_cursor-fetch stored procedure are performed at the end of processing all cursor rows and also to scroll backward to fetch the last row again. The use of the CacheSize property reduced the execution of the sp_cursorfetch stored procedure by fetching all the rows of the cursor in one round-trip. The effect of the CacheSize property becomes more significant as the number of rows in the cursor increases.

You can optimize the preceding costs associated with the API cursor by modifying the cursor characteristics to use a low-cost cursor:

- Use a client-side cursor to prevent the multiple network round-trips.

- Use a static cursor to prevent the overhead of modifying through the cursor. Perform the modification by executing a T-SQL UPDATE statement through the Connection object instead of modifying it through the Recordset object.

- Use read-only concurrency for the cursor, since the modification is not performed through the Recordset object.

The updated ASP file is as follows (corrected_analysis.asp in the download):

```
<%@ LANGUAGE="VBSCRIPT" %>
<HTML>
<HEAD><TITLE>Efficient use of Cursors</TITLE></HEAD>
<BODY>
<%
```

```
'Cursor constants
Const adUseClient = 3 'Server-side cursor NOT required
Const adOpenStatic = 3 'Dynamic cursor NOT required
Const adLockReadOnly = 1 'Optimistic concurrency model NOT required

'Cursor open
Dim Conn, Rs, strConn
strConn = "Provider=SQLOLEDB;" _
          & "Data Source=<Server Name>;" _
          & "Initial Catalog=Northwind;" _
          & "User ID=<User ID>; Password=<Password>;"
Set Conn = Server.CreateObject("ADODB.Connection")
Conn.Open strConn
Set Rs = Server.CreateObject("ADODB.Recordset")
'Declare and open an API cursor to retrieve shippers
'information
'Cursor location: Client-side
Rs.CursorLocation = adUseClient
'Cursor type: Static; Cursor concurrency: Read-only
Rs.Open "SELECT * FROM Shippers", Conn, adOpenStatic, adLockReadOnly
%>

<!--Display information of all Shippers-->
<TABLE BORDER="1">
   <TR><TH>Shipper ID</TH><TH>Company Name</TH></TR>
   <%Do While Not Rs.EOF%>
   <!--Display information of a shipper by processing one row at a time-->
   <TR><TD><%=Rs("ShipperID")%></TD><TD><%=Rs("CompanyName")%></TD></TR>
   <%
   Rs.MoveNext
   Loop
   %>
</TABLE>

<!--Display Company Name of last Shipper-->
<BR>Company name of the last shipper is
<%Rs.MovePrevious%>
<INPUT TYPE=TEXT VALUE="<%=Rs("CompanyName")%>" SIZE=40>

<%
'Update the last shipper's company name
'Modify the row directly using SQL statement without going
'through the cursor
Conn.execute "UPDATE Shippers " _
         & "SET CompanyName = '" & Left(Rs("CompanyName"),16) & CStr(now) & "' " _
         & "WHERE ShipperID = " & Rs("ShipperID")

'Close the cursor and release all resources assigned to the
'cursor
```

```
Rs.close
Set Rs = Nothing
Conn.close
Set Conn = Nothing
%>
</BODY>
</HTML>
```

Figure 14-7 shows the resultant Profiler trace output.

Figure 14-7. *Profiler trace output showing a minimal number of database requests made by an optimized API cursor*

You can see that modifying the cursor characteristics reduces both the network round-trips and the impact on server resources. Also, consider the fact that a significant cost overhead is associated with modifying a row through the cursor (or Recordset). Modifying a row directly using a T-SQL statement is always cheaper than modifying the row through the cursor.

Most of these cursor costs have been avoided in ADO.NET (the .NET version of ADO) by always disconnecting the Recordset object once the rows are fetched. The Recordset object implemented by ADO.NET is a disconnected record set. By using the disconnected record set, the client application can cache the records at the client side, and can thereby optimize the network round-trips and the impact on server resources. This can also be done with conventional ADO by initializing the CursorLocation to adUseClient and disconnecting the Recordset object immediately after the Recordset.Open method returns.

The Microsoft Knowledge Base article "How to Create ADO Disconnected Recordsets in VBA/C++/Java" (http://support.microsoft.com/default.aspx?scid=kb;en-us;Q184397) provides more information on how to do this.

Cursor Recommendations

As demonstrated in the example in the previous section, small changes to the cursor characteristics can make a big impact on performance. An ineffective use of cursors can degrade the application performance by introducing extra network round-trips and load on server resources. To keep the cursor cost low, try to follow these recommendations:

- Use set-based SQL statements over T-SQL cursors, since SQL Server is designed to work with sets of data.

- Use the least expensive cursor:

  - While using SQL Server cursors, use the FAST_FORWARD cursor type, which is generally referred to as the fast forward–only cursor.

  - While using the API cursors implemented by ADO, OLE DB, or ODBC, use the default cursor type, which is generally referred to as the default result set.

  - While using ADO.NET, use the DataReader object.

- Minimize impact on server resources:

  - Use a client-side cursor for API cursors.

  - Do not perform actions on the underlying table(s) through the cursor.

  - Always deallocate the cursor as soon as possible.

  - Redesign the cursor's SELECT statement (or the application) to return the minimum set of rows and columns.

  - Avoid T-SQL cursors by rewriting the cursor's SELECT statement as joins and/or subqueries, which are generally more efficient than cursors.

  - Use a TIMESTAMP column for dynamic cursors to benefit from the efficient version-based concurrency control compared to the value-based technique.

- Minimize impact on tempdb:

  - Minimize resource contention in tempdb by avoiding the static and keyset-driven cursor types.

  - Minimize latch contention in tempdb. When a static or keyset-driven cursor is opened in SQL Server, the tempdb database is used to hold either the keyset or the snapshot for the cursor management. It creates "worktables" in the tempdb database.

    Creating a lot of worktables can cause latch contention in the tempdb database on the Page Free Space (PFS) or Global Allocation Map (GAM) page. In that case, the output of the sysprocesses system table will show a lastwaittype of PAGELATCH_EX or LATCH_EX and the waitresource will show 2:1:1 (for PFS) or 2:1:2 (for GAM). Spreading the tempdb database among multiple files generally minimizes the contention on the GAM page.

    SQL Server uses GAM pages to record which extents have been allocated. Each GAM page covers 64,000 extents with a bit for each extent. A 1 in a bit position indicates that the extent is free. Otherwise, the extent has been allocated. Once an extent has been allocated to a database object, SQL Server uses PFS pages to record the use of pages in the extent. Each PFS page covers approximately 8,000 pages with a bitmap for each page recording whether the page is empty, 1–50% full, 51–80% full, 81–95% full, or 96–100% full. SQL Server uses this information to find a page with free space when a row is inserted.

- Avoid the dynamic cursor type, even though dynamic cursors do not contribute to PFS latch contention in the tempdb database as much as the static or keyset-driven cursors do. However, the amount of activity on the tempdb database with dynamic cursors is sufficient to bottleneck on allocation page latches.

- Reduce the autogrow overhead. Set the size of the tempdb database to the maximum size it may grow to. Generally, it is recommended that you keep this feature on and set the autogrow increment large enough for all databases, to reduce the autogrow overhead. For example, the autogrow feature of the tempdb database can be turned on as follows (autogrow.sql in the download):

```
ALTER DATABASE [tempdb] MODIFY FILE
( NAME = N'tempdev' --tempdb database-file name
  , MAXSIZE = UNLIMITED
  , FILEGROWTH = 10%
)
ALTER DATABASE [tempdb] MODIFY FILE
( NAME = N'templog' --tempdb log-file name
  , MAXSIZE = UNLIMITED
  , FILEGROWTH = 10%
)
GO
```

- Minimize blocking:

  - Use the default result set, fast forward–only cursor, or static cursor.

  - Process all cursor rows as quickly as possible.

  - Avoid SCROLL_LOCKS or pessimistic locking.

- Minimize network round-trips while using API cursors:

  - Use the CacheSize property of ADO to fetch multiple rows in one round-trip.

  - Use client-side cursors.

  - Use disconnected record sets.

Summary

As you learned in this chapter, a cursor is the natural extension to the result set returned by SQL Server, enabling the calling application to process one row of data at a time. Cursors add a cost overhead to application performance and impact the server resources.

You should always be looking for ways to avoid cursors. However, if the cursor operation is mandated, then choose the best combination of cursor location, concurrency, type, and cache size characteristics to minimize the cost overhead of the cursor.

In the next chapter, I will discuss the performance overheads of database connections and how to optimize these costs.

■■■

CHAPTER 15

Database Connection Performance Issues

If you want to execute T-SQL queries from an application, you will need to establish a connection between SQL Server and the application. The time required to open this connection adds to the overall response time of the database request. The connection will also consume server resources, impacting the scalability of the server. Thus, you need to know how to optimize the overhead associated with database connections, improving the performance and scalability of your application requests.

In this chapter, I cover the following topics:

- Costs associated with database connections

- The ODBC and OLE DB connection-pooling mechanisms for SQL Server

- The effect of ADO/ADO.NET's threading model on connection cost

- How to choose the data access layer

- How to choose the network transfer protocols

- Recommendations for optimizing the database connection cost

Database Connection Cost

The main server resource that database connections consume is the memory required to save the context information of the connection. SQL Server 2000 is very efficient in storing the context information, typically using 24KB of memory per context. This 24KB consists of a fixed 12KB, plus 3 times the network packet size, where the network packet size is the size of the Tabular Data Scheme (TDS) packets used by SQL Server to communicate between the client and the database server. The default network packet size is 4KB, and you can configure it using the sp_configure system stored procedure as follows:

```
sp_configure "network packet size", 4096
RECONFIGURE WITH OVERRIDE
GO
```

It is generally recommended that you stick with the default network packet size. You may increase the size if the application interacting with the server mostly sends/reads a large amount of data, reducing the number of network packets to be accessed.

For example, consider an administrative functionality that executes Data Transformation Services (DTS) packages to import (or export) a large amount of data from SQL Server. If this functionality is executed during off-peak hours, and the size of the data imported (or exported) is much greater than 4KB, then you can increase the network packet size so the work can be accomplished with fewer network reads and writes. But you should consider this change only if you are certain that an increase of the network packet size will benefit the application.

As usual, your best bet is to validate your prediction through testing. Keep in mind that the network packet size of 4KB usually works well for most applications.

Unlike memory, CPU cycles are not consumed for the complete duration for which a connection remains open. CPU cycles are mainly consumed during connection open and close requests. With proper use of connection pooling, which allows reuse of connections between multiple connection requests (as explained in the following section), the CPU cost overhead can be greatly optimized.

■**NOTE** The CPU cost overhead for database connections with and without reuse of connection is demonstrated through an example later in this chapter.

The other factor to consider is the time it takes to establish the connection context when a request to the database is made. Even for a simple query, the time required to open a connection to the database can be quite significant. Again, you can minimize this overhead by using connection pooling.

Connection Pooling

Connection pooling allows an inactive connection to be cached for reuse. When an application closes a connection, the connection pooling mechanism holds the connection in a pool, preventing the connection from actually closing. The next connection open request by the application can be served directly from the pool, without requesting a new connection to SQL Server. The connection pooling technique saves the time that would otherwise be required to establish new connections.

Both the OLE DB provider and ODBC driver for SQL Server provide connection pooling, which is enabled by default. When enabled, a request for a connection is handled in one of three ways:

- If there is no connection in the pool, a new connection is created and returned to the application.

- If a connection is available in the pool and the connection properties (User ID, Password, and so on) requested by the application match the connection properties of the pooled connection, the open connection from the pool is returned to the application.

- If connections exist in the pool, but the properties requested for the new connection do not match the properties of any of the connections in the pool, a new connection with the required properties is created and returned to the application.

Connection pooling has the following benefits:

- *Reduced connection open time*: It saves time otherwise required to establish a new connection on every `connection open` request.

- *Reduced network pressure*: Reusing a pooled connection reduces network latency, since the connection open request is served locally from the pool, without going across the network to establish a connection.

- *Reduced server memory and CPU pressure*: A limited number of pooled connections can be multiplexed among a large number of database functionalities. By not holding the connections, the application allows the connections to be returned to the pool to be reused by other database functionalities.

To benefit from connection pooling, always close a connection at the earliest possible opportunity. The sooner you close a connection, the sooner it will be available for reuse. It is important to avoid coding connection caching in the application—it is better to leave this to the OLE DB and ODBC data access layers, which can provide a connection pool across all applications.

ODBC Connection Pooling

With ODBC, connection pooling is enabled by default. You can configure it using the ODBC Data Source Administrator tool on the client by following these steps:

1. Open the ODBC Data Source Administrator tool by clicking the Start button and selecting Settings ➤ Control Panel ➤ Administrative Tools ➤ Data Sources (ODBC) on the client (see Figure 15-1).

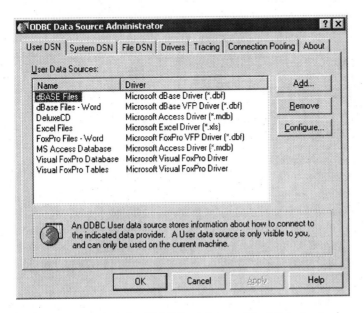

Figure 15-1. *Opening the ODBC Data Source Administrator tool*

2. On the Connection Pooling tab, double-click the name of the driver used by the application. In this case, it is SQL Server, as shown in Figure 15-2.

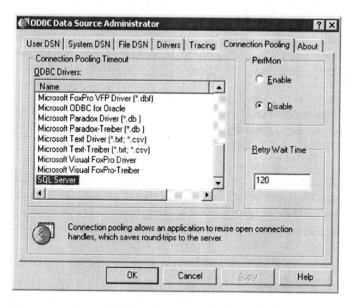

Figure 15-2. *Selecting the SQL Server ODBC driver*

3. In the Set Connection Pooling Attributes dialog box, ensure that the option "Pool Connections to this driver" is selected with a timeout value set to 60 seconds, as shown in Figure 15-3.

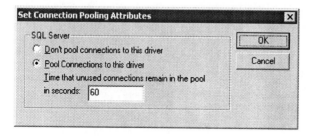

Figure 15-3. *Setting connection pooling attributes for SQL Server*

The option "Pool Connections to this driver" enables connection pooling for the database connections established using this ODBC driver. The time parameter for this option defines the time (in seconds) that an unused connection will remain in the pool. The other option, "Don't pool connections to this driver," is provided to disable connection pooling, if required. Generally, it is not recommended that you disable connection pooling.

4. Close all the dialog boxes by clicking the OK buttons.

Alternatively, if your version of the ODBC Data Source Administrator tool is below 3.5, then you can find the timeout value for the ODBC driver for SQL Server in the registry at the following registry key:

- *Key*: HKEY_LOCAL_MACHINE\SOFTWARE\ODBC\ODBCINST.INI\SQL Server
- *Name*: CPTimeout
- *Type*: REG_SZ
- *Data*: <Seconds>

The ODBC driver manager controls the number of connections in the pool based on the usage of the connections. A connection is dropped out of the pool if it is not used for more than the timeout setting for the driver. When the timeout for a connection expires, the ODBC driver manager requests SQL Server to close the connection and removes the closed connection from the pool. The timeout (CPTimeout) setting for an ODBC driver applies to all the connections. The default timeout value is 60 seconds. Setting the timeout value to 0 disables connection pooling. If the registry entry CPTimeout for an ODBC driver does not exist, the connection pooling will be disabled for that ODBC driver.

OLE DB Session Pooling

As with ODBC, OLE DB connection pooling, commonly referred to as *OLE DB session pooling*, is enabled by default. You can change (or add) the following registry entry for each individual OLE DB provider whose session pooling needs to be controlled (enabled/disabled):

- *Key*: HKEY_CLASSES_ROOT\CLSID\<CLSID of OLEDB Provider>
- *Name*: OLEDB_SERVICES
- *Type*: REG_DWORD
- *Data*: ffffffff

The OLEDB_SERVICES entry is a hex value, and you should set it to ffffffff to enable OLE DB session pooling for the provider. Setting the value to 0 disables session pooling for the provider.

Every OLE DB provider has a unique CLSID, which is defined in the registry under the HKEY_CLASSES_ROOT key. Within the HKEY_CLASSES_ROOT key, providers must have the following subkeys and values for the programmatic identifier (ProgID) of the OLE DB provider:

- *Key*: HKEY_CLASSES_ROOT\<ProgID of OLEDB Provider>
- *Name*: (Default)
- *Type*: REG_SZ
- *Data*: <Friendly name of OLE DB Provider>

The CLSID subkey values for the OLE DB provider's ProgID are as follows:

- *Key*: HKEY_CLASSES_ROOT\<ProgID of OLEDB Provider>\CLSID
- *Name*: (Default)
- *Type*: REG_SZ
- *Data*: <CLSID of OLE DB Provider>

For example, the entries for the OLE DB provider for SQL Server, SQLOLEDB, are as follows:

- *Key*: HKEY_CLASSES_ROOT\SQLOLEDB

- *Data*: Microsoft OLE DB Provider for SQL Server

The CLSID subkey values for the SQLOLEDB provider are as follows:

- *Key*: HKEY_CLASSES_ROOT\SQLOLEDB\CLSID

- *Data*: {0C7FF16C-38E3-11d0-97AB-00C04FC2AD98}

The properties of the OLE DB provider are defined under the HKEY_CLASSES_ROOT\CLSID key. The following are the CLSIDs for some of the commonly used Microsoft OLE DB providers:

- SQLOLEDB (SQL Server native provider): HKEY_CLASSES_ROOT\CLSID\{0C7FF16C-38E3-11d0-97AB-00C04FC2AD98}

- Microsoft.Jet.OLEDB.4.0 (Jet native provider): HKEY_CLASSES_ROOT\CLSID\{dee35070-506b-11cf-b1aa-00aa00b8de95}

- MSDAORA (Oracle native provider): HKEY_CLASSES_ROOT\CLSID\{e8cc4cbe-fdff-11d0-b865-00a0c9081c1d}

- MSDASQL (OLE DB Provider for ODBC): HKEY_CLASSES_ROOT\CLSID\{c8b522cb-5cf3-11ce-ade5-00aa0044773d}

The session pooling can also be controlled at the connection level—in other words, for a specific connection—by using the OLE DB Services flag in the connection string while establishing the OLE DB connection, as shown in this ASP code snippet:

```
<%
Dim strConn, Conn
strConn = "Provider=SQLOLEDB;" _
        & "Data Source=<Server Name>;" _
        & "Initial Catalog=Northwind;" _
        & "User ID=<User ID>; Password=<Password>;" _
        & "OLE DB Services=-1;"
Set Conn = CreateObject("ADODB.Connection")
Conn.Open strConn
%>
```

Setting the OLE DB Services flag to -1 enables OLE DB session pooling. A value of 0 for this flag disables the session pooling, and setting this flag in the connection string overrides what is set in the registry for OLEDB_SERVICES.

You can control the duration for which an OLE DB connection will be pooled through registry entries. There are two global entries for all OLE DB providers, one entry for each individual provider. You can add these entries to the registry manually.

The following registry entry should be created for each OLE DB provider whose session pooling timeout needs to be configured:

- *Key*: HKEY_CLASSES_ROOT\CLSID\<CLSID of OLEDB Provider>

- *Name*: SPTimeout

- *Type*: REG_DWORD

- *Data*: <Seconds>

The value of SPTimeout represents the number of seconds for which an unused OLE DB connection remains in the pool before timing out and closing. If the SPTimeout registry value for an OLE DB provider is not created, then the default timeout value will be 60 seconds.

The following two registry entries are global to all OLE DB providers:

- *Key*: HKEY_LOCAL_MACHINE\SOFTWARE\Microsoft\DataAccess\Session Pooling

- *Name*: Retry Wait

- *Type*: REG_DWORD

- *Data*: <Seconds>

The ExpBackOff entry is as follows:

- *Key*: HKEY_LOCAL_MACHINE\SOFTWARE\Microsoft\DataAccess\Session Pooling

- *Name*: ExpBackOff

- *Type*: REG_DWORD

- *Data*: <Seconds>

The Retry Wait entry is congruous to the ODBC Retry Wait Time setting. It determines the amount of time the OLE DB providers will wait in the event of a failed connection before attempting to contact the server again. It defaults to 64 seconds without the registry entry. The ExpBackOff entry determines the factor by which the OLE DB providers will increase the wait time between consecutive attempts to contact the server, in the event of a failed connection. It defaults to 2 seconds without the registry entry.

Effect of Session Pooling on Performance

OLE DB session pooling is useful if the client application is designed to benefit from pooling and reusing connections. However, if the application is designed (or configured) such that every connection request is different, then the connections—even if pooled—won't benefit the application, since the new connection request will be different from the existing connections in the pool.

For instance, consider an intranet web application using a SQL Server database with both the web application and SQL Server configured to use Windows authentication. Using Windows authentication to connect to the web application as well as the database provides an integrated security environment where the Windows credentials of a user are passed all the way back to the database without repetitive authentication at different stages. This single-point authentication sounds like a dream for many network/web/database administrators, since it reduces the administrative overhead of managing user accounts at different levels. Does the application design have any side effects?

Let's see! Consider a user, say NTUser1, accessing a web page, which in turn connects to the database. The database connection is established with the Windows login credentials for NTUser1. With OLE DB session pooling enabled, the connection returns to the pool when closed. Now a second user, NTUser2, accesses the web page, which subsequently requests a database connection. Since this time the database connection is requested with the Windows login credentials for NTUser2, the pooled connection (of NTUser1) cannot be reused.

If the web page is accessed by 1,000 users, then the connection created for a user, even though pooled by default, can't be reused by the other 999 users. In such situations, the connection, or a session pooling, can be more of an overhead than of any actual benefit to the application.

In this situation, one of the easiest solutions to improve performance can be to avoid the overhead of session pooling. But usually that's not the best thing to do. To see the effect of disabling session pooling, consider the following simple ASP page (disable_pooling.asp in the download), which requests 1,000 database connections in sequence with the OLE DB session pooling disabled:

```
<%@ LANGUAGE="VBSCRIPT" %>
<HTML>
<BODY>
<%
Dim StartTime, EndTime, strConn, Conn

'Disable OLE DB session pooling, and use Windows
'authentication
strConn = "Provider=SQLOLEDB;" _
        & "Data Source=DOPEY\DOPEY;" _
        & "Initial Catalog=Northwind;" _
        & "Integrated Security=SSPI;" _
        & "OLE DB Services=0;"
Set Conn = CreateObject("ADODB.Connection")

StartTime = Now()       'Now() is equivalent to the GETDATE()
                        'function of SQL Server
For NumberOfConn = 1 to 1000
  Conn.Open strConn     'Open a database connection
  Conn.Close            'Close the database connection
Next
EndTime = Now()

Response.Write "Time to open/close 1000 connections: " _
            & DateDiff("s", StartTime, EndTime) & " seconds."

Set Conn = Nothing
%>
</BODY>
</HTML>
```

You can analyze the overhead of database connections using the System Monitor tool with the performance counters shown in Table 15-1.

Table 15-1. *System Monitor Counters to Analyze the Effect of Session Pooling on Performance*

Performance Object	Counter	Instance
SQLServer:General Statistics	Logins/sec	
SQLServer:General Statistics	Logouts/sec	
SQLServer:General Statistics	User Connections	
Process	% Processor Time	sqlservr

TIP The name of a performance object for a default SQL Server setup includes the prefix SQLServer:, as shown in Table 15-1. For a SQL Server 2000 named instance (a nondefault setup), the prefix is MSSQL$<Instance Name>:, as shown in Figure 15-4. Also, since I run the ASP code on the same server as the SQL Server, I used the Process\%Processor Time[sqlservr] counter instead of the Processor/%Processor[_Total] counter to measure the CPU usage of SQL Server independently.

The System Monitor counter log for the preceding implementation of opening/closing 1,000 connections without OLE DB session pooling is shown in Figure 15-4, and a summary of the counter values is shown in Table 15-2.

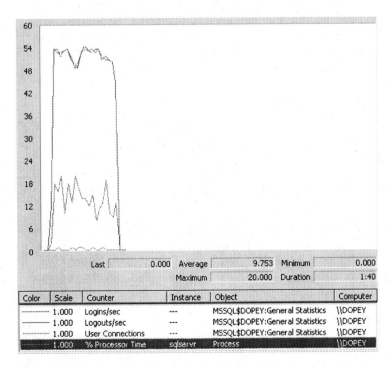

Figure 15-4. *System monitor counter log showing the system utilization without OLE DB session pooling*

Table 15-2. *System Monitor Counter Values Without OLE DB Session Pooling*

Performance Object\Counter[Instance]	Average Value
General Statistics\Logins/sec	35
General Statistics\Logouts/sec	35
General Statistics\User Connections	0.23
Process\% Processor Time[sqlservr]	9.75

From Figure 15-4, you can see that the rate of login (Logins/sec) is the same as the rate of logout (Logouts/sec). Without session pooling, a connection close request (Conn.Close) sends a logout request to the database. This closes the connection without it being made available (or pooled) for the next connection open request. Therefore, for every pair of connection open and close requests, a pair of login and logout requests is sent to the database.

Consequently, the maximum number of open connections is 1. This occurs between a pair of connection open and close requests. The number of open connections then remains at 0 until the next open connection request is issued. This is indicated by the average value of 0.23 for the User Connections counter. Since the connections are not pooled, every open and close request requires SQL Server to process the connection request, causing a CPU usage of 9.75% by SQL Server just to manage connections.

To avoid the preceding overhead of connections on SQL Server, you can enable session pooling and modify the application design to benefit from session pooling. You can use either a specific Windows user to connect to SQL Server or a SQL Server login with a specific SQL Server user for all users executing the ASP page. This will allow the connection close request to return the connection to the pool and make it available for the next connection request. To enable session pooling, modify the OLE DB Services flag to -1 as follows (pooling.asp in the download):

```
'Enable OLEDB session pooling, and use SQL Server login
strConn = "Provider=SQLOLEDB;" _
          & "Data Source=<Server Name>;" _
          & "Initial Catalog=Northwind;" _
          & "User ID=<User ID>; Password=<Password>;" _
          & "OLE DB Services=-1;"        'Or remove this flag
Set Conn = CreateObject("ADODB.Connection")
```

Since the session pooling is enabled by default, removal of the OLE DB Services flag from the connection string will also keep the session pooling ON (unless it is disabled through the registry, as explained earlier). Figure 15-5 shows the resultant System Monitor counter log and the Table 15-3 shows a summary of the counter values with and without OLE DB session pooling.

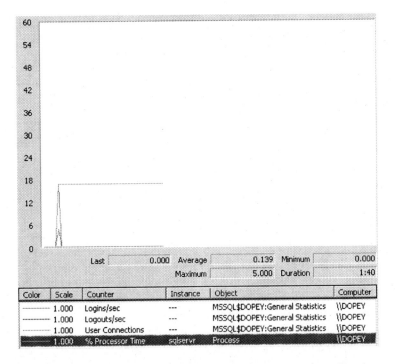

Figure 15-5. *System monitor counter log showing the system utilization with OLE DB session pooling*

▪TIP For a better comparison with the previous counter log, I've used the same Duration (0:42) for this counter log as that of the previous one.

Table 15-3. *System Monitor Counter Values with and Without OLE DB Session Pooling*

Performance Object\Counter[Instance]	Average Value	
	Session Pooling ON	**Session Pooling OFF**
General Statistics\Logins/sec	0.47	35
General Statistics\Logouts/sec	0	35
General Statistics\User Connections	14	0.23
Process\% Processor Time[sqlservr]	0.14	9.75

Table 15-4 shows the output of the ASP page.

Table 15-4. *Time to Open the Database Connections with and Without OLE DB Session Pooling*

Session Pooling	Time to Open/Close 1,000 Connections (s)
ON	2
OFF	37

From Figure 15-5, you can see that the value of Logouts/sec is 0, which means that none of the connection close requests by the ASP code were actually sent to SQL Server. With session pooling enabled, the connection close request allows the OLE DB provider for SQL Server to return the connection to the pool without sending a logout request to SQL Server. This allows the connections to be kept open and the next connection open request to be served from the pool without sending a login request to SQL Server. Consequently, the number of login requests represented by the Logins/sec counter is lower (0.47).

Since detaching a connection from a session (or a user), returning the connection to the pool, and making it available for the next connection open request takes a little while, a connection open request may not find the previous connection available for reuse immediately. Therefore, a few extra connections (User Connections = 14) are created to serve the 1,000 connection open requests. The reuse of the connection from the pool reduced the CPU usage of SQL Server to 0.14% during the same period of time compared to when session pooling was disabled. With the reduced cost overhead for the connections, the ASP page took only 2 seconds to open/close 1,000 connections.

ADO/ADO.NET Threading Model

Applications written in Microsoft development languages such as Visual Basic, or scripting languages such as VBScript (used in ASP), commonly use ADO to connect to SQL Server. ADO is a COM+ DLL (msado15.dll for ADO 2.7), and it provides database components such as Connection, Command, and Recordset to connect to the database, execute queries, and manage the returned result set. The performance of the queries executed through the ADO components depends on the threading model of ADO. The default threading model of ADO is Single Threaded Apartment (STA).

As you probably know, ASP.NET, the latest version of ASP, uses ADO.NET instead of the conventional ADO. An ASP.NET application can access SQL Server using ADO.NET classes found in the System.Data namespace (in the .NET class library) or by referencing the standard adodb .NET assembly (<Drive>:\Program Files\Microsoft.NET\Primary Interop Assemblies\ adodb.dll). If the adodb assembly is used to connect to SQL Server, then it also uses the latest version of the ADO's COM+ DLL under the hood, and thereby relies on the threading model of ADO.

The STA threading model of ADO causes some problems in the ASP.NET environment. ASP.NET uses the Multithreaded Apartment (MTA) threading model instead of the STA model. Consequently, the COM+ components referred by adodb should be configured to be free-threaded for ASP.NET applications; otherwise, a deadlock condition can occur. To avoid the possible deadlock, the .NET Framework and Visual Studio .NET setup programs automatically modify the ADO threading model when registering Aspnet_isapi.dll (a key component of ASP.NET). Another reason to manually convert ADO's threading model to free-threaded is that an instance of the ADO Connection can be cached safely by an ASP-based web application only when ADO is marked as free-threaded. But it may not be the best thing to do, as I'll discuss later in this section.

To manually configure ADO as free-threaded, use the Makfre15.bat file. This configuration file is located in the setup directory of ADO, which is typically <Drive>:\Program Files\ Common Files\System\ADO.

On a particular machine, if ADO is used in an ASP environment without being indirectly referred to (through the adodb .NET assembly) in the ASP.NET environment, then it is preferable to use the STA threading model for the ADO's COM+ DLL to improve the performance of ADO. Another reason to keep STA as the threading model of ADO is that accessing a Microsoft Access database through ADO configured as free-threaded can cause consistency issues. Furthermore, in a database application it is generally recommended that you not cache ADO Connection objects, as mentioned earlier in the connection pooling section.

In general, do not cache a part of an ADO component (say, the Connection object) globally and invoke methods on it concurrently from multiple threads. If each client request in the application invokes the Connection.Execute method on a globally cached Connection object, the application won't scale due to the synchronization overhead in the Connection.Execute method. Avoiding caching the ADO Connection eliminates the need to convert the ADO threading model to free-threaded.

The threading model of ADO can be converted to STA using the Makapt15.bat file. This configuration file is located in the same directory as Makfre15.bat, as installed by the ADO setup program.

Selecting the Data Access Mechanism

If a database application needs an extremely high degree of control over the data access mechanism, the best bet is to use ODBC and preferably OLE DB (as OLE DB is Microsoft's data access layer of choice). However, if a high degree of control is not required, or the database application uses a development language such as Visual Basic (or Visual Basic .NET), then ADO (or ADO.NET) is generally the preferred choice. Although the ADO (or ADO.NET) data access layer does not provide the maximum degree of control, it does provide a powerful and easy-to-use object model. Table 15-5 lists the available data access layers, along with their properties.

Table 15-5. *Data Access Layers and Their Properties*

Data Access Layer	Standard	Degree of Developer Control	Access to SQL Server Features
ADO.NET	Emerging	Moderate	Most
OLE DB	Emerging	High	All
ODBC	Existing	High	All
RDO	Existing	Moderate	Most
DAO	Legacy	Low	Limited
DB-Library	Legacy	High	Limited

The DB-Library data access layer is still supported in SQL Server 2000, but it has not been enhanced—it ships with the same features that shipped with SQL Server 7.0. This means that a DB-Library–based application can only connect to a default instance of SQL Server 2000; it can't connect to a SQL Server 2000 named instance. In addition, it doesn't understand any of the new features available in SQL Server 7.0 and later. Since the DB-Library data access layer isn't updated to benefit from the optimizations in SQL Server 2000 and 7.0, it isn't recommended that you use DB-Library while building a new database application.

In general, for a .NET application, ADO.NET is the preferred data access mechanism. Similarly, for a conventional application (a non-.NET application), ADO is preferred.

Selecting Network Transfer Protocols

The network transfer protocol between the client application and SQL Server affects the communication speed between the client and the server. SQL Server supports different protocols, including TCP/IP and Named Pipes, to establish a connection between the client and the server.

For best performance, follow these recommendations:

- *Client and server on different machines*: Use the TCP/IP protocol.

- *Client and server on the same machine*: Use the Named Pipes protocol.

You can create these configurations using the SQL Server Client Network Utility tool, as shown in Figure 15-6.

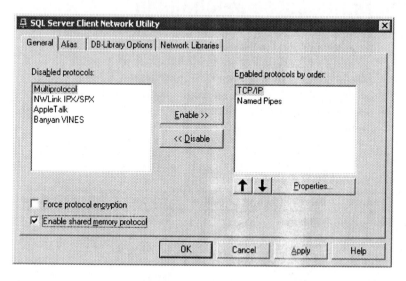

Figure 15-6. *SQL Server Client Network Utility tool*

You can install the Client Network Utility tool on a client machine by installing SQL Server Client Tools only. You can also install these tools on the server along with the SQL Server installation. When the SQL Server Client Utilities are installed on a client machine, SQL Server 2000 Setup configures the default client protocol for SQL Server–based applications to use TCP/IP. It also allows choosing a different network port for the database application and SQL Server to communicate, which is generally not required.

As shown in Figure 15-6, SQL Server 2000 (and 7.0) provides an additional Interprocess Communication (IPC) component for a local client to communicate with the server using the Shared Memory protocol. By default, a local client application and SQL Server on the same machine use this protocol. It is the most efficient communication mechanism between a client application and SQL Server on the same machine, since it uses Local Procedure Calls (LPCs) instead of Remote Procedure Calls (RPCs) to communicate.

RPCs are usually several times slower than LPCs. Also, since the Shared Memory protocol is used only for intracomputer communications, it is inherently secure and doesn't need resource-intensive encryption/decryption.

For a client application to communicate with SQL Server, the protocol used by the client application should be enabled at the server. The network protocols supported by SQL Server can be configured using the SQL Server Network Utility tool, as shown in Figure 15-7.

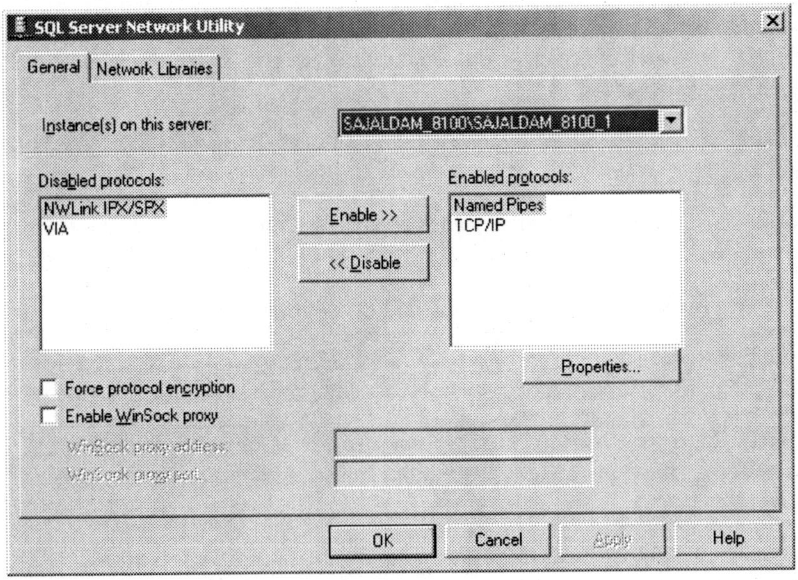

Figure 15-7. *SQL Server Network Utility tool*

SQL Server accepts communication through every protocol enabled on the server.

Database Connection Recommendations

Consider the following recommendations to reduce the overhead of the data access layer and thereby improve query performance:

- *Choose a system data source name (DSN) or DSN-less connection over a user DSN or a file DSN.* A system DSN is usually three times faster than a file DSN. You can create a system, user, or file DSN for an ODBC data source using the ODBC Data Source Administrator tool.

  Usually, a DSN-less method of specifying the connection string in the application itself (as shown in the preceding examples) is faster than using a system DSN. The DSN-less method avoids the overhead of determining the connection string from the ODBC layer. However, the system DSN method is generally preferred for its ease of reconfiguring the connection parameters and the login credentials.

- *Select a suitable network protocol.* Based on the proximity of the server and the data access tier, you should use different network protocols to communicate between the server and the data access tier, as explained in the "Selecting Network Transfer Protocols" section.

- *Reuse connections.* Use ODBC connection pooling or OLE DB session pooling, thereby reusing a locally maintained connection pool and saving the trip across the network to SQL Server for a new connection.

- *Design applications to benefit from connection pooling.* Here are some recommendations to accomplish this:

  - Open connections late and close them early to keep the connections available in the pool for reuse.

  - Always close a connection so that it is returned to the pool.

  - Avoid application-level connection caching, since both the OLE DB provider and the ODBC driver for SQL Server already automatically provide connection pooling.

  - Use a specific login credential to connect to SQL Server so that the connection requests by the application are always the same, allowing reuse of connections from the pool.

- *Use ADO.NET over ADO for .NET applications.* Being the latest data access layer, ADO.NET is more efficient than ADO. For non-.NET applications, ADO is still a good choice. For a detailed comparison between ADO.NET and ADO, please refer to the MSDN article "In-memory Representations of Data" (http://msdn.microsoft.com/library/en-us/vbcon/html/vbconADOPreviousVersionsOfADO.asp).

Summary

As described in this chapter, the cost of opening database connections affects the performance of the database requests. It also impacts the resource utilization of the server. Your selection of a data access layer should be based on the efficiency of the data access layer and the degree of flexibility required by the application. The connection pooling mechanism implemented by the ODBC driver and OLE DB provider for SQL Server helps optimize the cost overhead of database connections. To benefit from these connection pooling techniques, a database application must return connections to the pool at the earliest possible time. The threading model of ADO should also be reviewed to keep the cost of connections low.

In the next chapter, I describe how to use the performance techniques you have learned up to this point while analyzing the performance of a database workload. It's time to see the combined effect of the performance techniques and tools.

■■■

CHAPTER 16

Database Workload Optimization

Up to now, you have learned about a number of aspects that can affect query performance, the tools that you can use to analyze query performance, and the optimization techniques you can use to improve query performance. Now you need to learn how to apply this information to analyze, troubleshoot, and optimize the performance of database workload.

In this chapter, I cover the following topics:

- The characteristics of a database workload

- The steps involved in database workload optimization

- How to identify costly queries in the workload

- How to measure the baseline resource use and performance of costly queries

- How to analyze factors that affect the performance of costly queries

- How to apply techniques to optimize costly queries

- How to analyze the effects of the query optimization on the overall workload

Workload Optimization Fundamentals

Optimizing a database workload often fits the 80/20 rule: 80% of the workload consumes about 20% of server resources. Trying to optimize the performance of the majority of the workload is usually not very productive. So, the first step in workload optimization is to find the 20% of the workload that consumes 80% of the server resources.

Optimizing the workload requires a set of tools to measure the resource consumption and response time of the different parts of the workload. As you saw in Chapter 3, SQL Server provides a set of tools and utilities to analyze the performance of a database workload and individual queries.

In addition to using these tools, it is important to know how you can use different techniques to optimize a workload. The most important aspect of workload optimization to remember is that not every optimization technique is guaranteed to work on every performance problem. Many optimization techniques are specific to certain database application designs and database environments. Therefore, for each optimization technique, measure the performance of each part of the workload (that is, each individual query) before and after you apply the optimization technique. After this, measure the impact of the optimization on the complete workload.

It is not unusual to find that an optimization technique has little effect—or even a negative effect—on the other parts of the workload, which hurts the overall performance of the workload. For instance, a nonclustered index added to optimize a SELECT statement can hurt the performance of UPDATE statements that modify the value of the indexed column. The UPDATE statements have to update index rows in addition to the data rows. However, as demonstrated in Chapter 4, sometimes indexes can improve the performance of action queries, too. Therefore, improving the performance of a particular query could benefit or hurt the performance of the overall workload. As usual, your best course of action is to validate any assumptions through testing.

Workload Optimization Steps

The process of optimizing a database workload follows a specific series of steps. As part of this process, you will use the set of optimization techniques presented in previous chapters. Since every performance problem is a new challenge, a different set of optimization techniques may be used for troubleshooting different performance problems.

To understand the optimization process, you will simulate a sample workload using a set of queries. These are the optimization steps you will follow while optimizing the sample workload:

1. Capture the workload.

2. Analyze the workload.

3. Identify the costliest query.

4. Quantify the baseline resource use of costliest query:

   • Overall resource use

   • Detailed resource use

5. Analyze and optimize external factors:

   • Analyze the use of network protocol.

   • Analyze the effectiveness of statistics.

   • Analyze the need for defragmentation.

6. Analyze the internal behavior of the costliest query:

   • Analyze the query execution plan.

   • Identify the costly steps in the execution plan.

   • Analyze the effectiveness of the processing strategy.

7. Optimize the costliest query.

8. Analyze the effects of the changes on database workload.

9. Iterate through multiple optimization phases.

As explained in Chapter 1, performance tuning is an *iterative* process. Therefore, you should iterate through the performance optimization steps multiple times until the application performance targets are achieved, repeating the process after a certain time period when the workload on the database changes.

Sample Workload

To troubleshoot SQL Server performance, you need to know the SQL workload that is executed on the SQL Server. You can then analyze the workload to identify the cause of the poor performance and the applicable optimization steps. Ideally, you should capture the workload on the SQL Server facing the performance problems. You will use a set of queries to simulate a sample workload so that you can follow the optimization steps listed in the previous section. The sample workload used in this chapter consists of a combination of good and bad queries. For your convenience, you will execute the sample workload from Query Analyzer.

Also, you will set up the database objects for the sample workload so that the workload executes successfully and faces different performance overheads outside the queries. The following SQL statements create the database objects required by the queries of the sample workload (create_od.sql in the download):

```
USE Northwind
GO
--Create a test table
IF(SELECT OBJECT_ID('od')) IS NOT NULL
  DROP TABLE od
GO
SELECT * INTO od FROM [Order Details]
CREATE CLUSTERED INDEX i1 ON od(OrderID, ProductID)
ALTER TABLE od ADD Filler CHAR(50)
GO
UPDATE od SET Filler = '-1'
GO
--Create a test view
IF(SELECT OBJECT_ID('v1')) IS NOT NULL
  DROP view v1
GO
CREATE VIEW v1
AS
SELECT o.OrderID, od.ProductID, od.Quantity, od.UnitPrice
  FROM od, Orders o
  WHERE od.OrderID = o.OrderID
GO
```

This script creates a test table, od, and a test view, v1, that you can test your sample workload against. You need to use the Northwind database to populate table od.

The test workload is simulated by the following set of sample queries (workload.sql in the download) executed on the Northwind database:

```
SELECT p.SupplierID, SUM(p.UnitsInStock), SUM(p.UnitsOnOrder)
  FROM Products p
  WHERE p.SupplierID < 2
  GROUP BY p.SupplierID
GO
SELECT *
  FROM Orders o
  WHERE o.OrderID = 11070
GO
SELECT v1.OrderID, v1.ProductID, v1.Quantity, v1.UnitPrice
  FROM Products p, v1
  WHERE p.ProductID = v1.ProductID AND v1.UnitPrice < 3
  ORDER BY v1.UnitPrice
GO
SELECT od.OrderID, od.ProductID
  FROM od
  WHERE od.ProductID < 3
GO
SELECT od.OrderID, od.ProductID
  FROM od
  WHERE od.OrderID > 11000
  ORDER BY od.OrderID
GO
```

The sample workload consists of the different types of queries you usually execute on SQL Server:

- Queries using aggregate functions.

- Point queries that retrieve only one row or a small number of rows. Usually they are the best for performance.

- Queries joining multiple tables.

- Queries retrieving a narrow range of rows.

- Queries performing additional result set processing, such as providing a sorted output.

The first optimization step is to identify the worst-performing queries, as explained in the next section.

Capturing the Workload

As a part of the diagnostic-data collection step, you must trace the workload on the database server. You can trace the workload using the Profiler tool with the events and data columns as recommended in Chapter 3. To be able to follow the logical flow of execution for every SPID, do not use any filter on the Read and Duration columns (see PerformanceTraceForWorkload.pdf in the code download for this chapter). Tables 16-1 and 16-2 list some of the important events and data columns that you are specifically interested in to measure the resource intensiveness of the queries.

Table 16-1. *Events to Analyze Costly Queries*

Event Class	Event
Stored procedures	RPC:Completed
	SP:Completed
	SP:StmtCompleted
T-SQL	SQL:StmtCompleted

Table 16-2. *Data Columns to Analyze Costly Queries*

Data Columns	
Groups	
Columns	EventClass
	TextData
	CPU
	Reads
	Writes
	Duration
	SPID
	StartTime

■TIP To minimize the effect of the Profiler tool on the server performance, please follow the SQL Profiler recommendations described in Chapter 3.

As explained in Chapter 3, for production databases, it is recommended that you use the stored procedure technique of capturing the SQL trace instead of using the Profiler tool. To create the stored procedure–based SQL script file, you can script out the previous trace definition from Profiler as explained in Chapter 3. Use of the stored procedure technique of capturing the SQL workload has the following advantages over the use of Profiler:

- Since you intend to analyze the SQL queries once the workload is captured, you do not need to display the SQL queries while capturing them, as done by Profiler.

- If the database is already having performance issues, then using the stored procedure technique is more economical than using Profiler, since the stored procedure technique avoids the overheads of the Profiler tool, such as updating Profiler's display as the trace is captured.

- Profiler doesn't provide a very flexible timing control over the tracing process.

With regard to timing control, say you want to start tracing at 11:00 p.m. and capture the SQL workload for 24 hours. Profiler doesn't provide a provision to define the start time. On the other hand, since the stored procedure technique is based on SQL scripts, you can define the trace schedule by modifying the following lines of code in the SQL script file generated by Profiler:

```
-- Set the trace status to start
exec sp_trace_setstatus @TraceID, 1
```

Replace the preceding lines of code with the following lines:

```
-- Schedule the time window for tracing
-- Set these values as needed
DECLARE @StartTime DATETIME
DECLARE @Duration CHAR(5)
SET @StartTime = '23:00' -- 24 hour clock
-- To start immediately, comment the line above and uncomment the line below
--SET @StartTime = NULL -- Start immediately
SET @Duration = '24:00'
-- Start tracing at a scheduled start time
IF @StartTime IS NOT NULL
  WAITFOR TIME @StartTime
exec sp_trace_setstatus @TraceID, 1
-- Stop tracing after a scheduled duration
WAITFOR DELAY @Duration
EXEC sp_trace_setstatus @TraceID, 0
EXEC sp_trace_setstatus @TraceID, 2
```

If you want to stop the trace intermediately, you must follow these steps:

1. Determine the traceid for the running trace by using the built-in function fn_trace_getinfo:

   ```
   SELECT * FROM ::fn_trace_getinfo(default)
   ```

   From the output of the fn_trace_getinfo, determine the traceid referring to your trace file.

2. Subsequently, execute the following SQL queries to stop the trace:

```
EXEC sp_trace_setstatus <traceid>, 0
EXEC sp_trace_setstatus <traceid>, 2
```

To be able to use the stored procedure technique for the example, I have modified the SQL script file, setting @StartTime to NULL and @Duration to '00:01' (PerformanceTraceFor-Workload.sql in the download). Consequently, the trace operation will start immediately on execution of the SQL script file and will run for 1 minute.

Analyzing the Workload

Once the workload is captured in a trace file, you can analyze the workload either by using Profiler or by importing the content of the trace file into a database table.

The Profiler tool provides the following two methods of analyzing the content of the trace file, both of which are relatively straightforward.

- *Sort the trace output on a data column by altering the data column property of the trace (i.e., move the data column under the Groups category).* Profiler rearranges the content in an ascending order on the data column. For nested sorting, you may group the trace output on multiple columns. Sorting the trace output helps you to easily locate the slowest running queries and the costliest queries.

- *Filter the trace output to a selective list of data columns and events.* You may slice the trace output further by applying post filters, as explained in Chapter 3. Slicing the content helps you to focus on a selective part of the trace output.

Profiler provides limited ways of analyzing the traced output. For instance, if a query is executed frequently, then instead of looking at the cost of only the individual execution of the query, you should also try to determine the cumulative cost of the repeated execution of the query within a fixed period of time. Although the individual execution of the query may not be that costly, the query may be executed so many times that even a little optimization may make a big difference. The Profiler tool is not powerful enough to help analyze the workload in such advanced ways. For in-depth analysis of the workload, you must import the content of the trace file into a database table as follows:

```
IF(SELECT OBJECT_ID('TRACE_TABLE')) IS NOT NULL
  DROP TABLE TRACE_TABLE
GO
SELECT *, IDENTITY(INT, 1, 1) AS RowNumber INTO TRACE_TABLE
  FROM ::FN_TRACE_GETTABLE('<TraceFileName>', DEFAULT)
```

Once you have the traced content in a table, you can use SQL queries to analyze the workload, as you can do with Profiler. For example, to find the slowest queries, you may execute this SQL query:

```
SELECT *
  FROM TRACE_TABLE
  ORDER BY Duration DESC
```

Profiler does one good thing for you: it shows the name of the EventClass instead of showing the corresponding number, even though the trace file records the event number and not the event name. Thus, when you import the content of the trace file and use SQL queries to analyze the workload, you need to convert the event number to the event name to improve the trace's readability. So first build the event lookup table as follows:

```
--Bulk load trace event info into EVENT_TABLE
IF(SELECT OBJECT_ID('EVENT_TABLE')) IS NOT NULL
  DROP TABLE EVENT_TABLE
GO
CREATE TABLE EVENT_TABLE(
  EventNumber INT PRIMARY KEY,
  EventName VARCHAR(32),
  Description VARCHAR(275))
GO
BULK INSERT EVENT_TABLE FROM 'C:\Event_Table.bcp'
  WITH(FIELDTERMINATOR = '|', ROWTERMINATOR = '\n')
GO
```

NOTE The file Event_Table.bcp is included in the code download.

Subsequently, while analyzing the workload, you may join the TRACE_TABLE with the EVENT_TABLE:

```
SELECT EventName, TRACE_TABLE.*
  FROM TRACE_TABLE JOIN EVENT_TABLE
  ON TRACE_TABLE.EventClass = EVENT_TABLE.EventNumber
  ORDER BY Duration DESC
```

The objective of analyzing the workload is to identify the costliest query (or the costly queries), as explained in the following section.

Identifying the Costliest Query

As just explained, you can use Profiler or the stored procedure technique to identify the costly queries for different criteria. The queries in the workload can be sorted on the CPU, Reads, or Writes columns to identify the costliest query, as discussed in Chapter 3.

Since the total number of reads usually outnumbers the total number of writes by at least 7 to 8 times for even the heaviest OLTP database, sorting the queries on the Reads column usually identifies more bad queries than sorting on the Writes column. Also, since a query with even a small number of reads hurts performance much more than a query that consumes hundreds of CPU cycles, sorting on the Reads column generally identifies the worst queries. (The comparative effect between number of reads and CPU cycles on query performance is explained in Chapter 3.) You should identify and optimize the queries with the highest number of writes and CPU cycles only after you have optimized the queries performing excessive numbers of reads.

To analyze the sample workload for the worst-performing queries, you need to know how costly the queries are—say, in terms of number of reads. Since the number of reads performed by a query is known only after the query completes its execution, you are mainly interested in the completed events. (The rationale behind using completed events for performance analysis is explained in detail in Chapter 3.)

For presentation purposes, open the trace file in Profiler. The captured trace output, sorted on Reads, is shown in Figure 16-1.

Reads	EventClass	TextData	CPU	Writes	Duration
	TraceStart				
	ExistingConnection	-- network protocol: LPC set quoted_id...			
	SQLTransaction				
	SQLTransaction				0
	TraceStop				
2	SQL:StmtCompleted	SELECT * FROM Orders o WHERE o.O...	0	0	0
2	SQL:BatchCompleted	SELECT * FROM Orders o WHERE o.O...	0	0	0
9	SQL:StmtCompleted	SELECT p.SupplierID, SUM(p.UnitsInStoc...	0	0	0
9	SQL:BatchCompleted	SELECT p.SupplierID, SUM(p.UnitsInStoc...	0	0	0
10	SQL:StmtCompleted	SELECT od.OrderID, od.ProductID FRO...	0	0	0
10	SQL:BatchCompleted	SELECT od.OrderID, od.ProductID FRO...	0	0	0
40	SQL:StmtCompleted	SELECT od.OrderID, od.ProductID FRO...	10	0	10
40	SQL:BatchCompleted	SELECT od.OrderID, od.ProductID FRO...	10	0	10
175	SQL:StmtCompleted	SELECT v1.OrderID, v1.ProductID, v1.Qu...	10	0	10
175	SQL:BatchCompleted	SELECT v1.OrderID, v1.ProductID, v1.Qu...	10	0	10

```
SELECT v1.OrderID, v1.ProductID, v1.Quantity, v1.UnitPrice
  FROM Products p, v1
  WHERE p.ProductID = v1.ProductID AND v1.UnitPrice < 3
  ORDER BY v1.UnitPrice
```

Figure 16-1. *Profiler trace output showing the SQL workload sorted on the Reads data column*

■**TIP** To have a similar number of reads as shown in Figure 16-1, ensure that the Auto Stats properties for the database are kept in the default state—that is, ON—as recommended in Chapter 7. Even if the Auto Stats properties are left OFF, which in turn hurts the performance of one or more queries, you will be able to figure out the problem as you proceed through the optimization process.

The worst-performing query in terms of reads is highlighted in Figure 16-1 (you may have a different number of reads, but this will still be the worst-performing query) and is presented here for easy reference:

```
SELECT v1.OrderID, v1.ProductID, v1.Quantity, v1.UnitPrice
  FROM Products p, v1
  WHERE p.ProductID = v1.ProductID AND v1.UnitPrice < 3
  ORDER BY v1.UnitPrice
```

Once you've identified the worst-performing query, the next optimization step is to determine the resources consumed by the query.

Determining the Baseline Resource Use of the Costliest Query

The current resource use of the worst-performing query can be considered as a baseline figure before you apply any optimization techniques. You may apply different optimization techniques to the query, and you can compare the resultant resource use of the query with the baseline figure to determine the effectiveness of the individual optimization technique.

The resource use of a query can be presented in the following two categories:

- Overall resource use

- Detailed resource use

Overall Resource Use

The overall resource use of the query provides a gross figure for the amount of hardware resources consumed by the worst-performing query. The resource use of an optimized query can be compared with the overall resource use of the nonoptimized query, to ensure overall effectiveness of the performance techniques applied.

You can determine the overall resource use of the query from the workload trace. Table 16-3 shows the overall use of the query from the trace in Figure 16-1.

Table 16-3. *Data Columns Representing the Amount of Resources Used by a Query*

Data Column	Value	Description
Reads	175	Number of logical reads performed by the query. If a page is not found in memory, then a logical read for the page will require a physical read from the disk to fetch the page to the memory first.
Writes	0	Number of pages modified by the query.
CPU	10 ms	Amount of CPU used by the query.

The corresponding response time of the query as determined from the workload trace is

- Duration: 10 ms

NOTE In your environment, you may have different figures for the preceding data columns. Irrespective of the data columns' absolute value, it's important to keep track of these values so that you can compare them with the corresponding values later on.

Detailed Resource Use

You can break down the overall resource use of the query to locate the bottlenecks on the different database tables accessed by the query. This detailed resource use helps determine which table accesses are the most problematic. Optimizing the query that performs the maximum number of reads usually benefits performance the most.

As you saw in Chapter 3, the number of reads performed on the individual tables accessed by the query can be obtained from the STATISTICS IO output for the query. You can obtain this output by re-executing the query with the SET statements as follows (or by selecting the Set Statistics IO check box in Query Analyzer):

```
SET STATISTICS IO ON
GO
SELECT v1.OrderID, v1.ProductID, v1.Quantity, v1.UnitPrice
  FROM Products p, v1
  WHERE p.ProductID = v1.ProductID AND v1.UnitPrice < 3
  ORDER BY v1.UnitPrice
GO
SET STATISTICS IO OFF
GO
```

The STATISTICS IO output for the worst-performing query is as follows:

```
Table 'Orders'. Scan count 32, logical reads 67, physical reads 0, read-ahead⊘
 reads 0.
Table 'Products'. Scan count 32, logical reads 64, physical reads 0, read-ahead⊘
 reads 0.
Table 'od'. Scan count 1, logical reads 34, physical reads 0, read-ahead reads 0.
```

▓**TIP** To prevent the effect of first-time internal overhead, due to factors such as creation of missing statistics and creation of the execution plan on the actual number of reads performed by the query, execute the query with the SET STATISTICS IO statements twice.

The output of STATISTICS IO can be summarized as shown in Table 16-4.

Table 16-4. STATISTICS IO *Output*

Table	Reads
Orders	67
Products	64
od	34

Usually, the sum of the reads from the individual tables referred to in a query will be less than the total number of reads performed by the query, because additional pages have to be read to access internal database objects such as sysobjects, syscolumns, and sysindexes.

Once the worst-performing query is identified and its resource use is measured, the next optimization step is to determine the factors that are affecting the performance of the query. However, before you do this, you should check to see whether there are factors external to the query that might be causing the large number of reads.

Analyzing and Optimizing External Factors

Besides factors such as query design and indexing, external factors can affect query performance. Thus, before diving into the execution plan of the query, you should analyze and optimize the major external factors that can affect query performance. Here are some of those external factors:

- The network protocol used by the connection
- The statistics of the database objects accessed by the query
- The fragmentation of the database objects accessed by the query

Analyzing the Use of the Network Protocol

Choosing a proper network protocol between the server and the data access tier, as explained in Chapter 15, can keep the cost of the connection low. The protocol used by a client application (or data access tier) to connect to the server can be determined using Profiler. The Audit Login and ExistingConnection events flag the protocol used by the client application.

Since it is always recommended that you run SQL Server on a dedicated machine, client applications generally access the database remotely. As mentioned in Chapter 15, for best performance, you should always use TCP/IP for accessing SQL Server remotely. Sometimes you will access SQL Server through a Terminal Server session. Since accessing SQL Server through a Terminal Server session is not much different from accessing the SQL Server locally, you should use the Shared Memory protocol for the local clients.

In my test setup, both the client application (SQL Query Analyzer) and SQL Server are launched on the same machine. As you saw in Chapter 15, a local client application running on the same machine as SQL Server should use the Shared Memory protocol, which uses local procedure calls (LPCs) instead of remote procedure calls (RPCs). Since the current test setup has both the client application and SQL Server on the same machine, the Shared Memory protocol serves the best. Otherwise, the network protocol for the connection can be configured using the SQL Server Client Network Utility tool, as explained in Chapter 15.

Analyzing the Effectiveness of Statistics

The statistics of the database objects referred to in the query are one of the key pieces of information that the query optimizer uses to decide upon certain execution plans. As explained in Chapter 7, the optimizer generates the execution plan for a query based on the statistics of the objects referred to in the query. The optimizer looks at the statistics of the database objects referred to in the query to estimate the number of rows affected, and thereby determines the processing strategy for the query. If a database object's statistics are not accurate, then the optimizer may generate an inefficient execution plan for the query.

As explained in Chapter 7, you can determine the effectiveness of statistics for the objects referred in a query from the STATISTICS PROFILE output for the query. You can obtain the STATISTICS PROFILE output for the worst-performing query by re-executing the query with the SET statements as follows:

```
SET STATISTICS PROFILE ON
GO
SELECT v1.OrderID, v1.ProductID, v1.Quantity, v1.UnitPrice
  FROM Products p, v1
  WHERE p.ProductID = v1.ProductID AND v1.UnitPrice < 3
  ORDER BY v1.UnitPrice
GO
SET STATISTICS PROFILE OFF
GO
```

Figure 16-2 shows the output of the SET STATISTICS PROFILE statement for the worst-performing query.

	Rows	Executes	StmtText	S	N	P	P	L	A	D	EstimateRows	E	E	A	T	O	Warnings
1	32	1	SELECT v1.OrderID, v1.Product...	2	1	0	.	.	.	.	32.0	.	.	.	.	.	NULL
2	32	1	|--Sort(ORDER BY:([od].[Uni...	2	2	1	.	.	.	.	32.0	.	.	.	.	.	NULL
3	32	1	|--Nested Loops(Inner ...	2	4	2	.	.	.	.	32.0	.	.	.	.	.	NULL
4	32	1	|--Nested Loops(I...	2	6	4	.	.	.	.	32.0	.	.	.	.	.	NULL
5	32	1	| |--Clustered...	2	7	6	.	.	.	.	32.0	.	.	.	.	.	NULL
6	32	32	| |--Clustered...	2	8	6	.	.	.	.	1.0	.	.	.	.	.	NULL
7	32	32	|--Clustered Inde...	2	9	4	.	.	.	.	1.0	.	.	.	.	.	NULL

Figure 16-2. *SET STATISTICS PROFILE output for the query showing the textual execution plan of the query*

In the output of the SET STATISTICS PROFILE statement, use the following columns to determine the effectiveness of the statistics:

- Rows

- Executes

- EstimateRows

- Warnings

In Figure 16-2, the NULL values for all the steps in the Warnings column indicate that there are no missing statistics for any of the objects referred to in the query. If there are warnings, turn the auto create statistics property of the database on. In the graphical execution plan, the node accessing the database object with missing statistics is colored red. The missing statistics can be created from the graphical execution plan by selecting "Create missing statistics" from the context menu of the corresponding node. All these techniques for creating missing statistics are explained in Chapter 7.

You can determine whether or not the statistics are up to date from the Rows, Executes, and EstimateRows columns. The product of Executes and EstimateRows for a step represents the number of rows that SQL Server expects to be returned by the execution step. With up-to-date statistics, the value of the Rows column (the number of rows actually returned by a step) will be close to the product of the Executes and EstimateRows columns.

In our statistics profile, Rows = Executes × EstimateRows for all the rows. This indicates that the statistics are up to date for all the objects referred to in the query. If this is not the case, ensure that the auto update statistics property of the database is on.

Analyzing the Need for Defragmentation

As explained in Chapter 8, a fragmented table increases the number of pages to be accessed by a query. This adversely affects performance. For this reason, you should ensure that the database objects referred to in the query are not too fragmented.

You can determine the fragmentation of the three tables accessed by the worst-performing query using three DBCC SHOWCONTIG statements (showcontig.sql in the download), the first of which is as follows:

```
DBCC SHOWCONTIG(Orders)
```

The output of this DBCC SHOWCONTIG statement is as follows (you may have slightly different results, depending upon your previous use of the Northwind database):

```
DBCC SHOWCONTIG scanning 'Orders' table...
Table: 'Orders' (21575115); index ID: 1, database ID: 6
TABLE level scan performed.
- Pages Scanned................................: 20
- Extents Scanned..............................: 5
- Extent Switches..............................: 4
- Avg. Pages per Extent........................: 4.0
- Scan Density [Best Count:Actual Count].......: 60.00% [3:5]
- Logical Scan Fragmentation ..................: 0.00%
- Extent Scan Fragmentation ...................: 40.00%
- Avg. Bytes Free per Page.....................: 146.5
- Avg. Page Density (full).....................: 98.19%
DBCC execution completed. If DBCC printed error messages, contact your↵
 system administrator.
```

And next, here is the Products table:

```
DBCC SHOWCONTIG(Products)
```

```
DBCC SHOWCONTIG scanning 'Products' table...
Table: 'Products' (117575457); index ID: 1, database ID: 6
TABLE level scan performed.
- Pages Scanned................................: 1
- Extents Scanned..............................: 1
- Extent Switches..............................: 0
- Avg. Pages per Extent........................: 1.0
- Scan Density [Best Count:Actual Count].......: 100.00% [1:1]
- Logical Scan Fragmentation ..................: 0.00%
```

```
- Extent Scan Fragmentation ...................: 0.00%
- Avg. Bytes Free per Page....................: 3.0
- Avg. Page Density (full)....................: 99.96%
DBCC execution completed. If DBCC printed error messages, contact your⤶
 system administrator.
```

Finally, here is the od table:

```
DBCC SHOWCONTIG(od)
```

```
DBCC SHOWCONTIG scanning 'od' table...
Table: 'od' (1368391944); index ID: 1, database ID: 6
TABLE level scan performed.
- Pages Scanned...............................: 33
- Extents Scanned.............................: 8
- Extent Switches.............................: 23
- Avg. Pages per Extent.......................: 4.1
- Scan Density [Best Count:Actual Count].......: 20.83% [5:24]
- Logical Scan Fragmentation ..................: 51.52%
- Extent Scan Fragmentation ...................: 37.50%
- Avg. Bytes Free per Page....................: 2806.5
- Avg. Page Density (full)....................: 65.33%
DBCC execution completed. If DBCC printed error messages, contact your⤶
 system administrator.
```

From the output of the preceding DBCC SHOWCONTIG statements, the fragmentation of the
Orders and Products tables can be summarized as follows:

- Extent Switches = Extents Scanned – 1

- Logical Scan Fragmentation = 0%

As you saw in Chapter 8, the preceding two facts indicate that the Products and Orders
tables have almost no fragmentation.

However, the DBCC SHOWCONTIG output for the od table indicates that the table is highly
fragmented. This output can be summarized as follows:

- Extent Switches = 23, whereas Extents Scanned = 8

- Logical Scan Fragmentation = 51.52%

With the number of extents (Extents Scanned) being 8, the number of switches among
the extents (Extent Switches) should ideally be 7. The large number of extent switches indicates that the pages in the extents are not laid out in the proper order. The fragmentation of
table od is also indicated by the high value for Logical Scan Fragmentation. Both these factors
indicate that table od is highly fragmented.

You can resolve this fragmentation by using the DBCC DBREINDEX statement:

DBCC DBREINDEX(od)

Now if you run DBCC SHOWCONTIG(od) again, you get this:

```
DBCC SHOWCONTIG scanning 'od' table...
Table: 'od' (1368391944); index ID: 1, database ID: 6
TABLE level scan performed.
- Pages Scanned...............................: 22
- Extents Scanned.............................: 3
- Extent Switches.............................: 2
- Avg. Pages per Extent.......................: 7.3
- Scan Density [Best Count:Actual Count].......: 100.00% [3:3]
- Logical Scan Fragmentation ..................: 0.00%
- Extent Scan Fragmentation ...................: 0.00%
- Avg. Bytes Free per Page....................: 161.7
- Avg. Page Density (full)....................: 98.00%
DBCC execution completed. If DBCC printed error messages, contact your⏎
  system administrator.
```

The output of the DBCC SHOWCONTIG statement for the od table indicates that the fragmentation of the table is removed.

With the fragmentation of the tables analyzed and resolved, the number of reads for the tables accessed by the worst-performing query should be reduced. Now, you can run the query again:

```
SET STATISTICS IO ON
GO
SELECT v1.OrderID, v1.ProductID, v1.Quantity, v1.UnitPrice
  FROM Products p, v1
  WHERE p.ProductID = v1.ProductID AND v1.UnitPrice < 3
  ORDER BY v1.UnitPrice
GO
SET STATISTICS IO OFF
GO
```

The resultant STATISTICS IO output for the query is as follows:

```
Table 'Orders'. Scan count 32, logical reads 67, physical reads 0, read-ahead⏎
  reads 0.
Table 'Products'. Scan count 32, logical reads 64, physical reads 0, read-ahead⏎
  reads 0.
Table 'od'. Scan count 1, logical reads 23, physical reads 0, read-ahead reads 0.
```

■**NOTE** To prevent the effect of first-time internal overhead due to factors such as creation of missing statistics and creation of the execution plan (after defragmentation) on the actual number of reads performed by the query, execute the query with the SET STATISTICS IO statements twice.

The number of reads for the od table is reduced from 34 to 23. Once again, in your environment, the absolute figures may be different, but the important factor is the reduction in number of reads.

Once you've analyzed the external factors that can affect the performance of a query and resolved the nonoptimal ones, you should analyze internal factors such as improper indexing and query design.

Analyzing the Internal Behavior of the Costliest Query

Now that the statistics are up to date, you can analyze the processing strategy for the query chosen by the optimizer to determine the internal factors affecting the query's performance. Analyzing the internal factors that can affect query performance involves these steps:

- Analyzing the query execution plan

- Identifying the costly steps in the execution plan

- Analyzing the effectiveness of the processing strategy

Analyzing the Query Execution Plan

To see the execution plan, turn Query ➤ Show Execution Plan on. The graphical execution plan of the worst performing query is shown in Figure 16-3.

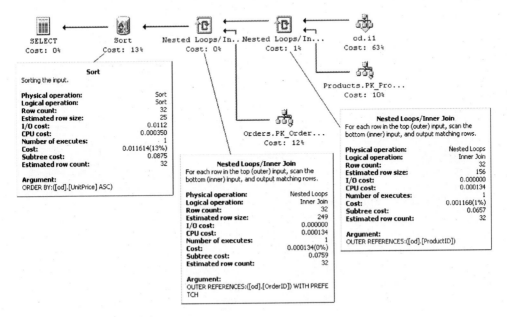

Figure 16-3. *Graphical execution plan of the query*

You can observe the following from this execution plan, as explained in Chapter 3:

- Data access:

  - Index scan on clustered index od.i1

  - Index seek on clustered index Products.PK_Products

  - Index seek on clustered index Orders.PK_Orders

- JOIN strategy:

  - Nested inner loop JOIN between the od and Products tables with the od table as the outer table

  - Nested inner loop JOIN between the od and Orders tables with the od table as the outer table

- Additional processing:

  - Sort on od.UnitPrice in ascending order

Identifying the Costly Steps in the Execution Plan

Once you understand the execution plan of the query, the next step is to identify the costly steps in the execution plan. The optimization of the costly steps usually benefits the query performance the most. You can see that the following are the two costliest steps:

- *Costly step 1*: Index scan on clustered index od.i1: 63%

- *Costly step 2*: Sort on od.UnitPrice: 13%

The next optimization step is to analyze the costly steps, determining whether these steps can be optimized through techniques such as redesigning the query or indexes.

Analyzing the Effectiveness of the Processing Strategy

Figure 16-4 presents a detailed description for costly step 1.

From this, you can see that the filter criterion for the data retrieval from the od table is on the UnitPrice column, as indicated by the WHERE clause. However, index i1 is on the OrderID and ProductID columns. This mismatch between the filter criterion and the index chosen indicates that the index on column UnitPrice is probably missing, which is true in the current situation. (Ways to analyze index effectiveness are explained in detail in Chapter 3.)

Costly step 2 performed a sort on column od.UnitPrice. If the data from the od table had been retrieved using an index on the od.UnitPrice column, then the retrieved data would have been presorted on column od.UnitPrice. The current data retrieval from the od table using index i1 caused the additional sort step on column od.UnitPrice.

```
                    Clustered Index Scan
Scanning a clustered index, entirely or only a range.

Physical operation:              Clustered Index Scan
Logical operation:               Clustered Index Scan
Row count:                                         32
Estimated row size:                                48
I/O cost:                                      0.0531
CPU cost:                                     0.00244
Number of executes:                                 1
Cost:                              0.055583(63%)
Subtree cost:                                  0.0555
Estimated row count:                               32

Argument:
OBJECT:([NWTest].[dbo].[od].[i1]), WHERE:([od].[UnitPri
ce]<3.00)
```

Figure 16-4. *Detailed description from the graphical plan of the data retrieval step od.i1*

TIP At times you may find no improvements can be made to the most costly step in a processing strategy. In that case, concentrate on the next most costly step to identify the problem. If none of the steps can be optimized further, then move on to the next costliest query in the workload.

Optimizing the Costliest Query

Once you've diagnosed the problems with the costly steps, the next stage is to implement the necessary corrections to reduce the cost of the query.

The corrective actions for a problematic step can have one or more alternative solutions. For example, should you create a new index on a limited number of columns or on a large number of columns? In such cases, prioritize the solutions based on their expected effectiveness. For example, if a narrow index can more or less do the job of a wider index, then it is usually better to prioritize the narrow index solution over the wider index solution.

Apply the solutions individually in the order of their expected benefit, and measure their individual effect on the query performance. You can finally apply the solution that provides the greatest performance improvement to correct the problematic step. Sometimes it may be evident that the best solution will hurt other queries in the workload. For example, a new index on a large number of columns can hurt the performance of action queries. However, since that's not always true, it's better to determine the effect of such optimization techniques on the complete workload through testing. If a particular solution hurts the overall performance of the workload, choose the next best solution, while keeping an eye on the overall performance of the workload.

Creating a New Index

It seems obvious from looking at the processing strategy that an index on od.UnitPrice will reduce the cost of both steps 1 and 2. Since the od table already has a clustered index, you will create a nonclustered index on column od.UnitPrice:

```
CREATE NONCLUSTERED INDEX UnitPrice ON od(UnitPrice)
```

Now run the costly query again, with STATISTICS IO switched on. The STATISTICS IO output is as follows:

```
Table 'Orders'. Scan count 32, logical reads 67, physical reads 0, read-ahead↵
  reads 0.
Table 'Products'. Scan count 32, logical reads 64, physical reads 0, read-ahead↵
  reads 0.
Table 'od'. Scan count 1, logical reads 23, physical reads 0, read-ahead reads 0.
```

The number of reads on the od table is the same as before. Figure 16-5 shows the corresponding execution plan.

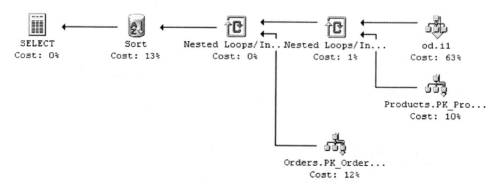

Figure 16-5. *Graphical execution plan of the query with a new nonclustered index on the column od.UnitPrice*

This is exactly the same result as before. This indicates that the optimizer finds using index i1 cheaper than using the newly created index. Consequently, you have the following two choices:

- Drop the new index and proceed with the next optimization step.

- Determine why the new index is not efficient.

The first choice is essentially a nice way of saying "Let's give up." So, let's opt for the second choice instead.

Analyzing Index Behavior with an Index Hint

You can find out how using the new index on od.UnitPrice is costlier than using index i1 by forcing the optimizer to use the new index. You can do this by re-creating view v1 with an index hint. The following code re-creates the view from create_od.sql with an index hint on the od table:

```
IF(SELECT OBJECT_ID('v1')) IS NOT NULL
  DROP view v1
GO
CREATE VIEW v1
AS
SELECT o.OrderID, od.ProductID, od.Quantity, od.UnitPrice
  FROM od WITH(INDEX(UnitPrice)), [Orders] o
  WHERE od.OrderID = o.OrderID
GO
```

Figure 16-6 shows the resultant execution plan for the worst-performing query.

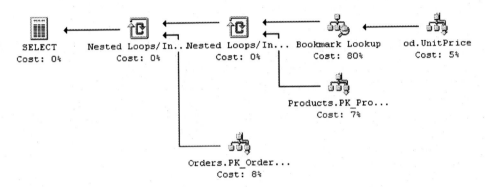

Figure 16-6. *Graphical execution plan of the query with an index hint to use the new nonclustered index*

From Figure 16-6, you can see that index od.UnitPrice is used. Since the data from table od is accessed through the index on the UnitPrice column, the data returned by the data-retrieval step is presorted on the UnitPrice column. Consequently, the sort step on od.UnitPrice is eliminated. However, accessing table od has introduced a bookmark lookup step with a relative cost of 80%. In terms of the number of reads, the resultant STATISTICS IO output for the query is as follows:

```
Table 'Orders'. Scan count 32, logical reads 67, physical reads 0, read-ahead⤶
  reads 0.
Table 'Products'. Scan count 32, logical reads 64, physical reads 0, read-ahead⤶
  reads 0.
Table 'od'. Scan count 1, logical reads 68, physical reads 0, read-ahead reads 0.
```

> **TIP** To prevent the effect of the graphical execution plan and the first-time internal overhead of the SET STATISTICS IO statement on the actual number of reads performed by the query, turn the graphical execution plan OFF and execute the query with the SET STATISTICS IO statements twice.

The number of reads for the od table has increased from 23 to 68. Once again, you may get different figures, but the important factor here is that there has been a substantial increase in the number of reads.

Using the new index on od.UnitPrice seems to be a bad choice. As a result, you have again two choices at this stage:

- Reinstate view v1 without the index hint and drop the new index created on the od.UnitPrice column.

- Analyze the cause of the bookmark lookup.

Once again, let's opt for the second choice.

Avoiding the Bookmark Lookup Operation

As explained in Chapter 6, a bookmark lookup operation helps retrieve columns from a table that are not available in the index. Therefore, the query under consideration must access columns besides the UnitPrice column from the od table. You can determine the columns returned by the bookmark lookup operation from the SHOWPLAN_ALL output for the query, as explained in Chapter 6. You can obtain the SHOWPLAN_ALL output for the query by re-executing the query with the SET statements as follows:

```
SET SHOWPLAN_ALL ON
GO
SELECT v1.OrderID, v1.ProductID, v1.Quantity, v1.UnitPrice
  FROM Products p, v1
  WHERE p.ProductID = v1.ProductID AND v1.UnitPrice < 3
  ORDER BY v1.UnitPrice
GO
SET SHOWPLAN_ALL OFF
GO
```

Figure 16-7 shows the output of the SHOWPLAN_ALL statement for the query.

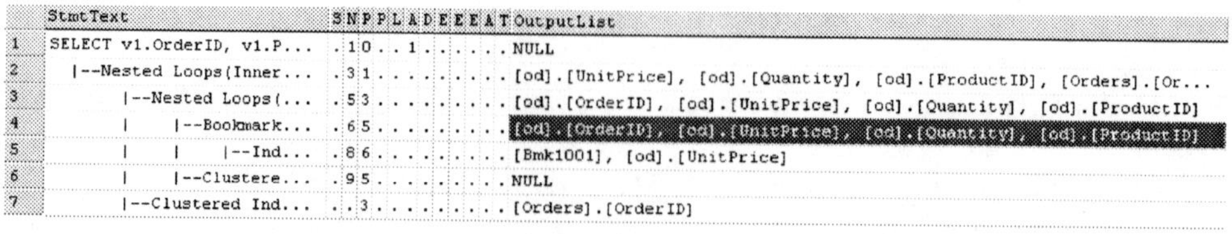

Figure 16-7. *Textual execution plan of the query with the index hint, showing the columns returned by the bookmark lookup step*

From the OutputList column, you can see that the bookmark lookup operation returned the following columns:

- od.OrderID

- od.UnitPrice

- od.Quantity

- od.ProductID

The bookmark lookup operation has returned three more columns, in addition to the UnitPrice column on which the new index was created. Going back to the query, you can figure out that these columns are referred to in the SELECT statement. As explained in Chapter 6, the columns may be referred to in any part of the query, not just select_list.

The columns may also be referred to in the views or the functions used in the query, which makes identifying the columns a little difficult. However, using SHOWPLAN_ALL reveals the columns accessed by an execution plan step, irrespective of where the columns are referred to in the query. Adding the columns accessed by the bookmark lookup operation to the new index will prevent the bookmark lookup operation, since all the required columns will be served by the modified index.

So, do you really have to add all three columns to the UnitPrice index to avoid the bookmark lookup operation? The answer is no. As explained in Chapter 4, every nonclustered index on a table with a clustered index contains the clustered index columns as the row locator. Since the od table has a clustered index on the OrderID and ProductID columns, the nonclustered index UnitPrice contains these two columns along with the UnitPrice column. Therefore, you only have to add the Quantity column to the new index to avoid the bookmark lookup:

```
CREATE NONCLUSTERED INDEX UnitPrice ON od(UnitPrice, Quantity) WITH DROP_EXISTING
```

Figure 16-8 shows what the resultant execution plan for the worst performing query becomes.

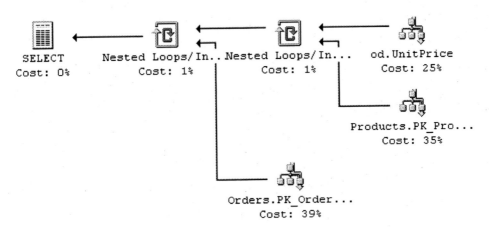

Figure 16-8. *Graphical execution plan of the query with the nonclustered index on od.UnitPrice and od.Quantity*

From this, you can see that the new index UnitPrice is used for the od table without the bookmark lookup operation. Note that the sort operation present in the original execution plan is avoided as well.

The resultant STATISTICS IO output for the query is as follows.

```
Table 'Orders'. Scan count 32, logical reads 67, physical reads 0, read-ahead⏎
 reads 0.
Table 'Products'. Scan count 32, logical reads 64, physical reads 0, read-ahead⏎
 reads 0.
Table 'od'. Scan count 1, logical reads 2, physical reads 0, read-ahead reads 0.
```

TIP To prevent the effect of the graphical execution plan and the first-time internal overhead of the SET STATISTICS IO statement on the actual number of reads performed by the query, turn the graphical execution plan OFF and execute the query with the SET STATISTICS IO statements twice.

The number of reads for the od table is significantly reduced, from 23 to 2.

You can pretty much wind up the optimization drill at this stage. However, before doing so, let's be sure that you have considered most of the optimization techniques you learned in the previous chapters.

Using Database Constraints

Recall that in Chapter 11 you learned about optimization techniques such as the use of declarative referential integrity (DRI). Let's establish the DRI among the tables by creating the following foreign keys on the od table (dri.sql in the download):

```
ALTER TABLE od
ADD
  CONSTRAINT FK_Orders FOREIGN KEY (OrderID)
    REFERENCES Orders(OrderID),
  CONSTRAINT FK_Products FOREIGN KEY (ProductID)
    REFERENCES Products(ProductID)
GO
```

NOTE Primary keys exist on the Products.ProductID and the Orders.OrderID columns in the respective tables.

Figure 16-9 shows the resultant execution plan for the query with DRI in place.

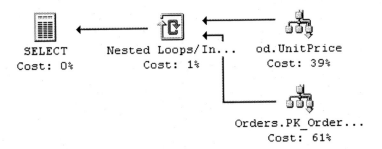

Figure 16-9. *Graphical execution plan of the query with DRI in place*

The resultant execution plan looks interesting. The Products table is not accessed by the query, even though it is referred to in the WHERE clause. This SQL Server behavior is explained in Chapter 11. The query uses only the ProductID column from the Products table to join with the view's column v1.ProductID. This column refers to the od.ProductID column in the view's SELECT statement.

The primary key/foreign key relationship between the Products table and the od table ensures that for every (non-null) od.ProductID column value, there will be at least one Products.ProductID column value. This allows the SQL Server optimizer to avoid joining the Products table, since no other column value is required from that table. Note that if the primary key/foreign key relationship were reversed between the two tables, then the Products table would have been accessed by the optimizer, as more than one row can be returned from the Products table.

Redesigning the Costliest Query

Taking the preceding explanation into account, let's look at the relationship between the od table and the Orders table. The relationship between them is the same as that between the od table and the Products table. So why is the Orders table still accessed by the optimizer? Well, the SELECT statement of the v1 view specifically requested the OrderID column value from the Orders table in the corresponding select_list. The obvious thing to do in that case is to use the OrderID column from the od table in the view's select_list instead, since it doesn't affect the result set returned by the view. Let's modify the view in create_od.sql accordingly:

```
IF(SELECT OBJECT_ID('v1')) IS NOT NULL
  DROP view v1
GO
CREATE VIEW v1
AS
SELECT od.OrderID, od.ProductID, od.Quantity, od.UnitPrice
  FROM od, [Orders] o
  WHERE od.OrderID = o.OrderID
GO
```

■**TIP** Remember to remove the index hint from the FROM od, [Orders] o line.

Figure 16-10 shows the resultant execution plan for the query.

```
SELECT                    od.UnitPrice
Cost: 0%                  Cost: 100%
```

Figure 16-10. *Graphical execution plan of a redesigned version of the query*

This execution plan looks wonderful. The query accesses neither the Products table nor the Orders table because of the DRI and the proper columns referred to in the SELECT statement. The resultant STATISTICS IO output for the query is as follows:

Table 'od'. Scan count 1, logical reads 2, physical reads 0, read-ahead reads 0.

The number of reads performed by the query can be summarized as shown in Table 16-5.

Table 16-5. *Number of Reads Performed by the Query Before and After Optimization*

Table	Reads Before Optimization	Reads After Optimization
Orders	67	0
Products	64	0
od	34	2

You have optimized the performance of the query enough so that it is one of the cheapest queries in the workload.

Analyzing the Effect on Database Workload

Once you've optimized the worst-performing query, you must ensure that it doesn't hurt the performance of the other queries; otherwise, your work will have been in vain.

To analyze the resultant performance of the overall workload, re-execute the complete workload in workload.sql and trace the overall performance using the stored procedure technique (PerformanceTraceForWorkload.sql in the download).

■**TIP** For proper comparison with the original Profiler trace output, please ensure that the graphical execution plan is turned OFF.

The corresponding trace output captured in a trace file is shown in Profiler in Figure 16-11. To identify the costliest query in terms of number of logical reads, the trace output has been sorted on the Reads column.

Reads	EventClass	TextData	CPU	Writes	Duration
	TraceStart				
	ExistingConnection	-- network protocol: LPC set quoted_id...			
	TraceStop				
2	SQL:StmtCompleted	SELECT * FROM Orders o WHERE o.O...	0	0	0
2	SQL:BatchCompleted	SELECT * FROM Orders o WHERE o.O...	0	0	0
2	SQL:StmtCompleted	SELECT vl.OrderID, vl.ProductID, vl.Qu...	0	0	0
2	SQL:BatchCompleted	SELECT vl.OrderID, vl.ProductID, vl.Qu...	0	0	0
4	SQL:StmtCompleted	SELECT od.OrderID, od.ProductID FRO...	0	0	0
4	SQL:BatchCompleted	SELECT od.OrderID, od.ProductID FRO...	0	0	0
9	SQL:StmtCompleted	SELECT p.SupplierID, SUM(p.UnitsInStoc...	10	0	10
11	SQL:StmtCompleted	SELECT od.OrderID, od.ProductID FRO...	10	0	10
11	SQL:BatchCompleted	SELECT od.OrderID, od.ProductID FRO...	10	0	10
82	SQL:BatchCompleted	SELECT p.SupplierID, SUM(p.UnitsInStoc...	10	0	10

```
SELECT vl.OrderID, vl.ProductID, vl.Quantity, vl.UnitPrice
  FROM Products p, vl
  WHERE p.ProductID = vl.ProductID AND vl.UnitPrice < 3
  ORDER BY vl.UnitPrice
```

Figure 16-11. *Profiler trace output showing the effect of optimizing the costliest query on the complete workload*

From this trace, the resource use and the response time (or Duration) of the query under consideration can be summarized as shown in Table 16-6.

Table 16-6. *Resource Usage and Response Time of the Optimized Query Before and After Optimization*

Column	Before Optimization	After Optimization
Reads	175	2
Writes	0	0
CPU	10 ms	0 ms
Duration	10 ms	0 ms

> ■**NOTE** The absolute values are less important than the relative difference between the "Before Optimization" and the corresponding "After Optimization" values. The relative differences between the values indicate the relative improvement in performance.

A comparison between the original and final Profiler trace output indicates that the previous optimization steps have also improved the performance of many of the other queries in the workload. *Note that this is not always expected.* It's possible that the optimization of the worst-performing query may hurt the performance of some other query in the workload. However, as long as the overall performance of the workload is improved, you can retain the optimizations performed on the query.

Iterating Through Optimization Phases

An important point to remember is that you need to iterate through the optimization steps multiple times to optimize the costly queries identified on the basis of not only reads, but also writes and CPU. In each iteration, you can identify one or more poorly-performing queries and optimize the query or queries to improve the performance of the overall workload. You must continue iterating through the optimization steps until you achieve the workload's performance target.

Besides analyzing the workload for resource-intensive queries, you must also analyze the workload for the following aspects:

- Long-running queries

- Error conditions

Long-Running Queries

One of the biggest performance issues in SQL Server is that the database requests block one another. Although a database request may not be very resource intensive, poor transaction management or a high level of transaction isolation used by the database request may cause many other queries to wait on the resources reserved by it. The wait time of the blocked queries increases the execution time or duration of those queries. A query with very high duration but relatively low CPU, reads, and writes is an indication that the query took a long time not because it was costly but for some other reason—blocking is the most common cause of such cases. Therefore, to identify such queries, use the following two procedures:

- Sort the trace on Duration data column.

- Look for Attention event in the trace.

In either case, you must analyze the workload for blocking scenarios. While analyzing a database workload, it is usually beneficial to turn on the blocker script execution loop, as explained in Chapter 12, along with tracing the workload. If you come across Attention events or queries with relatively high Duration values in the captured trace, you will be able to analyze the output of the blocker script. Use the EndTime data column of the Attention event or the long-running query as the reference point into the output of the blocker script and travel upward in the blocker script output to analyze the blocking condition for the corresponding SPID. The objective is to find whether or not the concerned SPID was waiting on any resource and, if it was, what caused the blocking scenario. For an in-depth explanation on how to analyze blocking, please refer to Chapter 12.

Error Conditions

While analyzing the workload, you must also look for error conditions that may be adding too much unproductive load to the database server. For example, if you try to insert duplicate rows into a table with its column protected by the unique constraint, SQL Server will reject the new rows and report an error condition to the application. Although the data was not entered into the table or no useful work was performed, still valuable resources were used to determine that the data was invalid and must be rejected.

To identify the error conditions caused by the database requests, look for the following events in the captured trace:

- Exception

- Execution Warnings

- Hash Warning

- Missing Column Statistics

- Missing Join Predicate

- Sort Warnings

For example, consider the following SQL queries:

```
USE Northwind
GO
INSERT INTO [Order Details]
  VALUES(11070, 1, 20.0, 10, 0.0)
GO
SELECT ProductName, CategoryName, Description
  FROM Products, Categories
  WHERE ProductID IS NOT NULL
GO
```

Figure 16-12 shows the corresponding Profiler trace output.

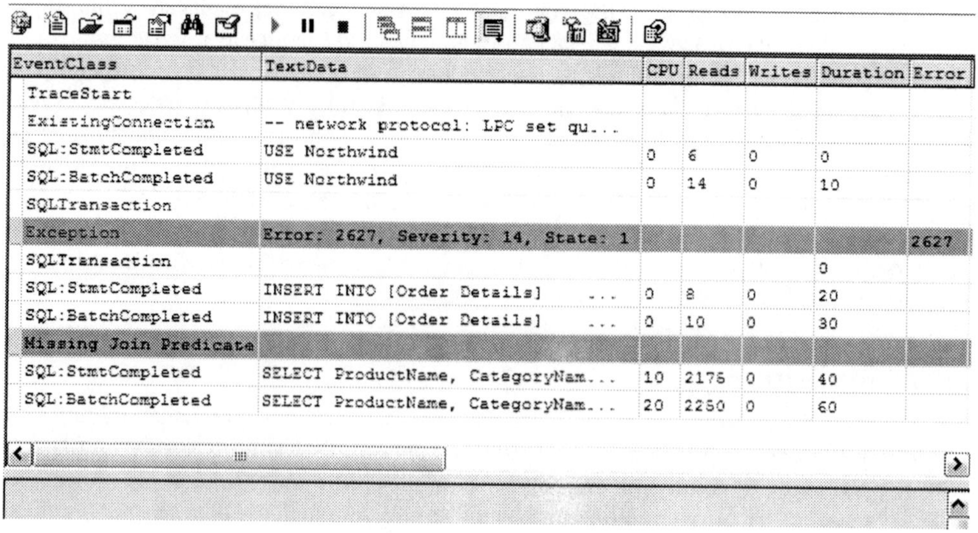

EventClass	TextData	CPU	Reads	Writes	Duration	Error
TraceStart						
ExistingConnection	-- network protocol: LPC set qu...					
SQL:StmtCompleted	USE Northwind	0	6	0	0	
SQL:BatchCompleted	USE Northwind	0	14	0	10	
SQLTransaction						
Exception	Error: 2627, Severity: 14, State: 1					2627
SQLTransaction					0	
SQL:StmtCompleted	INSERT INTO [Order Details] ...	0	8	0	20	
SQL:BatchCompleted	INSERT INTO [Order Details] ...	0	10	0	30	
Missing Join Predicate						
SQL:StmtCompleted	SELECT ProductName, CategoryNam...	10	2176	0	40	
SQL:BatchCompleted	SELECT ProductName, CategoryNam...	20	2250	0	60	

Figure 16-12. *Profiler trace output showing errors raised by a SQL workload*

From the Profiler trace output in Figure 16-12, you can see that the following two errors occurred:

- Exception

- Missing Join Predicate

The Exception error was caused by the INSERT statement, which tried to insert a duplicate row into the [Order Details] table. The [Order Details] table already has the OrderID, ProductID combination of 11070 and 1, and there is a primary key on these columns. From the Error data column, you can see that the error number is 2627. You can determine the error description for this error number from the master.dbo.sysmessages system table:

```
SELECT * FROM master.dbo.sysmessages
WHERE error = 2627
```

Figure 16-13 shows the error description from the sysmessages table.

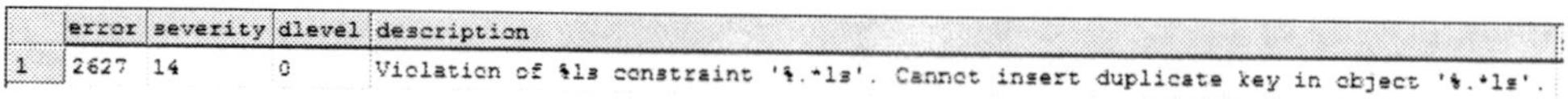

	error	severity	dlevel	description
1	2627	14	0	Violation of %ls constraint '%.*ls'. Cannot insert duplicate key in object '%.*ls'.

Figure 16-13. *sysmessages output showing the description of the error*

If too many exceptions are caused by the workload, then it is advantageous to import the content of the trace file into a table so that you can identify the different types of exceptions caused by the workload and the volume of the different exception types. You may execute a SELECT statement joining the TRACE_TABLE and the sysmessages system table:

```
SELECT E.[Count], E.Error, SUBSTRING(E.SQL,1,7)+Msg.Description 'ErrorDescription'
FROM (SELECT CAST(TextTData AS VARCHAR(100)) SQL, Error, COUNT(*) [Count]
      FROM TRACE_TABLE
      WHERE Error IS NOT NULL
      GROUP BY CAST(TextTData AS VARCHAR(100)), Error) E,
    master.dbo.sysmessages Msg
WHERE E.Error = Msg.Error
ORDER BY E.[Count] DESC
```

Once you identify an Exception event in the traced output, you must find the SQL query that caused the exception. To do so, follow the SPID in the trace output that caused the exception. The Completed event (i.e., SQL:StmtCompleted, SP:StmtCompleted, or RPC:Completed) for the SPID immediately after the Exception event represents the SQL query that caused the exception. For instance, in the preceding example, you can see that the SQL:StmtCompleted event for the INSERT statement represents the SQL query that caused the exception.

The second error, Missing Join Predicate, is caused by the SELECT statement:

```
SELECT ProductName, CategoryName, Description
  FROM Products, Categories
  WHERE ProductID IS NOT NULL
```

If you take a closer look at the SELECT statement, you will see that the query does not specify a JOIN clause between the two tables. A missing join predicate between the tables usually leads to an inaccurate result set and a costly query plan. You must identify the queries causing such Errors and Warnings events and implement the necessary resolutions. For instance, in the preceding SELECT statement, you should not join every row from the Categories table to every row in the Products table—you must join only the rows with matching CategoryID, as follows:

```
SELECT ProductName, CategoryName, Description
  FROM Products, Categories
  WHERE ProductID IS NOT NULL
    AND Products.CategoryID = Categories.CategoryID
```

Even after you thoroughly analyze and optimize a workload, you must remember that workload optimization is not a one-off process. The workload or data distribution on a database can change over time, so you should check periodically whether your queries are optimized for the current situation.

Summary

As you learned in this chapter, optimizing a database workload requires a range of tools, utilities, and commands to analyze different aspects of the queries involved in the workload. You can use the Profiler tool to analyze the big picture of the workload and identify the costly queries. Once you've identified the costly queries, you can use Query Analyzer and various SQL commands to troubleshoot the problems associated with the costly queries. Based on the problems detected with the costly queries, you can apply one or more sets of optimization techniques to improve the query performance. The optimization of the costly queries should improve the overall performance of the workload; if this does not happen, you should roll back the change.

In the next chapter, I'll cover a few database designs that usually present challenges in achieving database scalability unless designed with care.

■ ■ ■

CHAPTER 17

Scalability Scenarios

If your database performs well with only one user and a small dataset, this does not mean that it will scale well when queries are executed by multiple concurrent users, or on large datasets. In this chapter, you will look into some of the query design aspects that you should consider so that the database functionalities implemented using SQL queries are scalable. Specifically, you will consider the implementation of three commonly used database functionalities and apply the optimization techniques you learned in the previous chapters to improve scalability.

In this chapter, I will cover the following:

- Hit count measurement

- Large dataset migration

- Queue processing

Hit Count Measurement

Measuring the number of times a web page is accessed is a common functional requirement of many web applications. This requirement, often referred to as *hit count measurement*, is usually implemented using a database table to store the hit count value and a stored procedure to increment the value (create_HitCount.sql in the download):

```
--Table to store hit count value
IF(SELECT OBJECT_ID('HitCountTable')) IS NOT NULL
   DROP TABLE HitCountTable
GO
CREATE TABLE HitCountTable(HitCount INT)
INSERT INTO HitCountTable VALUES(0)
GO

--Stored procedure to increment hit count value
IF(SELECT OBJECT_ID('spHitCount_Original')) IS NOT NULL
   DROP PROC spHitCount_Original
GO
CREATE PROC spHitCount_Original
AS
SET NOCOUNT ON
```

```
UPDATE HitCountTable SET HitCount = HitCount + 1
SET NOCOUNT OFF
GO
```

Every time the web page is accessed, the stored procedure is executed, incrementing the hit count value by 1. You can determine the number of hits by executing the following SELECT statement:

```
SELECT HitCount FROM HitCountTable
```

Although this implementation of the hit count function is simple, it presents a scalability bottleneck when the web page is accessed by multiple users concurrently. Only one user can increment the hit count value at a time, and the rest of the users are forced to wait. The bottleneck developed on the hit count value can hurt the scalability of the application.

The amount of blocking caused by the preceding implementation of the hit count function can be analyzed by having multiple users execute the spHitCount_Original stored procedure simultaneously. To facilitate this kind of testing, you can simulate multiple users with a SQL load tool, such as the one included in the SQL Server 2000 Resource Kit called Database Hammer. (The previous version of SQL Server Resource Kit was included in the BackOffice 4.5 Resource Kit [BORK 4.5], and the corresponding tool was called SQL Load Simulator.) You can find out more information about these tools from the article "Assessing the New Microsoft SQL Server 2000 Resource Kit" (http://msdn.microsoft.com/library/en-us/dnsqlpro01/html/sql01f1.asp).

You will use the load simulation tool with the following configuration (as shown in Figure 17-1) to analyze the bottleneck caused by the preceding implementation of the hit count function:

- *Load simulation tool*: SQL Load Simulator

- *Number of users*: 60

- *Test duration*: 180 seconds

- *SQL batch* (batch.sql in the download):

```
--Increment HitCount for 180 seconds
DECLARE @start DATETIME
SELECT @start = GETDATE()
WHILE DATEDIFF(ms, @start, GETDATE()) < 180000
BEGIN
  EXEC spHitCount_Original
END
--Stop the virtual user
WAITFOR DELAY '01:00:00'
```

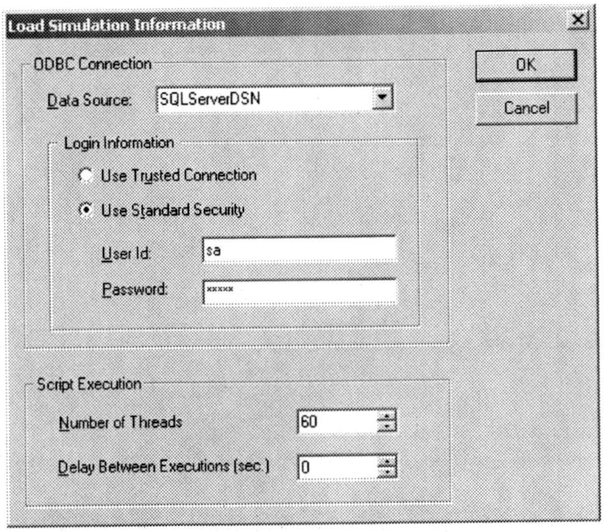

Figure 17-1. *Load Simulation Information dialog box*

The WHILE loop allows the virtual user to execute the stored procedure for 180 seconds. The WAITFOR statement stops the virtual users after 180 seconds by suspending the users for a period of time (1 hour).

The System Monitor counters that you can use to analyze the amount of blocking are shown in Table 17-1.

Table 17-1. *System Monitor Counters to Analyze Amount of Blocking*

Performance Object	Counter	Instance
SQLServer:Locks	Lock Waits/sec	_Total
SQLServer:Locks	Lock Wait Time (ms)	_Total
SQLServer:Databases	Transactions/sec	<Database Name>

■**TIP** The name of a performance object for default SQL Server setup includes the prefix SQLServer:, as shown in Table 17-1. For a SQL Server 2000 named instance (a nondefault setup), the prefix is MSSQL$<Instance Name>:, as shown in Figure 17-2.

The System Monitor log for the preceding implementation of the hit count function, with 60 concurrent users, is shown in Figure 17-2, and the summary of the counter values is shown in Table 17-2.

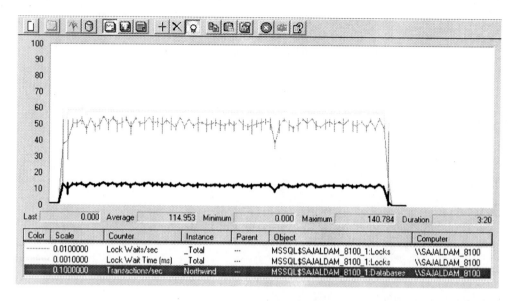

Figure 17-2. *System Monitor log showing the amount of blocking by the hit count implementation*

Table 17-2. *System Monitor Counter Values Showing the Amount of Blocking by the Hit Count Implementation*

Performance Object\Counter[Instance]	Average Value
Locks\Lock Waits/sec[_Total]	4,609
Locks\Lock Wait Time (ms)[_Total]	52,993
Databases\Transactions/sec[Northwind]	114

From this, you can see that the implementation of the hit count function causes a large amount of blocking, as multiple users attempt to increment the hit count value row at the same time. SQL Server serializes the users trying to update the hit count value into a synchronous queue, and this hurts concurrency. The preceding implementation of the hit count function performed 23,085 hits in 180 seconds. You can avoid the scalability bottleneck due to blocking by redesigning the function as follows:

- Let a user increment an existing hit count value if the hit count entry is not locked by other users.

- If a hit count entry is locked by a user, then allow the new user to skip the locked hit count entry (or entries):

  - If the new user finds a free hit count entry, let the new user increment the entry.

  - Otherwise, let the new user add a new hit count entry.

The total number of hit counts can be determined by adding the value of all the hit count entries. The new implementation of the hit count function prevents a user from being blocked by another user incrementing the hit count. The implementation of this new design is as follows (HitCountNew.sql in the download):

```
IF(SELECT OBJECT_ID('spHitCount_New')) IS NOT NULL
  DROP PROC spHitCount_New
GO
CREATE PROC spHitCount_New
AS
SET NOCOUNT ON
SET ROWCOUNT 1 --Allow user to increment only 1 row
--Increment the first free hit count entry
UPDATE HitCountTable SET HitCount = HitCount + 1
  FROM HitCountTable WITH(READPAST)
--If all hit count entries are locked, add a new entry
IF @@ROWCOUNT = 0
  INSERT INTO HitCountTable (HitCount) VALUES(1)
SET ROWCOUNT 0 --Reset the ROWCOUNT limitation
SET NOCOUNT OFF
GO
```

The SET ROWCOUNT statement causes SQL Server to stop processing the query after the specified number of rows is returned. For instance, in the preceding stored procedure, SET ROWCOUNT 1 causes SQL Server to stop processing the UPDATE statement after one row is returned. The default value of ROWCOUNT is 0, which means that a query is processed until all the rows affected by the query are returned. The effect of SET ROWCOUNT is connection-specific and remains in effect until it is modified or the connection is closed.

The READPAST locking hint allows a user to check the lock status of a row and skip the row if it is locked (without being blocked). The table schema of the HitCountTable remains the same. For a better comparison between the results of the new implementation and the original implementation, you should re-create the original table by rerunning create_HitCount.sql.

To analyze the scalability improvement of the new implementation, use the load simulation tool to execute the following SQL batch (with the new stored procedure) as 60 concurrent users for 180 seconds (batch2.sql in the download):

```
--Increment HitCount for 180 seconds
DECLARE @start DATETIME
SELECT @start = GETDATE()
WHILE DATEDIFF(ms, @start, GETDATE()) < 180000
BEGIN
  EXEC spHitCount_New
END
--Stop the virtual user
WAITFOR DELAY '01:00:00'
```

Figure 17-3 shows the System Monitor log for the new implementation of the hit count function with 60 concurrent users. The summary of the corresponding counter values is shown in Table 17-3.

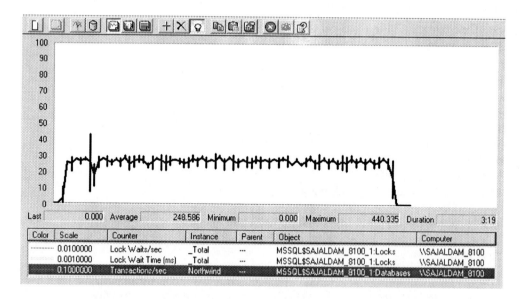

Figure 17-3. *System Monitor log showing the amount of blocking by the new implementation of the hit count*

Table 17-3. *System Monitor Counter Values Showing the Amount of Blocking by the New Implementation of the Hit Count*

Performance Object\Counter[Instance]	New Implementation (Avg. Value)	Original Implementation (Avg. Value)
Locks\Lock Waits/sec[_Total]	0	4,609
Locks\Lock Wait Time (ms)[_Total]	0	52,993
Databases\Transactions/sec[Northwind]	249	114

From this, you can see that the new implementation avoids the blocking that was such a problem in the original implementation. Consequently, the number of transactions started per second in the new implementation is much higher than in the original implementation.

An excerpt of the resulting data in the HitCountTable after the last test run with the new implementation is shown in Table 17-4.

Table 17-4. *Number-of-Hits Data Spread in Multiple Rows of HitCountTable*

Row Number	[HitCountTable]
1	3,908
2	3,877
3	3,635
4–30	…
31	417
32	399
33	379
34–57	…
58	115
59	108
60	97

Sixty row(s) are affected.

From this data, you can see that more increments are performed toward the top of the table, which is quite natural because the new implementation causes an increment of a lower row only if all the rows above it are locked. At the busiest time period, the sixtieth user finds that the remaining 59 users are incrementing the first 59 rows. It then skips the first 59 rows to either increment or add the final row.

The total number of hit counts with the new implementation can be determined by adding all the hit count entries:

```
SELECT SUM(HitCount) AS HitCount FROM HitCountTable
```

Table 17-5 shows the resulting number of concurrent hits the new implementation can support.

Table 17-5. *Number of Hit Counts Supported by the New vs. Original Implementation*

	New Implementation	Original Implementation
Total Number of Hits	49,725	23,085

As you can see, the new hit count implementation achieved a higher number of hits than the original implementation.

Large Dataset Migration

Another common functional requirement in database applications is to move a large amount of data from one table to another (preferably on a different data source). This is usually done for the following reasons:

- To regulate the size of a transactional table to maintain a satisfactory user experience

- To archive historical data

- For data analysis or reporting, and so forth

This kind of database functionality usually operates on a large dataset and involves the following steps:

- Selecting a large number of rows from a source table

- Inserting the rows in a destination table

- Deleting the rows from the source table

Data migration of a large dataset is affected by the number of transactions used to complete the task.

To analyze the effect of the number of transactions on performance, consider the following example. For simplicity, consider the INSERT operation on the destination table only and a small dataset of 256,000 rows. You will use a sample destination table as follows (create_t1.sql in the download):

```
IF(SELECT OBJECT_ID('t1')) IS NOT NULL
  DROP TABLE t1
GO
CREATE TABLE t1(c1 TINYINT)
CREATE CLUSTERED INDEX i1 ON t1(c1)
```

You can insert the 256,000 rows into the destination table as follows:

```
SET NOCOUNT ON
DECLARE @Start DATETIME
SET @Start = GETDATE()

--Insert 256000 rows
DECLARE @Count INT
SET @Count = 1
WHILE @Count <= 256000
BEGIN
  INSERT INTO t1 VALUES(@Count%256)
  SET @Count = @Count + 1
END

SELECT DATEDIFF(s, @Start, GETDATE()) AS ExecutionTime
SET NOCOUNT OFF
```

■**NOTE** On my test setup, with a 500 MHz CPU, 256MB RAM, and one disk, inserting 256,000 rows took 217 seconds.

In a real situation, the number of rows can be a few million, with additional SELECT and DELETE operations on the source table. A database function like this can take a very long time to complete. Since this database function operates on a transactional table, it is generally preferable to complete the operation as quickly as possible, to minimize the effect on the performance of user queries executed concurrently on the transactional table. So how do you improve the performance of this database function? Can you complete the functional requirement in a shorter time period on the same setup? First, you need to see if there are any bottlenecks in the function. Since the INSERT statement is very simple with no WHERE clauses involved, it won't be much use to look at the execution plan of the INSERT statement. Also, since only one user executes the function, the performance bottleneck can't be due to blocking. To analyze and optimize the performance of action queries such as the INSERT statement, you can use the System Monitor counters shown in Table 17-6.

Table 17-6. *System Monitor Counters to Analyze the Resource Pressure Caused by the INSERT Statement*

Performance Object	Counter	Instance	Description
PhysicalDisk	Disk Transfers/sec	_Total	Rate of read and write operations on the disk
SQLServer:Databases	Log Flushes/sec	<Database Name>	Number of log flushes per second
SQLServer:Databases	Transactions/sec	<Database Name>	Number of transactions started per second

Figure 17-4 shows the System Monitor log for the preceding implementation. The corresponding summary of the counter values is shown in Table 17-7.

Table 17-7. *System Monitor Counter Values Showing the Resource Pressure Created by the INSERT Statements*

Performance Object\Counter[Instance]	Average Value
PhysicalDisk\Disk Transfers/sec[_Total]	1,160
Databases\Log Flushes/sec[NWTest]	1,154
Databases\Transactions/sec[NWTest]	1,153

You can see that under the current implementation, inserting 256,000 rows caused a very high Disk Transfers/sec rate of 1,160 disk transfers per second. At the time of this writing, an average disk can sustain around 80–120 disk transfers per second—the amount of disk transfers per second here is way beyond the capacity of one hard disk. To improve performance, you need to eliminate this disk bottleneck.

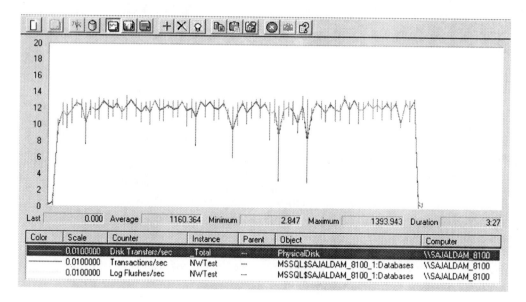

Figure 17-4. *System Monitor log showing the resource pressure created by the INSERT statements*

One solution to this performance issue is to add more disks to the disk subsystem, so that disk transfers per second per disk fall within the capacity of an individual disk. In the current scenario, you will need around 10–15 disks with all the disks working at their peak disk transfers per second capacity. But with so much disk activity, it will be quite difficult to achieve the desired performance target. Additionally, imagine the number of disks the database function will require to operate on a more realistic dataset size of a few million rows! Adding more disks would become prohibitively expensive, so for such database functions, it is important to identify the root cause of the disk bottleneck and resolve the root cause to improve performance.

Log Flushes/sec

From Table 17-7, you can see that Log Flushes/sec is 1,154. The Log Flushes/sec counter indicates the number of times per second the database log was flushed to the log disk. SQL Server 2000 uses a *write-ahead log* to maintain database integrity and durability. This ensures that no data modifications are written to the data disk before the associated log record is written to the log disk.

When data is modified by an action query, the data modification is made to a page in the in-memory SQL Server buffer cache, and a corresponding log record is built in the log cache to record the modification. The log record is written to the log on disk before the associated dirty page from the buffer cache is flushed to the data disk. At the end of a transaction, all pending log records for the transaction are flushed to the log disk. A log flush can cause one or more disk transfers on the log disk. Therefore, it can be inferred that the large Disk Transfers/sec value on the log disk is an outcome of the large Log Flushes/sec value.

Transactions/sec

From the preceding explanation, you can also infer that every transaction causes a log flush. If you consider the previous table with the strong correlation between log flushes and transactions, you have a pretty good idea that the large Log Flushes/sec value is caused by the large Transactions/sec value. Therefore, to decrease the disk bottleneck, you have to decrease the rate of database transactions.

Action Queries Treated As Separate Transactions

In SQL Server, by default every action query (including the INSERT statement) is treated as a separate transaction. This behavior of action queries is called *autocommit mode*, and you can modify it by starting explicit or implicit transactions as follows:

- *Explicit transaction*: A transaction is started explicitly by issuing a BEGIN TRANSACTION statement.

- *Implicit transaction*: The implicit transaction mode is enabled, through either an API function or the SET IMPLICIT_TRANSACTIONS ON SQL statement. The next SQL statement automatically starts a new transaction. When the transaction is completed, any further SQL statements start a new transaction.

A transaction started using one of these techniques can be completed using either the COMMIT or the ROLLBACK statement, marking the success or failure of the transaction, respectively.

You can reduce the number of transactions per second by modifying create_t1.sql to execute all 256,000 INSERT operations within a single explicit transaction, as follows:

```
SET NOCOUNT ON
DECLARE @Start DATETIME
SET @Start = GETDATE()

--Insert 256000 rows
DECLARE @Count INT
SET @Count = 1
BEGIN TRANSACTION
  WHILE @Count <= 256000
  BEGIN
    INSERT INTO t1 VALUES(@Count%256)
    SET @Count = @Count + 1
  END
COMMIT

SELECT DATEDIFF(s, @Start, GETDATE()) AS ExecutionTime
SET NOCOUNT OFF
```

With the preceding modification, the database function took only 23 seconds to insert all 256,000 rows, compared to 217 seconds for the original implementation.

Figure 17-5 shows the corresponding System Monitor log, and Table 17-8 shows the summary of the corresponding counter values.

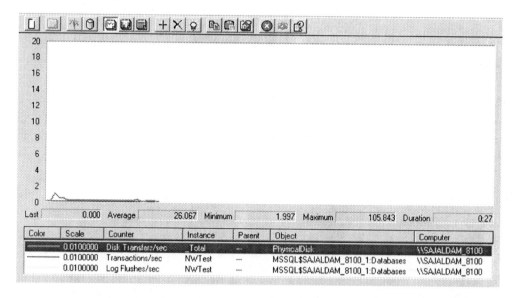

Figure 17-5. *System Monitor log showing the resource pressure created by the execution of all the INSERT statements in one transaction*

Table 17-8. *System Monitor Counter Values Showing the Resource Pressure Created by the Current vs. Original Implementation*

Performance Object\Counter[Instance]	Average Value (1 Tx)	Average Value (Original)
PhysicalDisk\Disk Transfers/sec[_Total]	26	1,160
Databases\Log Flushes/sec[NWTest]	14	1,154
Databases\Transactions/sec[NWTest]	0.115	1,153

Table 17-9 shows the execution time comparison between the current implementation and the original implementation.

Table 17-9. *Total Execution Time of the Current vs. Original Implementation*

Average Value (1 Tx) in Seconds	Average Value (Original) in Seconds
23	217

That's a wonderful performance improvement.

However, you still have other problems with the situation. In a real environment, as explained earlier, the database function will be selecting and deleting rows from the source table as well as inserting rows into the destination table. Furthermore, the dataset size could easily be a few million rows. Once these variables are factored in, all the corresponding queries may take an unacceptably long time to complete. During that time, the locks held by the transaction will prevent other concurrent operations on the resources involved in the transaction. This means that executing all the action queries within one transaction will hurt concurrency on a large dataset.

Originally, you were at one extreme, executing 256,000 transactions. Now, you are at the other extreme of executing only one transaction. Since you don't want to block other users for the entire duration of the transaction, you can break the 256,000 INSERT operations into multiple transactions. Although this may affect the overall performance of the database function up to a point, it will allow other users to work concurrently on the relevant database resources. In the resulting implementation, you break the single transaction into multiple transactions of the "right size," so that you get the best of both the worlds. To improve concurrency without sacrificing the performance of the database, you need to determine the maximum number of INSERT operations you can perform within one transaction.

Sizing the Transaction Correctly

Although only one transaction is used in the second implementation, it still performed more than one disk transfer. The number of disk transfers is related to the total amount of data inserted, which is 256,000 rows multiplied by the average row size. The sample destination table has only one column, with a TINYINT data type, making the average row size equal to 1 byte (excluding the internal overhead). Thus, the database function inserts around 256KB (256,000 rows × 1 byte) of data. This content is also written to the log disk by the write-ahead log behavior, as explained earlier.

A single transaction cannot write this large content to the log disk in one disk transfer, because the maximum size of a log block in SQL Server 2000 is 60KB. Therefore, multiple disk transfers are required for a single large transaction. If you resize a transaction to write in 60KB chunks, you will have a minimum number of disk transfers per transaction. You can then repeat the transaction the appropriate number of times to insert all 256,000 rows.

This technique will require almost the same number of disk transfers as used by the single transaction technique, and it may make the database functionality a little slower due to the overhead associated with managing multiple transactions. It won't, however, sacrifice the performance of the database function much compared to using only one transaction, because the major part (usually the cost of disk transfers) of the total cost can be kept low by sizing the transaction properly. Furthermore, correctly sizing the transaction allows the locks to be released in between the transactions. This new technique will not only keep the execution time low, but also allow other concurrent requests on the resource in between consecutive transactions.

Let's implement this new technique. Since the average row size is 1 byte, you will insert around 64,000 rows in one transaction and repeat the transaction four times:

```
--Prerequisite: Re-create the original table with the index
SET NOCOUNT ON
DECLARE @Start DATETIME
SET @Start = GETDATE()

DECLARE @Count INT, @CountOut INT
SET @CountOut = 1
WHILE @CountOut <= 4
BEGIN
  SET @Count = 1
```

```
  BEGIN TRANSACTION
    WHILE @Count <= 64000
    BEGIN
      INSERT INTO t1 VALUES(@Count%256)
      SET @Count = @Count + 1
    END
  COMMIT
  SET @CountOut = @CountOut + 1
END

SELECT DATEDIFF(s, @Start, GETDATE()) AS ExecutionTime
SET NOCOUNT OFF
```

TIP In one transaction, 64,000 rows are inserted for easy calculation. Also, the table should be re-created for better comparison with the previous implementation techniques. You can find the whole script in create_t1_final.sql in the code download.

With the new implementation technique, the database function took only 24 seconds to insert all 256,000 rows! Figure 17-6 shows the corresponding System Monitor log, and Table 17-10 shows the summary of the corresponding counter values.

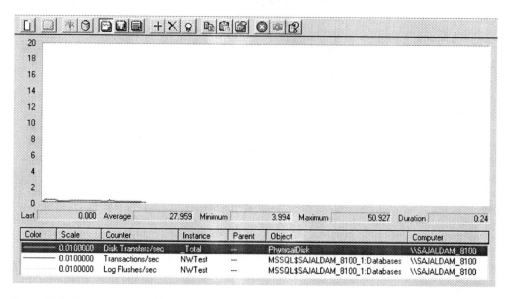

Figure 17-6. *System Monitor log showing the resource pressure created by the execution of multiple INSERT statements in a properly sized transaction*

Table 17-10. *System Monitor Counter Values Showing the Resource Pressure Created by the Different Implementations of the Large Dataset Migration*

Performance Object\Counter[Instance]	Avg. Value (4 Tx)	Avg. Value (1 Tx)	Avg. Value (Original)
PhysicalDisk\Disk Transfers/sec[_Total]	28	26	1,160
Databases\Log Flushes/sec[NWTest]	17	14	1,154
Databases\Transactions/sec[NWTest]	0.250	0.115	1,153

Table 17-11 shows the execution time comparison between the three techniques.

Table 17-11. *Total Execution Time of the Different Implementations of the Large Dataset Migration*

Value (4 Tx) in Seconds	Value (1 Tx) in Seconds	Value (Original) in Seconds
24	23	217

From Table 17-10, you can see that the current implementation technique greatly reduced the Disk Transfers/sec compared to that of the original implementation. This reduced the execution time from 217 to 24 seconds, as you can see in Table 17-11. The single transaction technique may have been marginally quicker, but the current technique releases the locks on the table after every 6 seconds (24 seconds/4 loops), improving concurrency.

As demonstrated, a properly sized transaction will optimize the performance and concurrency of a database function that executes a large number of action queries.

Calculating the Average Row Size of a Table

In the preceding optimization technique, determining the "right size" of the transaction depended upon knowing the average size of a row in the table. It was easy to work it out in the previous example, since the table contained only one column with the TINYINT data type. In the real world, table schemas are not so simple, and thus they require a little thought to determine the average row size.

One way to calculate the row size of a table is to sum up the defined size of all the columns of the table. SQL Server maintains column information of every table in the syscolumns system table. So, for example, the row size of the Orders table can be calculated as follows (rowsize.sql in the download):

```
SELECT SUM(LENGTH) AS [ROW-SIZE]
FROM syscolumns
WHERE id = OBJECT_ID('Orders')
```

This is the result:

```
ROW-SIZE = 364 bytes
```

This technique may not always yield satisfactory results, since it is quite common to find tables with variable-length columns, say VARCHAR(256). The average size of data in a variable-length column may be much smaller than the defined size of the column.

A better technique would be to determine the sum of actual DATALENGTH of all columns for every row in the table, and then find their AVG (average) as follows (datalength.sql in the download):

```
SELECT AVG(DATALENGTH(OrderID) + DATALENGTH(CustomerID)
           + DATALENGTH(EmployeeID) + DATALENGTH(OrderDate)
           + DATALENGTH(RequiredDate) + DATALENGTH(ShippedDate)
           + DATALENGTH(ShipVia) + DATALENGTH(Freight)
           + DATALENGTH(ShipName) + DATALENGTH(ShipAddress)
           + DATALENGTH(ShipCity) + DATALENGTH(ShipRegion)
           + DATALENGTH(ShipPostalCode) + DATALENGTH(ShipCountry)
         ) AS [ROW-SIZE]
FROM Orders
```

This is the result:

```
ROW-SIZE = 181 bytes
```

This technique of determining the average row size provides the best result. However, since it accesses the complete table and uses functions on every row-column value, it can consume a lot of system resources, especially if the table under consideration is large.

A better technique to determine the average row size of a table without consuming too many resources is to use the output of the DBCC SHOWCONTIG command. You can execute this on the Orders table as follows:

```
DBCC SHOWCONTIG('Orders')
```

Here is the output of this command for the Orders table:

```
DBCC SHOWCONTIG scanning 'Orders' table...
Table: 'Orders' (21575115); index ID: 1, database ID: 6
TABLE level scan performed.
- Pages Scanned................................: 20
- Extents Scanned..............................: 5
- Extent Switches..............................: 4
- Avg. Pages per Extent........................: 4.0
- Scan Density [Best Count:Actual Count].......: 60.00% [3:5]
- Logical Scan Fragmentation ..................: 0.00%
- Extent Scan Fragmentation ...................: 40.00%
- Avg. Bytes Free per Page.....................: 146.5
- Avg. Page Density (full).....................: 98.19%
```

NOTE The DBCC SHOWCONTIG command and its output are explained in Chapter 8.

You can then manually calculate the size of total data in the Orders table from this output.

Total data in Orders table
= Pages Scanned × Avg. Page Density (full) × **8,060 bytes**
= 20 × **98.19%** × **8,060**
= **158,282 bytes**
(where 8,060 is the bytes per page for SQL Server 2000)

Therefore:

Average row size of the Orders table
= **Total data / Number of rows**
= **(158,282 / 830) in bytes**
= **191 bytes**
(where 830 is the output of SELECT COUNT(*) FROM Orders**)**

The average row size value provided by this technique is quite close to the real row size value determined by the previous technique using the DATALENGTH function. The big advantage of this technique is that it is much cheaper than other techniques. Considering the fact that the preceding technique requires a little effort on the part of the database developer to calculate the row size, I've put together the following stored procedure (spRowSize in the download):

```
IF(SELECT OBJECT_ID('spRowSize')) IS NOT NULL
  DROP PROC spRowSize
GO
CREATE PROC spRowSize
@TableName VARCHAR(255)
AS
--Create a temporary table to hold DBCC SHOWCONTIG output for
--the input @TableName
CREATE TABLE #FragmentationResult(
ObjectName VARCHAR(255), ObjectId INT, IndexName VARCHAR(255)
, IndexId INT, [Level] INT, Pages INT, [Rows] INT
, MinimumRecordSize INT, MaximumRecordSize INT
, AverageRecordSize FLOAT, ForwardedRecords INT, Extents INT
, ExtentSwitches INT, AverageFreeBytes FLOAT
, AveragePageDensity FLOAT, ScanDensity FLOAT, BestCount INT
, ActualCount INT, LogicalFragmentation FLOAT
, ExtentFragmentation FLOAT
)

--Determine fragmentation of the input @TableName
INSERT INTO #FragmentationResult
  EXEC('DBCC SHOWCONTIG([' + @TableName + ']) WITH TABLERESULTS')
```

```
--Calculate the size of total data in the input @TableName
DECLARE @TotalSize INT
SELECT @TotalSize = Pages * (AveragePageDensity / 100) * 8060
  FROM #FragmentationResult

--Calculate the average row-size
SELECT @TotalSize / [Rows] AS RowSize
  FROM #FragmentationResult
GO
```

To determine the average row size of the Orders table, execute the stored procedure as follows:

```
EXEC spRowSize 'Orders'
```

This process is pretty straightforward, but in fact there is an even easier way to determine the average row size. You can just collect the value of the AverageRecordSize column from the output of the following DBCC SHOWCONTIG statement:

```
DBCC SHOWCONTIG('Orders') WITH TABLERESULTS
```

This is the result:

```
AverageRecordSize = 190 bytes
```

The DBCC SHOWCONTIG WITH TABLERESULTS statement does all of the calculations for you and directly provides you with the average row size.

As an aside, another technique that you can use to calculate the average row size is to first create a covering index on all the columns, and then execute the DBCC SHOW_STATISTICS command:

```
DBCC SHOW_STATISTICS(Orders, <Covering Index on All Columns>)
```

NOTE The DBCC SHOW_STATISTICS command and its output are explained in Chapter 7.

The Average key length value in the DBCC SHOW_STATISTICS output will provide the average row size of the table. However, this technique is only useful if there is already a covering index on all the columns—creating one is a costly process.

Queue Processing

Another common database functionality that, unless you are careful, can cause a scalability bottleneck is queue processing. *Queue processing* is often used by database applications when a group of writers and readers are required to work together to process records. A group of writers produce records based on some business decision, and a group of readers work on those records to take a business decision or process the records as needed. Instead of tying a reader to a writer to process the records produced by its own writer, it is usually efficient to allow any reader—whichever is free—to work on a record to be processed. Otherwise, there can be situations in which all the records produced by a writer are worked on by a single reader, with all other readers idling away because their corresponding writers are not producing any records.

To achieve a maximum combined throughput from the group of readers, the writers can put the records into a queue, and the readers can pick up the records from the queue for processing. This type of queue processing allows all the readers to work together in emptying the queue as quickly as possible, without being selective about who wrote the record.

One of the places where you can use queue processing is in a publisher/subscriber scenario:

- One or more publishers add rows to a queue (or table).

- Multiple subscribers work on the queue, processing the rows added by the publishers.

- As the subscribers process the queue, the rows move from one state to another for different kinds of processing. For example, if the rows have to be processed through multiple stages with a different process to be applied at each stage, then as a subscriber processes a row, the row moves from its current state to a new state for the next stage of processing.

You can implement the queue using a database table as follows (queue.sql in the download):

```
IF(SELECT OBJECT_ID('Queue')) IS NOT NULL
  DROP TABLE Queue
GO
CREATE TABLE Queue([id] INT IDENTITY, Data CHAR(10), Status INT)
CREATE CLUSTERED INDEX i1 ON Queue([id])
GO


--Add 1000 rows to the queue for processing
DECLARE @Count INT
SET @Count = 1
WHILE @Count <= 1000
BEGIN
  INSERT INTO Queue (Data, Status) VALUES('', 0)
  SET @Count = @Count + 1
END
```

A subscriber may poll the queue regularly to process any unprocessed rows from the queue. You can implement the processing part of the subscriber using a stored procedure (process_queue.sql in the download):

```
--Process a row from the queue
IF(SELECT OBJECT_ID('spProcessQueue')) IS NOT NULL
  DROP PROC spProcessQueue
GO
CREATE PROC spProcessQueue
AS
SET NOCOUNT ON
```

```
DECLARE @id INT
--Identify an unprocessed row
SELECT TOP 1 @id = [id] FROM Queue
  WHERE Status = 0
--Simulate processing time for the row
WAITFOR DELAY '00:00:30'
--Update the status of the row
UPDATE Queue
  SET Data = 'Modified', Status = 1
  WHERE [id] = @id AND Status = 0
SET NOCOUNT OFF
GO
```

The preceding stored procedure, which works as a subscriber, identifies an unprocessed row from the queue using the SELECT statement. The time required to process the row is simulated by using the WAITFOR DELAY statement. Once the row is processed, the subscriber updates the status of the row in the table so that the same row is not reprocessed the next time.

The preceding implementation of the subscriber takes around 30 seconds to process a row. This means that a single subscriber can process only two rows in 1 minute. The queue processing can be accelerated by having multiple subscribers work on the queue. To analyze the queue processing by multiple subscribers, let's simulate multiple subscribers (or users) using the load simulator tool:

- *Load simulation tool*: SQL Load Simulator

- *Number of users (or subscribers)*: 60

- *Test duration*: 180 seconds

- *SQL batch* (batch3.sql in the download):

  ```
  --Process queue for 180 seconds
  DECLARE @start DATETIME
  SELECT @start = GETDATE()
  WHILE DATEDIFF(ms, @start, GETDATE()) < 180000
  BEGIN
    EXEC spProcessQueue
  END
  --Stop the virtual user
  WAITFOR DELAY '01:00:00'
  ```

The WHILE loop allows a virtual user to execute the subscriber stored procedure for 180 seconds. The WAITFOR statement stops the virtual users after 180 seconds by suspending the users for a long time (1 hour).

Since processing a row requires 30 seconds, a single subscriber can process 6 rows in 180 seconds. Ideally, you might expect the 60 subscribers to process 360 rows in 180 seconds. Surprisingly, however, with the preceding implementation, the 60 subscribers process only 6 rows in 180 seconds!

Why is this the case? Poor application scalability is generally attributed to poor concurrency among multiple users. As explained in Chapter 12, blocking, the main cause of poor concurrency, can be analyzed using a blocker script (`blockerscript.sql` in Chapter 12's download):

```
WHILE 1=1
BEGIN
    EXEC master.dbo.sp_blocker_pss80 @fast=1
    WAITFOR DELAY '00:00:15'
END
```

However, in this case, the blocker script will not provide any blocking information. Why is this the case?

In the preceding implementation, blocking is not the primary cause of the poor scalability. The problem lies in the design.

All 60 subscribers access the topmost unprocessed row in the queue, since the (S) locks requested by the concurrent execution of the SELECT statement are compatible. This allows all the subscribers to pick up the same row from the queue. While updating the status of the row, only one subscriber can update the row at a time, since the (U) locks requested by the concurrent execution of the UPDATE statement are not compatible. Once a subscriber updates the status of the row, the UPDATE statement of the other subscribers will not find the row since the row is already processed. Thus, after the first round of 30 seconds, only 1 out of the 60 subscribers can actually process a row. This nullifies the benefit of executing multiple subscribers.

Since with the current implementation, all the subscribers picked up the same row, the processing effort of all but one subscriber is wasted. You can prevent multiple subscribers from accessing the same row by using the UPDLOCK locking hint:

```
--Process a row from the queue
IF(SELECT OBJECT_ID('spProcessQueue')) IS NOT NULL
    DROP PROC spProcessQueue
GO
CREATE PROC spProcessQueue
AS
SET NOCOUNT ON
DECLARE @id INT
BEGIN TRAN
    --Identify an unprocessed row
    SELECT TOP 1 @id = [id] FROM Queue WITH(UPDLOCK)
      WHERE Status = 0
    --Simulate processing time for the row
    WAITFOR DELAY '00:00:30'
    --Update the status of the row
    UPDATE Queue
      SET Data = 'Modified', Status = 1
    WHERE [id] = @id AND Status = 0
COMMIT
SET NOCOUNT OFF
GO
```

This hint allows a subscriber to retain a (U) lock on the row until the end of the transaction. Since two (U) locks are incompatible, other subscribers can't access the same row. Please don't use the HOLDLOCK or REPEATABLEREAD locking hint in this case, as these locking hints will allow a subscriber to retain an (S) lock on the row accessed by the SELECT statement. Since the same row is updated toward the end of the transaction, retaining an (S) lock instead of a (U) lock will cause the typical deadlock avoided by the internal implementation of an UPDATE statement.

NOTE This typical deadlock, which you can avoid by the internal implementation of the UPDATE statement by attaining a (U) lock instead of an (S) lock at the first internal step, is explained in Chapter 12.

To verify the scalability improvement of the current implementation technique, let's use the load simulation tool with the same settings as earlier to simulate 60 concurrent subscribers. The result of the current implementation technique is as follows:

- *Rows processed up to 180 seconds:* 6 rows

- *Total number of rows processed (allowing all 60 subscribers to finish)*: 65 rows

- *Total time taken for all 60 subscribers to finish*: 1,950 seconds (approximately)

You are still not seeing the ideal of 360 rows from 60 subscribers in 180 seconds. Why is this? You can analyze the poor scalability of the current implementation using the blocker script as explained previously. Figure 17-7 shows an excerpt from the blocker script output.

The blocking information provided by the blocker script output can be summarized as follows:

- At any point in time, only one subscriber was not blocked (SPID 120).

- Up to 180 seconds, 59 out of the 60 subscribers were blocked on the row accessed by the nonblocked subscriber.

- After 180 seconds, the nonblocked subscriber exited, leaving behind the remaining subscribers. However, at any point in time, only one subscriber was not blocked.

The cause of the blocking can be explained as follows.

The UPDLOCK locking hint allows only one subscriber to access a row and blocks the remaining 59 subscribers on the row accessed by the first subscriber. After 30 seconds, when the first subscriber finishes processing the topmost unprocessed row, the Status column value of the row gets modified to 1. As a result, the 59 subscribers until then blocked on that row move to the next unprocessed row (with Status = 0) in the queue. Meanwhile, the first subscriber loops back to join the other subscribers. Once again, the SELECT statement of only one of the subscribers attains a (U) lock on the new topmost unprocessed row from the queue. The remaining 59 subscribers are blocked on the new row. Thus, every 30 seconds, the 60 subscribers end up processing only one row.

```
SYSPROCESSES  DOPEY\DOPEY  134218262
spid   status                            blocked  open_tran  waitresource
------ -------------------------------   -------  ---------  ----------------------------
114    sleeping                          115      0          TAB: 20:229575856 [[COMPILE]]
115    sleeping                          120      0          TAB: 20:229575856 [[COMPILE]]
116    sleeping                          115      0          TAB: 20:229575856 [[COMPILE]]
118    sleeping                          115      0          TAB: 20:229575856 [[COMPILE]]
119    sleeping                          115      0          TAB: 20:229575856 [[COMPILE]]
120    runnable                          0        25         TAB: 20:229575856 [[COMPILE]]
121    sleeping                          115      0          TAB: 20:229575856 [[COMPILE]]
123    sleeping                          115      0          TAB: 20:229575856 [[COMPILE]]
126    sleeping                          115      0          TAB: 20:229575856 [[COMPILE]]
127    sleeping                          115      0          TAB: 20:229575856 [[COMPILE]]
128    sleeping                          115      0          TAB: 20:229575856 [[COMPILE]]
130    sleeping                          115      0          TAB: 20:229575856 [[COMPILE]]
131    sleeping                          115      0          TAB: 20:229575856 [[COMPILE]]
132    sleeping                          115      0          TAB: 20:229575856 [[COMPILE]]
133    sleeping                          115      0          TAB: 20:229575856 [[COMPILE]]
134    sleeping                          115      0          TAB: 20:229575856 [[COMPILE]]
136    sleeping                          115      0          TAB: 20:229575856 [[COMPILE]]
140    sleeping                          122      0          TAB: 20:229575856 [[COMPILE]]
141    sleeping                          122      0          TAB: 20:229575856 [[COMPILE]]
142    sleeping                          122      0          TAB: 20:229575856 [[COMPILE]]
143    sleeping                          122      0          TAB: 20:229575856 [[COMPILE]]
144    sleeping                          122      0          TAB: 20:229575856 [[COMPILE]]
```

Figure 17-7. *Blocker script output showing the blocking chain caused by the current implementation*

This process continues until the end of the first 180 seconds and yields only 6 processed rows. After 180 seconds, a subscriber, on finishing a row processing, goes to the stop state, leaving behind the remaining subscribers to come out of blocking and finish a row processing.

The concurrency of the queue processing can be improved by preventing a subscriber from blocking on a row being processed by another subscriber. A combination of UPDLOCK and READPAST locking hints can be used to give an exclusive modification right on a row to one subscriber, and allow other subscribers to skip the reserved row and move to the next unreserved row. The new implementation with the UPDLOCK and READPAST locking hints is as follows:

```
--Process a row from the queue
IF(SELECT OBJECT_ID('spProcessQueue')) IS NOT NULL
  DROP PROC spProcessQueue
GO
CREATE PROC spProcessQueue
AS
SET NOCOUNT ON
DECLARE @id INT
BEGIN TRAN
  --Identify an unprocessed row
  SELECT TOP 1 @id = [id] FROM Queue WITH(UPDLOCK, READPAST)
    WHERE Status = 0
  --Simulate processing time for the row
  WAITFOR DELAY '00:00:30'
  --Update the status of the row
  UPDATE Queue
```

```
    SET Data = 'Modified', Status = 1
  WHERE [id] = @id AND Status = 0
COMMIT
SET NOCOUNT OFF
GO
```

You can verify the concurrency of the current implementation by using the load simulation tool to simulate 60 concurrent users as explained previously. With the current implementation, the 60 subscribers processed 360 rows in 180 seconds. The UPDLOCK locking hint allowed only one subscriber to reserve a row or attain a (U) lock on the row. The READPAST locking hint allowed a subscriber to skip the reserved row(s) and work on a row not reserved by other subscribers. As a result, this implementation technique allowed all 60 subscribers to process the queue concurrently. As one subscriber can process 6 rows in 180 seconds, the 60 subscribers processed 360 rows in the same time period by working concurrently.

The concurrency of the various implementation techniques for the queue processing is summarized in Table 17-12.

Table 17-12. *Number of Rows Processed by the Different Queue-Processing Implementations*

Implementation Technique	Rows Processed in 180 Seconds
Original	6
With UPDLOCK locking hint	6 (65 total in 1,950 seconds)
With UPDLOCK and READPAST locking hints	360

Thus, as demonstrated, you can use a combination of locking hints to improve the concurrent processing of a queue implemented in a database.

Summary

As demonstrated in this chapter, when implementing database functionalities, you must consider the scalability of the functionality for large datasets as well as for multiple concurrent users. It is incorrect to assume that a functionality that performs well for a single user on a small dataset will scale well as the number of users or amount of data increases, unless you have actually tested such a scenario. All the optimization techniques you have learned so far in this book will be of no help to you unless you test the database functionalities for scalability.

So, use the techniques presented in this book wisely, test for scalability, and you will be well on your way to a high-performing, future-proofed database; happy customers; and a back-end process that's invisible to end users.

In the next chapter, I summarize the performance-related best practices in a nutshell for your ready reference.

CHAPTER 18

SQL Server Optimization Checklist

If you have read through the previous 17 chapters of this book, then by now you understand the major aspects involved in performance optimization, and that it is a challenging and ongoing activity.

What I hope to do in this chapter is provide a performance-monitoring checklist that can serve as a quick reference for database developers and DBAs when out in the field. The idea is similar to the notion of tear-off cards of "best practices." This chapter does not cover everything, but it does summarize, in one place, some of the major tuning activities that can have quick and demonstrable impact on the performance of your SQL Server systems.

I have categorized these checklist items into the following sections:

- Database design

- Query design

- Configuration settings

- Database administration

- Database backup

Each section contains a number of optimization recommendations and techniques and, where appropriate, cross-references specific chapters in this book that provide full details.

Database Design

Although database design is a broad topic and can't be given due justice in a small section in this query tuning book, I advise you to keep an eye on the following design aspects to ensure that you pay attention to database performance from an early stage:

- The balance between under- and overnormalization

- Benefits of using entity-integrity constraints

- Benefits of using domain and referential integrity constraints

- Index-design best practices

- Avoidance of the sp_ prefix for stored procedure names

Balance Between Under- and Overnormalization

While designing a database, you have the following two extreme options:

- Save the complete data in a single, flat table with little to no normalization.

- Save the data in fine-grained tables by exploding every attribute into its own table and thus allowing every attribute to save an unlimited number of multiple values.

Reasonable normalization enhances database performance. The presence of wide tables with a large number of columns is usually a characteristic of an undernormalized database. *Undernormalization* causes excessive repetition of data and often hurts query performance. For example, in an ordering system, you can keep a customer's profile and all the orders placed by the customer in a single table, as shown in Table 18-1.

Table 18-1. *Original Customers Table*

CustID	Name	Address	Phone	OrderDt	ShippingAddress
100	Liu Hong	Boise, ID, USA	123-456-7890	08-Jul-04	Boise, ID, USA
100	Liu Hong	Boise, ID, USA	123-456-7890	10-Jul-04	Austin, TX, USA

Keeping the customer profile and the order information together in a single table will repeat the customer profile in every order placed by the customer, making the rows in the table very wide. Consequently, fewer customer profiles can be saved in one data page. For a query interested in a range of customer profiles (not their order information), more pages have to be read compared to that in the design in which customer profiles are kept in a separate table. To avoid the performance impact of undernormalization, you must normalize the two logical entities (customer profile and orders), which have a one-to-many type of relationship, into separate tables, as shown in Tables 18-2 and 18-3.

Table 18-2. *New Customers Table*

CustID	Name	Address	Phone
100	Liu Hong	Boise, ID, USA	123-456-7890

Table 18-3. *Orders Table*

CustID	OrderDt	ShippingAddress
100	08-Jul-04	Boise, ID, USA
100	10-Jul-04	Austin, TX, USA

Similarly, overnormalization is also not good for query performance. *Overnormalization* causes excessive joins across too many narrow tables. To fetch any useful content from the database, a database developer has to join a large number of tables in the SQL queries. For example, if you create separate tables for a customer name, address, and phone number, then, to retrieve the customer information, you have to join three tables. If the data (e.g., the customer name and address) has a one-to-one or one-to-two type of relationship and is usually accessed together by the queries, then normalizing the data into separate tables hurts query performance.

Benefit from Entity-Integrity Constraints

Data integrity is essential to ensuring the quality of data in the database. An essential component of data integrity is *entity integrity*, which defines a row as a unique entity for a particular table. As per entity integrity, every row in a table must be uniquely identifiable. The column or columns serving as the unique row identifier for a table must be represented as the primary key of the table.

Sometimes, a table may contain an additional column that also can be used to uniquely identify a row in the table. For example, an Employee table may have the columns EmployeeID and SocialSecurityNumber. The column EmployeeID, which serves as the unique row identifier, can be defined as the primary key, and the column SocialSecurityNumber can be defined as the alternate key. In SQL Server, alternate keys can be defined using unique constraints, which are essentially the younger siblings to primary keys. In fact, both the unique constraint and the primary key constraint use unique indexes behind the scenes.

Besides maintaining data integrity, unique indexes—the primary vehicle for entity-integrity constraints—help the optimizer generate efficient execution plans. SQL Server can often search through a unique index faster than it can search through a nonunique index, because in a unique index each row is unique and, once a row is found, SQL Server does not have to look any further for other matching rows. If a column is used in sort (or GROUP BY or DISTINCT) operations, consider defining a unique constraint on the column (using a unique index), because columns with a unique constraint generally sort faster than ones with no unique constraint.

To understand the performance benefit of entity integrity or unique constraint, consider this example. You'll use a copy of the Northwind.dbo.Orders table as your test table:

```
--Create a copy of Northwind.dbo.Orders table
IF(SELECT OBJECT_ID('Order1')) IS NOT NULL
   DROP TABLE Order1
GO
SELECT * INTO Order1 FROM Northwind.dbo.Orders
CREATE NONCLUSTERED INDEX I1 ON Order1(OrderID)
```

The nonclustered index does not include the UNIQUE constraint. Therefore, although the OrderID column contains unique values, the absence of the UNIQUE constraint from the nonclustered index does not provide this information to the optimizer in advance. Now, let's consider the performance impact of the UNIQUE constraint (or a missing UNIQUE constraint) on the following SELECT statement:

```
SELECT DISTINCT(OrderID) FROM Order1
```

Figure 18-1 shows the execution plan of this SELECT statement.

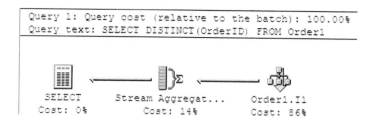

Figure 18-1. *Execution plan with no UNIQUE constraint on the OrderID column*

From the execution plan, you can see that the nonclustered index I1 is used to retrieve the data, and then a Stream Aggregate operation is performed on the data to group the data on the OrderID column so that the duplicate OrderID values can be removed from the final result set. The Stream Aggregate operation would not have been required if the optimizer had been told in advance about the uniqueness of the OrderID column by defining the nonclustered index with a UNIQUE constraint, as follows:

```
CREATE UNIQUE NONCLUSTERED INDEX I1 ON Order1(OrderID)
  WITH DROP_EXISTING
```

Figure 18-2 shows the new execution plan of the SELECT statement.

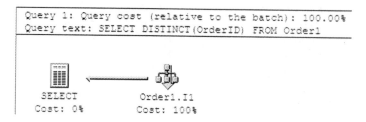

Figure 18-2. *Execution plan with a UNIQUE constraint on the OrderID column*

In general, the entity integrity constraints (i.e., primary keys and unique constraints) provide useful information to the optimizer about the expected results, assisting the optimizer in generating efficient execution plans.

Benefit from Domain and Referential Integrity Constraints

The other two important components of data integrity are *domain integrity* and *referential integrity*. Domain integrity for a column can be enforced by restricting the data type of the column, defining the format of the input data, and limiting the range of acceptable values for the column. SQL Server provides the following features to implement the domain integrity: data types, FOREIGN KEY constraints, CHECK constraints, DEFAULT definitions, and NOT NULL definitions. If an application requires that the values for a data column be restricted within a range of values, then this business rule can be implemented either in the application code or in the database schema. Implementing such a business rule in the database using domain constraints (such as the CHECK constraint) usually helps the optimizer generate efficient execution plans.

To understand the performance benefit of domain integrity, consider this example:

```
--Create two test tables
IF(SELECT OBJECT_ID('T1')) IS NOT NULL
  DROP TABLE T1
GO
CREATE TABLE T1(C1 INT, C2 INT CHECK(C2 BETWEEN 10 AND 20))
INSERT INTO T1 VALUES(11, 12)
GO
IF(SELECT OBJECT_ID('T2')) IS NOT NULL
  DROP TABLE T2
GO
CREATE TABLE T2(C1 INT, C2 INT)
INSERT INTO T2 VALUES(101, 102)
```

Now, execute the following two SELECT statements:

```
SELECT T1.C1, T1.C2, T2.C2
FROM T1 JOIN T2 ON T1.C1 = T2.C2 AND T1.C2 = 20
GO
SELECT T1.C1, T1.C2, T2.C2
FROM T1 JOIN T2 ON T1.C1 = T2.C2 AND T1.C2 = 30
```

The two SELECT statements appear to be the same except for the predicate values (20 in the first statement and 30 in the second). Although the two SELECT statements have exactly the same form, the optimizer treats them differently because of the CHECK constraint on the T1.C2 column, as shown in the execution plan in Figure 18-3.

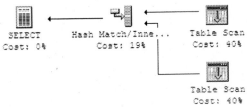

```
Query 1: Query cost (relative to the batch): 100.00%
Query text: SELECT T1.C1, T1.C2, T2.C2  FROM T1 JOIN T2 ON T1.C1 = T2.C2 AND T1.C2 = 20
```

SELECT   Hash Match/Inne...   Table Scan
Cost: 0%   Cost: 19%   Cost: 40%

Table Scan
Cost: 40%

```
Query 2: Query cost (relative to the batch): 0.00%
Query text: SELECT T1.C1, T1.C2, T2.C2  FROM T1 JOIN T2 ON T1.C1 = T2.C2 AND T1.C2 = 30
```

SELECT   Constant Scan
Cost: 0%   Cost: 100%

Figure 18-3. *Execution plans with predicate values within and outside the CHECK constraint boundaries*

From the execution plan, you can see that, for the first query (with T1.C2 = 20), the optimizer accesses the data from both tables. For the second query (with T1.C2 = 30), since the optimizer understands from the corresponding CHECK constraint on the column T1.C2 that the column can't contain any value outside the range of 10 to 20, the optimizer doesn't even access the data from the tables. Consequently, the relative cost of the second query is 0%.

I explained the performance advantage of referential integrity in detail in the section "Declarative Referential Integrity" of Chapter 11, and further demonstrated it in the section "Using Database Constraints" of Chapter 16.

Therefore, use domain and referential constraints not only to implement data integrity, but also to facilitate the optimizer in generating efficient query plans. To understand other performance benefits of domain and referential integrity, please refer to the section "Use Domain and Referential Integrity" of Chapter 11.

Adopt Index-Design Best Practices

The most common optimization recommendation, and usually the biggest contributor to good performance, is to implement the correct indexes for the database workload. Unlike tables, which are used to store data and can be designed even without knowing the queries thoroughly (as long as the tables properly represent the business entities), indexes must be designed by reviewing the database queries thoroughly. Except in common and obvious cases, such as primary keys and unique indexes, please don't fall into the trap of designing indexes without knowing the queries. Even for primary keys and unique indexes, I advise you to validate the applicability of those indexes as you start designing the database queries. Considering the importance of indexes for database performance, you must be very careful while designing indexes.

Although the performance aspect of indexes is explained in detail in Chapters 4, 6, and 7, I'll reiterate a short list of recommendations for easy reference:

- Choose narrow columns for indexes.

- Ensure that the selectivity of the data in the candidate column is very high or that the column has a large number of unique values.

- Prefer columns with the integer data type (or variants of the integer data type). Avoid indexes on columns with string data types such as VARCHAR.

- For a multicolumn index, consider the column with higher selectivity toward the leading end of the index.

- While deciding the columns to be indexed, pay extra attention to the queries' WHERE clause and join criteria columns, which can serve as the entry points into the tables. Especially if a WHERE clause criterion on a column filters the data on a highly selective value or constant, the column can be a prime candidate for an index.

- While choosing the type of an index (clustered or nonclustered), keep in mind the advantages and disadvantages of clustered and nonclustered index types. For queries retrieving a range of rows, usually clustered indexes perform better. For point queries, nonclustered indexes are usually better.

Be extra careful while designing a clustered index, since every nonclustered index on the table depends on the clustered index. Therefore, follow these recommendations while designing and implementing clustered indexes:

- Keep the clustered indexes as narrow as possible. You don't want to widen all your nonclustered indexes by having a wide clustered index.

- Create the clustered index first, and then create the nonclustered indexes on the table.

- If required, rebuild a clustered index in a single step using the DROP_EXISTING keyword in the CREATE INDEX command. You don't want to rebuild all the nonclustered indexes on the table twice: once when the clustered index is dropped and again when the clustered index is re-created.

- Do not create a clustered index on a frequently updateable column. If you do so, the nonclustered indexes on the table will have difficulty remaining in sync with the clustered index key values.

Do Not Use the sp_ Prefix for Stored Procedure Names

As a rule, don't use the sp_ prefix for user stored procedures, since SQL Server assumes that stored procedures with the sp_ prefix are system stored procedures, which are supposed to be in the master database. The use of sp or usp as the prefix for user stored procedures is quite common. The performance hit of the sp_ prefix is explained in detail in the section "Do Not Prefix a Stored Procedure Name with sp_" of Chapter 11.

Query Design

Here's a list of the performance-related best practices you should follow when designing the database queries:

- Use the command SET NOCOUNT ON.

- Explicitly define the owner of an object.

- Avoid nonindexable search conditions.

- Avoid arithmetic operators/functions on WHERE clause columns.

- Avoid optimizer hints.

- Minimize logging overhead.

- Adopt execution-plan reuse best practices.

- Adopt database transaction best practices.

- Reduce the overhead of database cursors.

I further detail each best practice in the following sections.

Use the Command SET NOCOUNT ON

As a rule, always use the command SET NOCOUNT ON as the first statement in stored procedures, triggers, and other batch queries to avoid the network overhead associated with the return of the number of rows affected, after every execution of a SQL statement. The command SET NOCOUNT is explained in detail in the section "Use SET NOCOUNT" of Chapter 11.

Explicitly Define the Owner of an Object

As a performance best practice, always qualify a database object with its owner to avoid the runtime cost required to verify the owner of the object. The performance benefit of explicitly qualifying the owner of a database object is explained in detail in the section "Avoid Implicit Resolution of Objects in Queries" of Chapter 9. The additional performance benefit of explicitly defining the owner of a stored procedure while executing the stored procedure is explained in detail in the section "Avoid Implicit Resolution of Stored Procedure Names" of Chapter 9.

Avoid Nonindexable Search Conditions

Be vigilant when defining the search conditions in your query. If the search condition on a column used in the WHERE clause prevents the optimizer from effectively using the index on that column, then the execution cost for the query will be high in spite of the presence of the correct index. The performance impact of nonindexable search conditions is explained in detail in the corresponding section of Chapter 11.

Additionally, please be careful while defining your application features. If you define an application feature such as "retrieve all products with product name ending in Sauce," then you will have queries scanning the complete table (or the clustered index). As you know, scanning a multimillion-row table will hurt your database performance. Unless you use an index hint, you won't be able to benefit from the index on that column. However, since the use of an index hint overrides the decisions of the query optimizer, it's generally not recommended that you use index hints either, as explained in Chapter 11. To understand the performance impact of such a business rule, consider the following SELECT statement:

```
SELECT * FROM Products WHERE ProductName LIKE '%Sauce'
```

Figure 18-4 shows the execution plan.

In Figure 18-4, you can see that the execution plan didn't use the index on the Product-Name column; the optimizer instead used the index PK_Products, which is on the ProductID column. Since an index on a column with character data types (such as CHAR and VARCHAR) sorts the data values for the column on the leading-end characters, the use of a leading % in the LIKE condition didn't allow a seek operation into the index. The matching rows may be distributed throughout the index rows, making the index noneffective for the search condition, and thereby hurting the performance of the query.

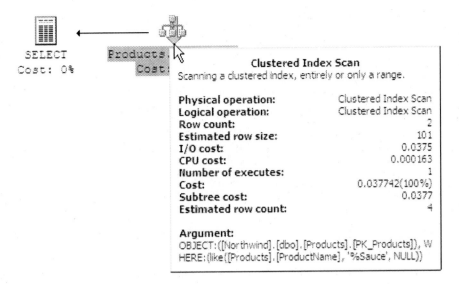

Figure 18-4. *Execution plan showing clustered-index scan caused by a nonindexable LIKE clause*

Avoid Arithmetic Operators/Functions on WHERE Clause Columns

Always try not to use arithmetic operators and functions on WHERE clause columns. The use of operators/functions on the WHERE clause columns prevents the use of indexes on those columns. The performance impact of using arithmetic operators on WHERE clause columns is explained in detail in the section "Avoid Arithmetic Operators on the WHERE Clause Column" of Chapter 11, and the impact of using functions is explained in detail in the section "Avoid Functions on the WHERE Clause Column" of the same chapter.

Avoid Optimizer Hints

As a rule, avoid the use of optimizer hints, such as index hints and join hints, because they overrule the decision-making process of the optimizer. In general, the optimizer is smart enough to generate efficient execution plans and works the best without any optimizer hint imposed on it. For a detailed understanding of the performance impact of optimizer hints, please refer to the corresponding section "Avoid Optimizer Hints" of Chapter 11.

Minimize Logging Overhead

As explained in the section "Large Dataset Migration" of Chapter 17, SQL Server maintains the old and new state of every atomic action (or transaction) in the transaction log to ensure database consistency and durability, creating a huge pressure on the log disk and often making the log disk a point of contention. Therefore, to improve database performance, you must try to optimize the transaction log overhead. Besides the hardware solutions discussed later in the chapter, you should adopt the following query-design best practices:

- Prefer table variables over temporary tables for small result set. The performance benefit of table variable is explained in detail in the section "Use Table Variables" of Chapter 10.

- Batch a number of action queries in a single transaction. You must be careful when using this option, because if too many rows are affected within a single transaction, the corresponding database objects will be locked for a long time, blocking all other users trying to access the objects. To determine the number of rows that may be affected in a single transaction, and thereby reduce logging overhead, please refer to the section "Sizing the Transaction Correctly" of Chapter 17.

Reuse Query Execution Plans

The best practices around optimizing the cost of plan generation can be broadly classified into two categories:

- Caching execution plans effectively

- Minimizing recompilation of execution plans

Caching Execution Plans Effectively

You must ensure that the execution plans for your queries are not only cached, but also reused often by adopting the following best practices:

- Avoid executing queries as nonparameterized, ad hoc queries. Instead, parameterize the variable parts of a query and submit the parameterized query using a stored procedure or the sp_executesql system stored procedure.

- Use the same environment settings (such as ANSI_NULLS) in every connection that executes the same parameterized queries, as the execution plan for a query is dependent on the environment settings of the connection.

- As explained earlier in the section "Explicitly Define the Owner of an Object," explicitly qualify the owner of the objects while accessing them in your queries.

The preceding aspects of plan caching are explained in detail in Chapter 9.

Minimizing Recompilation of Execution Plans

To minimize the cost of generating execution plans for stored procedures, you must ensure that the plans in the cache are not invalidated or recompiled for reasons that are under your control. The following recommended best practices minimize the recompilation of stored procedure plans:

- Do not interleave DDL and DML statements in your stored procedures. You must put all the DDL statements at the top of the stored procedures.

- In a stored procedure, avoid the use of temporary tables that are created outside the stored procedure.

- Avoid recompilation caused by statistics change on temporary tables by using the KEEPFIXED PLAN option.

- Prefer table variables over temporary tables for small data sets.

- Do not change the ANSI SET options within a stored procedure.

- If you really can't avoid a recompilation, then identify the stored procedure statement that is causing the recompilation and execute it either as a dynamic query or through the sp_executesql system stored procedure.

The causes of stored procedure recompilation and the recommended solutions are explained in detail in Chapter 10.

Optimize Database Transactions

The more effectively you design your queries for concurrency, the faster the queries will be able to complete without blocking one another. Consider the following recommendations while designing the transactions in your queries:

- Keep the scope of the transactions as short as possible. In a transaction, include only the statements that must be committed together for data consistency.

- Prevent the possibility of transactions being left open because of poor error-handling routines or application logic by using the following techniques:

  - Use SET XACT_ABORT ON to ensure that a transaction is aborted or rolled back on an error condition within the transaction.

  - After executing a stored procedure or a batch of queries containing a transaction from a client code, always check for an open transaction, and roll back any open transactions using the following SQL statement:

    ```
    IF @@TRANCOUNT > 0 ROLLBACK
    ```

- Use the lowest level of transaction isolation required to maintain data consistency. The amount of isolation provided by the read committed isolation level, the default isolation level, is sufficient most of the time. If an application feature (such as reporting) can tolerate dirty data, consider using the read uncommitted isolation level or the NOLOCK hint.

The impact of transactions on database performance is explained in detail in Chapter 12.

Reduce the Overhead of Database Cursors

Since SQL Server is designed to work with sets of data, processing multiple rows using DML statements is generally much faster than processing the rows one by one using database cursors. If you must use a database cursor, then use the database cursor with the least overhead, which is the FAST_FORWARD cursor type (generally referred to as the *fast forward–only cursor*), or use the equivalent DataReader object in ADO.NET.

The performance overhead of database cursors is explained in detail in Chapter 14.

Configuration Settings

Here's a checklist of the server and database configurations settings that have a big impact on database performance:

- Affinity mask

- Memory configuration options

- Database file layout

- Database file compression

I cover these settings in more detail in the sections that follow.

Affinity Mask

As explained in the section "Parallel Plan Optimization" of Chapter 9, affinity mask is a special configuration setting at the server level that you can use to restrict the specific CPUs available to SQL Server. It is recommended that you keep this setting at its default value of 0, which allows SQL Server to use all the CPUs of the machine.

Memory Configuration Options

As explained in the section "SQL Server Memory Management" of Chapter 2, it is strongly recommended that you keep the memory configuration of SQL Server at the default dynamic setting. For a dedicated SQL Server box, the max server memory setting may be configured to a nondefault value under the following two situations:

- *SQL Server cluster with active/active configuration*: In active/active configuration, both SQL Server nodes accept incoming traffic and remain available to run a second instance of SQL Server if the other node fails, accepting the incoming traffic for the other SQL Server. Since both nodes must be capable of running two instances of SQL Server, the max server memory setting for each SQL Server instance must be set to around 100MB less than the half of the physical memory so that both SQL Server instances can run simultaneously on a single node, when needed.

- *More than 4GB of physical memory*: If a SQL Server machine has more than 4GB of physical memory, and the PAE switch (in boot.ini) is set, then set the awe enabled parameter of SQL Server to allow SQL Server to access the memory beyond 4GB, and set the max server memory setting to a value approximately 200MB less than the physical memory. The PAE and AWE settings are explained in detail in the section "Using Extended Memory Within SQL Server" of Chapter 2.

Another memory configuration to consider for a SQL Server machine is the /3GB setting at the operating system level. If the machine has 4GB of physical memory, then you may add this setting to the boot.ini file, allowing SQL Server to use the physical memory up to 3GB. These memory configurations of SQL Server are explained in detail in the sections "Memory Bottleneck Analysis" and "Memory Bottleneck Resolutions" of Chapter 2.

Database File Layout

For easy reference, I'll list here the best practices you should consider when laying out database files:

- Place the data and transaction log files of a user database on different disks, allowing the transaction log disk head to progress sequentially without being moved randomly by the nonsequential I/Os commonly used for the data files.

  Placing the transaction log on a dedicated disk also enhances data protection. If a database disk fails, you will be able to save the completed transactions until the point of failure by performing a backup of the transaction log. By using this last transaction log backup during the recovery process, you will be able to recover the database up to the point of failure, also known as *point-in-time recovery*.

- Avoid RAID 5 for transaction logs because, for every write request, RAID 5 disk arrays incur twice the number of disk I/Os compared to RAID 1 or 10.

- You may choose RAID 5 for data files, since even in a heavy OLTP system the number of read requests is usually seven to eight times that of writes, and for read requests the performance of RAID 5 is similar to that of RAID 1 and RAID 10 with an equal number of total disks.

- If the system has multiple CPUs and multiple disks, spread the data across multiple data files distributed across the disks. SQL Server can take advantage of multiple files by performing parallel scans on the data files.

For a detailed understanding of database file layout and RAID subsystems, please refer to the section "Disk Bottleneck Resolutions" of Chapter 2.

Database File Compression

As a rule, do not compress the database files, even though the native file compression feature of Windows appears to be an appealing option to conserve disk space. The compression and decompression of the file contents by the operating system while SQL Server accesses the database files add a substantial overhead to the disk I/O operations for the database requests. Therefore, always ensure that the database files are not compressed.

Database Administration

For your reference, here is a short list of the performance-related database administrative activities that you should perform while managing your database server on a regular basis:

- Keep the statistics up to date.

- Maintain a minimum amount of index defragmentation.

- Update the stored procedure plans.

- Cycle the SQL error log file.

- Minimize the overhead of SQL tracing.

In the following sections, I detail these activities.

> ■**NOTE** For a detailed explanation of SQL Server 2000 administration best practices, please refer to the Microsoft TechNet article "SQL Server 2000 Operations Guide: System Administration" (http://www.microsoft.com/technet/prodtechnol/sql/2000/maintain/sqlops4.mspx).

Keep the Statistics Up to Date

Although the performance impact of database statistics is explained in detail in Chapter 7, here's a short list for easy reference:

- Allow SQL Server to automatically maintain the statistics of the data distribution in the tables by using the default settings for the configuration parameters AUTO_CREATE_STATISTICS and AUTO_UPDATE_STATISTICS.

- As a proactive measure, in addition to the continual update of the statistics by SQL Server, you can programmatically update the statistics of every database object on a daily basis during nonpeak hours. This practice partly protects your database from having outdated statistics in case the auto update statistics feature fails to provide a satisfactory result. In Chapter 7, I illustrate how to set up a SQL Server job to programmatically update the statistics on a regular basis.

▓**NOTE** Please ensure that the statistics update job is scheduled after the completion of the index defragmentation job, as explained later in the chapter.

Maintain a Minimum Amount of Index Defragmentation

The following best practices will help you maintain a minimum amount of index defragmentation:

- Defragment a database on a daily basis during nonpeak hours.

- On a daily basis, use the command DBCC INDEXDEFRAG. However, considering that DBCC INDEXDEFRAG is less effective in removing fragmentation than DBCC DBREINDEX, run DBCC DBREINDEX for the first time to establish a minimal-fragmentation starting point for the DBCC INDEXDEFRAG command by executing the following SQL statements:

```
--Bring all databases to minimal-fragmentation for DBCC INDEXDEFRAG
SET NOCOUNT ON

--Create a temporary table to hold all table names in a database
IF(SELECT OBJECT_ID('tempdb..#Tables')) IS NOT NULL
  DROP TABLE #Tables
GO
CREATE TABLE #Tables(
  TableName sysname,
  UserName sysname,
  TableID INT PRIMARY KEY
)

--Process all databases
DECLARE @DBName sysname, @DBObjectName sysname,
        @UserName sysname, @TableID INT
DECLARE DBNames CURSOR
  FOR SELECT name FROM master.dbo.sysdatabases WITH(NOLOCK)
      WHERE DATABASEPROPERTYEX(name,'Status') = 'ONLINE'
        AND name NOT IN ('tempdb', 'model') --Database exclusion list
OPEN DBNames
FETCH NEXT FROM DBNames INTO @DBName
WHILE @@FETCH_STATUS = 0
BEGIN
  --Identify all user tables in the database
  PRINT CHAR(10) + 'Database: ' + @DBName
  INSERT INTO #Tables
    EXEC('USE ' + @DBName + ' SELECT name, USER_NAME(uid), id
                    FROM sysobjects WITH(NOLOCK)
                    WHERE xtype = ''U'' ORDER BY id')
```

```
--Process all the user tables in the database
SET @TableID = 0
SELECT TOP 1 @DBObjectName = TableName, @UserName = UserName,
            @TableID=TableID
  FROM #Tables WHERE TableID > @TableID
WHILE @@ROWCOUNT = 1
BEGIN
  --Defragment the user table and all its indexes
  PRINT 'Executing DBCC DBREINDEX(''' + @DBName + '.' + @UserName +
    '.' + @DBObjectName + ''') ...'
  EXEC('DBCC DBREINDEX(''' + @DBName + '.' + @UserName +
    '.' + @DBObjectName + ''')')

  SELECT TOP 1 @DBObjectName = TableName, @UserName = UserName,
              @TableID=TableID
    FROM #Tables WHERE TableID > @TableID
END

  --Process the next database
  TRUNCATE TABLE #Tables
  FETCH NEXT FROM DBNames INTO @DBName
END
CLOSE DBNames
DEALLOCATE DBNames

SET NOCOUNT OFF
GO
```

Once the fragmentation in a database is brought down to a minimal level, DBCC
INDEXDEFRAG can continually chip off the fragmentation developed in the database
on a regular basis.

- To remove the maximum amount of fragmentation and yet minimize blocking during
  index defragmentation, on a monthly basis execute the command DBCC DBREINDEX on
  an index only if the index is fragmented significantly. Chapter 8 illustrates an effective
  way of defragmenting a database using DBCC DBREINDEX without causing excessive
  blocking.

Update the Stored Procedure Plans

Considering that the initiation of the automatic stored procedure recompilation and that of
the auto update statistics feature use the same algorithm, as a proactive measure you should
mark your database stored procedures for recompilation at a frequency similar to that for programmatic update of statistics, using the system stored procedure sp_recompile as explained
in the section "Explicit Call to sp_recompile" of Chapter 10.

▓**NOTE** Schedule the administrative routine for the automatic recompilation of stored procedures after the completion of the administrative jobs for index defragmentation and statistics update.

The recompilation of stored procedures is explained in depth in Chapter 10.

Cycle the SQL Error Log File

By default, the SQL Server error log file keeps growing until SQL Server is restarted. Every time SQL Server is restarted, the current error log file is closed and renamed errorlog.1, then errorlog.1 is renamed errorlog.2, and so on. Subsequently, a new error log file is created. Therefore, if SQL Server is not restarted for a long time, as expected for a production server, the error log file may grow to a very large size, making it not only difficult to view the file in an editor, but also very memory unfriendly when the file is opened.

SQL Server provides a system stored procedure, sp_cycle_errorlog, that you can use to cycle the error log file without restarting SQL Server. To keep control over the size of the error log file, you must cycle the error log file periodically by executing sp_cycle_errorlog as follows:

```
EXEC master.dbo.sp_cycle_errorlog
```

You can accomplish the same thing by executing the following DBCC command:

```
DBCC ERRORLOG
```

Use a SQL Server job to cycle the SQL Server log on a regular basis.

Minimize the Overhead of SQL Tracing

One of the most common ways of analyzing the behavior of SQL Server is to trace the SQL queries executed on SQL Server. For easy reference, here's a list of the performance-related best practices for SQL tracing:

- Capture trace output using stored procedures (not Profiler).

- Limit the number of events and data columns to be traced.

- Discard starting events while analyzing costly and slow queries.

- Limit trace output size.

- If you decide to run Profiler for very short tracing, run the tool remotely.

- Avoid online data column sorting while using Profiler.

These best practices are explained in detail in the section "SQL Profiler Recommendations" of Chapter 3.

Database Backup

Although database backup is a broad topic and can't be given due justice in this query optimization book, I suggest that, for database performance, you be attentive to the following aspects of your database backup process:

- Transaction log backup frequency

- Backup distribution

- Backup compression

The next sections go into more detail on these suggestions.

▧**NOTE** For a detailed explanation of backup and restore strategies, please refer to the article "Backup and Restore Strategies with SQL Server 2000" (http://www1.us.dell.com/content/topics/global.aspx/ power/en/ps4q00_martin?c=us&cs=04&l=en&s=bsd).

Transaction Log Backup Frequency

For an OLTP database, it is mandatory that the database be backed up regularly so that, in case of a failure, the database can be restored on a different server. Because for large databases the full database backup usually takes a very long time, full backups cannot be performed often. Consequently, full backups are performed at widespread time intervals, with transaction log backups scheduled more frequently between two consecutive full backups. With the frequent transaction log backups set in place, if a database fails completely, the database can be restored up to the last transaction log backup.

The frequent backup of the transaction log adds overhead to the server, even during peak hours. To minimize the performance impact of transaction log backup on incoming traffic, consider the following three aspects of transaction log backups:

- *Performance*: You may back up the transaction log only if the size of the log file is greater than 20% of the total size of all the data files. This option is best for the database performance, since the transaction log is backed up only when it is significantly full. However, this option is not good for minimizing data loss, and the amount of data loss (in terms of time) cannot be quantified, because if the log disk fails and the database needs to be recovered from backup, then the last log backup up to which the database can be recovered may be far in the past. Additionally, the delayed backup of the transaction log causes the log file to grow up to 20% of the total size of the data files, requiring a large log-disk subsystem.

- *Disk space*: You may back up the transaction log whenever the size of the log file becomes greater than 500MB. This option is good for disk space and may be partly good for performance, too, if the 500MB log space doesn't fill up quickly. However, as with the previous option, the amount of data loss (in terms of time) cannot be quantified, because it may take a random amount of time to fill the 500MB log. If the log disk fails, then the database can be recovered up to the last log backup, which may be far in the past.

- *Data loss*: To minimize and quantify the maximum amount of data loss in terms of time, back up the log frequently. If a business can withstand the maximum data loss of 60 minutes, then the interval of transaction log backup schedule must be set to less than 60 minutes.

Because, for most businesses, the acceptable amount of data loss (in terms of time) usually takes precedence over conserving the log-disk space or providing an ideal database performance, you must take into account the acceptable amount of data loss while scheduling the transaction log backup instead of randomly setting the schedule to a low time interval.

Backup Distribution

When multiple databases need to be backed up, you must ensure that all full backups are not scheduled at the same time so that the hardware resources are not pressurized at the same time. If the backup process involves backing up the databases to a central SAN disk array, then the full backups from all the database servers must be distributed across the backup time window so that the central backup infrastructure doesn't get slammed by too many backup requests at the same time. Flooding the central infrastructure with a great deal of backup requests at the same time forces the components of the infrastructure to spend a significant part of their resources just managing the excessive number of requests. This mismanaged use of the resources increases the backup durations significantly, causing the full backups to continue during peak hours, and thus affecting the performance of the end-user requests.

To minimize the impact of the full backup process on database performance, you must first determine the nonpeak hours when full backups can be scheduled, and then you distribute the full backups across the nonpeak time window as follows:

1. Identify the number of databases that must be backed up.

2. Prioritize the databases in order of their importance to the business.

3. Determine the nonpeak hours when the full database backups can be scheduled.

4. Calculate the time interval between two consecutive full backups as follows:

   Time interval = (Total backup time window) / (Number of full backups)

5. Schedule the full backups in order of the database priorities, with the first backup starting at the start time of the backup window, and the subsequent backups spread uniformly at time intervals as calculated in the preceding equation.

This uniform distribution of the full backups will ensure that the backup infrastructure is not flooded with too many backup requests at the same time, and thus reduce the impact of the full backups on the database performance.

Backup Compression

For relatively large databases, the backup durations and backup file sizes usually become an issue. Long backup durations make it difficult to complete the backups within the administrative time windows, and thus start affecting the end user's experience. The large size of the backup files makes space management for the backup files quite challenging, and it increases the pressure on the network when the backups are performed across the network to a central backup infrastructure.

The recommended way to optimize the backup duration, the backup file size, and the resultant network pressure is to use *backup compression*. Many backup tools are available that support backup compression. One such tool is SQL LiteSpeed from Imceda Software, Inc. Using this backup tool, you may be able to reduce the backup duration by 50–70% and the backup file size by 75–90%. Since the backup compression tools are highly CPU intensive, please ensure that the CPU utilization of SQL Server is below 50% during the backup window. For example, LiteSpeed may consume an additional 10–15% of CPU compared to the native backup of SQL Server. However, the 50–70% reduction in the backup durations makes the backup compression tool a viable backup solution.

NOTE For detailed information on enhancing the SQL Server backup and recovery process using SQL LiteSpeed, please refer to the article "SQL LiteSpeed 3.0—The Smarter DBA's Backup" (http://www.sql-server-performance.com/sql_litespeed_spotlight.asp).

Summary

Performance optimization is an ongoing process. It requires continual attention to database and query characteristics that affect performance. The goal of this chapter was to provide you with a checklist of these characteristics to serve as a quick and easy reference during the development and maintenance phase of your database applications.

Index

Printed in the United States
69770LV00004B/159-162